SYMBOLS USED IN THIS BOOK

SYMBOL	DEFINITION
R^2	Squared multiple correlation. The variance explained in a dependent variable by a set of independent variables
RMSEA	Root mean square error of approximation, a measure of fit in SEM
SD	Standard deviation
SE	Standard error, as in SE of a regression coefficients (SE_b)
sr	Semipartial correlation, equal to $\sqrt{\Delta R^2}$ when a variable is added last to a regression equation
SRMR	Standardized root mean square residual, a measure of fit in SEM
ss	Sums of squares, a measure of variation, used calculate R and determine the statistical significance of a regression equation
t	As in t-test. t-tests are used to test the statistical significance of regression coefficients, means, and many other parameters
T scores	Standardized scores with a $M = 50$ and $SD = 10$
TLI	Tucker-Lewis index, also known as the NNFI, the non-normed fit index, a measure of fit in SEM
u	Unique and error variance in SEM and CFA
V	Variance
X	An independent variable
Y	A dependent variable
Y'	The predicted Y
z scores	As in z-scores. Standardized scores with $M = 0$, $SD = 1$. The basis for all other types of standard scores
α	Alpha, the probability level
β	Beta, the standardized regression coefficient
Δ	Delta, used to symbolize change, as in ΔR^2
η^2	Eta-squared, a measure of effect size in ANOVA that is equivalent to R^2
χ^2	Chi-square, a common measure of fit in SEM models

MULTIPLE REGRESSION AND BEYOND

TIMOTHY Z. KEITH

University of Texas at Austin

Boston ■ New York ■ San Francisco
Mexico City ■ Montreal ■ Toronto ■ London ■ Madrid ■ Munich ■ Paris
Hong Kong ■ Singapore ■ Tokyo ■ Cape Town ■ Sydney

Executive Editor: *Susan Hartman*
Editorial Assistant: *Therese Felser*
Marketing Manager: *Karen Natale*
Editorial Production Service: *Tom Conville Publishing Services, LLC*
Manufacturing Buyer: *JoAnne Sweeney*
Electronic Composition: *Omegatype Typography, Inc.*
Cover Administrator: *Kristina Mose-Libon*

For related titles and support materials, visit our online catalog at www.ablongman.com.

Between the time Web site information is gathered and then published, it is not unusual for some sites to have closed. Also, the transcription of URLs can result in typographical errors. The publisher would appreciate notification where these occur so that they may be corrected in subsequent editions.

Library of Congress Cataloging-in-Publication Data

Keith, Timothy, 1952–
    Multiple regression and beyond / Timothy Z. Keith.
      p. cm.
    Includes bibliographical references.
    ISBN 0-205-32644-7
    1. Regression analysis.   I. Title.

HA31.3.K45   2005
519.5'36—dc22

                        2005041044

Printed in the United States of America

10 9 8   09

CONTENTS

CHAPTER THREE

Multiple Regression: More Detail   43

CHAPTER FOUR

Three and More Independent Variables and Related Issues   56

CHAPTER EIGHT

Continuous Variables: Interactions and Curves   161

CHAPTER NINE

Multiple Regression: Summary, Further Study, and Problems   180

PART II   BEYOND MULTIPLE REGRESSION   212

Multiple Regression and Beyond is designed to provide a conceptually oriented introduction to multiple regression along with more complex methods that flow naturally from multiple regression: path analysis, confirmatory factor analysis, and structural equation modeling. Multiple regression (MR) and related methods have become indispensable tools for modern social science researchers. MR closely implements the general linear model and thus subsumes methods, such as analysis of variance (ANOVA), that have traditionally been more commonplace in psychological and educational research. Regression is especially appropriate for the analysis of nonexperimental research, and with the use of dummy variables and modern computer packages, it is often more appropriate or easier to use MR to analyze the results of complex quasi-experimental or even experimental research. Extensions of multiple regression—particularly structural equation modeling (SEM)—partially obviate threats due to the unreliability of the variables used in research and allow the modeling of complex relations among variables. A quick perusal of the full range of social science journals demonstrates the wide applicability of the methods.

Despite its importance, MR-based analyses are too often poorly conducted and poorly reported. I believe one reason for this incongruity is inconsistency between how material is presented and how most students best learn.

Anyone who teaches (or has ever taken) courses in statistics and research methodology knows that many students, even those who may become gifted researchers, do not always gain conceptual understanding through numerical presentation. Although many who teach statistics understand the processes underlying a sequence of formulas and gain conceptual understanding through these formulas, many students do not. Instead, such students often need a thorough conceptual explanation to gain such understanding, after which a numerical presentation may make more sense. Unfortunately, many multiple regression textbooks assume that students will understand multiple regression best by learning matrix algebra, wading through formulas, and focusing on details.

At the same time, methods such as structural equation modeling (SEM) and confirmatory factor analysis (CFA) are easily taught as extensions of multiple regression. If structured properly, multiple regression flows naturally into these more complex topics, with nearly complete carry-over of concepts. Path models (simple SEMs) illustrate and help deal with some of the problems of MR, CFA does the same for path analysis, and latent variable SEM combines all the previous topics into a powerful, flexible methodology.

I have taught courses including these topics at four universities (the University of Iowa, Virginia Polytechnic Institute & State University, Alfred University, and the University of Texas). These courses included faculty and students in architecture, educational psychology, educational research and statistics, kinesiology, management, political science, psychology, and sociology. This experience leads me to believe that it is possible to teach these methods by focusing on the concepts and purposes of MR and related methods, rather than the derivation and calculation of formulas (what my wife calls the "plug and chug" method of learning statistics). Students generally find such an approach clearer, more conceptual, and less threatening than other approaches. As a result of this conceptual approach, students become interested in conducting research using MR, CFA, or SEM and are more likely to use the methods wisely.

THE ORIENTATION OF THIS BOOK

My overriding bias in this book is that these complex methods can be presented and learned in a conceptual, yet rigorous, manner. I recognize that not all topics are covered in the depth or detail presented in other texts, but I will direct you to other sources for topics for which you may want additional detail. My style is also fairly informal; I've written this book as if I were teaching a class.

Data

I also believe that one learns these methods best by doing, and the more interesting and relevant that "doing," the better. For this reason, there are numerous example analyses throughout this book that I encourage you to reproduce as you read. To make this task easier, the Web site that accompanies the book (www.ablongman.com/keith1e) includes the data in a form that can be used in common statistical analysis programs. Many of the examples are taken from actual research in the social sciences, and I've tried to sample from research from a variety of areas. In most cases simulated data are provided that mimic the actual data used in the research. You can reproduce the analyses of the original researchers and, perhaps, improve on them.

And the data feast doesn't end there! The Web site also includes data from a major federal data set: 1000 cases from the National Education Longitudinal Study (NELS) from the National Center for Education Statistics. NELS was a nationally representative sample of 8th grade students first surveyed in 1988 and resurveyed in 10th and 12th grades, and then twice after leaving high school. The students' parents, teachers, and school administrators were also surveyed. The Web site includes student and parent data from the base year (8th grade) and student data from the first follow-up (10th grade). Don't be led astray by the word Education in NELS; the students were asked an incredible variety of questions, from drug use to psychological well-being to plans for the future. Anyone with an interest in youth will find something interesting in these data. Appendix A includes information about all the data on the Web site.

Computer Analysis

Finally, I firmly believe that any book on statistics or research methods should be closely related to statistical analysis software. Why plug and chug—plug numbers into formulas and chug out the answers on a calculator—when a statistical program can do the calculations more quickly and accurately with, for most people, no loss of understanding? Freed from the drudgery of hand calculations, you can then concentrate on asking and answering important research questions, rather than on the intricacies of calculating statistics. This bias toward computer calculations is especially important for the methods covered in this book, which quickly become unmanageable by hand. Use a statistical analysis program as you read this book; do the examples with me and the problems at the end of the chapters, using that program.

Which program? I use SPSS as my general statistical analysis program, and you can get the program for a very reasonable price as a student in a university (approximately $200 for the "Grad Pack" as this is written). But you need not use SPSS; any of the common packages will do (e.g., SAS or SYSTAT). The output in the text has a generic look to it, which should be easily translatable to any major statistical package output. In addition, Appendix B includes sample multiple regression output from three major statistical packages: SPSS, SAS, and SYSTAT.

For the second half of the book, you will need access to a structural equation modeling program. Fortunately, student or tryout versions of many such programs are available free on the Internet. The student version of the program used extensively in this book, Amos, is available at amosdevelopment.com. As this is written, the full version of Amos is also included as a component of the SPSS Grad Pack. Amos is, in my opinion, the easiest SEM program to use (and it produces really nifty pictures). We'll talk more about SEM via Amos in Part 2 of this book.

Overview of the Book

This book is divided into two parts. Part 1 focuses on multiple regression analysis. We begin by focusing on simple, bivariate regression and then expand that focus into multiple regression with two, three, and four independent variables. We will concentrate on the analysis and interpretation of multiple regression as a way of answering interesting and important research questions. Along the way, we will also deal with the analytic details of multiple regression so that you understand what is going on when we do a multiple regression analysis. We will focus on three different types, or flavors, of multiple regression that you will encounter in the research literature, their strengths and weaknesses, and their proper interpretation. Our next step will be to add categorical independent variables to our multiple regression analyses, at which point the relation of multiple regression and ANOVA will become clearer. We will learn how to test for interactions and curves in the regression line and to apply these methods to interesting research questions.

Part 1 ends with a review chapter that summarizes and integrates what we have learned about multiple regression. Besides serving as a review for those who have gone through Part 1, it also serves as a useful introduction for those who are interested primarily in the material in Part 2. In addition, this chapter introduces several important topics not covered completely in previous chapters.

Part 2 focuses on structural equation modeling—the "Beyond" portion of the book's title. We begin by discussing path analysis, or structural equation modeling with measured variables. Simple path analyses are easily estimated via multiple regression analysis, and many of our questions about the proper use and interpretation of multiple regression will be answered with this heuristic aid. We will deal in some depth with the problem of valid versus invalid inferences of causality in these chapters. The problem of error ("the scourge of research") serves as our jumping off place for the transition from path analysis to methods that incorporate latent variables (confirmatory factor analysis and latent variable structural equation modeling). Confirmatory factor analysis (CFA) approaches more closely the constructs of primary interest in our research by separating measurement error from variation due to these constructs. Latent variable structural equation modeling (SEM) incorporates the advantages of path analysis with those of confirmatory factor analysis into a powerful and flexible analytic system that partially obviates many of the problems we discuss as the book progresses. We will discuss fairly sophisticated SEMs, and we also reiterate one more time the dangers of nonexperimental research in general and SEM in particular.

ACKNOWLEDGMENTS

This project could not have been completed without the help of many people. I began this book while I was at Alfred University, and I completed it at the University of Texas. I am grateful to both Universities for their support. Janet Van Brunt, Jennifer Phipps, and Teresa Reid were especially helpful with many of the multitude of details required in document preparation. I also owe a huge debt to the former and current students who "test drove" the manuscript in various forms. Students' questions and comments improved the book immeasurably! Jodene Fine, in particular, asked questions, spotted problems, and even drew some of the figures in the text. Matthew Reynolds graciously double-checked the SAS, LISREL, and Mplus examples in the Appendices.

I thank the hard-working editors and assistants at Allyn & Bacon for all of their assistance. I am especially grateful to Susan Hartman and Therese Felser for seeing this project to its completion. Robert Crutcher, University of Dayton; Dale Fuqua, Oklahoma State University; Betty Gridley, Ball State University; Mercedes Schneider, Ball State University; and Kusum Singh, Virginia Tech read earlier versions of text and provided excellent advice, encouragement, and feedback. The book is stronger as a result of their feedback. Laura Stapleton at the University of Texas was always gracious and helpful in answering questions and double-checking occasional details. I am especially grateful to Lee Wolfle. Lee read every page of an earlier version of this text and made comments on at least half of those pages. Lee, your suggestions, questions, comments, and knowledgeable asides were erudite, educational, entertaining; thank you! None of these individuals is responsible for any remaining deficiencies of the book, however.

Finally, a special thank you to my wife and sons. Davis, Scotty, and Willie, you are a constant source of joy and a great source of research ideas! Trisia provided advice, manuscript assistance, statistical assistance, examples, encouragement, and the occasional nudge, all as needed. Thank you, my love, I could not have done it without you!

PART I

MULTIPLE REGRESSION

CHAPTER ONE

■ ■ ■ ■ ■

INTRODUCTION AND SIMPLE (BIVARIATE) REGRESSION

This book is designed to provide a conceptually oriented introduction to multiple regression along with more complex methods that flow naturally from multiple regression: path analysis, confirmatory factor analysis, and structural equation modeling. In this introductory chapter, we begin with a discussion and example of simple, or bivariate, regression. For many readers, this will be a review, but, even then, the example and computer output should provide a transition to subsequent chapters and *multiple* regression. The chapter also reviews several other related concepts, and introduces several issues (prediction and explanation, causality) that we will return to repeatedly in this book. Finally, the chapter relates multiple regression (MR) to other approaches with which you may be more familiar, such as analysis of variance (ANOVA). I will demonstrate that ANOVA and regression are fundamentally the same process and that, in fact, regression subsumes ANOVA.

As I suggested in the Preface, we start this journey by jumping right into an example and explaining it as we go. In this introduction, I have assumed that you are fairly familiar with the topics of correlation and statistical significance testing and that you have some familiarity with statistical procedures such as the *t* test for comparing means and Analysis of Variance. If these concepts are not familiar to you a quick review is provided in Appendix E. This appendix reviews basic statistics, distributions, standard errors and confidence intervals, correlations, *t* tests, and ANOVA.

SIMPLE (BIVARIATE) REGRESSION

We start our adventure into the wonderful world of multiple regression with a review of simple, or bivariate, regression; that is, regression with only one influence (independent variable) and one outcome (dependent variable).[1] Pretend that you are the parent of an adolescent. As a parent, you are interested in the influences on adolescents' school performance: what's important and what's not? Homework is of particular interest, because you see your daughter Lisa struggle with it nightly and hear her complain about it daily. You keep up with the news, and you've noticed that in recent years both *Time* and *Newsweek* have published articles critical of homework (Begley, 1998; Ratnesar, 1999). So you wonder if homework is just busywork or is it a worthwhile learning experience? Enquiring minds want to know!

Example: Homework and Math Achievement

The Data.   Fortunately for you, your good friend is an 8th-grade math teacher, and you are a researcher; you have the means, motive, and opportunity to find the answer to your question. Without going into the levels of permission you'd need to collect such data, you devise a quick survey that you give to all 8th-graders. The key question on this survey is:

> Think about your math homework over the last month. Approximately how much time did you spend, per week, doing your math homework? Approximately _____ (fill in the blank) hours per week.

A month later, standardized achievement tests are administered; when they are available, you record the math achievement test score for each student. You now have a report of average amount of time spent on math homework and math achievement test scores for 100 8th-graders.

A portion of the data is shown in Figure 1.1. The complete data are on the Web site that accompanies this book, www.ablongman.com/keith1e, under Chapter 1, in several formats: as an SPSS System file (chap 1, ex 1, hmwk & ach.sav), as a Microsoft Excel file (chap 1, ex 1, hmwk & ach.xls), and as an ASCII, or plain text, file (chapter 1, example 1 data.txt). The values for time spent on Math Homework are in hours, ranging from zero for those who do no math homework to some upper value limited by the number of free hours in a week. The Math Achievement test scores have a national mean of 50 and a standard deviation of 10 (these are known as *T* scores, which have nothing to do with *t* tests).[2]

Let's turn to the analysis. Fortunately, you have good data analytic habits: you check basic descriptive data prior to doing the main, regression analysis. The frequencies and descriptive statistics for the Math Homework variable are shown in Figure 1.2. Reported Math Homework ranged from no time, or zero hours, reported by 19 students, to 10 hours per week. The range of values looks reasonable, with no excessively high or impossible values. For example, if someone had reported spending 40 hours per week on Math Homework, you might be a lit-

MATH HOMEWORK	MATH ACHIEVEMENT
2	54
0	53
4	53
0	56
2	59
0	30
1	49
0	54
3	37
0	49
4	55
7	50
3	45
1	44
1	60
0	36
3	53
0	22
1	56

(Data Continue)

**FIGURE 1.1   Portion of the Math Homework
and Achievement data. The complete data are on
the Web site under Chapter 1.**

tle suspicious and would check your original data to make sure you entered the data correctly
(e.g., you may have entered a "4" as a "40"). You might be a little surprised that the average
amount of time spent on Math Homework per week is only 2.2 hours, but this value is certainly
plausible. (As noted in the Preface, the regression and other results shown are portions of an
SPSS printout, but the information displayed is easily generalizable to that produced by other
statistical programs. Appendix B shows sample output from a variety of statistics programs.)

Next, turn to the descriptive statistics for the Math Achievement test (Figure 1.3).
Again, given that the national mean for this test is 50, the 8th-grade school mean of 51.41
is reasonable, as is the range of scores from 22 to 75. In contrast, if the descriptive statistics
had shown a high of, for example, 90 (four standard deviations above the mean), further
investigation would be called for. The data appear to be in good shape.

The Regression Analysis.   Next, you run the regression: you regress Math Achievement
scores on time spent on Homework (notice the structure of this statement: we regress the
outcome on the influence or influences). Figure 1.4 shows the means, standard deviations,
and the correlation between the two variables.

The descriptive statistics match those presented earlier, without the detail. The correlation between the two variables is .320, not large, but certainly statistically significant
($p < .01$) with this sample of 100 students. As you read articles that use multiple regression,
you may see this ordinary correlation coefficient referred to as a zero-order correlation
(which distinguishes it from first-, second-, or multiple-order partial correlations, to be discussed later in Appendix D).

MATHHOME Time Spent on Math Homework per Week

		Frequency	Percent	Valid Percent	Cumulative Percent
Valid	.00	19	19.0	19.0	19.0
	1.00	19	19.0	19.0	38.0
	2.00	25	25.0	25.0	63.0
	3.00	16	16.0	16.0	79.0
	4.00	11	11.0	11.0	90.0
	5.00	6	6.0	6.0	96.0
	6.00	2	2.0	2.0	98.0
	7.00	1	1.0	1.0	99.0
	10.00	1	1.0	1.0	100.0
	Total	100	100.0	100.0	

Statistics

MATHHOME Time Spent on Math Homework per Week

N	Valid	100
	Missing	0
Mean		2.2000
Median		2.0000
Mode		2.00
Std. deviation		1.8146
Variance		3.2929
Minimum		.00
Maximum		10.00
Sum		220.00

FIGURE 1.2   **Frequencies and descriptive statistics for Math Homework.**

Descriptive Statistics

	N	Range	Minimum	Maximum	Sum	Mean	Std. Deviation	Variance
MATHACH Math Achievement Test Score	100	53.00	22.00	75.00	5141.00	51.4100	11.2861	127.376
Valid N (listwise)	100							

FIGURE 1.3   **Descriptive statistics for Math Achievement test scores.**

Next, we turn to the regression itself; although we have conducted a simple regression, the computer output is in the form of multiple regression to allow a smooth transition. First, look at the model summary in Figure 1.5. It lists the R, which normally is used to designate the multiple correlation coefficient, but which, with one predictor, is the same as the simple Pearson correlation (.320).[3] Next is the R^2, which denotes the variance explained in the outcome variable by the predictor variables. Homework time explains, accounts for, or

Descriptive Statistics

	Mean	Std. Deviation	N
MATHACH Math Achievement Test Score	51.4100	11.2861	100
MATHHOME Time Spent on Math Homework per Week	2.2000	1.8146	100

Correlations

		MATHACH Math Achievement Test Score	MATHHOME Time Spent on Math Homework per Week
Pearson Correlation	MATHACH Math Achievement Test Score	1.000	.320
	MATHHOME Time Spent on Math Homework per Week	.320	1.000
Sig. (1-tailed)	MATHACH Math Achievement Test Score	.	.001
	MATHHOME Time Spent on Math Homework per Week	.001	.
N	MATHACH Math Achievement Test Score	100	100
	MATHHOME Time Spent on Math Homework per Week	100	100

FIGURE 1.4   Results of the regression of Math Achievement on Math Homework: descriptive statistics and correlation coefficients.

predicts .102 (proportion) or 10.2% of the variance in Math test scores. As you run this regression yourself, your output will probably show some additional statistics (e.g., the adjusted R^2); we will ignore these for the time being.

Is the regression, that is, the multiple R and R^2, statistically significant? We know it is, because we already noted the statistical significance of the zero-order correlation, and this "multiple" regression is actually a simple regression with only one predictor. But, again, we'll check the output for consistency with subsequent examples. Interestingly, we use an F test, as in ANOVA, to test the statistical significance of the regression equation:

$$F = \frac{ss_{\text{regression}}/df_{\text{regression}}}{ss_{\text{residual}}/df_{\text{residual}}}$$

Model Summary

Model	R	R Square
1	.320[a]	.102

a. Predictors: (Constant), MATHHOME Time
Spent on Math Homework per Week

ANOVA[b]

Model		Sum of Squares	df	Mean Square	F	Sig.
1	Regression	1291.231	1	1291.231	11.180	.001[a]
	Residual	11318.959	98	115.500		
	Total	12610.190	99			

a. Predictors: (Constant) MATHHOME Time Spent on Math Homework per Week

b. Dependent Variable: MATHACH Math Achievement Test Score

FIGURE 1.5   **Results of the regression of Math Achievement on Math Homework: statistical significance of the regression.**

The term $ss_{\text{regression}}$ stands for sums of squares regression and is a measure of the variation in the dependent variable that is explained by the independent variable(s); the ss_{residual} is the variance unexplained by the regression. The sums of squares for the regression versus the residual are shown in the ANOVA table. In regression, the degrees of freedom (df) for the regression are equal to the number of independent variables (k), and the df for the residual, or error, are equal to the sample size minus the number of independent variables in the equation minus 1 ($N - k - 1$); the df are also shown in the ANOVA table. We'll double-check the numbers:

$$F = \frac{1291.231/1}{11318.959/98}$$

$$= \frac{1291.231}{115.500}$$

$$= 11.179$$

which is the same value shown in the table, within errors of rounding. What is the probability of obtaining a value of F as large as 11.179, if these two variables were in fact unrelated in the population? According to the table (in the column labeled "Sig."), such an occurrence would occur only 1 time in 1000 ($p = .001$); it would seem logical that these two variables are indeed related. We can double-check this probability by referring to an F table under 1 and 98 df; is the value 11.179 greater than the tabled value? Instead, however, I suggest that you get a computer program to calculate these probabilities. Excel, for example, will find the probability for values of all the distributions discussed in this text. Simply put the calculated value of F (11.179) in one cell, the degrees of freedom for the regression (1) in the next, and the df for the residual in the next (98). Go to the next cell, then click on Insert, Function, and select the category of Statistical and scroll down until you find FDIST, for F distribution.

Click on it and point to the cells containing the required information. (Alternatively, you could go directly to Function and FDIST and simply type in these numbers.) Excel returns a value of .001172809, or .001, as shown in Figure 1.6. Although I present this method of determining probabilities as a way of double-checking the computer output at this point, at times your computer program will not display the probabilities you are interested in, and this method will be useful.[4]

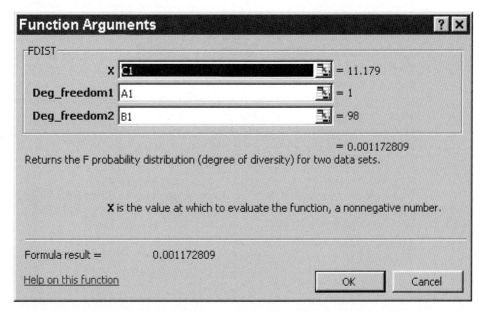

FIGURE 1.6   Using Excel to calculate probability: statistical significance of an F (1, 98) of 11.179.

There is another formula you can use to calculate F, an extension of which will come in handy later:

$$F = \frac{R^2/k}{(1 - R^2)/(N - k - 1)}$$

This formula compares the proportion of variance explained by the regression (R^2) with the proportion of variance left unexplained by the regression ($1 - R^2$). This formula may seem quite different from the one presented previously, until you remember that (1) k is equal to the df for the regression, and $N - k - 1$ is equal to the df for the residual, and (2) the sums of squares from the previous formula are also estimates of variance. Try this formula to make sure you get the same results (within rounding error).

I noted that the $ss_{regression}$ is a measure of the variance explained in the dependent variable by the independent variables, and also that R^2 denotes the variance explained. Given these descriptions, you may expect that the two concepts should be related. They are, and we can calculate the R^2 from the $ss_{regression}$: $R^2 = ss_{regression}/ss_{total}$. There is a certain amount of variance in the dependent variable, and the independent variables can explain a portion of this variance. The R^2 is a proportion of the total variance in the dependent variable that is explained by the independent variables. For the current example, the total variance in the dependent variable, Math Achievement (ss_{total}), was 12610.190 (Figure 1.5), and Math Homework explained 1291.231 of this variance. Thus,

$$R^2 = \frac{ss_{regression}}{ss_{total}} = \frac{1291.231}{12610.190} = .102$$

and Homework explains .102 or 10.2% of the variance in Math Achievement. Obviously, R^2 can vary between 0 and 1.

The Regression Equation.   Next, let's take a look at the coefficients for the regression equation, the notable parts of which are shown in Figure 1.7. The general formula for a regression equation is $Y = a + bX + e$, which, translated into English, says that a person's score on the dependent variable (in this case, Math Achievement) is a combination of a constant (a), plus a coefficient (b) times his or her value on the independent variable (Math Homework), plus error. Values for both a and b are shown in the second column (Unstandardized Coefficients, B). a is a constant, called the *intercept,* and its value is 47.032 for this homework–achievement example. *The intercept is the predicted score on the dependent variable for someone with a score of zero on the independent variable. b,* the unstandardized regression coefficient, is 1.990. Since we don't have a direct estimate of the error, we'll focus on a different form of the regression equation: $Y' = a + bX$, in which Y' is the *predicted* value of Y. The completed equation is $Y' = 47.032 + 1.990X$, meaning that to predict a person's Math Achievement score we can multiply his or her report of time spent on Math Homework by 1.990 and add 47.032.

Coefficients[a]

Model		Unstandardized Coefficients		Standardized Coefficients			95% Confidence Interval for B	
		B	Std. Error	Beta	t	Sig.	Lower Bound	Upper Bound
1	Intercept (Constant)	47.032	1.694		27.763	.000	43.670	50.393
	MATHHOME Time Spent on Math Homework per Week	1.990	.595	.320	3.344	.001	.809	3.171

a. Dependent Variable: MATHACH Math Achievement Test Score

FIGURE 1.7   Results of the regression of Math Achievement on Math Homework: regression coefficients.

Several questions may spring to mind after this last statement. Why, for example, would we want to *predict* a student's Achievement score (Y') when we already know the student's *real* Achievement score? The answer is that we want to use this formula to summarize the relation between homework and achievement for all students at the same time. We may also be able to use the formula for other purposes: to predict scores for another group of students or, to return to the original purpose, to predict Lisa's likely future math achievement, given her time spent on math homework. Or we may want to know what would likely happen if a student or group of students were to increase or decrease the time spent on math homework.

Interpretation.   But to get back to our original question, we now have some very useful information for Lisa, contained within the regression coefficient ($b = 1.99$), because this coefficient tells us the amount we can expect the outcome variable (Math Achievement) to change for each 1-unit change in the independent variable (Math Homework). Because the Homework variable is in hours spent per week, we can make this statement: "For each additional hour students spend on Mathematics Homework every week, they can expect to see close to a 2-point increase in Math Achievement test scores." Now, Achievement test scores are not that easy to change; it is much easier, for example, to improve grades than test scores (Keith et al., 1998), so this represents an important effect. Given the standard deviation of the test scores (10 points), a student should be able to improve his or her scores by a standard deviation by studying a little more than 5 extra hours a week; this could mean moving from average-level to high-average-level achievement. Of course, this proposition might be more interesting to a student who is currently spending very little time studying than to one who is already spending a lot of time working on math homework.

The Regression Line.   The regression equation may be used to graph the relation between Math Homework and Achievement, and this graph can also illustrate nicely the predictions made in the previous paragraph. The intercept (a) is the value on the Y (Achievement)-axis for a value of zero for X (Homework); in other words, the intercept is the value on the Achievement test we would expect for someone who does no homework. We can use the intercept as one data point for drawing the regression line ($X = 0$, $Y = 47.032$). The second data point is simply the point defined by the mean of X ($M_X = 2.200$) and the mean of Y ($M_Y = 51.410$). The graph, with these two data points highlighted, is shown in Figure 1.8. We can use the graph and data to check the calculation of the value of b, which is the *slope* of the regression line. The slope is equal to the increase in Y for each unit increase in X (or the rise of the line divided by the run); we can use the two data points plotted to calculate the slope:

$$b = \frac{\text{rise}}{\text{run}} = \frac{M_Y - a}{M_X - 0}$$

$$= \frac{51.410 - 47.032}{2.200}$$

$$= 1.990$$

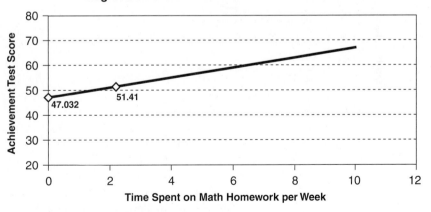

Regression of Math Achievement on Math Homework

FIGURE 1.8   Regression line for Math Achievement on Math Homework. The line is drawn through the intercept and the joint means of X and Y.

Let's consider for a few moments the graph and these formulas. The slope represents the predicted increase in Y for each unit increase in X. For this example, this means that for each unit—in this case, each hour—increase in Homework, Achievement scores increase, on average, 1.990 points. This, then, is the interpretation of an unstandardized coefficient: it is the predicted increase in Y expected for each unit increase in X. When the independent variable has a meaningful metric, like hours spent studying Mathematics every week, the interpretation of b is easy and straightforward. We can also generalize from this group-generated equation to individuals (to the extent that they are similar to the group that generated the regression equation). Thus the graph and b can be used to make predictions for others, such as Lisa. She can check her current level of homework time and see how much payoff she might expect for additional time (or how much she can expect to lose if she studies less). The intercept is also worth noting; it shows that the average Achievement test score for students who do no studying is 47.032, slightly below the national average.

Because we are using a modern statistical package, there is no need to draw the plot of the regression line ourselves; any such program will do it for us. Figure 1.9 shows the data points and regression line drawn using SPSS (using the Scatterplot command; see Appendix B for examples). The small circles in this figure are the actual data points; notice how variable they are. If the R were larger, the data points would cluster more closely around the regression line. We will return to this topic in a subsequent chapter.

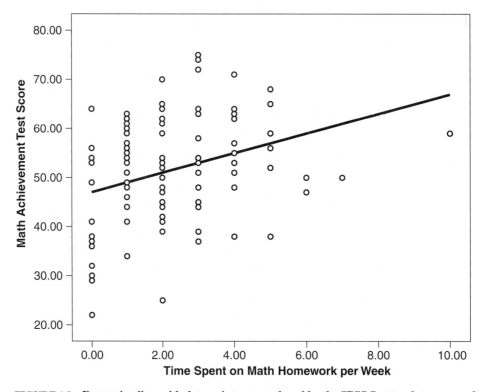

FIGURE 1.9   Regression line, with data points, as produced by the SPSS Scatterplot command.

Statistical Significance of Regression Coefficients.   There are a few more details to study for this regression analysis before stepping back and further considering the meaning of the results. With *multiple* regression, we will also be interested in whether each regression coefficient is statistically significant. Return to the table of regression coefficients (Figure 1.7), and note the columns labeled *t* and Sig. The values corresponding to the regression coefficient are simply the results of a *t* test of the statistical significance of the regression coefficient (*b*). The formula for *t* is one of the most ubiquitous in statistics (Kerlinger, 1986):

$$t = \frac{\text{statistic}}{\text{standard error of the statistic}}$$

or, in this case,

$$t = \frac{b}{SE_b} = \frac{1.990}{.595} = 3.345$$

As shown in the table, the value of *t* is 3.344, with $N - k - 1$ degrees of freedom (98). If we look up this value in Excel (using the function TDIST), we find the probability of obtaining such a *t* by chance is .001171 (a two-tailed test) rounded off to .001 (the value shown in the table). We can reject the null hypothesis that the slope of the regression line is zero. As a general rule of thumb, with a reasonable sample size (say 100 or more), a *t* of 2 or greater will be statistically significant with a probability level of .05 and a two-tailed (nondirectional) test.

This finding of the statistical significance of the regression coefficient for Homework does not tell us anything new with our simple regression; the results are the same as for the *F* test of the overall regression. You probably recall from previous statistics classes that $t^2 = F$; here t^2 indeed does equal *F* (as always, within errors of rounding). When we progress to multiple regression, however, this will not be the case. The overall regression may be significant, but the regression coefficients for some of the independent variables may not be statistically significant, whereas others are significant.

Confidence Intervals.   We calculated the *t* above by dividing the regression coefficient by its standard error. The standard error and the *t* have other uses, however. In particular, we can use the standard error to estimate a confidence interval around the regression coefficient. Keep in mind that *b* is an estimate, but what we are really interested in is the true value of the regression coefficient (or slope, or *b*) in the population. The use of confidence intervals makes this underlying thinking more obvious. The 95% confidence interval is also shown in Figure 1.7 (.809 to 3.171) and may be interpreted as "there is a 95% chance that the *true* (but unknown) regression coefficient is somewhere within the range .809 to 3.171" or, perhaps more accurately, "if we were to conduct this study 100 times, 95 times out of 100 the *b* would be within the range .809 to 3.171. The fact that this range does not include zero is equivalent to the finding that the *b* is statistically significant; if the range did include zero, our conclusion would be that we could not say with confidence that the coefficient was different from zero (see Thompson, 2002, for further information about confidence intervals).

Although the *t* tells us that the regression coefficient is statistically significantly different from zero, the confidence interval can be used to test whether the regression coefficient is different from any specified value. Suppose, for example, that previous research had shown a regression coefficient of 3.0 for the regression of Math Achievement on Math Homework for high school students, meaning that for each hour of Homework completed, their Achievement increased by 3 points. We might reasonably ask whether our finding for 8th-graders is inconsistent; the fact that our 95% confidence interval includes the value of 3.0 means that our results are *not* statistically significantly different from the high school results.

We also can calculate intervals for any level of confidence. Suppose we are interested in the 99% confidence interval. Conceptually, we are forming a normal curve of possible b's, with our calculated b as the mean. Envision the 99% confidence interval as including 99% of the area under the normal curve so that only the two very ends of the curve are not included. To calculate the 99% confidence interval, you will need to figure out the numbers associated with this area under the normal curve; we do so by using the standard error of b and the t table. Return to Excel (or a t table) and find the t associated with the 99% confidence interval. To do so, use the inverse of the normal t calculator, which will be shown when you select TINV as the function in Excel. This will allow us to type in the degrees of freedom (98) and the probability level in which we are interested (.01, or $1 - .99$). As shown in Figure 1.10, the t value associated with this probability is 2.627, which we multiply times the standard error ($.595 \times 2.627 = 1.563$). We then add and subtract this product from the b to find the 99% confidence interval: $1.990 \pm 1.563 = .427 - 3.553$. There is a 99% chance that the true value of b is within the range of .427 to 3.553. This range does not include a value of zero, so we know that the b is statistically significant at this level ($p < .01$) as well; and we can determine whether our calculated b is different from values other than zero, as well. (It is also possible to use the NCSS Probability Calculator to obtain this value.)

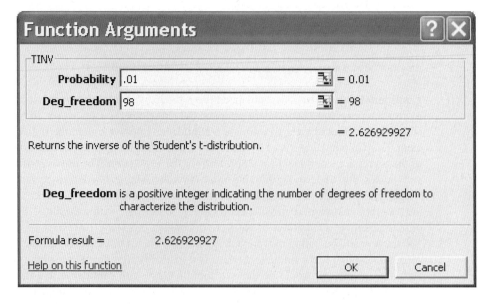

FIGURE 1.10   Using Excel to calculate a t value for a given probability level and degrees of freedom.

To review, we calculated the confidence intervals as follows:

1. Pick a level of confidence (e.g., 99%).
2. Convert to a probability (.99) and subtract that probability from 1 ($1 - .99 = .01$).
3. Look up this value with the proper degrees of freedom in the (inverse) t calculator or a t table. (Note that these directions are for a two-tailed test.) This is the value of t associated with the probability of interest.
4. Multiply this t value times the standard error of b, and add and subtract the product from the b. This is the confidence interval around the regression coefficient.

The Standardized Regression Coefficient.   We skipped over one portion of the regression printout shown in Figure 1.7, the standardized regression coefficient, or Beta (β). Recall that the unstandardized coefficient is interpreted as the change in the outcome for each unit change in the influence. In the present example, the b of 1.990 means that for each 1-hour change in Homework, predicted Achievement goes up by 1.990 points. The β is interpreted in a similar fashion, but the interpretation is in *standard deviation* (*SD*) units. The β for the present example (.320) means that for each SD increase in Homework, Achievement will, on average, increase by .320 standard deviation, or about a third of a SD. The β is same as the b with the independent and dependent variables standardized (converted to z scores).

It is simple to convert from b to β, or the reverse, by taking into account the SDs of each variable. The basic formula is

$$\beta = b \frac{SD_x}{SD_y} \qquad \text{or} \qquad b = \beta \frac{SD_y}{SD_x}$$

So, using the data from Figures 1.4 and 1.7,

$$\beta = 1.990 \frac{1.815}{11.286} = .320$$

Note that the standardized regression coefficient is the same as the correlation coefficient. This is the case with simple regression, with only one predictor, but will *not* be the case when we have multiple predictors (it does, however, illustrate that a correlation coefficient is also a type of *standardized* coefficient).

With a choice of standardized or unstandardized coefficients, which should you interpret? This is, in fact, a point of debate (cf., Kenny, 1979, chap. 13; Pedhazur, 1997, chap. 2), but my position is simply that both are useful at different times. We will postpone until later a discussion of the advantages of each and the rules of thumb for when to interpret each. In the meantime, simply remember that it is easy to convert from one to the other.

REGRESSION IN PERSPECTIVE

Relation of Regression to Other Statistical Methods

How do the methods discussed above and throughout this book fit with other methods with which you are familiar? Many users of this text will have a background with analytic methods, such as t tests and analysis of variance (ANOVA). It is tempting to think of these methods as doing something fundamentally different from regression. After all, ANOVA focuses on differences across groups, whereas regression focuses on the prediction of one variable from others. As you will learn here, however, the processes are fundamentally the same and, in fact, ANOVA and related methods are subsumed under multiple regression and can be considered special cases of multiple regression (Cohen, 1968). Thinking about multiple regression may indeed require a change in your *thinking,* but the actual statistical processes are the same.

Let's demonstrate that equivalence in two ways. First, most modern textbooks on ANOVA teach or at least discuss ANOVA as a part of the *general linear model.* Remember formulas along the lines of $Y = \mu + \beta + e$, which may be stated verbally as any person's score on the dependent variable Y is the sum of the overall mean μ, plus variation due to the effect of the experimental treatment (β), plus (or minus) random variation due to the effect of error (e).

Now consider a simple regression equation: $Y = a + bX + e$, which may be verbalized as any person's score on the dependent variable is the sum of a constant that is the same for all individuals (a), plus the variation due to the independent variable (X), plus (or minus) random variation due to the effect of error (e). As you can see, these are basically the same formulas with the same basic interpretation. The reason is that ANOVA is a part of the general linear model; multiple regression is virtually a direct implementation of the general linear model.

Second, consider several pieces of computer printout. The first printout, shown in Figure 1.11, shows the results of a *t* test examining whether boys or girls in the National Education Longitudinal Study (NELS) data score higher on the 8th-grade Social Studies Test (Appendix A provides more information about the NELS data). In other words, for this analysis, Sex is the independent variable, and the Social Studies Test score is the dependent variable. The results suggest no statistically significant differences between boys and girls: the *t* value was .689, and the probability that this magnitude of difference would happen by chance (given no difference in the population) was .491, which means that this difference is not at all unusual. If we use a conventional cutoff that the probability must be less than .05 to be considered statistically significant, this value (.491) is obviously greater than .05 and thus would not be considered statistically significant. For now, focus on this value (the probability level, labeled Sig.) in the printout.

Independent Samples Test

	t-test for Equality of Means		
	t	df	Sig. (2-tailed)
Social Studies Standardized Score	.689	959	.491

FIGURE 1.11   Results of a *t* test of the effects of sex on 8th-grade students' social studies achievement test scores.

The next snippet of printout (Figure 1.12) shows the results of a one-way analysis of variance. Again, focus on the column labeled Sig. The value is the same as for the *t* test; the results are equivalent. You probably aren't surprised by this finding, because you remember that with two groups a *t* test and an ANOVA will produce the same results and that, in fact, $F = t^2$. (Check the printouts; does $F = t^2$ within errors of rounding?)

ANOVA Table

			Sum of Squares	df	Mean Square	F	Sig.
Social Studies Standardized Score	Between Groups	(Combined)	44.634	1	44.634	.474	.491
	Within Groups		90265.31	959	94.124		
	Total		90309.95	960			

FIGURE 1.12   **Analysis of variance results of the effects of sex on 8th-grade students' social studies achievement test scores.**

Now, focus on the third snippet in Figure 1.13. This printout shows some of the results of a *regression* of the 8th-grade Social Studies Test score on student Sex. Or, stated differently, this printout shows the results of using Sex to predict 8th-grade Social Studies scores. Look at the Sig. column. The probability is the same as for the *t* test and the ANOVA: .491! (And check out the *t* associated with Sex.) All three analyses produce the same results and the same answers. The bottom line is this: the *t* test, ANOVA, and regression tell you the same thing.

Regression[a]

Model		Unstandardized Coefficients		Standardized Coefficients		
		B	Std. Error	Beta	t	Sig.
1	SEX	.431	.626	.022	.689	.491

a. Dependent Variable: Social Studies Standardized Score

FIGURE 1.13   **Results of the regression of 8th-grade students' social studies achievement test scores on sex.**

Another way of saying this is that multiple regression subsumes ANOVA, which subsumes a *t* test. And, in turn, multiple regression is subsumed under the method of structural equation modeling, the focus of the second half of this book. Or, if you prefer a pictorial representation, look at Figure 1.14. The figure could include other methods, and portions could be arranged differently, but for our present purposes the lesson is that these seemingly different methods are, in fact, all related.

In my experience, students schooled in ANOVA are reluctant to make the switch to multiple regression. And not just students; I could cite numerous examples of research by well-known researchers in which ANOVA was used to perform an analysis that would have been better conducted through multiple regression. Given the example above, this may seem reasonable; after all, they do the same thing, right? No. Regression subsumes ANOVA, is more general than ANOVA, and has certain advantages. We will discuss these advantages briefly, but will return to them as this book progresses.

Explaining Variance

The primary task of science, simply put, is to explain phenomena. In the social sciences, we ask such questions as "Why do some children do well in school, while others do poorly?" or "Which aspects of psychological consultation produce positive change?" We wish to explain the phenomena of school performance or consultation outcome. At another level, however, we are talking about explaining *variation: variation* in school performance, such

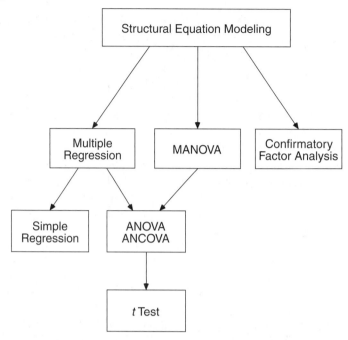

FIGURE 1.14   Relations among several statistical techniques. ANOVA may be considered a subset of multiple regression; multiple regression, in turn, may be considered a subset of structural equation modeling.

that some children perform well, while others do not, and *variation* in consultation outcome, with some consultees solving their presenting problem and learning a great deal versus those who make little progress.

And how do we seek to explain this variation? Through variation in *other* variables. We may reason that children who are more motivated will perform better in school, whereas those who are less motivated will not. In this case, we seek to explain *variation* in school performance through *variation* in motivation. In the consultation example, we may reason that consultants who go through the proper sequence of steps in the identification of the problem will be more successful in producing positive change than consultants who simply "wing it." Here we have posited *variation* in consultation implementation as explaining *variation* in consultation outcome.

Advantages of Multiple Regression

Our statistical procedures implement this explanation of variation in one variable via variation in another. In ANOVA, we seek to explain the variation in an outcome, or dependent, variable (e.g., consultation success) through variation in some treatment, or independent variable (e.g., training versus no training of consultants in problem identification). We do the same using regression; we may, for example, regress a measure of school performance (e.g., achievement test scores from high to low), our dependent variable, on a measure of academic motivation (with scores from high to low), our independent variable. One advantage of multiple regression over methods such as ANOVA is that we can use either categorical independent variables (as in the consultation example), or continuous variables (as in the motivation example), or both. ANOVA, of course, requires categorical independent variables. It is not unusual to see research in which a continuous variable has been turned into categories (e.g., a high-motivation group versus a low-motivation group) so that the researcher can use ANOVA in the analysis rather than regression. Such categorization is generally wasteful, however; it discards variance in the independent variable and leads to a weaker statistical test (Cohen, 1983).[5]

But why study only one possible influence on school performance? No doubt many plausible variables can help to explain variation in school performance, such as students' aptitude, the quality of instruction they receive, or the amount of instruction (cf. Carroll, 1963; Walberg, 1981). What about variation in these variables? This is where the *multiple* in multiple regression comes in; with MR we can use multiple independent variables to explain variation in a dependent variable. In the language of MR, we can regress a dependent variable on multiple independent variables; we can regress school performance on measures of motivation, aptitude, quality of instruction, and quantity of instruction, all at the same time. Here is another advantage of MR: It easily incorporates these four independent variables; an ANOVA with four independent variables would tax even a gifted researcher's interpretive abilities.

A final advantage of MR revolves around the nature of the research design. ANOVA is often more appropriate for *experimental* research, that is, research in which there is active manipulation of the independent variable and, preferably, random assignment of subjects to treatment groups. Multiple regression can be used for the analysis of such research (although ANOVA is often easier), but it can also be used for the analysis of *nonexperimental* research, in which the "independent" variables are not assigned at random or even manipulated in any way. Think about the motivation example again; *could* you assign students, at random, to different levels of motivation? No. Or perhaps you could try, but you would be deluding yourself by saying to normally unmotivated Johnny, "OK, Johnny, I want you to be highly motivated today." In fact, in this example, motivation was not manipulated at all; instead, we simply measured existing levels of motivation from high to low. This, then, was nonexperimental research. Multiple regression is almost always more appropriate for the analysis of nonexperimental research than is ANOVA.

We have touched on three advantages of multiple regression over ANOVA:

1. MR can use both categorical and continuous independent variables,
2. MR can easily incorporate multiple independent variables;
3. MR is appropriate for the analysis of experimental or nonexperimental research.

OTHER ISSUES

Prediction versus Explanation

Observant readers will notice that I use the term *explanation* in connection with MR (e.g., explaining variation in achievement through variation in motivation), whereas much of your previous experience with MR may have used the term *prediction* (e.g., using motivation to predict achievement). What's the difference?

Briefly, explanation subsumes prediction. If you can *explain* a phenomenon, you can predict it. On the other hand, prediction, although a worthy goal, does not necessitate explanation. As a general rule, we will here be more interested in explaining phenomena than in predicting them.

Causality

Observant readers may also be feeling queasy by now. After all, isn't another name for non-experimental research *correlational* research?[6] And when we make such statements as "motivation helps explain school performance," isn't this another way of saying that motivation is one possible *cause* of school performance? If so (and the answers to both questions are yes), how can I justify what I recommend, given the one lesson that everyone remembers from his or her first statistics class, the admonition "Don't infer causality from correlations!"? Aren't I now implying that you should break a cardinal rule of statistics?

Before I answer, I'd like you to take a little quiz. Are these statements true or false?

1. It is improper to infer causality from correlational data.
2. It is inappropriate to infer causality unless there has been active manipulation of the independent variable.

Despite the doubts I may have planted, you are probably tempted to answer these statements as true. Now try these:

3. Smoking increases the likelihood of lung cancer in humans.
4. Parental divorce affects children's subsequent achievement and behavior.
5. Personality characteristics affect life success.
6. Gravity keeps the moon in orbit around Earth.

I assume that you answered "true" or "probably true" for these statements. But if you did, your answers are inconsistent with answers of true to statements 1 and 2! Each of these is a causal statement. Another way of stating statement 5, for example, is "Personality characteristics partially cause life success." And each of these statements is based on observational or correlational data! I, for one, am not aware of any experiments in which Earth's gravity has been manipulated to see what happens to the orbit of the moon![7]

Now, try this final statement:

7. Research in sociology, economics, and political science is intellectually bankrupt.

I am confident that you should and did answer "false" to this statement. But if you did, this answer is again inconsistent with an answer of true to statements 1 and 2. True experiments are relatively rare in these social sciences; nonexperimental research is far more common.

The bottom line of this little quiz is this: We can and do make causal inferences from "correlational" (nonexperimental) data. Under certain conditions, we can make such inferences validly and with scientific respectability. In other cases, such inferences are invalid and misleading. What we need to understand, then, is *when* such causal inferences are valid and when they are invalid. We will return to this topic later; in the meantime, you should mull over the notion of causal inference. Why, for example, do we feel comfortable making a causal inference when a true experiment has been conducted, but may not feel so in non-experimental research? These two issues—prediction versus explanation and causality—are ones that we will return to throughout this text.

REVIEW OF SOME BASICS

Before turning to multiple regression in earnest, it is worth reviewing several fundamentals, things you probably know, but may need reminders about. The reason for this quick review may not be immediately obvious; but if you store these tidbits away, you'll find that occasionally they will come in handy as you learn a new concept.

Variance and Standard Deviation

First is the relation between a *variance* and a *standard deviation;* the standard deviation is the square root of the variance ($SD = \sqrt{V}$ or $V = SD^2$). Why use both? Standard deviations are in the same units as the original variables; we thus often find it easier to use SDs. Variances, on the other hand, are often easier to use in formulas and, although I've already promised that this book will use a minimum of formulas, some will be necessary. If nothing else, you can use this tidbit for an alternative formula for the standardized regression coefficient: $\beta = b \sqrt{V_x/V_y}$.

Correlation and Covariance

Next is a *covariance.* Conceptually, the variance is the degree to which one variable *varies* around its mean. A covariance involves two variables and gets at the degree to which the two variables vary *together.* When the two variables vary from the mean, do they tend to vary together or independently? A correlation coefficient is a special type of covariance; it is, in essence, a standardized covariance, and we can think of a covariance as an unstandardized correlation coefficient. As a formula,

$$r_{xy} = \frac{CoV_{xy}}{\sqrt{V_x V_y}} = \frac{CoV_{xy}}{SD_x SD_y}$$

Just as with standardized and unstandardized regression coefficients, if we know the standard deviations (or variances) of the variables, we can easily convert from covariances (unstandardized) to correlations (standardized) and back. Conceptually, you can think of a correlation as a covariance, but one in which the variance of X and Y are standardized. Suppose, for example, you were to convert X and Y to z scores ($M = 0$, $SD = 1$) prior to calculating the covariance. Since a z score has a SD of 1, our formula for converting from a covariance to a correlation then becomes

$$r_{xy} = \frac{CoV_{z_x z_y}}{1 \times 1} = CoV_{z_x z_y}$$

when the variables are standardized.

In your reading about multiple regression, and especially about structural equation modeling, you are likely to encounter variance–covariance matrices and correlation matrices. Just remember that if you know the standard deviations (or variances) you can easily convert from one to another. Table 1.1 shows an example of a covariance matrix and the corresponding correlation matrix and standard deviations. As is common in such presentations, the diagonal in the covariance matrix includes the variances.

WORKING WITH EXTANT DATA SETS

The data used for our initial regression example were not real, but were simulated (using the program DataSim; Bradley, 1988). The data were modeled after data from the National Education Longitudinal Study (NELS), a portion of which is on the Web site (www .ablongman.com/keith1e) that accompanies this book.

Already existing, or extant, data offer an amazing resource. For our simulated study, we pretended to have 100 cases from one school. With the NELS data included here, you have access to 1000 cases from schools across the nation. With the full NELS data set, the sample size is over 24,000, and the data are nationally representative. The students who were first surveyed in 8th grade were followed up in 10th and 12th grades and then twice since high school. If the researchers or organization that collected the data asked the questions you are interested in, then why reinvent the wheel only to get a small, local sample?

TABLE 1.1   Example of a Covariance Matrix and the Corresponding Correlation Matrix.

SAMPLE COVARIANCES

	Matrix	*Block*	*Similarities*	*Vocabulary*
Matrix	118.71			
Block	73.41	114.39		
Similarities	68.75	62.92	114.39	
Vocabulary	73.74	64.08	93.75	123.10

SAMPLE CORRELATIONS

	Matrix	*Block*	*Similarities*	*Vocabulary*
Matrix	1.00			
Block	0.63	1.00		
Similarities	0.59	0.55	1.00	
Vocabulary	0.61	0.54	0.79	1.00
Standard Deviations	10.90	10.70	10.70	11.10

For the covariance matrix, the variances are shown in the diagonal (thus it is a variance–covariance matrix); the standard deviations are shown below the correlation matrix.

The potential drawback, of course, is that the researchers who initially collected the data may not have asked the questions in which you are interested or did not ask them in the best possible manner. As a user of extant data, you have no control over the questions and how they were asked. On the other hand, if questions of interest were asked, you have no need to go collect additional data.

Another potential problem of interest is less obvious. Each such data set is set up differently and may be set up in a way that seems strange to you. Extant data are of variable quality; although the NELS data are very clean, other data sets may be quite messy and using them can be a real challenge. At the beginning of this chapter I mentioned good data analysis habits; such habits are *especially* important when using existing data.

An example will illustrate. Figure 1.15 shows the frequency of one of the NELS variables dealing with Homework. It is a 10th-grade item (the F1 prefix to the variable stands for first follow-up; the S means the question was asked of students) concerning time spent on math homework. Superficially, it was similar to our pretend Homework variable. But note that the NELS variable is not in hour units, but rather in blocks of hours. Thus, if we regress 10th-grade Achievement scores on this variable, we cannot interpret the resulting b as meaning "for each additional hour of Homework. . . ." Instead, we can only say something about each additional unit of Homework, with "unit" only vaguely defined. More importantly, notice that one of the response options was "Not taking math class," which was assigned a value of 8. If we analyze this variable without dealing with this value

F1S36B2 TIME SPENT ON MATH HOMEWORK OUT OF SCHL

		Frequency	Percent	Valid Percent	Cumulative Percent
Valid	0 NONE	141	14.1	14.9	14.9
	1 1 HOUR OR LESS	451	45.1	47.7	62.6
	2 2-3 HOURS	191	19.1	20.2	82.8
	3 4-6 HOURS	97	9.7	10.3	93.0
	4 7-9 HOURS	16	1.6	1.7	94.7
	5 10-12 HOURS	8	.8	.8	95.6
	6 13-15 HOURS	2	.2	.2	95.8
	7 OVER 15 HOURS	6	.6	.6	96.4
	8 NOT TAKING MATH	34	3.4	3.6	100.0
	Total	946	94.6	100.0	
Missing	96 MULTIPLE RESPONSE	8	.8		
	98 MISSING	19	1.9		
	System	27	2.7		
	Total	54	5.4		
Total		1000	100.0		

FIGURE 1.15   Time spent on Math Homework from the first follow-up (10th grade) of the NELS data. Notice the value of 8 for the choice "Not taking math class." This value would need to be classified as missing prior to statistical analysis.

(e.g., recoding 8 to be a missing value), our interpretation will be incorrect. When working with extant data, you should *always* look at summary statistics prior to analysis: frequencies for variables that have a limited number of values (e.g., time on Homework) and descriptive statistics for those with many values (e.g., Achievement test scores). Look for impossible or out of range values, for values that need to be flagged as missing, and for items that should be reversed. Make the necessary changes and recordings, and then look at the summary statistics for the new or recoded variables. Depending on the software you use, you may also need to change the value labels to be consistent with your recoding. Only after you are sure that the variables are in proper shape should you proceed to your analyses of interest.

Some of the variables in the NELS file on the accompanying Web site have already been cleaned up; if you examine the frequencies of the variable just discussed, for example, you find that the response "Not taking math class" has already been recoded as missing. But many other variables have not been similarly cleaned. The message remains: always check and make sure you understand your variables before analysis.

SUMMARY

Many newcomers to multiple regression are tempted to think that this approach does something fundamentally different from other techniques, such as analysis of variance. As we have shown in this chapter, the two methods are in fact both part of the general linear model. In fact, multiple regression is a close implementation of the general linear model and subsumes methods such as ANOVA and simple regression. Readers familiar with ANOVA may need to change their thinking to understand MR, but the methods are fundamentally the same.

Given this overlap, are the two methods interchangeable? No. Because MR subsumes ANOVA, MR may be used to analyze data appropriate for ANOVA, but ANOVA is not appropriate for analyzing all problems for which MR is appropriate. In fact, there are a number of advantages to multiple regression:

1. MR can use both categorical and continuous independent variables.
2. MR can easily incorporate multiple independent variables.
3. MR is appropriate for the analysis of experimental or nonexperimental research.

We will primarily be interested in using multiple regression for explanatory, rather than predictive, purposes. Thus, it will be necessary to make causal inferences, often from nonexperimental data. These are two issues that we will revisit often in subsequent chapters, in order to distinguish between prediction and explanation and to ensure that we make such inferences validly.

This chapter reviewed simple regression with two variables as a prelude to multiple regression. Our example regressed Math Achievement on Math Homework using simulated data. Using portions of a printout from a common statistical package, we found that Math Homework explained approximately 10% of the variance in Math Achievement, which is statistically significant. The regression equation was Achievement$_{(predicted)}$ = 47.032 + 1.990Homework, which suggests that, for each hour increase in time spent on Math Homework, Math Achievement should increase by close to 2 points. There is a 95% chance that the "true" regression coefficient is within the range from .809 to 3.171; such confidence intervals may be used to test both whether a regression coefficient differs significantly from zero (a standard test of statistical significance) and whether it differs from other values, such as those found in previous research.

Finally, we reviewed the relation between variances and standard deviations ($V = SD^2$) and between correlations and covariances (correlations are *standardized* covariances). Since many of our examples will use an existing data set, NELS, a portion of which is included on the Web site that accompanies this book, we discussed the proper use of existing, or extant, data. I noted that good data analytic habits, such as always examining the variables we use prior to complex analysis, are especially important when using extant data.

EXERCISES

Think about the following questions. Answer them, however tentatively. As you progress in your reading of this book, revisit these questions on occasion; have your answers changed?

1. Why does MR subsume ANOVA? What does that mean?

2. What's the difference between explanation and prediction? Give a research example of each. Does explanation really subsume prediction?

3. Why do we have the admonition about inferring causality from correlations? What is wrong with making such inferences? Why do we feel comfortable making causal inferences from experimental data, but not from nonexperimental data?

4. Conduct the regression analysis used as an example in this chapter (again, the data are found on the Web site under Chapter 1). Do your results match mine? Make sure you understand how to interpret each aspect of your printout.

5. Using the NELS data, regress 8th-grade Math Achievement (BYTXMSTD) on time spent on Math Homework (BYS79a). How do your results compare with those from the example used in this chapter? Which aspects of the results *can* be compared? Interpret your findings: What do they mean?

NOTES

1. Although I here use the terms *independent* and *dependent* variables to provide a bridge between regression and other methods, the term *independent variable* is probably more appropriate for experimental research. Thus, throughout this book I will often use the term *influence* or *predictor* instead of independent variable. Likewise, I will often use the term *outcome* to carry the same meaning as dependent variable.

2. Throughout this text I will capitalize the names of variables, but will not capitalize the constructs that these variables are meant to represent. Thus, Achievement means the variable achievement, which we hope comes close to achievement, meaning the progress that students make in academic subjects in school.

3. With a single predictor, the value of R will equal that of r, with the exception that r can be negative, whereas R cannot. If r were $-.320$, for example, R would equal .320.

4. Another possibility besides Excel is a free, complete, and easy to use probability calculator available from Number Cruncher Statistical Software (www.ncss.com); you can download the program, unzip it, and use it free of charge. The probability calculator can be used to check many different distributions, not just the F distribution.

5. You can, however, analyze both categorical and continuous variables in analysis of covariance, a topic for a subsequent chapter.

6. I encourage you to use the term *nonexperimental* rather than *correlational*. The term *correlational research* confuses a statistical method (correlations) with a type of research (research in which there is no manipulation of the independent variable). Using correlational research to describe nonexperimental research would be like calling experimental research ANOVA research.

7. Likewise, researchers have not randomly assigned children to divorced versus intact families to see what happens to their subsequent achievement and behavior, nor has anyone assigned personality characteristics at random to see what happens as a result. The smoking example is a little trickier. Certainly, *animals* have been assigned to smoking versus nonsmoking conditions, but I am confident that humans have not. These examples also illustrate that when we make such statements we do not mean that X is the one and only cause of Y. Smoking is not the only cause of lung cancer, nor is it the case that everyone who smokes will develop lung cancer. Thus, you should understand that *causality* has a probabilistic meaning. If you smoke, you will increase your probability of developing lung cancer.

MULTIPLE REGRESSION: INTRODUCTION

Let's return to the example that was used in Chapter 1, in which we were curious about the effect on math achievement of time spent on math homework. Given our finding of a significant effect, you might reasonably have a chat with your daughter about the influence of homework on achievement. You might say something like "Lisa, these data show that spending time on math homework is indeed important. In fact, they show that, for each additional hour you spend on math homework every week, your achievement test scores should go up by approximately 2 points. And that's not just grades, but *test scores*, which are more difficult to change. So, you say you are now spending approximately 2 hours a week on math homework. If you spent an additional 2 hours per week, your achievement test scores should increase by about 4 points; that's a pretty big improvement!"[1]

Now, if Lisa is anything like my children, she will be thoroughly unimpressed with any argument you, her mere parent, might make, even when you have hard data to back you up. Or perhaps she's more sophisticated. Perhaps she'll point out potential flaws in your reasoning and analyses. She might say that she cares not one whit whether homework affects achievement test scores; she's only interested in grades. Or perhaps she'll point to other variables you should have taken into account. She might say, "What about the parents? Some of the kids in my school have very well educated parents, and those are usually the kids who do well on tests. I'll bet they are also the kids who study more, because their parents think it's important. You need to take the parents' education into account." Your daughter has in essence suggested that you have chosen the wrong outcome variable and have neglected what we will come to know as a "common cause" of your independent and dependent variables. You suspect she's right.

A NEW EXAMPLE: REGRESSING GRADES ON HOMEWORK AND PARENT EDUCATION

Back to the drawing board. Let's take this example a little further and pretend that you devise a new study to address your daughter's criticisms. This time you collect information on the following:

1. Eighth-grade students' overall Grade-point average in all subjects (standard 100-point scale).
2. The level of Education of the students' parents, in years of schooling (i.e., a high school graduate would have a score of 12, a college graduate a score of 16). Although you collect data for both parents, you use the data for the parent with the higher level of education. For students who live with only one parent, you use the years of schooling for the parent the student lives with.
3. Average time spent on Homework per week, in hours, across all subjects.

The data are in three files on the Web site (www.ablongman.com/keith1e), under Chapter 2: chap2, hw grades.sav (SPSS file), chap2, hw grades.xls (Excel file), and chap2, hw grades data.txt (DOS text file). As in the previous chapter, the data are simulated.

The Data

Let's look at the data. The summary statistics and frequencies for the Parent Education variable are shown in Figure 2.1. As shown, parents' highest level of education ranged from 10th grade to 20 years, indicating a parent with a doctorate; the average level of education was approximately 2 years beyond high school (14.03 years). As shown in Figure 2.2, students reported spending, on average, about 5 hours (5.09 hours) on homework per week, with four students reporting spending 1 hour per week and one reporting 11 hours per week. The frequencies and summary statistics look reasonable. The summary statistics for students' GPAs are also shown in Figure 2.2. The average GPA was 80.47, a B minus. GPAs ranged from 64 to 100; again, the values look reasonable.

The Regression

Next we regress students' GPA on Parent Education and Homework. Both of the explanatory variables (Homework and Parent Education) were entered into the regression equation at the same time, in what we will call a *simultaneous* regression. Figure 2.3 shows the intercorrelations among the three variables. Note that the correlation between Homework and Grades (.327) is only slightly higher than was the correlation between Math Homework and Achievement in Chapter 1. Parent Education, however, is correlated with both time spent on

Statistics

PARED Parents' Education (highest)

N	Valid	100
	Missing	0
Mean		14.0300
Median		14.0000
Mode		13.00
Std. Deviation		1.9304
Variance		3.7264
Minimum		10.00
Maximum		20.00

PARED Parents' Education (highest)

		Frequency	Percent	Valid Percent	Cumulative Percent
Valid	10.00	4	4.0	4.0	4.0
	11.00	3	3.0	3.0	7.0
	12.00	13	13.0	13.0	20.0
	13.00	23	23.0	23.0	43.0
	14.00	19	19.0	19.0	62.0
	15.00	15	15.0	15.0	77.0
	16.00	12	12.0	12.0	89.0
	17.00	8	8.0	8.0	97.0
	18.00	2	2.0	2.0	99.0
	20.00	1	1.0	1.0	100.0
	Total	100	100.0	100.0	

FIGURE 2.1   Descriptive statistics for Parent Education for 8th-graders.

Homework (.277) and Grade-point average (.294). It will be interesting to see what the multiple regression looks like.

Multiple R.   Figure 2.4 shows the multiple correlation coefficient (denoted as a capital R, a value of .390, and sometimes referred to as the "mult R") and the squared multiple correlation, R^2, or .152, which shows that the two explanatory variables, Homework and Parent Education level, together account for 15.2% of the variance in students' GPAs.

Are you surprised that the R is not larger? Perhaps you expected that R might equal the sum of the correlations of the two explanatory variables with GPA (i.e., .294 + .327)? You cannot add correlation coefficients in this way, but you can sometimes add variances, or r^2's. But when you try adding variances, you find that $R^2 \neq r^2_{\text{ParEd}\cdot\text{GPA}} + r^2_{\text{HWork}\cdot\text{GPA}}$; that is, $.152 \neq .294^2 + .327^2$. Why not? The short answer is that R^2 is not equal to the sum of the r^2's because the two explanatory variables are also correlated with each other. Ponder why that might be while we look at the remainder of the regression results.

Statistics

HWORK Average Time Spent on
Homework per Week

N	Valid	100
	Missing	0
Mean		5.0900
Median		5.0000
Mode		5.00
Std. Deviation		2.0553
Variance		4.2241
Minimum		1.00
Maximum		11.00

HWORK Average Time Spent on Homework per Week

		Frequency	Percent	Valid Percent	Cumulative Percent
Valid	1.00	4	4.0	4.0	4.0
	2.00	8	8.0	8.0	12.0
	3.00	8	8.0	8.0	20.0
	4.00	18	18.0	18.0	38.0
	5.00	24	24.0	24.0	62.0
	6.00	12	12.0	12.0	74.0
	7.00	14	14.0	14.0	88.0
	8.00	8	8.0	8.0	96.0
	9.00	2	2.0	2.0	98.0
	10.00	1	1.0	1.0	99.0
	11.00	1	1.0	1.0	100.0
	Total	100	100.0	100.0	

Descriptive Statistics

	N	Minimum	Maximum	Mean	Std. Deviation	Variance
GRADES Grade Point Average	100	64.00	100.00	80.4700	7.6230	58.110
Valid N (listwise)	100					

FIGURE 2.2   Descriptive statistics for Homework and Grades for 8th-graders.

The ANOVA table, also shown in Figure 2.4, shows that the regression is statistically significant $F(2, 97) = 8.697, p < .001$. What does that mean? It means that taken together, in some optimally weighted combination, Homework and Parent Education level predict or explain students' Grades to a statistically significant degree. (We will examine what is meant by an optimally weighted combination in the next chapter.)

Correlations

		GRADES Grade Point Average	PARED Parents' Education (highest)	HWORK Average Time Spent on Homework per Week
Pearson Correlation	GRADES Grade Point Average	1.000	.294	.327
	PARED Parents' Education (highest)	.294	1.000	.277
	HWORK Average Time Spent on Homework per Week	.327	.277	1.000
Sig. (1-tailed)	GRADES Grade Point Average	.	.001	.000
	PARED Parents' Education (highest)	.001	.	.003
	HWORK Average Time Spent on Homework per Week	.000	.003	.
N	GRADES Grade Point Average	100	100	100
	PARED Parents' Education (highest)	100	100	100
	HWORK Average Time Spent on Homework per Week	100	100	100

FIGURE 2.3   Correlations among Grades, Parent Education, and Homework time.

Either of the two formulas from Chapter 1 for calculating F will work with multiple regression:

$$F = \frac{ss_{regression}/df_{regression}}{ss_{residual}/df_{residual}} \qquad \text{or} \qquad F = \frac{R^2/k}{(1 - R^2)/(N - k - 1)}$$

Recall that the df for the regression is equal to k, which is equal to the number of independent (predictor) variables, in this case 2. The df for the residual is equal to the total N, minus k, minus 1 (97). Try both of these formulas to make sure your answer is the same as that shown in the figure (within errors of rounding).

Regression Coefficients.   Next we turn to the regression coefficients (Figure 2.5). With simple regression, there was only one b, and its probability was the same as that of the overall regression equation. The corresponding β was equal to the original correlation. All this changes with multiple independent variables. With multiple regression, each independent

Model Summary

Model	R	R Square	Adjusted R Square	Std. Error of the Estimate
1	.390[a]	.152	.135	7.0916

a. Predictors: (Constant), HWORK Average Time Spent on Homework per Week, PARED Parents' Education (highest)

ANOVA[b]

Model		Sum of Squares	df	Mean Square	F	Sig.
1	Regression	874.739	2	437.369	8.697	.000[a]
	Residual	4878.171	97	50.290		
	Total	5752.910	99			

a. Predictors: (Constant), HWORK Average Time Spent on Homework per Week, PARED Parents' Education (highest)

b. Dependent Variable: GRADES Grade Point Average

FIGURE 2.4   Model summary and test of statistical significance of the regression of Grades on Parent Education and Homework.

variable has its own regression coefficient; the b for Parent Education is .871, and the b for Time Spent on Homework is .988; the intercept is 63.227. The regression equation is $Y = 63.227 + .871X_1 + .988X_2 + \text{error}$ or, for *predicted* Grades, $Grades_{(predicted)} = 63.227 + .871\text{ParEd} + .988\text{HWork}$. We could use this formula to predict any participant's GPA from his or her values on Homework and Parent Education. If a student spends 5 hours per week on homework and one of the parents completed college (16 years of education), his or her predicted GPA would be 82.103.

Coefficients[a]

Model		Unstandardized Coefficients		Standardized Coefficients			95% Confidence Interval for B	
		B	Std. Error	Beta	t	Sig.	Lower Bound	Upper Bound
1	(Constant)	63.227	5.240		12.067	.000	52.828	73.627
	PARED Parents' Education (highest)	.871	.384	.220	2.266	.026	.108	1.633
	HWORK Average Time Spent on Homework per Week	.988	.361	.266	2.737	.007	.272	1.704

a. Dependent Variable: GRADES Grade Point Average

FIGURE 2.5   Unstandardized and standardized regression coefficients for the regression of Grades on Parent Education and Homework.

With multiple regression, we can test each independent variable separately for statistical significance. It is not unusual, especially when we have a half-dozen or so variables in the regression equation, to have a statistically significant R^2, but to have one or more independent variables that are not statistically significant (an example is shown in Chapter 4). For the present case, note that the t $\left(t = b/se_b\right)$ associated with Parent Education is 2.266 ($p = .026$), and the 95% confidence interval for the b is $.108 - 1.633$. The fact that this range does not include zero tells us the same thing as the significance level of b: for a probability level of .05, the variable Parent Education is a statistically significant predictor of GPA. The regression coefficient (.871) suggests that, for each additional year of parental schooling, students' GPA will increase by .871, or close to one point on the 100-point GPA scale, once time spent on homework is taken into account.

Of greater interest is the regression coefficient for time spent on Homework, .988, which suggests that for each additional hour spent studying per week GPA should increase by close to 1 point (controlling for Parent Education). To increase GPA by 5 points, a student would need to spend a little more than 5 extra hours a week studying, or about an extra hour every night. As shown in the figure, this value is also statistically significant ($p = .007$).

You might wonder which of these two variables, Parent Education or Homework, has a stronger effect on Grades? You may be tempted to conclude that it is Homework, based on a comparison of the b's. You would be correct, but for the wrong reason. The Parent Education and Homework variables have different scales, so it is difficult to compare them. The b for Parent Education pertains to years of schooling, whereas the b for Homework pertains to hours of homework. If we want to compare the relative influence of these two variables we need to compare the β's, the *standardized* regression coefficients. When we do, we see that Homework ($\beta = .266$) is indeed a slightly more powerful influence on GPA than is Parent Education ($\beta = .220$). Each standard deviation increase in Homework will lead to .266 of a *SD* increase in Grades, whereas a standard deviation increase in Parent Education will result in .220 of a *SD* in Grades. Let's postpone asking whether this difference is statistically significant.[2]

As an aside, think about which of these two findings is more interesting. I assume most of you will vote for the homework finding, for the simple reason that homework time is potentially manipulable, whereas parent education is unlikely to change for most students. Another way of saying this is that the homework finding has implications for intervention, or school or home rules. Still another way to make a similar point is to note that our original interest was in the effect of homework on GPA, and we included the variable Parent Education in the analysis as a background or "control" variable.

Interpretations

Formal. Let's consolidate the interpretation of these findings and then move on to discuss several other issues. Our first, formal interpretation might be something along these lines:

> This research was designed to determine the influence of time spent on homework on 8th-grade students' Grade-point averages (GPAs), while controlling for parents' level of education. Students' 8th-grade GPAs were regressed on their average time spent on homework per week and the higher of their parents' levels of education. The overall multiple regression was

statistically significant ($R^2 = .152$, $F[2, 97] = 8.697$, $p < .001$), and the two variables (Homework and Parent Education) accounted for 15% of the variance in Grades. Each of the two independent variables also had a statistically significant effect on Grades. The unstandardized regression coefficient (b) for Parent Education was .871 ($t[97] = 2.266$, $p = .026$), meaning that for each additional year of parents' schooling, students' Grades increase by .871 points, controlling for time spent on homework. Of more direct interest was the b associated with time spent on Homework ($b = .988$, $t[97] = 2.737$, $p = .007$). This finding suggests that, for each hour students spend on Homework per week, their Grade-point average will increase by .988 points, controlling for parent education. (Although I have written this interpretation as it might appear in a journal, an example this simple would not be accepted for publication. It is included to illustrate the interpretation of regression results, however.)

We should take this interpretation a step further and discuss in English what these findings mean.

These results suggest that homework is indeed an important influence on students' grades and that this effect holds even after students' family backgrounds (parent education) are taken into account. Students who want to improve their grades may do so by spending additional time on homework. These findings suggest that each additional hour spent per week should result in close to a 1-point increase in students' overall GPA.

Real World.   I believe that it is important also to be able to provide a real-world (versus statistical) interpretation of these findings, in addition to the one that uses all the proper jargon. So, for example, here is how you might interpret these findings to a group of parents:

I conducted research to determine the influence on their grades of the time middle school students spend on homework. I also considered the students' parents' level of education as a background variable. As you might expect, the results indicated that parents' education indeed had an effect on students' grades. Parents with more education had students who earn higher grades. This may be related to the educational environment they provide or numerous other reasons. What is important, however, is that homework also had a strong and important effect on grades. In fact, it had a slightly stronger effect than did parent education levels. What this means is that students—no matter what their background—can perform at a higher level in school through the simple act of spending additional time on homework. The findings suggest that, on average, each additional hour per week spent on homework will result in a close to 1-point increase in overall grade-point average. So, for example, suppose your daughter generally spends 5 hours per week on homework and has an 80 average. If she spent an additional 5 hours per week on homework—or an additional 1 hour per weekday evening—her average should increase to close to 85. Please note that these are averages, and the effect of homework will vary for individual students.

Since our initial reason for completing this study was because of concerns about your daughter, you should develop an interpretation for her, as well. You might say something like:

You were right, Lisa, about parent education being important. Our new research shows that parents with higher education do indeed have children who earn higher grades in school. But homework is still important, even when you take parents' education into account. And homework is important for your grades in addition to test scores. Our new research shows that for each additional hour you spend per week on homework, your GPA should increase, on average, by close to 1 point. That may seem like a lot of work, but think about it: if you spend 2 hours on homework every night instead of 1 hour, your GPA should increase by close to 5 points. And that's your overall GPA, for the entire grading period, not just one test. It might be worth a try.

QUESTIONS

Controlling for . . .

For many of the interpretations listed above, you will notice remarks like "their Grade-point average will increase by .988 points, *controlling for Parent Education*" or "once variable *X* is taken into account." What do these statements mean? At the most basic level, we add these clarifications to indicate that we have taken into account variables other than the single predictor and single outcome that are being interpreted and thus differentiate this interpretation from one focused on zero-order correlations or simple, bivariate regression coefficients. The two (simple regression coefficient and multiple regression coefficient) are rarely the same, and the MR coefficients will often be smaller.

Another variation of these statements is "Grade-point average will increase by .988 points, *within levels of parent education.*" Consider if we were to regress Grades on Homework for students with parents with 10th-grade educations, and then for those whose parents completed the 11th grade, then for those whose parents completed high school, and so on, through students whose parents completed doctoral degrees. The .988 we calculated for the regression coefficient is conceptually equivalent to the average of the regression coefficients we would get if we were to conduct all these separate regressions.

Of course "control" in this nonexperimental research is not the same as control in the case of experimental research, where we may assign people who have a college education to one versus the other treatment, thus actually controlling which treatment they receive. Instead, we are talking about *statistical* control. With statistical control, we essentially take into account the variation explained by the other variables in the model. We take into account the variation explained by Parent Education when examining the effect of Homework on Grades, and we take into account the variation due to Homework when examining the effect of Parent Education on Grades.

I confess that I have mixed feelings about appending "controlling for . . ." to interpretive statements. On the one hand, these qualifications are technically correct and provide a sense of the other variables taken into account. On the other hand, if we are correct in our interpretation, that is, discussing the *effect* of homework on GPA, then effects are effects, regardless of what else is "controlled." Said differently, if we have controlled for the proper variables, then this is indeed a valid estimate of the effect of homework on GPA. If we have not controlled for the proper variables, then it is not a valid estimate. Figuring out the *proper variables* is an issue that we will return to repeatedly in this book and will finally resolve in the beginning chapters of Part 2. At any rate, perhaps these kinds of qualifications ("controlling for . . .") are more appropriate for a formal interpretation of results and less so for the English and real-world interpretations. If so, however, then it should be understood that for any interpretation that does not include a qualification like "controlling for *x*," we are also saying, perhaps under our breath, "assuming that I have included the correct variables in my regression equation." Again, what we mean by effects and when we are correct in such interpretations are topics that we will return to repeatedly in this book.

This discussion makes obvious the chief advantage of multiple, over simple, regression: it allows us to control for other relevant variables. When you conduct nonexperimental (or even experimental) research and try to tease out the effect of one variable on another, you will often be asked questions along the lines of "OK, but did you take into account (control for) variable *x*." We opened this chapter with such a question from Lisa, who argued that we needed to take parent education into account. Multiple regression allows you to take these other variables into account, to control for them statistically. The hard part is figuring out which variables need to be controlled! The other big advantage of multiple regression over simple regression is that, by controlling for additional variables, we increase the variance we are able to explain in the dependent variable; we are able to explain the phenomenon of interest more completely. This advantage was also illustrated with the current example.

Partial and Semipartial Correlations.   The preceding discussion has focused on the *effect* of one variable on another while taking a third variable into account. It is also possible to control for other variables without making assumptions about one variable influencing, affecting, or predicting another. That is, it is possible to calculate correlations between two variables, with other variables controlled. Such correlations are termed *partial correlations* and can be thought of as the correlation between two variables with the effects of another variable controlled, or removed, or "partialed" out. We could, for example, calculate the partial correlation between homework and grades, with the effects of parent education removed from homework and grades. We could have several such control variables, calculating, for example, the partial correlation of homework and grades while controlling for both parent education and previous achievement.

It is also possible to remove the effects of the control variable from only *one* of the two variables being correlated. For example, we could examine the correlation of homework (with parent education controlled) with grades. In this example, the effects of parent education are removed only from the homework variable, not the grades variable. This variation of a correlation coefficient is called a *semipartial* correlation. It is also referred to as a *part* correlation.

Although I will mention partial and semipartial correlations at several points in this text, they are not discussed in detail in the text itself, but rather in Appendix D. There are several reasons for this decision. First, the topic is somewhat of a detour from the primary topic of Part 1, multiple regression. Second, in my experience, different instructors like to fit this topic in at different places in their lectures. Putting the material in Appendix D makes such placement more flexible. Third, although the topic fits better conceptually in Part 1, I think that partial and semipartial correlations are much easier to explain and understand with reference to the figural, or path, models that are used throughout the text, but that are explained in depth in the beginning chapters of Part 2. Feel free to turn to Appendix D at any point that you want to learn more about part and partial correlations, however.

b versus ß

Believe it or not, the choice of interpreting the unstandardized versus the standardized regression coefficient can be controversial. It need not be. Briefly, *b* and β are both useful, but for different aspects of interpretation. As our examples have already illustrated, *b* can be very useful when the variables have a meaningful scale. In the present example, Homework time is measured in hours per week, and everyone is familiar with a standard 100-point grade scale. Thus, it makes a great deal of sense to make interpretations like "each hour increase in Homework per week should result in a .988-point increase in overall Grade-point average." Very often, however, the scales of our independent or dependent variables, or both, are not particularly meaningful. The test score metric used in Chapter 1 is probably not that familiar to most readers, except possibly measurement specialists who encounter *T* scores often. And the scale of the Parent Education variable used in the present example, although logical, is not very common; a much more common scale might be something along the lines of $1 = $ did not graduate from high school; $2 = $ high school graduate; $3 = $ some college; $4 = $ college graduate; and so on. This scale may be better from a measurement standpoint in dealing with cases such as someone who attends college for 6 years but never completes a degree, but it is not a readily interpretable metric. We will encounter many other variables without a meaningful metric. In these cases, it makes little sense to interpret b: "each 1-point increase in X should result in a 4-point increase in Y." What does a 1-point increase in X mean? What does a 4-point increase in Y mean? When the variables of interest do not have a meaningful metric, it makes more sense to interpret β: "each standard deviation increase in X should result in a .25-standard deviation increase in Y."

As we have already seen, β is generally our only interpretive choice when we want to compare the relative importance of several variables in a single regression equation. Different variables in a regression equation generally have different metrics, so it makes no sense to compare unstandardized regression coefficients; it is like comparing apples to oranges. The standardized coefficients place all variables on the same metric (standard deviation units) and thus may be compared in a qualitative manner. Of course, if the independent variables in a regression equation used the same metric, the b's for each could be compared, but this situation (variables sharing the same metric) is not very common.[3]

Often we are interested in the policy implications of our regression analyses. Using the present example, you want to give Lisa advice about the likely impact of completing more homework. More broadly, you may want to urge the local school board to encourage teachers to increase homework demands. When you are interested in making predictions about what will happen ("if you spend 5 more hours a week on homework . . . ") or are interested in changing or intervening in a system, or are interested in developing policy based on the findings of a regression analysis, then b is probably a better choice for interpretation *if* the variables have a meaningful metric.

Finally, we may want to compare our regression results with those from previous research. We may, for example, want to compare the effect of Homework in this example with the apparent effect of Homework in a published study. To compare across samples or populations, b is more appropriate. The reason for this rule of thumb is that different samples likely have different distributions for the same variables. If you measure Homework time in 8th grade and 4th grade, it is likely that the means and standard deviations for Homework will differ in the two grades. These differences in distributions—notably the standard deviations—affect the β's, but not the b's. To get an intuitive understanding of this point, look at the regression line shown in Figure 2.6. Assume that the b, which is the slope of the regression line, is .80 and that the β is also .80. (How could this be? The *SD*'s of the independent and dependent variables are equal.) Now assume that we remove the data in the areas that are shaded. With this new sample, the b could remain the same; the regression line remains the same, just shorter, so its slope remains the same. But what about the β?

Obviously, the *SD* of the independent variable has decreased, because we discarded all data from the shaded area. The *SD* of the dependent variable will also decrease, but not as much as the *SD* of the independent variable. Suppose the new *SD*'s are 7 for *X* and 9 for *Y*. Now recall from Chapter 1 how we can convert *b* to β: $\beta = b \dfrac{SD_x}{SD_y}$. So the new β is β = .80(7/9) = .62; the *b* remained the same, but the β changed. To return to the original point: to compare regression results across two different samples or studies, *b* is more appropriate. These rules of thumb are summarized in Table 2.1.

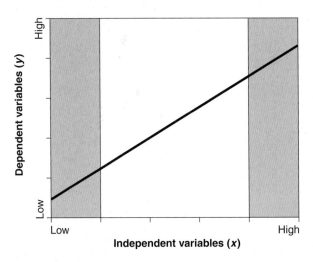

FIGURE 2.6   Effect of a change in variability on the regression coefficients. The figure shows the regression line from the regression of a hypothetical dependent variable on a hypothetical independent variable.

Again, you may read or hear strong defenses for the routine interpretation of *b* versus β, or vice versa. Just remember that with knowledge of the *SD*'s of the variables you can easily convert from one to another. Both are useful; they simply are useful for different purposes.

TABLE 2.1   Rules of Thumb for When to Interpret *b* versus ß

INTERPRET *b*:

When the variables are measured in a meaningful metric

To develop intervention or policy implications

To compare effects across samples or studies

INTERPRET β:

When the variables are not measured in a meaningful metric

To compare the relative effects of different predictors in the same sample

---

Comparison across Samples

I have mentioned comparison of regression coefficients across samples or studies. As an example, we might ask whether the effect of Homework on Grades in this chapter is consistent with the estimate we calculated in Chapter 1 examining the effect of Homework on achievement. Unfortunately, these two analyses used different dependent variables (Math Achievement test scores versus overall GPA), making such comparisons difficult. Instead, let's pretend that we redo the research, asking the same questions, on a sample of high school students. The descriptive statistics for this sample are shown in Figure 2.7, and the results of the multiple regression for this sample are shown in Figure 2.8

Descriptive Statistics

	Mean	Std. Deviation	N
GRADES	81.5348	7.46992	100
PARED	13.8300	2.04028	100
HWORK	6.9800	2.14608	100

Correlations

		GRADES	PARED	HWORK
Pearson Correlation	GRADES	1.000	.191	.354
	PARED	.191	1.000	.368
	HWORK	.354	.368	1.000
Sig. (1-tailed)	GRADES	.	.028	.000
	PARED	.028	.	.000
	HWORK	.000	.000	.
N	GRADES	100	100	100
	PARED	100	100	100
	HWORK	100	100	100

FIGURE 2.7   **Descriptive statistics and correlations among variables for high school students.**

The two estimates—1.143 for high school students versus .988 for 8th-graders earlier in this chapter—are obviously different, but are the differences statistically significant? There are several ways we might make this comparison. The easiest is to use the confidence intervals. Phrase the question this way: Is the present estimate of 1.143 (the value for the high school sample) significantly different from our earlier estimate of .988? Look at the 95% confidence interval for the regression coefficient for the 8th-grade sample (Figure 2.5): .272 to 1.704. The value of 1.143 falls within this range, so we can confidently say that our current value is *not* statistically different from our previous estimate.

Model Summary

Model	R	R Square	Adjusted R Square	Std. Error of the Estimate
1	.360[a]	.130	.112	7.03925

a. Predictors: (Constant), HWORK, PARED

ANOVA[b]

Model		Sum of Squares	df	Mean Square	F	Sig.
1	Regression	717.713	2	358.856	7.242	.001[a]
	Residual	4806.452	97	49.551		
	Total	5524.165	99			

a. Predictors: (Constant), HWORK, PARED

b. Dependent Variable: GRADES

Coefficients[a]

Model		Unstandardized Coefficients		Standardized Coefficients			95% Confidence Interval for B	
		B	Std. Error	Beta	t	Sig.	Lower Bound	Upper Bound
1	(Constant)	69.984	4.881		14.338	.000	60.297	79.671
	PARED	.258	.373	.071	.692	.490	-.482	.998
	HWORK	1.143	.355	.328	3.224	.002	.440	1.847

a. Dependent Variable: GRADES

FIGURE 2.8   Regression output for the Homework example for high school students.

Another way of making this determination is the good old t test. To ask whether our current value is different from some value other than zero, we make a minor change in the formula: $t = \frac{b - value}{SE_b}$, where *value* represents the other value to which we wish to compare b (Darlington, 1990, chap. 5). For the present example, the formula would be

$$t = \frac{.988 - 1.143}{.361}$$

$$= -.429$$

Using our rule of thumb (t's of 2 or greater are significant; ignore whether t is positive or negative), we again see that the high school value is not statistically significantly different at the .05 level from the value estimated for 8th-graders. Or, using the TDIST function in Excel, we see that this t would happen commonly by chance alone ($p = .669$, two-tailed, with 97 df; just use the value .429, without the negative sign, in Excel).

Note that this test compares our current estimate, with confidence intervals, to a specific value. It is also possible to compare the two regression estimates, considering the standard errors of both. The formula

$$z = \frac{b_1 - b_2}{\sqrt{SE_{b_1}^2 + SE_{b_2}^2}}$$

can be used to compare regression coefficients from two *separate* (independent) regression equations (Cohen & Cohen, 1983, p. 111). It doesn't matter which b goes first; it's easiest to make the larger one b_1. For the current example,

$$z = \frac{1.143 - .988}{\sqrt{.355^2 + .361^2}}$$

$$= \frac{.155}{\sqrt{.256}}$$

$$= .306$$

You can look this z value up in Excel (using the function NORMSDIST, for standard normal distribution). You will need to subtract the value returned (.620) from 1.0, for a probability of .38. The two regression coefficients are not statistically significantly different. Once more, note the difference in orientation between these comparisons. The first compared a coefficient to a specific number, taking that number as a given. It asked if the current estimate of the regression coefficient is different from a specific value. The second asks whether two regression coefficients are statistically significantly different.

Cautions.   Having gone through this illustration, we might be tempted to compare our results from this chapter with those from Chapter 1 using simple regression. I would not make this comparison because the two analyses used different dependent variables. In Chapter 1, our conclusion was that each additional hour of (math) Homework led to a 2-point increase in achievement test scores. In this chapter, our conclusion was that each additional hour of Homework led to a 1-point increase in Grades. Although Grades and test scores are certainly related, they are not the same thing; a 1-point increase in Grades is not the same as a 1-point increase in test scores.

In this example, I would be tempted instead to make a qualitative, rather than statistical, interpretation based on the standardized coefficients (β's), despite our rules of thumb. On the one hand, the two values are from separate regressions with different samples. On the other hand, at least with standardized coefficients, we have a chance of interpreting the same scale (standard deviation units). The β for Homework from Chapter 1 was .320; here it is .266. These values do not seem that different, so maybe the results are consistent after all.

DIRECT CALCULATION OF ß AND R^2

So far we have shown how to convert b to β and the reverse, but how could you calculate these values directly? We will focus on the direct calculation of β because it is instructive, and because it will be useful later in the book. It is fairly easy to calculate β with only two independent variables:

$$\beta_1 = \frac{r_{y1} - r_{y2}r_{12}}{1 - r_{12}^2} \quad \text{and} \quad \beta_2 = \frac{r_{y2} - r_{y1}r_{12}}{1 - r_{12}^2}.$$

Let's apply this formula to the 8th-grade Homework example:

$$\beta_{hwork} = \frac{r_{grades*hwork} - r_{grades*pared}r_{pared*hwork}}{1 - r^2_{pared*hwork}}.$$

Note that the β of Homework on Grades depends, in part, on the simple correlation between Homework and Grades. But it also depends on the correlation between Parent Education and Grades and the correlation between Homework and Parent Education. Calculate the β:

$$\beta_{hwork} = \frac{.327 - .294 \times .277}{1 - .277^2}$$

$$= \frac{.246}{.923}$$

$$= .267$$

which is, within errors of rounding, the same as the value calculated by SPSS (.266). From β we can calculate b:

$$b = \beta \frac{SD_y}{SD_x}$$

$$= .266 \frac{7.623}{2.055}$$

$$= .987$$

which again is equivalent to the value from SPSS. The important thing to keep in mind is that the value for each β (and b) depends not only on the correlation between the independent and dependent variable, but also on all the *other correlations* among the variables in the model. This is why one way to interpret the regression coefficients is a statement like this: Homework had a strong effect on Grades, even when parents' level of education was controlled. The regression coefficients take the other variables into account; thus, don't be tempted to interpret them as if they were correlations. At the same time, note that it would be computationally challenging to calculate regression coefficients in this manner with a half-dozen or so variables!

Likewise, it is worth noting various formulas for calculating R^2. To calculate R^2 from the sums of squares, $R^2 = ss_{regression}/ss_{total}$. To calculate R^2 using β's, $R^2_{y\cdot12} = \beta_1 r_{y1} + \beta_2 r_{y2}$. To calculate R^2 from the correlations,

$$R^2_{y\cdot12} = \frac{r^2_{y1} + r^2_{y2} - 2r_{y1}r_{y2}r_{12}}{1 - r^2_{12}}$$

Note, as we discovered at the beginning of this chapter, R^2 is not equal to the sum of the two r^2's; instead, it is reduced by a certain extent. Simply note for now that this reduction is related to the correlation between the two independent variables, r_{12}.

SUMMARY

This chapter introduced *multiple* regression, with two independent variables and one dependent variable. We conducted a regression designed to determine the effect of time spent on homework on grade-point average, controlling for parents' level of education. The regression equation was statistically significant. Unlike simple regression, with multiple regression it is possible for the overall regression to be statistically significant, but to have some independent variables be nonsignificant. Here, however, the regression coefficients showed that each variable—Parent Education and time spent on Homework—had an effect on students' GPAs. We interpreted the findings from a variety of orientations. Since all the variables in the equation used a meaningful scale, we focused our interpretation primarily on the unstandardized regression coefficients.

We examined how to calculate many of the important statistics in multiple regression for this simple example: β, b, and R^2. We discussed the pros and cons of interpreting standardized versus unstandardized regression coefficients. Both standardized and unstandardized coefficients are useful, but they serve different purposes. Unstandardized coefficients (b) are most useful when the variables are measured in a meaningful metric (e.g., hours of homework), when we wish to compare effects across studies, and when we are interested in developing policy or intervention implications from our research. Standardized coefficients (β) are more useful when the variables are not measured in a meaningful metric or when we are interested in comparing the relative importance of different predictors in the same regression equation. Rules of thumb for the use of regression coefficients are shown in Table 2.1.

Make sure you understand completely the topics presented in this chapter, because they form the foundation for much of the rest of the book. In the next chapter, we will delve deeper into this fairly simple multiple regression example.

EXERCISES

1. Conduct the Homework analysis from this chapter yourself.

2. Conduct a similar analysis using the NELS data set. Try regressing FFUGrad (GPA in 10th Grade) on BYParEd (Parents' highest level of education) and F1S36A2 (Time Spent on Homework out of School). Be sure to check descriptive statistics. Notice the scales for the independent variables. The dependent variable is the average of respondents' Grades in English, math, science, and social studies; for each of these subjects, the scale ranges from 1 = mostly below D to 8 = mostly A's.

3. Interpret the results of the regression in Exercise 2. Should you interpret the b's or the β's? Why would it be inappropriate to compare these results statistically with those presented in this chapter? Qualitatively, are the results similar to those presented with our simulated data?

4. The examples in this chapter suggest that students' home environments may affect their school performance. You may wonder, however, whether it is the educational environment of the home that is important or if it is the financial resources of the home that are important. The file "exercise 4, grades, ed, income.sav" has simulated data that will allow a test of this

question. (The data are on the Web site (www.ablongman.com/keith1e) under Chapter 2. Also included are Excel and plain text versions of the data.) Included are measures of grade-point average (Grades, a standard 100-point scale), parents' highest level of education (ParEd, in years), and family income (Income, in thousands of dollars). Regress Grades on Parent Education and Family Income. Be sure to also check the summary statistics. Is the overall regression statistically significant? Are both variables—Parent Education and Family Income—statistically significant predictors of students' Grades? Interpret the results of this regression. Interpret both the unstandardized and the standardized regression coefficients. Which interpretation is more meaningful, the *b*'s or the β's? Why? Which home variable appears to be more important for students' school performance?

NOTES

1. A reader felt uncomfortable with this individual interpretation of regression results, especially given the smallish R^2. Yet I think that translation of research results to the individual level is often among the most useful things we can do with them. The results of this hypothetical research were both meaningful and statistically significant and therefore (in my opinion) ripe for interpretation. Keep in mind, however, that not everyone feels comfortable on this point.

2. As you progress through the chapter, you may be tempted to use the *b*'s and their standard errors for such a comparison. These are good instincts, but it will not work, because the *b*'s are in different metrics. Some programs will produce standard errors of the β's which could be useful.

3. Although β is the most common metric for comparing the relative influence of the variables in a regression equation, it is not the only possible metric, nor is it without its problems (especially when the independent variables are highly correlated). Darlington (1990, chap. 9), for example, argued for the use of the semipartial correlations, rather than β, as measures of the relative importance of the independent variables. Yet β works well for most analyses, and it fulfills this role better than do other statistics that are commonly produced by statistics programs. We will continue to focus on β as providing information about the relative influence of different variables, at least for the time being. As already noted, partial and semipartial correlations are discussed in Appendix D.

MULTIPLE REGRESSION: MORE DETAIL

In this chapter we will delve into a little more detail about multiple regression and explain some concepts a little more fully. This chapter probably includes more formulas than in any other, but I will try to explain concepts several different ways to ensure that at least one explanation makes sense to every reader. The chapter is short, but if math and statistics do not come easily to you, you may need to read this chapter more than once. Your perseverance will pay off with understanding!

WHY $R^2 \neq r^2 + r^2$

I noted in the last chapter that, as a general rule, R^2 is not equal to $r^2 + r^2$ and briefly mentioned that this was due to the correlation between the independent variables. Let's explore this phenomenon in more detail. To review, in the example used in the beginning of Chapter 2, $r^2_{HWork \cdot Grades} = .327^2 = .107$, and $r^2_{ParEd \cdot Grades} = .294^2 = .086$.

The R^2 from the regression of GPA on Homework and Parent Education was .152. Obviously, $.152 \neq .107 + .086$. Why not? We'll approach this question several different ways.

First, recall one of the formulas for R^2:

$$R^2_{y \cdot 12} = \frac{r^2_{y1} + r^2_{y2} - 2r_{y1}r_{y2}r_{12}}{1 - r^2_{12}}$$

Note that the squared multiple correlation depends not only on the correlation between each independent variable and the dependent variable, but also on the correlation between the two independent variables, r_{12}, or, in this case $r_{HWork \cdot ParEd}$, a value of .277.

Next, look at Figure 3.1. The circles in the figure represent the variance of each variable in this regression analysis, and the areas where the circles overlap represent the shared variances, or the r^2's, among the three variables. The shaded area marked 1 (including the area marked 3) represents the variance shared by Grades and Homework, and the shaded area marked 2 (including the area marked 3) represents the variance shared by Parent Education and Homework. Note, however, that these areas of overlap also overlap each other in the doubly shaded area marked 3. This overlap occurs because Homework and Parent Education are themselves correlated. The combined area of overlap between Homework and Grades and between Parent Education and Grades (areas 1 and 2) represents the variance of Grades *jointly accounted* for by Homework and Grades, or the R^2. As a result of the joint overlap (3), however, the total area of overlap is not equal to the sum of areas 1 and 2; area 3 is counted once, not twice. In other words, R^2 is not equal to $r^2 + r^2$.

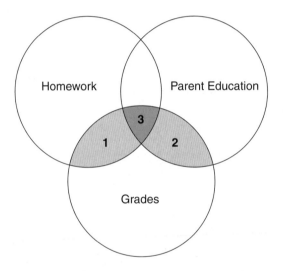

FIGURE 3.1   **Venn diagram illustrating the shared variance (covariance) among three variables. The shaded areas show the variance shared by each independent variable with the dependent variable. Area 3 shows the variance shared by all three variables.**

Using this logic, it follows that *if* the correlation between the two independent variables is zero then R^2 will equal $r^2 + r^2$. Such a situation is depicted in Figure 3.2, where the area of overlap is indeed equal to the sum of areas 1 and 2, because the two independent variables do not themselves overlap. Likewise, turning to the formula for R^2, you can see what happens when r_{12} is equal to zero. The formula is

$$R^2_{y\cdot 12} = \frac{r^2_{y1} + r^2_{y2} - 2r_{y1}r_{y2}r_{12}}{1 - r^2_{12}}$$

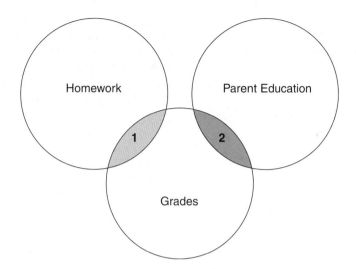

FIGURE 3.2   Venn diagram illustrating the shared variance among three variables. In this example, there is no correlation (and no shared variance) between the two independent variables.

When zero is substituted for r_{12},

$$R^2_{y \cdot 12} = \frac{r^2_{y1} + r^2_{y2} - 2r_{y1}r_{y2} \times 0}{1 - 0}$$

the formula reduces to $R^2_{y \cdot 12} = r^2_{y1} + r^2_{y2}$.

Let's double-check. Figure 3.3 shows the results of the regression of Grades on Homework and Parent Education in the (unlikely) event that the correlation between Homework and Parent Education is zero (the data are simulated). Note that the correlations between Parent Education and Grades (.294) and between Homework and Grades (.327) are the same as in Chapter 2, but that the correlation between Parent Education and Homework is now zero. And consistent with our reasoning above, R^2 now equals $r^2 + r^2$:

$$R^2_{\text{Grades} \cdot \text{HWork} \cdot \text{ParEd}} = r^2_{\text{Grades} \cdot \text{ParEd}} + r^2_{\text{Grades} \cdot \text{HWork}}$$
$$.193 = .294^2 + .327^2$$
$$.193 = .193$$

Also note that when the independent variables are uncorrelated, the β's are again equal to the correlations (as with simple regression). The reason why is, of course, that the formula for β,

$$\left(\beta_1 = \frac{r_{y1} - r_{y2}r_{12}}{1 - r^2_{12}} \right)$$

reduces to $\beta_1 = r_{y1}$ when $r_{12} = 0$.

Correlations

		GRADES	PARED	HWORK
Pearson Correlation	GRADES	1.000	.294	.327
	PARED	.294	1.000	.000
	HWORK	.327	.000	1.000
Sig. (1-tailed)	GRADES	.	.001	.000
	PARED	.001	.	.500
	HWORK	.000	.500	.
N	GRADES	100	100	100
	PARED	100	100	100
	HWORK	100	100	100

Model Summary

Model	R	R Square	Adjusted R Square	Std. Error of the Estimate
1	.440[a]	.193	.177	6.916656

a. Predictors: (Constant), HWORK, PARED

Coefficients[a]

Model		Unstandardized Coefficients		Standardized Coefficients	t	Sig.
		B	Std. Error	Beta		
1	(Constant)	58.008	5.382		10.778	.000
	PARED	1.161	.360	.294	3.224	.002
	HWORK	1.213	.338	.327	3.586	.001

a. Dependent Variable: GRADES

FIGURE 3.3   Multiple regression results when there is no correlation between the independent variables.

To reiterate, the R^2 depends not only on the correlations of the independent variable with the dependent variable, but also on the correlations among the independent variables. As a general rule, the R^2 will be less than the sum of the squared correlations of the independent variables with the dependent variable.[1] The only time R^2 will equal $r^2 + r^2$ is when the independent variables are uncorrelated, and this happens rarely in the real world.

PREDICTED SCORES AND RESIDUALS

It is worth spending some time examining more detailed aspects of multiple regression, such as the residuals and the predicted scores. Understanding these aspects will help you more completely understand what is going on in multiple regression and also provide a good foundation for topics that we will cover later.

Among other things, residuals (the error term from the regression equation) are useful for diagnosing problems in regression, such as the existence of outliers, or extreme values. We will address the use of residuals for diagnostic purposes in Chapter 9.

In Chapter 2 we saw how to use the regression equation to predict an individual's score on the outcome. Simply plug a person's values for the two independent variables (i.e., Parent Education and Homework time) into the regression equation and you get the person's predicted grade-point average. We also may be interested in the predicted outcomes for everyone in our data set. In this case, it is simple to have our statistics program calculate the predicted scores as a part of the multiple regression analysis. In SPSS, for example, simply click on the Save button in multiple regression and highlight Predicted Values; Unstandardized (see Figure 3.4). While we're at it, we'll also ask for the unstandardized residuals. In SYSTAT, check Save and highlight Residuals/Data (see Figure 3.5). In SAS, you can get predicted values and residuals using an OUTPUT statement.

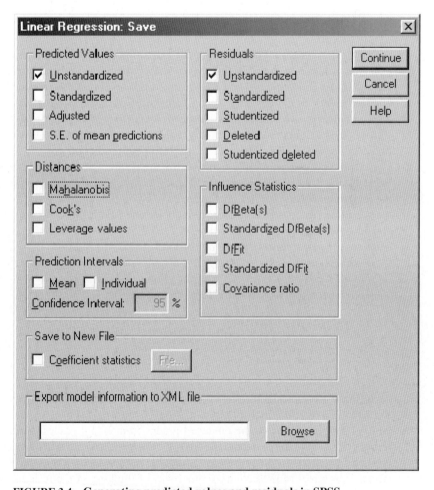

FIGURE 3.4   Generating predicted values and residuals in SPSS.

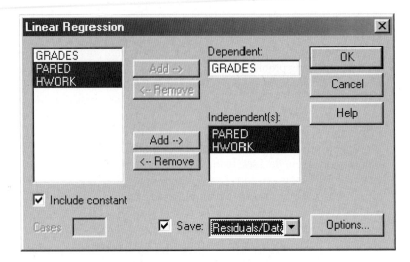

FIGURE 3.5   Generating predicted values and residuals in SYSTAT.

I again regressed Grades on Parent Education and Homework using the 8th-grade data from Chapter 2, but this time saved the predicted scores and residuals. Figure 3.6 shows Grades (first column) and the Predicted Grades (PredGrad) for the first 34 cases of our Homework & Grades data from Chapter 2. Note that for some students we predict higher grades based on the regression equation than they actually earned, whereas for other students their actual grades were higher than their predicted grades. Obviously, the prediction is not exact; in other words, there is error in our prediction.

The third column in this figure shows the residuals from this regression (Resid_1). What are the residuals? Conceptually, the residuals are what is left over or unexplained by the regression equation. They are the errors in prediction that we noticed when comparing the actual versus predicted Grades. Remember one form of the regression equation (with two independent variables): $Y = a + bX_1 + bX_2 + e$. In this equation, the residuals are equal to e, the error term from the regression.

Remember also the other form of the regression equation, using the *predicted* scores on Y (symbolized as Y'), in this case the predicted grades: $Y' = a + bX_1 + bX_2$. We can subtract this formula from the first formula to figure out how to solve for e, the residuals:

$$Y = a + bX_1 + bX_2 + e$$

$$\underline{-Y' = a + bX_1 + bX_2}$$

$$Y - Y' = e$$

Thus, in the present example, the residuals are simply the predicted grades subtracted from the actual grades. The final column in Figure 3.6 (Error_1) shows the results of $Y - Y'$, in which I simply subtracted the predicted grades from actual grades. Notice that this error term is identical to the residuals (RESID_1). The residuals are what are left over after the predicted outcome variable is removed from the actual outcome variable; they are the inaccuracies, or errors of prediction. Another way of thinking of the residuals is that they are

GRADES	PREDGRAD	RESID_1	ERROR_1
78.00	76.52082	1.47918	1.47918
79.00	81.34282	−2.34282	−2.34282
79.00	75.53297	3.46703	3.46703
89.00	79.48435	9.51565	9.51565
82.00	80.12053	1.87947	1.87947
77.00	78.49651	−1.49651	−1.49651
88.00	79.48435	8.51565	8.51565
70.00	77.50866	−7.50866	−7.50866
86.00	81.22560	4.77440	4.77440
80.00	80.35498	−.35498	−.35498
76.00	78.14484	−2.14484	−2.14484
72.00	79.48435	−7.48435	−7.48435
66.00	76.63804	−10.63804	−10.63804
79.00	79.36713	−.36713	−.36713
76.00	75.88464	.11536	.11536
80.00	86.56656	−6.56656	−6.56656
91.00	84.18914	6.81086	6.81086
85.00	83.08407	1.91593	1.91593
79.00	82.44789	−3.44789	−3.44789
82.00	78.37928	3.62072	3.62072
94.00	81.57727	12.42273	12.42273
91.00	79.60157	11.39843	11.39843
80.00	80.35498	−.35498	−.35498
73.00	82.33067	−9.33067	−9.33067
77.00	78.61373	−1.61373	−1.61373
76.00	82.09622	−6.09622	−6.09622
84.00	76.63804	7.36196	7.36196
81.00	82.09622	−1.09622	−1.09622
97.00	87.03545	9.96455	9.96455
80.00	82.21344	−2.21344	−2.21344
74.00	82.09622	−8.09622	−8.09622
83.00	87.15267	−4.15267	−4.15267
78.00	80.47220	−2.47220	−2.47220
64.00	84.94254	−20.94254	−20.94254

FIGURE 3.6   Partial listing comparing Grades (Y), Predicted Grades (Y'), the residuals as output by the computer program, and the error term (Y-Y').

equivalent to the original dependent variable (Grades) with the effects of the independent variables (Parent Education and Homework) removed.

Regression Line

With simple regression, we can also understand the predicted scores and residuals using the regression line. With simple regression, we find the predicted scores using the regression line: find the value of the independent variable on the X-axis, go straight up to the regression line, and then find the value of the dependent variable (Y-axis) that corresponds to that point on the regression line. The regression line, with simple regression, is simply a line connecting the predicted Y's for each value of X. With multiple regression, however, there are multiple regression lines (one for each independent variable). But wait; if the regression line is equivalent to the predicted scores, then the predicted scores are equivalent to the regression line. In other words, with multiple regression, we can, in essence, get an overall, single regression line by plotting the predicted scores (X-axis) against the actual scores (Y-axis). This has been done in Figure 3.7, which includes both the regression line of the plot of predicted versus actual GPA, and each data point.

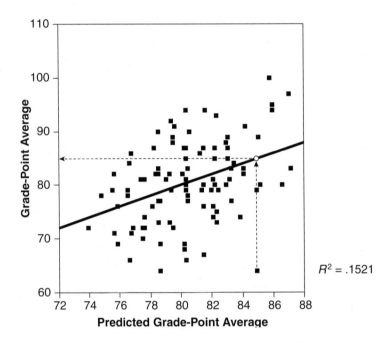

FIGURE 3.7   Plot, with regression line, of Grades (Y) versus Predicted Grades (Y').

First note that the r^2 (.1521, shown in the lower right of Figure 3.7) from the regression of Grades on Predicted Grades (with Grades predicted by Homework and Parent Education) is identical to the R^2 from the multiple regression of Grades on Homework and Parent Education (.1521), further evidence that this can be thought of as the overall regression line for our multiple regression of Grades on Homework and Parent Education. This finding also points to another way of thinking about R^2: as the correlation between the Y and predicted Y (Y').

If the line represents the predicted Grades, then the deviation of each actual Grade (each data point) from the line represents what? The residuals; if you subtract the value (on the Y-axis) of the *regression line* from the value of each *data point* (on the Y-axis), you will find the same values for the residuals as shown in Figure 3.6. Again, this is simply $Y - Y'$. You can see this most easily by focusing on the data point in the lower-right corner of the graph, defined as $X = 84.94$ and $Y = 64$. This is also the final data point in Figure 3.6. Follow the line from this point to the regression line and then over to the Y-axis. The value on the Y-axis is also 84.94. The residual is thus $64 - 84.92 = -20.94$, also the same value shown for the residual in Figure 3.6. (Here's an extra-credit question for you: since in this figure every point on the regression line has the same values for both the X- and the Y-axes, what is the value for b? Remember that b is the slope of the regression line.)

LEAST SQUARES

Recall that I said in Chapter 2 that the two independent variables were "optimally weighted." What does this mean? Why not just weight each of the two variables by ½ to predict GPA; in other words, why not just standardize the two independent variables, average them, and use that composite to predict GPA using simple regression? Or why not weight them in some other logical combination? The reason is that the prediction will not be as good, as accurate. The explained variance (R^2) will not be as high, and the unexplained variance ($1 - R^2$) will be higher. Another way of saying this is to state that the regression line shown in Figure 3.7 is the best fitting of all possible (straight) lines that could be drawn through these data points.

So what does *best fitting* mean? Again, it means the line that minimizes the error of prediction, or the unexplained variance. Take a look at the line again. Suppose you were to measure the distance from each data point to the regression line and subtract from it the corresponding point from the regression line. This is what we just did for a single data point (84.94, 64), and we found that these are the same as the residuals. These are the errors in prediction. If you were to sum these values, you would find that they summed to zero; the positive values will be balanced by negative values. To get rid of the negative values, you can square each residual and then sum them. If you do this, you will find that the resulting number is smaller than for *any other possible straight line*. This best fitting line thus minimizes the errors of prediction; it minimizes the squared residuals. You will sometimes hear simple or multiple regression referred to as *least squares regression* or OLS (ordinary least squares) regression. The reason is that the regression weights the independent variables so as to *minimize* the *squared* residuals, thus *least squares*.

Figure 3.8 displays descriptive statistics for some of the variables we have been discussing: Grades (Y), Predicted Grades (Y'), and the Residuals. Also shown are descriptive statistics for the *squared* Residuals (ResidSq). Note that the means and sums for Grades and Predicted Grades are the same. The Predicted Grades have a narrower range (73.91 to 87.15) than do the actual Grades (64 to 100) and a smaller variance (8.84 compared to 58.11), which should be obvious when looking at the figure that shows the regression line (Figure 3.7). The Y-axis on the figure has a much wider range than does the X-axis. Note that the sum of the residuals is zero. Note also the sum of the squared residuals: 4878.17. As mentioned in the previous paragraph, the regression line minimizes this number; any other possible straight line will result in a larger value for the sum of the squared residuals. If you turn back to Chapter 2, you can compare this number to the Sum of Squares for the residual in Figure 2.4; they are the same (4878.17). The residual sums of squares is just that: the sum of the squared residuals.

I argued that the independent variables are weighted so that this sum of squared residuals is minimized, and the R^2 is maximized. In our current example, Parent Education was weighted .220 (the standardized regression coefficient), and Homework was weighted by .266, close to a 50/50 ratio. What would happen if we chose a different weighting? Perhaps,

Descriptive Statistics

	N	Minimum	Maximum	Sum	Mean	Variance
GRADES Grade Point Average	100	64.00	100.00	8047.00	80.4700	58.110
PREDGRAD Unstandardized Predicted Value	100	73.90895	87.15267	8047.000	80.47000	8.836
RESID_1 Unstandardized Residual	100	-20.94254	14.18684	.00000	-8.8E-15	49.274
RESIDSQ	100	.01	438.59	4878.17	48.7817	4431.695
Valid N (listwise)	100					

FIGURE 3.8   **Descriptive statistics for Grades, Predicted Grades, the residuals, and the squared residuals.**

for some reason, you believe that Parent Education is not nearly as important as Homework for explaining Grades. Therefore, you decide to weight Parent Education by .25 versus .75 for Homework when predicting Grades. This solution may be satisfying in other ways, but the resulting prediction is not as accurate and is more error laden. Using the least squares solution of multiple regression in Chapter 2, we explained 15.2% of the variance in Grades ($R^2 = .152$). If, however, you regress Grades on a composite that weighted Parent Education by .25 and Homework by .75, our logically determined solution, you will find that this solution explains slightly less variance in Grades: 14% (see Figure 3.9). As noted previously, the error variance (residual sum of squares) was 4878.171 using the least squares solution. In contrast, using this 25/75 solution, the sum of squared residuals is larger: 4949.272 (Figure 3.9). The least squares, multiple regression, solution minimized the residual, or error, sums of squares and maximized the R^2, or the variance in Grades explained by Parent Education and Homework. As a result (and given the adherence to necessary assumptions), the estimates produced by the least squares solution will be the best possible estimates and the least biased (meaning the most likely to reproduce the population values).

Perhaps it is obvious that the variability of points around the regression line is closely related to the accuracy in prediction. The closer the data points in Figure 3.7 cluster around the regression line, the less error involved in prediction. In addition, the closer the data points are to the regression line, the more likely the regression is to be statistically significant, because this lowered variability will reduce the variation in residuals. The value of F depends, in part, on the variability in the residuals:

$$F = \frac{ss_{\text{regression}}/df_{\text{regression}}}{ss_{\text{residual}}/df_{\text{residual}}}$$

In addition, the variability in the residuals is related to the standard error of the regression coefficient (se_b), which is used to calculate the statistical significance of b ($t = b/se_b$).

REGRESSION EQUATION = CREATING A COMPOSITE?

These last few sections hint at a different way of conceptualizing what happens in multiple regression. We saw under Predicted Scores and Residuals that we could create a single

Model Summary

Model	R	R Square	Adjusted R Square	Std. Error of the Estimate
1	.374	.140	.131	7.1065

ANOVA [b]

Model		Sum of Squares	df	Mean Square	F	Sig.
1	Regression	803.638	1	803.638	15.913	.000
	Residual	4949.272	98	50.503		
	Total	5752.910	99			

b. Dependent Variable: GRADES Grade Point Average

FIGURE 3.9   Regression results with Parent Education weighted at 25% and Homework weighted at 75%. Note that the R^2 decreases, and the sum of squared residuals increases.

score, the predicted dependent variable (in this case, predicted Grades), that functions the same way in a simple regression analysis as do the multiple independent variables in a multiple regression analysis. We saw, for example, that the R^2 from multiple regression is the same as r^2 between Y and Y'. We hinted in the section Least Squares that we could also create such a single independent variable by weighting the multiple independent variables. Is it therefore possible to use this weighting method to create a single independent variable that matches the predicted score?

The answer is yes. Instead of weighting the standardized Homework and Parent Education variables by .75 and .25, we could have weighted them by β's from the multiple regression equation (.266 and .220) to create a composite. Even more directly, we could create a composite using the unstandardized values of Homework and Parent Education, weighting each according to its b from the multiple regression in Chapter 2 (.988 and .871, respectively). Either of these approaches would have created a composite of Homework and Parent Education that predicted Grades just as well as did our predicted Grades variable and just as well as did the original Homework and Parent Education variables.

I am not suggesting that you do this in practice; the multiple regression does it for you. Instead, you should understand that this is one way of thinking about how multiple regression works: MR provides an optimally weighted composite, a synthetic variable, of the independent variables and regresses the dependent variable on this single composite variable. This realization will stand you in good stead as you ponder the similarities between multiple regression and other statistical methods. In fact, this is what virtually all our statistical methods do, from ANOVA to structural equation modeling. "All statistical analyses of scores on measured/observed variables actually focus on correlational analyses of scores on synthetic/latent variables derived by applying weights to the observed variables" (Thompson, 1999, p. 5). Thompson goes on to note—tongue in cheek—what you may have long suspected, that we simply give these weights different names (e.g., factor loadings, regression coefficients) in different analyses so as to confuse graduate students.

ASSUMPTIONS OF REGRESSION AND REGRESSION DIAGNOSTICS

Given the conceptual nature of this book, I have just touched on the issues of residuals and least squares regression. Analysis of residuals is also a useful method for detecting violations of the assumptions underlying multiple regression and outliers and other problems with data. I want to postpone discussion of the assumptions underlying regression until you have a deeper understanding of how to develop, analyze, and interpret regression analyses. These assumptions are presented in Chapter 9 as an important topic and one worthy of additional study. Likewise, we will postpone discussion of the regression diagnostics until that time, along with diagnosis of other potential problems in regression (e.g., multicollinearity).

It is worth noting that residuals have other uses, as well. Suppose, for example, that you were studying student performance on a test across various age levels, but wanted to remove the effects of age from consideration in these analyses. One possible solution would be to regress the test scores on age, and use the residuals as age-corrected test scores (e.g., Keith, Kranzler, & Flanagan, 2001). Darlington (1990) discusses using residuals for other research purposes.

SUMMARY

This chapter has focused on some of the nitty-gritty of multiple regression analysis, including the nature of R^2 compared to r^2, the conceptual and statistical meaning of predicted scores and residuals, and the method by which multiple regression produces the "optimal" prediction. We found that R^2 depends not only on the original correlation of each independent variable with the dependent variable, but also on the correlations of the independent variables with each other. As a result, R^2 is usually less than the sum of the r^2's and only equals the sum of the r^2's when the independent variables are themselves uncorrelated. Likewise, the β's are not equivalent to and are usually smaller than the original r's. Only when the correlations among the independent variables are zero do the β's equal the r's.

Residuals are the errors in prediction of a regression equation and the result of subtracting the predicted scores on the dependent variable (predicted via the regression equation) from the actual values of participants on the dependent variable. Multiple regression works to minimize these errors of prediction so that the residual sums of squares, the sum of the squared residuals, is the smallest possible number. For this reason, you will sometimes see regression referred to as least squares regression. One way of thinking about multiple regression is that it is creating a synthetic variable that is an optimally weighted composite of the individual variables and using it to predict the outcome. This composite, weighting each independent variable by its regression weight, is then used to predict the outcome variable.

Do not be overly worried if all the concepts presented in this chapter are not crystal clear; opaque will do for now! I do encourage you, however, to return to this chapter periodically as you become more familiar and fluent in multiple regression; I believe this chapter will make more sense each time you read it and will also deepen your understanding of other topics.

EXERCISES

1. Use the Grades, Parent Education, and Homework example from Chapter 2; make sure you can reproduce the residual analyses from this chapter (i.e., those summarized in Figures 3.6 through 3.8). Output residuals and predicted scores, and examine their descriptive statistics and correlations with Grades and each other. Make sure you understand why you obtain the relations you find.

2. Create a composite variable weighting Parent Education and Homework by their regression weights as found in Exercise 1. Regress Grades on this composite. Note that you can weight the original variables using the unstandardized regression weights, or you can first standardize Parent Education and Homework (convert them to z scores) and then weight them by the appropriate β's. How do the R^2 and sums of squares compare to the multiple regression results?

3. Now try creating a composite that weights the Parent Education and Homework by some other values (e.g., 25% and 75%). Note that to do this you will need to standardize the variables first. What happens to the R^2 and sum of squared residuals?

4. Reanalyze the regression of Grades on Parent Education and Family Income from Chapter 2. Output the unstandardized predicted values and residuals. Compute the correlation between Grades and Predicted Grades. Is the value the same as the R from the multiple regression? Explain why it should be. Create a scatterplot of Predicted Grades with Grades, along with a regression line. Pick a data point in the raw data and note the actual value for Grades, Predicted Grades, and the Residual. Is the residual equal to Grades minus Predicted Grades? Now find the same data point on the scatterplot and mark the value on the graph for that person's Grades and Predicted Grades. Show graphically the residual.

NOTE

1. If the two independent variables are *negatively* correlated with each other, but correlate positively with the dependent variable, R^2 will actually be larger than $r^2 + r^2$. The β's will also be larger than the r's. This phenomenon may be considered a form of what is called statistical *suppression*. Suppression is discussed in more detail in several sources (e.g., Cohen & Cohen, 1983, chap. 3; Pedhazur, 1997, chap. 7; Thompson, 1999).

- - - - -

CHAPTER FOUR

THREE AND MORE INDEPENDENT VARIABLES AND RELATED ISSUES

This chapter will present two more examples of multiple regression, one using three independent variables and the other, four. The intent is to increase your comfort with running and interpreting multiple regression and to solidify the concepts presented so far. You will see that the addition of explanatory variables makes the regression no more difficult, with the exception that you have more to discuss when explaining the results. We will use these examples to confront several looming issues.

THREE PREDICTOR VARIABLES

Let's take our homework example a little further. Suppose that you become interested in the effects of homework completed in school versus the effects of homework completed out of school. I actually *did* become interested in this topic thanks to my children. When we would ask them if they had homework to complete, they began to respond "I did it in school." Our response, in turn, was "that's not homework, that's schoolwork!" Beyond our little parent–child exchanges, I began to wonder if "homework" completed in school had the same effects on learning and achievement as homework completed at home. The results of this research are described in Keith, Hallam, and Fine (2004); the research used structural equation modeling, rather than multiple regression, but MR could have been used.

    At any rate, suppose that you share at least some of my interest in this topic (we will switch to other examples in subsequent chapters). We will use the NELS data to examine the relative effects of homework completed in school versus homework completed out of school on students' grades. Our research question is something along these lines: Does homework completed in school have the same effect on high school students' grades as homework completed out of school? To answer the question, we regress Grades on a measure of time spent on Homework In School and a measure of time spent on Homework Out of School. As in the previous example, we control for Parents' level of Education. Grades (FFUGrad) in this example are an average of students' 10th-grade grades in English, Math, Science, and Social Studies. Parent Education (BYParEd) is education level of the father or mother (whichever is higher) for each student. The Homework variables are students' 10th-Grade reports of the amount of time they spend, on average, per week doing homework, across subjects, In School (F1S36A1) and Out of School (F1S36A2). All variables are included in your copy of the NELS data; you should examine the descriptive statistics for all these variables and may want to examine the frequencies of each predictor variable. It is good practice to run the multiple regression analysis, too! It might also be worth rereading Appendix A and its discussion of the NELS data set.

Figure 4.1 shows the frequencies of the independent variables. Notice that the scales of these variables are different from those in previous chapters. In the current example, Parent Education ranges from a value of 1, representing "Did not finish High School," up to a value of 6, representing an advanced graduate degree (PhD, MD, etc.). The Homework variables are no longer hours, but rather chunks of hours, ranging from 0 (No homework) to 7 (Over 15 hours per week). Figure 4.2 shows the descriptive statistics for the dependent variable, 10th-grade (First Follow-Up) Grade Average. Its scale has also changed, from the common 0 to 100 scale to a 1 to 8 scale, with 1 representing low grades and 8 representing high grades. The NELS developers had justifiable reasons for scaling these variables in this manner, but the variables no longer have the nice logical scales (e.g., years or hours) from the previous examples. This deficiency is more than made up for, in my opinion, by the fact that these are real and nationally representative data, whereas the previous examples had used simulated data. Figure 4.3 shows the correlations among these variables.

FIGURE 4.1   Frequencies for the independent variables in the three-predictor MR example.

BYPARED PARENTS' HIGHEST EDUCATION LEVEL

		Frequency	Percent	Valid Percent	Cumulative Percent
Valid	1 did not finish HS	97	9.7	9.7	9.7
	2 HS Grad or GED	181	18.1	18.1	27.8
	3 lt 4 year degree	404	40.4	40.4	68.3
	4 college grad	168	16.8	16.8	85.1
	5 M.A. or equiv.	86	8.6	8.6	93.7
	6 PhD., M.D. or other	63	6.3	6.3	100.0
	Total	999	99.9	100.0	
Missing	8 missing	1	.1		
Total		1000	100.0		

(Continued)

FIGURE 4.1   Continued

F1S36A2 TIME SPENT ON HOMEWORK OUT OF SCHOOL

		Frequency	Percent	Valid Percent	Cumulative Percent
Valid	0 NONE	63	6.3	6.7	6.7
	1 1 HOUR OR LESS	232	23.2	24.6	31.3
	2 2-3 HOURS	264	26.4	28.0	59.3
	3 4-6 HOURS	168	16.8	17.8	77.1
	4 7-9 HOURS	80	8.0	8.5	85.6
	5 10-12 HOURS	66	6.6	7.0	92.6
	6 13-15 HOURS	31	3.1	3.3	95.9
	7 OVER 15 HOURS	39	3.9	4.1	100.0
	Total	943	94.3	100.0	
Missing	96 MULTIPLE RESPONSE	7	.7		
	98 MISSING	17	1.7		
	System	33	3.3		
	Total	57	5.7		
Total		1000	100.0		

F1S36A1 TIME SPENT ON HOMEWORK IN SCHOOL

		Frequency	Percent	Valid Percent	Cumulative Percent
Valid	0 NONE	76	7.6	8.1	8.1
	1 1 HOUR OR LESS	341	34.1	36.5	44.6
	2 2-3 HOURS	242	24.2	25.9	70.5
	3 4-6 HOURS	158	15.8	16.9	87.4
	4 7-9 HOURS	42	4.2	4.5	91.9
	5 10-12 HOURS	37	3.7	4.0	95.8
	6 13-15 HOURS	14	1.4	1.5	97.3
	7 OVER 15 HOURS	25	2.5	2.7	100.0
	Total	935	93.5	100.0	
Missing	96 MULTIPLE RESPONSE	9	.9		
	98 MISSING	23	2.3		
	System	33	3.3		
	Total	65	6.5		
Total		1000	100.0		

Regression Results

Figure 4.4 shows some of the results of the regression analysis. As you can see, the three variables, Parent Education, time spent on Homework In School, and time spent on Homework Out of School explained 15.5% of the variance in students' 10th-grade GPA

Descriptive Statistics

	N	Minimum	Maximum	Mean	Deviation Std.	Variance
FFUGRAD ffu grades	950	1.00	8.00	5.6661	1.4713	2.165
Valid N (listwise)	950					

FIGURE 4.2   Descriptive statistics for the dependent variable Grades.

$(R^2 = .155)$, and the overall regression equation was statistically significant $(F[3, 905] = 55.450, p < .001)$. The third table in the figure, however, shows that not all the variables are important in this regression. In fact, Parent Education had a substantial and statistically significant effect on Grades $(b = .271, \beta = .234, p < .001)$, as did time spent on Homework Out of School $(b = .218, \beta = .256, p < .001)$. In contrast, the effect of time spent on Homework In School was tiny and was not statistically significant $(b = .012, \beta = .012, p = .704$. (When you do this regression yourself, you may get a value of 1.16E-02 in the b column. Don't panic; the coefficient is simply displayed as an exponential number; move the decimal point two places to the left, that is, .0116.). Note also the 95% confidence intervals for unstandardized coefficients. The CI for Homework In School encompasses zero; again, we cannot reject the hypothesis that the population value is different from zero.

The results are fairly similar to those we found using the simulated data in Chapter 2 (which were, of course, designed to mimic reality). Focusing on the β's, we conclude that each standard deviation increase in time spent on Homework Out of School led to a .256 SD increase in GPA, with Parent Education and In School Homework controlled. Each additional SD in Parent Education resulted in a .234 SD increase in student GPA (controlling for Homework). As noted earlier, the scales of the three independent variables (Homework and Parent Education) are not particularly meaningful. Parent Education ranged from 1 (did not finish high school) to 6 (PhD, MD, or other doctoral degree). The two Homework variables had values that ranged from 0, for "None" as the average amount of time spent on Homework per week, to 7 for "over 15 hours per week." Because the scales for these variables do

Correlations[a]

		FFUGRAD ffu grades	F1S36A1 TIME SPENT ON HOMEWORK IN SCHOOL	F1S36A2 TIME SPENT ON HOMEWORK OUT OF SCHOOL	BYPARED PARENTS' HIGHEST EDUCATION LEVEL
FFUGRAD ffu grades	Pearson Correlation	1	.096	.323	.304
	Sig. (2-tailed)	.	.004	.000	.000
F1S36A1 TIME SPENT ON HOMEWORK IN SCHOOL	Pearson Correlation	.096	1	.275	.059
	Sig. (2-tailed)	.004	.	.000	.075
F1S36A2 TIME SPENT ON HOMEWORK OUT OF SCHOOL	Pearson Correlation	.323	.275	1	.271
	Sig. (2-tailed)	.000	.000	.	.000
BYPARED PARENTS' HIGHEST EDUCATION LEVEL	Pearson Correlation	.304	.059	.271	1
	Sig. (2-tailed)	.000	.075	.000	.

a. Listwise N=909

FIGURE 4.3   Correlations among the independent and dependent variables.

Model Summary[b]

Model	R	R Square	Adjusted R Square	Std. Error of the Estimate
1	.394[a]	.155	.152	1.3500

a. Predictors: (Constant), F1S36A2 TIME SPENT ON HOMEWORK OUT OF SCHOOL, BYPARED PARENTS' HIGHEST EDUCATION LEVEL, F1S36A1 TIME SPENT ON HOMEWORK IN SCHOOL

b. Dependent Variable: FFUGRAD ffu grades

ANOVA

Model		Sum of Squares	df	Mean Square	F	Sig.
1	Regression	303.167	3	101.056	55.450	.000
	Residual	1649.320	905	1.822		
	Total	1952.486	908			

Coefficients[a]

Model		Unstandardized Coefficients		Standardized Coefficients			95% Confidence Interval for B	
		B	Std. Error	Beta	t	Sig.	Lower Bound	Upper Bound
1	(Constant)	4.242	.135		31.337	.000	3.977	4.508
	BYPARED PARENTS' HIGHEST EDUCATION LEVEL	.271	.037	.234	7.375	.000	.199	.343
	F1S36A1 TIME SPENT ON HOMEWORK IN SCHOOL	.012	.031	.012	.379	.704	-.048	.072
	F1S36A2 TIME SPENT ON HOMEWORK OUT OF SCHOOL	.218	.028	.256	7.780	.000	.163	.273

a. Dependent Variable: FFUGRAD ffu grades

FIGURE 4.4 Results of a multiple regression with three independent variables.

not follow any naturally interpretable scale, such as years for Education or hours for Homework, the *b*'s are not readily interpretable. We could say "each unit of Homework Time Out of School resulted in a .218-point increase in GPA," but this would not tell us much, since we would then need to explain what a "unit" increase in Homework meant. Likewise, it does not help that the scale used for Grades is nontraditional, as well (it ranges from 1, "Mostly below D" to 8 "Mostly A's"). When the scales of the variables are in a nonmeaningful metric, it makes more sense to interpret standardized regression coefficients, β's, than it does to interpret unstandardized regression coefficients, or *b*'s. You should still report both, however, along with standard errors or confidence intervals of the *b*'s. Such a practice will allow comparability with other studies using similar scales.

Interpretation

Assuming that you trusted these findings as reflecting reality, how might you interpret them to parents, or to high school students? The important finding, the finding of primary interest, is the difference in the effects of In School versus Out of School Homework. Parent Education was used primarily as a control variable that was included to improve the accuracy of our estimates of the effects of the Homework variables on GPA (see the original rea-soning for including this variable in Chapter 2); its interpretation is of less interest. With these caveats in mind, I might interpret these finding as follows:

> As you may know, many high school students complete a part or all of their homework while in school, whereas others complete all or most of their homework at home or out of school. Some do a little of both. I was interested in whether these two types of homework—in school versus out of school—were equally effective in producing learning. To find out, I conducted research to examine the relative influence of time spent on homework in school and out of school on high school students' grades in school. I also took the education of the parents into account. The results suggest that these two types of homework indeed have different effects. Homework completed In School had virtually no effect on students' Grades. In contrast, Homework completed Out of School, presumably at home, had a fairly strong effect on Grades; students who completed more Homework Out of School achieved higher Grades, even after the Education level of their parents was taken into account. I encourage you to encourage your high schoolers to complete their homework at home rather than in school. If they do, that homework is likely to show an important payoff in their grades: the more home-work they complete, the higher their grades are likely to be.

Again, this explanation would be worthwhile if you believed that these results explained the relations among these variables; as you will see, the findings from our next regression will create doubts about this. This explanation also side steps an important question: *why* does homework completed outside of school have an effect on GPA while homework completed in school does not? I can think of at least two possibilities. First, it may be that the process of doing homework out of school requires a greater degree of initiative and independence and that initiative and independence, in turn, improve grades. Second, it may be that when students complete homework in school that homework is essentially displacing instructional time, thus resulting in no net gain in time spent on learning. These possibilities are explored further in the research article (Keith et al., 2004), and you may have other ideas why this difference exists. These possible reasons for the difference are all testable in future research!

RULES OF THUMB: MAGNITUDE OF EFFECTS

Another issue that I should address is the criteria by which I argued that some effects were "tiny," whereas others were "substantial." One criticism of much research in psychology is that many researchers focus on and report only statistical significance, ignoring the magni-tude of effects (Cohen, 1994; Thompson, 1999). There is a growing consensus in psychol-ogy that researchers should report and interpret effect sizes in addition to statistical significance, and many journals now require such reporting. One advantage of multiple regression is that its statistics focus naturally on the magnitude of effects. R^2 and regression coefficients (b) can certainly be tested for their statistical significance. But R^2 and the regression coefficients (especially β) are scales that range from low to high, from zero to 1.0 for R^2 (and β usually, although not always, ranges between ± 1), and thus it is natural to focus on the magnitude of these effects. So, what constitutes a large versus a small effect? Although there are general rules of thumb for a variety of statistics (e.g., Cohen, 1988), it is also the case that Cohen and others have urged that each area of inquiry should develop its own criteria for judging the magnitude of effects.

Much of my research focuses on the influences on school learning, influences like homework, parent involvement, academic coursework, and so forth. Based on my research and reading in this area, I use the following rules of thumb for judging the magnitude of effects on learning outcomes (e.g., achievement, Grades). I consider β's below .05 as too small to be considered meaningful influences on school learning, even when they are statistically significant. β's above .05 are considered small but meaningful; those above .10 are considered moderate, and those above .25 are considered large (cf. Keith, 1999). Using these criteria, the β associated with time spent on Homework Out of School is large, whereas the β associated with time spent on Homework In School would be considered tiny, even if it were statistically significant. Keep in mind, however, that these rules of thumb apply to research on learning and achievement and that I have little idea how well they generalize to other areas. You will need to use your and others' expertise in your own area of research to develop similar guidelines.

FOUR INDEPENDENT VARIABLES

Our next example will also continue our exploration of the effects of time spent on homework on high school students' achievement. The purpose of this example is twofold. First, it will extend our analyses to an example with four independent variables; you should feel quite comfortable with this extension by now, because the analysis and interpretation are very similar to those completed previously. Second, however, this extension of our example will erect a few speed bumps in the merry analysis and interpretation road I have been leading you down. You should be troubled by the differences in these results and those presented previously. And although we will eventually resolve these problems, this example should begin to illustrate the importance of theory and thought in multiple regression analysis. On to the example.

Another Control Variable

For our previous examples, we have added a variable representing Parent Education to our regressions to "control," to some extent, students' family backgrounds. Our reasoning went something like this: parents who value education for themselves likely value education for their children, as well. Such parents are likely to emphasize learning, schooling, and studying more than are parents who place a lower value on education (Walberg, 1981, referred to such an orientation as the "curriculum of the home"). As a result, children in such homes are likely to spend more time studying; they are also likely to earn higher grades. I noted earlier that we needed to include Parent Education in the regression because, if our speculation about the effects of Parent Education is correct, it is a potential common cause of both Homework and Grades.

What about other potential common causes? It seems likely that students' academic aptitude, or ability, or previous achievement might also function in this manner. In other words, doesn't it seem likely that more able students should not only earn higher grades, but might also be inclined to spend more time studying? If so, shouldn't some measure of students' prior achievement be included in the regression as well?

Our next multiple regression example is designed with this speculation in mind. In it, I have regressed students' 10th-grade GPA (FFUGrade) on both In School (F1S36A1) and Out of School Homework (F1S36A2), as in the previous example. Also included is a measure of

Parents' highest level of Education (BYParEd), again as in the previous example. This new regression, however, also includes a measure of students' Previous Achievement (BYTests), an average of students' scores on a series of academic achievement tests in Reading, Mathematics, Science, and Social Studies administered in the 8th grade. This new regression, then, tests the effects on Grades of In School Homework versus Out of School Homework, while controlling for Parents' highest levels of Education and students' Previous Achievement.

Regression Results

The results of the multiple regression are shown in Figures 4.5 and 4.6. As shown in Figure 4.5, the linear combination of the variables representing parents' education, previous

Descriptive Statistics

	Mean	Std. Deviation	N
FFUGRAD ffu grades	5.7033	1.4641	879
BYPARED PARENTS' HIGHEST EDUCATION LEVEL	3.22	1.27	879
F1S36A1 TIME SPENT ON HOMEWORK IN SCHOOL	2.09	1.53	879
F1S36A2 TIME SPENT ON HOMEWORK OUT OF SCHOOL	2.55	1.72	879
BYTESTS Eighth grade achievement tests (mean)	51.9449	8.6598	879

Model Summary

Model	R	R Square	Adjusted R Square	Std. Error of the Estimate
1	.531	.282	.279	1.2432

ANOVA[b]

Model		Sum of Squares	df	Mean Square	F	Sig.
1	Regression	531.234	4	132.808	85.935	.000[a]
	Residual	1350.728	874	1.545		
	Total	1881.962	878			

a. Predictors: (Constant), BYTESTS Eighth grade achievement tests (mean), F1S36A1 TIME SPENT ON HOMEWORK IN SCHOOL, F1S36A2 TIME SPENT ON HOMEWORK OUT OF SCHOOL, BYPARED PARENTS' HIGHEST EDUCATION LEVEL

b. Dependent Variable: FFUGRAD ffu grades

FIGURE 4.5   Multiple regression with four independent variables: descriptive statistics and model summary.

Coefficients[a]

Model		Unstandardized Coefficients		Standardized Coefficients	t	Sig.
		B	Std. Error	Beta		
1	(Constant)	1.497	.257		5.819	.000
	BYPARED PARENTS' HIGHEST EDUCATION LEVEL	9.12E-02	.037	.079	2.443	.015
	F1S36A1 TIME SPENT ON HOMEWORK IN SCHOOL	-1.2E-02	.029	-.013	-.423	.672
	F1S36A2 TIME SPENT ON HOMEWORK OUT OF SCHOOL	.158	.027	.186	5.876	.000
	BYTESTS Eighth grade achievement tests (mean)	6.80E-02	.006	.402	12.283	.000

a. Dependent Variable: FFUGRAD ffu grades

FIGURE 4.6   Multiple regression with four independent variables: regression coefficients.

achievement, time spent on in school homework, and the time spent on out of school home-work accounted for 28.2% of the variance in 10th-grade GPA ($R^2 = .282$), which appears to be quite an improvement over the 15.5% of the variance explained by the previous multiple regression (in subsequent chapters we will learn how to test this change in R^2 for statistical significance). The overall regression, as in the previous example, is statistically significant ($F[4, 874] = 85.935, p < .001$).[1] Everything seems to be in order.

Trouble in Paradise

When we focus on Figure 4.6, however, we are led to different conclusions than in our previous analysis. Parents' Education level and time spent on Homework Out of School still had statistically significant effects on Grades, but the magnitude of these effects are very different. In the previous example, the unstandardized and standardized regression coefficients associated with Parent Education were .271 and .234, and now they are .091 and .079, respectively. Indeed, all the coefficients changed, as shown in Table 4.1, with the addition of the new independent variable.

What this means is that the conclusions we draw from these regressions will also be very different. Focusing on the variables of primary interest (the two Homework variables), we conclude from the three-independent-variable multiple regression that Homework time Out of School had a large effect on Grades, using my rules of thumb, but in the four-variable regression, we conclude that Homework had only a moderate effect on Grades. The effect of In School Homework was small and not statistically significant in both analyses, although the sign switched from positive to negative. What is going on? Were all our conclusions from the earlier analysis erroneous? (You may be tempted to conclude that we should instead focus only on statistical significance, since the same vari-

TABLE 4.1 **Comparison of Regression Coefficients for the Three-Variable versus Four-Variable Multiple Regression**

VARIABLE	THREE INDEPENDENT VARIABLES		FOUR INDEPENDENT VARIABLES	
	b (SE$_b$)	ß	b (SE$_b$)	ß
Parent Education	.271 (.037)	.234	.091 (.037)	.079
Previous Achievement	—	—	.068 (.006)	.402
In School Homework	.012 (.031)	.012	–.012 (.029)	–.013
Out of School Homework	.218 (.028)	.256	.158 (.027)	.186

ables remain statistically significant versus not statistically significant in the two regressions. This conclusion is incorrect, however, since it is not always the case that the same variables will remain statistically significant with the addition of new independent variables.)

You should be troubled by this development. It suggests that our conclusions about the effects of one variable on another change depending on which other variables are included in our analyses. Focusing on the three-variable regression, you would conclude that each additional unit (whatever it is) of time spent on Homework out of school results in a .218-point increase in GPA. If you believe the four-variable regression, however, you might argue that each additional unit of time spent on Homework out of school results in a .158-point increase in GPA. Which conclusion is correct?

This example illustrates a danger of multiple regression as illustrated so far: *The regression coefficients will often (although not always) change depending on the variables included in our regression equation.* This development certainly does not argue for the scientific respectability of our findings, however, nor does it bode well for the scientific respectability of multiple regression. If our conclusions change depending on the variables we include in our analyses, then knowledge and conclusions depend on our skill and honesty in selecting variables for analysis. Research findings should be more constant and less ephemeral if they are to form the basis for understanding, knowledge, and theory. Furthermore, this change in findings and conclusions means that, to some extent, we can find what we want by choosing the variables to include in our regression. Want to find that Parent Education has a moderate to strong effect on GPA? Don't include previous achievement in your analysis. Want to conclude, instead, that Parent Education only has a small effect? Then do include a measure of previous achievement in your regression.

It may be small comfort if I tell you that this danger is not entirely a result of multiple regression, per se. Instead, it is a danger in most nonexperimental research, whatever statistical technique is used for analysis. This conundrum is one reason that many researchers argue against making causal conclusions from nonexperimental research: the results change depending on the variables analyzed. Of course, an admonition against non-experimental research means that much scientific inquiry is simply not possible, because many worthy scientific questions—and especially questions in the behavioral sciences—are simply not testable through other means. This danger is also one reason that many researchers focus on prediction rather than explanation. We may be on slightly more stable ground if we make statements like "when GPA was regressed on Parent Education and Homework In and Out of School, Homework Out of School and Parent Education were statistically significant *predictors* of GPA, whereas Homework In School was not." Such a predictive conclusion avoids the implied causal connection in my statements [e.g., that time spent on Homework Out of School has a strong *effect* (as in cause and effect) on Grade-point average]. But a focus on prediction rather than explanation is also scientifically less valuable; it does not allow us to use our findings for the development of theory or to change the status quo. If all we can conclude is that homework predicts achievement, then we cannot legitimately encourage children, parents, or teachers to use homework as a method of improving learning. *Intervention thinking requires causal thinking!* Causal thinking, in turn, requires careful thought and knowledge of previous research and theory.

COMMON CAUSES AND INDIRECT EFFECTS

Fortunately, there is a resolution to this dilemma. Ironically, the solution requires additional, more formal, causal thinking, rather than less, and will be dealt with in depth in the beginning of Part 2. In the meantime, I will present a brief preview of what is to come, enough, I hope, to quell your fears to some extent.

Figure 4.7 shows a model of the thinking underlying our four-independent-variable multiple regression, with the arrows or paths in the model representing the presumed influence of one variable on another. The explicitness of the model may seem surprising, but it should not; most of the paths simply present in figural form my earlier explanations concerning the reasons for the variables included in the multiple regression. The inclusion of the four independent variables in the multiple regression implies that we believe these variables may affect Grades and that we want to estimate the magnitude of these effects; it makes sense, then, to include paths representing these possible effects in the model. This portion of the model is implied, whether we realize it or not, every time we conduct a multiple regression analysis. Recall that we included the variables Parent Education and Previous Achievement in our regression because we thought that these variables might affect both Grades and Homework, and thus the paths from these variables to the two Homework variables make sense as well. This reasoning accounts for all the paths except two: the path from Parent Education to Previous Achievement and the arrow from In School Homework to Out of School Homework. Yet it makes sense that if Parent Education affects Grades it should affect achievement as well. My reasoning for drawing the path from In School to Out of School Homework is that students who complete homework in school will take home homework that is not completed in school. Although not discussed here, most of these decisions are also supported by relevant theory.

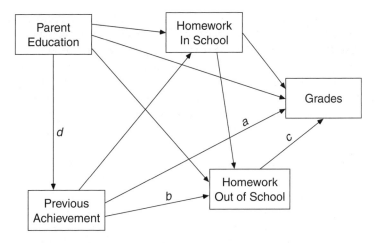

FIGURE 4.7   The causal model underlying our multiple regression example.

The paths labeled *a* and *b* make explicit what we mean by a *common cause:* Our model assumes that Previous Achievement affects Grades directly (path *a*) and that it also affects Homework completed out of school (path *b*). If so, if both of these paths are statistically significant and meaningful, then Previous Achievement *must* be included in the model to get an accurate estimate of the effects of Out of School Homework on Grades. *To interpret regression coefficients as effects, all common causes of the presumed cause and the presumed effect must be included in the model.* If they are not, then the regression coefficients will be inaccurate estimates of the effects; in many cases, they will be overestimates of these effects. This, then, was the reason for the drop in the apparent effect of Out of School Homework on Grades from the three-independent-variable regression to the four-independent-variable regression: Previous Achievement, a common cause of both Homework and Grades, was erroneously excluded from the three-independent-variable model. With this common cause included in the model, we get smaller and more accurate estimates of effects.

If you include in the regression a variable that logically is prior to Homework Out of School and Grades, but is *not* a common cause of Homework and Grades, the regression weight for Out of School Homework will *not* change. That is, a variable that affects only Out of School Homework but not Grades will not change the Homework regression coefficient. Likewise, a variable that affects Grades but not Out of School Homework will not change the Homework regression coefficient.[2]

There is a different reason for the drop in the apparent effects of Parent Education on Grades (from $b = .271$ to $b = .091$) in moving from the first to the second multiple regression. A portion of the effect we initially attributed to the effect of Parent Education on Grades now appears as an *indirect* effect. In our current model, Parent Education affects Previous Achievement (path *d*), and Previous Achievement affects Grades. Thus Parent Education affects Grades *indirectly* through Previous Achievement. Another way of saying this is that Previous Achievement is an *intervening* or *mediating* variable between Parent Education and

Grades. When we discuss structural equation modeling and path analysis, we will learn how to calculate these indirect effects, and you will find that for both models the *total* effects of Parent Education on Grades are the same. For now, just remember that it is not necessary to include mediating effects for multiple regression to provide accurate estimates of effects, but that the regression coefficients from simultaneous regression (the type of multiple regression we are currently doing) only focus on *direct,* not mediating, effects.

To reiterate, to interpret regression coefficients as the effects of one variable on another, the common causes of the presumed cause and presumed effect must be included in the regression. If your regression *does* include these common causes, you can indeed make such interpretations (well, there are a few other assumptions that we will deal with later in Chapter 9). You can thus rest somewhat easier, because this requirement, although difficult, is not impossible to satisfy. In contrast, it is not necessary to include intervening variables in your regression, although you should keep in mind that, if you do include mediating variables between your presumed cause and presumed effect, you are estimating only a portion of the total effect of one variable on another. We will deal with these topics more extensively in the next chapter and at the beginning of Part Two of this book.

THE IMPORTANCE OF R^2?

As we switched from a regression with three independent variables to one with four, we also noted that the R^2 increased; we explained more variance in students' GPAs. As you will discover in your reading, some researchers make much ado about the size of R^2 and try to explain as much variance as possible in any given regression. I do not, and with a little reflection on the previous few sections, you may understand why. It is relatively easy to increase R^2; just add more variables to the regression that predicts the outcome. In the current example, we could add previous GPA to the regression, which would likely lead to another healthy increase in the variance explained, and we might also add a measure of motivation, assuming that it, too, should increase the variance explained in students' Grades. But recall that our primary interest in these regressions was to understand the effects of In School and Out of School Homework on Grades. Indeed, it makes sense to add variables to the regression *if* these variables are common causes of Homework and Grades. In contrast, given our purpose, it makes little sense to add variables to the regression if they are not common causes of Homework and Grades. Thus, although we can inflate the R^2 by adding to the regression variables that affected students' Grades (but not Homework), such additions serve little purpose other than inflating the R^2; they will not help us to better understand the effects of Homework on Grades. We can also increase R^2 by adding intervening variables between Homework and Grades, but unless our interest is in understanding the indirect effects of Homework on Grades, this addition will also make little sense.

It is tempting to think that the more variance you have explained the closer you have come to understanding and explaining some phenomenon. But this is true only if you have included the proper variables in your regression. It is also tempting to think that if you find a high R^2 you must have included the proper variables in your regression. This is also not necessarily the case. Suppose you regress SAT (Scholastic Aptitude Test) scores of incoming students on the prestige of various colleges. You will likely get a fairly high R^2, but college rankings do not influence SAT scores (you have confused cause and effect). You have not explained the phenomenon. Or perhaps you decide to regress reading proficiency of elementary students on their shoe size. Again you would likely get a high R^2, but you have not explained reading skill, nor have you chosen the right variables for your regression. The high R^2 is the result of a spurious association (there is a common cause of reading proficiency and shoe size: growth or age). The high R^2 did not assure that you chose the correct variables for inclusion in the regression.

Should you then ignore R^2? No, of course not, and we have not done so here. My point is simply this: yes, other things being equal, the higher the R^2 the better; but a high R^2 is generally not the most important criterion if we are conducting regression for the purposes of explanation. What I suggest is that you make sure that R^2 is reasonable, which depends on the constructs you are studying and requires some knowledge of research in this area. For the dependent variable of Grades, for example, I generally expect to explain 25% or so of the variance in Grades, and our four-independent-variable regression is consistent with this expectation. If we are focusing on achievement test scores, I expect a higher R^2, whereas, if our dependent variable is self-concept, I expect to explain less variance. Some phenomena are easier to explain than others; more reliable dependent variables should also lead to more explained variance. Likewise, prior to interpretation you should make sure the other regression results are reasonable. Suppose in the Grades–Homework regression used in this chapter you found a negative regression coefficient associated with Previous Achievement. That result is so implausible that I likely would not interpret the findings no matter how high the R^2, and certainly not without additional investigation.

Are you surprised that I think it's reasonable to explain only 25% of the variance in Grades? This means that 75% of the variance in Grades is unexplained! I have several responses. First, yes, it's difficult to explain human behavior; we are unpredictable creatures. To put it differently, you'd probably be insulted if I declared that I could predict your behavior with a high degree of accuracy. If I rattle off the influences of your grades and tell you that I can predict your future grades very accurately from these variables, you might even feel angry or defeated. When you think of it this way, you might thus be relieved that we are explaining only 25% of the variance in Grades. Or, as Kenny put it, "human freedom may then rest in the error term" (i.e., the unexplained variance) (1979, p. 9).

I should also note for the benefit of those more familiar with ANOVA that we will generally consider explaining 25% of the variance in a dependent variable as a *large* effect size in an ANOVA. "A good rule of thumb is that one is fooling oneself if more than 50% of the variance is predicted" (Kenny, 1979, p. 9). It happens, but not often. When it does happen, it's often the case that we have analyzed longitudinal data with the same variable measured at two points in time (as both the dependent and an independent variable). Finally, I should note that others place a greater emphasis on R^2 than I do. Ask the instructor teaching your class: What's his or her position on the importance of R^2?

PREDICTION AND EXPLANATION

Let's spend a little more time on a topic that we have broached a few times so far: the distinction between prediction and explanation. The underlying purpose of our research for purposes of prediction or explanation has important implications for how we choose the variables for regression, conduct the analysis, and interpret the results. As you will see in

Chapter 5, some methods of multiple regression are better suited for one purpose than another. I am assuming that most readers will be interested in using multiple regression for explanatory purposes, and most of my examples have been set up accordingly. Many researchers blur these two purposes, however, and I may have done the same in previous chapters. It is time, however, to make the distinction sharper.

In most of the examples so far, we have been interested in the *effects,* or *influences,* of one or more variables on an outcome. Such an interest denotes an explanatory purpose; we want to *explain,* partially, how an effect comes about, and we use our independent, or explanatory, variables to accomplish this purpose. The explanatory intent of these examples is further revealed in our interpretations; we talk of the effects of homework, for example, on grades. Even more revealing, we discuss the probable results if students were to increase the time they spent on homework. Such an interpretation reveals a clear inference of cause and effect, and such an inference is the essence of explanation.

It is also possible to use multiple regression for the purpose of prediction. You may be an admissions officer of a college interested in predicting, in advance, which applicants to your college are most likely to perform well in school so that you can accept these students and reject those who are likely to perform poorly. In such an example, you have no real interest in explanation and no interest in making cause and effect interpretations. Your only interest is in making as accurate a prediction as is possible from the various predictor variables available to you. If prediction is your goal, you *will* want to maximize the R^2 (in contrast to our earlier discussion).

As discussed earlier in this chapter, if your interest is in explanation, you need to choose the variables for the regression equation very carefully. In addition to the dependent and independent variables of primary interest, your regression should include any likely common causes of these variables. At the same time, you should refrain from including any irrelevant variables (unless you wish to demonstrate that they are not common causes), because they are likely to dilute your power and muddy your findings. Because of the care needed in choosing the variables to include in an explanatory regression analysis, the researcher needs a firm grounding in relevant theory and previous research. Theory and previous research go far in telling you which variables should be included in such regressions.

If your interest is in prediction, however, you have much less need to fret over your selection of variables. Certainly, a knowledge of theory and previous research can help you maximize successful prediction, but it is not critical. In fact, if your purpose is simple prediction, then you could even use an "effect" to predict a "cause."

An example will help illustrate this point. Intelligence (or aptitude or previous achievement) commonly appears in theories of school learning as an important influence on students' learning. Thus, explanatory regressions with achievement tests, grades, or some other measure of learning as an outcome often include a measure of one of these constructs. It would make little sense to include a measure of grades as an independent variable in a regression analysis attempting to explain intelligence, because the analysis would reverse the "cause" and the "effect." If our interest were only in *predicting* intelligence, however, including grades among the predictors would be perfectly acceptable. If grades made prediction more accurate, why not use them?

As noted above, many researchers confuse these purposes, and thus don't think through the variables carefully when conducting an explanatory regression or end up using an approach more suited to prediction, when their real interest is in explanation. Even worse, it is not unusual for a researcher to set up and conduct a prediction-oriented regression, but then interpret the results in an explanatory fashion. For example, I have seen researchers speak of prediction throughout a research article, carefully eschewing any sort of causal language. But then, in the discussion, the researchers argue that programs or interventions are needed to change the level of a variable from their study to effect change in the outcome, and such an argument is predicated on causal, explanatory thinking. This bait and switch, while presumably unintentional, is poor practice and may lead to wildly erroneous conclusions (think about an erroneous, explanatory interpretation of our above prediction example). Don't fall prey to this danger in your own research or in reading the research of others. Be clear as to whether your purpose is explanatory or predictive, choose your method accordingly, and interpret your findings properly.[3]

SUMMARY

This chapter extended the example used in previous chapters to illustrate multiple regression with three and four independent variables. First, we regressed Grades on Parent Education, time spent on In School Homework, and time spent on Out of School Homework. The results suggested that Out of School Homework had a strong effect on Grades, whereas In School Homework had no such effect. In the second example, we added another variable to the regression, students' Previous Achievement. In this regression, Homework Out of School had only a moderate effect on Grades. As we have seen, the analysis and interpretation of these examples were very similar to those in earlier chapters. We can easily add additional independent variables, with straightforward analysis and interpretation.

We made a disturbing discovery, however: the regression coefficients changed in magnitude as we added new variables to the multiple regression equation. I argued, although not demonstrated, that there may be two reasons for such changes: first, if a common cause of a presumed cause and a presumed effect is included in a regression, the regression coefficients will change from those found when such a variable is excluded from the regression. Second, if an intervening variable is included in a regression between the presumed cause and the presumed effect, the regression coefficients will change in magnitude, because the regression coefficients focus only on direct effects. The first reason for the change in the regression coefficients constitutes a serious error in the analysis, but the second does not.

I discouraged a fixation on R^2, as well as a temptation to maximize R^2. We should include the relevant variables and not load up our regressions with irrelevant variables. You might, in fact, reasonably be suspicious when you obtain R^2's above .50.

These problems and concerns only apply to regression for which you are interested in explanation, that is, when you are interested in the magnitude of the effect of one variable on another. They are less applicable when your chief interest is in the simple prediction of one variable from a group of others. I have argued, however, that such simple prediction is scientifically less appealing, because it does not allow you to think in terms of theory, interventions, policy, or changes to the status quo. One thing you must *not* do is to pretend you are interested in simple prediction, but then switch to an explanatory conclusion (e.g., if you spent more time on homework out of school, your grades would likely improve). Unfortunately, such bait and switch tactics are depressingly common in the research literature. I have also argued that it is necessary to think causally to understand what is happening in explanatory analyses; path diagrams are a useful heuristic aid to such thinking. We will use such diagrams throughout this text to explicate important concepts. We will cover these topics in more detail in Part 2; for now, we will continue to focus on the proper analysis and interpretation of multiple regression. You have no doubt noticed that there are several topics, including prediction and explanation, understanding which variables should be included in a regression, and the proper interpretation of regression coefficients, that we will revisit on a regular basis. I believe these issues are important to introduce early to get you thinking about them. We will revisit them as your knowledge increases and eventually resolve them.

E X E R C I S E S

1. If you have not done so already, conduct the two multiple regression analyses presented in this chapter. Compare your results to mine. Analyze the descriptive statistics for the variables used (e.g., means, standard deviations, variances, minimum and maximum for all variables, frequency distributions of Parent Education, Homework In School, and Homework Out of School) to make sure you understand the metric of the variables.

2. Does the size of an adolescent's family influence his or her self-esteem? Does TV viewing affect self-esteem? Using the NELS data, regress 10th-graders' Self-Concept scores (F1Cncpt1) on Parent Education (BYParEd), Achievement (BYTests), Family Size (BYFamSiz), and TV Time (create a composite by calculation of the mean of BYS42A and BYS42B). Check the variables to make sure that you understand their metric (F1Cncpt1 has positive and negative values because it is a mean of z scores; positive scores represent more positive self-concept). Clean up the data, as needed, and run the multiple regression. Interpret your findings. Do any of your findings surprise you? Are you willing to interpret the regression coefficients as effects?

3. Does age affect eating disorders in women? Tiggemann and Lynch (2001) studied the effect of women's body image on eating disorders across the life-span. The file labeled "Tiggeman & Lynch simulated.sav" includes a simulated version of some of the variables from this research (the data are also contained in an Excel file and a text file with the same name, but the extension ".xls" or ".dat"). The variables in the file are Age (21 to 78), the extent to which the women habitually monitored their bodies and how it looked (Monitor), the extent to which the women felt shame when their bodies did not look the way they expected (Shame), the extent to which women felt anxiety about their bodies (Anxiety), and the extent to which the women endorsed eating disorder symptoms (Eat_Dis). Is the correlation between age and eating disorders statistically significant? When you regress eating disorders on Age and these other variables (Monitor, Shame, and Anxiety), does age have an effect on eating disorders? Which of these variables are most important for explaining eating disorders? Interpret your findings.

4. Conduct a multiple regression on four or five variables of your choice. Look through the NELS data and find a variable you are interested in explaining. Pick several independent variables you think may help in explaining this dependent variable. Examine descriptive statistics for these variables and frequencies for variables with a limited number of response options to make sure you understand their scales. Clean up the data as needed; that is, make sure the variables are coded in the proper order and that missing values are dealt with properly (e.g., "Don't know" responses are coded as missing, rather than as a value that will be analyzed). Conduct the multiple regression and interpret the results. Are there any threats to your analysis and interpretation (e.g., neglected likely common causes)?

NOTES

1. You may—and should—wonder about the substantial change in degrees of freedom. In the previous example, we had 3 and 905 degrees of freedom, with 3 degrees of freedom for the regression of Grades on three independent variables ($df = k = 3$) and 905 df for the residual ($df = N - k - 1 = 909 - 3 - 1 = 905$). Now we have 4 and 874 df. The 4 makes sense ($df = k = 4$), but the 874 does not. The reason is due to our treatment of missing data. All large-scale surveys have missing data, as does NELS. In these regressions I have used *listwise deletion* of missing data, meaning that any person who had any missing data on any one of the five variables in the analysis was not included in the analysis. Apparently, some students who had complete data when four variables were used (Grades, Parent Education, Homework In School, and Homework Out of School) had missing data for the new variable Previous Achievement. When this new variable was added, our sample size (using listwise deletion) decreased from 909 to 879, so our new residual degrees of freedom equals $879 - 4 - 1 = 874$. Listwise deletion is the default treatment of missing data in SPSS and most other programs, but there are other options as well.

2. To demonstrate why this is so, I need to skip ahead to some concepts presented in Part 2, Chapter 10. Our formula for calculating β from correlations [e.g., $\beta_1 = (r_{y1} - r_{y2}r_{12})/(1 - r_{12}^2)$] will not work because we are talking about *effects*, not correlations, equal to zero. Thus, you can either take these statements on faith for now or continue with this note. Focus on the model shown in Figure 4.8, a much simplified version of the model from Figure 4.7. The variables of primary interest are Homework Out of School (Homework) and Grades. The variable labeled X is a potential common cause of Homework and Grades. The paths are equivalent to β's. The path c is equal to the regression weight for Homework when Grades is regressed on X and Homework, and the path b is equal to the regression weight for X for this same regression. We will see in Chapter 10 that $r_{\text{Grades·Homework}} = c + ab$. But if X has no effect on Grades (the first way by which X would not be a common cause), then $b = 0$, and, as a result, $r_{\text{Grades·Homework}} = c$. In other words, in this case the β is the same as the r. This means that when X affects Homework but not Grades the β for Homework from the regression of Grades on Homework and X will be the same as the correlation between Grades and Homework. Recall from Chapter 1 that β is equal to r when there is only a single independent variable. Thus my comment "a variable that affected only Out of School Homework but not Grades would not change the Homework regression coefficient." My second statement was "a variable that affected Grades but not Out of School Homework would not change the Homework regression coefficient." In this case the path a would be equal to zero. Using the same formula as above ($r_{\text{Grades·Homework}} = c + ab$), if a were equal to zero, then $r_{\text{Grades·Homework}} = c$ again. If X has no effect on Homework, then with the regression of Grades on Homework and X, the regression coefficient for Homework will be the same as if X were not included in the regression. If a variable is not a common cause of Homework and Grades, then its inclusion in the regression will not change the regression coefficients.

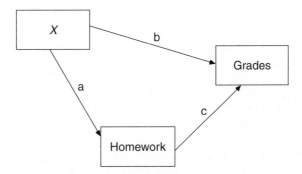

FIGURE 4.8   Simplified version of Figure 4.7, used to demonstrate what happens to regression coefficient equations in the absence of *common* causes.

3. To some extent, these distinctions overlap those made by Huberty (2003) between multiple *correlation* analysis and multiple *regression* analysis.

■ ■ ■ ■ ■

THREE TYPES OF
MULTIPLE REGRESSION

The type of multiple regression that we have been using so far in this book is one of three major types or flavors of multiple regression, commonly called simultaneous or forced entry regression. In this chapter, we will compare simultaneous regression to two other types of multiple regression, sequential (hierarchical) regression and stepwise regression. As you will see, the different types of multiple regression serve different purposes and have different interpretations and different strengths and weaknesses.

We will analyze one problem several different ways to illustrate the differences in the three regression approaches. Suppose you are interested in the effect of self-perceptions on some aspect of academic performance. Specifically, you are interested in achievement in Social Studies. We will use the NELS data and the 10th-grade achievement standardized scores on the History, Civics, and Geography (or Social Studies) test (F1TxHStd). For measures of self-perceptions, the examples will use a short measure of 10th-grade self-esteem (F1Cncpt2), made up of seven items such as "I feel I am a person of worth, the equal of other people" and "On the whole, I am satisfied with myself." The items were reversed, if necessary, so that high scores represented higher self-esteem. The items were converted to *z* scores and then averaged to create the composite. (NELS also includes another self-esteem variable, labeled F1Cncpt1, which uses fewer items than does the F2Cncpt2 composite that we are using.) Also included in the regressions is a short measure of locus of control (F1Locus2), a measure of the degree to which people believe they control their own destiny (an internal locus of control) versus the extent to which they believe external forces control them (an external locus). Sample items include "In my life, good luck is more important than hard work for success" and "Every time I try to get ahead, something or somebody stops me." F1Locus2 included six items, with higher scores representing a more internal locus of control.

In the regressions, we will also include two control variables in the spirit of our previous discussion of the importance of including common causes in our analyses. Instead of parent education level, we turn to a broader socioeconomic status (SES) variable (BySES). This SES variable includes a measure of the parents' level of education, but also includes measures of the parents' occupational status and family income. BySES is a mean of *z*-scores of these items. Such SES variables are common in regression analyses of educational outcomes, although they may go by the name of Family Background, rather than SES. We will call this variable SES for now; remember, however, that it is much more than a measure of income. Students' Grade-Point Average from grades 6 to 8 (ByGrads), on a standard 4.0 scale, was included in the regressions as a measure of students' previous academic performance. Descriptive statistics for the five variables are shown in Figure 5.1, and the correlation matrix of the variables is shown in Table 5.1.

Descriptive Statistics

	N	Minimum	Maximum	Mean	Std. Deviation	Variance
F1TXHSTD HIST/CIT/GEOG STANDARDIZED SCORE	923	28.94	69.16	50.9181	9.9415	98.834
BYSES SOCIO-ECONOMIC STATUS COMPOSITE	1000	-2.414	1.874	-3.1E-02	.77880	.607
BYGRADS GRADES COMPOSITE	983	.5	4.0	2.970	.752	.566
F1CNCPT2 SELF-CONCEPT 2	941	-2.30	1.35	3.97E-02	.6729	.453
F1LOCUS2 LOCUS OF CONTROL 2	940	-2.16	1.43	4.70E-02	.6236	.389
Valid N (listwise)	887					

FIGURE 5.1 Descriptive statistics for the NELS variables used in the chapter.

TABLE 5.1   **Intercorrelations among 10th-Grade Social Studies Test Score, Parent SES, Previous GPA, Self-Esteem, and Locus of Control**

VARIABLES		F1TXHSTD	BYSES	BYGRADS	F1CNCPT2	F1LOCUS2
F1TXHSTD	10th-Grade Standardized Test	1.000				
BYSES	Socioeconomic Status Composite	.430	1.000			
BYGRADS	Grades Composite	.498	.325	1.000		
F1CNCPT2	Self-Concept 2 Composite	.173	.132	.167	1.000	
F1LOCUS2	Locus of Control 2 Composite	.248	.194	.228	.585	1.000

SIMULTANEOUS MULTIPLE REGRESSION

The Analysis

In the type of multiple regression we have been using so far, all the independent variables were entered into the regression equation at the same time, thus the label *simultaneous regression.* This type of regression is also referred to as *forced entry regression,* because all variables are forced to enter the equation at the same time, or *standard* multiple regression. The simultaneous multiple regression results are shown in Figure 5.2. These are the type of results you are used to looking at, so we will not spend much time with them. First, we focus on the R and the R^2 and their statistical significance; the four explanatory variables in combination account for 34% of the variance in 10th-grade Social Studies test scores. The overall regression is statistically significant ($F = 112.846$ [4, 882], $p < .001$). The next step is to focus on the unstandardized regression coefficients, their statistical significance and confidence intervals, and the standardized regression coefficients. From this portion of Figure 5.2, you can see that all of the variables except Self-Esteem have a statistically significant effect on the Social Studies test score. SES and previous Grades have a strong effect, whereas Locus of Control has a small to moderate effect.

Purpose

Simultaneous regression is primarily useful for explanatory research to determine the extent of the influence of one or more variables on some outcome. In the present example, we could use simultaneous regression to determine the extent of the influence of Self-Esteem and Locus of Control on social studies achievement, while controlling for SES and previous academic performance. Simultaneous regression is also useful for determining the *relative* influence of each of the variables studied; indeed, it may be the best method for making this determination. As noted in the previous chapter, simultaneous regression estimates the direct effects of each independent variable on the dependent variable.

Because explanation subsumes prediction, however, simultaneous regression can also be used to determine the extent to which a set of variables *predicts* an outcome and the relative importance of the various predictors. For the current example, we can examine the β's to conclude that previous Grades is the best predictor among this set of variables, fol-

Model Summary

Model	R	R Square	Adjusted R Square	Std. Error of the Estimate
1	.582[a]	.339	.336	8.0412

a. Predictors: (Constant), F1LOCUS2 LOCUS OF CONTROL 2, BYSES SOCIO-ECONOMIC STATUS COMPOSITE, BYGRADS GRADES COMPOSITE, F1CNCPT2 SELF-CONCEPT 2

ANOVA[b]

Model		Sum of Squares	df	Mean Square	F	Sig.
1	Regression	29186.88	4	7296.721	112.846	.000[a]
	Residual	57031.03	882	64.661		
	Total	86217.92	886			

a. Predictors: (Constant), F1LOCUS2 LOCUS OF CONTROL 2, BYSES SOCIO-ECONOMIC STATUS COMPOSITE, BYGRADS GRADES COMPOSITE, F1CNCPT2 SELF-CONCEPT 2

b. Dependent Variable: F1TXHSTD HIST/CIT/GEOG STANDARDIZED SCORE

Coefficients[a]

Model		Unstandardized Coefficients		Standardized Coefficients			95% Confidence Interval for B	
		B	Std. Error	Beta	t	Sig.	Lower Bound	Upper Bound
1	(Constant)	35.517	1.226		28.981	.000	33.112	37.923
	SES	3.690	.378	.285	9.772	.000	2.949	4.431
	Previous Grades	5.150	.399	.380	12.910	.000	4.367	5.933
	Self-Esteem	.218	.501	.015	.436	.663	-.764	1.201
	Locus of Control	1.554	.552	.097	2.814	.005	.470	2.638

a. Dependent Variable: F1TXHSTD HIST/CIT/GEOG STANDARDIZED SCORE

FIGURE 5.2   Simultaneous regression of Social Studies test scores on SES, Previous Grades, Self-Esteem, and Locus of Control.

lowed by SES and Locus of Control. Simultaneous regression can also be used to develop a prediction equation; for the current example, the *b*'s could be used in an equation with a new sample of students to predict 10th-grade social studies achievement.

What to Interpret

In simultaneous multiple regression, the R^2 and associated statistics are used to determine the statistical significance and importance of the overall regression. The regression coefficients are used to determine the magnitude of effect of each variable (controlling for the other variables) and, as we have seen, can be used to make policy or intervention recommendations. Such recommendations are particularly useful when the variables used have a meaningful metric (unlike the current example), using the unstandardized regression coefficients. The standardized coefficients are useful for determining the *relative* importance of each explanatory variable.

Strengths and Weaknesses

As we will see, simultaneous MR is probably the most useful of the three regression approaches when the goal of research is explanation, because of the ability to focus on both the overall effect of all variables and the effect of each variable by itself. The regression coefficients are useful for making predictions concerning what would happen if interventions or policy changes were made (e.g., how much would achievement increase if one were able to effect a change in locus of control from external to internal), and the standardized coefficients can provide information concerning the relative importance of various influences. If one has used theory and previous research to choose the variables to include in the regression, simultaneous regression can indeed provide estimates of the effects of the independent on the dependent variables. We have already broached the primary weakness of simultaneous MR: the regression coefficients can change, perhaps drastically, depending on the variables included in the regression equation.

SEQUENTIAL MULTIPLE REGRESSION

Sequential (also called hierarchical) regression is another common method of multiple regression and, like simultaneous regression, is often used in an explanatory manner. We will spend considerable time discussing the method, its interpretation, strengths, and weaknesses. This discussion will also point toward similarities and differences with simultaneous regression. We will end with a summary of this presentation.

The Analysis

With sequential multiple regression, the variables are entered into the regression equation one at a time, in some order determined in advance by the researcher. For our current example, I entered SES into the equation in the first step, then previous GPA in the second step, then Self-Esteem, and finally Locus of Control. (Appendix B shows how this sequential approach is accomplished using various computer programs.)

The primary results of interest are shown in Figure 5.3. The first table in the figure shows that the variables were entered in four steps (rather than one) and the order of entry of the variables. The second portion of the figure provides the statistics related to each step of the sequential regression. With sequential regression, instead of focusing on the regression coefficients, we often focus on the change in R^2 (ΔR^2) to determine whether a variable is important and to test the statistical significance of each variable in the equation.

SES was the first variable entered, and the ΔR^2 associated with SES was .185 (.185 minus 0, since no variance was explained prior to the entry of SES into the equation). With the entry of previous Grades in the equation, the R^2 increased to .328, so ΔR^2 for previous Grades is .143 (.328 − .185), and the addition of Self-Esteem increased the variance explained by .5% ($\Delta R^2 = .005$), and so on.

Are these increases in explained variance statistically significant? The formula we use is a simple extension of one of our earlier formulas:

$$F = \frac{R_{12}^2 - R_1^2 / k_{12} - k_1}{1 - R_{12}^2 / (N - k_{12} - 1)}$$

Variables Entered/Removed [b]

Model	Variables Entered	Variables Removed	Method
1	BYSES SOCIO-ECONOMIC STATUS COMPOSITE [a]	.	Enter
2	BYGRADS GRADES COMPOSITE [a]	.	Enter
3	F1CNCPT2 SELF-CONCEPT 2 [a]	.	Enter
4	F1LOCUS2 LOCUS OF CONTROL 2 [a]	.	Enter

a. All requested variables entered.

b. Dependent Variable: F1TXHSTD HIST/CIT/GEOG STANDARDIZED SCORE

Model Summary

Added to the Model	R	R Square	Change Statistics				
			R Square Change	F Change	df1	df2	Sig. F Change
SES	.430[a]	.185	.185	200.709	1	885	.000
Previous Grades	.573[b]	.328	.143	188.361	1	884	.000
Self-Esteem	.577[c]	.333	.005	6.009	1	883	.014
Locus of Control	.582[d]	.339	.006	7.918	1	882	.005

a. Predictors: (Constant), BYSES SOCIO-ECONOMIC STATUS COMPOSITE

b. Predictors: (Constant), BYSES SOCIO-ECONOMIC STATUS COMPOSITE, BYGRADS GRADES COMPOSITE

c. Predictors: (Constant), BYSES SOCIO-ECONOMIC STATUS COMPOSITE, BYGRADS GRADES COMPOSITE, F1CNCPT2 SELF-CONCEPT 2

d. Predictors: (Constant), BYSES SOCIO-ECONOMIC STATUS COMPOSITE, BYGRADS GRADES COMPOSITE, F1CNCPT2 SELF-CONCEPT 2, F1LOCUS2 LOCUS OF CONTROL 2

FIGURE 5.3   Sequential regression of Social Studies test scores on SES, Previous Grades, Self-Esteem, and Locus of Control.

In other words, we subtract the R^2 from the equation with fewer variables from the R^2 with more variables (ΔR^2). This is divided by the unexplained variance (from the equation with more variables). The numerator uses the change in degrees of freedom (which is often 1), and the denominator uses the degrees of freedom for the equation with more variables. As in the earlier simultaneous regression, $N = 887$.

We'll use the formula to calculate the F associated with the final step of the sequential multiple regression:

$$F = \frac{R^2_{1234} - R^2_{123}/k_{1234} - k_{123}}{1 - R^2_{1234}/(N - k_{1234} - 1)}$$

$$= \frac{.339 - .333/1}{(1 - .339)/(887 - 4 - 1)}$$

$$= \frac{.006}{.661/882} = 8.006$$

which matches the value shown in the figure (7.918), within errors of rounding. In other words, the addition of Locus of Control to the equation leads to an increase in R^2 of .006, or a 6/10 of 1% increase, in explained variance. This seemingly tiny increase in variance explained is statistically significant, however ($F = 7.918$ [1, 882], $p = .005$).

Of course, we can also test the overall regression equation, with all variables entered, for statistical significance. The overall $R^2 = .339$, $F = 112.846$ [4, 882], $p < .001$, which is the same result we got with the simultaneous regression.

Comparison to Simultaneous Regression

It will be instructive to compare the results of our sequential regression to those of the simultaneous regression using the same variables (Figures 5.2 versus 5.3). One of the most striking differences is that for the simultaneous regression Self-Esteem was not statistically significant, whereas for the sequential regression it was statistically significant ($\Delta R^2 = .005$, $F = 6.009$ [1, 883], $p = .014$). Why do we get different answers with the different methods? The second difference is that the magnitude of effects, as suggested by the ΔR^2's in the sequential regression, seems so different and so much smaller than the effects suggested by the β's in the simultaneous regression. In the simultaneous regression, for example, we found a small to moderate effect for Locus of Control on the Achievement tests ($\beta = .097$), but in the sequential regression, Locus of Control accounted for only a .6% increase in the variance explained in Social Studies achievement, a seemingly minuscule amount. We will deal with the first problem (statistical significance) first and with the second issue (magnitude of effects) later.

The Importance of Order of Entry.   As you will soon discover, the statistical significance (and the apparent magnitude of effect) of the variables in a sequential regression depends on their order of entry into the equation. Look at Figure 5.4. In this sequential regression, the first two variables were entered in the same order, but Locus of Control was entered at step 3, and Self-Esteem at step 4. With this order of entry, the Self-Esteem variable was again not statistically significant ($p = .663$). The primary reason that Self-Esteem was statistically significant in one sequential regression and not the other is, of course, the difference in variance accounted for by Self-Esteem in one regression versus the other ($\Delta R^2 = .005$ in Figure 5.3 versus .001 in Figure 5.4).

Next, focus on Figure 5.5. For this regression, the order of entry into the sequential regression was Locus of Control, Self-Esteem, previous Grades, and SES. Notice the drastic change in the variance accounted for by the different variables. When entered first in the regression equation, SES accounted for 18.5% of the variance in Achievement (Figures 5.2 and 5.3), but when entered last, SES only accounted for 7.2% of the variance (Figure 5.5). The bottom line is this: with sequential multiple regression, the variance accounted for by each independent variable (i.e., ΔR^2) changes depending on the order of entry of the variables in the regression equation. Because the ΔR^2 changes depending on order of entry, variables will sometimes switch from being statistically significant to being not significant, or vice versa. Again, we have encountered a disconcerting discrepancy.

If the order of entry makes such a big difference in sequential regression results, what then is the *correct* order of entry? A cynical, unethical answer might be to enter the variables you want to show as important first in the regression equation, but this is an indefensible and inferior solution. What are the options? What was my thinking for various orders of entry in Figures 5.3 through 5.5? One common and defensible solution is to input the

Variables Entered/Removed [b]

Model	Variables Entered	Variables Removed	Method
1	BYSES SOCIO-ECONOMIC STATUS COMPOSITE[a]	.	Enter
2	BYGRADS GRADES COMPOSITE[a]	.	Enter
3	F1LOCUS2 LOCUS OF CONTROL 2 [a]	.	Enter
4	F1CNCPT2 SELF-CONCEPT 2 [a]	.	Enter

a. All requested variables entered.

b. Dependent Variable: F1TXHSTD HIST/CIT/GEOG STANDARDIZED SCORE

Model Summary

Added to the Model	R	R Square	Change Statistics				
			R Square Change	F Change	df1	df2	Sig. F Change
SES	.430[a]	.185	.185	200.709	1	885	.000
Previous Grades	.573[b]	.328	.143	188.361	1	884	.000
Locus of Control	.582[c]	.338	.010	13.797	1	883	.000
Self-Esteem	.582[d]	.339	.001	.190	1	882	.663

a. Predictors: (Constant), BYSES SOCIO-ECONOMIC STATUS COMPOSITE

b. Predictors: (Constant), BYSES SOCIO-ECONOMIC STATUS COMPOSITE, BYGRADS GRADES COMPOSITE

c. Predictors: (Constant), BYSES SOCIO-ECONOMIC STATUS COMPOSITE, BYGRADS GRADES COMPOSITE, F1LOCUS2 LOCUS OF CONTROL 2

d. Predictors: (Constant), BYSES SOCIO-ECONOMIC STATUS COMPOSITE, BYGRADS GRADES COMPOSITE, F1LOCUS2 LOCUS OF CONTROL 2, F1CNCPT2 SELF-CONCEPT 2

FIGURE 5.4   Sequential regression of Social Studies test scores on SES, Previous Grades, Locus of Control, and Self-Esteem. With sequential regression, the order of entry of the variables affects their apparent importance.

variables in order of presumed or actual time precedence. This was my thinking for the first example. SES, a parent variable largely in place when many children are born, should logically precede the student variables, measured in 8th and 10th grades. Previous Grades, from grades 6 through 8, is prior to both Self-Esteem and Locus of Control measured in 10th grade. Self-Esteem and Locus of Control are a little more difficult, but it seems to me that conceptions of one's worth should come about and thus be causally prior to conceptions of internal versus external control. It would also be possible to argue that one's conception of internal versus external control may be prior to feelings of self-worth, reasoning that was operationalized in the second sequential regression example of Figure 5.4. Beyond actual time precedence and logic, previous research can also help make such decisions. I know of one study that tested these competing hypotheses, and it supported either a reciprocal relation or self-esteem as prior to locus of control (Eberhart & Keith, 1989).

For Figure 5.5, variables were entered in possible *reverse* time precedence, with strikingly different findings. And there are undoubtedly other methods for deciding the order of

Model Summary

			Change Statistics				
Added to the Model	R	R Square	R Square Change	F Change	df1	df2	Sig. F Change
Locus of Control	.248[a]	.061	.061	57.867	1	885	.000
Self-Esteem	.250[b]	.063	.001	1.099	1	884	.295
Previous Grades	.517[c]	.267	.204	246.158	1	883	.000
SES	.582[d]	.339	.072	95.495	1	882	.000

a. Predictors: (Constant), F1LOCUS2 LOCUS OF CONTROL 2

b. Predictors: (Constant), F1LOCUS2 LOCUS OF CONTROL 2, F1CNCPT2 SELF-CONCEPT 2

c. Predictors: (Constant), F1LOCUS2 LOCUS OF CONTROL 2, F1CNCPT2 SELF-CONCEPT 2, BYGRADS GRADES COMPOSITE

d. Predictors: (Constant), F1LOCUS2 LOCUS OF CONTROL 2, F1CNCPT2 SELF-CONCEPT 2, BYGRADS GRADES COMPOSITE, BYSES SOCIO-ECONOMIC STATUS COMPOSITE

FIGURE 5.5   Sequential regression of Social Studies test scores on Locus of Control, Self-Esteem, Previous Grades, and SES. Again, the order of entry makes a big difference in the apparent effects of the variables with sequential regression.

entry: perceived importance, background variables versus variables of interest, static versus manipulable variables, and so on. But again, which method is correct? And why is order so important?

Why Is Order of Entry So Important?   One way of understanding why different orders of entry make such a difference in findings is through a return to Venn diagrams. Figure 5.6 shows the relations among three hypothetical variables: a dependent variable Y, and two independent variable X_1 and X_2. The areas of overlap represent the shared variance among the three variables. The shaded area of overlap marked 1 (including area 3) represents the variance shared by X_1 and Y, and the shaded area marked 2 (including area 3) represents the variance shared by X_2 and Y. But these variances overlap, and area 3 represents the variance shared by all three variables. It is the area of double shading (3) that is treated differently depending on the order of entry of the variables in sequential regression. If X_1 is entered first into the equation to predict Y, this variance (area 1 and area 3) is attributed to variable X_1. When variable X_2 is added, the ΔR^2 is equal to area 2 (excluding area 3). In contrast, if Y is first regressed on variable X_2, then both areas 2 and 3 will be attributable to variable X_2, and when variable X_1 is subsequently added, only the variance of area 1 (excluding area 3) will be attributed to it. This heuristic aid helps explain *why* order of entry makes a difference, but the question of which order is correct is still not answered.

Total Effects.   It is again useful to turn to path diagrams to further understand why we get a difference depending on order of entry and to help us to understand the proper order of entry. Figure 5.7 shows the model that represents the ordering used for the initial sequential analysis (Figure 5.3). The regression coefficients from the simultaneous multiple regression in fact are estimates of the direct paths, or direct effects, to the final outcome, Social Studies Achievement. These paths are marked a, b, c, and d, and we could simply insert the standardized or unstandardized coefficients from the simultaneous regression (Figure 5.2) in place of these letters. Simultaneous regression estimates the *direct* effects in such models.

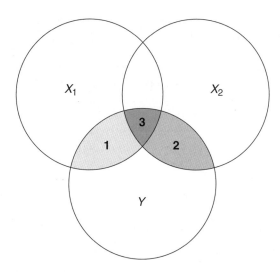

FIGURE 5.6   Venn diagram illustrating why the order of entry is so important in sequential regression. The variance shared by all three variables (area 3) is attributed to whichever variable is first entered in the MR.

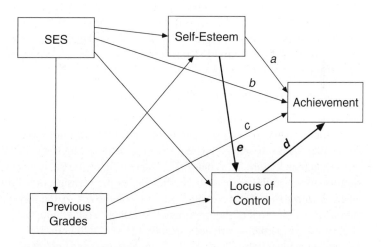

FIGURE 5.7   Path model illustrating the difference between sequential and simultaneous regression. Simultaneous regression estimates the direct effect of each variable on the outcome. Sequential regression estimates the total effects (direct + indirect).

Note, however, that there are also *indirect effects*. In addition to the possible direct effect of Self-Esteem on Achievement (path *a*), Self-Esteem also has an indirect effect on Achievement, through Locus of Control, symbolized by the heavier arrows in the figure (paths *e* and *d*). If we were to estimate path *e*, we could actually multiply path *e* times path *d* to produce an estimate of this indirect effect. And we could also sum the direct and indirect effects of Self-Esteem on Achievement to estimate the *total effect* of Self-Esteem on Achievement.

As it turns out, sequential multiple regression estimates the variance accounted for by these *total effects*. (Note that the ΔR^2's do *not* estimate the total paths directly, but rather the variance attributable to these total effects.) Thus the reason that sequential multiple regression may give us one answer concerning the importance of different variables and simultaneous multiple regression a different answer is that they focus on two different aspects of the multiple regression. Simultaneous regression focuses on estimates of *direct* effects, whereas sequential regression focuses on the variance accounted for by *total* effects.

Variables entered first in a sequential regression have larger effects, other things being equal, than do variables entered later in the equation, because there are many more (indirect) ways variables entered early can affect the final outcome. Thus SES, for example, seems to have a relatively large effect when entered first in a sequential regression, because it can thus affect Social Studies Achievement through Grades, Self-Esteem, and Locus of Control.

Armed with this understanding, the question of the proper order of entry becomes clearer. Whether we realize it or not, *any time* we use sequential regression in an explanatory manner, we have implied a model such as that shown in Figure 5.7! The *proper* order of entry is the order implied by our models. Thus, if you use sequential regression, you had better first spend some time thinking through the model that underlies your analysis. If you do not think through your model correctly, your analysis will produce inaccurate estimates of the effects of one variable on another. When variables are entered prematurely, sequential regression will overestimate their effects. The effects of variables that are entered later in the analysis than they should be will be underestimated. If you use sequential regression, you should be prepared to defend the model underlying this regression. As you read the results of others' sequential regressions, you should sketch out the models underlying these regressions to make sure they are reasonable.

Problems with R^2 as a Measure of Effect

We have discussed the problem of variables changing in apparent importance depending on their order of entry in a sequential regression. Let's now return to our second concern: why do all the effects in sequential regression appear so much smaller than in simultaneous regression (e.g., Figure 5.2 versus 5.3)? The reason, of course, is that in simultaneous regression we focus on the regression coefficients as the measure of the importance of effects, whereas with sequential regression, we focus on the ΔR^2's, the increments to the explained variance, as indicators of the importance of effects. And although variances have a number of desirable properties—variances are easy to work with in formulas, and they are a familiar metric—explained variance is a very stingy measure of the effect of one variable on another (Rosenthal & Rubin, 1979). There are many possible examples of this truism. For example, everyone knows the importance of smoking on lung cancer; smoking is one of the primary causes of lung cancer. How much variance, then, do you think smoking explains in lung cancer: 30%? 50%? No matter what your answer, you will be surprised: smoking explains 1% to 2% of the variance in lung cancer (Gage, 1978)! The point is not that smoking is unimportant; the point is that this seemingly small amount of variance is important.

What statistic comes closer to representing "importance" than R^2? Darlington (1990) suggested using the unsquared metric, rather than the squared metric. It does make a difference. A multiple correlation of .40 is twice as large as a multiple correlation of .20, but if we squared these correlations, the first accounts for four times the variance as the second (.16 versus .04). In sequential multiple regression, the unsquared counterpart to ΔR^2 is $\sqrt{\Delta R^2}$ (which is not the same as ΔR). $\sqrt{\Delta R^2}$, as it turns out, is equal to what is known as the *semipartial* correlation of Y with X, controlling for the other variables in the equation. Conceptually, a semipartial correlation is the correlation of Y with X_1, with the effects of X_2, X_3, and so on, removed from X_1. It may be symbolized as $sr_{y(1.23)}$, with the parentheses showing that the effects of X_2 and X_3 are removed from X_1, but not from Y. (Partial and semipartial correlations are presented in more depth in Appendix D.) Turning to the sequential regression from Figure 5.3, the $\sqrt{\Delta R^2}$'s will equal .430, .378, .071, and .077 for SES, Grades, Self-Esteem, and Locus of Control. These values are at least a little more consistent with the β's from Figure 5.2 than are the ΔR^2's.

There is another reason for preferring $\sqrt{\Delta R^2}$ to ΔR^2 (and R to R^2, and r to r^2, and so on): these unsquared coefficients generally come closer to representing most definitions of "importance" than do the squared coefficients (Darlington, 1990). Darlington provided several useful examples. To use one example (Darlington, p. 212), suppose I ask you to flip two coins, a dime and a nickel. If either coin comes up heads, I will pay you the amount of that coin (10 cents or 5 cents). Over a long series of coin flips, you will earn 5 cents 25% of the time (i.e., nickel = heads, dime = tails), 10 cents 25% of the time, 15 cents 25% of the time, and nothing 25% of the time (dime and nickel both = tails). Obviously, the dimes are twice as important in determining your earnings as the nickels, since dimes are worth twice as much as nickels. If you conduct a multiple regression of this problem, regressing your earnings on the results of each coin (heads = 1 and tails = 0; these are examples of *dummy* variables to be discussed in later chapters), the ΔR^2 associated with dimes will not be twice as large as that associated with nickels, but *four times as large* (ΔR^2 for nickels = .20, ΔR^2 for dimes = .80). The $\sqrt{\Delta R^2}$'s put importance back in the proper metric, however. The $\sqrt{\Delta R^2}$ associated with dimes (.894) is, in fact, twice as large as that associated with nickels (.447). These data are summarized in Table 5.2. In sequential multiple regression (and in other types of regression), the unsquared coefficient generally provides a better indicator of importance than does the squared coefficient. We will still test the statistical significance of ΔR^2, but if we are interested in comparing the magnitude of effects, we will use $\sqrt{\Delta R^2}$.[1]

TABLE 5.2   Comparison of R^2 versus $\sqrt{\Delta R^2}$ as Measures of the Importance of Effects

MEASURE OF IMPORTANCE	IMPORTANCE OF NICKELS	IMPORTANCE OF DIMES
ΔR^2	.200	.800
$\sqrt{\Delta R^2}$	.447	.894

Dimes are twice as important as nickels in determining the amount of money received; $\sqrt{\Delta R^2}$ demonstrates this importance, but ΔR^2 does not.

Other Uses of Sequential Regression

There are other ways of conducting sequential multiple regression; the method I have outlined here is, in my experience, far and away the most common method. You may see this method referred to as *variance partitioning* (Pedhazur, 1997) or *sequential variance decomposition* (Darlington, 1990).

Interpretation of Regression Coefficients　It is also possible to use regression coefficients from each step of the sequential regression as estimates of the *total* effects of each variable on the outcome. In this case, we would use the *b* or β associated with the variable entered at that step as the estimate of the total effect, ignoring the coefficients for variable entered at earlier steps in the equation. For example, Figure 5.8 shows a table of such coefficients as

Coefficients[a]

Model		Unstandardized Coefficients		Standardized Coefficients		
		B	Std. Error	Beta	t	Sig.
1	(Constant)	51.090	.299		170.745	.000
	BYSES SOCIO-ECONOMIC STATUS COMPOSITE	*5.558*	.392	*.430*	14.167	.000
2	(Constant)	34.793	1.218		28.561	.000
	BYSES SOCIO-ECONOMIC STATUS COMPOSITE	3.875	.377	.300	10.280	.000
	BYGRADS GRADES COMPOSITE	*5.420*	.395	*.400*	13.724	.000
3	(Constant)	35.138	1.223		28.734	.000
	BYSES SOCIO-ECONOMIC STATUS COMPOSITE	3.798	.377	.294	10.068	.000
	BYGRADS GRADES COMPOSITE	5.291	.397	.391	13.318	.000
	F1CNCPT2 SELF-CONCEPT 2	*1.016*	.414	*.069*	2.451	.014
4	(Constant)	35.517	1.226		28.981	.000
	BYSES SOCIO-ECONOMIC STATUS COMPOSITE	3.690	.378	.285	9.772	.000
	BYGRADS GRADES COMPOSITE	5.150	.399	.380	12.910	.000
	F1CNCPT2 SELF-CONCEPT 2	.218	.501	.015	.436	.663
	F1LOCUS2 LOCUS OF CONTROL 2	*1.554*	.552	*.097*	2.814	.005

a. Dependent Variable: F1TXHSTD HIST/CIT/GEOG STANDARDIZED SCORE

FIGURE 5.8　Sequential regression used to estimate the total effects of each variable on the outcome. The italicized boldface coefficients are estimates of total unstandardized and standardized effects.

generated by SPSS. The relevant coefficients are in italic boldface; these are the coefficients that I would report in a write-up of the research, perhaps accompanied by a table such as Table 5.3. I have rarely seen this approach used outside of path analysis, however, so we will discuss it in more detail when we get to that topic (see Chapter 10).

TABLE 5.3   Total Effects of SES, Previous Grades, Self-Esteem, and Locus of Control on 10th-Grade Social Studies Achievement, Estimated through Sequential Regression

VARIABLE	b (SE$_b$)	ß
SES	5.558 (.392)[a]	.430
Previous Grades	5.420 (.395)[a]	.400
Self-Esteem	1.016 (.414)[b]	.069
Locus of Control	1.554 (.552)[a]	.097

[a]$p < .01$.

[b]$p < .05$.

Block Entry.   It is possible to enter groups of variables in blocks, or groups of variables, as well as one at a time. A primary reason for entering variables in blocks might be to estimate the effect of a type or category of variables on the outcome. Using our current example, we might be interested in the effect of the psychological variables together, and above and beyond the effect of the background variables, on Achievement. If this were our interest, we could enter the two variables as a group, after accounting for the background variables. The statistical significance of the resulting ΔR^2 could be examined to determine whether these psychological variables explained statistically significantly more variance, and the resulting $\sqrt{\Delta R^2}$ could be examined to determine the relative importance of the effect of these psychological variables. Some of the output from such an analysis is shown in Figure 5.9. These results suggest that the two psychological variables, in combination, are important for Social Studies Achievement (the example will be interpreted in more detail later in this chapter). In essence, this example illustrates one possible combination of sequential and simultaneous regression. Another possible reason for entering variables in blocks is if you were unsure of the proper order of some of your variables. Using our current example, if we could not decide whether Self-Esteem should follow or precede Locus of Control, we might enter the two variables in the same block.

Unique Variance.   Another use of sequential regression is for researchers who wish to isolate the unique variance in a dependent variable accounted for by each variable in a regression, after taking all other variables into account. Return to the Venn diagram in Figure 5.6. If you are interested in the unique variance attributable to a variable, you will be interested in variance associated with area 1 (excluding area 3) as the unique variance attributable to variable X_1 and the variance associated with area 2 (excluding area 3) as the unique variance of variable X_2. Conceptually, this approach is like conducting a series of

Variables Entered/Removed[b]

Model	Variables Entered	Variables Removed	Method
1	BYSES SOCIO-ECONOMIC STATUS COMPOSITE[a]	.	Enter
2	BYGRADS GRADES COMPOSITE[a]	.	Enter
3	F1CNCPT2 SELF-CONCEPT 2, F1LOCUS2 LOCUS OF CONTROL 2[a]	.	Enter

a. All requested variables entered.

b. Dependent Variable: F1TXHSTD HIST/CIT/GEOG STANDARDIZED SCORE

Model Summary

			Change Statistics				
Added to the Model	R	R Square	R Square Change	F Change	df1	df2	Sig. F Change
SES	.430[a]	.185	.185	200.709	1	885	.000
Previous Grades	.573[b]	.328	.143	188.361	1	884	.000
Self-Esteem & Locus of Control	.582[c]	.339	.010	6.987	2	882	.001

a. Predictors: (Constant), BYSES SOCIO-ECONOMIC STATUS COMPOSITE

b. Predictors: (Constant), BYSES SOCIO-ECONOMIC STATUS COMPOSITE, BYGRADS GRADES COMPOSITE

c. Predictors: (Constant), BYSES SOCIO-ECONOMIC STATUS COMPOSITE, BYGRADS GRADES COMPOSITE, F1CNCPT2 SELF-CONCEPT 2, F1LOCUS2 LOCUS OF CONTROL 2

Coefficients[a]

Model		Unstandardized Coefficients		Standardized Coefficients		
		B	Std. Error	Beta	t	Sig.
1	(Constant)	51.090	.299		170.745	.000
	BYSES SOCIO-ECONOMIC STATUS COMPOSITE	5.558	.392	.430	14.167	.000
2	(Constant)	34.793	1.218		28.561	.000
	BYSES SOCIO-ECONOMIC STATUS COMPOSITE	3.875	.377	.300	10.280	.000
	BYGRADS GRADES COMPOSITE	5.420	.395	.400	13.724	.000
3	(Constant)	35.517	1.226		28.981	.000
	BYSES SOCIO-ECONOMIC STATUS COMPOSITE	3.690	.378	.285	9.772	.000
	BYGRADS GRADES COMPOSITE	5.150	.399	.380	12.910	.000
	F1CNCPT2 SELF-CONCEPT 2	.218	.501	.015	.436	.663
	F1LOCUS2 LOCUS OF CONTROL 2	1.554	.552	.097	2.814	.005

a. Dependent Variable: F1TXHSTD HIST/CIT/GEOG STANDARDIZED SCORE

FIGURE 5.9 Self-Concept and Locus of Control entered as a block in a sequential regression.

sequential regressions, entering each variable last in one of these equations. In practice, isolating the unique variance for a variable can be accomplished this way, but there are simpler methods. If your primary interest is the statistical significance of each unique variance, it is simpler to conduct a simultaneous regression. The statistical significance of the regression coefficients is equal to the statistical significance of the ΔR^2's, with each variable entered last in the regression equation. You can demonstrate this to yourself by comparing the statistical significance for the ΔR^2 from the last variable entered in Figures 5.3 through 5.5 with that of the regression coefficients from Figure 5.2. So, for example, with the simultaneous regression, Self-Esteem had a probability of .663. When entered last in a sequential regression (Figure 5.4), Self-Esteem had a probability of .663. Likewise, in Figure 5.2, the *t* associated with Self-Esteem was .436; in Figure 5.4, the *F* was .190 (recall that $t^2 = F$). Compare the *t* and *p* associated with SES in Figure 5.2 with the *F* and *p* associated with SES when it was entered last in a sequential regression (Figure 5.5). The equivalence of the statistical significance of variables in simultaneous regression with variables entered last in sequential regression will prove useful in later chapters.

If you are interested in the *values* of $\sqrt{\Delta R^2}$ for each variable when entered last in the regression equation, recall that these are equal to the semipartial correlations. Thus, if your computer program produces them, you can conduct a simultaneous regression requesting the semipartial correlations (also called *part* correlations). The last column of the table in Figure 5.10, for example, shows the semipartial correlations of each variable with the Social Studies test, controlling for all other variables (SPSS labels these as part correlations). If the program you use does not easily produce semipartial correlations, but you want information about unique variance, you can get this information by conducting a series of sequential regressions, entering, in turn, each variable last in the equation. I will refer to this approach as *sequential unique regression.*

Coefficients[a]

Model		Unstandardized Coefficients		Standardized Coefficients			Correlations		
		B	Std. Error	Beta	t	Sig.	Zero-order	Partial	Part
1	(Constant)	35.517	1.226		28.981	.000			
	BYSES SOCIO-ECONOMIC STATUS COMPOSITE	3.690	.378	.285	9.772	.000	.430	.313	*.268*
	BYGRADS GRADES COMPOSITE	5.150	.399	.380	12.910	.000	.498	.399	*.354*
	F1CNCPT2 SELF-CONCEPT 2	.218	.501	.015	.436	.663	.173	.015	*.012*
	F1LOCUS2 LOCUS OF CONTROL 2	1.554	.552	.097	2.814	.005	.248	.094	*.077*

a. Dependent Variable: F1TXHSTD HIST/CIT/GEOG STANDARDIZED SCORE

FIGURE 5.10   Semipartial (part) correlations of each variable with the Social Studies Achievement outcome. Semipartial correlations are equal to $\sqrt{\Delta R^2}$, with each variable entered last in a sequential regression.

Interactions and Curves.   Finally, we can use sequential regression to test for interactions and curves in the regression line by adding these terms last in a sequential regression. This is a common use and one we will discuss in later chapters.

Interpretation

Throughout this book, I've interpreted the results of a number of simultaneous regressions. Here is a brief interpretation of a sequential regression, one that also illustrates a plausible use of the methodology. For this analysis, we'll use the analysis and output from Figure 5.9. Here's a possible interpretation:

> The purpose of this research was to determine whether students' psychological characteristics have an effect on high school students' social studies achievement, even after controlling for the effects of relevant background variables. To accomplish this purpose, students' scores on a 10th-grade standardized social studies (history, citizenship, geography) were regressed on SES, previous (8th grade) Grades, and two psychological variables, Locus of Control and Self-Esteem, using a sequential multiple regression analysis.
>
> The results of the analysis are shown in Table 5.4. The first background variable entered in the regression, SES, resulted in a statistically significant increase in explained variable ($\Delta R^2 = .185$, $F[1, 885] = 200.709$, $p < .001$), as did the second background variable entered into the regression equation, Previous Grades ($\Delta R^2 = .143$, $F[1, 884] = 188.361$, $p < .001$). Of greater interest are the results of the third step of the sequential regression. In this step, the psychological variables of Locus of Control and Self-Esteem were entered as a block. As shown in the table, these psychological variables explained a statistically significant increase in the variance of Achievement ($\Delta R^2 = .010$, $F[2, 882] = 6.987$, $p = .001$). These findings suggest that personal, psychological variables may indeed be important for students' high school achievement. If so, focusing on high school students' psychological well-being may be important for their achievement as well as their well-being.

TABLE 5.4   Effects of SES, Previous Grades, Self-Esteem, and Psychological Characteristics on 10th-Grade Social Studies Achievement

BLOCK	ΔR^2	PROBABILITY
1 (SES)	.185	<.001
2 (Previous Grades)	.143	<.001
3 (Locus of Control and Self-Esteem)	.010	.001

In this interpretation, I could have included in the table the semipartial correlations (or $\sqrt{\Delta R^2}$) or the β's from each step or just the final step of the regression, but without a discussion and interpretation of total effects, I think these statistics would be more misleading than illuminating.

Summary: Sequential Regression

Analysis.   With sequential regression, variables are added one at a time or in blocks. The order of entry of the variables should be consistent with an underlying causal model, or the results will not provide accurate estimates of the effects of the variables on the outcome.

Purpose.   The primary purpose of sequential regression is explanation. A researcher is interested in determining which variables are important influences on some outcome. Given the adequacy of the underlying causal model, one can also use sequential regression to determine the extent of the total influence of each variable on the outcome. This use requires the use of the β's from each step in analysis, however, rather than the more common use of ΔR^2; it will be presented in more detail in Part 2 when we discuss path analysis (Chapter 10). Sequential unique regression can also be used to determine the unique contribution of each variable to some outcome, after controlling for the other variables in a model.

Sequential regression can also be used in the service of prediction, for example, to determine which variables are statistically significant predictors of some outcome. You may also be interested in rank ordering the importance of predictors. In this case, order of entry makes a difference, so the best approach is to add each variable last in the equation to determine its unique contribution to the prediction (sequential unique regression). For both of these purposes, however, simultaneous regression may accomplish the same goals more simply. The danger of using sequential regression for prediction is that you or the readers of your research may be sorely tempted to interpret the results in an explanatory fashion. Remember that any time you start thinking along the lines of "this means that if we were to increase X, then Y would increase" you have crossed the line from prediction to explanation.

What to Interpret.   In sequential regression, we generally focus on the statistical significance of the change in explained variance (ΔR^2) as the measure of the statistical significance of each variable. It is common to see ΔR^2 also used as an indicator of the importance of each variable, but, as we have seen, $\sqrt{\Delta R^2}$ is a better measure of importance. In addition, any reference to the relative importance of variables in sequential regression is implicitly or explicitly based on a causal model. It is also possible to interpret the regression coefficients associated with the variables entered at each step of a sequential regression.

The exception to the rule that sequential regression requires an implicit causal model is when each variable is added last to the equation to determine each variable's unique contribution to the outcome variable (sequential unique regression). This approach is analogous to simultaneous regression.

Strengths.   If based on a defensible model, sequential regression can provide good estimates of the *total* effects of a series of variables on some outcome (although examining β rather than ΔR^2). Sequential regression, with its focus on change in explained variance, may be more comfortable than simultaneous regression for those more familiar with ANOVA methods. Sequential regression is useful for determining whether some new variable improves the prediction of some outcome over and above an existing set of variables; we will use sequential regression in this fashion to test the statistical significance of interaction terms and curve components.

Weaknesses.   Sequential regression will give different estimates of the importance of variables in the regression depending on the order of entry of these variables. Other things being equal, variables entered earlier in a sequential regression will appear more important than those entered later. This is because sequential regression estimates total effects, including indirect effects through variables entered later in an analysis. If not based on an implicit, reasonable model sequential regression can give misleading estimates of effects. In my experience, the use of such models underlying sequential regression is rare. Sequential regression will underestimate effects entered too late and overestimate the effects of variables entered too early.

Conclusion.   As you can see, I have suggested fairly constrained uses for sequential multiple regression: testing the statistical significance of curves and interactions (discussed in more detail in Chapters 7 and 8), testing whether single variables or blocks of variables are important additions to a regression equation, and for calculating total effects within a causal model (discussed in more detail in Part 2). Why, then, have I spent so much time on the topic? The primary reason is that, depending on your area of research interest, you may encounter sequential regression very commonly in your research reading. Unfortunately, many such presentations will use sequential regression poorly and in ways I have argued against in this chapter. I have here tried to present the most common uses of sequential regression and explain why some are appropriate and others are not.

STEPWISE MULTIPLE REGRESSION

In your reading, you may encounter a multiple regression variation called stepwise regression (or one of its variations, e.g., forward selection or backward elimination). Unlike forced entry or sequential regression, stepwise multiple regression should only be used for prediction. Unfortunately, because of its apparent ease, stepwise regression is often used in attempts at explanation. I will admonish you over and over not to make this mistake and will generally discourage the use of stepwise methods. The presentation of stepwise regression will follow the format used for sequential regression, with an extended discussion followed by a summary.

The Analysis

Stepwise multiple regression is similar to sequential regression in that predictor variables are entered one at a time in a sequential order. The difference is that with stepwise multiple regression the computer chooses the order of entry, rather than the researcher.

Figure 5.11 shows the primary output from a stepwise regression using the variables and data used throughout this chapter. Previous Grades were entered at step 1, SES at step 2, and Locus of Control at step 3. Note from the model summary table that each of these additions to the equation resulted in a statistically significant increase in ΔR^2. Self-Esteem, in contrast, was not added to the equation because its addition would not have led to a statistically significant increase in R^2.

How Are Variables Added to the Equation?   As shown in the last column of the table labeled Variables Entered/Removed, variables are entered into the equation if the probability associated with the ΔR^2 is less than .05. If this were the only way variables could be included in the equation, we would call this *forward entry* (stepwise) regression. It is also possible, however, that the variance of a variable entered at one step of the equation is reproduced by that of several variables entered in later steps of the equation. If this occurs (it does not in the

Variables Entered/Removed [a]

Model	Variables Entered	Variables Removed	Method
1	BYGRADS GRADES COMPOSITE	.	Stepwise (Criteria: Probability-of-F-to-enter <= .050, Probability-of-F-to-remove >= .100).
2	BYSES SOCIO-ECONOMIC STATUS COMPOSITE	.	Stepwise (Criteria: Probability-of-F-to-enter <= .050, Probability-of-F-to-remove >= .100).
3	F1LOCUS2 LOCUS OF CONTROL 2	.	Stepwise (Criteria: Probability-of-F-to-enter <= .050, Probability-of-F-to-remove >= .100).

a. Dependent Variable: F1TXHSTD HIST/CIT/GEOG STANDARDIZED SCORE

Model Summary

Added to the Model	R	R Square	Adjusted R Square	R Square Change	F Change	df1	df2	Sig. F Change
				Change Statistics				
Previous Grades	.498[a]	.248	.247	.248	291.410	1	885	.000
SES	.573[b]	.328	.327	.080	105.682	1	884	.000
Locus of Control	.582[c]	.338	.336	.010	13.797	1	883	.000

a. Predictors: (Constant), BYGRADS GRADES COMPOSITE

b. Predictors: (Constant), BYGRADS GRADES COMPOSITE, BYSES SOCIO-ECONOMIC STATUS COMPOSITE

c. Predictors: (Constant), BYGRADS GRADES COMPOSITE, BYSES SOCIO-ECONOMIC STATUS COMPOSITE, F1LOCUS2 LOCUS OF CONTROL 2

ANOVA[d]

Model		Sum of Squares	df	Mean Square	F	Sig.
1	Regression	21357.16	1	21357.164	291.410	.000[a]
	Residual	64860.76	885	73.289		
	Total	86217.92	886			
2	Regression	28283.26	2	14141.630	215.781	.000[b]
	Residual	57934.66	884	65.537		
	Total	86217.92	886			
3	Regression	29174.59	3	9724.864	150.536	.000[c]
	Residual	57043.33	883	64.602		
	Total	86217.92	886			

a. Predictors: (Constant), BYGRADS GRADES COMPOSITE

b. Predictors: (Constant), BYGRADS GRADES COMPOSITE, BYSES SOCIO-ECONOMIC STATUS COMPOSITE

c. Predictors: (Constant), BYGRADS GRADES COMPOSITE, BYSES SOCIO-ECONOMIC STATUS COMPOSITE, F1LOCUS2 LOCUS OF CONTROL 2

d. Dependent Variable: F1TXHSTD HIST/CIT/GEOG STANDARDIZED SCORE

FIGURE 5.11   Stepwise regression of Social Studies Achievement on SES, Previous Grades, Self-Esteem, and Locus of Control.

current example) and the *p* associated with the earlier-entered variable increased to .10 or greater, this variable would be dropped from the regression equation. This is, of course, more likely in problems with many possible predictor variables. If this were the only approach to be used (i.e., all variables entered and the statistically not significant ones dropped), we would be conducting a *backward elimination* (stepwise) regression. The term *stepwise regression* usually refers to a combination of these two methods, but is also used to refer to the forward entry method alone. The probability values for entry and removal can be changed. It is also possible to limit the number of steps; we could have set a maximum of two steps, for example, thus allowing only Grades and SES to enter the equation.

How Does the Program Decide What Variable to Add at Each Step?   The first variable to enter is the variable with the largest correlation with the outcome variable. In the current example, Grades had the largest correlation with Social Studies Achievement and was the first variable to enter the equation. The program then calculates the semipartial correlation of each remaining variable with the outcome, controlling for the variable(s) already in the equation, and the variable with the largest semipartial correlation with the outcome is entered next. In the current example, SES had the largest semipartial correlation with Social Studies, after controlling for Grades. The program then continues to cycle through these steps—add a variable, compute semipartial correlations of the excluded variables controlling for the entered variables—until no more excluded variables fulfill the requirement for entry, or the maximum number of steps is reached. Since we know that the squared semipartial correlations are equal to the ΔR^2, this process is the same as calculating the possible ΔR^2 for each variable at each step.

Danger: Stepwise Regression
Is Inappropriate for Explanation

This sounds great, doesn't it? No more need to do the hard work of thinking through models, no more embarrassment if these models are proved wrong! All you have to do is decide which variables to include in the analysis, not which are important. Just let the computer decide! There are no substitutes for the hard work, however. Stepwise regression may indeed help you determine a useful subset of variables for predicting some outcome (and we will even question this statement later), but that is all. Stepwise regression cannot tell you which variables influence some outcome; to decide this, you must start with a defensible, theory- and research-derived notion of the plausible influences on some outcome, what we have been calling a model. Even with such a model, what a proper, explanatory, regression analysis reveals is the extent of the influence of one variable on another, *given the adequacy of your model.* In other words, an implicit or explicit model is required for explanatory interpretation of multiple regression, and such models do not come from statistics programs, but from knowledge of theory and research on a topic, combined with careful thought.

Perhaps the answer is to start with an informal explanatory model, one that includes the important, relevant variables, and then conduct a stepwise regression. This technique does not help either, since stepwise regression does nothing to tell you the proper order of the variables in the model. Yes, stepwise regression orders the variables, but only in reference to the degree to which the variables sequentially explain variance. This ordering may be entirely different from the *causal* ordering of variables. Note that the stepwise results in

Figure 5.11 don't tell us the proper time precedence of the variables (compare the results in Figure 5.11 with the model in Figure 5.7). And we can get even more ridiculous. We could just as easily regress Previous Grades on SES, self-perceptions, and 10th-grade Social Studies Achievement, and the stepwise regression would dutifully tell us that Social Studies achievement was the best single predictor of Grades, followed by SES, and so on, even though our predictor (Social Studies Achievement) happened after the criterion (Grades)! The bottom line is this: stepwise regression results do not help us understand how variables affect an outcome. For these reasons, methodologists routinely condemn stepwise regression as an explanatory method: "variables mindlessly enter into the analysis in the absence of theory and the results, therefore, are theoretical garbage" (Wolfle, 1980, p. 206). To make this point in class, I tell my students, tongue in cheek, that stepwise regression is a tool of the devil. Do *not* use stepwise regression if you wish to understand the influence of a group of variables on an outcome; do *not* use stepwise regression if you wish to make policy or intervention recommendations based on your results.

A Predictive Approach

What can stepwise regression tell you, then? Stepwise regression can tell you which subset of a group of predictors may be used to predict some criterion. It may be used to develop an equation to predict some criterion, using a given group of predictors. Stepwise regression may be used for prediction. Several examples will help illustrate these points. One of the most common uses of regression for prediction is in selection. Suppose, for example, you are a college admissions officer and want to improve your accuracy in admitting students who will do well at your college. Suppose further that you have a number of predictors available: high school grades, rank in class, SAT or ACT scores, participation in academic clubs and athletics, even personality measures. You could develop a prediction equation using your current student body by regressing students' current GPAs on this information, and you could then use this prediction equation as an aid in selecting new students. This equation will look just like the equations we developed earlier in this book:

$$\text{Grades (predicted)} = a + b_1\text{HSGrades} + b_2\text{HSRank} + b_3\text{SAT} + \cdots$$

Note that this example illustrates the use of simultaneous regression in the service of prediction. But suppose further that it is difficult to collect all this information, and it would be more cost effective if you could predict almost as well using fewer predictors. In this case, stepwise regression might be a method of reducing the number of variables in the equation while still improving prediction accuracy over the status quo.

Psychologists often use individually administered tests to select participants for a treatment (e.g., special education services or participation in intervention programs). These tests are expensive and time consuming. If shorter versions could be developed with little loss of reliability or validity, we might consider this a worthwhile trade-off. If so, you could use stepwise regression to find out which 4 of the 10 subtests, for example, best predicted the overall score on the test. Future selection could then use the generated equation to predict the overall score from these 4 tests.

Note that for these examples of prediction theories and models are unimportant. The admissions officer does not care which of these variables *affect* college success; she only cares that the prediction improves the admissions process. The psychologist who is searching for a valid, but shorter version of a test of intelligence does not care which subtests help in the prediction of the total score. Indeed, he would probably be willing to use an *achievement* test to aid in prediction, even though relevant theory would argue that intelligence affects achievement, rather than the reverse. Likewise, if you could develop a reliable method for predicting the future price of a stock or which horse would win a race, you probably would not care why your equation worked (at least until it stopped working). If our goal is simply prediction, the theoretical relation of the predictors to the criterion does not matter. What is important, however, is that we are not subsequently tempted to interpret our predictive results in an explanatory fashion. The college admissions officer is therefore not justified in telling a potential applicant that if he raises his High School GPA this, in turn, will likely improve his subsequent college GPA.

Cross-Validation

Just as the researchers in these examples don't care why the variables enter the equation in stepwise regression, neither does the program "care" why variables enter the equation. The variance that a predictor accounts for in a criterion may be reliable, valid variation, or it may be due to error, or chance variation. In other words, stepwise regression capitalizes on chance. As a result, the accuracy of prediction, as measured by the variance explained in the criterion by the predictors, or R^2, is likely to be inflated. Likewise, the regression coefficients used in subsequent prediction may be less accurate than is acceptable.

One way of exploring and improving such prediction is through a method called *cross-validation.* In this method, one sample is used to develop the regression equation, which is then cross-validated on a second sample. The two samples can be separate samples from the same population, or one larger sample split at random. The regression equation from the first sample is used to create a composite, a weighted predicted criterion score, for the second sample (e.g., via a "compute" statement in SPSS). This is similar to the composite variable creation we did in Chapter 3. This predicted criterion is then correlated with the actual criterion in the second sample. If this correlation is considerably smaller than the R from the initial equation, it means that the equation does not generalize and is therefore suspect. Double cross-validation is also possible, in which each sample is used to generate an equation that is then tested in the other sample. If the cross-validation is successful (the r for the second regression is close to the R from the first regression), it is common to combine the two samples to generate even more stable regression weights.

We could split our NELS data set into two samples of 500. For the first exploratory sample, we could use stepwise regression to predict Social Studies Achievement from SES, Grades, Self-Esteem, and Locus of Control. The generated regression equation could then be used to create a composite predicted Social Studies Achievement score in the second, or cross-validation, sample. We could then compare the correlation of this composite with actual Social Studies Achievement in the cross-validation sample with the value of the R for the exploratory sample. If the two were close, we could have confidence that the b's in Figure 5.11 can be used in another sample to predict the Social Studies Achievement score. It is also common to split the samples in a ratio of two-thirds (exploratory) and one-third (cross-validation).[2]

Obviously, cross-validation requires a larger sample (or second samples). Ironically, the way to ensure that regression weights are stable, that equations generalize, is through large samples and fewer predictors. This, then, should be another major lesson of stepwise regression: use large samples and relatively few predictors. Unfortunately, this advice often runs counter to the use of stepwise regression in practice.

Adjusted R^2

Just as R^2 is likely to be smaller in a new sample, it is also likely to be smaller in the population than in the sample. There are a number of methods for estimating the population R^2 from the sample R^2. A common formula is:

$$R^2_{\text{adjusted}} = R^2 - \frac{k(1 - R^2)}{N - k - 1}$$

If you do the calculations, you will see this is the "adjusted R^2" reported in the table in Figure 5.11 (and it appears to be the one used by most computer programs). It is also possible to estimate, from a single sample, the *expected* R^2 that you get if you cross-validate with another sample (see Darlington, 1990, Chap. 6 for example; also see Raju, Bilgic, Edwards, and Fleer, 1999, for a comparison of methods). The point I want to make is this: the R^2 we would likely get in the population and the one that we would likely get upon cross-validation depend on sample size and the number of predictors used. Other things being equal, your results will be more stable with larger samples and fewer predictors.

I should note that neither of these issues, cross-validation or adjusted R^2, apply only to stepwise regression or even to regression in the service of prediction. Although less common, we could just as easily and fruitfully cross-validate explanatory regression results. Indeed, such cross-validation can be considered a form of replication, both of which should be conducted more commonly than they are.

Additional Dangers

I hope I have succeeded in convincing you that you should not use stepwise regression in explanatory research. Unfortunately, there are also dangers when using stepwise regression in the service of prediction. I will outline a few of them briefly here; for a more complete treatment, see Thompson (1998).

Degrees of Freedom.   At each step in stepwise regression, the program examines *all* variables in the set of predictors, not just the variable added in that step. The degrees of freedom for the regression and residual *should* recognize this use of the data, but computer programs generally print degrees of freedom as if only one variable had been considered, ignoring all the variables that were considered but not entered into the equation. In other words, the degrees of freedom for every step of the regression shown in Figure 5.11 should be 4 and 882, because four variables were either entered or evaluated at every step (and these same *df*s apply to the final equation, even though only three variables were used in the final equation). The result of such adjustments is that the actual F values are smaller than that listed on most printouts. Likewise, the *adjusted R^2* should take into account the total number of predictors used. If sample size is small and the number of predictors large, the actual adjusted R^2 may be much smaller than that shown on the printout.

Not Necessarily the Best Predictors.   Stepwise regression is commonly used when the researcher wishes to find the best subset of predictors to accomplish the prediction (indeed, this was the reasoning behind my prediction examples above). Yet, because of the way stepwise regression works, entering one variable at a time, the final set of predictors may not even be the "best" subset. That is, it may not be the subset with the highest R^2. Thompson illustrates this point nicely (1998).

Lack of Generalizability   More than other regression methods, stepwise regression is especially likely to produce coefficients and equations that generalize poorly to other samples or situations. Cross-validation is especially important for stepwise regressions.

Alternatives to Stepwise Regression

In my experience, most researchers who use stepwise regression are interested in finding which variables are "most important," in some vague sense, for the outcome. If one digs deeper, it usually turns out that the intended purpose is explanatory in nature. As we have already discussed, simultaneous regression or sequential regression are more appropriate for explanation.

In cases where prediction is the goal, stepwise regression may be acceptable. As noted by Cohen and Cohen (1983, p. 125), the problems of stepwise regression become less severe when the researcher is interested only in prediction, the sample size is large and the number of predictors relatively small, and the results are cross-validated. Even in these cases, there may be better alternatives.

I have already argued that both simultaneous and sequential regression can be used for prediction. If a researcher is interested in developing an equation from a set of predictors, this can be obtained via simultaneous regression. If used for purposes of prediction, one could enter variables in a sequential regression based on the ease of obtaining them, using the coefficients from the final equation to develop the prediction equation.

Even when one simply wants to get the "best" subset of predictors from among a larger group, there are alternatives. *All subsets* regression, for example, will test all possible subsets of a set of predictors to determine which subset offers the best prediction. Say you want the best 10 out of 25 predictors for some outcome; all subsets regression will likely give you this information more accurately than will stepwise regression. This method is one of the options for variable selection in SAS (MaxR). It can be conducted manually in other statistical programs by using a series of regressions and comparing the variance explained by all possible subsets of variables.

Summary: Stepwise Regression

Analysis.   In stepwise regression, variables are added one at a time. The order of entry of the variables is controlled by the statistics program; the variable that will lead to the largest increase in ΔR^2 is entered at each step. If an earlier variable becomes statistically not significant with the addition of later variables, it can be dropped from the equation.

Purpose.   The primary purpose of stepwise regression is prediction. It is often used to select a subset of available variables that provides efficient prediction of some criterion. Stepwise regression should not be used when you want to understand the effect of a group of variables on some outcome (explanation).

What to Interpret   The statistical significance associated with the change in variance explained (ΔR^2) is the primary focus with stepwise regression. You may also use the produced regression coefficients (b's) in subsequent prediction equations.

Strengths.   Stepwise regression may be useful when you have a large number of possible predictors and don't know which you should keep and which you should discard (of course you should also have a large N). Stepwise regression can help you reduce the number of predictors and still predict the outcome efficiently. It is tempting to think that stepwise regression's ability to choose predictors, thus allowing you to avoid a lot of difficult thinking, is a strength of this method. I believe it is, instead, a weakness.

Weaknesses.   It should be obvious that I am no fan of stepwise regression. It should not be used for explanatory research and, if it is used in this manner, the results will likely be useless. Stepwise regression can be used for predictive research, but even then other approaches may be more productive. I believe there are few uses for this method.

Why spend time discussing this method when I and many others discourage its use? In my experience, the use of stepwise regression, although diminishing, is still all too common. And this assessment is not confined to the areas of research with which I am most familiar. As part of the preparation for this chapter, I conducted a series of literature searches for the word *stepwise,* and it was amazing how often the term showed up in connection with stepwise regression. It appears stepwise regression is common in all areas of psychology that use regression, in education, other social sciences, and even medicine. I present, but condemn, stepwise regression because you are likely to encounter it in your reading. I want to discourage you from using the method, however, so I do not present an interpretation here or demonstrate its setup with various programs in Appendix B.

THE PURPOSE OF THE RESEARCH

This chapter introduced two new flavors of multiple regression, sequential and stepwise regression, and compared them to simultaneous regression and to each other. We focused on the method of analysis, interpretation, purpose, strengths, and weaknesses of each method. The three general regression approaches, their purposes, strengths, and weaknesses, are summarized in Table 5.5.

Now, the important question: How should you decide which approach to use? The first step is careful thinking about your purpose in conducting the research. What do you want to be able to say about your findings; how do you plan to use them? An examination of your intended purpose will first help you understand whether you are interested in explanation or in prediction. Following this decision, you can focus on more specific questions to help you make an informed choice as to the most appropriate method.

Explanation

Are you interested in understanding some phenomenon? Do you want to be able to explain how something comes about? Do you wish to make policy recommendations based on your research? Do you want to be able to provide information on what variables should be

TABLE 5.5   Three Types of Multiple Regression: Summary Table

METHOD	SIMULTANEOUS	SEQUENTIAL	STEPWISE
Procedure	All variables forced to enter the regression equation at the same time	*Researcher* enters one variable at a time based on previous knowledge or theory	*Computer* enters one variable at a time based on increases in variance explained
Purpose	*Explanation:* relative importance, effects of each variable *Prediction:* generating prediction equations	*Explanation:* Is variable important for the outcome? *Explanation:* test for statistical significance of interaction, curve components *Prediction:* Does variable aid in prediction?	*Prediction:* Which variables help predict criterion?
What to Interpret	Overall R^2, statistical significance of b's, magnitude of b's and ß's	Statistical significance of ΔR^2, magnitude of $\sqrt{\Delta R^2}$	Statistical significance of ΔR^2
Strengths	1. Very useful for explanation when combined with theory 2. Allows conclusions about relative effects of variables 3. Allows conclusions about policy, intervention implications 4. Estimates direct effects in implied model 5. Order of variables in implied model unimportant	1. Useful for explanation if combined with theory 2. Useful for testing for curves and interactions 3. Estimates total effects in implied model (see Part 2 of this book for more information)	1. May tell you which variables can be used for efficient prediction 2. Doesn't require thought or theory
Weaknesses	1. Regression weights can change depending on which variables are entered 2. Implies a theoretical model 3. Estimates only direct effects	1. ΔR^2 changes depending on the order of entry of variables 2. Can over- or underestimate the importance of variable depending on order of entry 3. Order of entry implies an ordered, theoretical model 4. Estimates only total effects	1. Doesn't require thought or theory 2. Give up control to computer 3. Cannot use for explanation 4. "Theoretical garbage"

I am grateful to Bettina Franzese, who developed the original version of this table.

changed to maximize some worthwhile outcome? Do you want to describe the likely effects of increasing (or decreasing) a variable?

If any of these questions describe your research focus, then you are primarily interested in the goal of explanation, and either simultaneous regression or sequential regression may be an appropriate method. As a general rule, I find simultaneous regression more often useful than sequential regression, but there is also considerable overlap between the two methods and the information they provide (more so than most researchers realize). They do have distinct advantages and disadvantages for different problems, however.

I have argued that explanatory research implies a causal model and that you will be on much firmer ground if you think through this causal model prior to conducting research. One way that simultaneous and sequential regression differ is that they focus on different portions of this implied model. Simultaneous regression estimates the *direct* effects from this model, whereas sequential regression focuses on the *total* effects. As a result, the order of the variables in the model and in the regression is very important for sequential regression, but unimportant for simultaneous regression. The practical upshot of this difference is that if you are confident about which variables should appear in your model, but less sure about their ordering, simultaneous regression will be more appropriate. If you are confident in the ordering, either approach can be used, depending on whether your interest is in direct or total effects. In Part 2 of this book we will focus on estimating both direct and total effects in a single model.

Are you interested in the effects of one variable on another, for example, so that you can make statements about what happens if we change a key variable (as in our earlier homework–achievement examples)? If so, the unstandardized regression coefficients from simultaneous regression are probably your primary interest. The β's from simultaneous regression can be used to determine the relative importance of the variables in the model.

Are you interested in the unique variance accounted for by a variable? Said differently, perhaps you wonder if a variable is important, after controlling for some already existing variables. Sequential regression is the common method for answering these types of questions, although, as we have seen, simultaneous regression can provide the same information.

Prediction

If your primary interest is prediction, you have more options, including all three methods of multiple regression. I encourage you to spend some time thinking through this basic question, however, because it is often the case that researchers assume they are interested in prediction when, if fact, their real interest is in explanation.

Are you simply interested in generating a prediction equation for a set of variables? In this case, the regression coefficients from simultaneous regression should work well. Are you interested in whether a new variable improves prediction over and above that offered by a given set of predictors? Either sequential or simultaneous regression will work.

Or are you interested in finding a smaller subset of predictors that works well? If so, is it possible to rank order them on some relevant criteria (e.g., ease of cost of obtaining measures of these predictors)? If you can accomplish such rank ordering, sequential regression may be your best bet, with the ranking providing you information on the order of entry. If not, if you simply have a group of variables from which you want a smaller subset for prediction, stepwise regression may fit the bill (but all subsets regression would probably work better).

COMBINING METHODS

This chapter has necessarily focused on three methods as distinct categories of multiple regression. It is also quite possible to combine the approaches, however. We already broached this topic in the discussion of sequential regression, when we added two variables (simultaneously) in one step of a sequential analysis. Other combinations are possible, as well. We could force one group of variables into a regression equation and then use step-wise regression to choose one additional variable from several possibilities. *Blocks* of variables can be added at every step of a sequential regression.

The important lesson, whatever your approach, is to make sure you understand thoroughly your intent in conducting the research. Once you have this understanding, make sure that your regression method allows you to fulfill your purpose.

SUMMARY

In this chapter we expanded our repertoire of MR methods. The method that we have been using for MR so far—simultaneous or forced entry regression—is, in fact, one of several types of MR. Other methods include sequential (or hierarchical) MR and stepwise MR. With simultaneous MR, all variables are entered into the regression equation at the same time. The overall R^2 and the regression coefficients are generally used for interpretation. The b's and β's in simultaneous regression represent the direct effects of the variables on the outcome, with the other variables in the equation taken into account. Simultaneous regression is very useful for explanatory research and can provide estimates of the relative effects of the variables on the outcome. Simultaneous regression can also be used for prediction, in which case the standardized regression coefficients estimate the relative importance of the predictors. The primary weakness of simultaneous regression is that the regression coefficients may change depending on the variables entered in the regression.

In sequential or hierarchical multiple regression, variables are entered in steps or blocks predetermined by the researcher; time precedence is a common basis for such order of entry. The change in R^2 from one step to the next is generally used to test the statistical significance of each variable, and $\sqrt{\Delta R^2}$ may be interpreted as the measure of the relative importance of each variable's total effect (given the correct order of entry of the variables). The regression coefficients from each step of the regression may be interpreted as the total effects of each variable on the outcome, if the variables have been entered in accordance with a theoretical model. A variation, sequential unique MR, is used to determine whether one or several variables are important (explain additional variance) after taking an original set of variables into account. This form of sequential regression is commonly used to test the statistical significance of interactions and curves in the regression line. Sequential regression may be useful for explanation, if the variables are entered in accordance with theory; it can also be used to determine if a variable is useful in prediction. The primary weakness of sequential regression is that the ΔR^2 changes depending on the order of entry of the variables, and thus it can over- or underestimate the importance of variables, depending on the order of entry of variables in the regression.

In stepwise multiple regression and its variations, variables are also entered one at a time, but the computer program chooses the order of entry based on the degree to which each variable increases ΔR^2. Although this solution may seem to avoid problems in simultaneous or sequential regression, it does not, because using ΔR^2 as a measure of the importance of variables is predicated on the assumption that the variables have been entered in the correct order. It would be circular reasoning to also use ΔR^2 to determine the order of entry.

For this reason, stepwise regression should not be used for explanation. Stepwise regression is only appropriate when the purpose is prediction and, even then, simultaneous and sequential regression may be more appropriate. ΔR^2 and its statistical significance are the primary focus of interpretation in stepwise regression. If used to develop a prediction equation, the b's from the final regression equation will also be used.

It is also possible, and indeed common, to combine these methods. In the next few chapters, for example, we will combine simultaneous and sequential regression to test for interactions and curves. The chapter ended with a plea that you thoroughly understand your purpose for using multiple regression. This purpose, in turn, will help you decide which method or methods of MR you should use.

EXERCISES

1. Choose an outcome variable from NELS and four or five variables you think may help explain this outcome. Conduct a simultaneous regression, a sequential regression, and a stepwise regression using your variables. Provide an appropriate interpretation of each regression. Make sure you understand and can explain any differences in the three solutions.

2. Pair with a classmate; analyze his or her variables from Exercise 1 in your own sequential regression. Did you both choose the same ordering? Make sure you can explain to your partner the reasons for choosing your ordering. Draw a "model" that explains the ordering you chose for your problem.

3. In an interesting study of a controversial topic, Sethi and Seligman studied the effect of religious fundamentalism on optimism (1993). Think about this problem: are religious fundamentalists likely to be less optimistic or more so than those with a more "liberal" religious orientation? Perhaps fundamentalists have a strict and stern religious orientation that will lead to greater pessimism (and thus less optimism). Or perhaps those with more fundamentalist views decide to let God worry about the problems of the world, thus leading to a more optimistic view. What do you think?

   The files titled "Sethi & Seligman simulated" (there are SPSS, Excel, and text [.dat] files) are designed to simulate the Sethi & Seligman data from a MR perspective.[3] The primary variables of interest are Fundamentalism (coded so that a high score represents high religious fundamentalism, a low score religious liberalism) and Optimism (high score = optimistic, low score = pessimistic). Also included are several measures of religiosity: the extent of influence of religion in one's daily life (Influenc), religious involvement and attendance (Involve), and religious hope (Hope). It may be important to control for these variables in examining the effect of Fundamentalism on Optimism.

   Regress Optimism on these variables, using both simultaneous and sequential regression. For the sequential regression, design your regression to determine whether Fundamentalism affects Optimism above and beyond the effects of Involvement, Hope, and Influence. Could you get the same information from the simultaneous regression? Interpret your results.

4. Use a library research database (e.g., PsycINFO, Sociological Abstracts, ERIC) to find an article in your area of interest that used stepwise regression in the analysis. Read the article: Are the authors more interested in prediction or explanation? Pay special attention to the Discussion: Do the authors make inferences from their regression that if a predictor variable

were increased or reduced then people would change on the outcome? Was stepwise regression appropriate? Would some other method have been more appropriate?

NOTES

1. In fact, Darlington recommends that semipartial correlations (also known as *part* correlations) be used to compare the effects of different variables in simultaneous regression, as well, and instead of β's. You can request that semipartial correlations be produced as part of the output for some computer programs, but others do not routinely provide them. Semipartial correlations can be calculated from the values of t given for each regression coefficient, however: $sr_{y(1.234)} = t\sqrt{(1-R^2)/(N-k-1)}$ (Darlington, 1990, p. 218).

2. I have greatly simplified the issue of cross-validation and recommend additional reading if you use the methodology. There are actually a number of different formulas for estimating the true R^2 and the likely cross-validation R^2; Raju and colleagues (1999) compared these empirically. Even more interesting, this and other research suggests that equal weighting of predictors often produces better cross-validations than do those based on MR estimates!

3. In the original study, members of nine religious groups were categorized into a Fundamentalist, Moderate, or Liberal categorical variable and the results analyzed via ANOVA. For this MR simulation, I instead simulated a continuous Fundamentalism variable. The results, however, are consistent with those in the original research. I used simulation provided by David Howell as the starting point for creating my own simulation data (www.uvm.edu/~dhowell/StatPages/Examples.html). Howell's Web pages have numerous excellent examples.

■ ■ ■ ■ ■

ANALYSIS OF CATEGORICAL VARIABLES

Our analyses to this point have focused on explaining one continuous dependent variable by regressing it on one or more continuous independent variables. In Chapter 1, however, I argued that a major advantage of multiple regression is that it can be used to analyze both continuous and categorical independent variables. We begin our analysis of categorical independent variables in this chapter.

Categorical variables are common in research. Sex, ethnic origin, religious affiliation, region of the country, and many other variables are often of interest to researchers as potential influences or control variables for a multitude of possible outcomes. We may be interested in the effects of sex or ethnic origin on children's self-esteem or in the effects of religious affiliation or place of residence on adults' voting behavior.[1] Yet these variables are substantively different from the variables we have considered in our MR analyses to this point. Those variables—Homework, SES, Locus of Control, and so on—are continuous variables, ranging from low (e.g., no homework) to high (e.g., 15 hours of homework). Variables such as sex or ethnic origin have no high or low values, however. Certainly we can assign "boys" a value of 0 and "girls" a value of 1, but this assignment makes no more sense than assigning boys a value of 1 and girls a value of 0. Likewise, we can assign values of 1, 2, 3, and 4 to Protestant, Catholic, Jewish, and other religions, respectively, but any other ordering will make just as much sense. These variables each use a nominal, or naming, scale; names make more sense for the values of the scales than do numbers. How, then, can we analyze such variables in multiple regression analysis?

DUMMY VARIABLES

Simple Categorical Variables

As it turns out, we can analyze such categorical variables by creating a series of scales in which we assign values of 1 for membership in a category and values of 0 for nonmembership. Thus, our initial coding of the sex variable (boys = 0, girls = 1) can be thought of as a "girl" variable, with membership coded as 1 and nonmembership (i.e., boys) coded as 0. Such coding is called *dummy coding,* creating a dummy variable.[2]

Figure 6.1 shows the results of a *t* test comparing the 8th-grade reading achievement of girls and boys using the NELS data. For this analysis, I recoded the existing sex variable (Sex, boys = 1, girls = 2) into NewSex, with boys = 0 and girls = 1. The average score for boys on the Reading test was 49.58 versus 52.62 for girls. This difference of 3 points is relatively small; measures of effect size, for example, are $d = .304$, and $\eta^2 = .023$. Nevertheless, the difference is statistically significant ($t = 4.78$, $df = 965$, $p < .001$); girls score statistically significantly higher on the 8th-grade Reading tests than do boys.

Group Statistics

	NEWSEX Sex	N	Mean	Std. Deviation	Std. Error Mean
BYTXRSTD READING STANDARDIZED SCORE	1.00 Female	464	52.61781	9.83286	.45648
	.00 Male	503	49.58206	9.90667	.44172

Independent Samples Test

	t-test for Equality of Means						
						95% Confidence Interval of the Difference	
	t	df	Sig. (2-tailed)	Mean Difference	Std. Error Difference	Lower	Upper
BYTXRSTD READING STANDARDIZED SCORE	4.778	965	.000	3.03576	.63540	1.78884	4.28268

FIGURE 6.1   *t* **Test analyzing Reading test score differences for boys and girls.**

Now turn to Figure 6.2. For this analysis, I regressed the 8th-grade Reading test score on the NewSex dummy variable. As you can see by comparing Figure 6.2 with Figure 6.1, the results of the regression are identical to those of the *t* test. The *t* associated with the New-Sex regression coefficient was 4.78, which, with 965 degrees of freedom, is statistically significant ($p < .001$).

These figures include additional information, as well. Note that the R^2 is equal to the η^2 I reported above (.023); in fact, η^2 is a measure of the variance accounted for in a dependent variable by one or more independent variables (i.e., R^2). In other words, the η^2 com-

Model Summary

Model	R	R Square	Adjusted R Square	Std. Error of the Estimate
1	.152[a]	.023	.022	9.87132

a. Predictors: (Constant), NEWSEX Sex

ANOVA[b]

Model		Sum of Squares	df	Mean Square	F	Sig.
1	Regression	2224.300	1	2224.300	22.827	.000[a]
	Residual	94032.55	965	97.443		
	Total	96256.85	966			

a. Predictors: (Constant), NEWSEX Sex

b. Dependent Variable: BYTXRSTD READING STANDARDIZED SCORE

Coefficients[a]

	Unstandardized Coefficients		Standardized Coefficients			95% Confidence Interval for B	
	B	Std. Error	Beta	t	Sig.	Lower Bound	Upper Bound
(Constant)	49.582	.440		112.650	.000	48.718	50.446
NEWSEX Sex	3.036	.635	.152	4.778	.000	1.789	4.283

a. Dependent Variable: BYTXRSTD READING STANDARDIZED SCORE

FIGURE 6.2   Regression of Reading test scores on Sex. The results are the same as for the *t* test.

monly reported as a measure of effect size in experimental research is equivalent to the R^2 from MR. Turn next to the table of coefficients in Figure 6.2. Recall from Chapter 1 that the intercept (constant) is equal to the predicted score on the dependent variable for those participants with a score of zero on the independent variable(s). When dummy coding is used, the intercept is the mean on the dependent variable for the group coded 0 on the dummy variable. When dummy variables are used to analyze the results of experimental research, the group coded 0 is often the control group. In the present example, boys were coded 0; thus the mean Reading score for boys is 49.58. The *b,* in turn, represents the deviation from the intercept for the other group; in the present example, then, girls (the group coded 1) scored 3.04 points higher on the Reading test than did boys (the group coded 0). Again, the results match those of the *t* test.

More Complex Categorical Variables

The same technique works with more complex categorical variables, as well. Consider a question about religious affiliation. We could ask "What is your religious affiliation?" and then list the possibilities, as shown in the top of Table 6.1. Alternatively we could ask a series of three questions, with yes or no answers, to get the same information, as shown in the bottom of Table 6.1. The two methods are equivalent. If you considered yourself to have some other religious affiliation than those listed, you would choose the final option for the first method or simply answer no to each question for the second method. Essentially, we do something similar to analyze categorical variables in multiple regression by changing them into a series of yes or no, or dummy, variables. An example research study will illus-

TABLE 6.1   Two Different Methods of Asking (and Coding) Religious Affiliation

WHAT IS YOUR RELIGION?

1. Protestant

2. Catholic

3. Jewish

4. Islam

5. Other (or none)

ARE YOU:	YES	NO
Protestant?	1	0
Catholic?	1	0
Jewish?	1	0
Muslim?	1	0

trate the coding and analysis of dummy variables; we will then use the same study to illustrate other possible coding methods.

False Memory and Sexual Abuse

Considerable controversy surrounds adult self-reports of previous childhood sexual abuse: do such reports represent valid, but repressed, memories, or are they false memories (cf., Lindsay & Read, 1994)? Bremner, Shobe, and Kihlstrom (2000) investigated memory skills in women with self-reported sexual abuse and posttraumatic stress disorder (PTSD). Briefly, women who had and had not been sexually abused as children were read lists of words and were later given a list of words, including words they had heard along with words *implied* by, but not included on, the original lists ("critical lures," or false positives). Figure 6.3 shows the (simulated) percentage of these false positives remembered by Abused women with PTSD, Abused women without PTSD, and Nonabused, non-PTSD women.[3] The data are also on the Web site ("false memory data, 3 groups.sav" or "false.txt"). As the figure shows, Abused, PTSD women falsely recognized more words not on the list than did non-PTSD and Nonabused women; in fact, they "recalled" almost 95% of the false critical lures as being on the lists. The differences are striking, but are they statistically significant?

ANOVA and Follow-Up.   The most common way of analyzing such data is through analysis of variance. Such an analysis is shown in Figure 6.4. As the figure shows, there

Report

FALSEPOS percent of false positives

GROUP group membership	Mean	N	Std. Deviation
1.00 Abused, PTSD women	94.6000	20	10.3791
2.00 Abused, Non-PTSD women	68.0500	20	39.3800
3.00 Non-abused, non-PTSD women	63.5500	20	27.9143
Total	75.4000	60	31.2395

FIGURE 6.3   Descriptive statistics for the false memory data.

were indeed statistically significant differences in the percentages of false recalls across the three groups ($F = 6.930$ [2, 57], $p = .002$). Although not shown in the figure, the difference across groups represented a medium to large effect size ($\eta^2 = .196$), one that would presumably be apparent to a careful observer (cf. Cohen, 1988).

ANOVA

FALSEPOS percent of false positives

	Sum of Squares	df	Mean Square	F	Sig.
Between Groups	11261.70	2	5630.850	6.930	.002
Within Groups	46316.70	57	812.574		
Total	57578.40	59			

Multiple Comparisons

Dependent Variable: FALSEPOS percent of false positives
Dunnett t (2-sided)[a]

(I) GROUP group membership	(J) GROUP group membership	Mean Difference (I-J)	Std. Error	Sig.	95% Confidence Interval	
					Lower Bound	Upper Bound
1.00 Abused, PTSD women	3.00 Non-abused, non-PTSD women	31.0500*	9.0143	.002	10.6037	51.4963
2.00 Abused, Non-PTSD women	3.00 Non-abused, non-PTSD women	4.5000	9.0143	.836	-15.9463	24.9463

*. The mean difference is significant at the .05 level.

a. Dunnett t-tests treat one group as a control, and compare all other groups against it.

FIGURE 6.4   Analysis of variance of the false memory data, with Dunnett's test as a follow-up.

Also shown in Figure 6.4 are the results of Dunnett's test, which is a post hoc test used to compare several groups to one group, usually several experimental groups to a single control group. Here our interest was to compare Abused women (with and without PTSD) to women who had not been abused. As shown in the figure, Abused, PTSD women had statistically significantly more false positives than did women who were not abused, but the difference between Abused (Non-PTSD) and Nonabused women was not statistically significant.

Regression Analysis with Dummy Variables.   Our real interest, of course, is not in the ANVOA tables, but in how to conduct such an analysis via multiple regression; the ANOVA is included for comparison purposes. The three groups may be considered a single, categorical variable with three categories: 20 participants form the Abused, PTSD group, coded 1; 20 participants form the Abused, Non-PTSD group, coded 2; and so on. We need to convert the categorical Group variable into dummy variables.

To include all the information contained in a single categorical variable, we need to create as many dummy variables as there are categories, **minus 1.** The example includes three categories, or groups, so we need to create two $(g - 1)$ dummy variables. Each dummy variable should represent membership in one of the groups. Table 6.2 shows how I translated the original single categorical variable into two dummy variables. The first dummy variable, AbusePTS (meaning Abused, PTSD) has values of 1 for members of the Abused, PTSD group, and thus contrasts members of this group with all others. The second dummy variable (No_PTSD) is coded so that members of the Abused, Non-PTSD group were coded 1, while all other participants were coded 0. The actual computer manipulations to create these dummy variables can be accomplished via RECODE or IF commands, depending on your computer program.

TABLE 6.2   Converting a Group Variable with Three Categories into Two Dummy Variables

GROUP		ABUSEPTS	NO_PTSD
1	Abused, PTSD	1	0
2	Abused, Non-PTSD	0	1
3	Nonabused, Non-PTSD	0	0

You may wonder why there is no third dummy variable that compares the Nonabused, Non-PTSD group with the other two groups. But such a third dummy variable is not needed; it would be redundant. Consider that in multiple regression we examine the effect of each variable, with the other variables in the equation *held constant.* If we regress the proportion of false positives on only the first dummy variable, our results will highlight the comparison of Abused, PTSD participants against the other two groups. We will use *multiple* regression, however, and control for the second dummy variable at the same time, which means the first dummy variable will show the effect of Abuse and PTSD, while controlling for Abuse, Non-PTSD. The result is that in the multiple regression the first dummy variable will contrast the Abused, PTSD group with the Nonabused (and Non-PTSD) group, whereas the second dummy variable will compare the Abused, Non-PTSD with the Nonabused group. We will return to this question (the number of dummy variables) later in the chapter.

Figure 6.5 shows a portion of the data. It is always a good idea to check the raw data after recoding or creating new variables to make sure the results are as intended. Figure 6.5 shows that the two dummy variables were created correctly. For the multiple regression, I regressed the percentage of false positives on these two dummy variables; the results are shown in Figure 6.6, where these two variables account for 19.6% of the variance in the number of false positives, and this R^2 (.196) matches the η^2 from the analysis of variance. Likewise, the F associated with the regression (6.930 [2, 57], $p = .002$) matches that from the ANOVA.

GROUP	ABUSE PTS	NO_PTSD
1.00	1.00	.00
1.00	1.00	.00
1.00	1.00	.00
1.00	1.00	.00
1.00	1.00	.00
2.00	.00	1.00
2.00	.00	1.00
2.00	.00	1.00
2.00	.00	1.00
2.00	.00	1.00
3.00	.00	.00
3.00	.00	.00
3.00	.00	.00
3.00	.00	.00

FIGURE 6.5   Portions of the false memory data showing the Group variable converted into two dummy variables, AbusePTS and No_PTSD.

Post Hoc Probing.   The regression coefficients, also shown in Figure 6.6, may be used to perform post hoc comparisons. As in the simpler example, the intercept (constant) provides the mean score on the dependent variable (percentage of false positives) for the group that was assigned zeros for *both* dummy variables. Again, this is often the "control" group and, in this case, is the mean score for those participants who were neither abused nor suffered from PTSD ($M = 63.55$). The regression coefficients, in turn, represent the *deviations* from this mean for *each* of the other two groups. Women who were abused and suffer from PTSD had an average of 94.60 false positives (63.55 + 31.05), and abused, non-PTSD women had an average of 68.05 false positives (63.55 + 4.50). Compare these calculations of the mean scores for each group with those shown in Figure 6.3.

Dunnett's Test.   The t's associated with the dummy variables can be used in several ways. First, we can use them for Dunnett's test, as we did with the ANOVA. To do so, you need to ignore the probabilities associated with the t's on the printout; instead look up those values of t in Dunnett's table in a statistics book that contains a variety of such tables (e.g., Howell, 2002; Kirk, 1995). The critical values for three treatment groups and 60 degrees of freedom (the closest value in the table to the actual value of 57 *df*) are 2.27 ($\alpha = .05$) and 2.90 ($\alpha = .01$) (two-tailed test, Table E.7, Kirk, 1995; it is also quite easy to find this and other tables on the Web; just search for Dunnett test). Thus, the regression results are again identical to those

Model Summary

Model	R	R Square	Adjusted R Square	Std. Error of the Estimate
1	.442[a]	.196	.167	28.5057

a. Predictors: (Constant), NO_PTSD Abused, non-PTSD vs other, ABUSEPTS Abused, PTSD vs other

ANOVA[b]

Model		Sum of Squares	df	Mean Square	F	Sig.
1	Regression	11261.70	2	5630.850	6.930	.002[a]
	Residual	46316.70	57	812.574		
	Total	57578.40	59			

a. Predictors: (Constant), NO_PTSD Abused, non-PTSD vs other, ABUSEPTS Abused, PTSD vs other

b. Dependent Variable: FALSEPOS percent of false positives

Coefficients[a]

Model		Unstandardized Coefficients		Standardized Coefficients	t	Sig.	95% Confidence Interval for B	
		B	Std. Error	Beta			Lower Bound	Upper Bound
1	(Constant)	63.550	6.374		9.970	.000	50.786	76.314
	ABUSEPTS Abused, PTSD vs other	31.050	9.014	.472	3.445	.001	12.999	49.101
	NO_PTSD Abused, non-PTSD vs other	4.500	9.014	.068	.499	.620	-13.551	22.551

a. Dependent Variable: FALSEPOS percent of false positives

FIGURE 6.6   Multiple regression analysis of the false memory data using the two dummy variables.

from the ANOVA: the data suggest that Abused, PTSD participants have statistically significantly more false memories of words than do nonabused women, whereas the difference between Abused and Nonabused women without PTSD is not statistically significant.

Why not simply use the probabilities associated with the t's in Figure 6.6? And why do these probabilities differ from those shown in Figure 6.4? Simply put, Dunnett's test takes into account the number of comparisons made in an effort to control the total family-wise error rate. Recall that if you conduct, for example, 20 t tests, each with an error rate of .05, you would likely find one of these comparisons to be statistically significant by chance alone. Many post hoc tests control for this increase in family-wise error rate resulting from multiple comparisons, and Dunnett's test is one such post hoc comparison. The probabilities associated with the t's in the regression do not take the family-wise error rate into account; but when we look up the t's in Dunnett's table, we do take these error rates into account.[4]

Other Post Hoc Tests.   We could also simply focus on the t's and associated probabilities in the regression output, uncorrected for the family-wise error. Given the statistical significance of the overall regression, this procedure is equivalent to the Fisher least significant difference (LSD) post hoc procedure. Alternatively, we can use the Dunn–Bonferroni procedure to control the family-wise error rate. That is, we set the overall alpha to .05 and decide to make two comparisons. We would then look at the probabilities associated with each dummy variable and count any with $p < .025$ ($.05/2$) as statistically significant. With the current example, all three approaches (Dunnett, multiple t tests, and Dunn–Bonferroni) give the same answer, although with different levels of probability. This will not always be the case. The Dunn–Bonferroni procedure is more conservative (meaning that it is least likely to be statistically significant) than is the use of multiple t tests, among the most liberal procedures. Dunnett's test is more conservative than the LSD procedure, but is fundamentally different in that it only makes a subset of all possible comparisons.

What if we were interested in the third possible comparison, whether the difference between Abused, PTSD and Abused, Non-PTSD participants was statistically significant? Using the regression results, you can calculate the mean difference between the two results ($94.60 - 68.05 = 26.55$). As long as the n's in each group are the same, the standard error of this difference is the same for all three possible comparisons; as shown in Figure 6.6, the standard error is 9.014.[5] Thus the t associated with a comparison of the AbusePTS and the No_PTSD groups is $26.55/9.014 = 2.95$ ($p = .005$). We then either use this value in an LSD-type post hoc comparison or compare it to $\alpha = .0167$ ($.05/3$) in a Dunn–Bonferroni comparison. In either case, we conclude that abused women with PTSD also have statistically significantly more false memories of words than do abused women without PTSD. Try conducting an ANOVA on these data, followed by both the LSD and Dunn–Bonferroni post hoc analyses to check the accuracy of these statements. Of course, to make this final comparison in MR, you could also simply redo the dummy coding making, for example, group 1 the comparison group to find this final comparison.

Demonstration of the Need for Only $g - 1$ Dummy Variables.   I argued earlier that we only need $g - 1$ dummy variables because this number of dummy variables captures all the information contained in the original categorical variable. In the present example, we only need two dummy variables to capture all the information from the three categories used in the research. You may be skeptical that $g - 1$ dummy variables indeed include all the information of the original categorical variable, but we can demonstrate that equivalence easily. To do so, I regressed the original Group variable used in the ANOVA analysis against the two dummy variables that I claim capture all the information contained in that Group variable. If the two dummy variables do indeed include all the information from the original categorical variable, then the dummy variables should account for 100% of the variance in the Group variable; R^2 will equal 1.0. If, however, a third dummy variable is needed to contrast the three groups, then the R^2 should equal something less than 1.0.

Figure 6.7 shows the results of such a multiple regression: the two created dummy variables do indeed explain all the variation in the original categorical variable. Thus, we only need $g - 1$ dummy variables to correspond to any categorical variable (indeed, if we use g dummy variables, our MR would encounter problems).

Was Multiple Regression Necessary?   Now, was there any reason to use multiple regression to analyze the results of this research? No; for this problem, it would be easier to analyze the data using ANOVA. The simple example is included for several reasons, however. First, it is important to understand the continuity between multiple regression and ANOVA. Second, you may well encounter or develop more complex experimental designs in which it makes more sense to conduct the analysis via MR than ANOVA. Third, you need to

Variables Entered/Removed [b]

Model	Variables Entered	Variables Removed	Method
1	NO_PTSD Abused, non-PTSD vs other, ABUSEPTS Abused, PTSD vs other [a]	.	Enter

a. All requested variables entered.

b. Dependent Variable: GROUP group membership

Model Summary

Model	R	R Square	Adjusted R Square	Std. Error of the Estimate
1	1.000[a]	1.000	1.000	.0000

a. Predictors: (Constant), NO_PTSD Abused, non-PTSD vs other, ABUSEPTS Abused, PTSD vs other

FIGURE 6.7   **Multiple regression demonstrating the need for only $g - 1$ dummy variables. These dummy variables explain 100% of the variance of the original Group variable.**

understand how to analyze categorical variables in MR as a foundation for conducting MR analyses that include both categorical and continuous variables.

This final reason is, I think, paramount. Most of us will likely rarely use MR to analyze either simple or complex experimental data. We will, however, use MR to analyze a mix of continuous and categorical variables. A thorough understanding of the analysis of categorical variables provides a foundation for this type of analysis.

OTHER METHODS OF CODING CATEGORICAL VARIABLES

There are other methods of coding categorical variables besides dummy coding. We will review a few of these briefly. What is important to keep in mind is that these different methods all lead to the same overall outcome (i.e., the same R^2 and level of statistical significance). In other words, the model summary and ANOVA table will be the same across the methods. Different methods, however, can produce differences in the coefficients, in part because the comparisons being made are different. I will use our current example to illustrate several other methods of coding categorical variables.

Effect Coding

Effect coding is another method of coding categorical variables so that they can be analyzed in multiple regression. Recall that in dummy coding one group ends up being assigned zeros on all dummy variables. Effect coding is similar in that there is this contrast group, but with effect coding this group is assigned –1 on both effect variables, rather than 0. The contrast group is usually the last group.

Table 6.3 shows effect coding for the three groups for the Abuse/PTSD example. For the first effect variable, the Abused/PTSD group is coded 1 and all other groups are scored 0, except for the final group, which is scored –1. (In this example, these "all other groups" only includes 1 group, Abused/Non-PTSD, but if we had, say, 6 groups and 5 effect coded variables, 4 groups would be coded 0 on this first effect variable.) For the second effect variable, the Abused, Non-PTSD group was coded 1 and all other groups were coded 0, except for the final group, which was coded –1.

TABLE 6.3   Converting a Group Variable with Three Categories into Two Effect Coded Variables

GROUP	EFFECT 1	EFFECT 2
1 Abused, PTSD	1	0
2 Abused, Non-PTSD	0	1
3 Nonabused, Non-PTSD	–1	–1

Figure 6.8 shows the results of the regression of the percentage of false positives on the two effect variables. The same percentage of variance was accounted for as in the previous regression (19.6%), with the same resulting F and probability. The only differences show up in the table of coefficients.

Why the differences? The intercept and b's highlight different comparisons for effect than for dummy coding. Recall that the intercept is the predicted score on the dependent variable for those with a score of zero on all independent variables. But with effect coding no group is coded zero on all the effect variables. With effect coding, the intercept (constant) shown in Figure 6.8 is the *grand* mean of all three groups on the dependent variable (percentage of false positives). The intercept, representing the grand, or overall, mean is 75.40; note that this value is the same as the overall mean listed in Figure 6.3. The b's, in turn, are the deviation for each group from the grand mean. The b associated with the first effect variable, representing the first group, was 19.20, and the mean for this group on the dependent variable was 94.60 (75.40 + 19.20). The mean for the second group was 68.05 (75.40 + [–7.35]). If we want to find the mean score for the third group, we simply sum the two b's (19.20 + [–7.35] = 11.85) and change the sign (–11.85). This is the deviation of the third group from the grand mean, so the mean of group 3 is 63.55 (75.40 + [–11.85]). The reason why is because the intercept is the grand mean, and each b represents each group's deviation from the mean. The three deviations from the mean must sum to zero, and thus the third deviation has the same absolute value as the sum of the other two deviations, but with a reversed sign. This way the three deviations do sum to zero (19.20 − 7.35 − 11.85 = 0).

The t's in this coding method represent the statistical significance of the difference between each group and the overall mean. That is, does each group differ at a statistically significant level from all other groups? This is an uncommon post hoc question, but it may be of interest in some applications. It is possible, of course, to calculate other post hoc comparisons using the group means (cf. Pedhazur, 1997, Chap. 11).

Model Summary

Model	R	R Square	Adjusted R Square	Std. Error of the Estimate
1	.442[a]	.196	.167	28.5057

a. Predictors: (Constant), EFFECT_2, EFFECT_1

ANOVA[b]

Model		Sum of Squares	df	Mean Square	F	Sig.
1	Regression	11261.70	2	5630.850	6.930	.002[a]
	Residual	46316.70	57	812.574		
	Total	57578.40	59			

a. Predictors: (Constant), EFFECT_2, EFFECT_1

b. Dependent Variable: FALSEPOS percent of false positives

Coefficients[a]

Model		Unstandardized Coefficients		Standardized Coefficients	t	Sig.	95% Confidence Interval for B	
		B	Std. Error	Beta			Lower Bound	Upper Bound
1	(Constant)	75.400	3.680		20.489	.000	68.031	82.769
	EFFECT_1	19.200	5.204	.506	3.689	.001	8.778	29.622
	EFFECT_2	-7.350	5.204	-.194	-1.412	.163	-17.772	3.072

a. Dependent Variable: FALSEPOS percent of false positives

FIGURE 6.8   **Multiple regression analysis of the false memory data using two effect coded variables.**

Recall that in earlier chapters I discussed ANOVA as a part of the general linear model, with formulas like $Y = \mu + \beta + e$. This formula may be stated as follows: any person's score on the dependent variable Y is the sum of the overall mean μ, plus (or minus) variation due to the effect of the treatment (β), plus (or minus) random variation due to the effect of error (e). We would interpret the regression equation ($Y = a + bX + e$) using effect coding in the exact same manner: a person's score on the dependent variable is the sum of the overall mean (a), plus (or minus) variation due to their group, plus (or minus) random variation due to error. One advantage of effect coding is that it illustrates nicely the general linear model in analysis of variance.

Criterion Scaling

Suppose you have a large number of categories for a categorical variable and are only interested in the *overall* effects of the categorical variable, not any subsequent post hoc comparisons. As an example, the controversial book *More Guns: Less Crime* (Lott, 1998) made extensive use of multiple regression. One categorical independent variable of interest was the 50 states, which could be represented by 49 dummy variables. There is an easier way to take the various states into account, however, through a method called *criterion scaling.*

With criterion scaling, a *single* new variable is created to replace the $g - 1$ dummy variables. For this single variable, each member of each group is coded with that group's mean score on the dependent variable. Thus, for the present example, using the group means displayed in Figure 6.3, all members of the Abused, PTSD group are assigned a score of 94.60 on this new variable, whereas members of the Abused, Non-PTSD group are assigned values of 68.05, and so on. Figure 6.9 shows a portion of the data following the creation of this criterion scaled variable (Crit_Var).

FALSEPOS	GROUP	CRIT_VAR
55.00	1.00	94.60
93.00	1.00	94.60
89.00	1.00	94.60
98.00	1.00	94.60
96.00	1.00	94.60
100.00	2.00	68.05
100.00	2.00	68.05
16.00	2.00	68.05
7.00	2.00	68.05
73.00	2.00	68.05
61.00	2.00	68.05
100.00	3.00	63.55
61.00	3.00	63.55
27.00	3.00	63.55
10.00	3.00	63.55
96.00	3.00	63.55

FIGURE 6.9   Portions of the false memory data showing the group variable converted into a single criterion coded variable.

The dependent variable, percentage of false positive memories, was regressed on Crit_Var, and the results are shown in Figure 6.10. Note that the explained variance is identical to the previous printouts. Also note, however, that the F and its associated probability are different (and incorrect). When criterion scaling is used, the degrees of freedom associated with the criterion scaled variable will be incorrect. Even though we have collapsed $g - 1$ dummy variables into a single criterion scaled variable, this variable still represents the g groups in the original categorical variable, and the df associated with it should be $g - 1$. In the present example, Crit_Var still represents three groups, and the df for the regression should still be 2 (and not 1). And because the df for the regression is incorrect, the df for the residual is incorrect, and the F is incorrect as well. The bottom line is that when you use criterion scaling you need to recalculate F using the printed sums of squares, but the corrected degrees of freedom.

Model Summary

Model	R	R Square	Adjusted R Square	Std. Error of the Estimate
1	.442[a]	.196	.182	28.2589

a. Predictors: (Constant), CRIT_VAR

ANOVA[b]

Model		Sum of Squares	df	Mean Square	F	Sig.
1	Regression	11261.70	1	11261.700	14.102	.000[a]
	Residual	46316.70	58	798.564		
	Total	57578.40	59			

a. Predictors: (Constant), CRIT_VAR

b. Dependent Variable: FALSEPOS percent of false positives

FIGURE 6.10   **Multiple regression results using criterion coding. The ANOVA table needs to be corrected for the proper degrees of freedom.**

UNEQUAL GROUP SIZES

For the PTSD example used in this chapter, there were equal numbers of women in each of the three PTSD/Abuse groups. In the real world of research, however, there are often different numbers of participants in different levels of an independent variable; unequal n's are especially common in nonexperimental research. Naturally occurring groups (ethnic group membership, religious affiliation) rarely conform to our research desire for equal numbers from each group (the variable sex is sometimes an exception, since this variable is close to evenly split at many ages). If we conduct our research by simply sampling from the population, our samples will reflect this difference in sample sizes across groups. Even in experimental research, where participants are assigned at random to different groups, we have participants who drop out of the research, and this participant mortality often varies by group. The result is unequal sample sizes by group.[6]

As you will see, having equal numbers in groups makes it easier to interpret the results of the regression. An example from NELS will illustrate the differences.

Family Structure and Substance Use

Does family structure affect adolescents' use of dangerous and illegal substances? Are adolescents from intact families less likely to use alcohol, tobacco, and drugs? To examine these questions, I analyzed the effect of Family Structure (coded 1 for students who lived with both parents, 2 for students who lived with one parent and one guardian or step-parent, and 3 for students who lived with a single parent) on Substance use, a composite of students' reports of their use of cigarettes, alcohol, and marijuana.[7] The descriptive statistics for the two variables are shown in Figure 6.11. As you would expect, there were unequal numbers of students from households with two parents, a single parent, and so on. The Substance Use variable was a mean of z scores, with negative scores representing little use of substances and positive scores representing more common use of substances.

FAMSTRUC Family Structure

		Frequency	Percent	Valid Percent	Cumulative Percent
Valid	1.00 Two-parent family	677	67.7	69.7	69.7
	2.00 One parent, one guardian	118	11.8	12.1	81.8
	3.00 Single-parent family	177	17.7	18.2	100.0
	Total	972	97.2	100.0	
Missing	System	28	2.8		
Total		1000	100.0		

Descriptive Statistics

	N	Minimum	Maximum	Mean	Std. Deviation
SUBSTANC Use of alcohol, drugs, tobacco	855	-.81	3.35	-.0008	.77200
Valid N (listwise)	855				

FIGURE 6.11   Descriptive information about the Family Structure and Substance Use variables created using the NELS data.

Figure 6.12 shows the results of an ANOVA using Substance Use as the dependent variable and Family Structure as the independent variable. As the figure shows, the effect of Family Structure was statistically significant ($F[2, 830] = 7.252$, $p = .001$), although the effect was small ($\eta^2 = .017$). The graph in the figure shows the mean levels of Substance Use by group: Students from intact families are less likely, on average, to use substances than are those from families with one parent and one guardian, and students from families with one parent and one guardian are less likely to use substances than those from single-parent families.

Post hoc tests (Fisher's LSD, Dunn–Bonferroni, and Dunnett's test) are shown in Figure 6.13. According to the LSD procedure, the differences between students from intact families and those from single-parent and parent–guardian families were both statistically significant. The difference between parent–guardian and single-parent families was not statistically significant. The comparison between students from two-parent and single-parent families was the only statistically significant difference according to the Dunn–Bonferroni post hoc comparison. For Dunnett's test, two-parent families were used as the reference (or "control") group. Dunnett's test also suggested that students from single-parent homes use statistically significantly more substances than those from two-parent homes, but that the difference between two-parent and parent–guardian homes was not statistically significant.

Descriptive Statistics

Dependent Variable: SUBSTANC Use of alcohol, drugs, tobacco

FAMSTRUC Family	Mean	Std. Deviation	N
1.00 Two-parent family	-.0585	.72621	597
2.00 One parent, one guardian	.1196	.76153	94
3.00 Single-parent family	.1918	.93617	142
Total	.0043	.77554	833

Tests of Between-Subjects Effects

Dependent Variable: SUBSTANC Use of alcohol, drugs, tobacco

Source	Type III Sum of Squares	df	Mean Square	F	Sig.	Partial Eta Squared
FAMSTRUC	8.594	2	4.297	7.252	.001	.017
Error	491.824	830	.593			
Corrected Total	500.418	832				

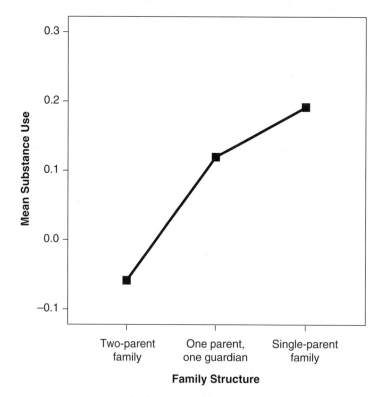

FIGURE 6.12   Analysis of Variance of the effects of family structure on adolescents' use of dangerous substances.

Multiple Comparisons

Dependent Variable: SUBSTANC Use of alcohol, drugs, tobacco

	(I) Family Structure	(J) Family Structure	Mean Difference (I-J)	Std. Error	Sig.	95% Confidence Interval Lower Bound	Upper Bound
LSD	1.00 Two-parent family	2.00 One parent, one guardian	-.1780*	.08542	.037	-.3457	-.0103
		3.00 Single-parent family	-.2503*	.07187	.001	-.3914	-.1092
	2.00 One parent, one guardian	1.00 Two-parent family	.1780*	.08542	.037	.0103	.3457
		3.00 Single-parent family	-.0723	.10236	.480	-.2732	.1286
	3.00 Single-parent family	1.00 Two-parent family	.2503*	.07187	.001	.1092	.3914
		2.00 One parent, one guardian	.0723	.10236	.480	-.1286	.2732
Bonferroni	1.00 Two-parent family	2.00 One parent, one guardian	-.1780	.08542	.112	-.3829	.0269
		3.00 Single-parent family	-.2503*	.07187	.002	-.4227	-.0779
	2.00 One parent, one guardian	1.00 Two-parent family	.1780	.08542	.112	-.0269	.3829
		3.00 Single-parent family	-.0723	.10236	1.000	-.3178	.1733
	3.00 Single-parent family	1.00 Two-parent family	.2503*	.07187	.002	.0779	.4227
		2.00 One parent, one guardian	.0723	.10236	1.000	-.1733	.3178
Dunnett t (2-sided)[a]	2.00 One parent, one	1.00 Two-parent family	.1780	.08542	.073	-.0132	.3692
	3.00 Single-parent family	1.00 Two-parent family	.2503*	.07187	.001	.0894	.4112

Based on observed means.

*. The mean difference is significant at the .05 level.

a. Dunnett t-tests treat one group as a control, and compare all other groups against it.

FIGURE 6.13   Post hoc analyses of the effect of three types of family structures on substance use.

Before reading further, take a minute to consider how you could analyze these data using MR. Consider how you would convert Family Structure into dummy variables (and how many dummy variables you would need). How would you convert Family Structure into effect variables? I present the results of such regressions only briefly, but ask you to delve more deeply into the analyses in Exercise 2.

Dummy Variable Coding and Analysis.   Two dummy variables are needed to capture the information contained in the three categories of the Family Structure variable. Table 6.4 shows my conversion of the Family Structure variable into two dummy variables. As in the Dunnett comparison, I used two-parent families as the reference group for comparison with other family structures. It seems to me that our primary questions of interest in such an analysis will be whether other family structures are comparable to two-parent families. The first dummy variable (Step) contrasts students from parent–guardian families with those from two-parent families, and the second dummy variable (Single) contrasts students from single-parent families with those from two-parent families.

Figure 6.14 shows the results of a MR of Substance Use on these two dummy variables. The two Family Structure dummy variables accounted for 1.7% of the variance in Substance Use ($R^2 = \eta^2 = .017$). Given the large sample, this value was statistically significant ($F[2, 830] = 7.252, p = .001$). The values match those from the ANOVA.

Next, focus on the table of coefficients shown in Figure 6.14. The intercept (constant) is equal to the mean score on Substance Use of the contrast group, the group coded zero in

TABLE 6.4   Converting the Family Structure Variable into Two Dummy Variables

GROUP	STEP	SINGLE
1 Two-parent family	0	0
2 One parent, one guardian	1	0
3 Single-parent family	0	1

Model Summary

Model	R	R Square	Adjusted R Square	Std. Error of the Estimate
1	.131[a]	.017	.015	.76978

a. Predictors: (Constant), SINGLE, STEP

ANOVA[b]

Model		Sum of Squares	df	Mean Square	F	Sig.
1	Regression	8.594	2	4.297	7.252	.001[a]
	Residual	491.824	830	.593		
	Total	500.418	832			

a. Predictors: (Constant), SINGLE, STEP

b. Dependent Variable: SUBSTANC Use of alcohol, drugs, tobacco

Coefficients[a]

Model		Unstandardized Coefficients		Standardized Coefficients			95% Confidence Interval for B	
		B	Std. Error	Beta	t	Sig.	Lower Bound	Upper Bound
1	(Constant)	-.058	.032		-1.855	.064	-.120	.003
	STEP	.178	.085	.073	2.084	.037	.010	.346
	SINGLE	.250	.072	.121	3.483	.001	.109	.391

a. Dependent Variable: SUBSTANC Use of alcohol, drugs, tobacco

FIGURE 6.14   Analysis of the Substance Use data using multiple regression with dummy variables.

both dummy variables, that is, students from two-parent families. As in the earlier example, the b's represent the deviation for each group from the mean of the contrast group. So, for example, students from single-parent families had mean Substance Use scores of .1918 (Figure 6.12). From the table of regression coefficients in Figure 6.14, we can calculate the mean score on the dependent variable for students from single-parent families as $-.058 + .250 = .192$, the same value, within errors of rounding.

The interpretation of the t values and their statistical significance is the same as in the earlier example. We could look up the t values in a Dunnett's table and find that the Single dummy variable was statistically significant, whereas the Step dummy variable was not.

These finding are also consistent with the findings from the ANOVA and suggest that students from single-parent families use statistically significantly more dangerous substances than do students from two-parent families, but that the difference between parent–guardian families and two-parent families is not statistically significant.

We can also use the t values and their associated statistical significance as the basis for a series of LSD or Dunn–Bonferroni post hoc comparisons. Using Fisher's LSD, we would simply use the statistical significance of the t's as listed in the MR output. We would conclude that students from both single-parent and parent–guardian families are more likely to use dangerous substances than those from traditional two-parent families.

It would be easy to calculate the b associated with the third possible comparison, that between single-parent and parent–guardian families. We know the means for the two groups. If one of these groups was used as the comparison group (e.g., the Parent–Guardian group), the b for the other group (the Single-parent group) would be equal to the difference between these two means. That is, Single – (Parent–Guardian) = .1918 – .1196 = .0722. Unfortunately, with unequal sample sizes, the standard errors associated with each group are different (you can see this by comparing the standard errors associated with Single and Step in the table of coefficients in Figure 6.14). You can calculate the standard error for this comparison using the formula

$$SE_b = \sqrt{MS_r \times \left(\frac{1}{n_1} + \frac{1}{n_c}\right)}.$$

The MS_r is the mean square for the residual from the ANOVA table in Figure 6.14, and the n's are the sample sizes for the two groups (the single-parent and parent–guardian groups). For this comparison, SE_b is equal to .102. The value for t ($t = b/SE_b$) is .705, and the probability of obtaining this t by chance alone is .481. Note that this is the same value for the standard error and significance shown in the LSD post hoc comparisons in Figure 6.13. This comparison shows no statistically significant differences in substance use for students from single-parent compared to parent–guardian families. You should perform these calculations yourself to make sure you get the same results that I did.

If you don't trust yourself to make these calculations by hand, it is easy to get these same results by rerunning the MR. Simply create new dummy variables using the parent–guardian group as the reference group and conduct the regression using these dummy variables. The dummy variable associated with the comparison between the single-parent group and the parent–guardian group should provide the same standard error, t, and p as we calculated above. Whichever method you use, you can use these same t and p values to make post hoc comparisons using a Dunn–Bonferroni correction. For example, you can set the overall family-wise error rate at .05, meaning that each of three comparisons will need to have a probability of less than .0167 ($\alpha = \frac{.05}{.3}$) to be considered statistically significant.

Effect Variable Coding and Analysis.   With effect coding, one group is assigned values of –1 for all effect coded variables. As shown in Table 6.5, I chose to make single-parent families the group assigned –1's. Figure 6.15 shows the results of the regression of Substance Use on the two effect coded variables, TwoEff (for two-parent families) and StepEff (for parent–guardian families).

TABLE 6.5   Converting the Family Structure Variable into Two Effect Coded Variables

GROUP		TWOEFF	STEPEFF
1	Two-parent family	1	0
2	One parent, one guardian	0	1
3	Single-parent family	−1	−1

Model Summary

Model	R	R Square	Adjusted R Square	Std. Error of the Estimate
1	.131[a]	.017	.015	.76978

a. Predictors: (Constant), STEPEFF, TWOEFF

ANOVA[b]

Model		Sum of Squares	df	Mean Square	F	Sig.
1	Regression	8.594	2	4.297	7.252	.001[a]
	Residual	491.824	830	.593		
	Total	500.418	832			

a. Predictors: (Constant), STEPEFF, TWOEFF

b. Dependent Variable: SUBSTANC Use of alcohol, drugs, tobacco

Coefficients[a]

Model		Unstandardized Coefficients		Standardized Coefficients	t	Sig.	95% Confidence Interval for B	
		B	Std. Error	Beta			Lower Bound	Upper Bound
1	(Constant)	.084	.036		2.362	.018	.014	.154
	TWOEFF	-.143	.040	-.141	-3.563	.000	-.221	-.064
	STEPEFF	.035	.058	.024	.607	.544	-.079	.149

a. Dependent Variable: SUBSTANC Use of alcohol, drugs, tobacco

FIGURE 6.15   Multiple regression analysis of Substance Use differences for students from three family types using effect variables.

With unequal numbers in the three groups, the interpretation of the multiple regression is only slightly different from the interpretation with equal n's. With equal sample sizes, the intercept is equal to the overall mean, across groups, on the dependent variable. With unequal sample sizes, the intercept is equal to the mean of means, or the unweighted means of the three groups. In other words, average the three means shown in Figure 6.12 without respect to the differences in the n's of the three groups: $(-.0585 + .1196 + .1918)/3 = .0843$. As before, the b's are the deviation from the mean of the group coded 1 in the effect variable. Thus, the mean on Substance Use for students from two-parent families is $.084 + (-.143) = .059$. Again, you will delve deeper into this analysis in Exercise 2.

ADDITIONAL METHODS AND ISSUES

There are still additional methods for coding simple or complex categorical variables. Like the methods illustrated here, the various methods produce the same overall results, such as R^2 and its statistical significance, but enable different contrasts among the different levels of the categorical variable. Orthogonal or contrast coding produces orthogonal contrasts among the levels of the categorical variable (usually an a priori rather than a post hoc test). Sequential coding can be used to compare categories that can be ranked in some way, nested coding can be used to compare categories within categories, and there are other possible coding schemes beyond these.

In addition, we can have multiple categorical variables, as in a factorial design, and can test for possible interactions among these variables. However, dummy coding does not work well for testing interactions in experimental factorial designs unless you center the dummy variables (we will discuss both interactions and centering in the next chapter).

Which method of coding should you use? I expect that in most cases our interest in categorical variables will be to include such variables in a regression analysis along with other, continuous variables. Very often, these categorical variables will be "control" variables, which we need to take into account in our regression, but which are not of central interest. Sex, region of the country, and ethnic origin often are used in regression analyses as such control variables. Under these circumstances, the simple methods of coding presented here are sufficient, and simple dummy coding will often work well. Dummy coding is also useful if you have an obvious contrast group (such as a control group) to which you wish to compare other groups.

Effect coding is useful when you wish to compare each group with the overall mean of all groups. Suppose, for example, you were interested in whether self-esteem differed across different religious groups. If you wanted to determine whether each religious group differed from the average, overall level of self-esteem, effect coding is a good choice for coding the religion variable. Criterion scaling is especially useful for categorical variables that have numerous categories. Other books may be consulted for further information about some of the more complex coding schemes mentioned (e.g., Cohen, Cohen, West, & Aiken, 2003; Darlington, 1990; Pedhazur, 1997).

SUMMARY

This chapter introduced the analysis of categorical variables in multiple regression. Categorical, or nominal, variables are common in research, and one advantage of MR is that it can be used to analyze continuous, categorical, or a combination of continuous and categorical independent variables.

With dummy coding, a common method of dealing with categorical variables in MR analyses, the categorical variable is converted into as many dummy variables as there are group categories, minus one $(g - 1)$. Thus, if the categorical variable includes four groups, three dummy variables are needed to capture the same information for analysis in MR. Each such dummy variable represents membership (coded 1) versus nonmembership (coded 0) in some category. As a simple example, a Sex variable could be converted into a dummy variable in which girls are assigned 1 and boys assigned 0; thus the variable represents membership in the category girls. As shown in the chapter, the results of an analysis of the effects of a categorical independent variable (in the example used here, abuse and posttraumatic stress) on a continuous dependent variable are the same whether analyzed via ANOVA or MR. The F associated with the two procedures is the same, and the effect size η^2 from ANOVA is identical to the R^2 from MR. The table of coefficients from the MR may be used to perform post hoc comparisons using several different post hoc procedures.

Dummy coding is not the only method of dealing with categorical variables so that they can be analyzed in MR. With effect coding, one group, often the final group, is assigned values of -1 on all effect coded variables; in contrast, with dummy coding this group is assigned all zeros. Effect coding contrasts each group's mean on the dependent variable with the grand mean. For criterion scaling, each group is assigned its mean value on the dependent variable as its value on a single criterion scale. So, for example, if boys achieved an average score of 50 on a reading test and girls a score of 53, a criterion scaled version of the Sex variable will assign all boys a value of 50 and all girls a value of 53 in a regression of Reading test scores on Sex. Criterion scaling is useful when there are many categories, because only one variable is needed, rather than $g - 1$ variables. When criterion scaling is used, however, you must correct the ANOVA table produced by the regression because the df will be incorrect (the df still equals $g - 1$). The interpretation of the intercept and regression coefficients for these three methods of coding is summarized in Table 6.6.

TABLE 6.6 Interpretation of Intercepts and Regression Coefficients Using Different Methods of Coding Categorical Variables

CODING METHOD	INTERCEPT	b
Dummy	Mean on the dependent variable of the reference group (the group coded zero on all dummy variables)	Deviation from the mean for the group coded 1
Effect	Unweighted mean, or mean of the means of the groups on the dependent variable	Deviation from the unweighted mean by the group coded 1
Criterion	Not of interest	Not of interest

Although it is possible to analyze the results of simple and complex experiments in which all independent variables are categorical using multiple regression, it is generally easier to do so via ANOVA. A more common use of categorical variables (and dummy and other coding) in MR analysis is when categorical variables are analyzed in combination with continuous variables in nonexperimental research. A researcher might want to control for Sex, for example, in an analysis of the effects of achievement on self-esteem. This analysis of both categorical and continuous variables in MR is the focus of the next chapter. Before analyzing both types of variables, however, it is necessary to understand how to analyze categorical variables in MR; the present chapter thus served as an introduction to this topic.

EXERCISES

1. The file "false memory data, 4 groups.sav" (or, .xls, or "false2.txt"), available on the Web site (www.ablongman.com/keith1e), includes the false memory simulated data analyzed in this chapter, plus data from a fourth group, men who were neither abused nor suffered from PTSD (the four groups from Bremner et al., 2000). For comparison purposes, analyze the data via ANOVA, with follow-up via Fisher's LSD test, the Dunn–Bonferroni procedure, and Dunnett's test (with men as the control group).

    a. Convert the group variable into $g - 1$, or three, dummy variables and analyze the data with MR. Use the table of coefficients to conduct the three post hoc procedures. Compare the results with the ANOVA.

    b. Convert the group variable into three effect coded variables and analyze the data with MR. Compare the results with the ANOVA and with the dummy coded solution.

    c. Convert the group variable into a single criterion scaled variable and conduct the MR using it. Correct the ANOVA table from the MR for the correct degrees of freedom and compare the results with the other analyses of the same data.

2. Conduct the analyses of the effect of Family Structure on students' Substance Use as outlined in this chapter using the NELS data. This is one of the more complex exercises you will do, because it requires the creation of several new variables. It is also probably one of the more realistic examples. I suggest you team up with a classmate as you work on it.

    a. Create the Family Structure and Substance Use variables (see note 7). Examine descriptive statistics for each variable, and compute means and standard deviations of Substance Use by Family Structure.

    b. Create dummy variables contrasting students from two-parent families with those from parent–guardian families and those from single-parent families. Regress Substance Use on these dummy variables. Interpret the overall regression. Use the table of coefficients to conduct post hoc testing. Make sure you compare single-parent families and parent–guardian families.

    c. Create effect variables with single-parent families as the group coded –1 on all variables. Regress Substance use on these effect variables and interpret the regression results.

    d. Convert the Family Structure variable into a single criterion scaled variable and conduct the MR using it. Correct the ANOVA table from the MR for the correct degrees of freedom and compare the results with the other analyses of the same data.

NOTES

1. For now, we will postpone exploring what it means to say that sex affects self-esteem or religious affiliation influences voting behavior. We will address this issue in the next chapter.

2. Why the name "dummy" variables? Dummy means a stand-in, representation, a copy. Think of a store mannequin, rather than the slang usage of dummy.

3. The actual study included other measures of memory, an additional group (Nonabused, non-PTSD men) and unequal n's across groups. The data presented here are simulated, but are designed to mimic those in the original article (Bremner et al., 2000).

4. This discussion should make it obvious that our normal interpretation of the t's associated with regression coefficients does not make adjustments for the number of comparisons. Darlington (1990, p. 257) noted that normal multiple regression practice falls under the "Fisher Protected t" method, whereby if the overall R^2 is statistically significant we can make all the individual comparisons represented by the t tests of each regression coefficient. Our discussion of post hoc tests and correcting for error rates is intended as a brief introduction only. Darlington is an excellent resource for more information about multiple comparison procedures in MR.

5. If there are different numbers of cases for each category, the standard errors of the b's will differ for each comparison.

6. Astute readers will recognize that the PTSD example is actually an example of nonexperimental research, since women were not assigned to the different groups, but were sampled from preexisting groups. In the actual research, there were unequal numbers of participants in each category (Bremner et al., 2000).

7. Both variables were created from other NELS variables. Substance use (Substance) was the mean of variables F1S77 (How many cigarettes smoked per day), F1S78a (In lifetime, number of times had alcohol to drink), and F1S80Aa (In lifetime, number of times used marijuana). Because these variables used different scales, they were standardized (converted to z scores) prior to averaging. Family Structure (FamStruc) was created from the NELS variable FamComp (Adult composition of the household). FamComp was coded 1 = Mother & father, 2 = Mother and male guardian, 3 = Female guardian and father, 4 = Other two-adult families, 5 = Adult female only, and 6 = Adult male only. For Family Structure, category 1 was the same as for FamComp, categories 2 and 3 were combined, categories 5 and 6 were combined, and category 4 was set to a missing value.

- - - - - ━━━━━━━━━━━━━━━━━━━━━━━━━━━━━━━━━━━━━

CATEGORICAL AND CONTINUOUS VARIABLES

You should now have a firm grasp on how to analyze continuous variables using multiple regression, along with a new appreciation of how to analyze categorical variables in MR. In this chapter we will combine these two types of variables to analyze both categorical and continuous variables in a single MR. Our discussion starts with the straightforward analysis of both types of variables in a single multiple regression. We then turn to focus on the addition of *interactions* to such analyses. Specific types of interactions between continuous and categorical variables are often of particular interest to psychologists and other social science researchers: aptitude–treatment interactions and bias in the predictive validity of tests. We cover examples of such analyses. In the next chapter we will expand our discussion of interactions to cover interactions of two continuous variables and the analysis of potential curvilinear effects.

SEX, ACHIEVEMENT, AND SELF-ESTEEM

Much has been written about differences in self-esteem among adolescents; conventional wisdom is that girls' self-esteem suffers, compared to boys, during adolescence (Kling, Hyde, Showers, & Buswell, 1999). Will we find self-esteem differences between 10th-grade boys and girls in the NELS data? Will any differences persist once we take into account previous achievement?

To address these questions, I regressed 10th-grade self-esteem scores (F1Cncpt2) on Sex (Sex) and Previous Achievement (ByTests). (Question: Is it necessary to include ByTests for the regression to be valid?) Sex was converted into a dummy variable, NewSex, coded 0 for boys and 1 for girls (although the original coding 1 for male and 2 for female would have worked as well). For this analysis, I also converted the existing Self-Esteem variable (which was a mean of z scores) into T scores ($M = 50$, $SD = 10$); the new variable is named S_Esteem in subsequent figures (it is not on the Web site, but you can easily create it[1]).

Figure 7.1 shows the basic descriptive statistics for the variables in the regression. All statistics are consistent with the intended coding of the variables. Figure 7.2 shows some of the results of the simultaneous regression of Self-Esteem on Achievement and Sex. The interpretation of the regression is straightforward and consistent with our previous such interpretations. The two independent variables explained 2.6% of the variance in Self-Esteem, which, although small, is statistically significant ($F = 12.077$ [2, 907], $p < .001$). Achievement had a moderate, statistically significant, effect on Self-Esteem. The Sex

Descriptive Statistics

	N	Minimum	Maximum	Mean	Std. Deviation
S_ESTEEM	910	15.23	69.47	49.9602	10.0181
NEWSEX sex as dummy variable	910	.00	1.00	.4912	.5002
BYTESTS Eighth grade achievement tests (mean)	910	29.35	70.24	51.5758	8.7671
Valid N (listwise)	910				

Correlations

		S_ESTEEM	NEWSEX sex as dummy variable	BYTESTS Eighth grade achievement tests (mean)
Pearson Correlation	S_ESTEEM	1.000	-.106	.114
	NEWSEX sex as dummy variable	-.106	1.000	.064
	BYTESTS Eighth grade achievement tests (mean)	.114	.064	1.000

FIGURE 7.1   Descriptive statistics for the regression of Self-Esteem on Sex and Previous Achievement.

Model Summary

Model	R	R Square	Adjusted R Square	Std. Error of the Estimate
1	.161[a]	.026	.024	9.8983

a. Predictors: (Constant), BYTESTS Eighth grade achievement tests (mean), NEWSEX sex as dummy variable

ANOVA[b]

Model		Sum of Squares	df	Mean Square	F	Sig.
1	Regression	2366.444	2	1183.222	12.077	.000[a]
	Residual	88863.78	907	97.976		
	Total	91230.23	909			

a. Predictors: (Constant), BYTESTS Eighth grade achievement tests (mean), NEWSEX sex as dummy variable

b. Dependent Variable: S_ESTEEM

Coefficients[a]

Model		Unstandardized Coefficients		Standardized Coefficients	t	Sig.	95% Confidence Interval for B	
		B	Std. Error	Beta			Lower Bound	Upper Bound
1	(Constant)	43.924	1.969		22.306	.000	40.059	47.788
	NEWSEX sex as dummy variable	-2.281	.658	-.114	-3.468	.001	-3.572	-.990
	BYTESTS Eighth grade achievement tests (mean)	.139	.038	.121	3.698	.000	.065	.212

a. Dependent Variable: S_ESTEEM

FIGURE 7.2   Simultaneous regression results: Self-Esteem on Sex and Previous Achievement.

dummy variable was also statistically significant, and its negative sign ($b = -2.281$) means that girls indeed scored lower than boys on the measure of Self-Esteem, even after controlling for Achievement (recall that the NewSex variable was coded so that boys = 0 and girls = 1). The value for the Sex variable suggests that girls scored, on average, 2.28 points lower than did boys (after Achievement is controlled). Concerning our question of interest, the findings suggest that 10th-grade girls do have slightly lower self-esteem than do boys at the same grade level (although the findings do not help us understand why this difference exists).

In Chapter 6 we focused on the meaning of the intercept and the b's using dummy variables. For the present example, with one categorical and one continuous variable, the intercept was 43.924. As in previous examples, the intercept represents the predicted Self-Esteem for those with a value of zero on each predictor variable. Thus the intercept represents the predicted Self-Esteem score of boys (coded zero) with a score of zero on the Achievement test. The intercept is not particularly useful in this case, however, since the actual range of the achievement test was only approximately 29 to 70, with no scores of zero. The b for NewSex of –2.281 means, again, that girls scored an average of 2.28 points lower than boys on the Self-Esteem measure. This integration of categorical and continuous variables is straightforward.

INTERACTIONS

As you will discover in this section, it is also possible using MR to test for potential inter-actions between categorical and continuous variables (and also between several categorical variables or several continuous variables). Interactions are those instances when the effect of one variable depends on the value of another variable. In experimental research, we may find that the effect of a treatment depends on the sex of the participant; a cholesterol drug may be more effective in lowering the cholesterol of males than females, for example. To use an example from earlier chapters, we may find that homework is more effective for stu-dents with high levels of academic motivation compared to those with lower levels of moti-vation. In other words, the effect of one variable (homework) depends on the value of another variable (academic motivation).

What might such interactions look like? In our previous example, we found that 10th-grade girls had slightly, but statistically significantly, lower self-esteem than did boys in the same grade. Previous Achievement also had an apparent effect on 10th-grade Self-Esteem. Could it be, however, that there are different *effects* for achievement on self-esteem for boys as compared to girls? For example, perhaps girls' self-image is closely related to their school performance, with higher achievement leading to higher self-esteem. In contrast, it may be that achievement works differently for boys and that their self-esteem is unrelated to their school performance.

This type of differential relation between achievement and self-esteem is illustrated (in an exaggerated way) in Figure 7.3. In the figure, the two lines represent the regression lines from the regression of Self-Esteem on Achievement for boys and girls, respectively. Such graphs are an excellent way to understand interactions. The graph also illustrates that interactions occur when the slope of the regression line for one independent variable (Achievement) differs depending on the value of the other independent variable (Sex). Again, the graph illustrates a potential *interaction* between Sex and Achievement in their effects on Self-Esteem: For girls, Achievement has a strong effect on Self-Esteem, whereas

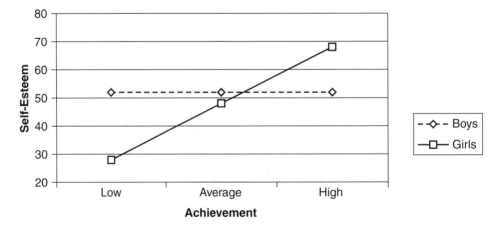

FIGURE 7.3   Graphic display of a possible interaction between Sex and Achievement on Self-Esteem.

it has no effect for boys. There are several ways to describe such an interaction. We could say that Sex and Achievement *interact* in their effect on Self-Esteem; that Achievement has differential effects on Self-Esteem depending on the Sex of the student; that Achievement has stronger effects on the Self-Esteem of girls than of boys; or that Sex *moderates* the effect of Achievement on Self-Esteem (cf. Baron & Kenny, 1986). A colleague of mine notes that most interactions can be described using the phrase "it depends." Does achievement affect self-esteem? It depends; it depends on whether you are a boy or a girl.

Methodologists often distinguish between ordinal and disordinal interactions. Interactions in which the regression lines cross within the effective range of the independent variable are often referred to as *disordinal* interactions. Figure 7.3 illustrates a disordinal interaction; the two lines cross within the effective range of the independent variable (Achievement). With an *ordinal* interaction, the lines representing the effects do not cross within the effective range of the independent variable. Figure 7.15 illustrates an ordinal interaction.

Testing Interactions in MR

We test such interactions in multiple regression by creating cross-product variables and testing whether these cross-product terms are statistically significant when added to the regression equation. Cross-product terms are created by multiplying the two variables of interest (Cohen, 1978); in this case we would create the cross product by multiplying the NewSex variable and the Achievement variable.[2] Although this product term will work as an interaction term, there are statistical and interpretive advantages to first *centering* the continuous variables prior to multiplication (Aiken & West, 1991; Cohen et al., 2003; Darlington, 1990; the advantages of centering will be illustrated in the following examples). Centering is most easily accomplished by subtracting the mean score of the variable from that variable (e.g., using a compute statement in SPSS), thus resulting in a new variable with a mean of zero and a standard deviation equal to the original standard deviation.

Centering and Cross Products: Achievement and Sex.   For the current example, in which the interest was testing the possible interaction between Sex and Achievement on Self-Esteem, I created two new variables. Ach_Cent was created as a centered version of the base year achievement tests by subtracting the mean for ByTests (51.5758, as shown in Figure 7.1) from each person's score on ByTests. Thus, students with an original achievement score of, for example, 30 will have a score of −21.5758 on Ach_Cent, whereas those with an original score of 70 will have a score of 18.4242 on Ach_Cent. Sex_Ach, the interaction term, was created by multiplying NewSex (the sex dummy variable) and Ach_Cent.

Figure 7.4 shows the descriptive statistics for these new variables; as you can see, the mean of Ach_Cent is effectively zero (−.00005). Also shown in the figure are the correlations among the variables. The centered variable has the same correlations with the other variables as does the original, uncentered variable (Figure 7.1). The interaction term (Sex_Ach), however, correlates at different levels with components (the Sex and Achievement variables) than does an interaction created from a noncentered variable. For example, an interaction term built on the uncentered Achievement variable correlated .975 with Sex, whereas the interaction term built on the centered Achievement variable correlated .048 with Sex (Figure 7.4). The excessively high correlation between these two predictor variables (termed

multicollinearity) can result in strange coefficients and large standard errors and make interpretation difficult. Indeed, this reduction in multicollinearity is a prime reason for centering.
The topic and effects of multicollinearity will be discussed in more depth in Chapter 9.

Descriptive Statistics

	Mean	Std. Deviation	N
S_ESTEEM	49.9602	10.0181	910
NEWSEX sex as dummy variable	.4912	.5002	910
ACH_CENT BY achievement, centered	-5.0E-05	8.7671	910
SEX_ACH Sex by Achieve interaction	.2814	5.9197	910

Correlations

		S_ESTEEM	NEWSEX sex as dummy variable	ACH_CENT BY achievement, centered	SEX_ACH Sex by Achieve interaction
Pearson Correlation	S_ESTEEM	1.000	-.106	.114	.103
	NEWSEX sex as dummy variable	-.106	1.000	.064	.048
	ACH_CENT BY achievement, centered	.114	.064	1.000	.677
	SEX_ACH Sex by Achieve interaction	.103	.048	.677	1.000

**FIGURE 7.4   Descriptive statistics for the test of a possible interaction
between Sex and Achievement in their effects on Self-Esteem.**

The MR Analysis.   To test the statistical significance of the interaction, Self-Esteem was
first regressed on Sex and Achievement. These variables were entered using simultaneous
multiple regression, a step similar to the first example from this chapter, but this was also
the first step in a sequential multiple regression. As shown in Figure 7.5, these variables
accounted for 2.6% of the variance in Self-Esteem (the same as in Figure 7.2). In the second step in this sequential regression, the interaction term (Sex_Ach) was added to the
equation. As shown, the addition of the interaction term did not lead to a statistically significant increase in R^2 ($\Delta R^2 = .001$, $F[1, 906] = 1.218$, $p = .270$). This means that the
interaction is not statistically significant: the interaction term does not help explain Self-
Esteem beyond the explanation provided by Sex and Achievement. We cannot reject the
null hypothesis that Achievement has the same effect for girls as for boys. Thus, contrary to
our speculation, there appears to be no differential effect for Achievement on the Self-
Esteem of girls as compared to boys; Achievement has the same magnitude of effect on
boys' and girls' achievement.

Model Summary

Model	R	R Square	R Square Change	Change Statistics			Sig. F Change
				F Change	df1	df2	
1	.161[a]	.026	.026	12.077	2	907	.000
2	.165[b]	.027	.001	1.218	1	906	.270

a. Predictors: (Constant), ACH_CENT BY achievement, centered, NEWSEX sex as dummy variable

b. Predictors: (Constant), ACH_CENT BY achievement, centered, NEWSEX sex as dummy variable, SEX_ACH Sex by Achieve interaction

FIGURE 7.5   **Test of the interaction between Sex and Achievement in their effects on Self-Esteem.**

How, you may wonder, does this method of testing an interaction relate to our graphical display of an interaction, such as that shown in Figure 7.3? The figure essentially shows separate regression lines for boys and girls, but we have not conducted separate regressions for the two groups. The method of testing an interaction illustrated here is *equivalent* to conducting separate regressions for boys and girls. We could, for example, regress Self-Esteem on Achievement separately for boys and girls and then compare the regression coefficients for Achievement for boys versus girls. If the interaction is statistically significant, these coefficients will be very different for boys versus girls; in Figure 7.3, for example, the regression coefficient for girls will be large and statistically significant, whereas the coefficient for boys will be small and not statistically significant. The fact that the interaction in the current example is not statistically significant means that, in fact, the *regression lines for boys and girls are parallel.* (The lines are parallel, but not identical, because the intercepts differ. This difference is not tested in the interaction term, which simply tests whether the lines are parallel.) The addition of an interaction term to the model is equivalent to testing separate models for different groups. The method of testing a cross product does this in one step, however, and also tests the statistical significance of the interaction.

Interpretation

Given that the interaction was not statistically significant, I would focus my interpretation on the coefficients from the first step of the multiple regression, prior to the addition of the interaction term. I would certainly report that the interaction was tested for statistical significance, as above, and found lacking, but then would turn my interpretation to the equation without the interaction term, as shown in Figure 7.6. With the centering of the Achievement variable, the intercept for the regression equation has changed. The intercept still represents the predicted Self-Esteem score for someone with zeros on each independent variable, but with centering a score of zero on the Achievement test represents the overall mean of Achievement for this group. Thus, the intercept now represents the predicted Self-Esteem score for boys who score at the mean (for the total sample) on the Achievement test (this ease of interpretation is another advantage of centering). The regression coefficients are the

Coefficients[a]

Model		Unstandardized Coefficients		Standardized Coefficients	t	Sig.	95% Confidence Interval for B	
		B	Std. Error	Beta			Lower Bound	Upper Bound
1	(Constant)	51.081	.460		110.929	.000	50.177	51.984
	NEWSEX sex as dummy variable	-2.281	.658	-.114	-3.468	.001	-3.572	-.990
	ACH_CENT BY achievement, centered	.139	.038	.121	3.698	.000	.065	.212

a. Dependent Variable: S_ESTEEM

FIGURE 7.6   Regression coefficients: effects of Sex and Achievement on Self-Esteem.

same as those shown in Figure 7.2, because centering does not change the standard deviations of the variables [and $b = \beta \, (SD_x)/(SD_y)$]. Here's a potential interpretation of these findings:

This research had two purposes. First, we were interested in the effect of sex on 10th-grade students' self-esteem. In particular, we tested whether girls have lower self-esteem in 10th-grade than do boys, after controlling for prior achievement. Previous research has suggested that achievement has differential effects on the achievement of boys versus girls (not really, I just made this up)—that achievement influences the self-esteem of girls, but not boys. The second purpose of this research was to test for this possible differential effect.

Self-Esteem was regressed on Sex and prior Achievement to address the first purpose of this research. A cross-product term (Sex × Achievement) was added next to the model to test the possible interaction between Sex and Achievement in their effects on Self-Esteem (cf. Aiken & West, 1991; Cohen, 1978); the Achievement variable was centered.

Sex and prior Achievement together accounted for 2.6% of the variance in 10th-grade Self-Esteem ($F[2, 907] = 12.077, p < .001$). The interaction was not statistically significant, however ($\Delta R^2 = .001, F[1, 906] = 1.218, p = .270$), suggesting that Achievement has the same effect on the Self-Esteem of both boys and girls.

TABLE 7.1   Effects of Sex and Achievement on the Self-Esteem of 10th-Graders

VARIABLE	ß	$b \, (SE_b)$	p
Sex	−.114	−2.281 (.658)	.001
Achievement	.121	.139 (.038)	<.001

The regression coefficients in Table 7.1 show the extent of the influence of Sex and Achievement on Self-Esteem. The effect of Sex on Self-Esteem was indeed statistically significant, and girls scored, on average, 2.28 points lower on the Self-Esteem scale than did boys, even after prior Achievement was controlled statistically. This effect of Sex can be considered a small to moderate effect. Although these results show that adolescent girls have lower self-esteem than do boys, the results do not illuminate why this may be so or what aspect of being a girl as opposed to a boy leads to lower self-esteem. Achievement also had a moderate and statistically significant effect on subsequent Self-Esteem. Thus, Achievement appears to have the same effect on the Self-Esteem of boys and girls and this effect is of moderate magnitude and statistically significant for both groups.

This example illustrates the basic method of testing interactions in multiple regression. And, although I have introduced the method in the context of an interaction between a categorical and a continuous variable, the method is the same for testing interactions between *continuous* variables (as illustrated in the next chapter) or between categorical variables. The example also illustrates the simple fact that such interactions are not very common in nonexperimental research, especially with small to medium sample sizes. There are several reasons for the infrequent finding of interactions in nonexperimental research. First, the nature of testing for interactions focuses on the *unique* effects attributable to the interaction after the variation due to the original variables has been statistically removed (e.g., in a sequential regression). Second, it is also the case that measurement error (unreliability and invalidity) reduces the statistical power to detect interactions in MR (Aiken & West, 1991); the unreliability of the interaction term is a product of the unreliability of both its components. As a result, tests of interactions in MR are simply less sensitive than tests to detect main effects. Third, simulation research has shown that when the assumption of homogeneity of error variances across groups is violated (such assumptions will be discussed in more detail in Chapter 9), the power to detect interactions can vary considerably. This variability can be especially problematic when sample sizes vary across groups (Alexander & DeShon, 1994). Finally, "it may be that substantial interaction simply does not often exist in the real world" (Darlington, 1990, p. 320). For these reasons, I recommend testing for interactions primarily when testing *specific* hypotheses. That is, I do not recommend testing all possible interactions, but instead testing those suggested in previous research or those designed to answer specific research questions. So, for example, in their examination of the effects of parent involvement, homework, and TV viewing on achievement, Keith, Reimers, Fehrmann, Pottebaum, and Aubey (1986) tested the interaction between TV viewing and ability because previous research had suggested the presence of such an interaction (this example is discussed in more detail in the next chapter). Adequate to large sample sizes are also needed (Alexander & DeShon, 1994).

A STATISTICALLY SIGNIFICANT INTERACTION

Another example will illustrate a statistically significant interaction. Based on theory, previous research, or even persuasive argument, we might suspect that achievement interacts with students' ethnic origin (rather than sex) in its effect on subsequent self-esteem. Just as we speculated for boys versus girls, we might speculate that achievement has a positive effect on the self-esteem of White youth, but little or no effect on the self-esteem of youth from various minority groups. To test this hypothesis, the Race variable in the NELS data was recoded into a new majority–minority (Maj_Min) variable with White non-Hispanic students coded 1 and members of all other ethnic groups coded 0. Maj_Min and a centered version of the Achievement variable (Test_Cen2) were multiplied to create an Ethnic origin by previous Achievement cross-product term.

Does Achievement Affect Self-Esteem? It Depends

Figure 7.7 shows some of the results of the sequential regression to test the significance of the interaction. In the first block, Self-Esteem was regressed on Ethnic origin (Maj_Min) and previous Achievement (Ach_Cen2); in the second step, the Ethnic–Achievement interaction term was entered (Eth_Ach). The addition of the interaction term resulted in a statistically significant increase in variance explained ($\Delta R^2 = .008$, $F[1, 896] = 7.642$, $p = .006$); in other words, the interaction is statistically significant.

Model Summary

Model	R	R Square	R Square Change	F Change	df1	df2	Sig. F Change
			Change Statistics				
1	.148[a]	.022	.022	10.089	2	897	.000
2	.174[b]	.030	.008	7.642	1	896	.006

a. Predictors: (Constant), ACH_CEN2 Achievement, centered, MAJ_MIN Majority versus minority

b. Predictors: (Constant), ACH_CEN2 Achievement, centered, MAJ_MIN Majority versus minority, ETH_ACH Ethnicity achievement interaction

FIGURE 7.7   Test of the interaction between Ethnic origin and Achievement in their effects on Self-Esteem using sequential regression.

Understanding an Interaction

Given a statistically significant interaction, what does it mean? Probably the easiest way to understand an interaction (in multiple regression or ANOVA) is to graph it. Recall that an interaction between a categorical and continuous variable in multiple regression represents different regression coefficients for the two (or more) groups. When we say that Achievement and Ethnicity interact in their effect on Self-Esteem, we mean that Achievement has different effects on the Self-Esteem for (in this example) White and minority adolescents. These different effects mean the regression coefficients (b's) associated with Achievement will be different for the two groups if we conduct separate regressions (Self-Esteem regressed on Achievement) for White and minority youth. Different regression coefficients further mean that the slopes of the regression lines will be different for the two groups (because the b is the slope of the regression line). What we need, then, is a graph of the regression lines of Self-Esteem on Achievement for White youth and minority youth separately.

Fortunately, it is relatively easy to produce such graphs using standard statistical analysis programs. Figure 7.8 shows such separate regression lines for White and Non-White youth, (created using the SPSS Scatterplot command, followed by some touch-up). As shown in the graph, it indeed appears that Achievement has a positive effect on the Self-Esteem of White non-Hispanic youth, but that it has little effect, or perhaps a small negative effect, on the Self-Esteem of minority group youth. If these findings are correct, they suggest that improving the achievement of White adolescents will result in increased self-esteem. For minority youth, however, it appears that increased achievement will result in no increases in self-esteem.

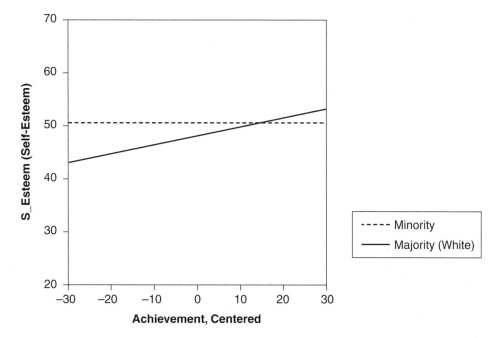

FIGURE 7.8   Regression lines illustrating the interaction of Ethnic origin and Achievement in their effects on Self-Esteem.

Further Analysis.   We are now faced with additional questions; although we know that the interaction is statistically significant, and we have an understanding of the nature of the interaction, we don't know whether the effects of Achievement on Self-Esteem are statistically significant for the two groups. This lack of clarity is especially obvious when looking at the regression line for minority students; does Achievement have no statistically significant effect on Self-Esteem for minority students, or does it actually have a negative effect? To investigate further, we can easily conduct the two separate regression analyses represented by the regression lines in Figure 7.8 (this is similar to conducting a test of simple main effects in ANOVA to probe a statistically significant interaction). If we conduct separate regressions, we find that the regression of Self-Esteem on Achievement was statistically significant for white adolescents, but not statistically significant for minority youth.

It is also possible to calculate the coefficients for these separate regression equations from the coefficients from the overall regression including the interaction term (Figure 7.9). The *intercept* for the regression with the interaction term is equivalent to the intercept for a *separate* regression of Self-Esteem on Achievement for the group coded zero. Thus, the intercept for the regression of Self-Esteem on Achievement for minority students is 50.877. The intercept for the group coded 1 is equal to the overall intercept plus the coefficient for the Maj_Min dummy variable (50.877 + [−1.627] = 49.250). So, if we were to conduct separate regressions, the intercept for minority students would be 50.877, and the intercept for majority students would be 49.250. Likewise, the b for Achievement in a separate regression for the group coded zero is equal to the b for Achievement for the overall regression with the interaction term. Thus, the b for minority students is the same as the b for

Achievement in Figure 7.9 (−.0067). The *b* for White students (the group coded 1), in turn, is equal to the *b* for Achievement from Figure 7.9 plus the *b* associated with the interaction term (−.007 + .237 = .230). Thus, if we were to conduct separate regressions for majority and minority youth, the equation for minority youth would be Self-Esteem$_{predicted}$ = 50.877 − .007 Achievement, and the equation for majority students would be Self-Esteem$_{predicted}$ = 49.250 + .230 Achievement. Try conducting separate regressions of Self-Esteem on Achievement by ethnic origin to see if your results match these. It is also possible to calculate the statistical significance of these separate regression coefficients from the overall regression output, but these calculations are more involved (see Aiken & West, 1991, for more information); it is generally easier to simply conduct the separate regressions.

Coefficients^a

Model		Unstandardized Coefficients		Standardized Coefficients			95% Confidence Interval for B	
		B	Std. Error	Beta	t	Sig.	Lower Bound	Upper Bound
2	(Constant)	50.877	.681		74.661	.000	49.540	52.215
	MAJ_MIN Majority versus minority	-1.627	.786	-.072	-2.069	.039	-3.170	-.084
	ACH_CEN2 Achievement, centered	-6.7E-03	.072	-.006	-.093	.926	-.148	.135
	ETH_ACH Ethnicity achievement interaction	.237	.086	.169	2.764	.006	.069	.405

a. Dependent Variable: S_ESTEEM

FIGURE 7.9   Regression coefficients: effects of Ethnic origin, Achievement, and their interaction on Self-Esteem.

Extensions and Other Examples

Note that I have illustrated the simplest of examples, one with a single continuous variable and a single categorical variable; the categorical variable also included only two categories. Extensions are straightforward. We could easily have included several other variables in the analysis, such as students' SES, or their sex as well as their ethnic origin. We could have included interaction terms with these variables as well (e.g., Achievement × SES or Sex × Ethnic Origin). Recall, however, that I earlier recommended that you not conduct a "fishing expedition" for interactions, but only include those terms that you are specifically interested in testing and have some reason to test (e.g., to test a specific hypothesis). Likewise, we could have left the ethnic origin variable as a multicategorical variable (Asian–Pacific Islander, Hispanic, Black not Hispanic, White not Hispanic, and American Indian–Alaskan Native), in which case we would have needed to create four dummy variables and four interaction terms (each dummy variable multiplied times the centered achievement variable). These four interaction terms would then have been added in one block in the second step of a sequential regression to test the statistical significance of the interaction. The essentials of the analysis would be the same in these cases.

You should be aware that social scientists may test for such interactions without labeling them as such. For example, Krivo and Peterson (2000) investigated whether the variables that affect violence (homicide rate) have the same magnitude of effect for African Americans and Whites. In other words, the authors tested whether ethnic origin interacted with a series of influences in their effects on violence, but they did not label these as tests of potential interactions. Yet anytime researchers suggest a difference in magnitude on effects (b's) across groups, they are, in fact, suggesting a potential interaction between a categorical and continuous variable(s). This example is interesting in a number of other ways as well. To test the primary questions, the authors conducted separate regressions across groups, rather than using a series of interaction terms, presumably because they were interested in the potential interaction of all variables with Race. The authors (correctly) used the *unstandardized* coefficients to compare the influences across groups. Within the separate models for African American participants, however, the authors added several interaction (cross-product) terms and labeled them as such.

Testing Interactions in MR: Summary

As a review, these are the steps involved in testing for an interaction in multiple regression:

1. Center the continuous variable expected to interact with a categorical variable by creating a new variable in which the mean of this variable is subtracted from each person's score on the variable.
2. Multiply the centered variable by the dummy variable(s) to create cross-product (interaction) terms (other types of coding, such as effect coding, can also be used, although the interpretation will be different).
3. Regress the outcome variable on the independent variables of interest using simultaneous regression. Use the centered versions of relevant variables, but exclude the interaction terms.
4. Add, in a sequential fashion, the interaction term(s). Check the statistical significance of the ΔR^2 to determine whether the interaction is statistically significant. If the ΔR^2 is statistically significant, conduct separate regressions for each level of the categorical variable. Graph the interaction.
5. If the ΔR^2 is not statistically significant, interpret the findings from the first portion of the multiple regression (before the addition of the interaction term).

SPECIFIC TYPES OF INTERACTIONS BETWEEN CATEGORICAL AND CONTINUOUS VARIABLES

Several specific types of interactions between categorical and continuous variables are often of interest in psychology, education, public policy, and other social sciences. A psychologist may be interested in whether a psychological test is biased against minority students in predicting various outcomes. More broadly, a policy maker may be interested in whether women are underpaid compared to men with the same level of experience and productivity. Finally, an educator may be interested in whether an intervention is more effective for teaching children who have high aptitude in some area versus those with lower aptitude in the same area. Each example can be examined via multiple regression by testing for an interaction between a categorical and a continuous variable.

Test (and Other) Bias

Psychological, educational, and other tests should be unbiased and fair for all people who take them. One type of bias to be avoided is bias in predictive validity; in other words, if a test is designed to predict some related outcome, it should predict that outcome equally well for all groups to which it may be given. The Scholastic Aptitude Test (SAT), for example, is designed, in large part, to determine which students will do well in college and which will not, and thus colleges use the SAT to select students based on its predictive power. If the SAT were a better predictor of college GPA for girls than for boys, then a potential student would have a differential chance of being selected for a given college based on sex, which should be irrelevant. In this case, we would be justified in saying that the SAT was biased. Likewise, an intelligence test may be used to select children for participation (or nonparticipation) in a program for gifted students. If the intelligence test is a better predictor for White than for minority students, the test is biased.[3]

Psychometric researchers can evaluate this type of bias using multiple regression. In essence, what we are saying is that a biased test has different regression lines for the groups (males and females, majority and minority); we can therefore conceive of bias in predictive validity as a problem of the possible interaction of a categorical (e.g., male versus female) and a continuous variable (e.g., the SAT) in their effect on some outcome (e.g., college GPA). Let's flesh out this example a little more fully, after which we will turn to a research example of predictive bias.

Predictive Bias.   Assume you are in charge of admissions for a selective college and that one type of information you use to select students is their scores on the SAT. Figure 7.10 shows your likely, albeit exaggerated, expectation of the relation between the SAT and college GPA. Based perhaps on data collected during a period of open admissions, you know that students with low SAT scores generally perform poorly in your college, whereas those with high SAT scores generally go on to perform well, with high grades in most courses. In addition, the graph shows that this ability of the SAT to predict future GPA is equal for males

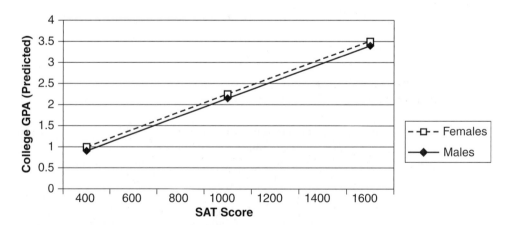

FIGURE 7.10   Possible regression lines: the SAT predicts College GPA equally well for boys and girls.

and females. If you decide to use a cutoff, for example, of 1000, you will be equally fair (or unfair) to both males and females. The females you accept with a SAT of, for example, 1200, will likely perform at the same level at your college as males with a score of 1200.

Figure 7.11, however, shows a different possibility. In this example, the regression lines are parallel, but the line for females is higher than that for males. What this means is that if you, as the admissions officer, use the common regression line (not taking into account sex) you will in essence treat males and females differently. Using a cutoff of 1000 for admissions, you will end up selecting a group of males who will likely perform at a lower level than the females, while rejecting females who will likely perform as well or better than the males. Follow the dotted line line vertically from the point on the *X*-axis representing a SAT score of 1000 up to the regression line for males and then horizontally across to the *Y*-axis. As you can see, a cutoff of 1000 on the SAT means you will be admitting males for whom their predicted college GPA is about 1.75. Yet, in this made-up example, you could admit females scoring around 500 on the SAT who will likely achieve at that same level in college (a GPA of 1.75). If you use the common regression line (instead of separate regression lines) to make admissions decisions, you have discriminated against females who scored above 500 but below 1000. If this is the case, the SAT will be biased when used for such purposes. This type of bias is termed *intercept bias* because the intercepts for the two groups are substantially different.

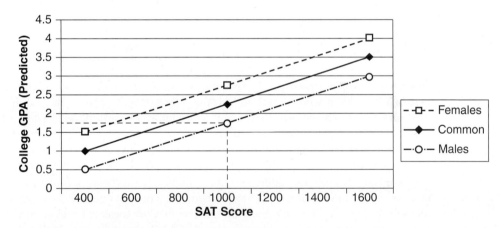

FIGURE 7.11   Possible regression lines: intercept bias in the use of the SAT to predict College GPA.

Figure 7.12 shows yet another possibility, in which the slopes for the regression line for males and females are different. As shown, the SAT has a steeper slope in predicting college GPA for males than for females. This example illustrates *slope bias.* In this example, the use of the common regression line will be biased against either males or females, depending on where we drew the SAT cutoff for admission. At a value of 800, our admissions will be biased against females, because we would not admit some qualified females (those expected to perform as well as some of the males admitted). If the cutoff were 1200, however, the use of the common regression line (instead of separate regression lines) will be biased against males, because some of the males rejected would likely perform as well or better than some of the females accepted. In some sense, slope bias is more problematic than intercept bias. With intercept bias we can have faith that our selection is fair if we use separate regression lines for the two groups. With slope bias, however, even if we use separate regression lines, our prediction is often simply better for one group than another.

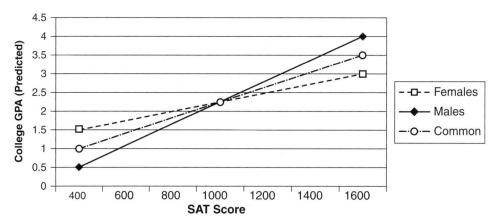

FIGURE 7.12   Possible regression lines: slope bias in the SAT in its prediction of College GPA for boys and girls.

Research Example: Investigating Test Bias.   One common duty of school psychologists is to assess children who are having learning or behavioral problems in school, with the assessment results being used, along with other information, to develop interventions to ameliorate these problems. One possible outcome of such assessment is placement in a special education program. Curriculum-based assessment (CBA), or measurement (CBM), is a relatively new method of assessment in which a student's curriculum materials are used in assessing a student. For a reading CBM, for example, the psychologist might have a student read passages from his or her reading textbook and count the number of words read correctly in 2 minutes. One advantage of CBM is that the measures are short and can be repeated frequently, even several times a week. CBMs, therefore, are especially useful for determining whether an academic intervention is working.

   Although there is ample evidence that CBMs can be reliable and valid (Shinn, 1989), there is little research addressing potential bias in CBMs. Kranzler, Miller, and Jordan (1999) examined a set of reading CBMs for potential racial–ethnic and sex bias in predictive validity. Their research included children in grades 2 through 5, and used reading CBMs to predict Reading Comprehension scores on the California Achievement Test (CAT). Their results suggested possible intercept bias (for race–ethnicity) at grade 4, and both intercept (for sex and race–ethnicity) and slope bias (for sex) at grade 5.

   The data set "Kranzler et al simulated data.sav" or "Kranzler.txt" includes data designed to simulate those reported in Kranzler and colleagues (1999) for boys and girls in grade 5. We will use these simulated data to go through the steps needed to test for predictive bias. Figure 7.13 shows the summary statistics for the total sample and for boys and girls in the sample.

Report

SEX		CAT California Achievement Test, Reading Comprehension	CBM Curriculum based measurement, reading
.00 girls	Mean	631.9200	118.8000
	N	50	50
	Std. Deviation	47.26384	68.10916
	Minimum	499.00	3.00
	Maximum	732.00	258.00
1.00 boys	Mean	790.6000	123.7800
	N	50	50
	Std. Deviation	69.13548	49.22306
	Minimum	673.00	29.00
	Maximum	985.00	228.00
Total	Mean	711.2600	121.2900
	N	100	100
	Std. Deviation	99.14530	59.17331
	Minimum	499.00	3.00
	Maximum	985.00	258.00

FIGURE 7.13   Descriptive data for the Kranzler et al. (1999) simulated data.

The multiple regression to test for bias in predictive validity is similar to the more generic test for interactions between categorical and continuous variables. In the first step, CAT scores were regressed on Sex (coded 1 for boys and 0 for girls) and the predictor variable, centered Reading CBM scores (the example departs from the article on this point; Kranzler et al., 1999, did not center the CBM scores). In the second step, a CBM (centered) by Sex cross product was added to the regression equation to test for a possible interaction (i.e., slope bias) between Sex and CBM. The basic results of the multiple regression are shown in Figure 7.14.

The regression of CAT Reading Comprehension on Reading CBM, Sex, and the interaction term was statistically significant ($R^2 = .763$, $F = 103.177$ [3, 96], $p < .001$). Furthermore, the addition of the Sex by CBM cross product led to a statistically significant increase in explained variance ($\Delta R^2 = .067$ [1, 96], $p < .001$), meaning that the interaction between Sex and CBM scores was statistically significant. This statistically significant interaction, in turn, suggests that Reading CBMs (in these simulated data) may indeed show sex-related slope bias for 5th-graders when predicting Reading Comprehension. (Note that the same story is told by the statistically significant b for the cross product in the second half of the table of coefficients: $b = .915$, $t = 5.217$, $p < .001$.)

For the next step, given the statistically significant interaction, I graph the interaction to understand it more completely, as well as conduct separate regressions, by Sex, to determine

Model Summary

Mode l	R	R Square	Change Statistics				
			R Square Change	F Change	df1	df2	Sig. F Change
1	.834[a]	.696	.696	111.123	2	97	.000
2	.874[b]	.763	.067	27.217	1	96	.000

a. Predictors: (Constant), CBM_CEN CBM, centered, SEX

b. Predictors: (Constant), CBM_CEN CBM, centered, SEX, SEX_CBM Sex by centered CBM crossproduct

ANOVA[c]

Mode l		Sum of Squares	df	Mean Square	F	Sig.
1	Regression	677467.0	2	338733.520	111.123	.000[a]
	Residual	295682.2	97	3048.270		
	Total	973149.2	99			
2	Regression	742778.7	3	247592.898	103.177	.000[b]
	Residual	230370.5	96	2399.693		
	Total	973149.2	99			

a. Predictors: (Constant), CBM_CEN CBM, centered, SEX

b. Predictors: (Constant), CBM_CEN CBM, centered, SEX, SEX_CBM Sex by centered CBM crossproduct

c. Dependent Variable: CAT California Achievement Test, Reading Comprehension

Coefficients[a]

Mode l		Unstandardized Coefficients		Standardized Coefficients			95% Confidence Interval for B	
		B	Std. Error	Beta	t	Sig.	Lower Bound	Upper Bound
1	(Constant)	632.847	7.812		81.014	.000	617.344	648.351
	SEX	156.826	11.052	.795	14.190	.000	134.890	178.761
	CBM_CEN CBM, centered	.372	.094	.222	3.968	.000	.186	.559
2	(Constant)	632.065	6.932		91.174	.000	618.305	645.826
	SEX	156.110	9.807	.791	15.918	.000	136.644	175.577
	CBM_CEN CBM, centered	5.84E-02	.103	.035	.568	.571	-.146	.262
	SEX_CBM Sex by centered CBM crossproduct	.915	.175	.320	5.217	.000	.567	1.263

a. Dependent Variable: CAT California Achievement Test, Reading Comprehension

FIGURE 7.14   Regression results for the simulated Kranzler et al. (1999) predictive bias study.

whether Reading CBMs are worthwhile predictors for both groups. Although we know that the slopes and the b's are different for the two groups, it might be that CBMs are significant predictors for both groups, but are simply better for one group compared to the other. The graph is shown in Figure 7.15, and it suggests that Reading CBMs are strongly related to Reading Comprehension for 5th-grade boys, but are not as good predictors for 5th-grade girls. This interpretation of the graph is confirmed by the results of the separate regressions of Reading Comprehension on Reading CBMs for girls and boys, partial results of which are shown in Figure 7.16. The regression of Reading Comprehension was statistically significant for boys, but not for girls. The results thus suggest that Reading CBMs are excellent predictors of Reading Comprehension for boys ($r = .693, r^2 = .480$), but poor predictors for girls. In other words, Reading CBMs appear valid for boys, but not for girls at this age (remember these are simulated data).

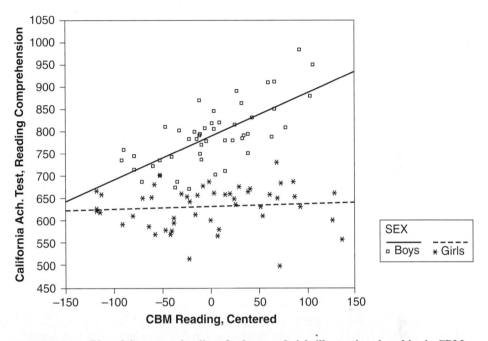

FIGURE 7.15   Plot of the regression lines for boys and girls illustrating slope bias in CBMs.

Return to Figure 7.14 to review what all the coefficients in the table of coefficients mean. For the bottom portion of the table (the portion that includes the interaction term):

1. The constant, or intercept, represents the value, on the predicted dependent variable, for the group coded 0, for a value of zero on the continuous (centered) independent variable. On the graph, this represents the predicted CAT score (632.065) for girls who have a score of zero on the centered CBM score. The centered CBM score, in turn, represents the overall mean of the original CBM variable.

2. The coefficient for Sex represents the *change* in intercept for the group scored 1 on the dummy variable. Thus, the predicted CAT score for boys scoring at the mean on the CBM variable is 156.110 points higher than for girls.

3. The coefficient for the continuous variable represents the slope of the regression line for those with a score of 0 on the dummy variable. Thus, the slope of the regression of CAT on centered CBM for girls is .058.

4. The coefficient for the interaction term is the change for the regression line for the group scored 1 on the dummy variable. Thus, a separate regression line for boys will

Coefficients[a,b]

Model		Unstandardized Coefficients		Standardized Coefficients			95% Confidence Interval for B	
		B	Std. Error	Beta	t	Sig.	Lower Bound	Upper Bound
1	(Constant)	632.065	6.734		93.862	.000	618.526	645.605
	CBM_CEN CBM, centered	5.84E-02	.100	.084	.585	.561	-.142	.259

a. Dependent Variable: CAT California Achievement Test, Reading Comprehension

b. Selecting only cases for which **SEX = .00 girls**

Coefficients[a,b]

Model		Unstandardized Coefficients		Standardized Coefficients			95% Confidence Interval for B	
		B	Std. Error	Beta	t	Sig.	Lower Bound	Upper Bound
1	(Constant)	788.176	7.130		110.546	.000	773.840	802.511
	CBM_CEN CBM, centered	.974	.146	.693	6.662	.000	.680	1.267

a. Dependent Variable: CAT California Achievement Test, Reading Comprehension

b. Selecting only cases for which **SEX = 1.00 boys**

FIGURE 7.16   Separate regressions of the California Achievement Test on CBMs for boys and girls.

have a slope of .973. (.915 + .058). Compare these values with the values shown for the intercepts and slopes using separate regressions (Figure 7.15); they should match within errors of rounding.

Should you interpret the statistically significant coefficient associated with Sex in the presence of an interaction? Maybe. On the one hand, this value suggests the presence of intercept bias in addition to slope bias. On the other hand, you may recall from previous exposure to ANOVA the rule of thumb that one should interpret main effects very cautiously if there is an interaction. (To complicate the matter further, as you will see in the exercises, the statistical significance of the difference in intercepts may also depend on whether the continuous variable was centered or not). I suggest examining the graph again to help make this decision (Figure 7.15). For these data, it seems obvious that, even with the differences in slope taken into account, the regression line for boys is generally higher than that for girls. Focus also on Figure 7.17, which shows the separate regression lines for boys and girls along with the common regression line. To return to our original entrance into the discussion of bias, if we use the common regression line for prediction, we will generally underestimate the CAT performance of boys, but overestimate the CAT performance of girls. Thus, in this case, I believe it makes sense to focus on the differences in intercepts even with the statistically significant interaction. It is also obvious, however, that this over- and underprediction becomes larger the better these children are in reading (slope bias). In this case, I will likely focus on both phenomena. In contrast, if the graphs looked more like those shown in Figure 7.12, there is no generalized difference in intercepts, and the primary story is that of slope bias. Thus, I probably would not interpret a difference in intercepts in the presence of differences in slope (although for Figure 7.12 there will likely be no statistically significant differences in intercepts). To summarize, if the primary story told by the data and the graph is one of differences in slope, then I will not interpret a difference in intercepts in the presence of an interaction. In contrast, if it is clear from the analyses and graphs that there are differences in the elevations of the regression lines above and beyond the differences in slope, I believe you should interpret the differences in intercepts in the presence of a significant interaction. We will return to this issue when we discuss aptitude treatment interactions, where this discussion may make more sense.

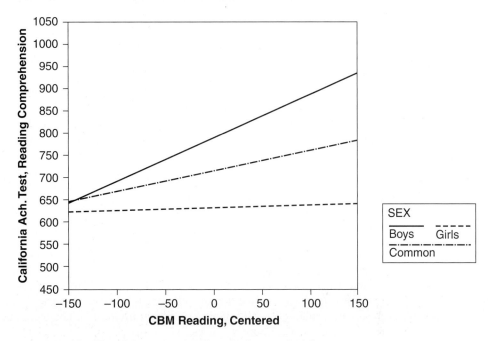

FIGURE 7.17   Plot of the regression lines for boys and girls for the CBM data. Also shown is the common regression line.

In contrast, if we had found no slope bias in this example (a statistically nonsignificant interaction), we would have focused on the first step of the regression equation, without the interaction term, to determine whether there was a difference in intercepts for the two groups (the top half of the table of coefficients). This would have been evidence for intercept bias, by itself.

Suppose our bias research focused on more than two groups; we will then have more than one dummy variable. We can determine whether intercept bias exists in this case by adding the dummy variables in a block, in a combination simultaneous and sequential regression. For example, in the first block we enter the continuous variable; in the second block, the dummy variables representing the categorical variables; and in the third block, the set of interaction terms.

Predictive Bias: Steps.   Let me summarize the steps for investigating predictive bias using multiple regression (summarized, with modifications, from Pedhazur, 1997, chap. 14):

1. Determine whether the variance accounted for by the regression including all three terms (the categorical variable, the continuous variable, and the interaction) is statistically significant and meaningful. If not, it makes little sense to proceed. If R^2 is meaningful, go to step 2.

2. Determine whether the interaction is statistically significant. The most general method for doing so is to conduct a simultaneous regression using the categorical and continuous variable and then sequentially add the cross-product (interaction) term(s). If ΔR^2 for the cross product is statistically significant, then the interaction between the categorical and continuous variable is statistically significant; in the context of predictive bias, this suggests the presence of slope bias. If the interaction is statistically significant, go to step 3. If the interaction is not statistically significant (suggesting a lack of slope bias), go to step 5.

3. Graph the interaction and conduct separate regressions for each group (e.g., boys and girls) of the outcome variable on the continuous variable. These steps will help you determine the nature of the interaction and the slope bias. Go to step 4.

4. It may be worthwhile to focus on whether the intercepts are also different for the two groups. Given that the interaction was statistically significant, determine whether the ΔR^2 associated with the categorical variable (with the continuous variable and the interaction term already in the regression equation) is statistically significant. The most general method for doing so is to do a simultaneous regression of the outcome on the continuous variable and the interaction, sequentially adding the categorical variable to the equation. With only two categories, and thus one dummy variable, this same information can be garnered from the statistical significance of the b of the categorical variable with all three terms in the regression equation. If the categorical variable is statistically significant, you should next focus on the graph of the interaction. If it makes sense to interpret the differences in intercept, do so. If the categorical variable is not statistically significant, or this difference is not interpretable, focus only on the slope bias. Stop.

5. Determine whether the continuous variable is statistically significant across groups (without the cross-product term in the equation). You can do this in two ways. You can regress the outcome on the categorical variable and then add the continuous variable to the regression equation, focusing on ΔR^2 and the associated test of statistical significance. Alternatively, you can focus on the statistical significance of the b associated with the continuous variable with the categorical variable in the equation (in the present example, the b associated with CBM in the top of the table of coefficients in Figure 7.14). If the continuous variable is statistically significant, meaning that the test is a valid predictor of the outcome across groups, go to step 6. If not, meaning a lack of predictive validity across groups, go to step 7.

6. Determine whether the intercepts are different for the groups with the continuous variable in the equation. Most generally, you could regress the outcome on the continuous variable, sequentially adding the categorical variable and focusing on the ΔR^2 and its statistical significance. In the present example, with only two categories and one dummy variable, we could garner the same information by focusing on the statistical significance of the b associated with the categorical variable (Sex) in the top half of the table of coefficients shown in Figure 7.14. A difference in intercepts suggests intercept bias, whereas no difference suggests a lack of intercept bias. If

there is no intercept or slope bias, then a single regression equation functions equally well for all groups; go to step 7.

7. Determine whether the groups differ without the continuous variable in the equation. Regress the outcome on the categorical variable alone and check for statistical significance. If the categorical variable is statistically significant, this means that the groups have different means, which does not constitute bias.

Before proceeding to the next section, I should note that findings of slope bias (like findings of more general interactions of categorical and continuous variables) are relatively uncommon (Jensen, 1980). I also know of no other evidence suggesting slope bias for CBMs, although, as already noted, very little research has been conducted concerning bias in curriculum-based assessment; I know of one other study suggesting no such bias (Hintze, Callahan, Matthews, Williams, & Tobin, 2002). This example was chosen because it *does* illustrate this special type of interaction and because it was a well-executed, well-written study.

Although I have discussed the narrow issue of bias in predictive validity here, it is also worth noting that this methodology extends to other types of bias beyond *test* bias. Suppose, for example, you were interested in the existence and nature of pay disparities between male and female college professors. Whether such disparities represent bias is also addressable through multiple regression using continuous and categorical variables. You could, for example, regress Salaries on variables representing experience, productivity, and sex, as well as cross-product terms (Sex by Experience, Sex by Productivity). Differences in slopes and differences in intercepts across groups would suggest inequities in salaries (cf. Birnbaum, 1979).

Aptitude–Treatment Interactions

Psychologists and educators often develop interventions and treatments with the belief that the effectiveness of these interventions depends, in part, on the characteristics of those receiving the interventions. Children may be placed in different reading groups (high, medium, low) based on their prior reading achievement with the belief that one teaching method is more effective with one group, whereas another method is more effective with another. A psychologist may use one type of therapy with clients who are depressed, but believe a different approach is more effective for those without depression. These are examples of potential Aptitude–Treatment Interactions (ATIs), also known as Attribute–Treatment Interactions (ATIs) or Trait–Treatment Interactions (TTIs). Whatever the terminology, ATIs are interactions between some characteristic of the individual with a treatment or intervention so that the treatments have differential effectiveness depending on the characteristics, attributes, traits, or aptitudes of the person. These attributes can generally be measured on a continuous scale (e.g., reading skill, depression), whereas the treatments are often categorical variables (e.g., two different reading approaches, two types of therapy).

ATIs are, then, generally an interaction between a categorical and continuous variable. Thus, they are properly tested using multiple regression in the same way we test for potential predictive bias, by testing the statistical significance of a cross-product term. An example will illustrate.

Verbal Skills and Memory Strategies.   Do children with lower verbal reasoning skills profit more from learning different memorization methods than do children with good verbal reasoning skills? For example, will children with lower verbal reasoning skills be more accurate in memorization if they use a visual mapping strategy as a memory aid (as opposed to a verbal rehearsal strategy)? In contrast, will children with higher verbal reasoning skills show greater accuracy using a verbal rehearsal memorization strategy? To answer these questions, you could develop an experiment to test for this possible attribute–treatment interaction. You could, for example, assess children's verbal reasoning skills, rank ordering the children based on their scores on the verbal reasoning measure. Take the first pair of students (the one with highest score and the one with the second highest score) and assign one (at random) to the verbal rehearsal group and one to the visual matching group. Continue with each pair of children, down through the lowest scoring child and the second lowest scoring child, assigned at random to one group or the other. Children in the verbal rehearsal group are taught to memorize things (e.g., words, lists) using a memory strategy based on verbal rehearsal, while those in the visual mapping group are taught a memory strategy in which they memorize by visualizing the placement of the objects to be memorized in stops in a map.

"ATI Data.sav" is a data set designed to simulate the possible results of such an experiment (the data are loosely based on Brady & Richman, 1994). If our speculation is correct, the verbal rehearsal strategy should be effective for children with high verbal skills, and the visual mapping strategy should be more effective for children with lower verbal skills. The data are plotted in Figure 7.18; it certainly appears that our speculation is correct: there is an interaction between the attribute (Verbal Reasoning) and the treatment (type of Memory Strategy) in their effect on Visual Memory skills. Let's test the statistical significance of the interaction (I displayed the graph prior to the testing of the interaction to give you a sense of the data).

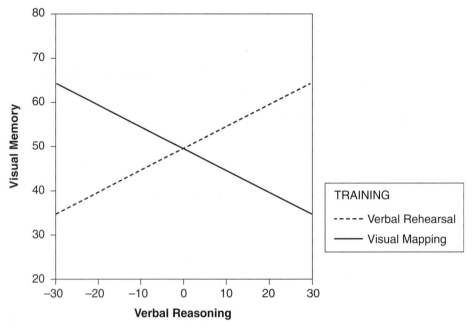

FIGURE 7.18   Plot of regression lines illustrating an aptitude treatment interaction. Verbal Reasoning is the aptitude, and type of Memory Strategy taught is the treatment.

The process of testing for an ATI is the same as testing for predictive bias. Visual Memory (expressed as a T score) was regressed on Memory Strategy (verbal rehearsal, coded 0, or visual mapping, coded 1) and Verbal Reasoning (T score, centered) in a simultaneous regression. In a second step, the cross product (Memory Strategy multiplied by Verbal Reasoning) was added sequentially to the regression to test for the statistical significance of the interaction. Relevant portions of the printout are shown in Figure 7.19. We can use the same basic steps for evaluating the results that we used for our analyses of bias, although the interpretation is slightly different.

Model Summary

Model	R	R Square	Change Statistics				
			R Square Change	F Change	df1	df2	Sig. F Change
1	.015[a]	.000	.000	.011	2	97	.989
2	.529[b]	.280	.280	37.332	1	96	.000

a. Predictors: (Constant), TRAINING Type of Memory Strategy, VERBAL Verbal Reasoning

b. Predictors: (Constant), TRAINING Type of Memory Strategy, VERBAL Verbal Reasoning, V_TRAIN Training by Verbal crossproduct

Coefficients[a]

Model		Unstandardized Coefficients		Standardized Coefficients	t	Sig.	95% Confidence Interval for B	
		B	Std. Error	Beta			Lower Bound	Upper Bound
1	(Constant)	50.000	1.421		35.178	.000	47.179	52.821
	VERBAL Verbal Reasoning	-1.49E-02	.102	-.015	-.147	.884	-.216	.187
	TRAINING Type of Memory Strategy	.000	2.010	.000	.000	1.000	-3.989	3.989
2	(Constant)	50.000	1.212		41.244	.000	47.594	52.406
	VERBAL Verbal Reasoning	.514	.122	.514	4.199	.000	.271	.757
	TRAINING Type of Memory Strategy	.000	1.714	.000	.000	1.000	-3.403	3.403
	V_TRAIN Training by Verbal crossproduct	-1.058	.173	-.748	-6.110	.000	-1.402	-.714

a. Dependent Variable: VIS_MEM Visual Memory

FIGURE 7.19   Regression of Visual Memory on an aptitude (Verbal Reasoning), a treatment (Memory Strategy), and their interaction.

Testing for ATIs

1. Is the overall regression meaningful? R^2 is indeed meaningful and statistically significant ($R^2 = .280$, $F[3, 96] = 12.454$, $p < .001$). We go to step 2.
2. Is the interaction term statistically significant? The addition of the cross-product term to the regression equation resulted in a statistically significant increase to ΔR^2 (.280, $F[1, 96] = 37.332$, $p < .001$), suggesting the statistical significance of the interaction.

In the context of ATIs, this suggests that the Attribute–Treatment Interaction is statistically significant. In the current example, the finding of an interaction suggests that the two memory strategies are indeed differentially effective depending on the verbal skills of the children (go to step 3).

3. Follow up the statistically significant interaction. The interaction is already graphed in Figure 7.18. Separate regressions (not shown) showed that Visual Memory regressed on Verbal Reasoning was statistically significant for both groups (both treatments). For those trained in verbal rehearsal as a memory strategy, the slope (b) of the regression line shown in the figure was .514 ($b = .514$, t [48] = 4.153, $p < .001$). For those in the visual mapping group, the slope was negative ($b = -.544$, t [48] = 4.492, $p < .001$). What do these findings mean (assuming they represent real, rather than simulated, data)? One way to interpret the findings is that for children taught to use verbal rehearsal to memorize lists verbal reasoning skills are useful, but for those taught to use visual maps as a memory aid verbal reasoning ability is a hindrance to effective memorization. I don't find this interpretation particularly helpful. Instead, a more useful interpretation is that visual mapping strategies are more effective for children with difficulties in verbal reasoning, whereas verbal rehearsal memory strategies appear more useful for students with good verbal reasoning skills. For students with average-level verbal reasoning skills, the approaches appear equally effective. We go to step 4.

4. Are the intercepts statistically significantly different, controlling for the statistically significant interaction? Does it make sense to interpret the difference? The intercept is not statistically significant with the interaction term in the equation. Focus on the bottom half of the table of coefficients in Figure 7.19: the b associated with Training was 0. What this means in the context of ATIs is that one treatment is not generally more effective than the other. Suppose that both the interaction and the intercept were statistically significant, and the graph looked more like Figure 7.15. This would suggest that the effectiveness of the memory strategy depended, in part, on the verbal reasoning skills of the children (the interaction), but that one method was also generally more effective than the other.

5. Had the interaction not been statistically significant, we would have gone to step 5 in the previous list (the statistical significance of the continuous variable), followed by step 6 (the statistical significance of the categorical variable). In the context of ATIs, the statistical significance of the continuous variable and the categorical variable are analogous to tests of the main effects in ANOVA. I assume that the statistical significance of the categorical variable will generally be of greater interest than that of the continuous variable.

Although multiple regression is ideal for the analysis of ATIs, its use is much too uncommon. Faced with the example above, many researchers try to fit the data into a classic ANOVA design by categorizing the continuous variable. That is, the researcher not familiar with this proper analysis of ATIs might place anyone scoring below the median on the verbal reasoning scale in a "low verbal" group and anyone above the median in a "high verbal" group, analyzing the data with a 2 by 2 Analysis of Variance. This approach, at minimum, ignores and discards variation in the continuous variable, thus reducing the power of the statistical analysis. Unfortunately, in my experience this improper approach is more common than is the more proper, more powerful MR approach outlined here. Be warned: you now know better.

The search for ATIs is most common in psychology and education; indeed, much of special education is predicated on the assumption that ATIs are important. Children with learning problems are sometimes placed in different classes (e.g., classes for children with mild mental retardation versus classes for children with learning disabilities) based in part on the assumption that different teaching methods should be used with the two groups. But these designs are applicable to other research areas as well. Are two different types of psychotherapy (treatment) differentially effective for depressed versus nondepressed (attribute) clients? Is one management style (treatment) more effective with less productive (attribute) employees, with a different style being more effective with more productive employees? ATI designs have wide applicability. For more information, Cronbach and Snow (1977) is the definitive source on ATIs and their analysis.

ANCOVA

Suppose you are interested in the effectiveness of Internet-based instruction in research methodology. Is, for example, an Internet-based research course as effective as traditional face to face instruction? One way of studying this problem would be via a classic pretest–posttest control group design. That is, you might assign, at random, students entering a course in research methodology to an Internet-based course versus a traditional classroom course. Because you believe the effectiveness of the coursework may depend, in part, on participants' prior knowledge, you give participants a pretest on research methodology knowledge. After the course completion, participants are given another measure of knowledge of research methodology. One straightforward method of analysis of the results of this experiment would be through analysis of covariance (ANCOVA), where the pretest serves as the covariate, and assignment to the Internet versus regular coursework is the independent variable of interest. ANCOVA is used to examine the effects of course type on research knowledge, controlling for participants' prior knowledge of research methodology. ANCOVA serves to reduce error variance by controlling for participants' individual differences and thus provides a more sensitive statistical test than does a simple ANOVA.[4]

I hope that it is obvious that ANCOVA can also be conceived as a multiple regression analysis with a continuous and a categorical variable. MR subsumes ANCOVA; if you analyze these same data using a simultaneous multiple regression, your results will be the same as those from the ANCOVA. There is, however, an advantage to analysis via MR. One assumption underlying analysis of covariance is that the regression lines of the dependent variable on the covariate are parallel for the different groups (e.g., Internet versus traditional course). In other words, ANCOVA assumes, but does not generally test for, the nonexistence of an interaction between the independent (or categorical) variable and the covariate (continuous variable). It might well be that Internet-based instruction is more effective for students with strong prior knowledge, but less effective for students whose prior research knowledge is weak. If this is the case, a graph of your findings might look something like Figure 7.20, which is simply one more illustration of an interaction between a categorical and continuous variable. Obviously, you can test this assumption using multiple regression,

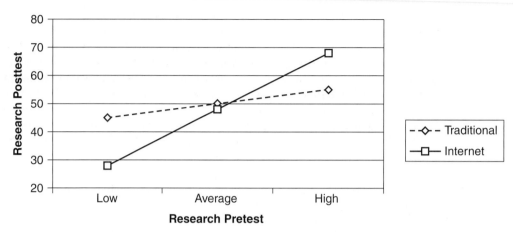

FIGURE 7.20   A potential interaction in a pretest–posttest control group design.

using the same method explained throughout this chapter, whereas most software packages ignore the interaction in ANCOVA.

One way of thinking about ATIs and ANCOVAs is this: If the interaction is not statistically significant in an ATI design, you can think of it as being a simple ANCOVA analysis. If in a pretest–posttest design the pretest (covariate) interacts with the treatment, you can consider it an ATI design and analyze it accordingly.

CAVEATS AND ADDITIONAL INFORMATION

"Effects" of Categorical Subject Variables

In this chapter and elsewhere, I have discussed the effects of variables such as Sex and Ethnic origin on outcomes such as Self-Esteem. Yet I hope it is obvious that these types of variables and others (e.g., rural and urban, region of the country, and religious affiliation) are very broad categories and can mean many different things. If we say that Sex affects Self-Esteem, what does this mean? That the biological differences between boys and girls result in different levels of self-esteem? Or that the way boys and girls are socialized results in differences in self-esteem? Or some other of the myriad of differences that are associated with being a boy or a girl? We just don't know (although when we discuss testing for indirect effects in structural equation modeling, you will have a tool that you can use to investigate some of the possibilities). All it means, really, is that *something* about being a boy versus being a girl results in differences in self-esteem. Similarly, if we say that sex and achievement interacted in their effects on self-esteem or that achievement had different effects on self-esteem for boys versus girls, we will be left to speculate about the many possible reasons that such an interaction might happen and what it might mean. "Big" categorical variables like Sex and Ethnic origin carry a lot of baggage, and sometimes, when we discover an interaction between them and some other variable, we are confronted with many new questions about meaning.

Some methodologists see this as a major problem. I don't. I think it's okay to say that sex affects self-esteem, as long as you know that this statement means "there is something—we don't know what—about being a boy versus being a girl that results in differences in self-esteem." Likewise, I think it is fine to say that Ethnic origin and Achievement interact in their effects on Self-Esteem, as long as you know that what this means is for some reason—unknown at this point—achievement has a different effect on self-esteem for adolescents of one group versus another. Understand the meaning behind such statements and then maybe the next step can be hypothesizing and testing why such effects come about.

Interactions and Cross Products

In an earlier footnote, I discussed the distinction between cross-product terms and interactions. Strictly speaking, the *partialed* cross product (controlling for the two variables used in the cross product) is an interaction term. Of course, these variables are controlled when all are entered into a multiple regression equation, either simultaneously or sequentially (the cross product entered last), so many researchers use the terms interchangeably.

Further Probing of Statistically Significant Interactions

Suppose, as in several of the examples in this chapter, you find a statistically significant interaction between a categorical variable and a continuous variable. How can you explore that interaction in more depth? Here I have suggested graphing the interaction and then conducting separate regressions across the different categories of the categorical variable. Yet further exploration is possible. You might be interested in knowing whether the regression lines are statistically significantly different for a specific value of the continuous variable. In our ATI example, you might wonder for a student with a verbal score of 10 whether the two approaches are really different or not. You may also be interested in the regions of significance; in other words, the point at which the two lines become statistically significantly different.

These are worthwhile topics, but they are beyond the scope of this text. Some references given throughout this chapter provide additional detail for how to probe a significant interaction in more depth than is discussed here (Aiken & West, 1991; Cohen & Cohen, 1983; Cronbach & Snow, 1977; Darlington, 1990; Pedhazur, 1997). Some of the procedures are relatively complex. If you are faced with an interaction that requires more complex probing, I recommend these sources.

It is relatively easy, however, to develop a less formal sense of answers to these kinds of questions, using the graphing features of common statistical programs. Figure 7.21, for example, shows another version of the graph of the ATI example originally shown in Figure 7.18. In this version, however, I asked for the 95% confidence interval around the two regression lines, which provides at least a general sense of where, at what points, the lines become significantly different from one another.

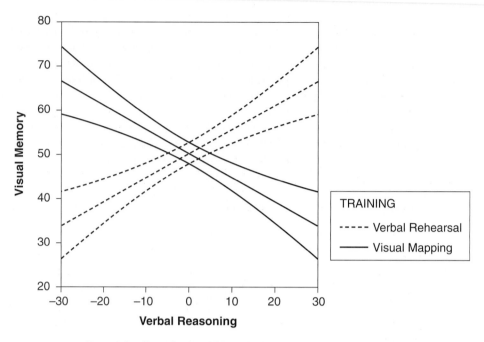

FIGURE 7.21   Regression lines for the ATI analysis, with 95% confidence intervals.

SUMMARY

In this chapter we focused on the analysis of categorical and continuous variables in the same multiple regression. Our first example examined the effect of Sex and Achievement on adolescents' Self-Esteem. As the example illustrated, analyses including both categorical and continuous variables are analytically and conceptually little different from those including only continuous variables. When the categorical variable is a single dummy variable, the b associated with it represents the difference, on the dependent variable, between the two groups, controlling for the other variables in the equation.

It is possible to test for interactions between variables by multiplying the two variables that may interact and entering this cross-product term in the regression equation along with the two original variables. It is desirable to center any continuous variables used to create such a cross product by subtracting the mean of that variable from each person's score on the variable. The ΔR^2 (if sequential regression is used) or the t associated with the cross-product term (if simultaneous regression is used with a single cross product) is used to test the statistical significance of the interaction. The same procedure works to test the interaction between two categorical variables, two continuous variables, or a categorical variable and a continuous variable. This chapter illustrated several examples of interactions between categorical and continuous variables. We found no statistically significant interaction between Sex and Achievement in their effect on Self-Esteem, but did find a statistically significant interaction between Ethnic origin and Achievement on Self-Esteem. Graphs and separate regressions across groups were used to probe the statistically significant interaction. It appears that Achievement affects the Self-Esteem for White adolescents, but not adolescents from various minority groups. In answer to the question "Does Achievement affect Self-Esteem?" we would need to answer "It depends. . . ." The phrase "it depends" is generally a clue that we are describing the presence of an interaction. Interactions are not common in nonexperimental research.

A few specific research questions are best conceived of as interactions between categorical and continuous variables. These include investigations of predictive bias and attribute or aptitude treatment interactions (ATIs). Examples were given of each, using simulated data designed to mimic previous research. Analysis of covariance (ANCOVA) can also be considered as a multiple regression analysis involving both continuous (the covariate) and categorical (the treatment or independent variable) variables. One potential advantage of using MR to analyze ANCOVAs is that it is possible to test for an interaction between the covariate and the treatment, whereas this is simply assumed for most ANCOVAs.

I noted that it is loose usage to discuss the "effects" of broad, existing categorical variables, such as Sex, on various outcomes, because of all the things that may be subsumed under the meaning of such categorical variables. My belief is that such usage is acceptable if you are clear as to the meaning. Likewise, a cross product is not strictly an interaction term, even though it is used to test for an interaction, but many people use these terms interchangeably. Finally, I discussed several additional sources for more detail on testing for interactions in MR.

EXERCISES

1. Conduct the first three examples used in this chapter that used the NELS data: the regression of Self-Esteem on Sex and Achievement, the same analysis with the addition of an Achievement by Sex cross product, and the regression of Self-Esteem on Ethnic origin, Achievement, and an Ethnic by Achievement cross product. Make sure your results match those presented in the chapter.

2. Use the "Kranzler et al simulated data.sav" (or "Kranzler et al simulated.xls" or "Kranzler.txt") data set found on the Web site (www.ablongman.com/keith1e). Center the CBM scores and create a Sex by CBM cross product using the centered variable. Conduct an analysis for predictive bias using the centered data. Do the results match those presented here? Try conducting the analysis using the uncentered data (and cross product based on uncentered data), as was done in Kranzler et al. (1999). Compare the coefficients and correlations from the two analyses. Would your interpretation be the same? You should find that the intercepts are not statistically significantly different without centering, but that they are different using the centered continuous variable and the interaction term created from the centered continuous variable. Compare the two printouts; see if you can develop a sense of why this difference occurs. (*Hint*: I recommend you focus on the correlation matrices and then the standard errors of the regression coefficients. Reread the section discussing the advantages of centering.)

3. Is the NELS math test biased against girls? Conduct an analysis of predictive bias using the base year test (ByTxMStd) and Sex, with 10th-grade Math GPA as the outcome (F1S39a). Make sure you convert Sex into a dummy variable and center the Math test score.

4. The file "ATI Data b.sav" (or the Excel or plain text versions of these data) includes another, perhaps more realistic, simulated data set for the attribute–treatment interaction problem illustrated in the chapter. Perform an ATI analysis and interpret the results.

5. The file "ancova exercise.sav" includes simulated data for the ANCOVA example presented in the chapter (see also the Excel or plain text versions of this file). This was a pretest–posttest two-group design in which 60 students registered for a course in research methodology were assigned, at random, to a traditional version of the class or an Internet version of the class. All students attended an orientation session in which they were given a pretest of their research knowledge. The posttest scores are students' grades for the class. Analyze the results of the experiment using multiple regression analysis. Test for the presence of an interaction between the pretest and the treatment (type of class). Conduct an ANCOVA and compare the results of this analysis with those of the multiple regression.

NOTES

1. For example, in SPSS, you could create this variable from the original z score using the following compute statement: COMPUTE S_ESTEEM=((F1CNCPT2*10)+50).

2. These cross products are often referred to as interaction terms. Strictly speaking, this multiplication of the two variables should be referred to as a cross-product term, rather than an interaction term. To create a pure interaction term, we need to remove the variance attributable to the categorical and continuous variables from the cross product (e.g., regress the cross product on the categorical and continuous variables and save the residuals as an interaction variable). The testing process is identical, however, and I will generally use the terms cross product and interaction interchangeably. Of course, the effects of these variables are also removed in the MR regression analysis when they are entered simultaneously or prior to the cross product.

3. Note that predictive bias is only one of several types of potential bias. It is also referred to as the regression model of bias, or Cleary's definition of test bias, after the late T. Anne Cleary who explicated the nature of bias in prediction (Cleary, 1968). My purpose here is not the exhaustive discussion of test bias, but to illustrate one instance of the wide applicability of testing interactions in regression. For more information on the topic of test bias, one classic source is Jensen (1980).

4. My example illustrates the most appropriate use of ANCOVA. A less appropriate, but more common, use is to attempt to equate existing groups in the absence of random assignment (e.g., a nonequivalent control group design).

CHAPTER EIGHT

CONTINUOUS VARIABLES: INTERACTIONS AND CURVES

As noted in Chapter 7, it is possible to have interactions between two or more continuous variables. This chapter will discuss such interactions, as well as regression in which there is a curve in the regression line. As we will see, such curves can be considered cases in which a variable interacts with itself in its effect on some outcome variable.

INTERACTIONS BETWEEN CONTINUOUS VARIABLES

Conceptually, there is little difference between testing an interaction between two continuous variables and testing an interaction between a categorical and continuous variable. Although the probing of a statistically significant interaction is slightly more complex when both variables are continuous, the basic steps are the same. With two continuous variables, both variables are centered, and then the centered variables are multiplied to create a cross-product term. The outcome variable is regressed on the two centered continuous variables (plus any other variables you wish to take into account) in a simultaneous regression. In a second, sequential step, the cross-product (interaction) term is entered into the regression. If the addition of the cross product leads to a statistically significant increase in R^2, the interaction is statistically significant. An example will illustrate the process.

Effects of TV Time on Achievement

In Chapter 7 I mentioned research testing for an interaction between TV viewing and ability in their effects on achievement (Keith et al., 1986). The primary purpose of this study was to assess and compare the effects of parent involvement, homework, and TV viewing on achievement. Previous research, however, had suggested that TV viewing may interact with Ability in their effects on Achievement (Williams, Haertel, Haertel, & Walberg, 1982). TV viewing appears to have a negative effect on achievement, but the extent of the effect may depend on the ability level of the student watching TV (remember, "it depends" often signals an interaction). Specifically, TV viewing may be especially detrimental for high-ability youth and less detrimental for low-ability youth (Williams et al.). Keith et al. (1986) sought to test the possible interaction between hours spent watching TV and intellectual Ability on adolescents' academic Achievement.

The Data: Centering and Cross Products. The data sets "tv ability interact2.sav," "tv ability interact2.xls," and "tv_abil.txt" include 500 cases of data designed to simulate the results of Keith et al. (1986). Variables in the data set include Ability (a composite of six verbal and non-verbal tests, each with a mean of 100 and a $SD = 15$), TV (average time per day, in hours, spent watching TV), and Achieve (an Achievement composite of Reading and Math, expressed as a T score). Also included is the background variable SES (in z score format: a combination of parents' educational attainment, parents' occupational status, family income, and possessions in the home). From these data, I created centered versions of each continuous independent variable (TV_Cen and Abil_Cen) and the cross product of the centered TV and Ability variables (TV × Abil). The descriptive statistics for these variables are shown in Figure 8.1.

Descriptive Statistics

	N	Minimum	Maximum	Mean	Std. Deviation
SES Familty Background	500	-2.84	3.12	.1099	1.01568
ABILITY Ability	500	75.00	130.00	100.4040	9.47504
TV TV Time, weekdays	500	0	8	4.01	1.754
ABIL_CEN Ability (centered)	500	-25.40	29.60	.0000	9.47504
TV_CEN TV Time, weekdays (centered)	500	-4.01	3.99	.0000	1.75445
TVXABIL TV by Ability crossproduct	500	-74.53	58.37	-2.9192	16.46830
ACHIEVE Achievement Test Score	500	29.00	75.00	50.0960	8.71290
Valid N (listwise)	500				

FIGURE 8.1 Descriptive statistics for the "tv ability interact.sav" data.

You may wonder why I did not create and use cross products reflecting interactions between TV viewing and SES, or between SES and Ability, and so on. Recall that in Chapter 7 I argued that you should only test specific interactions, those designed to test specific hypotheses of interest in research, rather than wholesale testing of all possible interactions. The current example exemplifies this approach by testing only the interaction of interest and suggested by previous research.

The Regression.   Achievement was regressed on SES, Ability (centered), and TV viewing (centered) in a simultaneous regression, with the Ability–TV cross product in a second, sequential step. Some of the regression results are shown in Figure 8.2. As shown in the model summary, the initial three independent variables accounted for 51% of the variance in Achievement ($F[3, 496] = 172.274$, $p < .001$), and the addition of the Ability–TV cross product explained an additional 4.4% of the variance in Achievement, a statistically significant increase ($F[1, 495] = 49.143$, $p < .001$). The interaction between ability and time spent watching TV is statistically significant.

Model Summary

Model	R	R Square	Change Statistics				
			R Square Change	F Change	df1	df2	Sig. F Change
1	.714[a]	.510	.510	172.274	3	496	.000
2	.745[b]	.555	.044	49.143	1	495	.000

a. Predictors: (Constant), TV_CEN TV Time, weekdays (centered), SES Familty Background, ABIL_CEN Ability (centered)

b. Predictors: (Constant), TV_CEN TV Time, weekdays (centered), SES Familty Background, ABIL_CEN Ability (centered), TVXABIL TV by Ability crossproduct

Coefficients[a]

Model		Unstandardized Coefficients		Standardized Coefficients	t	Sig.	95% Confidence Interval for B	
		B	Std. Error	Beta			Lower Bound	Upper Bound
1	(Constant)	49.937	.275		181.324	.000	49.396	50.479
	SES Familty Background	1.442	.294	.168	4.909	.000	.865	2.020
	ABIL_CEN Ability (centered)	.561	.032	.610	17.794	.000	.499	.623
	TV_CEN TV Time, weekdays (centered)	-.423	.159	-.085	-2.655	.008	-.737	-.110
2	(Constant)	49.616	.267		185.892	.000	49.092	50.140
	SES Familty Background	1.373	.281	.160	4.892	.000	.822	1.925
	ABIL_CEN Ability (centered)	.555	.030	.604	18.427	.000	.496	.614
	TV_CEN TV Time, weekdays (centered)	-.278	.154	-.056	-1.806	.072	-.580	.024
	TVXABIL TV by Ability crossproduct	-.113	.016	-.213	-7.010	.000	-.144	-.081

a. Dependent Variable: ACHIEVE Achievement Test Score

FIGURE 8.2   Regression results testing for an interaction between time spent watching TV and Ability in their effects on Achievement.

The table of coefficients, also shown in Figure 8.2, provides additional information about the effects of TV viewing on Achievement. As shown in the top portion of the table, prior to consideration of the cross product, each independent variable had a statistically significant effect on Achievement. Indeed, Ability had a large effect on Achievement (more able students achieve at a higher level), SES had a moderate effect (more advantaged students achieve at a higher level), and TV viewing had a small to moderate negative effect on Achievement. Other things being equal, the more time adolescents spend watching TV, the lower their academic achievement. The lower portion of the table again shows the statistical significance of the interaction.

Probing an Interaction between Continuous Variables.   With interactions between categorical and continuous variables, it is relatively easy to probe the interaction through graphing, because one variable already represents a limited number of categories. These categories can thus be plotted as separate lines in a graph of the dependent variable on the other (continuous) independent variable, and separate regression can be run across the different categories. It is slightly more complex to investigate further a statistically significant interaction between two continuous variables. I will outline several methods by which you can get a sense of the nature of interactions between continuous variables and will briefly mention methods for more complete post hoc probing of such interactions.

One relatively easy method of getting a sense for such interactions involves converting (for the purposes of follow-up) one continuous variable into a limited number of ordered categories and conducting the same sorts of analyses that we used when one variable was categorical. For the current example, I converted the Ability variable into a new, trichotomized Ability variable (Abil_3, which is also included in the data set). On this new Abil_3 variable, a value of 1 included approximately the lowest 33% of participants (on the Ability variable). The middle third of participants on the Ability variable was coded 2 on Abil_3. The top third of those on Ability was assigned a value of 3 on the Abil_3 variable. Thus scores of 1, 2, and 3 on the Abil_3 variable represent low, middle, and high ability, respectively.

Figure 8.3 shows three separate regression lines for the regression of Achievement on TV time for these three levels of Ability (SES is not taken into account in the graph). The graph clearly shows the nature of the interaction. It appears that TV viewing is considerably more detrimental for the achievement of high-ability youth than for other youth, in that each additional hour spent viewing TV appears to result in considerably lowered achievement

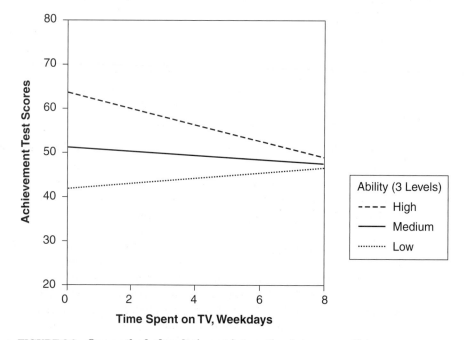

FIGURE 8.3   One method of exploring an interaction between continuous variables: regression of Achievement on TV for three levels of Ability.

for high-ability youth. In contrast, for students of average or lower ability, TV viewing seems to have little effect on their achievement. The results are consistent with previous research on the effects of TV viewing (e.g., Williams et al., 1982).

It is also possible to plot mean Achievement scores by levels of time spent on TV and (trichotomized) Ability (cf. Keith et al., 1986), as was done in Figure 8.4, to get a general sense of the nature of the interaction. Although this approach has some advantages—the variation in the lines is interesting—these lines represent means, not regression lines, and thus the nature of the difference in regression lines is less obvious. Also note that this procedure will only work if there are a limited number of possibilities for the independent variable being plotted on the *X*-axis, or the samples are large, or both. The present example fulfills these requirements, because there are only eight levels of the TV viewing variable.

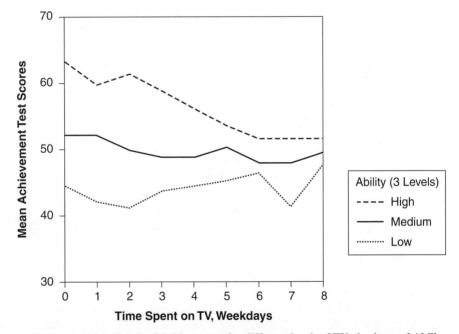

FIGURE 8.4   Mean levels of Achievement for different levels of TV viewing and Ability.

It is also possible to calculate the regression equation for any given value of Ability using the overall regression equation by substituting the desired values of Ability in the equation. The regression equation is

$$\text{Achieve}_{\text{predicted}} = 49.616 + 1.373\text{SES} + .555\text{Ability} - .278\text{TV} - .113\text{TV} \times \text{Ability}.$$

What values should be substituted? Common values are –1 *SD*, the mean, and +1 *SD* on the continuous independent variable (Aiken & West, 1991; Cohen & Cohen, 1983). In the present analysis, these would be values of approximately –9, 0, and 9 on the centered Ability variable (the mean and *SD* are shown in Figure 8.1). Other values are also possible, including clinically relevant values or commonly used cutoffs. So, for example, if you are especially interested in the implications of this research for low-ability students, you will probably want to calculate a regression equation for students whose ability is a standard deviation or more below the mean.

If you substitute values of 9, 0, and –9 for Ability (and in the Ability by TV interaction) in the above equation, you generate three new equations. The equation for high-ability youth is

$$\text{Achieve}_{\text{predicted}} = 49.616 + 1.373\,(0) + .555\,(9) - .278\text{TV} - .113\text{TV}\,(9).$$

Again, for this equation, +9 was substituted for Ability wherever it occurred in the overall regression equation. I also substituted a value of zero for SES (the population mean) to simplify the equations. The equation is simplified as

$$\text{Achieve}_{\text{predicted}} = 49.616 + 4.995 - .278\text{TV} - 1.017\text{TV}$$
$$= 54.611 - 1.295\text{TV}$$

For middle-ability youth, a value of zero is substituted for Ability. The regression equation is

$$\text{Achieve}_{\text{predicted}} = 49.616 + 1.373\,(0) + .555\,(0) - .278\text{TV} - .113\text{TV}\,(0)$$
$$= 49.616 - .278\text{TV}$$

For low-ability youth, a value of –9 is substituted, resulting in this regression equation:

$$\text{Achieve}_{\text{predicted}} = 49.616 + 1.373\,(0) + .555\,(-9) - .278\text{TV} - .113\text{TV}\,(-9)$$
$$= 49.616 - 4.995 - .278\text{TV} + 1.017\text{TV}$$
$$= 44.621 + .739\text{TV}$$

These, then, are the regression equations for the regression of Achievement on TV time for high-, middle-, and low-ability youth. These equations can then be plotted (Figure 8.5) to demonstrate the nature of the interaction. Although slightly more complex than the other methods outlined, this method has the advantage of being based on the original regression equation (rather than three new equations). In addition, it is possible to test the statistical significance of the slopes of the calculated regression equations. This topic is beyond the scope of this book, but is presented in detail in Aiken and West (1991), who also show how to calculate the new equations and test their statistical significance using a statistical analysis program.

To reiterate, there are several possibilities for exploring, through graphing, a statistically significant interaction with two continuous variables. They are (in reverse order):

1. Use the original regression equation to graph lines for different levels of one continuous variable. You can substitute, for example, values representing +1 *SD*, the mean, and –1 *SD* for one interacting variable to develop three regression equations representing participants who have high, medium, and low values on this variable.
2. Divide the sample into categories (e.g., lowest, middle, and high categories) on one of the interacting variables. Alternatively, you could make this division at +1 *SD*, the

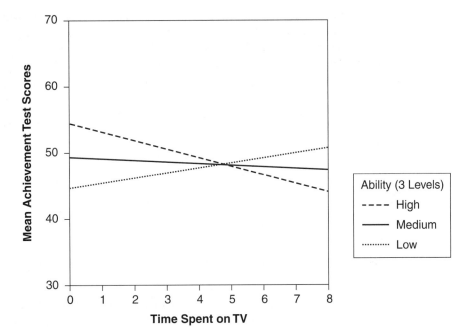

FIGURE 8.5   Using the overall regression equation to plot the effects of TV on Achievement for different levels of Ability.

mean, and −1 *SD*. Plot a line for each category showing the mean level of the dependent variable for each level of the other interacting variable. This procedure requires large samples and a limited number of levels of the other interacting variable.

3. Divide the sample into categories (e.g., lowest, middle, and high categories) on one interacting variable. Alternatively, you could make this division at +1 *SD,* the mean, and −1 *SD,* or other clinically significant values. Plot a regression line, with the outcome variable regressed on the other interacting variable, for each category.

Points to Consider.   Several aspects of these examples are worth noting. First, you should consider which continuous variable to categorize. We could have focused just as easily on high, medium, and low levels of TV viewing instead of high, medium, and low ability. In this case, our graph would have shown the regression of Achievement on Ability for low, medium, and high levels of TV viewing. Such a presentation strikes me as considerably less useful than the one presented; it would, for example, provide little illumination for parents wondering whether they should worry about their children's TV consumption. Basically, the way you choose to graph and analyze such interactions should depend on the questions you are interested in addressing. Different presentations answer different questions, so you should be clear about the questions you want to address and set up your graphs and additional analyses appropriately.

Second, note that for the graphs I used the original metric of TV viewing, rather than the centered metric. Either will work, but since the metric of TV viewing is meaningful (hours per day), I didn't want to waste the interpretive advantages of this metric. If I were graphing a variable without such a meaningful metric, say self-esteem, I would probably choose the centered version of the variable.

Third, you may wonder if I have here adopted a practice that I previously criticized: the mind-set that sometimes leads researchers to categorize continuous variables so that they may be analyzed by AVOVA. Here, however, I seem to be advocating such categorization. Note, however, that I did not categorize Ability prior to the test of the interaction. The continuous variable was only converted to categories after a statistically significant interaction was found and as an aid to probing the nature of this interaction. My harsh criticism of categorizing continuous variables prior to analysis still stands.

MODERATION, MEDIATION, AND COMMON CAUSE

This chapter and the previous one have focused on interactions in multiple regression. As noted, interactions can go by another label, moderation. I want to briefly draw the distinction between moderation and two other concepts we have discussed throughout this portion of the book, mediation and common cause (see especially Chapter 4). I hope these three concepts are clear in your mind, but, in my experience, students often confuse the nature of these three concepts and how they show up in multiple regression.

Moderation

Moderation means the same thing as interaction. When we say that ability *moderates* the effect of TV viewing on achievement, this is the same as saying that ability and TV viewing interact in their effect on achievement. Likewise, it is equivalent to saying that the effect of TV viewing differs for different levels of ability or that TV viewing has different effects for those of high ability versus those of low ability. Because regression coefficients represent the slope of the regression line, interactions–moderations are often described as differences in slopes across groups. Interactions, or moderation, can often be described using the statement "it depends." When you hear the term "moderated regression," it simply means to test for moderation–interaction using the regression procedures outlined in these chapters.

Mediation

The term mediation means the same thing as an indirect effect. When we say that motivation affects achievement through homework, this is the same as saying that motivation has an indirect effect on achievement through homework or that homework mediates the effect of motivation on achievement. We can describe this relation by explaining that more motivated students complete more homework and that homework, in turn, increases their achievement. We can also explain this mediation, or indirect effect, via a diagram such as that shown in Figure 8.6.

Although we have discussed mediation or indirect effects, we have not really discussed how to test for mediation using multiple regression. In the classic article on this topic, Baron and Kenny (1986) showed that mediation can be assumed to exist under the following conditions:

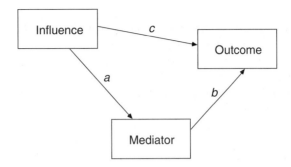

FIGURE 8.6 Mediation.

1. In a regression of Outcome on Influence (using the labels from Figure 8.6), the effect of Influence on Outcome is statistically significant. This regression does not include the mediating variable.
2. The regression of the Outcome on the Mediator results in a statistically significant effect.
3. The regression of Outcome on both Influence and the Mediator results in a reduction in the effect of Influence from step 1. In other words, the effect represented by path c in Figure 8.6 is smaller than would be the effect without the Mediator in the regression.

Complete mediation exists when the addition of the Mediator to the regression reduces the coefficient c to zero; partial mediation exists when the effect is simply reduced.

More directly, what is being evaluated in a test of mediation is the magnitude and statistical significance of the indirect effect of Influence on Outcome *through* Mediator. The statistical significance of this indirect effect can be calculated from the coefficients and standard errors from the regression of Outcome on Influence and Mediator (coefficient b) and the regression of the Mediator on the Influence (coefficient a). As of this writing, there is a Web page that will perform the calculations for you interactively (www.unc.edu/~preacher/sobel/sobel.htm).

Much has been written about mediation in the years since the Baron and Kenny (1986) article (for recent methodological articles, see MacKinnon, Lockwood, Hoffman, West, & Sheets, 2002; Shrout & Bolger, 2002). As you might guess from my (and others') reliance on path diagrams to explain mediation, it is most easily understood within the context of path and structural equation models. Indeed, most structural equation modeling programs easily calculate indirect effects and their statistical significance. For this reason, we will delve deeper into the topic in Part 2.

Common Cause

A common cause is a variable that affects both a presumed influence and its presumed outcome. If the coefficients represented by paths b and c in Figure 8.6 are both statistically significant, the variable Influence is a common cause of the Mediator and the Outcome. Common causes may also be referred to as confounding variables. As noted in Chapter 4, important common causes must be included in a regression for the regression coefficient to provide valid estimates of the effect of one variable on another. Analyses in which such common causes are not included are sometimes referred to as misspecified analyses or models. We will spend considerable time on the issue of common causes in Part 2.

CURVILINEAR REGRESSION

All the regression lines we have encountered so far have been straight lines. Indeed, as you will see in Chapter 9, linearity is one of the basic assumptions of regression. But it is also possible for a regression line to have curves in it. As an example, think of the likely relation of anxiety to test performance. If you have no anxiety at all about an upcoming exam, you likely will not study for it nor take it very seriously while it is being administered; the likely result is that you will not perform particularly well on the exam. At the other end of the anxiety spectrum, if you are extremely anxious about the same exam, your high anxiety will also likely inhibit your performance. Some middle level of anxiety should be most benefi-cial: enough anxiety to motivate you to study and perform well, but not so high as to inter-fere with your performance. If this expectation about anxiety and test performance is accurate (Teigen, 1995), the proper graph of test performance on anxiety might look some-thing like that shown in Figure 8.7.

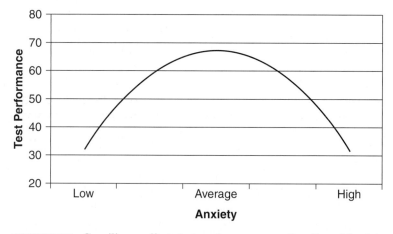

FIGURE 8.7   Curvilinear effect: test performance as a function of Anxiety.

Using normal linear regression, we would likely explain none of the variance in test performance based on anxiety; the regression line would be straight and flat. But it *is* pos-sible to take into account possible curves in the regression line. How? Recall how we described the results of interactions by saying "it depends." If asked to describe the effect of anxiety on test performance, we need to use this same language. What type of effect does anxiety have on test performance? It depends; it depends on the level of anxiety. For low levels of anxiety, anxiety has a positive effect on test performance, whereas for high levels of anxiety, anxiety has a negative effect on test performance. If the use of the term "it depends" signals a possible interaction, then in essence what we are saying is that anxiety interacts with *itself* in its effects on test performance. And if a curve in a regression line can be described as the interaction of a variable with itself on another variable, then the method of analysis also becomes clear: multiply the two variables that interact—in this case, multiply anxiety times anxiety—and enter the cross product in the regression equation following the original variable. Let's turn to real data to illustrate the method.

Curvilinear Effects of Homework on GPA

We have examined in several ways the effect of homework on achievement and grades. But doesn't it seem likely that homework's effect on learning should be curvilinear? Certainly, homework improves learning, but don't you think that there will be diminishing returns for each additional hour of homework completed? In other words, shouldn't the payoff for learning be greater when going from zero to 1 hour per week than when going from, say, 10 to 11 hours per week? In fact, research on homework suggests exactly this type of curvilinear relation: there are diminishing returns for the effects of homework on learning (cf. Cooper, 1989; Fredrick & Walberg, 1980).

The Data: Homework and Homework Squared.   This expectation for diminishing returns for homework is in fact built into the NELS data, at least to some extent. Look at the values of the homework variable, shown in Figure 8.8. Note that for lower values of homework the increment is 1 hour or less (e.g., from zero hours to 1 hour or less), whereas for later values the increment is greater (e.g., a value of 6 is used to describe 13, 14, or 15 hours of homework). This compression of the homework scale at the upper end may take some of the likely curvilinear effect of homework on learning into account. We'll see here if the effect is still curvilinear.

F1S36A2 TIME SPENT ON HOMEWORK OUT OF SCHOOL

		Frequency	Percent	Valid Percent	Cumulative Percent
Valid	0 NONE	63	6.3	6.7	6.7
	1 1 HOUR OR LESS	232	23.2	24.6	31.3
	2 2-3 HOURS	264	26.4	28.0	59.3
	3 4-6 HOURS	168	16.8	17.8	77.1
	4 7-9 HOURS	80	8.0	8.5	85.6
	5 10-12 HOURS	66	6.6	7.0	92.6
	6 13-15 HOURS	31	3.1	3.3	95.9
	7 OVER 15 HOURS	39	3.9	4.1	100.0
	Total	943	94.3	100.0	
Missing	96 MULTIPLE RESPONSE	7	.7		
	98 MISSING	17	1.7		
	System	33	3.3		
	Total	57	5.7		
Total		1000	100.0		

FIGURE 8.8   **The scale of the Homework time variable in NELS.**

Let's be a little more explicit: we will test the effect of time spent on out of school Homework in grade 10 on students' 10th-grade GPA. We are interested in testing for possible curvilinear effects for Homework, so we will use both the Homework variable and a Homework-squared variable in the regression. Just as in our tests for interactions, we will first center the continuous Homework variable prior to squaring it and will use centered Homework and centered Homework squared in the regression. We will also control for students' family background, or Socioeconomic Status, and Previous Achievement, with the thinking that SES and Previous Achievement may affect both Homework and subsequent Grades.

Figure 8.9 shows the descriptive statistics and correlations for the variables used in the analysis. All these variables are included in your version of the NELS data, except two: HW_Cen and HW_Sq. HW_Cen is the centered version of the Homework variable, created by subtracting the mean of F1S36A2 from F1S36A2 [e.g., compute Hw_Cen=(F1S36A2-2.544642857143)]. HW_Sq was created by squaring HW_Cen. Note the correlation between HW_Sq and HW_Cen: .582. Had we not centered the Homework variable prior to squaring it, the correlation between Homework and Homework squared would have been .953.

Tenth-grade GPA was regressed on SES, Previous Achievement, and HW_Cen in one step, and HW_Sq was sequentially added in a second step in the regression. Note that we could

Descriptive Statistics

	Mean	Std. Deviation	N
FFUGRAD ffu grades	5.6866	1.4726	896
BYSES SOCIO-ECONOMIC STATUS COMPOSITE	2.17E-02	.77097	896
BYTESTS Eighth grade achievement tests (mean)	51.8150	8.7000	896
HW_CEN Homework out of school, centered	-1.5E-13	1.7110	896
HW_SQ Homework centered, squared	2.9243	4.3862	896

Correlations

	FFUGRAD ffu grades	BYSES SOCIO-ECONOMIC STATUS COMPOSITE	BYTESTS Eighth grade achievement tests (mean)	HW_CEN Homework out of school, centered	HW_SQ Homework centered, squared
Pearson Correlation	1.000	.311	.494	.325	.097
	.311	1.000	.467	.285	.134
	.494	.467	1.000	.304	.138
	.325	.285	.304	1.000	.582
	.097	.134	.138	.582	1.000

FIGURE 8.9   Descriptive statistics for the variables used in the curvilinear regression example.

just as easily have added all variables in a single step to determine the statistical significance of the curve in the regression line (using the t test of the HW_Sq regression coefficient).[1]

The Regression.   Figure 8.10 shows the results of the multiple regression. As shown in the Model Summary, the addition of the HW_Sq term to the regression resulted in a statistically significant increase in the variance explained by the regression ($\Delta R^2 = .008$, $F = 10.366$ [1, 891] $p = .001$). There is a statistically significant curve in the regression line. Of course, the statistical significance of the HW_Sq variable in the lower half of the table of coefficients leads to the same conclusion.

Graphing the Curve.   The curved regression line is shown in Figure 8.11 (created by specifying a quadratic fit line as chart option in SPSS's scatterplot command; SES and

Model Summary[c]

Model	R	R Square	R Square Change	F Change	df1	df2	Sig. F Change
			Change Statistics				
1	.531[a]	.282	.282	116.543	3	892	.000
2	.538[b]	.290	.008	10.366	1	891	.001

a. Predictors: (Constant), HW_CEN Homework out of school, centered, BYSES SOCIO-ECONOMIC STATUS COMPOSITE, BYTESTS Eighth grade achievement tests (mean)

b. Predictors: (Constant), HW_CEN Homework out of school, centered, BYSES SOCIO-ECONOMIC STATUS COMPOSITE, BYTESTS Eighth grade achievement tests (mean), HW_SQ Homework centered, squared

c. Dependent Variable: FFUGRAD ffu grades

Coefficients[a]

Model		Unstandardized Coefficients B	Std. Error	Standardized Coefficients Beta	t	Sig.	95% Confidence Interval for B Lower Bound	Upper Bound
1	(Constant)	2.115	.290		7.296	.000	1.546	2.683
	BYSES SOCIO-ECONOMIC STATUS COMPOSITE	.133	.062	.069	2.132	.033	.011	.255
	BYTESTS Eighth grade achievement tests (mean)	6.89E-02	.006	.407	12.421	.000	.058	.080
	HW_CEN Homework out of school, centered	.156	.026	.181	5.993	.000	.105	.207
2	(Constant)	2.258	.292		7.741	.000	1.686	2.831
	BYSES SOCIO-ECONOMIC STATUS COMPOSITE	.128	.062	.067	2.074	.038	.007	.250
	BYTESTS Eighth grade achievement tests (mean)	6.82E-02	.006	.403	12.359	.000	.057	.079
	HW_CEN Homework out of school, centered	.214	.031	.248	6.786	.000	.152	.275
	HW_SQ Homework centered, squared	-3.8E-02	.012	-.112	-3.220	.001	-.060	-.015

a. Dependent Variable: FFUGRAD ffu grades

FIGURE 8.10   Regression results testing for a curvilinear effect of Homework on GPA.

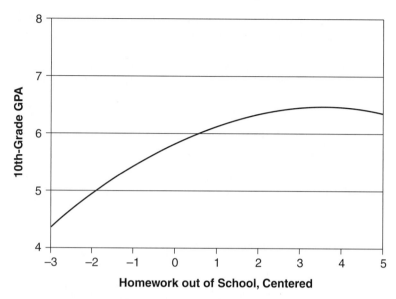

FIGURE 8.11   Plot of the curvilinear effect of Homework on 10th-grade GPA, using the centered Homework variable.

Previous Achievement are not controlled in this graph). Our findings are consistent with previous research, and it appears our speculation was correct: for lower levels of home-work, grades improve fairly quickly for each unit increase in homework, but these increases quickly flatten out; so for students already completing substantial amounts of homework, a unit increase in homework has little or no effect on GPA. This initial graph uses the centered homework variable, but the regression line using the uncentered data is shown in Figure 8.12. Note that the two graphs are essentially the same, with the only difference being the scale of the X-axis.

Note the shape of the regression line: primarily upward, with a convex shape. This shape is also revealed by the regression coefficients in the bottom half of the table of coefficients in Figure 8.10. The *positive* coefficient for HW_Cen suggests the general upward trend of the regression line, whereas the negative coefficient for the curve component (HW_Sq) suggests the gradually flattening, convex shape. In contrast, a negative coefficient for the independent variable suggests a generally downward trend to the regression line, and a positive coefficient for the squared independent variable suggests a concave shape. These relations between regression coefficients and the regression line are summarized in Table 8.1. Given this description, what do you think the coefficients associated with Figure 8.7 might be? The coefficient for Anxiety would be zero, and the coefficient for anxiety squared would be negative.

Controlling for Other Variables.   In the multiple regression, we controlled for SES and Previous Achievement when examining the linear and curvilinear effect of homework on GPA, but SES and Previous Achievement were not considered in the graphs. It is also possible to take

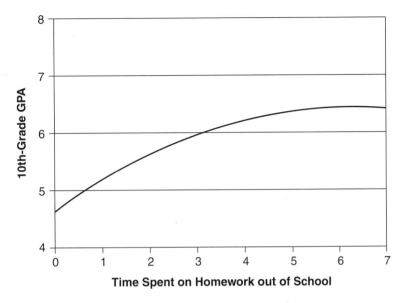

FIGURE 8.12   Another plot of the curvilinear effect of Homework on 10th-grade GPA, using the original Homework variable.

SES and Previous Achievement into account in these graphs. Recall in our discussion of residuals we found that residuals could be considered as the dependent variable with the effects of the independent variables removed. In the present case we are interested in plotting the effects of homework on GPA, with the effects of Previous Achievement and SES removed from GPA. Thus, we can easily regress GPA on SES and Previous Achievement, saving the residuals, which now represent GPA with SES and Previous Achievement taken into account. Figure 8.13 shows the curvilinear regression line for GPA, with SES and Previous Achievement removed, on Homework. The variable now labeled 10th-Grade GPA (SES, Ach removed) is, in turn, the saved residuals from the regression of GPA on SES and Previous Achievement.

TABLE 8.1   Relation between Regression Coefficients in a Curvilinear Regression and the Trend and Shape of the Regression Line

COEFFICIENT ASSOCIATED WITH:	WHAT IT DESCRIBES	IS THE VALUE:	
		Positive	*Negative*
Unsquared variable	Trend of the regression line	Upward trend	Downward trend
Squared variable (curve component)	Shape of the regression line	Concave shape	Convex shape

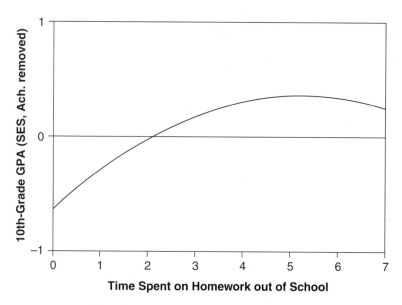

FIGURE 8.13   Plot of the curvilinear effect of Homework on 10th-grade GPA; SES and Previous Achievement are also controlled.

Testing Additional Curves.   Is it possible to have more than one curve in the regression line? Yes; for example, consider the possible effects of student employment during the school year on achievement. It may be that working a few hours a week is actually beneficial to student achievement, but that as students work beyond these few hours, their achievement suffers (this describes one curve in the regression line). Beyond a certain number of hours, however, additional hours may have no effect, and therefore the line would flatten out (where the slope changes from negative to flat describes another curve). Figure 8.14 illustrates such a possibility (cf. Quirk, Keith, & Quirk, 2001).

To test for additional curves, we simply test additional powers of the independent variable. To test for one curve in the regression line, we add the centered independent variable squared (a quadratic term) to the regression equation. To test for two curves, we additionally add a cubed version of the centered independent variable to the equation; to test for three curves, we add the independent variable to the fourth power, and so on. Figure 8.15 shows some of the results from the regression of GPA on the control variables, Homework, Homework squared, and Homework cubed. As shown, the cubic term entered at the third step was not statistically significant. There is only one curve in the regression line, and the shape of the regression line was adequately graphed in previous figures. It may be worthwhile to test such higher-order terms until statistical nonsignificance is found.

There are other methods of transforming data beyond the power transformations (X-squared, X-cubed, etc.) discussed in this chapter. For example, logarithmic transformations are possible, as are square root transformations. According to Cohen and colleagues (2003, p. 221), one major reason for such transformations is to simplify the relation between the predictor and outcome variables. For example, it is common to use a logarithmic transformation of income in regression rather than income, per se. Other reasons

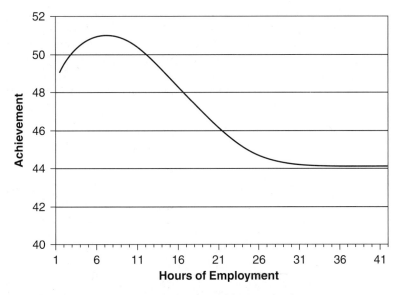

FIGURE 8.14   Graph of a regression line with two curves. These curves can be tested by adding variables representing Employment-squared and Emploment-cubed to the regression equation.

Model Summary

Model	R	R Square	Change Statistics				
			R Square Change	F Change	df1	df2	Sig. F Change
1	.531[a]	.282	.282	116.543	3	892	.000
2	.538[b]	.290	.008	10.366	1	891	.001
3	.539[c]	.290	.000	.364	1	890	.547

a. Predictors: (Constant), HW_CEN Homework out of school, centered, BYSES SOCIO-ECONOMIC STATUS COMPOSITE, BYTESTS Eighth grade achievement tests (mean)

b. Predictors: (Constant), HW_CEN Homework out of school, centered, BYSES SOCIO-ECONOMIC STATUS COMPOSITE, BYTESTS Eighth grade achievement tests (mean), HW_SQ Homework centered, squared

c. Predictors: (Constant), HW_CEN Homework out of school, centered, BYSES SOCIO-ECONOMIC STATUS COMPOSITE, BYTESTS Eighth grade achievement tests (mean), HW_SQ Homework centered, squared, HW_CUBE Homework centered, cubed

FIGURE 8.15   Testing for two curves in the regression equation.

involve dealing with threats to regression assumptions: homoscedasticity and normal distributions of residuals (these topics are discussed in Chapter 9). Finally, for complex nonlinear models, there is the method of nonlinear regression that can go well beyond the simple modeling of curves in a regression line that we are able to accomplish with ordinary multiple regression.

As with interactions in multiple regression, curves in regression lines are relatively rare, especially regression lines with more than one curve. As with interactions, it may be that curvilinear effects are rare or that straight lines are simply reasonably good approximations in most cases. It is also the case, however, that these tests are less often statistically significant because of their lower power. In addition, unusual data points can sometimes trick you into thinking you have a curve in your regression line. You should always inspect your data for such anomalies. These outliers will be discussed in more detail in Chapter 9.

SUMMARY

This chapter extended our discussion of testing for interaction in multiple regression to interactions involving continuous variables. Simulating data from published research, we regressed Achievement on Ability, time spent in leisure TV viewing, and a cross product of TV and Ability to determine whether TV viewing interacts with Ability in its effect on Achievement. The findings indeed suggested the presence of an interaction. We discussed several methods for exploring the nature of such interactions. First, we divided the Ability variable into three categories and graphed regression lines of Achievement on TV viewing for these three levels of Ability. Second, we plotted mean levels of Achievement by each level of TV and Ability. Third, we used the overall regression equation and substituted values representing low, medium, and high ability (–1 *SD,* the mean, and +1 *SD*) into the equation to generate three regression equations. These three equations were also plotted to explore the nature of the interaction. These methods should help you understand and describe the nature of any interaction that you do find.

We introduced regression lines including curves in this chapter, as well, and conceptualized such curve components as an interaction of a variable with itself in its influence on some outcome. Returning to an earlier example, we showed that Homework may, in fact, have a curvilinear effect on GPA, such that each additional hour spent on homework has a smaller effect on GPA than did the previous hour. We uncovered this curvilinear effect by adding a Homework-squared variable to the regression equation and testing its statistical significance. Higher-order terms (e.g., Homework cubed) could be added to test for additional curves in the regression line. Again, graphs were used to understand the nature of the curvilinear effect.

E X E R C I S E S

1. If you have not done so already, conduct the multiple regression testing the interaction of TV and Ability on Achievement conducted earlier in this chapter. Compare your results to mine. Make sure you are able to correctly center the variables and create the interaction term. Try the different methods for graphing the interaction. The data are on the Web site (www .ablongman.com/keith1e) ("tv ability interact2.sav," "tvability interact2.xls," and "tv_abil.txt").

2. Conduct a similar analysis using the NELS data. Try using F1S45A as the measure of time spent watching TV and a mean of the 10th-grade test scores (F1TxRStd, F1TxMStd, F1TxSStd, F1TxHStd) as the outcome. Because NELS did not include measures of ability,

test the interaction of TV and Previous Achievement (ByTests). Also control for base year SES (BySES). Is the interaction statistically significant? Graph the interaction (or the lack of an interaction). How do you account for the differences between these findings and those from Exercise 1?

3. Conduct the multiple regression testing the curvilinear effect of Homework on Grades conducted earlier in this chapter. Compare your results to mine. Make sure you are able to correctly center the variables and create the Homework squared term. Graph the curved regression line.

4. Does TV viewing have a curvilinear effect on Grades? Spend a few minutes thinking about this question. If you believe TV viewing has such an effect, what do you think will be the shape of the regression line: negative and concave; negative and convex? Use NELS to test this question. Use F1S45A as a measure of TV viewing and FFUGrad as a measure of 10th-grade GPA. Also control for SES and Previous Achievement (BySES and ByTests).

5. Use a literature research database to find an article in an area of interest to you with the word *mediation* in either the title or the abstract. Read the abstract to make sure the term mediation refers to statistical mediation (rather than, say, legal mediation). Read the article. Do the authors also refer to mediation as an indirect effect? How do they test for mediation? Do they use steps similar to those described in this chapter, or do they use structural equation modeling? Do you understand the test that was used?

6. Search for an article in your area of interest with the words *moderation* or *moderated regression* in the title or abstract. Read the abstract to make sure regression was used. Read the article. Is moderation also referred to as an interaction? Which variables interact? Were they continuous or categorical? Did the authors use techniques like those described in Chapter 7 and this chapter? Were the variables of interest centered prior to creating a cross product? Was the article understandable in light of this chapter and Chapter 7?

N O T E

1. Technically, because there are additional independent variables, we are not testing for a curve in a line, but rather a curve in a regression plane.

CHAPTER NINE

MULTIPLE REGRESSION: SUMMARY, FURTHER STUDY, AND PROBLEMS

You should now have a reasonably complete, conceptual understanding of the basics of multiple regression analysis. This chapter will begin by summarizing the topics covered in Part 1. I will touch on some issues that you should investigate and understand more completely to become a sophisticated user of MR and will close the chapter with some nagging problems and inconsistencies that we have discussed off and on throughout Part 1 (and will try to resolve in Part 2).

SUMMARY

"Standard" Multiple Regression

For social scientists raised on statistical analyses appropriate for the analysis of experiments (ANOVA and its variations), multiple regression often seems like a different animal altogether. It is not. MR provides a close implementation of the general linear model, of which ANOVA is a part. In fact, MR subsumes ANOVA, and as shown in several places in this portion of the book, we can easily analyze experiments (ANOVA-type problems) using

MR. The reverse is not the case, however, because MR can handle both categorical and continuous independent variables, whereas ANOVA requires categorical independent variables. Those with such an experimental background may need to change their thinking about the nature of their analyses, but the underlying statistics are not fundamentally different. In my experience, this transition to MR tends to be more difficult for those with a background in psychology or education; in other social sciences, such as sociology and political science, experimentation (i.e., random assignment to treatment groups) is less common.

In early chapters we covered how to calculate the fundamental statistics associated with multiple regression. More practically, we discussed how to conduct, understand, and interpret MR using statistical analysis programs. R is the multiple correlation coefficient, and R^2 the squared multiple correlation. R^2 is an estimate of the variance explained in the dependent variable by all the multiple independent variables in combination; an R^2 of .2 means that the independent variables jointly explain 20% of the variance in the dependent variable. In applied social science research, R^2's are often less than .5 (50% of the variance explained), unless some sort of pretest is included as a predictor of some posttest outcome, and R^2's of .10 are not uncommon. A high R^2 does not necessarily mean a good model; it depends on the dependent variable to be explained. R^2 may be tested for statistical significance by comparing the variance explained (regression) to the variance unexplained (residual) using an F table, with degrees of freedom equal to the number of independent variables (k) and the sample size minus this number, minus 1 ($N - k - 1$).

R^2 provides information about the regression as a whole. The MR also produces information about each independent variable alone, controlling for the other variables in the model. The unstandardized regression coefficients, generally symbolized as b (or sometimes as B), are in the original metric of the variables used, and the b can provide an estimate of the likely change in the dependent variable for each 1-unit change in the independent variable (controlling for the other variables in the regression). For example, Salary, in thousands of dollars a year, may be regressed on Educational Attainment, in years, along with several other variables. If the b associated with Educational Attainment is 3.5, this means that for each additional year of schooling salary would increase, on average, by 3.5 thousand dollars per year. The b is equal to the slope of the regression line. The b's may also be tested for statistical significance using a simple t test $\left(t = \dfrac{b}{SE_b} \right)$, with the df equal to the df residual for the overall F test. This t simply tests whether the regression coefficient is statistically significantly different from zero. More interestingly, it is also possible to determine whether the b differs from values other than zero, either using a modification of the t test or by calculating the 95% (or 90%, or some other level) confidence interval around the b's. Suppose, for example, that previous research suggests that the effect of Educational Attainment on Salary is 5.8. If the 95% CI around our present estimate is 2.6 to 4.4, this means that our present estimate is statistically significantly lower than are estimates from previous research. The use of confidence intervals is increasingly required by journals (see, for example, American Psychological Association, 2001).

We can also examine the standardized regression coefficients associated with each independent variable, generally symbolized as β. β's are in standard deviation units, thus allowing the comparison of coefficients that have different scales. A β of .30 for the effect of Educational Attainment on Salary would be interpreted as meaning that each standard deviation increase in Educational Attainment should result in a .30 *SD* average increase in Salary.

The standardized and unstandardized regression coefficients serve different purposes and have different advantages. Unstandardized coefficients are useful when the scales of the independent and dependent variables are meaningful, when comparing results across samples and studies, and when we wish to develop policy implications or interventions from our research. Standardized coefficients are useful when the scales of the variables used in the regression are not meaningful or when we wish to compare the relative importance of variables in the same regression equation.

The regression analysis also produces an intercept or constant. The intercept represents the predicted score on the dependent variable when all the independent variables have a value of zero. The regression coefficients and the intercept can be combined into a regression equation (e.g., $Y_{predicted} = \text{intercept} + b_1 X_1 + b_2 X_2 + b_3 X_3$), which can be used to predict someone's score on the outcome from the independent variables.

The regression equation, in essence, creates an optimally weighted composite of the independent variables to predict the outcome variable. This composite is weighted so as to maximize the prediction and minimize the errors of prediction. We can graph this prediction by plotting the outcome (*Y*-axis) against the predicted outcome (*X*-axis). The spread of data points around the regression line illustrates the accuracy of prediction and the errors of prediction. Errors of prediction are also known as residuals and may be calculated as outcome scores minus predicted outcome scores. The residuals may also be considered as the outcome variable with the effects of the independent variables statistically removed.

Explanation and Prediction

MR may serve a variety of purposes, but these generally fall under one of two broad categories: prediction or explanation. If our primary interest is in explanation, then we are interested in using MR to estimate the effects or influences of the independent variables on the dependent variable. Underlying this purpose, whether we admit it or not, is an interest in cause and effect. To estimate such effects validly, we need to choose carefully the variables included in the regression equation; it is particularly important that we include any common causes of our presumed cause and presumed effect. An understanding of relevant theory and previous research can help one choose variables wisely. Throughout this text, I have assumed that in most instances we are interested in using MR in the service of explanation, and most of the examples have had an explanatory focus.

In contrast, MR may also be used for the general purpose of prediction. If prediction is our goal, we are not necessarily interested in making statements about the effect of one variable on another; rather, we only want to be as accurate as possible in predicting some outcome. A predictive purpose is often related to selection; a college may be interested in predicting students' first-year GPAs as an aid in determining which students should be admitted. If prediction is the goal, the larger the R^2 the better. One does not need to worry about common causes, or even cause and effect, if one's interest is in prediction, and thus variable selection for prediction is less critical. It may even be perfectly acceptable to have an "effect" predicting a "cause" if prediction is the goal. Theory and previous research can certainly help you choose the variables that will predict your outcome successfully, but they are not critical to the interpretation of your findings as they are when MR is used for explanation. If your interest is in prediction, however, you must refrain from making statements or coming to conclusions about the effects of one variable on another (an explanatory purpose). It is unfortunately common to see research in which the purpose is supposedly prediction, but then when you read the discussion you find explanatory (causal) conclusions are being made. Any time you wish to use MR to make recommendations for intervention or change (if we increase X, Y will increase), your primary interest is in explanation, not prediction. Explanation subsumes prediction. If you can explain a phenomenon well, then you can generally predict it well. The reverse does not hold, however; being able to predict something does not mean you can explain it.

Three Types of Multiple Regression

There are several types, or varieties, of multiple regression. The type of MR used in the earlier chapters of this book is generally referred to as simultaneous, or forced entry, or standard multiple regression. In *simultaneous regression,* all independent variables are entered into the regression equation at the same time. The regression coefficients and their statistical significance are used to make inferences about the importance and relative importance of each variable. Simultaneous regression is useful for explanation or prediction. When used in an explanatory context, the regression coefficients from simultaneous regression provide estimates of the direct effects of each independent variable on the outcome (taking the other independent variables into account); this is one of this method's major advantages. Its chief disadvantage is that the regression coefficients may change depending on which variables are included in the regression equation; this disadvantage is related to the exclusion of relevant common causes or the presence of intervening or mediating variables.

In sequential, or hierarchical, regression, each variable [or group (block) of variables] is entered separately into the regression equation, in steps, in an order determined by the researcher. With *sequential regression,* we generally focus on ΔR^2 from each step to judge the statistical significance of each independent variable. ΔR^2 is a stingy and misleading estimate of the *importance* of variables, however; the square root of ΔR^2 provides a better estimate of the importance of each variable (*given* the order of entry). Order of entry is critical with sequential regression, because variables entered early in the sequential regression will appear, other things being equal, more important than variables entered later. Time precedence and presumed causal ordering are common methods for deciding the order of entry. The regression coefficients for each variable from the step in which it enters a sequential regression may be interpreted as the *total* effect of the variable on the outcome, including any indirect or mediating effects through variables entered later in the regression. To interpret sequential regression results in this fashion, variables must be entered in their correct causal order. Causal, or path, models are useful for both sequential and simultaneous regression and will be explored in more depth in Part 2. Sequential regression may be used for explanation or prediction. An advantage is that it can provide estimates of the total effects of one variable on another, given the correct order of entry. A chief disadvantage is that the apparent importance of variables changes depending on the order in which they are entered in the sequential regression equation.

Simultaneous and sequential regression may be combined in various ways. One combination is a method sometimes referred to as *sequential unique regression.* It is commonly used to determine the "unique" variance accounted for by a variable or a group of variables, after other relevant variables are accounted for. In this method, the other variables are entered in a simultaneous block, and a variable or variables of interest are entered sequentially in a second block. If a single variable is of interest, simultaneous regression may be used for the same purpose; if the interest is in the variance accounted for by a block of variables, this combination of simultaneous and sequential regression should be used. We made extensive use of this sort of combination of methods when we tested for interactions and curves in the regression line.

A final general method of multiple regression is stepwise regression and its variations. *Stepwise regression* operates in a similar fashion to sequential regression, except that the computer program, rather than the researcher, chooses the order of entry of the variables; it does so based on which variable will lead to the greatest single increment in ΔR^2 at each step. Although this solution seems a blessing—it avoids lots of hard thinking and potentially embarrassing statements about causal ordering—it is not. Using ΔR^2 or $\sqrt{\Delta R^2}$ as a measure of the importance of variables is predicated on the assumption that the variables have been entered in the regression equation in the proper order. To also use ΔR^2 to determine the order of entry thus requires circular reasoning. For this reason, stepwise methods should be used only for prediction, not explanation. In the words of my friend Lee Wolfle, stepwise regression is "theoretical garbage" (1980, p. 206), meaning that its results will mislead rather than inform if you try to use it in explanatory research. And, in fact, stepwise regression may not be a particularly good choice even for prediction. If your interest is simply selecting a subset of variables for efficient prediction, stepwise regression may work (although I still wouldn't recommend it); large samples and cross-validation are recommended. Whatever method of MR you use, be sure you are clear on the primary purpose of your research and choose your regression method to fulfill that purpose.

Categorical Variables in MR

It is relatively easy to analyze categorical, or nominal, variables in multiple regression. One of the easiest ways is to convert the categorical variable into one or more *dummy variables.* With dummy variables, a person is assigned a score of 1 or 0, depending on whether the person is a member of a group or not a member. For example, the categorical variable sex can be coded so that males are scored 0 and females 1, essentially turning it into a "female" variable on which those who are members of the group (females) receive a score of 1 and those who are not members (males) receive a score of 0. For more complex categorical variables, multiple dummy codes are required. We need to create as many dummy variables as there are categories, minus 1 ($g - 1$). When a categorical variable has more than two categories, thus requiring more than one dummy variable, one group will be scored 0 on all the dummies; this is essentially the reference group, or often the control group. When dummy variables are analyzed in MR, the intercept is equal to the mean score on the dependent variable for the reference group, and the b's are equal to the mean deviations from that group for each of the other groups.

We demonstrated that MR results match those of ANOVA when the independent variables are all categorical: the F from the two procedures is the same, and the effect size η^2 from ANOVA is equal to the R^2 from MR. The coefficients from MR may be used to perform various post hoc procedures. There are other methods besides dummy coding for coding categorical variables for analysis in MR; we illustrated effect coding and criterion scaling. The different methods will provide the same overall results, but different contrasts from the regression coefficients.

Categorical and Continuous Variables, Interactions, and Curves

Our primary interest in discussing the analysis of categorical variables in MR was as preparation for combining categorical and continuous variables together in MR analyses. Analyses including both categorical and continuous variables are conceptually and analytically little different from those including only continuous variables. It is also possible to test for interactions between categorical and continuous variables. To do so, we centered the continuous variable and created a new variable that was the cross product of the dummy variable and the centered continuous variable. If there are multiple dummy variables, then there will also be multiple cross products. These cross products are then entered as the second, sequential step in a regression following the simultaneous regression with all other independent variables (including the categorical and continuous variables used to create the cross products). The statistical significance of the ΔR^2 associated with the cross products is the test of the statistical significance of the interaction. With multiple dummy variables, and thus multiple cross products, the ΔR^2 associated with the *block* of cross products is used to determine the statistical significance of the interaction.

Given the presence of a statistically significant interaction, the next step is to graph the interaction to provide an understanding of its nature, perhaps followed by separate regressions across the values of the categorical variable or other post hoc probing. Tests of predictive bias and attribute–treatment interactions are specific examples of analyses that should use this MR approach. ANCOVA can also be considered as MR with categorical and continuous variables, but researchers using MR can also test for possible interactions between the covariate and the treatment.

It is equally possible to test for interactions between two continuous variables in MR. The same basic procedure is used: the continuous variables are centered and multiplied, and this cross product is entered sequentially in a regression equation. Follow-up of this type of interaction may be a little more difficult, but the first step again is generally to graph the interaction. Several methods were discussed for graphing and exploring interactions between continuous variables. All types of interactions are often well described using the phrase "it depends."

A special type of interaction between continuous variables is when a variable interacts with itself, meaning that its effects depend on the *level* of the variable. For example, we found that the effect of homework depends on the amount of homework being discussed; homework has a stronger effect on achievement for fewer hours of homework than for higher levels of homework. This type of interaction shows up as curves in the regression line. We test for curves in the regression line by multiplying a variable times itself and then entering this squared variable last in a combined simultaneous–sequential regression. We can test for more than one curve by entering additional product terms (variable-cubed, to the fourth power, etc.). Again, graphs were recommended as a method for understanding the nature of these curvilinear effects.

ASSUMPTIONS AND REGRESSION DIAGNOSTICS

We have postponed discussion of several important topics until you had a more complete understanding of multiple regression and how to conduct and interpret results of multiple regression analyses. Now it is time to discuss assumptions underlying our multiple regressions, as well as how to diagnose various problems that can affect regression analyses and what to do about these problems. References are given to sources that provide more detail about these topics.

Assumptions Underlying Regression

What assumptions underlie our use of multiple regression? If we are to be able to trust our MR results and interpret the regression coefficients, we should be able to assume the following:

1. The dependent variable is a linear function of the independent variables.
2. Each person (or other observation) should be drawn independently from the population. Recall one general form of the regression equation: $Y = a + bX_1 + bX_2 + e$. This assumption means that the errors (e's) for each person are independent from those of others.
3. The variance of the errors is not a function of any of the independent variables. The dispersion of values around the regression line should remain fairly constant for all values of X. This assumption is referred to as homoscedasticity.
4. The errors are normally distributed.

The first assumption (linearity) is the most important. If it is violated, then all of the estimates we get from regression—R^2, the regression coefficients, standard errors, tests of statistical significance—may be biased. To say the estimates are biased means that they will likely not reproduce the true population values. When assumptions 2, 3, and 4 are violated, regression coefficients are unbiased, but standard errors, and thus significance tests, will not be accurate. In other words, violation of assumption 1 threatens the meaning of the parameters we estimate, whereas violation of the other assumptions threatens interpretations from these parameters (Darlington, 1990, p. 110). Assumptions 3 and 4 are less critical, because regression is fairly robust to their violation (Kline, 1998). The violation of assumption 4 is only serious with small samples. We have already discussed methods of dealing with one form of nonlinearity (curvilinearity) and will discuss here and later methods for detecting and dealing with violations of the other assumptions.

In addition to these basic assumptions, to interpret regression coefficients as the *effects* of the independent variables on the dependent variable, we need to be able to assume that the errors are uncorrelated with the independent variables. This assumption further implies the following:

5. The dependent variable does not influence any of the independent variables. In other words, the variables we think of as causes must in fact be the causes, and those that we think of as the effects must be the effects.
6. The independent variables are measured without error, with perfect reliability and validity.
7. The regression must include all common causes of the presumed cause and the presumed effect.

We have already discussed assumptions 5 and 7 and will continue to develop them further in Part 2. Assumption 6 is a concern, because in the social sciences we rarely have perfect measurement. Again, we will discuss the implications of violation of this assumption in Part 2. There are a number of very readable, more detailed explanations of these seven assumptions. Allison (1999), Berry (1993), and Cohen and colleagues (2003) are particularly useful.

Regression Diagnostics

Here and in earlier chapters I noted that a good habit in any data analysis is to examine the data to make sure the values are plausible and reasonable. Regression diagnostics take this examination to another level and can be used to probe violations of assumptions and spot impossible or improbable values and other problems with data. In this section I will briefly describe regression diagnostics, illustrate their use for the data from previous chapters, and discuss what to do with regression diagnostic results. I will emphasize a graphic approach.

Diagnosing Violations of Assumptions.

Nonlinearity.   In Chapter 8, we examined how to deal with nonlinear data by adding powers of the independent variable to the regression equation. In essence, by adding both Homework and Homework^2 to the regression equation, we turned the nonlinear portion of the regression line into a linear one and were thus able to model the curve effectively using MR.

This approach thus hints at one method for determining whether we have violated the assumption of linearity: If you have a substantive reason to suspect that an independent variable may be related to the outcome in a curvilinear fashion, add a curve component (variable^2) to the regression equation to see whether this increases the explained variance.

The potential drawback to this approach is that the curve modeled by variable^2 may not adequately account for the departure from linearity. Therefore, it is useful to supplement this approach with a more in depth examination of the data using scatterplots. Rather than plotting the dependent variable of interest against the independent variable, however, we will plot the *residuals* against the independent variables; the residuals should magnify departures from linearity. Recall that the residuals represent the predicted values of the dependent variable minus the actual values of the dependent variable ($Y' - Y$). They are the errors in prediction.

To illustrate, we will use the example from Chapter 8 that was used to illustrate testing for curves in MR: the regression of Grades on SES, previous Achievement, and time spent on Homework out of school. The addition of a Homework^2 variable was statistically significant, indicating (and correcting) a departure from linearity in the regression. Let's see if we can pick up this nonlinearity using scatterplots.

I reran the initial regression (without the Homework^2 variable and using the original uncentered metric) and saved the residuals (regression programs generally allow you to save unstandardized residuals as an option). Figure 9.1 shows the plot of the residuals against the original variable Homework. Note the two lines in the graph. The straight, horizontal line is the mean of the residuals. The line should also represent the regression line of the residuals on Homework. That line would be horizontal because the residuals represent Grades with the effects of Homework (and the other independent variables) *removed*. Because Homework has been removed, it is no longer related to the residuals. Recall that when two variables are unrelated our best prediction for Y is its mean for all values of X. The regression line is thus equal to the line drawn through the mean of the residuals. The other, almost straight line is what is called a *lowess* (or *loess*) fit line, which represents the *nonparametric* best fitting line, one that does not impose the requirement of linearity. Most computer programs can easily add this line to a regression scatterplot.

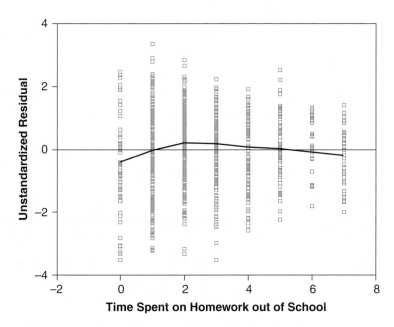

FIGURE 9.1   Plot of the unstandardized residuals against one independent variable (Homework). The lowess line is fairly straight.

If there is no departure from linearity in the data, we would expect the lowess line to come close to the regression line; Cohen and colleagues note that the lowess line should look like "a young child's freehand drawing of a straight line" (2003, p. 111). With a significant departure from linearity, you would expect the lowess line to be curved, something more similar to the curvilinear regression lines shown in Chapter 8 (e.g., Figure 8.13), but without the upward slope. The lowess line in this plot indeed approaches the straight regression line. Figure 9.2 shows another useful plot: the residuals and the predicted values for the Grades dependent variable. Recall in Chapter 3 that we demonstrated that the predicted Y is an optimally weighted composite of the independent variables. It is, then, a variable that represents

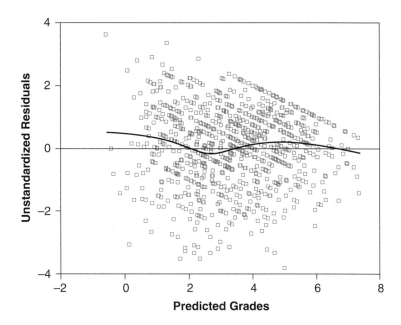

FIGURE 9.2   Plot of unstandardized residuals against the predicted Grades (a composite of the independent variables).

all independent variables in combination. Again, the lowess line comes close to the regression line and does not suggest a departure from linearity.

In this example, the test of the addition of a curve component (Chapter 8) was more successful in spotting a departure from linearity than was the inspection of data through scatterplots. This will not always be the case, and thus I recommend that you use both methods if you suspect a violation of this assumption. If theory or inspection suggests a departure from linearity, a primary method of correction is to build nonlinear terms into the regression (e.g., powers, logarithms). The method is discussed in Chapter 8; see also Cohen and colleagues (2003) and Darlington (1990) for more depth.

Nonindependence of Errors.   When data are not drawn independently from the population, we risk violating the assumption that errors (residuals) will be independent. As noted in the section on Hierarchical Linear Modeling later in this chapter, the NELS data, with students clustered within schools, risks violation of this assumption. Violation of this assumption does not affect regression coefficients, but does affect standard errors. When clustered as described, we risk underestimating standard errors and thus labeling variables as statistically significant when they are not. This danger is obviated, to some degree, with large samples like the NELS data used here, especially when we are more concerned with the magnitude of effects than with statistical significance.

Are the residuals from the regression of Grades on SES, Previous Achievement, and Homework nonindependent? Is there substantial variation within schools? Unfortunately, this assumption is difficult to test with the NELS data included on the Web site because, with the subsample of 1000 cases, few of the schools had more than one or two students.

Therefore, I used the original NELS data and selected out 414 cases from 13 schools. I conducted a similar regression analysis (Grades on SES, Previous Achievement, and Homework) and saved the residuals.

One way to probe for the violation of this assumption is through a graphing technique called *boxplots.* The boxplots of residuals, clustered by schools, are shown in Figure 9.3. The center through the boxplot shows the median, with the box representing the middle 50% of cases (from the 25th to the 75th percentile). The extended lines show the high and low values, excluding outliers and extreme values. For the purpose of exploring the assumption of independence of errors, our interest is in the variability of the boxplots. There is some variability up and down by school, and thus this clustering may indeed be worth taking into account. Another, quantitative test of the independence of observations uses the intraclass correlation coefficient, which compares the between-group (in this case, between-schools) variance to the total variance (for an example, see Stapleton, in press). The intraclass correlation could be computed on the residuals or on a variable (e.g., Homework) that you suspect might vary across schools.

One option for dealing with a lack of independence of errors is to include categorical variables (e.g., using criterion scaling; see Chapter 6) that take the clustering variable into account. Another option is the use of hierarchical linear modeling, discussed briefly later in this chapter. This assumption can also be violated in longitudinal designs in which the same tests or scales are administered repeatedly. We will deal with this issue briefly in Part 2.

Homoscedasticity.   We assume that the variance of errors around the regression line is fairly consistent across levels of the independent variable. In other words, the residuals should spread out consistently across levels of *X*. Violation of this assumption affects standard errors and thus statistical significance (not the regression coefficients), and regression

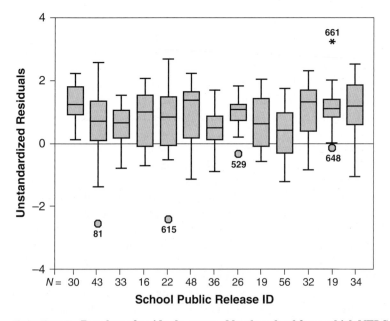

FIGURE 9.3   Boxplots of residuals, grouped by the school from which NELS students were sampled. The data are 414 cases from the full NELS data.

is fairly robust to its violation. Scatterplots of residuals with independent variables or predicted values are also helpful for examining this assumption.

Return to Figure 9.1, the scatterplot of Homework with the Residuals from the regression of Grades on SES, Previous Achievement, and Homework. Although the residuals are spread out more at lower levels of homework than at upper levels, the difference is slight; visual inspection suggests that heteroscedasticity (the opposite of homoscedasticity) is not a problem. A common pattern of heteroscedasticity is a fan shape with, for example, little variability at lower levels of Homework and large variability at higher levels of Homework. Butterfly shapes are also possible (residuals constricted around the middle level of Homework), as is the opposite shape (a bulge in the middle).

Focus again on Figure 9.2. Notice how the residuals bunch up at higher levels of the Predicted *Y;* the plot has something of a fan shape, narrowing at upper levels of the predicted values. Do these data violate the assumption of homoscedasticity? To test this possibility, I collapsed the predicted Grades into five equal categories so that we can compare the variance of the residuals at each of these five levels. The data are displayed in Figure 9.4 as

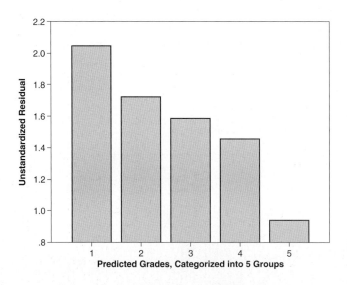

Report

RES_2 Unstandardized Residual

NPRE_2 predicted	Mean	N	Std. Deviation	Variance
1	.1813529	173	1.43089123	2.047
2	-.2252563	178	1.31232697	1.722
3	-.0820244	182	1.25877627	1.585
4	.0519313	182	1.20728288	1.458
5	.0784449	181	.96944000	.940
Total	.0000000	896	1.24815811	1.558

FIGURE 9.4   Comparison of the variance of residuals for different levels of predicted Grades.

both a bar chart and table. As shown in the table, for the lowest category of predicted values, the variance of the residuals was 2.047, versus .940 for the highest category. There is a difference, but it is not excessive. One rule of thumb is that a ratio of high to low variance of less than 10 is not problematic. Statistical tests are also possible (Cohen et al., 2003).

Normality of Residuals.   The final assumption we will deal with is that the errors, or residuals, are normally distributed. What we are saying with this assumption is that if we plot the values of the residuals they will approximate a normal curve. This assumption is fairly easily explored because most MR software has tools built in to allow such testing.

Figure 9.5 shows such a plot: a bar graph of the residuals from the NELS regression of Grades on SES, Previous Achievement, and Homework (this graph was produced as one of the plot options in regression in SPSS). The superimposed normal curve suggests that the residuals from this regression are indeed normal. Another, more exacting, method is what is known as a q–q plot (or, alternatively, a p–p plot) of the residuals. A q–q plot of the residuals shows the value of the residuals on one axis and the expected value (if they are normally distributed) of the residuals on the other. Figure 9.6 shows the q–q plot of the residuals from the Grades on SES, Previous Achievement, Homework regression. If the residuals are normally distributed, the thick line (expected versus actual residuals) should come close to the diagonal straight line. As can be seen from the graph, the residuals conform fairly well to the superimposed straight line. The reason this method is more exact is

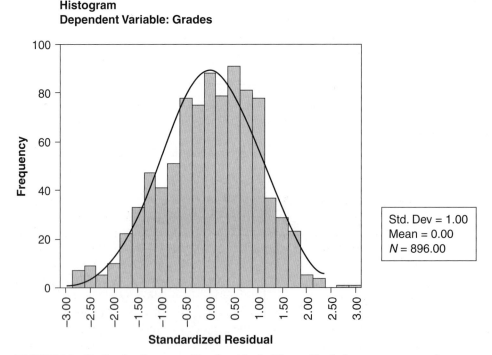

FIGURE 9.5   Testing for the normality of residuals. The residuals form a near normal curve.

that it is easier to spot a deviation from a straight line than a normal curve (Cohen et al., 2003). Some programs (e.g., SPSS) produce a p–p plot of the residuals as an option in multiple regression. A p–p plot uses the cumulative frequency and is interpreted in the same fashion (looking for departures from a straight line).

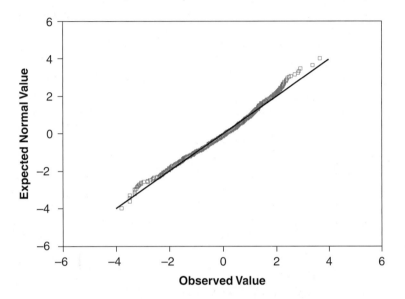

FIGURE 9.6   A q–q plot of the residuals. The residuals' adherence to a nearly straight line supports their normality.

Excessive heteroscedasticity and nonnormal residuals can sometimes be corrected through transformation of the dependent variable. Eliminating subgroups from the regression may also be useful. Finally, there are alternative regression methods (e.g., weighted least squares regression) that may be useful when these assumptions are seriously violated (see Cohen et al., 2003, and Darlington, 1990, for more information).

Diagnosing Data Problems.   Regression diagnostics for spotting problematic data points focus on three general characteristics: distance, leverage, and influence. Conceptually, how would you spot unusual or problematic cases, commonly referred to as outliers or as extreme cases? Focus on Figure 9.7, a reprint of the earlier Figure 3.7. The figure is a by-product of the regression of students' Grades on Parent Education and Homework. Recall that we saved the variable Predicted Grades, which I demonstrated was an optimally weighted composite of the two independent variables, weighted so as to best predict the outcome. The figure shows students' GPA plotted against their Predicted GPAs. Note the case circled in the lower right of the figure. This case is among the farthest from the regression line; this is one method of isolating an extreme case, called *distance. Leverage* refers to an unusual pattern on the independent variables and does not consider the dependent variable. If you were using homework in different academic areas to predict overall GPA, it would not be unusual to find a student who spent 1 hour per week on math homework nor would it be unusual to find a student who spent 8 hours per week on English homework. It would likely be unusual to find a student who combined these, who spent only 1 hour per week on math while spending 8 hours per week on English. This case would likely have high leverage. Because leverage is not calculated with respect to the dependent variable, the graph shown here may not be informative as to leverage; a graph of the two independent variables may be more useful (as we will soon see). The final characteristic of interest is *influence*. As the name implies, a case that has high influence is one that, if removed from the regression, results in a large change on the regression results. Cases with high influence are those that are high on both distance and leverage. The circled case would likely fit this description as well. If it were deleted from the regression, the regression line would likely be somewhat steeper than it is in the figure.

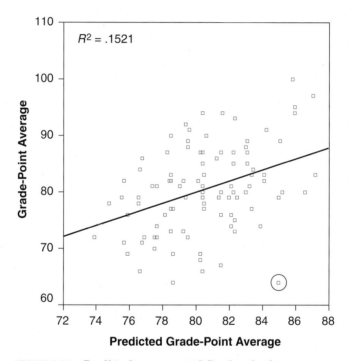

FIGURE 9.7   Predicted versus actual Grades plot from Chapter 3. The circled case is a potential extreme case, a long distance from the regression line.

Distance.   Common measures of distance are derived from the residuals. In Figure 9.7, the residual for the circled case is the point on the regression line above the case (approximately 85) minus the actual value of the case (64). This definition matches well the conceptual definition of distance given above.

In practice, the unstandardized residuals are less useful than are standardized versions of residuals. Table 9.1 shows some of the cases from this data set. The first column

TABLE 9.1 Regression Diagnostics for the Regression of Grades on Parent Education and Homework

					ZRE_1	SRE_1	SDR_1	COO_1	LEV_1	SDB0_1	SDB1_1	SDB2_1
											Standardized DF Beta	
CASENUM	GRADES	PARED	HWORK	PREDGRAD	Standardized residual	Studentized t residual	t resid, deleted	Cook	Leverage	intercept	pared	hwork
12.00	72.00	13.00	5.00	79.48435	−1.05539	−1.06231	−1.06302	0.00495	0.00299	−0.07044	0.05836	−0.01163
13.00	66.00	12.00	3.00	76.63804	−1.50010	−1.52071	−1.53122	0.02134	0.01693	−0.19095	0.12503	0.11783
14.00	79.00	14.00	4.00	79.36713	−0.05177	−0.05211	−0.05184	0.00001	0.00303	−0.00098	−0.00072	0.00287
15.00	76.00	10.00	4.00	75.88464	0.01627	0.01673	0.01664	0.00001	0.04405	0.00377	−0.00347	0.00009
16.00	80.00	20.00	6.00	86.56656	−0.92597	−0.98069	−0.98049	0.03901	0.09848	0.30209	−0.32258	0.04489
17.00	91.00	15.00	8.00	84.18914	0.96042	0.97535	0.97510	0.00994	0.02038	−0.04474	0.01145	0.13224
32.00	83.00	15.00	11.00	87.15267	−0.58558	−0.61536	−0.61338	0.01317	0.08446	0.03559	0.01979	−0.18448
33.00	78.00	13.00	6.00	80.47220	−0.34861	−0.35156	−0.34996	0.00070	0.00669	−0.02205	0.02422	−0.02180
34.00	64.00	17.00	7.00	84.94254	−2.95316	−3.00886	−3.14360	0.11492	0.02668	0.45737	−0.42923	−0.16864
35.00	82.00	13.00	4.00	78.49651	0.49404	0.49765	0.49571	0.00121	0.00448	0.03455	−0.02020	−0.01998
36.00	81.00	17.00	1.00	79.01546	0.27984	0.29462	0.29322	0.00313	0.08776	−0.03788	0.06746	−0.07800
37.00	73.00	13.00	4.00	78.49651	−0.77508	−0.78075	−0.77917	0.00298	0.00448	−0.05430	0.03175	0.03141
80.00	72.00	10.00	5.00	76.87248	−0.68708	−0.70760	−0.70576	0.01012	0.04714	−0.15793	0.15778	−0.04060
81.00	79.00	17.00	4.00	81.97900	−0.42008	−0.42961	−0.42780	0.00283	0.03391	0.05808	−0.07712	0.04376
82.00	93.00	14.00	7.00	82.33067	1.50451	1.51942	1.52989	0.01533	0.00954	0.01337	−0.04408	0.15087
83.00	100.00	18.00	7.00	85.81316	2.00052	2.05698	2.09249	0.08073	0.04414	−0.41586	0.40491	0.08101
84.00	90.00	13.00	4.00	78.49651	1.62214	1.63401	1.64841	0.01307	0.00448	0.11487	−0.06717	−0.06645
85.00	69.00	10.00	4.00	75.88464	−0.97082	−0.99817	−0.99815	0.01898	0.04405	−0.22643	0.20833	−0.00511

Data from Chapter 3.

shows the case number, followed by the dependent variable Grades and the two independent variables Parent Education and Homework. Column five shows the Predicted Grades
used to create the graph in Figure 9.7. The remaining columns show various regression
diagnostics. The first row of the table shows the names assigned these variables in SPSS,
under which I have included a brief explanation. Column six, labeled ZRE_1, shows the
standardized residuals, which are the residuals standardized to approximately a normal distribution. Think of them like z scores, with values ranging from 0 (very close to the regression line) to ± 3 or more. The next column (SRE_1) represents the standardized residuals
converted to a t distribution (the t distribution is also referred to as Student's t, hence the S),
which are generally called the studentized or t residuals. The advantage of this conversion
is that the t residuals may be tested for statistical significance (see Darlington, 1990,
p. 358). In practice, however, researchers often simply examine large positive or negative
standardized or studentized residuals or, with reasonable sample size, those greater than an
absolute value of 2 (with very large samples, there may be many of these).

The cases shown in Table 9.1 were chosen for display because they have high values
for distance, leverage, or influence. As shown in the table, cases 34 (–3.01) and 83 (2.06)
show high values for studentized residuals.

Figure 9.8 shows the same plot of Predicted and actual Grades, with a few of the cases
identified. Note the case that was originally circled is case number 34, the highest negative studentized (and standardized) residual. As can be seen, case 83, with a high positive standardized
residual, is also far away from the regression line. It might be worth investigating these cases
with high residuals further to make sure that they have been coded and entered correctly.

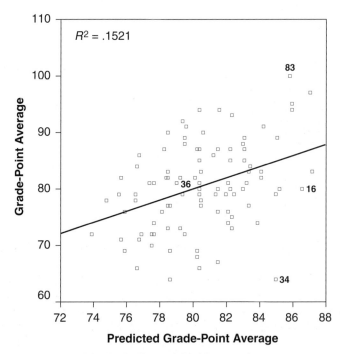

**FIGURE 9.8   Plot from Figure 9.7 with several
noteworthy cases highlighted.**

Leverage.   Leverage gets at the unusualness of a pattern of independent variables, without respect to the dependent variable. The column in Table 9.1 labeled LEV_1 provides an estimate of leverage (this measure is also often referred to as *h*). Leverage ranges from 0 to 1, with an average value of $(k + 1)/n$ (k = number of independent variables); twice this number has been suggested as a rule of thumb for high values of leverage (Pedhazur, 1997, p. 48). Case 16 in the table had the highest value for leverage (.098), followed by cases 36 (.088) and 32 (.084). All these values are higher than the rule of thumb would suggest:

$$2\left(\frac{k + 1}{N}\right) = 2\left(\frac{3}{100}\right) = .06.$$

As can be seen in Figure 9.8, you might suspect that case 16 was unusual from a visual display (because it is on one edge of the graph), but case 36 is right in the middle of the graph. Recall, however, that leverage does not depend on the dependent variable. Figure 9.9 shows a plot of the two independent variables. Cases 16, 36, and 32 are outside the "swarm" of most of the cases; they indeed represent an unusual combination of independent variables. These cases may also be worth checking.

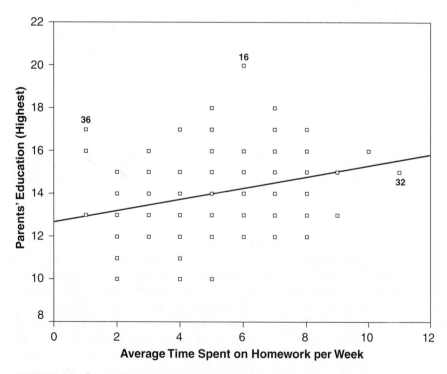

FIGURE 9.9   Leverage.

Influence.   Influence means what the name suggests: a case that is highly influential on the intercept or the regression line. The column labeled Coo_1 (for Cook's Distance) in Table 9.1 provides values of an estimate of influence; cases with large values are worth inspecting. The cases with the largest Cook's D values were cases 34 (.115) and 83 (.081). The regression plane would move the most if these cases were omitted.

Most computer programs also compute estimates of *partial* influence (as in influence, with the effects of the other independent variables accounted for). The DF Betas, standardized, listed in the last three columns are estimates of partial influence. The first of these columns (SDB0_1) pertains to the regression intercept, the second (SDB1_1) to the first independent variable (Parent Education), and the third (SDB2_1) to the second independent variable (Homework). The values shown are the change in each parameter, if a particular case were removed. A negative value means that the particular case lowered the value of the parameter, whereas a positive value means that the case raised the parameter. So, for example, case 34 had standardized DF Beta values of .457, –.429, and –.169. Case 34 served to raise the intercept and lower the regression coefficient for Parent Education and Homework. Although the unstandardized DF Betas are not shown in Table 9.1, they were 2.29, –.158, and –.058. If you run the regression without case 34, you will find that the intercept reduces by 2.29, the Parent Education *b* increases by .158, and the Homework *b* increases by .058.

An inspection of the standardized DF Betas showed large negative values by case 83 for the intercept (–.416) and large positive value for case 34 (.457). These two cases were also very influential for the Parent Education regression coefficient, although reversed: case 34 (–.429), case 83 (.405). The partial influence values for the Homework variable were considerably smaller. Cases 21 and 29 had the highest values (.334 and .335).

Uses.   What do these various regression diagnostics tell us? In the present example, cases 34 and 83 showed up across measures; it would certainly be worth inspecting them. But inspecting them for what? Sometimes these diagnostics can point out errors or misentered data. A simple slip of the finger may cause you to code 5 hours of homework as 50. This case will undoubtedly show up in the regression diagnostics, thus alerting you to the mistake. Of course, a simple careful inspection of the data will likely spot this case as well! Think about the example I used initially to illustrate leverage, however, someone who reports 1 hour of Math Homework and 8 hours of English Homework. This case will not show up in a simple inspection of the data, because these two values are reasonable, taken by themselves, and only become curious when taken together. The case will likely be spotted in an analysis of both leverage and influence; we might well discover that errors were made in entering this datum as well.

If there are not obvious errors for the variables spotted via regression diagnostics, then what? In our present example, cases 34 and 83, although outliers, are reasonable. A check of the raw data shows that case 34 had well-educated parents, higher than average homework, but poor grades. Case 83 simply had an excellent GPA and higher than average homework. On further investigation, I might discover that case 34 had a learning disability, and I might decide to delete this case and several other similar cases. Or I might decide that the variation is part of the phenomenon I am studying and leave case 34 in the analysis. Another option is additional analysis. If a number of outliers share characteristics in common and are systematically different from other cases, it may suggest that a different regression is needed for these participants or the advisability of including an interaction term in the analysis (e.g., Disability Status by Parent Education).

Obviously, unless clear-cut errors are involved, considerable judgment is involved in the inspection of regression diagnostics. Note that deletion of case 34 will increase the regression weight for Homework; if I did delete this case, I will need to be sure that my deletion is based on a concern about its extremity rather than a desire to inflate the apparent importance of my findings. If you do delete cases based on regression diagnostics, you should note this in the research write-up and the reasons for doing so. With the present example and after examining cases with high values on all the regression diagnostics, I would first double-check each of these values against the raw data, but would likely conclude in the end that all the cases simply represented normal variation. I would then leave the data in their present form.

Again, I have barely scratched the surface of an important topic; it is worth additional study. Darlington (1990, chap. 14), Fox (1997), and Pedhazur (1997) each devote chapters to regression diagnostics and are worth reading.

Multicollinearity.   I mentioned briefly when discussing interactions the potential problem of multicollinearity (also called collinearity). Briefly, multicollinearity occurs when several independent variables correlate at an excessively high level with one another or when one independent variable is a near linear combination of other independent variables. Multicollinearity can result in misleading and sometimes bizarre regression results.

Figure 9.10 shows some results of the regression of a variable named Outcome on two independent variables, Var1 and Var2. The correlations among the three variables are also shown. The results are not unusual and suggest that both variables have positive and statistically significant effects on Outcome.

Correlations

		OUTCOME	VAR1	VAR2
Pearson Correlation	OUTCOME	1.000	.300	.200
	VAR1	.300	1.000	.400
	VAR2	.200	.400	1.000
Sig. (1-tailed)	OUTCOME	.	.000	.000
	VAR1	.000	.	.000
	VAR2	.000	.000	.
N	OUTCOME	500	500	500
	VAR1	500	500	500
	VAR2	500	500	500

Coefficients[a]

Model		Unstandardized Coefficients		Standardized Coefficients			95% Confidence Interval for B		Collinearity Statistics	
		B	Std. Error	Beta	t	Sig.	Lower Bound	Upper Bound	Tolerance	VIF
1	(Constant)	64.286	5.133		12.524	.000	54.201	74.370		
	VAR1	.262	.046	.262	5.633	.000	.171	.353	.840	1.190
	VAR2	9.52E-02	.046	.095	2.048	.041	.004	.187	.840	1.190

a. Dependent Variable: OUTCOME

FIGURE 9.10   Regression of Outcome on Var1 and Var2. The results are reasonable.

Now focus on Figure 9.11. For this analysis, the two independent variables correlated at the same level with the dependent variable as in the previous example (.3 and .2). However, in this example, Var1 and Var2 correlate .9 with each other (versus .4 in the previous example). Notice the regression coefficients. Even though all variables correlate positively with one another, Var1 seems to have a positive effect on Outcome, whereas Var2 has a negative effect. As noted above, multicollinearity can produce strange results such as these; standardized regression coefficients greater than 1 are also common. Notice also that the standard errors of the *b*'s are also considerably larger for the second example than for the first. Multicollinearity also inflates standard errors; sometimes two variables will correlate at similar levels with an outcome, but one will be a statistically significant predictor of the outcome, while the other will not, as a result of multicollinearity.

Correlations

		OUTCOME	VAR1	VAR2
Pearson Correlation	OUTCOME	1.000	.300	.200
	VAR1	.300	1.000	.900
	VAR2	.200	.900	1.000
Sig. (1-tailed)	OUTCOME	.	.000	.000
	VAR1	.000	.	.000
	VAR2	.000	.000	.
N	OUTCOME	500	500	500
	VAR1	500	500	500
	VAR2	500	500	500

Coefficients[a]

Model		Unstandardized Coefficients		Standardized Coefficients	t	Sig.	95% Confidence Interval for B		Collinearity Statistics	
		B	Std. Error	Beta			Lower Bound	Upper Bound	Tolerance	VIF
1	(Constant)	73.684	4.373		16.848	.000	65.092	82.277		
	VAR1	.632	.097	.632	6.527	.000	.441	.822	.190	5.263
	VAR2	-.368	.097	-.368	-3.807	.000	-.559	-.178	.190	5.263

a. Dependent Variable: OUTCOME

FIGURE 9.11   Regression of Outcome on Var1 and Var2 when Var1 and Var2 are very highly correlated (collinear). The results are puzzling, and the interpretation will likely be misleading.

Conceptually, multicollinearity suggests that you are trying to use two variables in a prediction that overlap completely or almost completely with one another. Given this definition, it makes intuitive sense that multicollinearity should affect standard errors: the more that variables overlap, the less we can separate accurately the effects of one versus the other. Multicollinearity is often a result of a researcher including multiple measures of the same construct in a regression. If this is the case, one way to avoid the problem is to combine the overlapping variables in some way, either as a composite or, as is done in Part 2, using the variables as indicators of a latent variable. Multicollinearity is also often a problem when researchers use a kitchen-sink approach: throwing a bunch of predictors into regression and using stepwise regression, thinking it will sort out which are important and which are not.

Given the example, you may think you can spot multicollinearity easily by examining the zero-order correlations among the variables, with high correlations alerting you to potential problems. Yet multicollinearity can occur even when the correlations among variables are not excessive. A common example of such an occurrence is when a researcher, often inadvertently, uses both a composite and the components of this composite in the same regression. For example, in Figure 9.12 I regressed BYTests on grades in each academic area, in addition to a composite Grades variable (BYGrads). Notice the results: the overall R^2 is statistically significant, but none of the predictors is statistically significant.

Model Summary

Model	R	R Square	Adjusted R Square	Std. Error of the Estimate
1	.558[a]	.311	.307	7.10940

a. Predictors: (Constant), BYGRADS GRADES COMPOSITE, BYS81B math88-grades, BYS81A English88-grade, BYS81D sstudies88-grades, BYS81C science88-grades

ANOVA[b]

Model		Sum of Squares	df	Mean Square	F	Sig.
1	Regression	20119.51	5	4023.903	79.612	.000[a]
	Residual	44579.48	882	50.544		
	Total	64699.00	887			

a. Predictors: (Constant), BYGRADS GRADES COMPOSITE, BYS81B math88-grades, BYS81A English88-grade, BYS81D sstudies88-grades, BYS81C science88-grades

b. Dependent Variable: BYTESTS Eighth grade achievement tests (mean)

Coefficients[a]

Model		Unstandardized Coefficients		Standardized Coefficients			Collinearity Statistics	
		B	Std. Error	Beta	t	Sig.	Tolerance	VIF
1	(Constant)	33.123	5.370		6.168	.000		
	BYS81A English88-grade	8.19E-02	1.501	.009	.055	.956	.027	36.744
	BYS81B math88-grades	-.698	1.490	-.077	-.469	.639	.029	34.153
	BYS81C science88-grades	.767	1.499	.090	.511	.609	.025	39.871
	BYS81D sstudies88-grades	-.125	1.487	-.015	-.084	.933	.026	38.350
	BYGRADS GRADES COMPOSITE	6.241	6.008	.538	1.039	.299	.003	343.374

a. Dependent Variable: BYTESTS Eighth grade achievement tests (mean)

FIGURE 9.12   Another cause of multicollinearity. A composite and its components are both used in the regression.

How can you avoid the effects of multicollinearity? Computer programs provide, on request, collinearity diagnostics. Such statistics are shown in Figures 9.10 through 9.12. Tolerance is a measure of the degree to which each variable is independent of (does not overlap with) the other independent variables (Darlington, 1990). Tolerance can range from 0 (no independence from other variables) to 1 (complete independence); larger values are desired. The variance inflation factor (VIF) is the reciprocal of tolerance and is "an index of the amount that the variance of each regression coefficient is increased" over that with uncorrelated independent variables (Cohen et al., 2003, p. 423). Small values for tolerance and large values for VIF signal the presence of multicollinearity. Cohen and colleagues (2003, p. 423) note that a common rule of thumb for a large value of VIF is 10, which means that the standard errors of b are more than three times as large as with uncorrelated variables ($\sqrt{10} = 3.16$), but that this value is probably too high. Note that use of this value will lead to an inspection and questioning of the results in Figure 9.12, but not those in Figure 9.11. Values for the VIF of 6 or 7 may be more reasonable as flags for excessive multicollinearity (cf. Cohen et al., 2003). These values of the VIF correspond to tolerances of .10 (for a VIF of 10), .14 (VIF of 7), and .17 (VIF of 6), respectively.

Factor analysis of independent variables and "all subsets" regression can also be useful for diagnosing problems. When you get strange regression results, you should consider and investigate multicollinearity as a possible problem. Indeed, it is a good idea to routinely examine these statistics. A method known as ridge regression can be used when data are excessively collinear.

Obviously, I have just touched the surface of this important topic; it is worth additional study. Pedhazur (1997) presents a readable, more detailed discussion of the topic, as does Darlington (1990, chaps. 5, 8).

TOPICS FOR ADDITIONAL STUDY

Sample Size and Power

"How large a sample do I need?" Anyone who has advised others on the use of multiple regression (or any other statistical method) has heard this question more times than he or she can count. This question may mean several things. Some who ask it are really asking, "Is there some minimum sample size that I can't go below in MR?" Others are looking for a rule of thumb, and there is a common one: 10 to 20 participants for each independent variable. Using this rule, if your MR includes 5 independent variables, you need at least 50 (or 100) participants. I've heard this rule of thumb many times, but have no idea where it comes from. We will examine it shortly to see if it has any validity for the types of MR problems we have been studying. Finally, more sophisticated researchers will ask questions about what sample size they need to have a reasonable chance of finding statistical significance.

I hope you recognize this final version of the question as one of the *power* of MR. I have alluded to power at several points in this text (e.g., in the discussion of interactions in MR), but, as you will see, we have really sidestepped the issue until this point by our use of the NELS data. With a sample size of 1000, we had adequate power for all the analyses conducted. You can't always count on sample sizes in the thousands, however, so let us briefly turn to the issue of power and sample size.

Briefly, power generally refers to the ability correctly to reject a false null hypothesis. It is a function of the magnitude of the effect (e.g., whether Homework has a small or a large effect on Grades); the alpha, or probability level chosen for statistical significance (e.g., .05, .01, or some other level); and the sample size used in the research. Likewise, the necessary sample size depends on effect size, chosen alpha, and desired power. The needed sample size increases as desired power increases, effect size decreases, and alpha gets more stringent (i.e., as the probability chosen gets smaller). Common values for power are .8 or .9, meaning that given a particular effect size one would like to have an 80% or 90% chance of rejecting a false null hypothesis of no effect. Like alpha, and despite conventions, power levels should be chosen based on the needs of a particular study.

This short section is, of course, no treatise on power analysis. What I do plan to do here is to examine power and sample size for the rule of thumb given above, as well as some of the examples we have used in this book, to give you some sense of what sorts of sample sizes are needed with the kinds of problems used in this book. Fortunately, there are some excellent books on power analysis, including Cohen's classic book on the topic (1988). The short text by Kraemer and Thiemann is also useful (1987), as is Cohen and colleagues (2003); for experimental research, I found Howell's (2002) introduction to power especially clear. If you intend to conduct research using MR (or other methods), I recommend that you read further on this important issue. If you are lucky, you also have access to a program for conducting power analysis. The examples that follow use SamplePower 2.0 (Borenstein, Rothstein, & Cohen, 2003), an easy to use program from SPSS. I have also used the PASS (Power Analysis and Sample Size; Hintze, 2002) program from NCSS (www.ncss.com), which also works well. In addition, as a student you can get a substantial discount on PASS 2002 ($50 or less at this writing with a student discount). You may also be able to find free power programs and interactive applications on the Web.

First, let's examine several of the examples in this text. In Chapter 4, we regressed GPA in 10th grade on Parent Education, In School Homework, and Out of School Homework. The R^2 for the overall regression was .155, with a sample size of 909. What sort of power did we have with this simultaneous regression? According to SamplePower, this example had a power of 1.0 (for this and the other examples, I will assume an alpha of .05) for the overall regression. Indeed, as shown in Figure 9.13, this example, with three variables and an R^2 of .15, will have a power of .8 with approximately 50 participants and a power of .9 with approximately 60 to 65 participants. The graph shows power (Y-axis) as a function of sample size, given an alpha of .05 and an R^2 of .15.

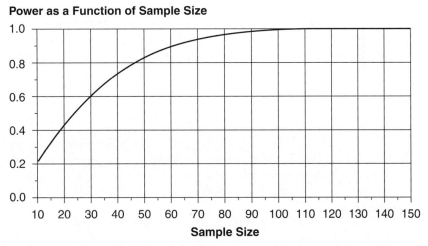

FIGURE 9.13   Power curve for a simultaneous regression example from Chapter 4.

We often are interested in the power of the addition of one variable or a block of variables to the regression equation, with other variables (background variables or covariates) controlled. For example, in Chapter 5 we considered the sequential regression in which we added Locus of Control and Self-Esteem to the regression, with SES and Previous Grades already in the equation. The R^2 with two variables in the equation was .328, and the psychological variables added another .01 to the R^2. What sort of power was associated with this block? Given the sample size of approximately 890, this final block in the regression had a power of .96; given this information, we had a 96% chance to reject correctly a false null hypothesis of no effect for the psychological variables. As shown in Figure 9.14, a sample size of 520 is needed for a power .80 and sample size of 700 for a power of .90 for this block.

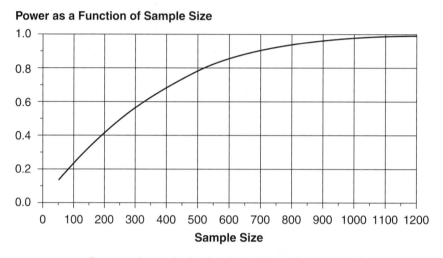

Power as a Function of Sample Size

FIGURE 9.14   Power and sample size for the addition of a block of two variables in a sequential regression. The example is from Chapter 5.

Consider the regressions in which we added interaction terms to the regression. In Chapter 7 we tested the interaction of Previous Achievement and Ethnicity in their possible effect on Self-Esteem. The categorical and continuous variable accounted for 2% of the variance in Self-Esteem, and the cross product added another .8% (which I will round off to 1%) to the variance explained, with a sample size of approximately 900. In this example, the test of the interaction term had a power of .86. Although the test of the interaction has lower power than the initial variables, with this sample size we still had plenty of power to examine the statistical significance of the interaction (see Figure 9.15).

Finally, consider the 10 to 20 participants per independent variable rule of thumb. Let's model this on some of the other regressions discussed here. Suppose four independent variables account for 20% of the variance in the outcome, a value that seems reasonable given our examples. Will a sample size of 40 to 80 produce adequate power? Forty cases will produce a total power of only .65, but 80 cases will result in a power of .95. If the R^2 for these four variables was .30 instead of .20, then the power associated with 40 cases is .89. The relevant graphs are shown in Figure 9.16. The top graph shows the power for sample sizes with $R^2 = .20$ and the bottom graph, for

Power as a Function of Sample Size

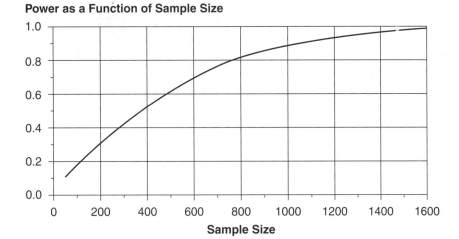

FIGURE 9.15   **Power curve for the sequential addition of an interaction term to the regression. The example is from Chapter 7.**

$R^2 = .30$. Suppose instead that you were interested in the power associated with one variable that increased the R^2 by .05 above an $R^2 = .20$ from the first four variables in the regression. You will need a sample size of 124 to have a power of .80 for this final variable (no graph shown). It appears that this rule of thumb, although sometimes accurate, will produce low power in many real-world research problems.[1]

In real-world research, you will, of course, conduct these power calculations prior to the research to make sure you collect data on the needed number of participants. You will not know the exact effect size, but can generally estimate effect sizes from previous research and your knowledge of relevant theory in the area. Most programs use R^2 or ΔR^2 as the measure of effect size (as in the examples above). You can, of course, get estimates of ΔR^2 if researchers have used sequential regression or by squaring the semipartial correlations (which you can calculate using t values, if necessary). If you have no previous research to go on, you can use common rules of thumb (e.g., ΔR^2's of .02, .13, and .26 represent small, medium, and large effects in the social sciences; Cohen et al., 2003). A medium effect size is generally recognized as one noticeable to a knowledgeable viewer (Howell, 2002).

As you plan your own research, I encourage you to investigate power more completely and spend some time estimating the sample size you will need in your research (assuming you are not using a large data set like NELS). You don't want to be filled with regrets after having conducted the research and finding nothing of statistical significance and then wishing that you had collected data from 10, or 100, additional participants!

Related Methods

Logistic Regression and Discriminant Analysis.   In all our regression examples in this book, the outcome variable has been continuous. Achievement test scores, Grades, Self-Esteem ratings, and so on, are all continuous variables. But we learned that it is possible

Power as a Function of Sample Size

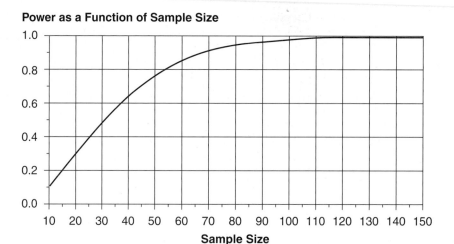

Power as a Function of Sample Size

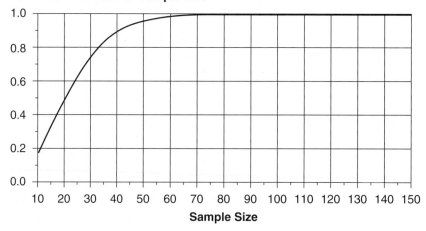

FIGURE 9.16   Power curves examining a common rule of thumb for sample sizes. The top graph is for a total $R^2 = .20$, whereas the lower graph is for $R^2 = .30$.

to include categorical independent variables in MR; what about categorical *dependent* variables?

There are two common methods for analyzing categorical dependent variables in a MR fashion: logistic regression and discriminant analysis. Logistic regression is the more popular method at the current time, in part because much of what you have learned about multiple regression is directly applicable to logistic regression. Logistic regression also has an advantage over discriminant analysis in that it can include both categorical and continuous variables as independent variables, whereas, strictly speaking, discriminant analysis should include only continuous independent variables. Discriminant analysis had been a better choice for categorical variables that included more than two categories, but up to date logistic regression programs can also handle polytomous, in addition to dichotomous, categorical variables. The Sage Quantitative Applications in the Social Science series includes good introductions to both methods (Klecka, 1980; Menard, 1995).

Hierarchical Linear Modeling.   One assumption briefly discussed earlier in this chapter is that the observations are drawn independently from the population. As shown, one way this assumption can be violated is for some observations to be related to one another, to overlap or cluster in some way. Think, for example, about the NELS data. The design of the full NELS survey was to select schools from a national list and then to select, at random, approximately 24 students per school for inclusion in the sample. We have treated the NELS participants as if they were unrelated; but if you think about it, you will probably expect that students will be somewhat more similar to other students within their same school than to students from other schools. This similarity probably becomes stronger when we focus on variables (like homework?) that may be controlled, in part, by the schools. What this means is that the NELS observations are not quite as independent as we would like, which, in turn, may deflate the standard errors of the regression coefficients and make variables seem statistically significant when they are not. To use a more striking example, suppose we were to regress a measure of marital satisfaction on variables such as age, educational attainment, and occupational status. Imagine, however, that we have collected data from couples—both husbands and wives. A wife and husband are likely more similar to one another than are two strangers on all these characteristics, and thus these observations are not independent.

One method of dealing with such problems is through a method known as hierarchical linear modeling (HLM) or, more generally, multilevel models. HLM is a regression method that can take into account data that are clustered in some way—students in schools, men and women in couples, and so on. To use the NELS example, with HLM we could examine the effects of homework on achievement at both an individual level and school level. In addition to dealing with the problem of lack of independence of observations, multilevel models can also provide a richer understanding of how group-level variables can affect individual-level variables. For more information, see Bryk and Raudenbush (1992).

PROBLEMS WITH MR?

Let's revisit some of the interpretive problems we've dealt with throughout this part of the book. I conducted three multiple regressions of high school Achievement on Family Background (SES), Intellectual Ability, Academic Motivation, and Academic Coursework in high school. Our interest is in the effects of these variables on students' high school achievement. We will briefly examine the results of a simultaneous, a sequential, and a stepwise multiple regression, with a focus on the different conclusions we can reach using the different methods. Because our primary interest is in the differences across methods, I won't define the variables in any more detail. The data are taken from Keith and Cool (1992), however, if you are interested in learning more. For this example, rather than simulating the data, I have conducted the regressions using a portion of the correlation matrix as presented in the article. The file "problems w MR 3.sps" illustrates how to conduct a MR using a correlation matrix in SPSS. You may want to print this file; it's a useful method and one you can use to reanalyze any published correlation matrix.

Figure 9.17 shows the primary results from a simultaneous MR of Achievement on the four explanatory variables. The regression is statistically significant, and over 60% of the variance in Achievement is explained by these four variables ($R^2 = .629$). The table of coefficients in the figure provides information about the relative influence of the variables. All the variables appear important, with the exception of Academic Motivation. The effects of Motivation appear very small ($\beta = .013$) and are not statistically significant. Motivation, it seems, has no effect on high school Achievement. Turning to the other variables and based on the β's, Ability appears the most important influence, followed by high school Coursework; both effects were large. Family Background, in contrast, had a small, but statistically significant, effect on Achievement.

Model Summary

Model	R	R Square	Change Statistics				
			R Square Change	F Change	df1	df2	Sig. F Change
1	.793[a]	.629	.629	421.682	4	995	.000

a. Predictors: (Constant), COURSES, FAM_BACK, MOTIVATE, ABILITY

Coefficients[a]

Model		Unstandardized Coefficients		Standardized Coefficients			95% Confidence Interval for B	
		B	Std. Error	Beta	t	Sig.	Lower Bound	Upper Bound
1	(Constant)	6.434	1.692		3.803	.000	3.114	9.753
	FAM_BACK	.695	.218	.069	3.194	.001	.268	1.122
	ABILITY	.367	.016	.551	23.698	.000	.337	.398
	MOTIVATE	1.26E-02	.021	.013	.603	.547	-.028	.054
	COURSES	1.550	.120	.310	12.963	.000	1.315	1.785

a. Dependent Variable: ACHIEVE

FIGURE 9.17   Simultaneous regression of Achievement on Family Background, Ability, Motivation, and Academic Coursework.

Figure 9.18 shows the same data analyzed via sequential MR. For this problem, the explanatory variables were entered in the order of presumed time precedence. Parents' background characteristics generally come prior to their children's characteristics; Ability, a relatively stable characteristic from an early age, comes prior to the other student characteristics; Motivation determines in part the courses students take in high school; and these courses, in turn, determine in part a high school student's Achievement. Thus, achievement was regressed on Family Background, then Ability, then Motivation, and finally Coursework. Relevant results of this regression are shown in Figure 9.18.

Model Summary

Model	R	R Square	Change Statistics				
			R Square Change	F Change	df1	df2	Sig. F Change
1	.417[a]	.174	.174	210.070	1	998	.000
2	.747[b]	.558	.384	865.278	1	997	.000
3	.753[c]	.566	.009	19.708	1	996	.000
4	.793[d]	.629	.063	168.039	1	995	.000

a. Predictors: (Constant), FAM_BACK

b. Predictors: (Constant), FAM_BACK, ABILITY

c. Predictors: (Constant), FAM_BACK, ABILITY, MOTIVATE

d. Predictors: (Constant), FAM_BACK, ABILITY, MOTIVATE, COURSES

Coefficients[a]

Model		Unstandardized Coefficients		Standardized Coefficients	t	Sig.	95% Confidence Interval for B	
		B	Std. Error	Beta			Lower Bound	Upper Bound
1	(Constant)	50.000	.288		173.873	.000	49.436	50.564
	FAM_BACK	*4.170*	.288	*.417*	14.494	.000	3.605	4.735
2	(Constant)	4.557	1.559		2.923	.004	1.498	7.617
	FAM_BACK	1.328	.232	.133	5.729	.000	.873	1.782
	ABILITY	*.454*	.015	*.682*	29.416	.000	.424	.485
3	(Constant)	.759	1.766		.430	.667	-2.706	4.224
	FAM_BACK	1.207	.231	.121	5.221	.000	.753	1.661
	ABILITY	.445	.015	.667	28.768	.000	.414	.475
	MOTIVATE	*9.53E-02*	.021	*.095*	4.439	.000	.053	.137
4	(Constant)	6.434	1.692		3.803	.000	3.114	9.753
	FAM_BACK	.695	.218	.069	3.194	.001	.268	1.122
	ABILITY	.367	.016	.551	23.698	.000	.337	.398
	MOTIVATE	1.26E-02	.021	.013	.603	.547	-.028	.054
	COURSES	*1.550*	.120	*.310*	12.963	.000	1.315	1.785

a. Dependent Variable: ACHIEVE

FIGURE 9.18   Sequential regression results for the same data.

There are several differences in these results and those from the simultaneous MR. What is more disturbing is that we will likely come to different conclusions depending on which printout we examine. First, with the sequential regression and focusing on the statistical significance of ΔR^2 for each step, it now appears that Academic Motivation *does* have a statistically significant effect on Achievement ($\Delta R^2 = .009$, $F[1, 996] = 19.708$, $p < .001$). Second, although we still conclude that Ability was the most important variable, we now conclude that Family Background was second in importance ($\sqrt{\Delta R^2} = .620, .417,$ .251, .095, for Ability, Family Background, Coursework, and Motivation, respectively; of course this rank order would stay the same if we were to focus on ΔR^2 instead).

Figure 9.19 shows the results from a stepwise regression of these same variables. Again, Academic Motivation appears unimportant, since it never entered the regression equation. And again, the order of "importance" changed. In the stepwise regression, Ability entered the equation first, followed by Coursework, followed by Family Background. The stepwise regression thus seems to paint yet another picture of the importance of these variables for Achievement.

Model Summary

Model	R	R Square	Adjusted R Square	R Square Change	F Change	df1	df2	Sig. F Change
				Change Statistics				
1	.737[a]	.543	.543	.543	1186.615	1	998	.000
2	.791[b]	.625	.624	.082	217.366	1	997	.000
3	.793[c]	.629	.628	.004	10.453	1	996	.001

a. Predictors: (Constant), ABILITY

b. Predictors: (Constant), ABILITY, COURSES

c. Predictors: (Constant), ABILITY, COURSES, FAM_BACK

FIGURE 9.19   Stepwise regression of Achievement on the same four school learning variables.

How do we resolve these differences? First, we can ignore the results of the stepwise regression, because this is an explanatory problem and stepwise regression is not appropriate for explanatory research. But we still have the differences between the simultaneous and the sequential regressions, both of which are appropriate for explanation.

We have touched on these differences in previous chapters. As noted primarily in Chapter 5, simultaneous regression focuses the *direct* effects of variables on an outcome, whereas sequential regression focuses on *total* effects. Thus, the two approaches may well produce different estimates, even when they are based on the same underlying model and even when one interprets the same statistics. Table 9.2 shows the relevant regression coefficients from Figures 9.17 (simultaneous regression) and 9.18 (sequential regression). For

TABLE 9.2   Regression Coefficients from the Simultaneous versus Sequential Regression of Achievement on Family Background, Ability, Academic Motivation, and Academic Coursework

VARIABLE	SIMULTANEOUS REGRESSION	SEQUENTIAL REGRESSION
Family Background	.695 (.218) .069	4.170 (.288) .417
Ability	.367 (.016) .551	.454 (.015) .682
Academic Motivation	.013 (.021) .013	.095 (.021) .095
Academic Coursework	1.550 (.120) .310	1.550 (.120) .310

Note. The first row for each variable shows the unstandardized coefficient followed by the standard error (in parentheses). The second row includes the standardized coefficient.

the sequential regressions, the coefficients are from the step at which each variable was entered (shown in italic boldface in the table of coefficients in Figure 9.18). Note the differences in the coefficients; many of them are large. Family Background, for example, has an effect of .069 in the simultaneous regression versus .417 in the sequential regression.

Again, these differences are not so startling if we know that the simultaneous regression focuses on direct effects versus total effects for sequential regression. But many users of multiple regression seem unaware of this difference. Likewise, many users of MR seem unaware that their regression, when used for explanatory purposes, implies a model and that this model should guide the analysis. In Part 2 of this book we will develop such models in considerably more detail and, along the way, gain a deeper understanding of MR and our current difficulties in interpretation. Even if you are using this book for a class in MR only and focusing on Part 1 only, I urge you to read Part 2 (at least the first two chapters). I think you will find they help you resolve many of the issues that have vexed us in our use and interpretation of multiple regression. If nothing else, these chapters will give you a more complete heuristic aid in understanding MR results.

EXERCISES

1. Return to the first regression we did with the NELS data. Regress 10th-grade GPA (FFU-Grad) on Parent Education (BYParEd) and Time Spent on Homework Out of School (F1S36A2) (see the exercises in Chapter 2). Save the unstandardized residuals and predicted values. Use the residuals to test for linearity in the Homework variable and for the overall regression. Are the residuals normally distributed? Is the variance of the errors consistent across levels of the independent variables (to conduct this final analysis, I suggest you reduce the Predicted Grades variable into a smaller number of categories).

2. Rerun the regression; save standardized and studentized residuals, leverage, Cook's Distance, and standardized DF Betas. Check out any outliers and unusually influential cases. Do these cases look okay on these and other variables? What do you propose to do? Discuss your options and decisions in class. (To do this analysis, you may want to create a new variable equal to the case number [e.g., COMPUTE CASENUM=$CASENUM in SPSS]. You can then sort the cases based on each regression diagnostic to find high values, but still return the data to their original order.)

3. Do the same regression, adding the variable BYSES to the independent variables (F YParEd is a component of BYSES). Compute collinearity diagnostics for this example. Do ̦ ou note any problems?

NOTE

1. Two slightly more sophisticated rules of thumb are $N \geq 50 + 8k$ for calculating the N needed for adequate power in an overall regression and $\geq 104 + k$ for the testing the statistical significance of a single variable (with k representing the number of independent variables). Green (1991) evaluated these and other rules of thumb and, although they work somewhat better than the simple $N \geq 10k$ rule mentioned in this chapter, they also fall short, because they do not take effect sizes into account. Indeed, the second rule would underestimate the sample size needed for the final example given here. Green also developed several additional rules of thumb that take effect size into account and are therefore more useful. If you do not have access to a power analysis program, I recommend this article.

PART II

BEYOND MULTIPLE REGRESSION

CHAPTER TEN

PATH MODELING: STRUCTURAL EQUATION MODELING WITH MEASURED VARIABLES

In this chapter, we continue our journey beyond multiple regression and begin discussing structural equation modeling (SEM). This chapter focuses on the technique of path analysis, which can be considered the simplest form of SEM. As you will see, many path analyses can be solved using multiple regression analysis, although we will soon begin using specialized structural equation modeling software for both simple and complex path models.

In the final chapter of Part 1, we reviewed one of the difficulties with multiple regression analysis, the fact that we can come to different conclusions about the effects of one variable on another depending on which type of multiple regression we use and which statistics from the analysis we interpret. (If you are beginning the book here, I recommend that you read Chapter 9 as a review of multiple regression.) As you will see, this difficulty is obviated in path analysis and structural equation modeling, where it is natural to focus not only on direct effects, but also on indirect and total effects (total effects are the sum of direct and indirect effects). We will use both simultaneous and sequential MR in path analysis, an exercise that will clarify the relation between these two methods. In the process, we will focus more explicitly on explanation, and on the issues of cause and effect. I think that path analysis makes many aspects of multiple regression more understandable, and it is often a better choice for the explanatory analysis of nonexperimental data.

Before we begin, let's deal with a little jargon. The general type of analysis discussed in this part of the book, SEM, is also referred to as analysis of covariance structures, or causal analysis. Path analysis, one form of SEM, is the subject of this and the next two chapters; it may also be considered as a component of SEM. Confirmatory factor analysis (CFA) is another component. More complex forms of SEM are often referred to as latent variable SEM, or simply as SEM. SEM is also sometimes referred to as LISREL analysis, which is actually the first computer program for conducting latent variable SEM and stands for *linear structural rel*ations. We will discuss these and other topics in subsequent chapters, including this and other SEM computer programs. Now we introduce path analysis.

INTRODUCTION TO PATH ANALYSIS

A Simple Model

Let's return to the example we used in Chapter 9, in which we were interested in the effects of Family Background, Ability, Academic Motivation, and Academic Coursework on high school Achievement. For the sake of simplicity, we will focus on only three of the variables: Ability, Motivation, and Achievement. Suppose, then, we are interested in the effects of Motivation on Achievement. Although presumably motivation is manipulable, it is not a variable that you can assign at random, and thus you will probably need to conduct a non-experimental analysis, as was done in Chapter 9. Intellectual Ability is included in the model to control for this variable. More specifically, we believe that Ability may affect both Motivation and Achievement, and we know that it is important to control for such *common causes* if we are to estimate accurately the effects of one variable on another.

Figure 10.1 illustrates the data we collected. Motivation is a composite of items reflecting academic motivation (student ratings of their interest in school, willingness to work hard in school, and plans for post-high school education); Achievement is a composite of achievement tests in reading, math, science, civics, and writing. We also collected data on Intellectual Ability (a composite of two verbal ability tests), with the notion that ability should be controlled because it may affect both Motivation and Achievement. The curved lines in the figure represent correlations among the three variables. The figure essentially presents the correlation matrix in graphic form. The correlation between Ability and Motivation, for example, is .205. (The data are from the correlation matrix used in Chapter 9.)

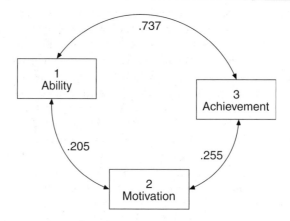

FIGURE 10.1   Correlations among Ability, Motivation, and Achievement. An "agnostic" model.

Unfortunately, the data as presented in Figure 10.1 do little to inform our question of interest: understanding the effects of Motivation on Achievement. The correlations are statistically significant, but we have no information on the effects of one on the other. We can think of this figure, then, as an "agnostic" model. In Figure 10.2 we take the first bold step in solving this dilemma by drawing arrows or paths from presumed causes to presumed effects. The purpose of this research was to determine the *effect* of Motivation on Achievement, so it certainly makes sense to draw a path from Motivation to Achievement. Ability was included in the research because we worried that it might *affect* both Motivation and Achievement; therefore, paths drawn from Ability to Motivation and Achievement are the embodiment of this supposition. Our drawing of the paths asserting presumed cause and effect was not so bold after all; it simply made obvious the reasoning underlying our study and the data we collected.

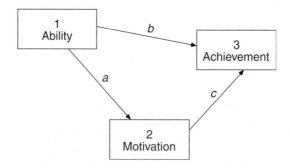

FIGURE 10.2   Presumed causal structure of the three variables. The assumptions about causal direction were not based on the correlations.

What exactly do these paths mean? They assert what is called a *weak causal ordering,* meaning that the path from Motivation to Achievement does not assert that Motivation directly causes Achievement, but rather that *if* Motivation and Achievement are causally related the cause is in the direction of the arrow, rather than the reverse. Note that we did not use the correlations or the data to make these inferences about causality; indeed, our informal causal thinking guided the data we collected and used! Figure 10.2 formalizes our notions of how these three variables are related and thus represents our model of the nature of the relations among these three variables.

The data shown in Figure 10.1 may be used to solve for the paths in the model shown in Figure 10.2. The easiest way to do so is to use the tracing rule: "the correlation between two variables X and Z is equal to the sum of the product of all paths from each possible tracing between X and Z [in Figure 10.2]. These tracings include all possible routes between X and Z, with the exceptions that (1) the same variable is not entered twice per tracing and (2) a variable is not both entered and exited through an arrowhead" (Keith, 1999, p. 82; cf. Kenny, 1979, p. 30). Thus, the correlation between Ability and Achievement (r_{13}) would be equal to path b plus the product of path a times path c: $r_{13} = b + ac$. Two other formulas (for the other two correlations) may be derived: $r_{23} = c + ab$ and $r_{12} = a$. You may wonder why the third equation does not include the tracing bc. The reason is that this tracing would violate the second exception (the same variable was entered and exited through an arrowhead).

We now have three equations and three unknowns (the three paths). If you recall high school algebra, you can use it to solve for the three unknowns:[1]

$$a = r_{12}$$

$$b = \frac{r_{13} - r_{12}r_{23}}{1 - r_{12}^2}$$

$$c = \frac{r_{23} - r_{12}r_{13}}{1 - r_{12}^2}$$

(If you don't recall high school algebra, note 1 shows how these three equations were generated!) Substituting the actual correlations in these equations, we calculate

$$a = .205$$

$$b = \frac{.737 - .205 \times .255}{1 - .205^2} = .715$$

$$c = \frac{.255 - .205 \times .737}{1 - .205^2} = .108$$

The solved paths are included in the model in Figure 10.3. The model may be interpreted as demonstrating the effects of Ability and Motivation on Achievement, along with the effects of Ability on Motivation (given several assumptions). The paths shown are the standardized path coefficients and are interpreted in standard deviation units. Thus, the path from Motivation to Achievement of .108 suggests that, given the adequacy of our model, each *SD* increase in Motivation will result in a .108 increase in Achievement.[2]

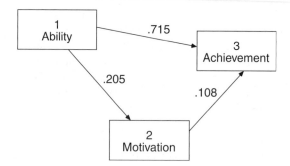

FIGURE 10.3   We used the data from Figure 10.1 to solve for the paths from Figure 10.2. The paths represent the standardized effect of one variable on another, given the adequacy of the model.

If this sounds familiar, it should. This type of interpretation is the same as that for standardized regression coefficients. A closer inspection of the formulas above will show striking similarity to those in Chapter 2 for regression coefficients. In fact, these formulas *are* the formulas for standardized regression coefficients. We don't need to use algebra to solve for the paths; we can use good old multiple regression analysis!

To solve for the paths using multiple regression, regress Achievement on Ability and Motivation. The β's from this regression are equal to the standardized paths, calculated above, from Ability and Motivation to Achievement. The path from Ability to Motivation is estimated through the regression of Motivation on Ability. Relevant portions of the output are shown in Figure 10.4. The first table of coefficients is from the first regression and estimates the paths to Achievement; the second table of coefficients is from the second regression and shows the path to Motivation. Compare the results to those shown in Figure 10.3.

We can use and interpret that printout and model in the same fashion as we previously did with multiple regression. The model thus suggests that Motivation has a moderate effect (using the rules of thumb from Chapter 4) on Achievement, after taking students' Ability into account.[3] Ability, in turn, has a moderate to large effect on Motivation and a very large effect on Achievement. We can use the rest of the regression output as we have previously. Just as in other forms of MR, the unstandardized regression coefficients—used as estimates of the unstandardized paths—may be more appropriate for interpretation, for example, when the variables are in a meaningful metric. In the present example, the standardized coefficients are probably more interpretable. (You may wonder why the unstandardized and standardized paths from Motivation to Achievement are the same. The reason is because the *SD*s for the two variables are the same.) In addition, we can use the *t*'s and standard errors from the output to determine the statistical significance of the path coefficients, as well as confidence intervals around the paths. The 95% confidence interval around the (unstandardized) path from Motivation to Achievement was .066 to .151.

The model shown in Figure 10.3 is not entirely complete. Conceptually and statistically, it should be clear that the model does not include all influences on Achievement or Motivation. You can no doubt think of many other variables that should affect high school

Model Summary

Model	R	R Square	F	df1	df2	Sig. F
1	.745[a]	.554	620.319	2	997	.000

a. Predictors: (Constant), MOTIVATE, ABILITY

Coefficients[a]

Model		Unstandardized Coefficients		Standardized Coefficients			95% Confidence Interval for B	
		B	Std. Error	Beta	t	Sig.	Lower Bound	Upper Bound
1	(Constant)	-3.075	1.627		-1.890	.059	-6.267	.118
	ABILITY	.477	.014	.715	33.093	.000	.448	.505
	MOTIVATE	.108	.022	.108	5.022	.000	.066	.151

a. Dependent Variable: ACHIEVE

Model Summary

Model	R	R Square	F	df1	df2	Sig. F
1	.205[a]	.042	43.781	1	998	.000

a. Predictors: (Constant), ABILITY

Coefficients[a]

Model		Unstandardized Coefficients		Standardized Coefficients			95% Confidence Interval for B	
		B	Std. Error	Beta	t	Sig.	Lower Bound	Upper Bound
1	(Constant)	36.333	2.089		17.396	.000	32.235	40.432
	ABILITY	.137	.021	.205	6.617	.000	.096	.177

a. Dependent Variable: MOTIVATE

FIGURE 10.4   Using simultaneous multiple regression to solve the paths.

achievement: family background, coursework, homework, and others. And what about effects on Motivation; if Ability only affects Motivation at a level of .205, obviously many influences are unaccounted for. The model shown in Figure 10.5 rectifies these deficiencies by including "disturbances" in the model, symbolized as d1 and d2. Disturbances represent *all other* influences on the outcome variables other than those shown in the model. Thus, the circled variable d2 represents all influences on Achievement other than Ability and Motivation. The disturbances are enclosed in circles or ellipses to signify that they are *unmeasured* variables. We obviously don't measure all variables that affect Achievement and include them in the model; the disturbances, then, are unmeasured, rather than measured variables.

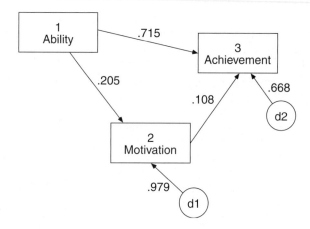

**FIGURE 10.5   The full, standardized, solved model,
including disturbances of the presumed effects.
Disturbances represent all other, unmeasured
variables that affect a variable other than the
variables already pointing to it.**

When I say that the disturbances represent all other influences on the outcomes
besides the variables in the model, this explanation may ring a bell, as well. You might think
that the disturbances should somehow be related to the residuals, which we at one point
described as what was left over or unexplained by the variables in the model. If you had this
sense, then reward yourself with a break or a chocolate, because the disturbances are basically the same as the residuals from MR. You have probably encountered instances in
research and statistics where two different names are used to describe the same concept;
this is another instance of this practice. Although many sources use the term disturbances to
describe these other influences (e.g., Bollen, 1989; Kenny, 1979), others continue to use
the term *residual,* and others simply refer to these outside influences as *errors.* The paths
associated with the disturbances are calculated as the square root of $1 - R^2$ ($\sqrt{1 - R^2}$) from
each regression equation. Focus again on Figure 10.4. For the first equation, the regression
of Achievement on Ability and Motivation, R^2 was equal to .554, and thus $\sqrt{1 - R^2} = .668$,
the value shown for the path from d2 to Achievement. Take a moment to calculate the disturbance for Motivation.

Cautions

With all this talk of cause and effect, you may feel a little queasy. After all, aren't we here
breaking the one cardinal rule of elementary statistics: Don't infer causation from correlations? If you are having such misgivings, I first urge you to revisit the short quiz on this
same topic in Chapter 1. Second, I point out that, no, we did not infer causality from the correlations. Yes, we had the correlations, but recall that they did not lead to or even enter into
our causal inferences. We made the inference of causality when we drew paths from one

variable to another, and we drew these paths *without* reference to the correlations. Neither the magnitude nor the sign (positive or negative) of the correlations entered our consideration of cause and effect.

How did we, and how could we, make these inferences of cause and effect? Several lines of evidence can be used to make such inferences and thus to draw the paths. First is *theory*. School learning theories generally include both motivation and ability (or some similar construct) as influences on academic achievement and thus justify the paths from Ability and Motivation to Achievement (Walberg, 1986). And even when formal theory is not available, informal theory can often inform such decisions. Talk to an observant teacher and he or she will tell you that if you can increase a child's level of motivation his or her achievement will increase.

Second, we should attend to *time precedence.* As far as we know, causality cannot operate backward in time and so, if we can establish that one variable occurs prior to another in time, it makes it easier to draw the path. This is one reason that longitudinal data are so valued in research; we can feel more confident about inferring cause and effect when our "effect" is measured after our "cause." Yet even with cross-sectional data it is often possible to determine logical time precedence. In the current example, it is well known that ability is a relatively stable characteristic, for most people, from about the time children start school. Logically, then, Ability, stable from an early age, occurs prior to high school motivation and achievement, and thus it makes sense to draw a path from Ability to both Motivation and Achievement. For an even more striking example, consider if we had the variable Sex in our model. For almost everyone (excepting those who have sex change operations!), Sex is stable from conception on. Thus, no matter when Sex is measured, we can feel confident placing it prior to variables that logically occur after conception.

Third, you should have a competent understanding of the relevant research. Previous research may well highlight the proper causal inference. Even if it doesn't—even if you find that other researchers have had to make these same inferences—previous research may help you understand the logic by which others have decided that A affected B rather than B affecting A.

Our fourth and final line of evidence we'll call logic, although it is probably a combination of logic, observation, understanding, and common sense. Go back to the illustration of what I termed informal theory. Teachers observe children every day in their classes; they are keen observers of the process of learning. If you were to ask a teacher, "Which is more likely, an increase in students' levels of motivation affecting their learning or an increase in their learning affecting their motivation?" most would pick the former possibility. You can use the same sort of process to make such inferences. Imagine the ways in which A could affect B, and then imagine the ways in which B could affect A. If you are familiar with the phenomena you are considering, if you have observed them carefully, you will often find it easy to imagine the cause going in one direction, but may require mental gyrations to imagine it going in the other. This logical exercise, then, will often suggest that one direction of causation is much more plausible than the other.

Again, these lines of evidence are how we make such inferences of cause and effect. Once we have made those inferences, the correlations merely provide fuel for our calculations.

More formally, three conditions are necessary before we can make a valid inference of causality (see Kenny, 1979, or Kline, 1998, for additional discussion of these conditions;

for a considerably expanded discussion of the concept of causality, see Pearl, 2000). First, there must be a relation between the variables being considered. If two variables are unrelated, then they are also *causally* unrelated. This condition is generally satisfied by the presence of a correlation between the variables (although there are exceptions). Second, and as already discussed, the presumed cause must have time precedence over the presumed effect. Causality does not operate backward in time. Third, the relation between the variables must be a true, rather than a spurious, relation. This is the hardest condition to satisfy and gets to the heart of what we have been calling the problem of omitted common causes. We will delve into this problem more deeply in the next chapter, but for now simply note that this condition means that all common causes are taken into account. Given that these three conditions are satisfied, it is perfectly reasonable to make an inference of cause and effect. What makes nonexperimental research so interesting and challenging is that we can often be very confident that we have satisfied these three conditions, but never completely sure. (As it turns out, however, we can never be sure in experimental research either.)

Just to make sure we are all on the same page, let's be completely clear as to what we mean by cause. When we say one variable "causes" another, we do *not* mean that one variable directly and immediately results in change in another. When we say, for example, that smoking causes lung cancer, we do not mean that every person who smokes will necessarily and quickly develop lung cancer. What we mean is that if you smoke you will, as a result of smoking, increase your probability of developing lung cancer. The term cause is thus a probabilistic statement.

Jargon and Notation

I've been sneaking some of the jargon of SEM into the chapter as we introduce path analysis. Before we move to an expanded example, let's spend a little time going over such jargon so that it will be familiar. I have already noted that the variables representing other influences from outside the model are often called disturbances in path analysis, although many researchers use the term with which you are already familiar, residuals. In addition, I have noted that variables that we wish to symbolize, but which we have not measured (unmeasured variables) are generally enclosed in circles or ovals. In contrast, measured variables, variables that we have measured in our data, are generally enclosed in rectangles. Paths or arrows represent influences from presumed cause to presumed effect, whereas curved, double-headed arrows represent correlations without an inference of causality.

Recursive and Nonrecursive Models. The models shown in Figures 10.2 and 10.3 are called *recursive* models, meaning that paths, and presumed causes, go in one direction only. It is also possible to have feedback loops in a model, to specify that two variables affect each other in a reciprocal fashion. Such models are termed *nonrecursive;* an example is shown in Figure 10.6, where Variable 2 is assumed to both affect (path *c*) and be affected by Variable 3 (path *d*). You cannot solve for the equations for nonrecursive models using the tracing rule, although you can generate the correct equations using the first law. Likewise, nonrecursive models cannot be estimated through multiple regression (you can estimate such models with MR, but the results will be incorrect). It is possible to estimate nonrecursive models using specialized SEM software or through a method called two-stage least squares regression, although such estimation is often tedious (and, as we will see momentarily, *this* model could not be estimated). It is tempting, especially for those new to SEM, to solve difficult questions of presumed cause and effect by deciding that such effects are reciprocal. Can't decide whether Motivation affects Achievement or Achievement affects Motivation? Draw paths in both directions! Generally, however, this is equivocation rather than decision. Nonrecursive models require additional constraints to avoid underidentification (see below) and, in my experience, often end up suggesting that the effect is indeed in the direction we would have guessed had we done the difficult work of making such decisions. I am not suggesting that you develop a cavalier attitude toward making decisions about the correct direction of causality; it often requires tough work and deep thought. Instead, I am arguing that you should not try to avoid this work by defaulting to nonrecursive models. Save such models for those instances when you have real, substantive questions about causal direction or when effects really appear to go in both directions. Some authors (e.g., Kenny, 1979) refer to recursive models as hierarchical models and nonrecursive models as nonhierarchical, but such usage may be confusing because sequential regression is also often termed hierarchical regression.

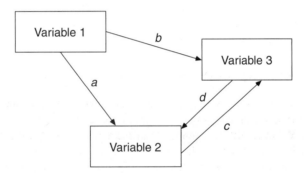

FIGURE 10.6   Nonrecursive model. The model is also underidentified and cannot be solved without additional assumptions.

Identification.   The model shown in Figure 10.3 is also a *just-identified* model. In a simplistic sense, what this means is that we had just enough information to estimate the model. Focus again on the Figures 10.1 through 10.3. We had three unknowns (the three paths in Figure 10.2), and we solved for these three paths using the three correlations from Figure 10.1. We had just enough information to solve for the paths. In addition to being a nonrecursive model, the model shown in Figure 10.6 is an *underidentified* model. For this model, we still have three correlations, but we now have four paths that we need to estimate. Unless we make some additional assumptions (e.g., assuming that paths *d* and *c* are equal), we cannot solve for the paths in this model.

The model shown in Figure 10.7, in contrast, is *overidentified*. For this model, we have more correlations than paths. The result is that we could, in fact, develop two separate sets of equations to solve for paths a and b. Consider the three equations generated from the tracing rule:

$$r_{13} = b \qquad r_{12} = a \qquad r_{23} = ab$$

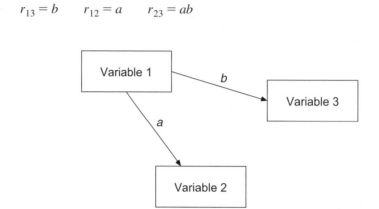

FIGURE 10.7   Overidentified model. The paths can be estimated more than one way.

Using these equations to solve for a (and substituting for b), for example, we could generate the equations $a = r_{12}$ and $a = r_{23}/r_{13}$. And for b, $b = r_{13}$ and $b = r_{23}/r_{12}$. At first blush, the possibility of calculating two different estimates of each path might seem a problem. But consider for a minute what it would mean if our two estimates of the same path were very close to one another versus considerably divergent? Wouldn't you be more likely to believe a model in which you could estimate a path several different ways and always get the same result? We won't explore this topic in any greater depth right now, but will return to it later. In the meantime, simply recognize that overidentified models are not problematic, but, rather, overidentification may help us evaluate the quality of our models.

This discussion has been a necessary simplification of the topic of identification, which can be much more complex than has been presented here. For example, it is possible for portions of a model to be overidentified and other portions to be underidentified. The primary rule presented for determining identification—comparing the number of correlations to the number of unknown paths—is really more of a necessary but insufficient condition for identification. Nevertheless, this rule generally works well for the simple path models of the type presented in this and the next chapter. For a more detailed discussion of the topic of identification with simple or complex models, see Bollen (1989).

Exogenous and Endogenous Variables.   In SEM, the presumed causes (e.g., Ability in Figure 10.3) in a model are often referred to as *exogenous* variables. In medicine or biology, exogenous means "having a cause external to the body" (Morris, 1969, p. 461). An exogenous variable has causes outside the model or not considered by the model. Or, more simply, exogenous variables are ones that have no arrows pointing toward them. In contrast, variables that are affected by other variables in the model, variables that have arrows pointed toward them, are termed *endogenous* variables (meaning, loosely, from within). In Figure 10.3, Motivation and Achievement are endogenous variables.

Measured and Unmeasured Variables.   In the discussion of disturbances, I noted that we generally symbolize unmeasured variables in path models by enclosing them in circles or ellipses. Unmeasured variables are variables that we wish to include in a path model, but we have no measures of these variables in our data. For now, the only unmeasured variables we will deal with are disturbances, but in later chapters we will focus on other types of unmeasured variables. Unmeasured variables are also known as *latent* variables or *factors*.

Variables enclosed in rectangles are measured variables for which we have actual measures in our data. These include all sorts of items, scales, and composites. Indeed, all the variables we have discussed so far in this book, with the exception of disturbances and residuals, are measured variables. Measured variables are also known as *manifest* variables.

A MORE COMPLEX EXAMPLE

Now that you have a handle on the basics of path analysis, let's expand our example to a more realistic level. We will now focus on the effects of Family Background characteristics, Ability, Motivation, and Academic Coursework on High School Achievement. These are, then, the same data and the same example from Chapter 9, but in path analytic form. The comparison of the results of the path analysis to the results for the different forms of multiple regression will be instructive and help illustrate important concepts about both methods.

Steps for Conducting Path Analysis

Here are the steps involved in conducting a path analysis (Kenny, 1979; Kline, 1998).

Develop the Model.   The first step in path analysis is to develop and draw the model based on formal and informal theory, previous research, time precedence, and logic. Figure 10.8 shows my model, or theory, of how these variables are related to one another. School learning theories consistently include variables reflecting Ability (e.g., ability, aptitude, previous achievement), Motivation (internal motivation, perseverance), and Coursework (quantity of instruction, time spent learning, opportunity to learn) as influences on learning and achievement (e.g., Walberg, 1986). School learning theory, therefore, supports our drawing paths from Ability, Motivation, and Coursework to Achievement. You can probably easily justify these paths in other ways, as well.

Family Background is basically a background variable. By this I mean that it is included in the model because it seems needed to make the model valid (i.e., I think it may be a common cause of some of the variables and Achievement), but I'm not really interested in its effects on any of the other variables in the model. The fact that I consider this a background variable is not, however, justification for placing it first in the model. The likelihood that Family Background occurs before the other variables in time can be used to draw such paths, however, and you may find that the notion of *background variable* often is related to time. In the present case, Family Background is a parent variable, and most of its components—parents' level of education, occupational status—were likely in place, for many families, before children were even born. Even in cases in which parents were still in school or not yet employed when their children were born, time precedence would seem to flow from Family Background to the other variables in the model. Think about it: Is it more likely that parents' SES will affect

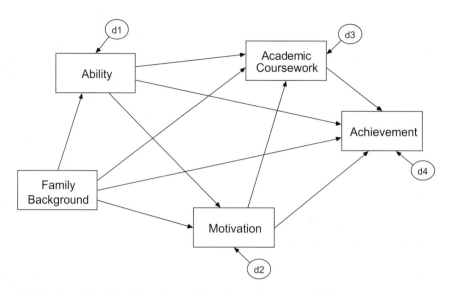

FIGURE 10.8 Model of the effects of Family Background, Ability, Motivation, and Academic Coursework on Achievement.

their child's ability (or motivation, etc.) or that a child's ability will affect his or her parents' SES? I suppose the second option is possible (children's ability affecting parents' SES), but it requires some mental gyrations to come up with plausible scenarios. Such reasoning may be used to draw paths from Family Background to each of the other variables in the model.

Time precedence, along with previous research, may also be used to justify the paths from Ability to each subsequent variable in the model. Ability, intelligence, or academic aptitude is relatively stable from an early elementary level on, and there is ample evidence that Ability affects many aspects of life and schooling, from Motivation to Achievement (Jensen, 1980, 1998).

This leaves the path from Motivation to Coursework. Imagine two high school students of equal ability and background. It is not hard to imagine one student taking a relatively easy mix of courses in high school and the other taking courses like pre-calculus, physics, and advanced English. Academic Motivation—the desire to work hard and persevere in school, the expectation that schooling and what is learned in school will be important for the future—is likely a key difference between these students. Many of you can probably think of such examples in your own family, siblings or children who were highly motivated taking tough courses versus just getting by. In essence, it makes a great deal of sense to posit that students with high levels of academic motivation will, other things being equal, take a tougher mix of academic courses than will students with lower levels of motivation. (Keith and Cool, 1992, further bolstered this time precedence by measuring Motivation 2 years prior to Coursework.)

This reasoning justifies the directions of the paths in the model, but what about the *variables* in the model? In particular, are there variables that should be included in the model that have not been included? That is, have I neglected an important common cause? Are there variables in the model that are unnecessary? I will postpone in-depth discussion of these issues until the next chapter. For now, I simply note that theory and previous research can help answer these questions, as well.

Check the Identification Status of the Model.   Make sure that the model is either just-identified or overidentified so that the model may be estimated. The model shown in Figure 10.8 is just-identified. The correlation matrix includes 10 correlations, and there are 10 paths to be solved for. The model appears to be just-identified and can probably be estimated.

Measure the Variables in the Model.   We next need to decide how to measure the variables in the model. This may mean selecting tests and items designed to measure the constructs of interest and then administering these measures to a sample of participants. When using existing data, such as the NELS data, this may mean seeing if items that measure the variables of interest have already been administered to a sample of participants. In the present case, the variables in the model were already measured in the High School and Beyond data set; the authors selected items and composites to measure these constructs.

Estimate the Model.   Our next step is to estimate the model. We are currently discussing how to estimate such models using multiple regression analysis; in subsequent chapters we will learn how to estimate such models using SEM software. To estimate the paths to Achievement using MR, we regress Achievement on Family Background, Ability, Motivation, and Academic Coursework. Partial results of this regression are shown in Figure 10.9. The b's and β's from the regression are the estimates of the unstandardized and standardized path coefficients, respectively, from each variable to Achievement. The R^2 is used to calculate the path from the disturbance (d4) to Achievement: $\sqrt{1 - R^2} = \sqrt{1 - .629} = .609$.

Model Summary

Model	R	R Square	Adjusted R Square	Std. Error of the Estimate
1	.793[a]	.629	.627	6.103451

a. Predictors: (Constant), COURSES, FAM_BACK, MOTIVATE, ABILITY

Coefficients[a]

Model		Unstandardized Coefficients B	Std. Error	Standardized Coefficients Beta	t	Sig.	95% Confidence Interval for B Lower Bound	Upper Bound
1	(Constant)	6.434	1.692		3.803	.000	3.114	9.753
	FAM_BACK	.695	.218	.069	3.194	.001	.268	1.122
	ABILITY	.367	.016	.551	23.698	.000	.337	.398
	MOTIVATE	1.26E-02	.021	.013	.603	.547	-.028	.054
	COURSES	1.550	.120	.310	12.963	.000	1.315	1.785

a. Dependent Variable: ACHIEVE

FIGURE 10.9   Using simultaneous regression to estimate the paths to Achievement.

The paths to Academic Coursework are estimated by regressing Courses on Family Background, Ability, and Motivation, and the path from d3 to Coursework is estimated from the R^2 from that regression ($R^2 = .348$). Results from this regression are shown in Figure 10.10. The paths to Motivation are estimated from the regression of Motivation on Family Background and Ability, and the path from Family Background to Ability is estimated through the regression of Ability on Family Background. The relevant regression results are shown in Figure 10.11.

Model Summary

Model	R	R Square	Adjusted R Square	Std. Error of the Estimate
1	.590[a]	.348	.346	1.617391

a. Predictors: (Constant), MOTIVATE, FAM_BACK, ABILITY

Coefficients[a]

Model		Unstandardized Coefficients		Standardized Coefficients	t	Sig.	95% Confidence Interval for B	
		B	Std. Error	Beta			Lower Bound	Upper Bound
1	(Constant)	-3.661	.433		-8.454	.000	-4.511	-2.811
	FAM_BACK	.330	.057	.165	5.827	.000	.219	.442
	ABILITY	4.99E-02	.004	.374	13.168	.000	.042	.057
	MOTIVATE	5.34E-02	.005	.267	10.138	.000	.043	.064

a. Dependent Variable: COURSES

FIGURE 10.10   Estimating the paths to Academic Coursework through simultaneous multiple regression.

Figure 10.12 shows the path model with all the standardized path coefficients added. You should compare the model to the regression results to help you understand where each path came from, including those from the disturbances.

Interpretation: Direct Effects

So, what do these findings tell us? If you focus first on the paths to Achievement, you will see these findings and their interpretation are the same as those from the simultaneous multiple regression of Achievement on these four variables in Chapter 9. Ability and Academic Coursework each had a strong effect on Achievement (.551 and .310, respectively), whereas Family Background had a small, but statistically significant effect (.069). As in the simultaneous regression of these same data in Chapter 9, the effect of Motivation on Achievement was small and not statistically significant.

The path model includes much more than this single simultaneous regression, however, because it also includes information about the effects *on* Coursework, Motivation, and Ability. Which of these variables affect the courses students take in high school? As hypothesized (and given the adequacy of the model), students' level of Academic Motivation had

Model Summary

Model	R	R Square	Adjusted R Square	Std. Error of the Estimate
1	.235[a]	.055	.053	9.729581

a. Predictors: (Constant), ABILITY, FAM_BACK

Coefficients[a]

Model		Unstandardized Coefficients		Standardized Coefficients	t	Sig.	95% Confidence Interval for B	
		B	Std. Error	Beta			Lower Bound	Upper Bound
1	(Constant)	39.850	2.279		17.488	.000	35.379	44.322
	FAM_BACK	1.265	.339	.127	3.735	.000	.601	1.930
	ABILITY	.101	.023	.152	4.495	.000	.057	.146

a. Dependent Variable: MOTIVATE

Model Summary

Model	R	R Square	Adjusted R Square	Std. Error of the Estimate
1	.417[a]	.174	.173	13.640426

a. Predictors: (Constant), FAM_BACK

Coefficients[a]

Model		Unstandardized Coefficients		Standardized Coefficients	t	Sig.	95% Confidence Interval for B	
		B	Std. Error	Beta			Lower Bound	Upper Bound
1	(Constant)	100.000	.431		231.831	.000	99.154	100.846
	FAM_BACK	6.255	.432	.417	14.494	.000	5.408	7.102

a. Dependent Variable: ABILITY

FIGURE 10.11   Estimating the paths to Motivation and Ability.

a strong effect on Coursework (.267); students who are more motivated take a more academic mix of courses than do students with lower levels of motivation. The largest effect on Coursework was from Ability (.374); more able students also take more academic courses in high school. Finally, Family Background also had a moderate effect on Coursework (.165), meaning that students from more advantaged backgrounds are more likely to take academic courses in high school than are students from less advantaged backgrounds.

The solved model also speaks to the extent to which Family Background and Ability affect Motivation; higher levels of both Ability and Family Background lead to higher levels of Academic Motivation. In addition, students from more advantaged backgrounds also show higher levels of Ability.

As an aside, notice the paths from the disturbances to each of the endogenous variables. As a general rule, these get smaller the farther to the right in the model. Don't read too much into this phenomenon. Achievement has four paths pointing toward it, four

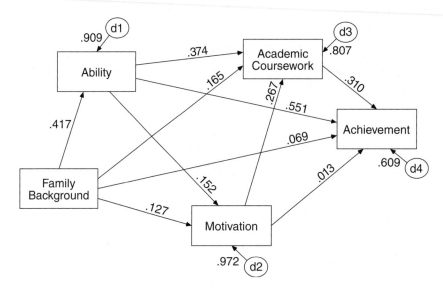

FIGURE 10.12   Solved model explaining Achievement, showing all standardized paths and disturbances.

variables explaining it in the model, whereas Ability has only one explanatory variable (Family Background) pointing toward it. Other things being equal, it is natural that our model should explain more of the variance of Achievement than Ability, and thus the paths from the disturbances from Achievement should be smaller.

Indirect and Total Effects

The model (Figure 10.12) includes other information, beyond what we would get in the usual MR (e.g., Chapter 9), as well. The results of this analysis suggest that Motivation affects Coursework, which in turn affects Achievement. This makes sense: More motivated students take more academic courses in high school, and this coursework, in turn, improves their achievement. Thus, although Motivation has little direct effect on Achievement, it does have an indirect effect, through Coursework. In fact, we can easily calculate this indirect effect: multiply the path from Motivation to Coursework times the path from Coursework to Achievement ($.267 \times .310 = .083$), which is the indirect effect of Motivation on Achievement through Coursework. We can also add the direct and indirect effects to determine the *total* effect of Motivation on Achievement ($.083 + .013 = .096$).[4]

It is slightly more complex to calculate the indirect and total effects of Ability or Family Background, because the farther back you go in the model, the more possible indirect effects there are. To calculate the indirect effect of Ability on Achievement, for example, you would need to calculate the indirect effect through Coursework ($.374 \times .310 = .116$), Motivation ($.152 \times .013 = .002$), and both Motivation and Coursework ($.152 \times .267 \times .310 = .013$). These indirect effects are then summed to calculate the total indirect effect, .131, and added to the direct effect (.551) to calculate the total effect, .682. Table 10.1 shows the standardized direct, indirect, and total effects for each variable on Achievement.

Calculate the indirect and total effects of Family Background on Achievement to see if your results match mine. Note also that there are no indirect effects for Coursework on Achievement. This is, of course, because our model includes no intervening variables between Coursework and Achievement. If it did, there would be indirect effects for Coursework as well.

TABLE 10.1   Standardized Direct, Indirect, and Total Effects of School Learning Variables on High School Achievement

VARIABLE	DIRECT EFFECT	INDIRECT EFFECT	TOTAL EFFECT
Academic Coursework	.310	—	.310
Motivation	.013	.083	.096
Ability	.551	.131	.682
Family Background	.069	.348	.417

Using Sequential Regression to Estimate Total and Indirect Effects.   Recall that in Part 1 of this book we focused on differences in findings from simultaneous (or forced entry) and sequential (hierarchical) regression. I noted at the time that the reason for this difference is that simultaneous regression focuses on direct effects, whereas sequential regression focuses on total effects. We have seen in this chapter that the b's and β's from simultaneous regression may be used as estimates of the direct effects in path analysis. Figure 10.13 shows some of the output for the sequential regression of Achievement on the variables in the school learning model, reproduced from Chapter 9. The figure shows the table of coefficients, with the variables entered into the equation based on their order of appearance in the model; that is, the first (exogenous) variable (Family Background) was entered first, followed by Ability, and so on. Focus on the standardized coefficients, β's, as each variable is added to the model; these coefficients are in italic boldface in the figure. Compare these coefficients to the total effects shown in Table 10.1 and you will see that they are the same, within errors of rounding. Thus, sequential regression may be used to estimate the *total effects* of each variable on the outcome for a path model. To do so, regress the endogenous variable of interest on each presumed cause in the order of their appearance in the model. The β for the variable entered at each step is the estimate of the variable's *total standardized effect* on the endogenous variable. The b for the variable entered at each step is the estimate of the variable's total unstandardized effect. If you are interested in the statistical significance of the total effects, however, you need to correct the degrees of freedom, using the value with all variables in the model. That is, look up the statistical significance of the t's using 995 df (total $N - k - 1$), rather than the df from each equation. Using this method, we can calculate the indirect effects via simple subtraction: we subtract the direct effect from the total effect to estimate the total indirect effects of each variable on the outcome. Try this subtractive method to calculate the indirect effects in Table 10.1. (To calculate the standard errors, confidence intervals, and statistical significance of indirect effects you will need to do a little hand calculation [Baron & Kenny, 1986], although as I write this there is a Web page that will do these calculations for you:

www.unc.edu/~preacher/sobel/sobel.htm. Alternatively, you can estimate the model with a SEM program, which will calculate standard errors of direct, indirect, and total effects.)

Coefficients[a]

Model		Unstandardized Coefficients		Standardized Coefficients			95% Confidence Interval for B	
		B	Std. Error	Beta	t	Sig.	Lower Bound	Upper Bound
1	(Constant)	50.000	.288		173.873	.000	49.436	50.564
	FAM_BACK	4.170	.288	*.417*	14.494	.000	3.605	4.735
2	(Constant)	4.557	1.559		2.923	.004	1.498	7.617
	FAM_BACK	1.328	.232	.133	5.729	.000	.873	1.782
	ABILITY	.454	.015	*.682*	29.416	.000	.424	.485
3	(Constant)	.759	1.766		.430	.667	-2.706	4.224
	FAM_BACK	1.207	.231	.121	5.221	.000	.753	1.661
	ABILITY	.445	.015	.667	28.768	.000	.414	.475
	MOTIVATE	9.53E-02	.021	*.095*	4.439	.000	.053	.137
4	(Constant)	6.434	1.692		3.803	.000	3.114	9.753
	FAM_BACK	.695	.218	.069	3.194	.001	.268	1.122
	ABILITY	.367	.016	.551	23.698	.000	.337	.398
	MOTIVATE	1.26E-02	.021	.013	.603	.547	-.028	.054
	COURSES	1.550	.120	*.310*	12.963	.000	1.315	1.785

a. Dependent Variable: ACHIEVE

FIGURE 10.13   Using sequential multiple regression to estimate the total effects of each variable on Achievement. The indirect effects are then calculated through subtraction (total – direct).

Note we could also calculate the total effects of each variable on each of the other endogenous variables in the model. To estimate the total effects of each variable on Coursework, for example, we sequentially regress Coursework on Family Background, followed by Ability, and followed by Motivation. The coefficient for the variable entered at each step equals its total effect on Coursework. The coefficients for the final step equal the direct effects for each variable on Coursework. We can calculate the indirect effects by subtracting the direct from the total effect for each variable.

Even with only five variables in the path model, it soon becomes tedious to solve for indirect and total effects directly, that is, by multiplying and summing paths. There are several possible shortcuts for doing such calculations. The one we have illustrated here—using sequential regression to estimate total effects and then calculating indirect effects by subtraction—is one of the easiest and has the advantage of illuminating the previously puzzling relation between sequential and simultaneous regression. The reason these methods tell different stories is because they focus on different questions; simultaneous regression focuses on direct effects, whereas sequential regression focuses on total effects. I hope the method also illustrates the importance of proper order of entry in sequential regression. If you wish to interpret sequential regression results in a causal fashion, you must enter the variables in their proper causal order.

It should be clear that this method of estimating total and indirect effects *does* work, but it may not be clear *why* it works. Recall that for the next to last variable in the causal chain (Coursework) the direct effects were equal to the total effects. The reason, of course, is there are no intervening or mediating variables between Coursework and Achievement and thus no possible indirect effect. The total and direct effects for Coursework on Achievement are the same. All the effect of one variable on another, then, is a direct effect *when there are no intervening variables.* It then stands to reason that one way of calculating total effects is to remove intervening variables.

In essence, what we have done with our sequential regression is to temporarily remove the intervening variables. Focus on Figures 10.14 through 10.16. The first step in the sequential regression, in which Achievement was regressed on Family Background, operationalized the model shown in Figure 10.14. In this model, all intervening variables between Family Background and Achievement are removed. The total effect of Family Background remains the same whether there are no intervening variables or whether there are three, or even 30, intervening variables; the total effects *are always the same.* Therefore, when we estimated *this* model, with the intervening variables removed, the direct effects and total effects are the same. The regression coefficient from this regression (.417) can then be used as an estimate of the total effect for the full model with all intervening variables. Figure 10.15 removes the intervening variables between Ability and Achievement. The second step in the sequential regression, in which Achievement is regressed on Family Background and Ability, operationalizes the model in Figure 10.15, and because there are no intervening variables between Ability and Achievement, the regression coefficient for Ability estimates the total effect of Ability on Achievement. Finally, the model shown in Figure 10.16, the third step in the sequential regression, provides the estimate of the total effect of Motivation on Achievement.

FIGURE 10.14   "Model" used to estimate the total effect of Family Background on Achievement.

Interpretation.   Let's take a few minutes to interpret these findings and, at the same time, further understand the relation between simultaneous and sequential regression. Focus on Motivation in Figure 10.12. The path model and Table 10.1 suggest that Motivation's effects on Achievement are primarily indirect, not direct. Motivation influences Achievement by influencing the courses students take in high school. Highly motivated students take more academically oriented courses, and these courses, in turn, improve their Achievement. In contrast, Ability's effects on Achievement are primarily direct. A portion of the effect of Ability is indirect, through Motivation and Coursework—more able students are more highly motivated and take more academic coursework, on average, than less able

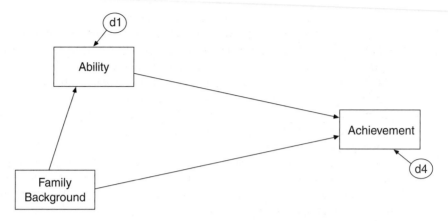

FIGURE 10.15   Estimating the total effect of Ability on Achievement. The total effect is estimated from the ß from this stage of the sequential regression.

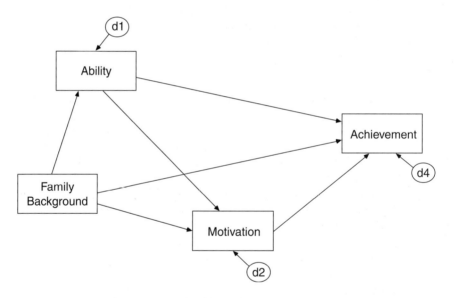

FIGURE 10.16   Estimating the total effect of Motivation on Achievement.

students—but the majority of the effect is direct: more able students also have higher academic Achievement. Again, the simultaneous regressions focused on direct effects and the sequential regressions focused on total effects.

I hope this discussion has illustrated some of the heuristic beauty of path models. They allow us to focus on both direct and indirect effects. Indirect effects, also known as mediating effects, are often vital for understanding how an influence comes about. *How* does Motivation affect Achievement? One important way is by influencing the courses students choose to take in high school. More motivated students take more academic coursework, and this coursework raises achievement. We generally miss understanding these indirect effects when we analyze our data with ordinary MR without path models. When you conduct path analysis, make sure to calculate and interpret all three types of effects. When you find a direct effect and wonder how it comes about, try incorporating several plausible mediating variables in a path model to see if you can understand how these effects happen. Suppose you find, for example, that physical abuse affects children's later social status. You may wonder whether these children's social behaviors (e.g., aggression) mediate, and thus partially explain, this effect. That is, are abused children more likely to be aggressive, with the aggression leading to a reduction in their subsequent social status (Salzinger, Feldman, Ng-Mak, Mojica, & Stockhammer, 2001)?

Path analysis has other advantages over multiple regression. A figure often makes it more obvious than does a table of regression coefficients exactly what are the presumed causes and the presumed effects. I think that the obviousness of the figural, causal assumptions in path analysis makes it more likely that the researchers will consider causal assumptions, as well as the basis for making these assumptions (theory and previous research). If nothing else, the drawing of the path model is at least an informal theory of cause and effect. As already discussed, path analysis makes use of the different stories told by simultaneous and sequential regression. For these reasons, I believe that path analysis (and SEM) is often the best method of analysis for nonexperimental research.

SUMMARY

We have covered a lot of material in this chapter, and I hope the chapter has both covered new ground and made clear some loose ends from our adventures in MR. This chapter introduced path analysis, which is the simplest form of structural equation modeling, or SEM.

We introduced the chapter with a simple model involving Ability, Motivation, and Achievement. Our initial, agnostic model simply showed the correlations among these three variables, a less than satisfying solution since it did not inform our research question of interest, which was understanding the influence of Motivation on Achievement. Thinking through our research interest and using a combination of theory, logic, and previous research, we were able to make some general causal statements: (1) if Motivation and Achievement are causally related, Motivation affects Achievement, rather than the reverse, and (2) Ability may affect both Motivation and Achievement. These statements, a weak causal ordering, were translated into a path model in which Ability was assumed to affect both Motivation and Achievement and Motivation was assumed to affect Achievement. The correlations, notably, were not used to draw the paths. We now had three unknowns (three paths) and three pieces of data (the correlations), and through the use of algebra we were able to generate equations for and solve for the paths.

Although we can solve for the paths using algebra, for simple recursive models the paths are equal to the standardized or unstandardized coefficients from a series of simultaneous regressions. For the three-variable model, we regressed Achievement on Ability and Family Motivation, with the β's providing estimates of the standardized paths from Ability and Motivation (or the b's estimating the unstandardized paths). A second regression of Motivation on Ability provided the estimate of the path from Ability to Motivation. The influences of the disturbances (or residuals) were estimated by $\sqrt{1 - R^2}$ from each regression equation. Disturbances represent all other influences on the effects in the model other than the variables in the model, and were symbolized by variables enclosed in circles or ovals.

What evidence was used to make the inferences of causality? It was not the correlations. Instead, we focused on formal and informal theory, time precedence, an understanding of the phenomenon being studied, and logic. At a more formal level, three conditions are required to make a valid inference of cause and effects: there must be a functional relation between the variables, the cause must precede the effect in time (either actually or logically), and the relation must be nonspurious.

We dealt with some jargon you are likely to encounter in path analysis. Measured variables, those measured in your research, are symbolized by rectangles. Unmeasured, or latent variables, are symbolized by circles or ovals. Disturbances represent unmeasured variables not considered in the model; disturbances may also be referred to as residuals or errors. Recursive models have arrows flowing in only one direction, whereas nonrecursive models have feedback loops, or arrows pointing in two directions. Just-identified models are those for which we have just enough information to solve for the paths, and overidentified models are those for which we have more information than we need and can thus estimate some of the paths in more than one way. Underidentified models are those for which we have more paths than we have information to estimate the paths; they are therefore not solvable without the addition of extra constraints. Exogenous variables are causes, variables with no paths pointing towards them. Endogenous variables are effects; they have paths pointing to them in the model. Most of this jargon is summarized in Figure 10.17.

We conducted a path analysis using the data from Chapter 9, where the data were used to highlight the differences in findings from simultaneous and sequential regression. We developed a model of the effects of Family Background, Ability, Motivation, and Coursework on Achievement based on theory, time precedence, previous research, and logic. Paths and disturbances were estimated via a series of simultaneous multiple regressions. Given the accuracy of the model, the results suggested that Ability and Coursework had strong effects on Achievement, Family Background had a small effect, and Motivation had no appreciable effect. Further inspection of the model showed that Motivation had a strong effect on the Coursework students take in high school, so Motivation should have an indirect effect on Achievement through Coursework. We were able to calculate these indirect effects by multiplying together the two paths. We added this indirect effect to the direct effect to estimate the total effect of Motivation on Achievement. When we focused on the total effect, Motivation did indeed have an influence on Achievement and one that makes sense: more motivated students, it appears, take more advanced coursework, and this coursework, in turn, improves their achievement.

An easier way to estimate total effects is through sequential regression. To do so, we regressed Achievement on Family Background and then added Ability, then Motivation, and then Coursework. The β associated with each variable, when entered, represents its total standardized effect. Thus, when Motivation was added to the model, its β was .096, its total effect. This procedure works because the total effects are the same whether or not there are intervening variables between the variable of interest and the outcome. If we remove the intervening variables, the total effects are equal to the direct effects. We then estimated the indirect effects by subtracting the direct from the total effects.

In addition to illustrating the basics of path analysis, this chapter tied together a major loose end of Part 1, the apparent inconsistency between simultaneous and sequential regres-

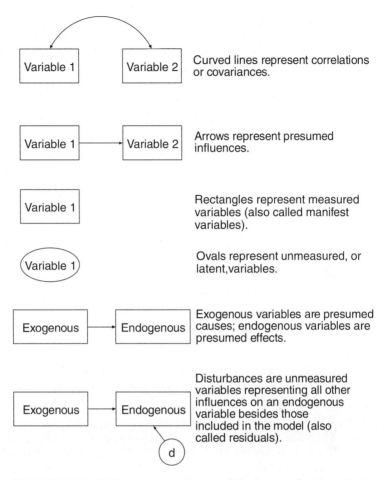

FIGURE 10.17   Quick summary of some of the jargon of path analysis.

sion results. I argued that path analysis is particularly useful because it allows us to focus on both direct and indirect effects and that indirect effects are useful in explaining how an effect works. Intervening or mediating variables can thus be added to models to help understand how an effect comes about. Path models are also useful because they make explicit what is too often left vague: the researcher's theory of how variables are causally related. In my opinion, path analysis is the best use of MR for explanatory, nonexperimental research.

EXERCISES

1. Table 10.2 shows the means, standard deviations, and correlations among the variables used in this chapter's example. Reanalyze the five-variable path model. (For users of SPSS, the file "motivate 5 var path.sps" on the Web site (www.ablongman.com/keith1e) shows how to analyze such a matrix using this program.) Calculate all paths and disturbances to create a table of direct, indirect, and total effects. Make sure your results match mine.

TABLE 10.2   Means, Standard Deviations, and Correlations among the School Learning Variables

	FAMILY BACKGROUND	ABILITY	MOTIVATION	COURSEWORK	ACHIEVEMENT
N	1000	1000	1000	1000	1000
Mean	0	100	50	4	50
SD	1	15	10	2	10
Family Background	1				
Ability	.417	1			
Motivation	.190	.205	1		
Coursework	.372	.498	.375	1	
Achievement	.417	.737	.255	.615	1

2. Construct a path model using the variables Family Background, 8th-grade GPA, 10th-grade Self-Esteem, 10th-grade Locus of Control, and 10th-grade Social Studies achievement test scores. How did you make the decisions on which variable affected which? Which of these decisions were the most difficult? What sources could you use to better inform your decisions?

3. What is the identification status of your model: just-identified, overidentified, or underidentified? If your model is underidentified, see if you can make it into a just-identified model so that you can estimate it.

4. Select the variables BYSES, BYGrads, F1Cncpt2, F1Locus2, and F1TxHStd from the NELS data. Check the variables (e.g., descriptive statistics) to make sure you understand the scales of the variables. Also make sure that any values that should be coded as missing values are so coded.

5. Estimate your model using the variables from NELS (Exercise 4). Calculate the direct effects and disturbances, and put them into your model. Calculate total effects and create a table of direct, indirect, and total effects. Interpret the model; focus on direct, indirect, and total effects.

6. Compare your model and interpretation with others in your class. How many classmates drew the model in the same way you did? How many drew it differently? What difference did these different models make in results and interpretation?

NOTES

1. Here's more detail in solving the paths using algebra. The three equations were $a = r_{12}$, $b = r_{13} - ac$, and $c = r_{23} - ab$. We will solve the equation for b by substituting the first and third equations (for a and c, respectively) into the second equation:

$$b = r_{13} - r_{12}(r_{23} - r_{12}b)$$
$$= r_{13} - (r_{12}r_{23} - r_{12}^2 b)$$
$$= r_{13} - r_{12}r_{23} + r_{12}^2 b$$
$$b - r_{12}^2 b = r_{13} - r_{12}r_{23}$$
$$b(1 - r_{12}^2) = r_{13} - r_{12}r_{23}$$
$$b = \frac{r_{13} - r_{12}r_{23}}{1 - r_{12}^2}$$

See if you can use the same approach to solve for c.

2.   The other method of developing equations to solve for paths is called the *first law* of path analysis (Kenny, 1979, p. 28). The correlation between Y (a presumed effect) and X (r_{xy}) is equal to the sum of the product of each path (p) from all causes of Y times the correlation of those variables with X: $r_{yx} = \sum p_{yz} r_{xz}$. Using the first law, the correlation between Motivation and Achievement is $r_{32} = br_{12} + cr_{22}$, which reduces to $r_{32} = br_{12} + c$ (description and equation adapted from Kenny, 1979, p. 28). The advantage of the first law is that it can be used to generate equations for any type of model, whereas the tracing rule works only with simple recursive models.

3.   These rules are that standardized coefficients above .05 could be considered small; those above .10, moderate; and those above .25, large. These rules apply primarily to manipulable influences on school learning.

4.   Total effects are sometimes referred to as total causal effects. It is also possible to subtract the total causal effects from the original correlation to determine the noncausal (or spurious) portion of the correlation.

PATH ANALYSIS: DANGERS AND ASSUMPTIONS

Path analysis is not magic; it does not prove causality. It does not make a silk purse out of a sow's ear; it cannot turn poor data into valid causal conclusions. Like multiple regression, there are assumptions underlying path analysis and the use of multiple regression to estimate paths. Like multiple regression, path analysis is open to abuse. This chapter will discuss these assumptions and the dangers of path analysis; it will also discuss how to avoid the dangers of the method.

ASSUMPTIONS

Because we have so far been using multiple regression to estimate path models, it should not be surprising that the basic assumptions of multiple regression also apply to path analysis. As discussed in Chapter 9, these include the following:

1. The dependent variable is a linear function of the independent variables.
2. Each person (or other observation) should be drawn independently from the population.
3. The errors are normally distributed and relatively constant for all values of the independent variable.

Multiple regression analysis assumes that the errors are uncorrelated with the independent variables or, in the jargon of path analysis, the disturbances are uncorrelated with the exogenous variables. Therefore, the causal mechanism underlying our path analysis (or multiple regression) model needs to conform to these same constraints in order for the regression coefficients to provide accurate estimates of the effects of one variable on another. This assumption also implies several additional assumptions; to the extent that the following conditions are violated, the paths (regression coefficients) may be inaccurate and misleading estimates of the effects.

1. There is no reverse causation; that is, the model is recursive.
2. The exogenous variables are perfectly measured, that is, they are completely reliable and valid measures.
3. "A state of equilibrium has been reached" (Kenny, 1979, p. 51). This assumption means that the causal process has had a chance to work.
4. No common cause of the presumed cause and the presumed effect has been neglected; the model includes all such common causes (Kenny, 1979).

If these sound a lot like the assumptions from Chapter 9, you are perceptive; they are virtually the same, but rewritten in path analytic lingo. These assumptions are also required any time we wish to interpret regression coefficients in a causal, or explanatory, fashion.

The first assumption (of the second set) is really twofold. It first means that we have paths drawn in the correct direction. We have already discussed how this is done and will continue to discuss this critical issue in this and later chapters. This assumption also means, as indicated, that the model is recursive, with no feedback loops or variables both causing and affecting other variables. There are methods for estimating such models, but ordinary multiple regression is not a valid method for nonrecursive models.

The second assumption is one we can only approximate. We all know there is no such thing as perfect measurement, especially in the social sciences. When we begin discussing latent variable SEM, we will see how serious our violation of this assumption is and what can be done about it. For now, I will simply note that if our exogenous variables are reasonably reliable and valid little harm is done, meaning our estimates of effects are not overly biased.

The third assumption is that the causal process has had a chance to work. If motivation affects achievement, this process presumably takes a certain amount of time, and this time must have elapsed. This assumption applies to all causal research. Consider an experiment in which children are given some treatment and subsequently measured on a dependent variable. If you make these measurements too soon, not allowing the treatment to work, you will miss spotting any real effects your treatment may have. The amount of time needed depends on the process being studied.

The final assumption is the most crucial, and it is one we have returned to over and over in this book. We will now explore it in more depth, because the danger of omitted common causes is the biggest threat to the causal conclusions we reach from path analysis, in particular, and nonexperimental research in general. Again, I remind you that these assumptions apply to *any* explanatory use of MR.

THE DANGER OF COMMON CAUSES

Suppose I were to go into my local elementary schools and ask every student to read the Gettysburg Address, and I scored each student on the number of words he or she read correctly within 2 minutes. Suppose that I also measured each child's shoe size. If we correlate these two variables (reading skill and shoe size), we likely will find a substantial correlation between them. This correlation is illustrated in the top of Figure 11.1 by the curved line between the two variables. It is foolish, however, to conclude that shoe size affects reading skill (as is done in the middle portion of the figure), and it is equally foolish to conclude that reading skill affects shoe size. The reason is that there is a third variable—age or growth—that affects both shoe size and reading skill, as symbolized by the bottom portion of Figure 11.1. Older students, on average, are larger (and thus have larger shoes) and read better than do younger students. The bottom of the figure illustrates the true causal relation among these variables; shoe size and reading skill are correlated only because the two are affected by age. The correlation between shoe size and reading skill is the essence of what we call a spurious correlation. The term *spurious correlation* means that two variables are not related by one variable affecting the other, but are the result of a third variable affecting both (cf. Simon, 1954).

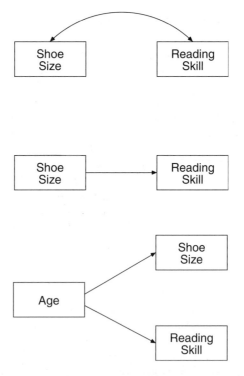

FIGURE 11.1   Spurious correlation in path form. Although shoe size and reading skill are correlated, shoe size does not cause reading skill, nor does reading skill cause shoe size. There is a third variable, age or growth, that affects both reading skill and shoe size. This common cause of shoe size and reading skill is why the two variables are correlated.

This example also illustrates the essence of the problem we have been referring to as that of a neglected common cause. If we set up a path analysis of the reading–shoe size data in which we assumed shoe size affected reading skill (as in the middle of Figure 11.1), the results do not tell us we were foolish, but instead suggest that shoe size has a substantial impact on reading skill. The reason, again, is that we neglected to control for age, the common cause in our analysis. If we control for age, we will see the apparent effect of shoe size on reading skill diminish to zero. The model is crucial; for the estimates to be accurate, we must control for important common causes of our presumed cause and presumed effect. This problem is referred to as omitted common causes, spurious correlation, or the third-variable problem.

A Research Example

A more realistic example will further illustrate the problem. There is ample evidence that involvement by parents in education improves students' learning (Christenson, Rounds, & Gorney, 1992), but estimates of the effects of parent involvement on learning vary widely across studies. Figure 11.2 shows a plausible model of the effects of Parent Involvement on 10th-grade GPA. For this model, Parent Involvement was defined as a combination of parents' educational aspirations for their children and communication between parents and their children about school. Background variables—potential common causes of Parent Involvement and 10th-Grade GPA—include students' Ethnic origin, their Family Background characteristics, and their previous school performance (Previous Achievement). Let's concentrate on this final variable. Previous Achievement should certainly affect students' current academic performance, since it forms a basis for all future learning. But should students' previous academic performance also affect the degree to which parents are involved in students' schooling? I think it should; it should affect both parent involvement, in general, and more specifically parents' aspirations for their children's future educational

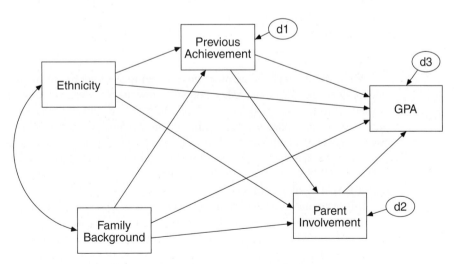

FIGURE 11.2   Model of the effects of Parent Involvement on high school GPA. The model is just-identified and recursive.

attainment (one of the components of parent involvement). We could turn to previous research and determine that students' previous performance or aptitude indeed affects their parents' level of involvement. In other words, Previous Achievement, or aptitude, appears to be a likely common cause of both Parent Involvement and current GPA.

I estimated the model using the NELS data; the results are shown in Figure 11.3. Parent Involvement appears to have a moderate effect on student GPA ($\beta = .160$). The results show that our supposition about Previous Achievement was also correct: Given the adequacy of the model, the results suggest that Previous Achievement had a large effect on both GPA (.417) and Parent Involvement (.345). Previous Achievement thus appears to be an important common cause of Parent Involvement and current Grades.

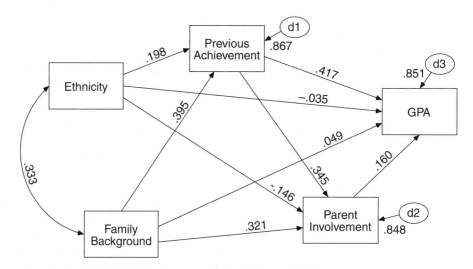

FIGURE 11.3   Parent Involvement model estimated through multiple regression analysis. Note the effect of Previous Achievement on Parent Involvement and GPA.

What would happen if we were not attuned to the importance of students' previous school performance? What if we had not built Previous Achievement into our model? What if we had neglected this important common cause? The results of such neglect are shown in Figure 11.4. In this model, Previous Achievement was not included; this important common cause was not controlled. The result is that the model substantially overestimates the effect of Parent Involvement on GPA: the effect in this model is .293, as opposed to .160 in the previous model. With the omission of this important common cause, we overestimated the effect of Parent Involvement on GPA.

This example illustrates the importance of including known common causes in path models. The example also illustrates the most frequent consequence of neglecting these common causes: When a common cause is omitted from a model, we often end up overestimating the magnitude of the effect of one variable on another.[1] Finally, the example illustrates one possible reason for the variability in findings concerning the effect of parent involvement on school performance: not all research has controlled for previous achieve-

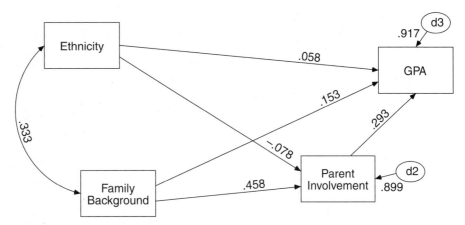

FIGURE 11.4   Previous Achievement, a common cause of Parent Involvement and GPA, is not included in this model. Notice the inflation of the path from Involvement to GPA.

ment (and there are other possible explanations, as well). Research on parent involvement is not the only area in which researchers have likely overestimated effects by ignoring important common causes. For example, Page and Keith (1981) showed how Coleman and colleagues (Coleman, Hoffer, & Kilgore, 1981) had overestimated the effects of private schooling on student achievement by ignoring student ability as a potential common cause of achievement and private school attendance. In fact, if you are suspicious of the findings of nonexperimental research, you should probably first look for neglected common causes as the reason for misleading findings.

Note that there was nothing in the analysis summarized in Figure 11.4 that told us we had missed an important common cause. The analysis did not explode; no alarm bells went off. How then do you know that you have included all relevant common causes in your research? A good understanding of relevant theory and previous research are the keys to avoiding this deadly sin, just as they are for drawing the model in the first place.

Common Causes, Not All Causes

Unfortunately, many neophytes to path analysis (and nonexperimental research in general), terrified of neglecting a common cause of a presumed cause and a presumed effect, include every variable they can think of that might be such a common cause. Others misunderstand the admonition about *common* causes and try to include all possible causes of *either* the presumed cause or the presumed effect. Both approaches lead to overloaded and less powerful analyses (by reducing degrees of freedom in the regression), ones that are more likely to confuse than inform (and see Darlington, 1990, chap. 8, for additional dangers with including too many variables).

I demonstrated in note 2 in Chapter 4 that the inclusion of a noncommon cause in a regression does not change the estimates of regression coefficients. Here we will demonstrate this truism again using the current example. Focus again on Figure 11.3. For this model, we do not need to include all causes of Parent Involvement in the model, nor do we need to include all causes of GPA in the model. This is fortunate, because there must be hundreds of variables that affect GPA alone! All we need to include in the model are *common* causes of Parent Involvement and GPA. Note the effect of Ethnicity on Parent Involvement and GPA. Ethnicity affects Parent Involvement; other things being equal, minority students report greater involvement than do majority students (majority students are coded 1 and minority students coded 0). But once the other variables in the model are controlled, Ethnicity had no meaningful effect on GPA ($\beta = -.035$). Despite its inclusion in the model, it appears that Ethnicity is not a common cause of Parent Involvement and GPA. If my argument is correct, if variables need not be included in a model unless they are common causes, then the exclusion of Ethnicity from the model should have little effect on our estimate of the magnitude of influence of Parent Involvement on GPA. As shown in Figure 11.5, the exclusion of Ethnicity had only a minor effect on this estimate, which changed from .160 to .165. We could exclude Ethnicity from this model without seriously affecting the estimate of the influence of Parent Involvement on GPA. To reiterate, models must include common causes of the presumed cause and the presumed effect if they are to be valid, but they need not include *all* causes.[2]

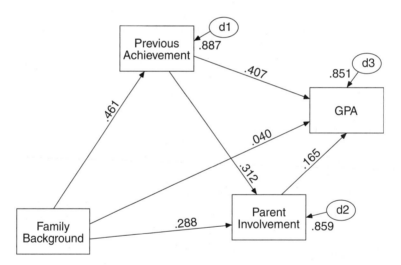

FIGURE 11.5 In this model, Ethnicity was excluded. But Ethnicity was not a meaningful common cause; it affected only Parent Involvement, not GPA, in Figure 11.3. Thus, its exclusion in this model has little effect on the estimate of the effect of Parent Involvement on GPA.

True Experiments and Common Causes. The elimination of the danger of omitted common causes is the reason that true experiments allow such a powerful inference of cause and effect. As a general rule, experimental research, in which participants are *assigned at random* to experimental versus treatment groups, has a higher degree of internal validity than does nonexperimental research, meaning that it is often less dangerous to make an inference of cause and effect with a true experiment. Figure 11.6 helps illustrate the reason for this power. Suppose you conduct an experiment in which you assign, at random, children with behavior disorders to two types of treatments: group therapy or behavior modification, with some measure of behavior improvement as the dependent variable. Figure 11.6 illustrates this experiment in path analytic form, with the path from the dummy variable Group Therapy versus Behavior Modification to Behavior providing the estimate of the relative effectiveness of the two treatments. But a multitude of variables affect children's behavior, from parents to friends to teachers, and many more. Why don't we have to consider these variables when we conduct our analysis of the experiment? The reason we don't have to consider these Other Influences on Behavior is because they are not *common* causes of assignment to treatment groups and Behavior. Although these Other Influences affect Behavior, they did not affect assignment to the Therapy versus Behavior Modification groups because assignment to the treatment groups was random, based on the flip of a coin. This, then, is why true experiments are so powerful. True experiments still require an inference of cause and effect, but we can make that inference so powerfully because the act of random assignment effectively excludes all possible common causes of the presumed cause and the presumed effect. Random assignment assures that no other variables affect the presumed cause.

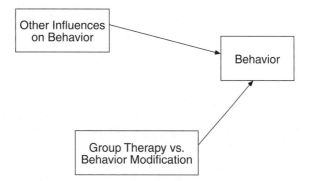

FIGURE 11.6   A true experiment in path form. Due to random assignment to groups (Therapy versus Behavior Modification), the variables that affect Behavior (the effect) do not affect the cause (treatment group). Random assignment rules out common causes, which is why we don't need to control for the multitude of other influences on Behavior in our analysis.

INTERVENING (MEDIATING) VARIABLES

Given the admonition that models must include all common causes of the presumed cause and presumed effect, you may wonder how this applies to intervening or mediating variables. Do you also need to include all variables that *mediate* the effect of one variable on another? The answer is no; mediating variables are interesting because they help explain how an effect comes about, but they are not necessary for the model to be valid; in short, they are gravy. It is good that mediating variables are not required to make the model valid, because you could always include another layer of mediating variables. In the present example, you might wonder if Homework and TV viewing time mediate the effects of Parent Involvement on GPA (cf. Keith et al., 1993). That is, do parents influence their adolescents' learning, in part, by influencing them to complete more homework and watch less TV? Suppose you found that these variables indeed mediated the influence of Parent Involvement on GPA; you might then wonder if the effects of Homework were mediated by time on task, and so on. Even with a seemingly direct relation, say the effect of smoking on lung cancer, we could posit and test indirect effects—the effect of smoking on buildup of carcinogens in the lungs, the effect of these chemicals on the individual cells, and so on. Again, it is not necessary to include indirect effects for models to be valid, but such indirect effects can help you understand how effects come about.

In our current example, suppose that our central interest was the effect of Previous Achievement on GPA. If we were to conduct an analysis examining the direct effect of Previous Achievement on GPA without the intervening variable of Parent Involvement, the standardized direct (and total effect) would be .472. If you conduct the calculations for the indirect and total effects, you will find that the total effect of Previous Achievement on GPA for Figure 11.3 is also .472. When mediating or intervening variables are included in the model, the total effects do not change (although direct effects do); indirect effects are unnecessary for model validity.

I stress again, however, that although unnecessary for valid models indirect effects are often very illuminating. Our current example suggests that Parent Involvement has a positive effect on GPA. But how does that effect come about? Previous research that tested for possible mediation by homework and TV viewing suggests that homework, in fact, partially mediates the effect of parent involvement on learning, but that TV viewing does not (Keith et al., 1993). Parents who are more involved encourage, cajole, or force their children to do more homework, and this homework, in turn, raises their achievement. Although parents who are involved also influence their adolescents to spend less time watching TV, TV viewing appears to have little effect on achievement. Thus, leisure TV viewing does not appear to mediate the effect of parent involvement on achievement. As you become more expert in a particular area of research, you will likely find yourself asking questions about indirect or mediating effects. Indeed, even for those conducting experiments, indirect effects may often be of interest. Suppose you find that your experimental treatment (e.g., a new versus an established type of consultation) is effective; you may next reasonably wonder why. Is it because the new consultation method improved problem identification, or speeded the time to intervention, or made evaluation more complete? Another advantage of mediating variables is that they can help strengthen the causal inferences embedded in path models. Logically, if you can explain both which variables affect an outcome and the mechanism *by which that effect occurs,* your causal claims are more believable. If we can demonstrate the indirect effect of smoking on lung cancer through the buildup of carcinogens in the lungs, it strengthens the case for smoking, as opposed to other characteristics of smokers, being a cause of lung cancer (Pearl, 2000). For additional information on testing mediating variables, see Baron and Kenny (1986), MacKinnon, Warsi, and Dwyer (1995), or Shrout and Bolger, 2002; see also the earlier discussion of mediation in Chapter 8.

OTHER POSSIBLE DANGERS

Paths in the Wrong Direction

Another possible danger in path analysis (and nonexperimental research in general) is that you may draw a path in the wrong direction. The implications of this danger depend on where this mistake takes place.

Figure 11.7 shows a model in which I erroneously assumed that 10th-grade GPA affected 8th-grade Parent Involvement. This model is clearly impossible, since it violates one of our primary assumptions, that cause cannot happen backward in time. The GPA variable occurs in 10th grade (although it is actually a measure of 9th- and 10th-grade GPA), whereas the Parent Involvement variable occurs in 8th grade. The model is clearly impossible. There is, however, nothing in the multiple regression analyses and nothing in the figure that would alert you to the fact that your model is incorrect. Indeed, the model leads you to completely erroneous conclusions about the moderate effect of 10th-grade GPA on 8th-grade Parent Involvement. Obviously, if the arrow between the two variables of prime interest is drawn in the wrong direction, the results will be completely and totally misleading.

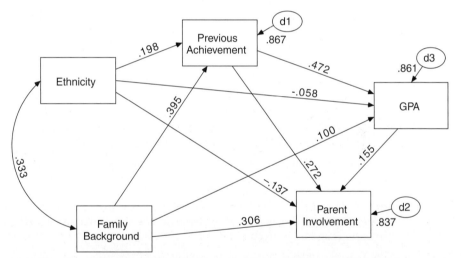

FIGURE 11.7   In this model the path between GPA and Parent Involvement is drawn in the wrong direction. There is nothing in the results to indicate that you are wrong.

In contrast, Figure 11.8 shows a model in which the path between Previous Achievement and Parent Involvement is drawn in the wrong direction. Previous Achievement was included in the model as a potential common cause of Parent Involvement and GPA, so the model in Figure 11.8 no longer controls for this variable as a *common* cause. Again, there is nothing in any of the analyses to suggest that our model is incorrect. In this case, however, with the mistaken path being between our primary causal variable and a "control" variable, the findings are not quite as misleading. In fact, the direct effects of each variable in the model are the same as they were with the "correct" model shown in Figure 11.3. This makes sense when you realize that all paths to GPA are estimated via simultaneous MR, and for the models shown in Figures 11.3 and 11.8, both simultaneous regressions regressed GPA on each of the four variables in the model. What are incorrect in Figure 11.8 are the *total* effects. In Figure 11.3, Previous Achievement has an indirect effect on GPA through Parent Involvement, and thus its total effect is .472, compared to a direct effect of .417. In Figure 11.8, Previous Achievement is the next to last variable in the causal chain, so it has no indirect effect on GPA; its direct and total effects are both .417. For Parent Involvement, the reverse is true. In the "correct" model (Figure 11.3), Involvement had no indirect effect on GPA, so its direct and total effects were both equal to .160. In Figure 11.8, Involvement has an indirect effect on GPA through Previous Achievement, and thus we overestimate its total effect as .294. You should calculate the indirect and total effects yourself to make sure your estimates agree with mine.

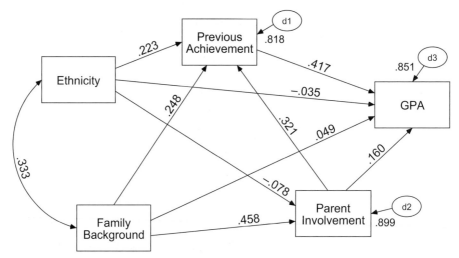

FIGURE 11.8   In this model the path between Parent Involvement and Previous Achievement is drawn in the wrong direction. The direct effects remain the same, but the indirect and total effects differ.

If the variables with paths drawn in the wrong direction are two of the less central variables, there should be little or no effect on the estimates of the primary variables of interest. For example, suppose the current example included a path from Ethnicity to Family Background, rather than a correlation. Suppose further that we erred by drawing that path in the wrong direction (from Family Background to Ethnicity). This mistake will have no effect on the estimates of the direct, indirect, or total effects of Parent Involvement on GPA.

To summarize, if the effect, the final endogenous variable, is in the wrong position, estimates of all effects will be erroneous. If the primary causal variable has paths drawn in the wrong direction (but not the primary *effect* of interest), estimates of direct effects may still be accurate, but indirect and total effects will likely be incorrect. If background variables have paths drawn in the wrong direction, this error will likely not affect estimates of effects from the main cause variable to the main effect. These comments apply to just-identified models estimated through multiple regression, but are not too far off for other, more complex models.

Reciprocal Causal Relations?   Given the problems resulting from paths drawn in the wrong direction, you may be tempted to be open-minded and proclaim that the variables are causally related in a reciprocal fashion, that not only does *a* affect *b,* but *b* also affects *a.* Don't succumb to this temptation at this stage of your development! Although it is indeed possible to estimate such nonrecursive models, you cannot do so using multiple regression. You can estimate nonrecursive models using the SEM programs discussed in subsequent chapters, but such models are neither easy nor their results always illuminating. In my experience, reciprocal effects are also relatively uncommon. Reserve the use of nonrecursive models for those cases in which you really think reciprocal effects may exist or for which you have legitimate, substantive questions about causal direction, not those for which you are simply unsure.

An even worse solution to this dilemma is to try to conduct the regression–path analysis both ways to see which "works best." You have already seen that the results of simple path analyses do not tell you when you have a path in the wrong direction. Likewise, the results of the analyses do not inform you as to which direction is best. Once again, theory, previous research, and logic are the appropriate tools for making such judgments.

I should note that, although the results of just-identified path analyses estimated through multiple regression cannot inform decisions about causal direction, properly over-identified models estimated through an SEM program may indeed be able to help with such decisions. In addition, well thought out nonrecursive models estimated via SEM programs can also be very informative about the nature and process of how one variable affects another. We will discuss these issues in later chapters.

Unreliability and Invalidity

One assumption underlying the causal interpretation of regression and path coefficients is that the exogenous variables are measured with near perfect reliability and validity. With our current model, Ethnicity may come close to meeting this assumption, but the variable Family Background, a composite of Parent Education, Parent Occupational Status, and Family Income, certainly does not. We obviously regularly violate this assumption, but will postpone until later chapters a discussion of the effects of this violation and possible solutions.

DEALING WITH DANGER

The two primary dangers of path analysis are (1) that you have neglected to include in your model an important common cause of the variable you think of as your primary cause and the variable you think of as your primary effect and (2) that you have drawn paths in the wrong direction; that is, you have confused cause and effect. In the jargon of SEM, these are generally termed specification errors, or errors in the model. Of these two, I consider the first the most common and insidious. In most cases, it should be pretty obvious when you draw a path in the wrong direction. What can you do to avoid these errors?

My first response is to say, "Welcome to the dangerous world of structural equation modeling; join us SEMers on the wild side!" More seriously, I again remind you that these same dangers apply to *any* nonexperimental research, no matter how that research is analyzed. One advantage of path analysis and structural equation modeling, in my opinion, is the requirement of a theory, generally expressed figurally in a path model, prior to analysis. It is much easier to spot missing common causes and causal assumptions in the wrong direction when examining such a model than it is when reading the description of, say, a MR analysis. Furthermore, these dangers apply to *all* research, experimental or nonexperimental, in which we wish to infer cause and effect. A true experiment allows a powerful inference of cause and effect by knocking one leg out from under the danger of common causes, but the farther we stray from the true experimental ideal of random assignment to treatment groups, the more real this danger becomes. Indeed, many concerns with quasi-experimental research (e.g., research using matched groups rather than random assignment) boil down to concerns over unmeasured common causes. With a true experiment we also actively manipulate the independent variable, the presumed cause, thus making true experiments less likely to confuse causal direction, as well.

We have seen that the analyses themselves do not guard against these errors; they do not tell us when our models are wrong or when we have neglected an important common cause. How, then, to avoid these specification errors? I come back to the same refrain: understand relevant theory; be familiar with the research literature; spend time puzzling over your model, especially thinking about potential common causes and potential problems in direction; and draw your model carefully.

These same concerns and dangers apply when you are a consumer and reader of others' research. As you read others' nonexperimental research, you should ask yourself whether the researchers neglected to include any important common causes of their presumed cause and presumed effect. If so, the results of the research will be misleading and likely overestimate (or underestimate) the effect of one variable on another. Arm-chair analysis is not sufficient, however; it is not valid to simply say, "Well, I think variable Z is a probable common cause of variables X and Y," and expect to have your concerns taken seriously. You should be able to demonstrate, through theory, previous research, or analysis, that variable Z is indeed a likely and important common cause. Likewise, as you read nonexperimental research, you should be attuned to whether any of the causal assumptions are reversed. Again, you should be able to demonstrate this incorrect causal direction through theory, research, logic, or your own analyses.

We will revisit the danger of measurement error and its effects. For the time being, you should simply strive to make sure that all your variables, and especially your exogenous variables, are as reliable and valid as possible.

REVIEW: STEPS IN A PATH ANALYSIS

Let's review the steps involved in path analysis now that we've carefully considered the dangers.

1. First, spend some time thinking about the problem; how might these variables of interest be causally related?

2. Draw a tentative model.
3. Study relevant theory and research. Which variables must be included in the analysis? You must include the relevant common causes, but not every variable under the sun. The relevant theory and research, along with careful thought, will also help you resolve questions of causal direction. "The study of structural equation models can be divided into two parts: the easy part and the hard part" (Duncan, 1975, p. 149). This step is the hard part of SEM.
4. Revise the model. It should be lean, but include all necessary variables.
5. Collect a sample and measure the variables in the model, or find a data set in which the variables are already measured. Use reliable and valid instruments.
6. Check the identification status of the model.
7. Estimate the model.
8. Fill in the model estimates (paths and disturbances) in your figure. Are the paths more or less as expected? That is, are the paths you expected to be positive in fact positive; those you expected to be negative, negative, and those that you expected to be close to zero in fact close to zero? Meeting such expectations allows more confidence in your model.
9. Write up the results and publish them.

Some writers recommend *theory trimming* in between my steps 8 and 9. Theory trimming means deleting statistically insignificant paths and reestimating the model. I do not recommend this step, especially when using multiple regression to solve for the paths. We will return to this issue in the next chapter.

SUMMARY

The chapter began by reiterating the basic assumptions of multiple regression: linearity, independence, and homoscedasticity. For regression coefficients to provide accurate estimates of effects, the disturbances should be uncorrelated with the exogenous variables. This assumption will likely be fulfilled if there is no reverse causation, the exogenous variables are perfectly measured, equilibrium has been achieved, and there are no omitted common causes in the model.

These assumptions led to a discussion of the dangers of path analysis. When a common cause (a variable that affects both a presumed cause and a presumed effect) is omitted from a model, this omission changes the estimate of the influence of one variable on another. The most common result is that we end up overestimating the effect, although underestimation is also possible. The dreaded *spurious correlation* is a result of an omitted common cause, and thus omitted common causes are the primary reason for the admonition about inferring causation from correlations. I illustrated the effects of omitting a common cause through a research example testing the effects of Parent Involvement on 10th-grade GPA. When Previous Achievement, a common cause of Involvement and GPA, was omitted from the model, we overestimated the effect of Parent Involvement on GPA. Omitted common causes may be a reason for variability in research findings in nonexperimental research.

The warning to include common causes should not be interpreted as a mandate to include all causes of the presumed cause and the presumed effect. Only variables that affect both the presumed cause and presumed effect must be included. We illustrated the difference between a cause and a common cause by deleting Ethnicity from the model. Ethnicity affected Parent Involvement but not GPA, and thus was not a *common cause* of the two variables. As a result, when Ethnicity was removed from the model, the estimate of the effect of Involvement on GPA barely changed. The main reason that true experiments allow such a powerful inference of causality is because, through the act of random assignment, such research rules out possible common causes of the independent (cause) and dependent (effect) variable, even though experiments do not rule out all causes of the dependent variable.

The warning to include common causes also does not extend to mediating or intervening variables. When an intervening variable is included in the model, the total effects remain the same, but a portion of the direct effect of *X* on *Y* becomes indirect effect through the mediating variable. Intervening variables help explain *how* an effect comes about, but do not need to be included for the model to be valid.

Estimates of effects are also incorrect when paths are drawn in the wrong direction, although the extent of the problem depends on the paths involved. If the incorrect path is from the effect to the cause, the results will obviously be incorrect and completely misleading. If the incorrect path involves the primary causal variable and one of the other causal variables in the model, this error will affect the total effects, but not the direct effects. If the incorrectly drawn path involves some of the background variables in the model, this error should have little effect on the estimates of primary interest (although it will make attentive readers less trusting of your results!). We will revisit and address this danger in subsequent chapters.

How, then, can you be sure that your model is correct? Have a good understanding of relevant theory and previous research. Think about the variables in your model, how they are related to one another. If necessary, bolster causal assumptions (e.g., *a* affects *b,* rather than *b* affects *a*) through the use of longitudinal data. Think about possible common causes and investigate them in the research literature. If necessary, test common causes in the research itself. In fact, most of what you should do to ensure the adequacy of your model boils down to the same advice for drawing a model in the first place: theory, previous research, and logic.

I also noted that, as a reader or reviewer of others' nonexperimental research, it is not enough to guess about neglected common causes; you should be able to demonstrate such criticisms through theory, previous research, or independent analysis. Finally, I noted again that these dangers apply to all nonexperimental research, no matter how it is analyzed. One advantage of path models is that the figural display of one's model (in essence a mini-theory) often makes errors and assumptions more obvious and therefore more likely to be corrected. We postponed dealing with the violation of the assumption of perfect measurement until later chapters.

EXERCISES

1. Conduct each of the parent involvement analyses reported in this chapter, using the NELS data. The variables, as listed in NELS, are: Ethnicity = Ethnic; Family Background = BySES; Previous Achievement = ByTests; Parent Involvement = Par_Inv; and GPA = Ffu-Grad. Compare your results to mine.

   a.   Make sure you understand what happens when a common cause is omitted versus a simple cause of only one of the variables of interest (Figures 11.3 through 11.4). Is Family

Background a common cause or a simple cause of Parent Involvement and GPA? Try deleting it from the model; what happens to the path from Involvement to GPA?

b. Analyze a model without Parent Involvement. Calculate direct, total, and indirect effects for each variable on GPA. Do the same for the model shown in Figure 11.3. Compare the tables of direct, indirect, and total effects.

c. Analyze a model like Figure 11.3, but in which a path is drawn from Ethnicity to Family Background. Now analyze a model in which the path is drawn from Family Background to Ethnicity. Which model is correct? How did you make this decision? What effect, if any, did this change in direction have on the estimate of the effect of Parent Involvement on GPA?

2. Find an article that uses path analysis or explanatory multiple regression on a research topic with which you are familiar and interested. If the authors' model is not drawn in the article, see if you can draw it from their description. How do the authors justify their causal assumptions or their paths? Do you agree, or do you think some of the paths are drawn in the wrong direction? Do you think there are any obvious common causes that have not been included in the model? Can you demonstrate that there are common causes that have been neglected? If the authors included a correlation matrix with their article, see if you can reproduce their results. Draw the estimated model.

3. In Chapter 10, you constructed and tested a path model using the variables Family Background (BYSES), 8th-grade GPA (BYGrads), 10th-grade Self-Esteem (F1Concpt2), 10th-grade Locus of Control (F1Locus2), and 10th-Grade Social Studies Achievement (F1TxHStd). Refer to or redo the analysis. For the sake of consistency, make sure you have Social Studies Achievement as the final endogenous variable.

a. Notice the direct effects of Self-Esteem and Locus of Control on Social Studies Achievement. Focus on the effect of GPA on Self-Esteem and Locus of Control. Is 8th-grade GPA a common cause of these variables and Social Studies Achievement? Now remove the 8th-grade GPA variable from the model. What happens to direct effects of Self-Esteem and Locus of Control on Social Studies Achievement? Explain the difference in effects from the original model.

b. Did you draw a path from Self-Esteem to Locus of Control or Locus of Control to Self-Esteem? Calculate the direct, indirect, and total effects of these two variables on Social Studies Achievement. Whichever way you drew the path, now reverse the direction and reestimate the model. Recalculate the direct, indirect, and total effects of these variables on Social Studies. Explain the differences you find.

N O T E S

1. If the common cause has positive effects on both the presumed cause and the presumed effect, its neglect will lead to an overestimate of the effect of the presumed cause on the presumed effect. If a common cause has a negative effect on either variable, its omission will lead to an underestimate, and if it has a negative effect on both, its omission will result in an overestimate.

2. There may be other advantages for including a variable in the model that is not a common cause. For example, if you include in the model a strong influence on GPA that did not affect Parent Involvement, this inclusion will reduce the standard errors of the path from Parent Involvement to Grades and thus make statistical significance more likely. Inclusion of noncommon causes also results in overidentified models, the advantages of which we will discuss in the following chapter.

ANALYZING PATH MODELS USING SEM PROGRAMS

To this point I have used multiple regression for the analysis of path models (as well as multiple regression models). It is also possible to use dedicated structural equation modeling (SEM) programs for such analysis. We make that switch in this chapter. As you will see, the results of simple path analyses are identical using SEM or MR analysis, but SEM programs can analyze more complex models and have real advantages when analyzing overidentified models.

SEM PROGRAMS

Numerous SEM programs are available, all of which are capable of analyzing everything from simple path models through latent variable structural equation models. LISREL (*Linear Structural Relations*; Jöreskog & Sörbom, 1996) was the first such program and is still widely used. Other common programs include EQS (pronounced "X"; Bentler, 1995) and M-Plus (Muthén & Muthén, 1998). Each such program has its own advantages (M-Plus, for example, has sophisticated routines for analyzing categorical variables) and generally cost $500 to $600 for those in academia. There is one free SEM program that I know of, Mx (Neale, Boker, Xie, & Maes, 1999), available as of this writing as a download at www.vcu.edu/mx.

Amos

My favorite program is one called Amos (*Analysis of Mo*ment *S*tructures; Arbuckle, 2003; Arbuckle & Wothke, 1999). Amos uses a graphic approach and is one of if not the easiest SEM program to use. It produces attractive path diagrams (all the path models you have seen so far were produced by Amos) and can be used both to draw the diagram and analyze it. Even better for you, there is a free student version of Amos available at www .amosdevelopment.com. The student version of Amos is the same as the full version, with the exceptions that it cannot analyze models with more than eight measured variables and more than 54 parameters. It can view (but not analyze) models of any size, however. You will be able to analyze most of the problems in the rest of this book using the Amos student version. As of this writing, the full version of Amos is also included in the SPSS Gradpack. Of course, you can analyze these problems using any SEM program, so if you have another program available, you may want to use it. There are also student or demo versions available of the other commercial SEM programs.

Brief examples of Amos output, as well as output from other SEM programs, are shown in Appendix C. Whatever program you use, you should purchase the user's manual, which provides the basics for the use of the program. There are numerous other sources of information about various SEM programs, as well. If you use Amos, for example, I recommend you download the tutorial from the Amos Web site (given above); another helpful Amos tutorial can be found at www.utexas.edu/cc/stat/tutorials/amos. You can likely find similar resources for other SEM programs. Although I will use Amos to estimate subsequent models, the next section also applies to SEM programs in general.

Basics of SEM Programs.   Everything you have learned about path analysis so far will transfer to Amos and other SEM programs. Figure 12.1 shows a basic SEM (Amos) version of the parent involvement model first presented in Chapter 11. As in all previous examples, rectangles represent measured variables, and ovals represent unmeasured or latent variables (in this example, the disturbances). Straight arrows represent paths, or presumed influences, and curved, double-headed arrows represent correlations (or, with unstandardized coefficients, covariances). The one new aspect of Figure 12.1 is the value of 1 beside the paths from the disturbances to the endogenous variables. These paths simply set the scale of measurement for the disturbances. Unmeasured variables have no natural scale. When we set the path from the disturbances, which are unmeasured variables, to the measured variables to 1.0, we are merely telling the SEM program that the disturbance should have the same scale as the measured variable. (In reality, any number could be used: .80, 2.0, but 1.0 is the most common and most straightforward.) We will use the same rule of thumb when we begin using other latent variables: we will set one path from each latent variable to 1.0 to set the scale of the latent variable. At a practical level, the model would be underidentified without this constraint (or some other way of setting the scale of the disturbances).

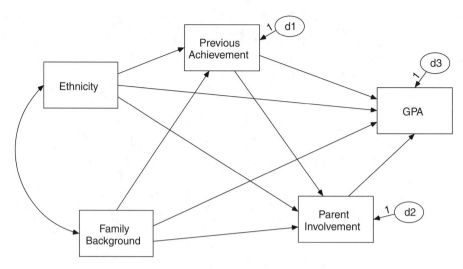

FIGURE 12.1 Parent Involvement model from Chapter 10, as drawn in the Amos SEM program.

We could also set the scale by fixing the variance of the disturbance to 1.0; all substantive results would be the same. In fact, this is what we did with multiple regression, even though we did not realize that we were doing so. When we use multiple regression to estimate the paths, the variances of the disturbances are set to 1.0, and the program estimates the paths from the disturbances to the endogenous variables (when we set the path to 1.0, the program estimates the variance of the disturbance). We can choose either method with most SEM programs; I here set the paths to 1.0 because that is the most common method.

REANALYSIS OF THE PARENT INVOLVEMENT PATH MODEL

The model shown in Figure 12.1 provides the basic input for analysis by Amos (the model is on the Web site, www.ablongman.com/keith1e, as "PI Example 1.amw"); add data and you can conduct the analysis. Most SEM programs, including Amos, can use the correlation matrix and standard deviations as input for the analysis. The matrix for this example is saved as both an SPSS (PI matrix, listwise.sav) and an Excel file (PI matrix, listwise.xls). The matrix is also shown in Table 12.1; the variable names are as in the NELS raw data. The SPSS commands I used to create the matrix using the NELS data are in the file "create corr matrix in spss.sps."

Estimating the Parent Involvement Model via Amos

With the model and the data, we can estimate the model via Amos (or any other SEM program). The standardized output for this model is shown in Figure 12.2. Compare the results with your results from Chapter 11; with the exception of the lack of a number associated with the paths from disturbances to endogenous variables, the results should be identical. Figure 12.3 shows the unstandardized output for the model. Recall that we set the paths

TABLE 12.1   Means, Standard Deviations, Sample Sizes, and Correlations among the Variables for the Parent Involvement Path Example

VARIABLE	ETHNIC	BYSES	BYTESTS	PAR_INV	FFUGRAD
ETHNIC	1.000	.333	.330	.075	.131
BYSES	.333	1.000	.461	.432	.299
BYTESTS	.330	.461	1.000	.445	.499
PAR_INV	.075	.432	.445	1.000	.364
FFUGRAD	.131	.299	.499	.364	1.000
M	.793	.047	52.323	.059	5.760
SD	.406	.766	8.584	.794	1.450
N	811.000	811.000	811.000	811.000	811.000

from disturbances to endogenous variables to 1.0 and estimated the variances of the disturbances. The numbers next to the disturbances are the estimates of their variances. The numbers above the two exogenous variables are their variances. Again, the results should match those from your regression analysis in Chapter 11.

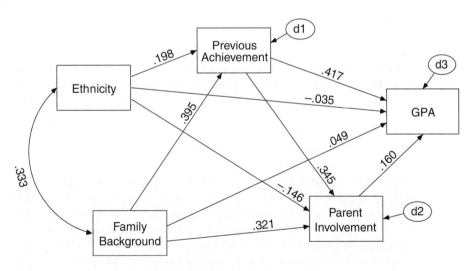

FIGURE 12.2   Parent Involvement model estimated via Amos. The standardized results are the same as those in Chapter 10 when the model was estimated via multiple regression

Of course, you will get more detailed output than just these diagrams from your SEM program. Figure 12.4 shows one portion of the printout; this and all subsequent printouts show Amos output, but you will get something similar with any of the SEM programs. The top portion of the output (Regression Weights) shows the unstandardized path coefficients, listed under the column Estimate. For example, the first row shows that the unstandardized

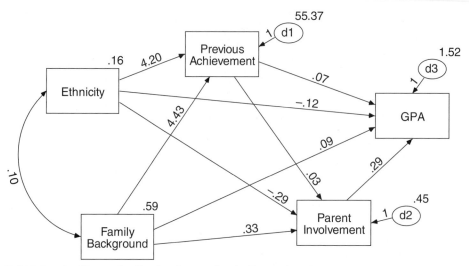

FIGURE 12.3   Unstandardized estimates for the Parent Involvement model.

path from BYSES (Family Background) to bytests (Previous Achievement) is 4.431. The S.E. column shows the standard errors of the coefficients, the column labeled C.R. (for critical ratio) shows the t's for each coefficient. (Recall that t = coefficient/$SE_{coefficient}$ and that with large samples t's greater than approximately 2 are statistically significant. The values are actually z statistics, but they are essentially the same with the sample sizes we are using.) The column labeled P shows the probability associated with each path, with values less than .001 indicated by ***. The next portion of the figure (Standardized Regression Weights) shows the standardized paths. Again, the output should match the SPSS output from Chapter 11. This portion is followed by the covariance and correlation between the two exogenous variables and the variances of the two exogenous variables, and the disturbances of the three endogenous variables.

SEM programs will also produce tables of direct, indirect, and total effects for both the standardized and unstandardized solution. The tables for the current example are shown in Figure 12.5. The tables are read from column to row; thus the total unstandardized effect of Family Background (BYSES) on GPA (ffugrad), as shown in the bottom left of the first table, is .544. Take some time to compare these results with those from the previous chapter.

It is also possible to evaluate the statistical significance of the indirect and total effects; in Amos this is done through a bootstrapping procedure. (*Bootstrapping* is a procedure in which one takes repeated, smaller random samples of an existing sample. With bootstrapping, it is possible to develop empirical estimates of standard errors of any parameter, even, for example, standard errors of standard errors.) Figure 12.6, for example, shows the indirect effects for the variables in the Parent Involvement model, followed by their standard errors. You can use this information to calculate the t values for each indirect effect to determine its statistical significance. Thus, SEM programs allow a more direct test of the statistical significance of mediation than do most regression results (see in Chapter 8 the section on Mediation). Amos also provides the *standardized* effects and their standard errors (the standardized indirect effects are shown in the figure).

Regression Weights

	Estimate	S.E.	C.R.	P	Label
bytests <--- BYSES	4.431	.362	12.229	***	
bytests <--- Ethnic	4.195	.684	6.131	***	
par_inv <--- bytests	.032	.003	10.034	***	
par_inv <--- Ethnic	-.286	.063	-4.525	***	
par_inv <--- BYSES	.333	.036	9.345	***	
ffugrad <--- bytests	.070	.006	11.406	***	
ffugrad <--- par_inv	.292	.064	4.528	***	
ffugrad <--- BYSES	.093	.069	1.354	.176	
ffugrad <--- Ethnic	-.124	.117	-1.057	.290	

Standardized Regression Weights

	Estimate
bytests <--- BYSES	.395
bytests <--- Ethnic	.198
par_inv <--- bytests	.345
par_inv <--- Ethnic	-.146
par_inv <--- BYSES	.321
ffugrad <--- bytests	.417
ffugrad <--- par_inv	.160
ffugrad <--- BYSES	.049
ffugrad <--- Ethnic	-.035

Covariances

	Estimate	S.E.	C.R.	P	Label
Ethnic <--> BYSES	.103	.011	8.996	***	

Correlations

	Estimate
Ethnic <--> BYSES	.333

Variances

	Estimate	S.E.	C.R.	P	Label
Ethnic	.164	.008	20.125	***	
BYSES	.586	.029	20.125	***	
d1	55.370	2.751	20.125	***	
d2	.452	.022	20.125	***	
d3	1.521	.076	20.125	***	

FIGURE 12.4   Output from the SEM program (Amos) showing unstandardized coefficients (e.g., regression weights), their standard errors, and critical ratios, along with standardized coefficients.

Total Effects

	BYSES	Ethnic	bytests	par_inv
bytests	4.431	4.195	.000	.000
par_inv	.474	-.153	.032	.000
ffugrad	.544	.127	.080	.292

Standardized Total Effects

	BYSES	Ethnic	bytests	par_inv
bytests	.395	.198	.000	.000
par_inv	.458	-.078	.345	.000
ffugrad	.287	.035	.472	.160

Direct Effects

	BYSES	Ethnic	bytests	par_inv
bytests	4.431	4.195	.000	.000
par_inv	.333	-.286	.032	.000
ffugrad	.093	-.124	.070	.292

Standardized Direct Effects

	BYSES	Ethnic	bytests	par_inv
bytests	.395	.198	.000	.000
par_inv	.321	-.146	.345	.000
ffugrad	.049	-.035	.417	.160

Indirect Effects

	BYSES	Ethnic	bytests	par_inv
bytests	.000	.000	.000	.000
par_inv	.141	.134	.000	.000
ffugrad	.450	.251	.009	.000

Standardized Indirect Effects

	BYSES	Ethnic	bytests	par_inv
bytests	.000	.000	.000	.000
par_inv	.136	.068	.000	.000
ffugrad	.238	.070	.055	.000

FIGURE 12.5   Total, indirect, and direct effects of variables on each other in the Parent Involvement model.

ADVANTAGES OF SEM PROGRAMS

Overidentified Models

Figure 12.7 shows a potential model of the effect of Homework on GPA. The data are from NELS (the larger NELS data, not those on the Web site). For this model, Ethnicity, Family Background, and Previous Achievement were measured in 1988 and are defined in the way

Indirect Effects

	BYSES	Ethnic	bytests	par_inv
bytests	.000	.000	.000	.000
par_inv	.141	.134	.000	.000
ffugrad	.450	.251	.009	.000

Indirect Effects: Standard Errors

	BYSES	Ethnic	bytests	par_inv
bytests	.000	.000	.000	.000
par_inv	.018	.025	.000	.000
ffugrad	.045	.065	.002	.000

Standardized Indirect Effects

	BYSES	Ethnic	bytests	par_inv
bytests	.000	.000	.000	.000
par_inv	.136	.068	.000	.000
ffugrad	.238	.070	.055	.000

Standardized Indirect Effect: Standard Errors

	BYSES	Ethnic	bytests	par_inv
bytests	.000	.000	.000	.000
par_inv	.017	.013	.000	.000
ffugrad	.023	.018	.013	.000

FIGURE 12.6   Indirect effects (both unstandardized and standardized) and their standard errors for the Parent Involvement model.

we have in the past (Ethnicity = majority vs. minority, Family Background = BYSES, Previous Achievement = BYTests). Homework was based on student reports of time spent on homework in each academic area, measured in both 1988 and 1990; it may be considered a measure of average homework over time. Grades are students' GPAs (English, Math, Science, and Social Studies) from 10th grade.

Note that several potential paths are not drawn: there are no paths from Ethnicity and Family Background to Grades. Just as it means something to draw a path, it means something to not draw a path and, in fact, it is often a *stronger statement* than drawing a path. When we draw a path, we are stating that one variable may have some effect on another. What the *lack of path* from Family Background to Grades means is that I believe the path from Background to Grades is a value of zero. Indeed, not drawing a path is the same as drawing a path and fixing or constraining that path to a value of zero. This model also makes explicit the notion that the only way Ethnicity and Family Background affect Grades is through Homework and Previous Achievement, that they have no direct effect on Grades, only indirect effects through other variables in the model. I developed this hypothesis in the usual way, based on previous research and logic. Indeed, you will even find support for the exclusion of paths from Ethnicity and Family Background to Grades based on our Parent Involvement models, which showed only small direct effects for these variables on Grades.

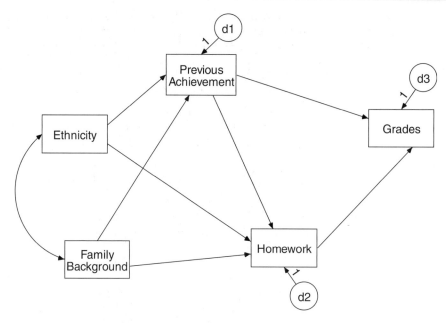

FIGURE 12.7   Overidentified model testing the effects of Homework on students' Grades in High School.

You know from Chapter 10 that this is an overidentified model, meaning that we have more information than we need to solve for the paths. Note that there are 10 correlations among variables, but we are solving for only eight parameters (seven paths and one correlation). Recall also that if we were solving for the paths using algebra we could come up with different formulas for solving some of the paths. I argued in Chapter 10 that this approach may have advantages, because similarity in path estimates calculated two different ways can give us additional confidence in our model, whereas dissimilarity might make us wonder about the veracity of the model.

One advantage of SEM programs is that they provide this type of feedback about overidentified models. The method is not as described above; the programs do not estimate the paths several different ways and allow you to compare the different estimates. Instead, the programs compare matrices and provide measures of the fit of the model to the data. We'll see how this process works when we analyze the model in Figure 12.7.

The data (correlation matrix, standard deviations, and *N*) are contained in both an Excel and an SPSS file ("homework overid 1.xls" and "homework overid 1.sav"); the data are also shown in Table 12.2.[1] The model shown in the figure was used as input to Amos and is in the file "homework path 1.amw" on the accompanying Web site.

Figure 12.8 shows the solved, standardized path model. Using our rules of thumb, it appears Homework has a moderate effect (.15) on 10th-grade GPA. Previous Achievement had a strong effect on Homework, suggesting a "rich get richer" sort of effect: students who achieve at a high level do more homework, and this homework, in turn, improves their subsequent school performance. Family Background also had a moderate effect on Homework, but Ethnicity had no substantive effect.

TABLE 12.2   Contents of the Excel File for the Homework Path Example

ROWTYPE_	VARNAME_	ETHNICITY	FAMBACK	PREACH	HOMEWORK	GRADES
n		1000	1000	1000	1000	1000
corr	Ethnicity	1				
corr	FamBack	0.3041	1			
corr	PreAch	0.3228	0.4793	1		
corr	Homework	0.0832	0.2632	0.2884	1	
corr	Grades	0.1315	0.2751	0.489	0.2813	1
stddev		0.4186	0.8311	8.8978	0.8063	1.479

The matrix is in the format required for analysis in Amos.

The file includes standard deviations, sample sizes, and correlations.

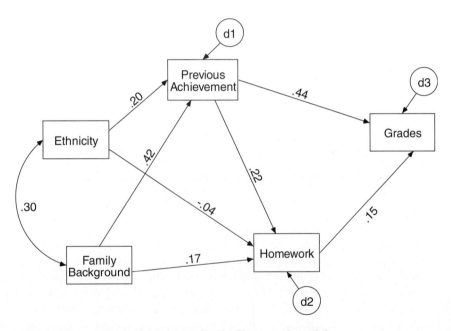

FIGURE 12.8   Standardized output for the Homework model.

How can we use the overidentification status of the model to assess the model? Recall how we solved for the paths in our first example of path analysis: through the use of algebra and the correlations among the variables. Amos is essentially doing the same thing here: the model specification and the correlation matrix (actually the covariance matrix, but we will address this point later) were used as input, and the program used these pieces of information to solve for the paths. If we can solve for the paths using the correlations, why can't we do the reverse: solve for the correlations using the paths? In fact, we can do exactly that. You could, and SEM programs do, use the solved path model (e.g., Figure 12.8) to calculate an expected, or predicted, correlation matrix, the matrix implied by the model. With overidentified models, this implied matrix (also known as the predicted matrix) and the input matrix will differ to some degree. The actual correlation matrix and the implied correlation matrix from the Amos output are shown in Figure 12.9. Notice that most of the correlations are the same, but that the values in the lower left—the correlations of Grades with Ethnicity and Family Background—differ slightly between the actual and the implied matrices. SEM programs use this degree of similarity or nonsimilarity between the two matrices to assess and measure the fit of the model to the data.

Sample Correlations

	Ethnic	FamBack	PreAch	Homework	Grades
Ethnic	1.000				
FamBack	.304	1.000			
PreAch	.323	.479	1.000		
Homework	.083	.263	.288	1.000	
Grades	.132	.275	.489	.281	1.000

Implied (for All Variables) Correlations

	Ethnic	FamBack	PreAch	Homework	Grades
Ethnic	1.000				
FamBack	.304	1.000			
PreAch	.323	.479	1.000		
Homework	.083	.263	.288	1.000	
Grades	.156	.253	.489	.281	1.000

FIGURE 12.9   The sample (input) correlation matrix compared to the matrix implied by the Homework model.

Correlations versus Covariances.   Before going any further, it is time to switch from thinking in terms of correlation matrices to thinking about covariance matrices. Most SEM programs are set up to analyze covariance rather than correlation matrices. For some SEM problems you will get the same substantive answer no matter which type of matrix you analyze, but for others you should analyze covariance matrices (see Cudeck, 1989, or Steiger, 2001, for further discussion about this issue). An easy solution is simply to get in the habit of analyzing covariance, rather than correlation, matrices. (An alternative is to use a program, such as SEPATH, a part of the Statistica package, designed specifically to analyze correlation matrices.)

Recall from Chapter 1 that we can easily calculate covariances from correlations if we know the variances or standard deviations of the variables, because $CoV_{xy} = r_{xy} \times SD_x SD_y$. Indeed, this is what Amos did; we input the correlations and standard deviations, and the program generated the covariance matrix from that input. The covariance matrix is shown at the top portion of Figure 12.10. The covariances are shown below the diagonal, and the variances are shown in the diagonal. Another way of thinking of covariance versus correlation matrices is to recall that correlation matrices are standardized covariance matrices, with all variables converted to z scores.

Sample Covariances

	Ethnic	FamBack	PreAch	Homework	Grades
Ethnic	.175				
FamBack	.106	.690			
PreAch	1.201	3.541	79.092		
Homework	.028	.176	2.067	.649	
Grades	.081	.338	6.429	.335	2.185

Implied (for All Variables) Covariances

	Ethnic	FamBack	PreAch	Homework	Grades
Ethnic	.175				
FamBack	.106	.690			
PreAch	1.201	3.541	79.092		
Homework	.028	.176	2.067	.649	
Grades	.097	.311	6.429	.335	2.185

Residual Covariances

	Ethnic	FamBack	PreAch	Homework	Grades
Ethnic	.000				
FamBack	.000	.000			
PreAch	.000	.000	.000		
Homework	.000	.000	.000	.000	
Grades	−.015	.027	.000	.000	.000

Standardized Residual Covariances

	Ethnic	FamBack	PreAch	Homework	Grades
Ethnic	.000				
FamBack	.000	.000			
PreAch	.000	.000	.000		
Homework	.000	.000	.000	.000	
Grades	−.776	.662	.000	.000	.000

FIGURE 12.10   Sample and implied covariance matrices and residual and standardized residual matrices for the Homework model.

Model Fit and Degrees of Freedom.   SEM programs, then, generally compare the actual covariance matrix to the implied covariance matrix. Some of the relevant output from Amos is shown in Figure 12.10: the actual covariance matrix, the implied matrix, and the residual covariance matrix. The residual covariance matrix is the result of subtracting the implied matrix from the actual matrix; intuitively, large differences between these matrices and large residuals should signal problems with the model. More helpful are the *standardized* residuals, in which the residuals have been converted to a common, standardized metric.

Although this matrix is not particularly useful in the present example in which only two paths have been constrained, as we begin to focus on more complex and latent variable models the standardized residual covariances will be useful for determining *where* there is misfit in our models. I focused on the actual, implied, and residual matrices now, however, because this difference between the actual and implied matrix is the source of other measures of the fit of the model.

We can and will quantify the *degree* to which a model is overidentified. The current model has two paths that could have been drawn to make the model just-identified (paths from Ethnicity and Family Background to Grades). The model thus has two degrees of freedom. More exactly, we can calculate the degrees of freedom using the following steps:

1. Calculate the number of variances and covariances in the matrix using the formula $[p \times (p + 1)]/2$ where p is equal to the number of variables in the model. For the current model, there are 15 variances and covariances: $[5 \times (5 + 1)]/2 = 15$.
2. Count the number of parameters that are estimated in the model. Don't forget covariances between exogenous variables, variances of the exogenous variables, and variances of the disturbances. For the current model, we estimated seven paths, one covariance between the exogenous variables, the variances of the two exogenous variables, and the variances of the three disturbances, for a total of 13 estimated parameters.
3. The degrees of freedom are calculated by subtracting the number of estimated parameters from the number of variances and covariances. The present model has two degrees of freedom $(15 - 13 = 2)$.

The degrees of freedom for a model provide information about the degree to which the overall model is overidentified. The degrees of freedom also provide a handy index of the parsimony of the model. In science, we value parsimony: if two explanations for a phenomenon are equally good (or, in SEM, fit equally well), we generally prefer the simplest or more parsimonious explanation. Degrees of freedom are an index of the parsimony of a path model: the more degrees of freedom, the more values constrained (to zero or some other value) prior to estimation, and thus the greater the parsimony.

The difference between the actual and implied matrices provides evidence of the degree to which the model is a good explanation of the data. This difference is used to generate a multitude of fit statistics or fit indexes for overidentified models. There are literally dozens of such fit indexes, with different indexes focusing on slightly different aspects of fit. We will focus on a few common such indexes here; there are also numerous sources for more information about fit indexes (e.g., Fan, Thompson, & Wang, 1999; Hoyle, 1995; Hu & Bentler, 1998, 1999).

Chi-square (χ^2) is the most commonly reported measure of fit.[2] Chi-square has the advantage of allowing a statistical test of the fit of the model; it can be used with the degrees of freedom to determine the probability that the model is "correct" (to be explained later). Interestingly, in SEM we want a small χ^2 and one that is not statistically significant. For our current example, $\chi^2 = 2.166$, with 2 *df* and a probability of .338. What does this mean? It means that the actual and the implied matrix are not statistically significantly different from one another, and thus the model and the data are consistent with one another. If the model and the data are consistent, the model could have generated the data and thus may provide a good approximation of how the phenomenon being studied works. In other words, the model may approximate reality, it may be "correct." Given all the "mays" and "coulds" in this explanation, you may be disappointed; this is hardly the kind of evidence of the quality of the model you were hoping for! Sorry; fit statistics do *not* prove that a model is true and do *not* prove causality. If the fit indexes are good, they suggest that a model may provide a reasonable, tentative explanation of the data. I'll simply note that this is better than nothing and more feedback than we've had in previous chapters about the quality of our explanations of our data.

Figure 12.11 shows the fit indexes output by Amos; other SEM programs will provide an equally intimidating listing of indexes of fit, many of which will be the same (although some may be labeled differently). Focus on the first few rows and columns. The model that is being estimated (i.e., the model in Figure 12.7) is labeled the Default model. The first column of numbers shows the number of parameters (NPAR) that are estimated in the model (remember we calculated 13 parameters being estimated), and the second shows the χ^2 (labeled CMIN, a value of 2.166). These are followed by the degrees of freedom (2) and the probability associated with the χ^2 and df (.338).

The rows labeled Saturated model pertain to a just-identified model. A just-identified model will estimate 15 parameters and thus have zero df. With a just-identified model, the implied covariance matrix will be identical to the actual matrix, and thus χ^2 associated with a just-identified model is equal to zero. In other words, a just-identified model will provide a perfect fit to the data. Why not, then, continue to estimate just-identified models, as we have done previously? The reason, again, is that we value parsimony. An overidentified model is more parsimonious than a just-identified model; our present overidentified model fits as well as a just-identified model (another interpretation of the statistically not significant χ^2). Because this model fits as well but is more parsimonious, it is a preferable model from a scientific standpoint.

The rows labeled Independence model refer to a model in which the variables in the model are assumed to be independent of one another. This model, also called a *null* model, could be represented by the five variables, with no paths or correlations drawn (and thus for this model all we would estimate would be the five variable variances). It could also be represented by constraining all paths and correlations in the current model to zero. Again, the null model assumes the variables are unrelated. The saturated and independence models essentially provide two endpoints with which we can compare our theoretical model. The saturated model provides a best fitting model and the independence model a very poorly fitting model. Some of the other fit indexes make use of these endpoints.

Other Measures of Fit. χ^2 seems to fill our need for assessing model fit: if it is not statistically significant, we have evidence that our model may explain reality, and if it is statistically significant, our model does not explain the data. Why do we need other fit indexes? Unfortunately, χ^2 has some problems as a measure of fit. First, χ^2 is related to sample size; indeed, χ^2 is calculated as $N - 1$ times the minimum value of the fit function (FMIN on the Amos output). Thus, given the same matrix and a sample size of 10,000 instead of 1000, the χ^2 would be approximately 10 times larger than the current value of 2.166. A χ^2 of 21.66 (actually 21.68, because $N - 1$ rather than N is used in the calculations), again with 2 df, will be statistically significant ($p < .001$), and thus we would reach

Model Fit Summary

CMIN

Model	NPAR	CMIN	DF	P	CMIN/DF
Default model	13	2.166	2	.338	1.083
Saturated model	15	.000	0		
Independence model	5	817.868	10	.000	81.787

RMR, GFI

Model	RMR	GFI	AGFI	PGFI
Default model	.008	.999	.994	.133
Saturated model	.000	1.000		
Independence model	1.998	.715	.572	.477

Baseline Comparisons

Model	NFI Delta1	RFI rho1	IFI Delta2	TLI rho2	CFI
Default model	.997	.987	1.000	.999	1.000
Saturated model	1.000		1.000		1.000
Independence model	.000	.000	.000	.000	.000

Parsimony-Adjusted Measures

Model	PRATIO	PNFI	PCFI
Default model	.200	.199	.200
Saturated model	.000	.000	.000
Independence model	1.000	.000	.000

NCP

Model	NCP	LO 90	HI 90
Default model	.166	.000	8.213
Saturated model	.000	.000	.000
Independence model	807.868	717.735	905.396

FMIN

Model	FMIN	F0	LO 90	HI 90
Default model	.002	.000	.000	.008
Saturated model	.000	.000	.000	.000
Independence model	.819	.809	.718	.906

RMSEA

Model	RMSEA	LO 90	HI 90	PCLOSE
Default model	.009	.000	.064	.854
Independence model	.284	.268	.301	.000

FIGURE 12.11   Fit indexes for the Homework model.

FIGURE 12.11   Continued

AIC

Model	AIC	BCC	BIC	CAIC
Default model	28.166	28.324	91.967	104.967
Saturated model	30.000	30.181	103.616	118.616
Independence model	827.868	827.929	852.407	857.407

ECVI

Model	ECVI	LO 90	HI 90	MECVI
Default model	.028	.028	.036	.028
Saturated model	.030	.030	.030	.030
Independence model	.829	.738	.926	.829

HOELTER

Model	HOELTER .05	HOELTER .01
Default model	2763	4248
Independence model	23	29

the conclusion that the model did not fit the data, an opposite conclusion from the one we reached with the sample size of 1000. (Note, if it is not already obvious, with SEM the *df* depend on the number of model constraints, not the sample size.) This weakness of χ^2 is one reason alternative measures of fit have been developed.

The Goodness of Fit Index (GFI) is analogous to R^2 in multiple regression analysis; it provides an estimate of the total covariance accounted for by the model (Tanaka, 1993). A number of fit indexes compare the fit of the existing model with that of the null, or independence model. The comparative fit index (CFI) and the Tucker–Lewis index (TLI, also known as the nonnormed fit index, or NNFI) are two common such indexes. The CFI provides a population estimate of the improvement in fit over the null model (although null models are the most common comparison, the CFI can also be calculated with more restricted but substantively meaningful models). The TLI provides a slight adjustment for parsimony and is relatively independent of sample size (Tanaka, 1993). Although neither the GFI nor the CFI are independent of sample size (Tanaka, 1993), they are much less affected by it than is χ^2. For all three indexes, values approaching 1.0 suggest a better fit; common rules of thumb suggest that values over .95 represent a good fit of the model to the data, and values over .90 represent an adequate fit (cf. Hayduk, 1996, p. 219; Hu & Bentler, 1999).

Another problem with χ^2 and its associated probability is that *p* is the probability that a model fits perfectly in the population, even though most researchers argue that a model is designed only to approximate reality. The root mean square error of approximation (RMSEA) is designed to assess the *approximate* fit of a model and may thus provide a more reasonable standard for evaluating models. RMSEAs below .05 suggest a "close fit of the model in relation to the degrees of freedom" (Browne & Cudeck, 1993, p. 144), in other words a good approximation. Browne and Cudeck further speculated that models with RMSEAs below .08 represented a reasonable fit, with those above .10 representing a poor fit. Research with the RMSEA supports these rules of thumb (i.e., values below .05 suggesting a good fit; Hu & Bentler, 1999), as well as its use as an overall measure of model fit (Fan, Thompson, & Wang, 1999). Other advantages of RMSEA include the ability to calculate confidence intervals around RMSEA, the ability to use RMSEA "to test a null hypothesis of *poor* fit" (Loehlin, 2004, p. 69), and the ability to conduct power calculations using RMSEA (MacCallum, Browne, & Sugawara, 1996). Conceptually, you can think of RMSEA as representing the degree of misfit per degree of freedom.

One final, useful measure of fit (or misfit) is the standardized root mean square residual (SRMR). We approached the topic of fit by discussing the difference between the actual covariance matrix used to estimate a model and the covariance matrix implied by the model. If you average these differences, you get the root mean square residual. (To keep the negative values from canceling out the positive values, you'd need to first square the values and then take the square root of the final average number.) The SRMR is the standardized version of the root mean square residual. Because correlations are standardized versions of covariances, the SRMR is conceptually equivalent to the average difference between the actual correlations among measured variables and those predicted by the model. Hu and Bentler's (1998, 1999) simulation research suggests SRMR as among the best of the fit indexes, with values below about .08 suggesting a good fit of the model to the data. The SRMR is not produced automatically in Amos, but is easily obtained (select the Tools menu, then Macro, then Standardized RMR).

I currently use RMSEA for my primary measures of the fit of a single model, supplemented by SRMR, CFI, TLI, and GFI, or sometimes other indexes. As we will soon see, it is also possible, indeed desirable, to compare the fit of competing models; we will use different fit indexes for this purpose. Note, however, that thinking and research about fit indexes are in a constant state of development. The advice I (or others) give as this is written is different from what I would have given 5 years ago and may well be different from what I will advise 5 years in the future. Because of this state of flux, and because much advice about fit indexes is based on the experience of the user, my advice may also be different from that of others.

Focus again on Figure 12.11. The RMSEA for our Homework model was .009, with a 90% confidence interval of .000 to .064 (Lo 90 to Hi 90 in the figure). The CFI, TLI, and GFI were 1.0, .999, and .999, respectively. Although not shown in the figure, the SRMR for this model was .0085, suggesting an average difference between the actual and predicted correlations of only .0085. All indexes suggest a good fit of the model to the data; the model could indeed have generated the data.

Comparing Competing Models

Another major advantage of SEM programs is that we can use them to compare competing theoretical models (and the hypotheses embedded in these competing models) via the fit statistics. An example will illustrate.

Suppose in your reading of the literature on the effects of homework you came across evidence that homework and school learning are unrelated. Perhaps the evidence is in the form of research that suggests that homework has no real effects on achievement or grades. Or perhaps the evidence is in the form of informal theory that suggests that home-work really should not affect learning, or vice versa. Whichever is the case, we could test these hypotheses by comparing models embodying them with our initial model (Figures 12.7 and 12.8). One such model will delete the paths from Previous Achievement to Homework and from Homework to Grades. This model asserts that students' previous achievement has no effect on the time they spend working on homework, and such time spent on homework also has no effect on students' grades. Stated differently, this model embodies the hypothesis that homework is unrelated to academic performance, either as an effect (the path from Previous Achievement to Homework) or as an influence (the path from Homework to Grades).

The standardized results of this model are shown in Figure 12.12, which also shows some of the relevant fit indexes. We will focus primarily on the RMSEA (.128), which suggests a poor fit of this model to the data. This assessment is supported by the TLI of .797 and the statistically significant χ^2 of 69.61 with 4 degrees of freedom. The CFI (.919), in contrast, suggests a so-so model, whereas the GFI (.974) suggests a good model. The model is, among other things, a good illustration that the various fit statistics often present different pictures and lead to different conclusions if used in isolation. Nevertheless, with our primary focus on RMSEA, we conclude that this model does not fit the data well, and we will likely reject the model as a good explanation of the relations between homework and learning.

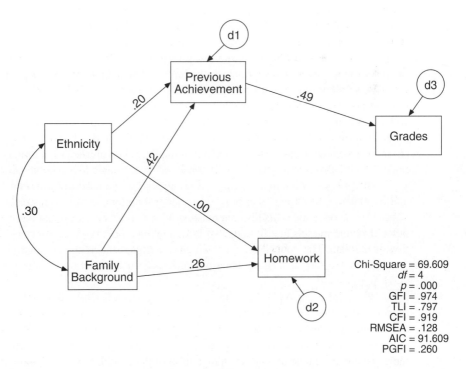

FIGURE 12.12   Does Homework indeed affect Grades? Compare the fit of this model with the earlier Homework model.

We can address our primary questions more directly, however, by comparing the results of this model with the results of our initial model. That model fit well, whereas this model did not; but are the *differences* between the fits of the two models meaningful or statistically significant? We can use the fit indexes to make these comparisons, as well. Interestingly, although χ^2 has problems as a measure of fit of a single model (what I will henceforth call a "stand-alone" measure of fit), it often works well for comparing competing models (Keith, 1999; Loehlin, 2004). Furthermore, if the models are nested (meaning that one can be derived from the other by deleting paths), this comparison can be statistical rather than qualitative.

When two models are nested, the more parsimonious model (the model with fewer free, or estimated, parameters) will have a higher *df* (recall that *df* is a measure of parsimony) and a larger χ^2. The χ^2 and *df* for the less parsimonious model can be subtracted from those of the more parsimonious. The resulting change in χ^2 ($\Delta\chi^2$) is also a χ^2 distribution and may be compared to the change in *df* for the two models. Again, models are nested when one can be derived from the other by deleting paths or correlations. This second model—the one with one or more paths deleted and the higher *df*—will be a subset of the first and nested within the first model.

The model shown in Figure 12.12 (no-homework-effects model) is a more parsimonious, more constrained version of the model shown in Figure 12.7 (the initial model); two paths that were estimated in the initial model were constrained to zero in the no-homework-effects model. This model is nested within the initial model. The no-homework-effects model had a χ^2 of 69.609, with 4 *df*. We subtract the corresponding values for the initial model ($\chi^2 = 2.166$, *df* = 2) from those for the no-homework-effects model to obtain a $\Delta\chi^2$ of 67.443, with a Δ *df* of 2. If you look up these values in the probability calculator or spreadsheet,[3] you will find an associated probability of $< .001$; the additional constraints on the no-homework-effects model resulted in a statistically significant increase in $\Delta\chi^2$.

This finding, that the $\Delta\chi^2$ is statistically significant, means that not only does the no-homework-effects model fit worse than the initial model, but it fits statistically significantly worse. Although the no-homework-effects model is more parsimonious than the initial model, the parsimony comes at too great a cost in terms of model fit, and we reject these constraints on the model and stick with the initial model. What this means, in turn, is that we can reject the hypothesis that time spent on homework is unrelated to academic performance.

The process of comparing competing models can be used to test competing models and hypotheses, but it can also bolster, or undermine, our faith in our preferred models. "The fact that one model fits the data reasonably well does not mean that there could not be other, different models that fit better. At best, a given model represents a tentative explanation of the data. The confidence with which one accepts such an explanation depends, in part, on whether other, rival explanations have been tested and found wanting" (Loehlin, 2004, p. 61).

We can also use $\Delta\chi^2$ to test the assumptions we made when we developed our initial model. Recall that we assumed that Ethnicity and Family Background had no direct effect on students' Grades, but that their effects were indirect through Previous Achievement and Homework. We could test whether these assumptions are, in fact, supported by freeing these parameters and studying the change in fit of the model. Table 12.3 shows fit statistics for the two models already discussed, plus a model labeled Background Effect, in which the path from Family Background to Grades was freed, or estimated. As you can see, this model is less parsimonious than the initial model. The $\Delta\chi^2$ for this model was .837 with 1 *df;* the $\Delta\chi^2$ is not statistically significant. In this case, the two models had nearly equivalent fit. The more relaxed (background effect) model did not fit statistically significantly better; the more parsimonious (initial) model did not fit statistically significantly worse. In other words, the models had equivalent fit. In this case, we favor the more parsimonious of the two models, the initial model. Therefore, our initial assumption that Family Background would affect Grades only through other variables was supported.

TABLE 12.3   Comparison of Fit Indexes for Alternative Models of the Effects of Homework on High School Students' Grades

MODEL	χ^2	*df*	$\Delta\chi^2$	Δdf	*p*	AIC	PCFI	RMSEA (90% CI)
Initial	2.166	2				28.166	.200	.009 (.000–.064)
No Homework Effects	69.609	4	67.443	2	<.001	91.609	.368	.128 (.103–.155)
Background Effect	1.329	1	.837	1	.360	29.329	.100	.018 (.000–.089)

Note that we could also have evaluated the statistical significance of the path from Family Background to Grades by focusing on the CR (critical ratio, or *t*) in the Amos print-out. The *t* was .915, which is not statistically significant, thus also supporting our initial assumption of the lack of direct effect of Family Background on Grades. When single parameters are tested, $\Delta\chi^2$ and *t* will usually, but not always, give the same answer. $\Delta\chi^2$ can be used to test the statistical significance of multiple changes to a model, whereas *t* focuses on only one parameter at a time.

We could have freed both paths that were constrained to zero in the initial model (Family Background to Grades and Ethnicity to Grades). In this case, the new model will be just-identified, with χ^2 and the *df* both equal to zero. Thus, the $\Delta\chi^2$ comparing this model with the initial model equals the value for the χ^2 for the initial model (2.166, *df* = 2), which was not statistically significant (*p* = .338). Perhaps this comparison makes it obvious that, strictly speaking, what we are testing with overidentified models is the overidentifying restrictions (constraints) on the model, *not* the model as a whole.

We can also use fit statistics to clean up our models. Note that the path from Ethnicity to Homework was not statistically significant in the initial homework model. One alternative model worth investigating is one in which this path is deleted. With this change, $\Delta\chi^2$ is statistically not significant; this more parsimonious model thus fits as well as does the initial model. Although it is perfectly reasonable to use $\Delta\chi^2$ and other fit statistics to clean up models, keep in mind that this process is fundamentally different from the other model comparisons we have made. Our previous model comparisons were designed to test hypotheses drawn from theory and previous research. Model modifications to remove statistically nonsignificant paths are not theoretical; instead, they are based on the data themselves. They should not be accorded the same weight as theoretically derived model modifications until they are tested against new data. If you do a lot of data-based model revisions, you should recognize that you are conducting exploratory, rather than theory testing, research.

To reiterate, our rule of thumb is that if $\Delta\chi^2$ is statistically significant it means that the more parsimonious model has a statistically significantly worse fit than does the less parsimonious model. If you use this methodology, you would then reject the more parsimonious model in favor of the less parsimonious one. If, on the other hand, the $\Delta\chi^2$ is not statistically significant, then this means that the two models fit equally well (within a reasonable margin of error). Because we value parsimony, in this case, you would reject the less parsimonious model in favor of the more parsimonious one.

Table 12.3 also includes several other fit indexes that can be used to compare competing models. The first, the Akaike Information Criterion (AIC) is a useful cross-validation index in that it tends to select models that would be selected if results were cross-validated to a new sample (Loehlin, 2004). Another useful feature of AIC is that it can be used to compare competing models that are not nested. Smaller values of AIC are better, and thus if we use the AIC to compare the models in Table 12.3, we will continue to favor the initial model over its competitors. Another, related measure is the Bayes Information Criterion (BIC in the Amos output); the BIC includes a slightly stronger adjustment for parsimony than does the AIC.

Recall that the *df*s are a measure of the parsimony of a model. We may also be interested in the *relative* parsimony of a model. The most parsimonious version of the present model is the independence or null model, with 10 *df*, as shown in Figure 12.11. We can therefore use these two values in a parsimony ratio that provides an index of the relative parsimony of a model compared to the maximum parsimony (2 *df*/10 *df* for the initial model; James, Mulaik, & Brett, 1982); this value can then be used to weight other fit indexes for parsimony. Table 12.3 shows the Parsimony CFI, which is the CFI weighted by the Parsimony Ratio. Larger values of parsimony fit indexes are better, and they can also be used to compare nonnested models. Interestingly, if we use the PCFI to compare competing models, we will favor the no-homework-effects model. The parsimony ratio is also often used to weight the GFI, for a PGFI index.

Finally, the table shows the values for the RMSEA, along with its 90% confidence interval. These values can also be used to compare competing models either informally, by choosing the model with the lowest RMSEA, or more formally, by comparing the point value for one model with the 90% CI for another model. Using either approach, we will favor the initial model as being better fitting than the no-homework-effects model and more parsimonious (but equivalent fitting) compared to the background effect model.

I currently use $\Delta\chi^2$ as my primary index for comparing competing models if these models are nested and given a reasonable sample size (say 150 to 1000). For nonnested models, the AIC has worked well in my experience. In my experience, the parsimony fit indexes often place too high a premium on parsimony and lead to poor fitting but parsimonious models (as would be the case in the present example).

MORE COMPLEX MODELS

Equivalent and Nonequivalent Models

Equivalent Models.   We saw in Chapter 11 that with just-identified models path directions could be reversed, leading to very different conclusions, without any warning that one model was correct and the other incorrect. In other words, these models (e.g., Figures 11.3 and 11.7) are equivalent; we cannot differentiate them by their fit. This makes sense, because just-identified models fit perfectly, and thus we cannot differentiate them by their fit.

We have seen in this chapter that one advantage of overidentified models analyzed through SEM programs is that they provide measures of fit of the model to the data. We can use these fit indexes to compare models, to reject those that fit less well and tentatively accept those with better fit. What may not be obvious is that it is also possible, in fact likely, to have equivalent overidentified models. Equivalent models are those that produce the same fit statistics as the original model and thus cannot be differentiated from that model based on fit. It is often possible to reverse a path or to replace a path with a correlation without any change in the fit of the model. For example, Figure 12.13 shows the results of an analysis in which the path from Homework to Previous Achievement was reversed (compared to Figure 12.8). As can be seen in Figure 12.13, the χ^2, df, and RMSEA are all the same as in the initial analyses of this model (Figure 12.11; and although not shown, the rest of the fit indexes are also identical). The two models, with the path between Homework and Previous Achievement drawn in opposite directions, are statistically equivalent and cannot be differentiated. There are, in fact, numerous equivalent models to most target models, and you should consider them as you focus on a particular model.

Stelzl (1986) and Lee and Hershberger (1990) provided rules for generating equivalent models. The main gist of these rules is summarized briefly here. For this presentation, I have assumed that the beginning models are recursive.

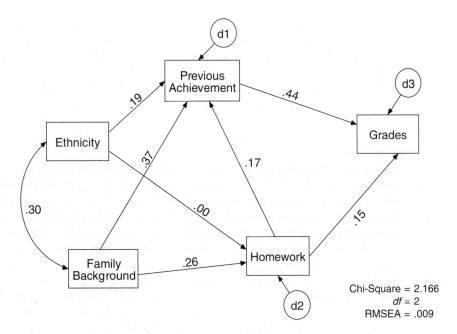

FIGURE 12.13   An equivalent model. Note that the Previous Achievement to Homework path is reversed, but the fit indexes are identical to those of the initial Homework model.

1. For a just-identified model, a path from *a* to *b* (symbolized as ⟶) may be replaced by a path from *b* to *a* (⟵) or by a correlation between *a* and *b* (if *a* and *b* are exogenous). Endogenous variables may not have simple correlations, but their disturbances may be correlated.[4] Thus, a path from endogenous variable *a* to endogenous variable *b* may be replaced by a correlation between the disturbances of *a* and *b* (I will symbolize both types of correlations by ⌢ for this discussion). All these possibilities are equivalent, meaning you can also replace ⌢ with ⟶ . This is simply another way of stating that all just-identified models are statistically equivalent because they all fit the data perfectly.

2. More importantly, for overidentified models, portions of these models may be just-identified. For the just-identified portions of models, these same rules apply. That is, you can replace ⟶ by ⟵ or by ⌢ (or vice versa), and the model will be equivalent. So, for example, in Figure 12.13 the model is just-identified through the variable Homework. This is why we can reverse the Homework–Previous Achievement path and still have an equivalent model.

3. For portions of the model that are overidentified, if *a* and *b* have the same causes, ⟶ may be replaced by ⌢ or by ⟵. Thus, for the model in Figure 12.7, reversing the path from Homework to Grades will not result in an equivalent model, because the two variables do *not* have the same causes.

4. For portions of the model that are overidentified, when *a* and *b* do *not* have the same causes, the substitutions are slightly more complex. A path from *a* to *b* may be replaced by ⌢ if the causes of *b* *include* all the causes of *a*. You could not replace the path from Homework to Grades with a correlated disturbance between d2 and d3 because the causes of Grades do not include all the causes of Homework. Ethnicity and Family Background are influences on Homework, but not Grades. In addition, correlated disturbances can be replaced by a path from *a* to *b* if *b* includes all causes of *a*.

Figure 12.14 shows several equivalent models to our original Homework model (from Figure 12.7, also shown as model A in Figure 12.14). Make sure you understand why each is equivalent to the original model. It is worth noting that these rules can be applied repeatedly, which is how the final model (model F) is derived. The derivation of each model is explained in note 5.

It should be obvious from a study of Figure 12.14 that the presence of equivalent models may threaten the causal conclusions from our research. If all these models are statistically equivalent to our preferred model, how can we assert, for example, that Previous Achievement affects Homework, rather than Homework affecting Previous Achievement? I encourage you to generate and consider alternatives to your model of choice. You may discover alternatives that make as much sense as your original model, or you may begin to feel more comfortable with your initial model. It is certainly better to consider equivalent models and either revise your models or defend your reasoning prior to publication rather than after! But, in reality, the answer to the threat of equivalent models is the same as the method of devising strong models to begin with: consider logical and actual time precedence, build in relevant theory and research, and carefully consider the variables involved.

What should we do, however, when equivalent models remain plausible even after such considerations? As we will see, one possible solution is to devise *non*equivalent models that evaluate the different possibilities; another possibility is the use of longitudinal data.

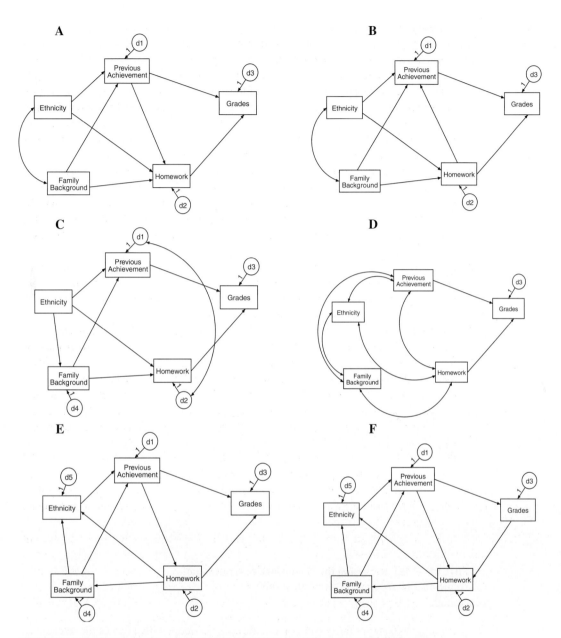

FIGURE 12.14   Equivalent models. All the models are equivalent to Model A and cannot be differentiated from it based on fit.

The Lee and Hershberger rules apply to portions of nonrecursive models as well, but the rules presented here will cover most models of interest in this text. See Lee and Hershberger (1990) for more information; the rules are also summarized and well illustrated by Kline (1998). MacCallum, Wegener, Uchino, and Fabrigar (1993) illustrated problems that arise from not considering equivalent models.

Directionality Revisited.   If some overidentified models are equivalent, it follows that some overidentified models are not equivalent and that we can use the same rules to generate nonequivalent models. These, in turn, may help us deal with one problem we encountered with simple just-identified models: uncertainty concerning causal direction.

Figure 12.15 shows one more version of the homework model, one in which the path from Homework to Grades is reversed, replaced by a path from Grades to Homework. This direction does not make sense based on time precedence (Homework includes information from 8th and 10th grades, whereas Grades are from 10th grade). Still, as demonstrated in Chapter 11, if we estimate a just-identified version of this model, there will be nothing in our analysis to tell us that it is incorrect. The current version is overidentified. More importantly, this model is not equivalent to the original model. Grades and Homework do not have the same causes (rule 3), and thus the reversal of the path does not result in an equivalent model. If the models are not equivalent, does that mean that the fit indexes may help spot the error in our model? In a word, yes.

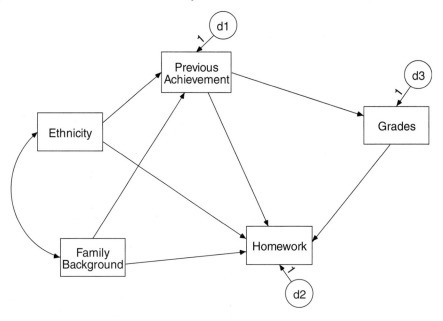

FIGURE 12.15   Reversing the Homework to Grades path results in a nonequivalent homework model.

Figure 12.16 shows the solved "wrong direction" model with a few of the relevant fit indexes. Note that if we look at the RMSEA (or other stand-alone fit indexes), this model will be deemed acceptable. Of more interest, however, is to compare this model with the initial "correct" homework model. We can't use $\Delta\chi^2$ because the two models are not nested; you cannot arrive at one by deleting paths from the other. Indeed, the models are equally parsimonious (they have the same *df*). We can still use the AIC to compare nonnested models, however. As you can see, if you compare the AIC from Figure 12.16 with the fit indexes for the original model (shown in Figure 12.11), the AIC for the original model is smaller. The rule of thumb for AIC is to favor the model with the lower value; we would thus favor the original model over the model with the Homework–Grades path drawn in the wrong direction. The judicious use of nonequivalent models may indeed help us answer nagging questions of directionality.

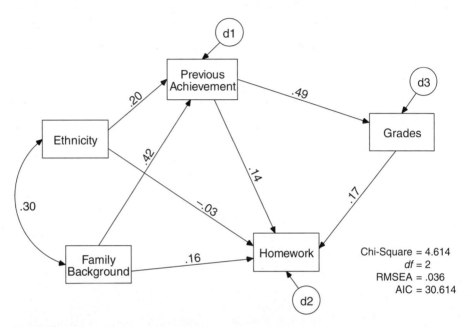

FIGURE 12.16   The nonequivalent homework model demonstrated a worse fit to the data.

You may wonder why this should work. Recall the genesis of the fit indexes: a comparison of the actual correlation–covariance matrix with the matrix implied by the model. Quite simply, Figure 12.16 implies a slightly different covariance matrix than does the model shown in Figure 12.8, and the matrix implied by the model shown in Figure 12.8 comes closer to the actual matrix.

Practically, the easiest way to develop such nonequivalent models is to include variables that uniquely cause one of the variables in question. That is, include variables in the model that are influences of the presumed cause but not the presumed effect and variables that are influences on the presumed effect but not the presumed cause. In other words, include some relevant *non*common causes in the model. Thus, although we saw in Chapter 11 that noncommon causes are not required for the model to be valid, we now see they may help in dealing with other problems. Likewise, intervening variables can help in the development of nonequivalent models and thus may be valuable for this purpose as well.

Nonrecursive Models

Another advantage of SEM programs is that they can be used to analyze nonrecursive models, or models with feedback loops. Suppose you were interested in the influences on partners' levels of trust in marriage and other close male–female relationships. It makes sense that my level of trust in my wife may be affected, in part, by my own personal and psychological characteristics. My trust may also be affected by my wife's level of trust in me, however, and vice versa. If I trust my wife more, she will likely trust me more, and so on. Trust likely has reciprocal effects. Your theoretical model might look something like that shown in Figure 12.17. The model posits that one's trust in his or her partner is affected by one's own characteristics (self-esteem and perception of the partner's desire for control), as well as by the partner's own level of trust. This model is a smaller version of one posited and tested by John Butler (2001).

Recall that the tracing rule does not work with nonrecursive models, but that we can develop formulas for the paths using the first law of path analysis. If you develop equations for the model shown in Figure 12.17, you find that, unlike recursive models, the formulas no longer are equivalent to those for regression coefficients from multiple regression. This is simply a convoluted way of saying that with nonrecursive models you cannot use ordinary multiple regression to estimate the paths.

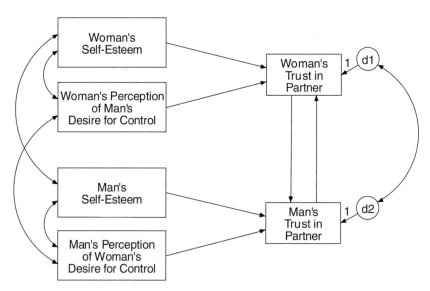

FIGURE 12.17   Nonrecursive model to test the reciprocal effects of partners' trust in each other.

It is possible, however, to use SEM programs to estimate models such as those shown in Figure 12.17. Some results of such an analysis are shown in Figure 12.18; they suggest that each partner's trust is indeed affected by the other's trust. Self-Esteem had a positive effect on Trust, and Perception of Control had a negative effect, although the relative magnitudes of these effects were different for men and women. You will have a chance to return to this model in the exercises. (The data that produced these results are simulated because the original article did not include the correlation or covariance matrix. These simulated findings are consistent with those of the original article, however.)

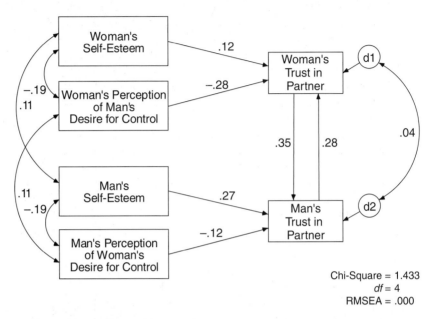

FIGURE 12.18   Standardized solution, partner trust model. The data are simulated, but based on research reported by Butler (2001).

I have presented this model as an example of the use of nonrecursive models to answer questions in which we expect there to be reciprocal effects. These are common in analyses of data from couples or other pairs of people. One of the best-known nonrecursive models, extensively analyzed and used as an example in many SEM manuals, was devised by sociologist Otis Dudley Duncan and colleagues to estimate the effects of friends on each other's occupational and educational aspirations (Duncan, Haller, & Portes, 1971). As you might expect, nonrecursive models are also used to settle questions of causal sequence (e.g., Reibstein, Lovelock, & Dobson, 1980).

Nonrecursive models are considerably more complex than this simple overview, however, and are beyond the scope of this book. If you are interested in pursuing nonrecursive models, you will need to study such models in considerably more depth. Kline (1998) and Loehlin (2004) provide a more detailed introduction, Rigdon (1995) presents a detailed discussion of identification issues for nonrecursive models, and Hayduk (1996) presents interesting issues related to nonrecursive models.

Longitudinal Models

Another method of answering questions about the reciprocal effects of variables on one another is through longitudinal models. Indeed, if you focus on our homework models, you will see that they take advantage of this technique. These models focus on the effects of homework on learning in later grades (subsequent Grades), while controlling for achievement in previous grades (Previous Achievement).

Do job stress and emotional exhaustion (or burnout) have reciprocal effects? Figure 12.19 shows a longitudinal model designed to answer this question for physicians surveyed in the United Kingdom (McManus, Winder, & Gordon, 2002). The physicians were surveyed in 1997 and again in 2000; the variables in the model should be self-explanatory. The data (stress burnout longitudinal.xls) and this model are on the Web site www.ablongman.com/keith1e (stress burnout longitudinal 5.amw).

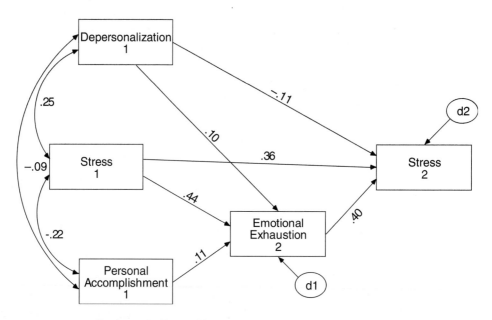

FIGURE 12.19   Reciprocal effects of Stress and Emotional Exhaustion, estimated via longitudinal data. The model is based on research with physicians (McManus et al., 2002).

The model is barely overidentified (with 1 *df*); there is no path from Personal Accomplishment at time 1 to Stress at time 2. The results suggest that Stress and Emotional Exhaustion indeed have reciprocal effects. Stress increases Exhaustion, which, in turn, increases subsequent Stress. It is worthwhile to compare this model to one in which it is assumed that Stress affects future Stress only via the indirect effect through Exhaustion.

Longitudinal models can also help bolster the reasoning behind the paths we draw, even in the presence of equivalent models. If Emotional Exhaustion is measured in 1997 and Stress in 2000, it is easier to argue that the proper direction is from Exhaustion to Stress than if they are measured concurrently. Still, I don't want to oversell the ability of nonrecursive and longitudinal models to answer questions about the direction of influence; the results are not always as clear as we would like them to be. I have provided fairly clean and clear-cut examples here to illustrate the possibilities.

There are also other reasons to analyze longitudinal models via SEM programs. Consider the model shown in Figure 12.20. This longitudinal model, also called a *panel model,* could be tested with the NELS full data (including the 12th-grade data, not included in our NELS subsample). Note that the Achievement tests (the same or very similar tests) are administered three times. One assumption of the model shown is that the residuals (disturbances) are uncorrelated with one another. The disturbances represent all the influences on a variable from outside the model; these include other variables, along with errors of measurement. If a variable is measured repeatedly, however, it is likely that some of the influences represented by the disturbances at each time point will be the same as those at other time points. In other words, with longitudinal models in which the same variable is measured repeatedly, we should no longer assume that the disturbances will be uncorrelated. Using a SEM program, we could easily add curved, double-headed arrows between disturbances to represent correlations between disturbances.

Self-Concept and Achievement
Model Specification

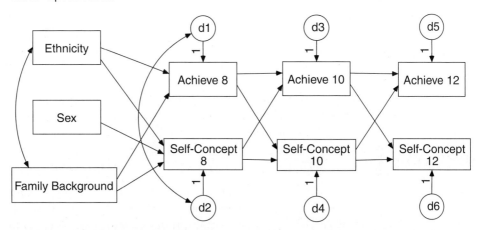

FIGURE 12.20   Potential longitudinal panel model designed to determine the extent of the effect of self-concept on achievement, and vice versa.

ADVICE: MR VERSUS SEM PROGRAMS

We have seen that with just-identified models SEM programs provide the same information for a path analysis as we get with multiple regression programs. With overidentified models, however, there are advantages in using SEM programs. If you have a choice, which should you use? Here's my advice:

1. If you plan to analyze a single, just-identified recursive model, either MR or a dedicated SEM program will work just fine.
2. If you plan to analyze an overidentified model or compare several competing models, use a SEM program. If you plan to analyze a nonrecursive model, use a SEM program.

From another perspective:

1. If you are using a MR program to conduct a path analysis, there is no real benefit in specifying overidentified models. Instead, what I suggest is a more qualitative evaluation of fit. By this I mean that prior to analysis you should try to predict, based on previous research and theory, which paths will be close to zero, which should be large, which should be positive, which should be negative, and so on. I'm not suggesting that you necessarily need to make these as formal predictions, but you should spend some time thinking about what you expect each path to look like. After conducting the analysis, see how your predictions fared. If the paths you thought should be close to zero were, in fact, close to zero, and so on, you can have much more faith that your model may be a faithful approximation of the way the phenomenon you are studying actually works. If, on the other hand, many of your predictions were wrong, you should be more cautious in your interpretation and should rethink you model and double-check your analyses.

2. If you are using a SEM program to conduct a path analysis, it is worthwhile to try to specify overidentified models rather than just-identified models. Again, spend some time comparing your model to what you know based on theory and previous research. Are there paths that you can set to zero based on such information? If so, delete them from your model (you can always test these no-effect hypotheses in subsequent models). Again, it is preferable to specify these no-effect hypotheses prior to analyzing the data, rather than after running a just-identified model and noting which paths were statistically insignificant. If you are using a SEM program, you should also consider the substantive hypotheses you can test by comparing competing models.

SUMMARY

We covered a great deal of ground in this chapter; a review is needed. In this chapter we made the transition from estimating path models using multiple regression analysis to estimating these models with programs specifically designed for structural equation modeling (SEM). Several such programs are available, each with its own advantages. Most programs have student, or demonstration, versions available, downloadable from the Web; these student versions work the same as do the full-featured programs, but generally limit the number of variables that can be analyzed. There is at least one completely free SEM program, Mx. I have used the Analysis of Moment Structures (Amos) program to illustrate SEM programs, and the student version of Amos is available at amosdevelopment.com. The illustrations and explanations should translate easily to other SEM programs, and Appendix C illustrates input and output from several SEM programs.

All our previous discussions of path analysis translate directly to path analysis via SEM programs. To illustrate, we reestimated the parent involvement path model from Chapter 11 using Amos. One advantage of Amos is that a drawing of a path model is used as the specification of the model, and the drawing, along with the data, is sufficient for conducting the analysis. The input drawing for reanalysis of the parent involvement example was similar to the conventions we have used previously for developing path models. The one difference was that, by convention, we set the paths from the disturbances to the endogenous variables to 1, which allowed us to estimate the variance of the disturbance. (In multiple regression the variance of the disturbance was assumed to be 1, but the path was estimated.) We will follow this convention with other unmeasured–latent variables as well: setting the scale of the unmeasured variable by setting the path from it to a measured variable to 1; this convention merely says the scale of the unmeasured variable is the same as that of the measured variable.

Output from the SEM program (in this case Amos) included standardized and unstandardized path models, as well as detailed output. The more detailed output included standard errors of unstandardized coefficients and their associated t (or z) statistics, as well as tables of direct, indirect, and total effects.

Our next example was an overidentified model designed to determine the extent of the influence of Homework time on high school Grades. The model did not include all the paths that could have been drawn, a specification that is the same as drawing the paths but constraining them to a value of zero. The solved model suggested that Homework had a moderate effect on Grades, and Previous Achievement and Family Background had moderate to strong effects on time spent on Homework.

In earlier chapters I noted that overidentified models can be used to provide feedback about the adequacy of the model. A chief advantage of SEM programs is that they naturally provide such feedback. We can solve for paths using covariances, but we can also do the reverse: solve for the covariances. When models are overidentified, these two matrices (the actual and the implied covariance matrices) will differ to some degree. Fit statistics or indexes describe this degree of similarity or dissimilarity and provide feedback as to the adequacy of the model in explaining the data.

The degrees of freedom for a model describe the extent to which it is overidentified, or the parsimony of the model. The Homework model had 2 degrees of freedom; there were two paths we could have drawn but did not. The more we constrain values in the model to zero (or some other value), the more parsimonious the model and the larger its degrees of freedom.

Numerous fit indexes are provided by SEM programs. We focused on the Root Mean Square Error of Approximation (RMSEA) as a primary index of fit for a single model; RMSEAs of .05 or less suggest a good fit, with values of .08 or less suggesting an adequate fit (cf. Browne & Cudeck, 1993). I also discussed using the Goodness of Fit Index (GFI), the Comparative Fit Index (CFI), and the Tucker–Lewis Index (TLI) as methods of assessing the fit of a single model. For these indexes, values above .95 suggest a good fit, and values above .90 suggest an adequate fit. χ^2, along with the df and its associated probability, may be used to assess the fit of a model, with statistically significant values suggesting a lack of fit and statistically not significant values suggesting a good fit of the model to the data. Although common, χ^2 has problems as a measure of the fit of a single model.

A major advantage of SEM programs and measures of fit is that they may be used to compare competing theoretical models. We compared the fit of the initial Homework model to several competing models; these comparisons tested basic hypotheses embodied in these models. Although I discouraged the use of χ^2 as the measure of fit of a single model, I argued that if models are nested (one is a more constrained version of the other) χ^2 can be a useful method of comparing the two models. The more parsimonious model (the one with the larger df) will also have a larger χ^2. If the change in χ^2 is statistically significant compared to the change in *df*, our rule of thumb is to prefer the less parsimonious model; but if the $\Delta\chi^2$ is statistically not significant, our preference is for the more parsimonious model. Other fit indexes for comparing competing models are the Akaike Information Criterion (AIC) and the Bayes Information Criterion (BIC), in which smaller values are better, and various parsimony fit indexes (e.g., PGFI), for which larger values are better.

Although overidentified models allow us to compare competing models, representing competing hypotheses about the effects of variables on each other, there may be several or many models that are equivalent to our preferred model. These equivalent models may also represent competing hypotheses about effects, but are statistically indistinguishable from our preferred model. I briefly explained and illustrated the rules for generating equivalent models, and noted that you should consider such equivalent models as you develop your own models. You can guard against the threat represented by equivalent models in the same way you build valid models in the first place, through careful consideration of theory, previous research, time precedence, and so on.

The flip side of equivalent models is that there are other overidentified but nonnested models that are not equivalent with the model under consideration. Such models can be very useful for testing and rejecting threats to path models. Knowing the rules for generating equivalent models also allows us to develop nonequivalent models. We illustrated this value by testing a nonequivalent version of the Homework model with the path from Homework to Grades reversed.

Other advantages of SEM programs are that they can be used to analyze nonrecursive models and can provide for more powerful analysis of longitudinal models. Longitudinal data may also be useful for overcoming some challenges posed by equivalent models by clarifying causal direction. I briefly illustrated such models, but did not delve into them in detail.

We now have two methods for analyzing path models: multiple regression analysis via a generic statistical analysis program or SEM programs. If you are using MR to conduct path analysis, there is no real benefit for developing overidentified models. If you are using a SEM program, however, it is worth developing overidentified models when possible, because of the fit information the programs provide. Similarly, if you are interested in overidentified models, comparing competing models, or in more complex forms of path models, I encourage you to use a SEM program to estimate these models.

EXERCISES

1. Reproduce the Homework models used in this chapter. Make sure your results match mine (note there may be minor differences in estimates if you are using programs other than Amos). Are there additional models that you might test?

2. Try estimating a similar homework model using your NELS data.

3. In the section introducing overidentifying models, I stated that "not drawing a path is the same as drawing a path and fixing or constraining that path to a value of zero." Demonstrate the truth of this statement. Using the homework model, constrain, for example, the path from Previous Achievement to Grades to zero and check the fit of the model. Now delete that same path. Is the fit the same? Are the parameter estimates the same for the two models?

4. Focus on the equivalent models in Figure 12.14. Note the difference between these and the initial model (model A). Which rule or rules were used to produce each equivalent model? Check your answers against those in note 5. Try estimating one or two of these models to demonstrate that they are indeed equivalent.

5. Henry, Tolan, and Gorman-Smith (2001) investigated the effect of one's peers on boys' later violence and delinquency. Figure 12.21 shows one model drawn from their study, their "fully mediated" model. Family Relationships is a composite of measures of family cohesion, beliefs about family, and family structure, with high scores representing a better functioning family; the violence and delinquency variables are measures of the frequency of violent and nonviolent delinquent offenses for peers and individuals. The model is longitudinal, with Family Relationships measured at age 12, Peer variables at age 14, and Individual variables at age 17. The model is also contained in the file "henry et al.amw" on the Web site.

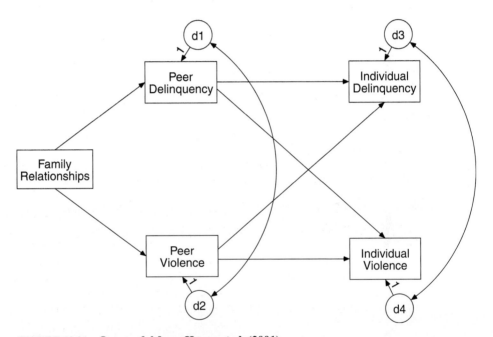

FIGURE 12.21   One model from Henry et al. (2001).

Data consistent with those reported in the original article are in the SPSS file "Henry et al.sav" or the Excel file "Henry et al.xls." Analyze and interpret this model. Which variable had a more important effect on boys' delinquency: peers who are delinquent or peers who are violent? Which variable was more important for boys' violence? What were the indirect effects of Family Relationships on Individual's Violence and Delinquency? Test an alternative model to determine whether Family Relationships directly affect the outcome variables.

(The Henry et al., 2001, article reported correlations among variables. The data used in this example were simulated data designed to mimic these correlations. The Family Relationships variable used here was a combination of three variables from the original article.)

6. Estimate the nonrecursive trust model from Figure 12.17. The model (trust nonrecursive model 1.amw) and the data (trust norec sim data.xls) are included on the accompanying Web site (www.ablongman.com/keith1e). Second, assume that the Man's Trust affects his partner, but not the reverse: delete the path from Woman's Trust to Man's Trust, along with the correlated disturbance. Are these models nested? Why? Compare the fit of the two models. What conclusions do you reach from these model comparisons?

NOTES

1. We could also analyze the NELS raw data, but would then need to consider methods of dealing with missing data in more depth than I want to right now. We will return to this issue in the final chapter.

2. I know, properly it should be chi-squared, but, by convention, it's chi-square.

3. For example, type the χ^2 and *df* into two cells in Excel. Click on another cell, then Insert, Function. Click on CHIDIST and follow the directions to obtain the probability associated with χ^2 with the indicated *df*.

4. What do correlated disturbances mean? Focus on model C in Figure 12.14, which shows a correlated disturbance between d1 and d2. The disturbances represent all other influences on the corresponding variables other than those shown in the model. The correlation between d1 and d2 in this model suggests that the other influences (other than Ethnicity and Family Background) on Previous Achievement and Homework may be correlated. What this means, in turn, is that there may be other common causes of Previous Achievement and Homework not included in the model. Correlated disturbances can also be used to denote an agnostic causal relation; that is, we think that Previous Achievement and Homework are causally related, but don't know the direction.

5. Model B and Models C and D resulted from the application of rule 2. Model E, with the paths between Homework and Ethnicity and Homework and Family Background reversed, also resulted from the application of this rule. Model F builds on Model E. Note that with model E Homework and Grades now have the same causes. We can therefore apply rule 3 to Model E and reverse the path from Grades to Homework. It may not be obvious, but Models E and F are nonrecursive models. Note that in Model F, for example, Homework affects Background, which affects Previous Achievement, which affects Homework, and so on.

ERROR: THE SCOURGE
OF RESEARCH

Recall the assumptions required to interpret regression coefficients (paths) as estimates of effects of one variable on another:

1. There is no reverse causation; that is, the model is recursive.
2. The exogenous variables are perfectly measured, that is, they are completely reliable and valid.
3. A state of equilibrium has been reached. This assumption means that the causal process has had a chance to work.
4. No common cause of the presumed cause and the presumed effect has been neglected; the model includes all such common causes (Kenny, 1979, p. 51).

We have dealt with several of these assumptions, such as the effect of neglecting a common cause, and I promised we would return to assumption 2: the assumption of perfect or near perfect measurement of the exogenous variables. Obviously, this assumption is violated routinely—perfect measurement is rare to impossible—but what effect does this violation have on our research? In addition, inaccurate measurement of the endogenous variables also affects estimates in path models.

It is worth noting that issues of reliability and validity of measurements affect *all* research, not just that based on path analysis and multiple regression. Many of us think of measurement as separate from statistics, but they are inexorably intertwined. In a laboratory experiment our experimental conditions (the exogenous variable) may be clear-cut and thus perfectly measured (e.g., treatment versus control), but the dependent (endogenous variable) (e.g., a measure of self-esteem) may be considerably less reliable. This lack of reliability may result in an underestimation of the effect of the experimental treatment, with even a truly meaningful finding showing up as statistically nonsignificant. In applied research, there may be variations in the treatments by those responsible for providing the experimental treatment. Teachers in an experiment designed to compare the effects of two methods for teaching reading may use other methods outside the experimental procedure. This variation is, in fact, unreliability and invalidity in the independent–exogenous variable, which will also cloud the results of the research. In fact, the effect of measurement on decision making affects *every* aspect of life. Your physician may prescribe or not prescribe medication for high blood pressure depending on her measurement of your blood pressure; if her measurements are unreliable, however, you may receive unnecessary treatment or not receive needed treatment. You may have costly repairs completed on your car based on unreliable measurement, and so on. Measurement accuracy affects all research and all decisions made from these measurements. Why, you may wonder, does it?

EFFECTS OF UNRELIABILITY

The Importance of Reliability

In classic measurement theory, we might administer a test, or survey, or other measurement to a group of people. There will be variation in their scores; some people will score high, some low. We also know that there will be error in their scores; all measurement involves error. This aspect of scores is represented in Figure 13.1. V represents the total variation in a set of scores on some measurement. This total variance can be divided into variation due to error (V_e) and true score variation (V_t): $V = V_t + V_e$. Using this definition, reliability is the proportion of the true score variance to the total variance: $\frac{V_t}{V}$. This makes sense: the greater the error in a set of scores, the less a person's score on that measure is a result of true variation and the less reliable the measurement.

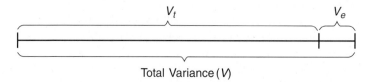

FIGURE 13.1   **Variance definition of reliability. Reliability is the proportion of true score variance to total variance ($\frac{V_t}{V}$).**

Figure 13.2 illustrates the effects of unreliability in path analytic format. In this graphic, a person's score on any measurement is affected both by the person's *true score* and by *errors* of measurement. In this graphic, error is equivalent to V_e and the true score to V_t. Note that the actual, measured score is the only measured variable in this model; both the true score and the error are unmeasured and unknown.

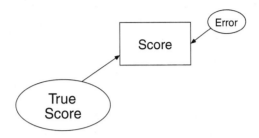

FIGURE 13.2   Path analytic definition of reliability; a person's score on a test or measurement is affected by their true, but unknown, score and by error.

The reliability of a test, scale, survey, or other measure places an upper limit on the correlation that the measurement can have with any other measurement. As a general rule, a second variable will correlate with the true score rather than the measured score. That is, other variables will generally correlate with the V_t portion of the variable illustrated in Figure 13.1, not the V_e portion. This, then, is the reason that measurement quality affects statistics and research: a less reliable measurement limits the correlations a variable can have with any other variable. Since correlations are the statistic underlying multiple regression, path analysis, ANOVA, and other derivatives of the general linear model, unreliable measurement causes us to underestimate the effects of one variable on another in *all* these methodologies.

Effects of Unreliability on Path Results

What effect does measurement error have on path analytic results? Figure 13.3 shows the results for the homework model from Chapter 12. In this model, whether we realize it or not, we are assuming that all the variables in the model are measured without error, with perfect reliability. As researchers, we may recognize that the variables in the model are measured with different degrees of error, but the model assumes they are all error free.

Focus on the variable of homework. Homework is based on student self-report of the average amount of time students spend on homework in several academic areas. Undoubtedly, error is inherent in this variable, not only because of the self-report nature of the questions, but also because, perhaps more importantly, students were asked to approximate their average amount of time per week. I would not be surprised to discover that this variable had a reliability of only about .70, with a corresponding error of 30%. If we build such estimates into the path model, what will be the effect on the estimates of paths?

Figure 13.4 shows a model that recognizes this unreliability (reliability = .70, error = .30) in the Homework variable. Note the increase in the apparent effect of Homework on

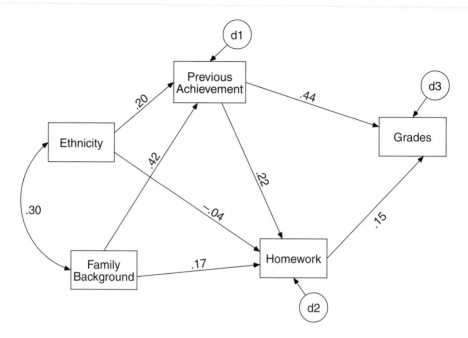

FIGURE 13.3   Homework model from Chapter 12 revisited.

Grades, from .15 in Figure 13.3 to .19 in Figure 13.4. What this means is that when we assumed that the error-laden Homework variable was perfectly reliable, as in Figure 13.3, we *underestimated* the true effect of Homework on Grades. In contrast, when we recognize the error inherent in this variable, we obtain a more realistic and larger estimate of the effect. This is also the most common effect of error in models: unreliability artificially reduces our estimates of the effects of one variable on another.

Note also that many of the other paths in the model are different from those in Figure 13.3. Indeed, all paths to Homework increased in magnitude, and the path from Achievement to Grades decreased slightly. Recognition of the error that exists in the Homework variable resulted in changes in many of the paths in the model.

But Homework is not the only less than perfectly reliable variable in the model. What about Grades? Grades were also based on student self-report, plus there are well-known problems with Grades as measures of student learning, including variations in grading standards from teacher to teacher, the unreliability of teacher-made tests and other components of grades, and the likely clouding of other variables (e.g., students' apparent interest) in teachers' grading practices. Given these deficiencies of Grades, it is probably reasonable to estimate their reliability at a maximum of .80 (and 20% of the variation in scores due to error).

Figure 13.5 shows the results of recognition of this level of error for the Grades variable (assuming perfect reliability for the other variables in the model). In this model, compared to Figure 13.3, the magnitude of the paths to Grades from both Previous Achievement (from .44 to .50) and Homework (from .15 to .17) increased.

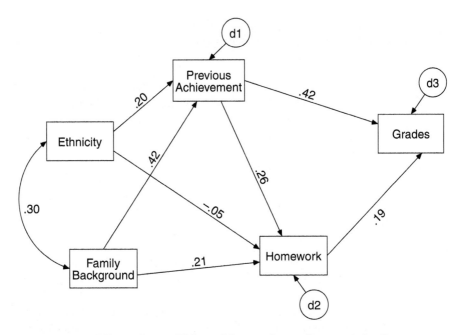

FIGURE 13.4 Effects of error. This model recognizes and accounts for the unreliability in the Homework variable; with this recognition, the apparent effect of Homework on Grades increases.

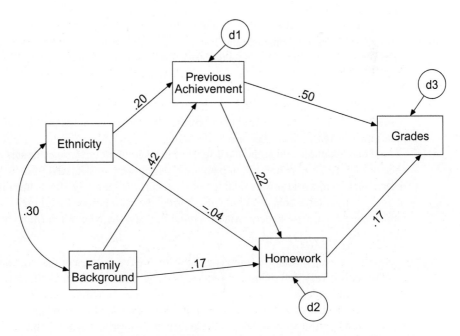

FIGURE 13.5 Effects of error. This model shows the result of recognizing the error inherent in the Grades variable.

Although it is not obvious from these figures, the effects of unreliability are different depending on whether the variable in question is exogenous or endogenous. Briefly, error in an exogenous variable affects both the standardized and unstandardized paths, as well as their statistical significance. Paths from other exogenous variables (in addition to the error-laden one) may be affected. In contrast, error in an endogenous variable affects only *standardized* estimates of effects, leaving unstandardized effects unchanged. The unstandardized paths for the model shown in Figure 13.5 would be the same as those for the model shown in 13.3, despite the differences in the standardized paths. This difference is why error in exogenous variables is more consequential than error in endogenous variables. When a variable is in the middle of a model—exogenous in relation to some variables, endogenous for others—the results of error are more complex, as in the example recognizing error in Homework (Figure 13.4). The bottom line is that measurement error affects estimates of effects, but is more serious for exogenous variables [for more information, see Bollen, 1989 (chap. 5); Rigdon, 1994; or Wolfle, 1979].

These examples have corrected for unreliability in a single variable. What would happen if we were to recognize the unreliability in *all* the variables in the model? If you think about it, all the variables in the model are unreliable to one degree or another. Even Ethnic orientation, probably the most reliable variable, likely has some error. Students may not read the survey question accurately, students who could legitimately claim to belong to more than one ethnic group are allowed only one answer, some students simply knowingly mark the wrong response, and there may be errors in coding of students' responses. For whatever the reason, even this variable likely includes some error.[1]

The model shown in Figure 13.6 attempts to recognize the error inherent in every variable in the model. For this example, I assumed that error was responsible for 30% of the variability for Homework, 20% for Grades, 5% for Ethnicity, 20% for Family Background, and 10% for Previous Achievement. These are plausible estimates. Note that every parameter estimate in the model changed from those shown in Figure 13.3. Most estimates increased in magnitude, but one, the path from Ethnicity to Previous Achievement, decreased (from .20 in Figure 13.3 to .17 in Figure 13.6). Recognition of the error inherent in the variables in our models will often, although certainly not always, result in larger estimates of the effects of one variable on another. With such complex patterns of errors, estimates may increase, decrease, or stay the same.

These examples illustrate the effects of measurement error on estimates of the influence of one variable on another in path analysis (as well at MR, ANOVA, etc.). What can researchers do to avoid misestimating such effects? We can strive for better measures, but no measures are error free. We could also correct the correlations for all the variables in the model using estimates of each variable's reliability and the common formula for correcting for attenuation, $r_{T_1T_2} = r_{12}/\sqrt{r_{11} \times r_{22}}$, where $r_{T_1T_2}$ is the corrected, or "true" correlation, r_{12} is the original correlation, and r_{11} and r_{22} are the reliabilities of the two variables. This solution is not very satisfying for several reasons. First, it divorces the correction from model testing; indeed, the process smacks of statistical voodoo. Second, when there are multiple estimates of reliability, such as with several studies providing estimates, it is unclear which estimate should be used. Conversely, no estimates of reliability may be available for a given measure. Finally, although this method might deal with unreliability of measures, it ignores problems of invalidity.

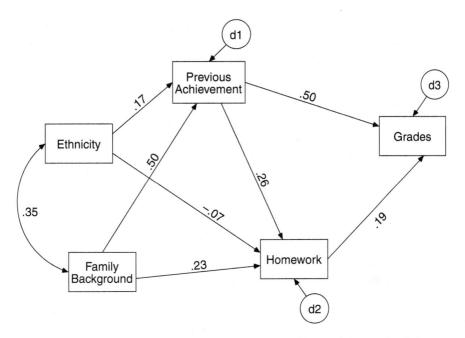

FIGURE 13.6   Effects of error. This model recognizes the error inherent in all the variables in the model. Compare the coefficients here with those shown in Figure 13.3.

EFFECTS OF INVALIDITY

The Meaning and Importance of Validity

What effect does invalidity have on estimates of effects? In classic measurement theory, validity may be considered as a subset of reliability. An example will illustrate how these measurement concepts are related. Suppose that you are interested in the effects of reading comprehension on subsequent delinquent behavior. One task is to measure reading comprehension. You will find that different tests of reading comprehension use different methods of measurement. Test 1, for example, asks research participants to read a passage on one page and then point to one picture (out of four choices) on the next page that best illustrates what they read in the passage. Test 2, in contrast, asks participants to read a passage (e.g., "stand up, walk around the table, then sit down") and then do what the passage requested. Test 3 uses a "cloze" procedure; the participant reads a passage with one or several words missing and then supplies the missing words based on the meaning of the text.

It is clear that each of these tests measures reading comprehension to some degree. But each test also measures something else, something other than reading comprehension. Test 1 also measures the ability to translate something read into a picture; Test 2 measures the ability to act out something read; Test 3 measures the ability to pick from one's knowledge store the word or words that will make the most sense when inserted in a passage. Each test may measure these unique skills reliably, but these skills are not the same as reading comprehension.

We are also not interested in the variation in scores due to these unique skills. We are interested in the effects of reading comprehension on delinquent behavior, not the effects of the ability to translate text into mental pictures (Test 1) or the unique skills measured by other tests on delinquent behavior. This variation due to these unique skills will not be removed through correction for attenuation, however, since these skills are measured reliably and are not due to error.

As shown in Figure 13.7, it is possible to extend the earlier variance definition of reliability. The true score variation (reliability) can be divided further. Using the reading comprehension example, one component of the true score variation for each test is the variance that these three tests have in common, the common variance, or V_c. What do the three Reading Comprehension Tests measure in common: reading comprehension! Each test also measures something unique or specific, however, and this component of the true score reliability is symbolized as V_s, for specific variance. The common variance, V_c, is an estimate of the validity of each test and thus demonstrates that validity is a subset of reliability. The V_s, the unique or specific variance of each test, is sometimes called the *specificity,* or the unique variance. For our present purposes, it represents invalidity and needs to be taken into account in our research on the effects of reading comprehension on delinquent behavior.

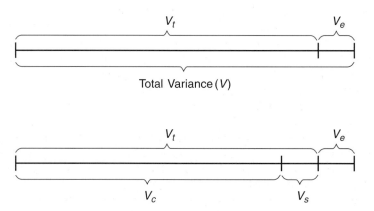

FIGURE 13.7   True score variance may be further subdivided into common variance (V_c) and specific or unique variance (V_s). Validity is related to common variance.

Accounting for Invalidity

How can we take this invalidity into account? Another way of conceptualizing the problem is as a path model, as shown in Figure 13.8. The diagram illustrates the influences on individuals' scores on the three Reading Comprehension Tests. Each person's score on each test is first affected by his or her level of reading comprehension. Reading Comprehension—the true level of reading comprehension—is an unmeasured or latent variable and is thus enclosed in an oval. Each person's scores on each test are also affected by error (unreliability) and by that person's level of the unique skills measured by each test (one's ability to translate text into pictures, and so on). These are also unmeasured variables. Our primary interest, of course, is in the Reading Comprehension latent variable.

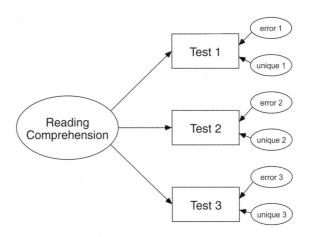

**FIGURE 13.8   Using path models to understand validity.
Individuals' scores on three tests of Reading Comprehension
are affected by their true level of Reading Comprehension
and by error and the unique aspects of each test.**

Figure 13.8 is a path model, and we can solve it in much the same way we solved the first path models in Chapter 10. Figure 13.9 shows a slight revision of the model, with the error and unique variances combined for each variable and the paths labeled to help develop equations. Figure 13.10 shows the correlations among the three tests. As in Chapter 10, we can use the tracing rule to develop equations:

$$r_{12} = ab,$$

$$r_{13} = ac, \quad \text{and}$$

$$r_{23} = bc.$$

If we combine the first two equations, we get $r_{12}r_{13} = abac$, which can be simplified as $a^2bc = r_{12}r_{13}$, or $a^2 = r_{12}r_{13}/bc$. Because $bc = r_{23}$ from the third equation, $a^2 = r_{12}r_{13}/r_{23}$ and $a = \sqrt{r_{12}r_{13}/r_{23}}$. We can also solve for b and c: $b = \sqrt{r_{12}r_{23}/r_{13}}$ and $c = \sqrt{r_{13}r_{23}/r_{12}}$. If you substitute the correlations in these equations, $a = .716$, $b = .894$, and $c = .839$. Figure 13.11 shows the model with the path estimates inserted.

Interestingly, what we have done by solving for the paths in Figure 13.11 is a simple (confirmatory) factor analysis. Figure 13.12 shows output from a factor analysis of these three items in SPSS; the factor loadings from the output are the same as the paths from the Reading Comprehension latent variable to the three reading Tests.[2] The example nicely illustrates the thinking underlying factor analysis: there is a latent, or unmeasured, variable, or factor, that affects individuals' scores on these three Tests and does so to different degrees. The example also illustrates the equivalence of several terms. What we have been referring to as latent or unmeasured variables are equivalent to the *factors* from factor analysis. These latent variables or factors are also much closer to the *constructs* we are interested in than are our normal, error-laden measurements.

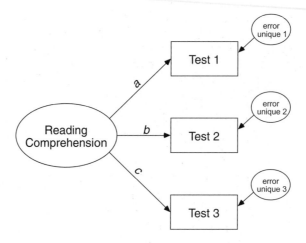

FIGURE 13.9 Reading Comprehension measurement model; we can generate equations to solve for the paths from Reading Comprehension to the three Tests.

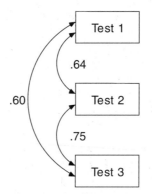

FIGURE 13.10 Correlations among the three Tests used to solve for the paths.

Our primary interest, of course, was the influence of Reading Comprehension on Delinquent Behavior. Because we can solve the model to estimate the Reading Comprehension latent variable, we could also use the latent variable in an analysis of the effects of Reading Comprehension on Delinquent Behavior, as in Figure 13.13 (once we were able to measure Delinquent Behavior).

LATENT VARIABLE SEM AND ERRORS OF MEASUREMENT

To return to our more general problem, perhaps this means that the solution to the problem of less-than-perfect measurement is not to correct all the correlations for attenuation, but to

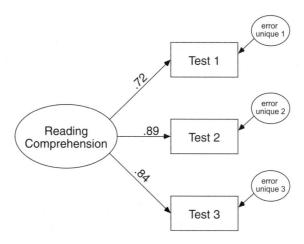

FIGURE 13.11   Solved Reading Comprehension measurement model.

Factor Matrix[a]

	Factor
	1
TEST_1	.716
TEST_2	.893
TEST_3	.839

Extraction Method: Principal Axis Factoring.
  a. 1 factors extracted. 11 iterations required.

FIGURE 13.12   Reading Comprehension measurement model solved via factor analysis. Our measurement model is a (confirmatory) factor analysis.

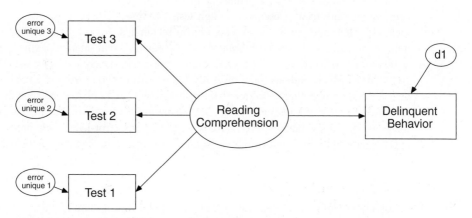

FIGURE 13.13   We could use the Reading Comprehension factor, or latent variable, in a structural equation to more accurately determine the effect of Reading Comprehension on Delinquent Behavior.

obtain multiple measures of each construct in our path model, separately factor analyze these items, and then use the factor scores in our path analyses, rather than the original items or tests. This process will rid our measures of both invalidity and unreliability (because ridding the measure of invalidity will subsume unreliability) and will allow us to get closer to the constructs we are interested in. Although this solution makes sense conceptually, it too has drawbacks. The multistep process separates the different factor analyses (the measurement model) from the testing of the path model (the structural model). It would be preferable to be able to conduct *all* analyses simultaneously.

This is what latent variable SEM does: it performs confirmatory factor analysis and a path analysis of the resulting factors at the same time. In the process, latent variable SEM removes the effects of unreliability and invalidity from the estimation of the effect of one variable on another. By doing so, the method gets closer to constructs we are really interested in. Thus, instead of doing research on the effects of a measure of Reading Comprehension on a measure of Delinquent Behavior, we can come closer to studying the effect of *true* Reading Comprehension on *true* Delinquent Behavior. Alternatively, if we are interested in the effects of income on job satisfaction, we are not interested in the effects of reported income (the number someone reports on a survey) on perceptions of job satisfaction. Instead, we are interested in the effects of *true* income on *true* job satisfaction. In other words, we want to strip away the fog of invalidity and measurement error and get at the true constructs of interest. Likewise, if we are studying the effect of social skills on peer acceptance, we are not really interested in the effects of someone's perceptions of peoples' social skills on their perceptions of acceptance; we are interested in the effects of *real* social skills on *real* acceptance. Latent variable SEM helps us get closer to this level of analysis.

The Latent SEM Model

Figure 13.14 illustrates a generic latent variable structural equation model. To refresh our jargon, latent variables are the same as unmeasured variables or factors. Latent variables are inferred from the measured variables, and they more closely approach the constructs of true interest in the research. Latent variables are enclosed in circles or ovals. Measured variables are also known as observed variables or manifest variables. They are the variables that we actually measure in our research through tests, surveys, observations, interviews, or other methods. Measured variables are enclosed in rectangles. Scores on a reading test, survey items concerning time spent on homework, records of social interactions from playground observations, and a count of errors on a computer task are all examples of measured variables. Actual reading comprehension, time really spent on homework, true social acceptance, and actual mental processing speed are the latent variables we hope to determine through these measured variables. In research we are almost *always* interested in the latent rather than the measured variables, but we often have to settle for the error-laden measured variables as approximations of the latent variables. Not necessarily so with latent variable SEM!

Understanding the Model.   The system of paths from the latent to the measured variables is sometimes referred to as the *measurement model*. It is a simultaneous confirmatory factor analysis of all the latent variables in the model. The system of paths and correlations among the latent variables is often referred to as the *structural model*. You can think of it as a path analysis of the latent variables.

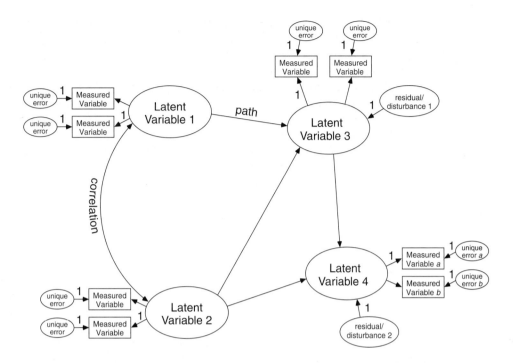

FIGURE 13.14   Latent variable structural equation model. The model includes a confirmatory factor analysis of the latent and measured variables, as well as a path analysis of the effects of one latent variable on another.

You may find it confusing at first glance that both the measured variables and the endogenous latent variables have smaller latent variables pointing to them, but you will soon see that these have previously been defined. Recall that endogenous variables (effects) in a path model have latent variables pointing toward them; these latent variables are generally called either residuals or disturbances. The disturbances represent all *other* influences on the endogenous variables other than those shown in the model. It is the same with *latent* endogenous variables. We need to account for all other influences on the latent variables besides those shown in the model; again we do so with other latent variables known as disturbances or residuals. The small latent variables pointing to the measured variables represent the unique and error variances that we wish to remove from consideration in the SEM as we focus on the true effects of one (latent) variable on another. These unique and error variances are often simply referred to as error or occasionally by Greek letters (e.g., theta delta, theta epsilon), a convention from LISREL. More generally, both types of variables (errors and disturbances) are sometimes referred to as errors.

In fact, you can think of errors and disturbances in the same way. Latent Variable 2 and Latent Variable 3 are not the only influences on Latent Variable 4; there may be a multitude of other such influences outside the model. Residual/Disturbance 2 represents all the other influences on Latent Variable 4. Likewise, Latent Variable 4 is not the only influence on Measured Variable *a*; unique and error variances also affect this and other Measured Variables. "Unique error *a*" represents these influences. Although I will continue to treat disturbances and errors as different, you can thus think of them as "all other influences" on the measured and latent variables.

Figure 13.15 shows a latent variable SEM version of the homework model used in the last few chapters. Note that each variable in the model, except Ethnicity, was measured via multiple measured variables and thus can be estimated by a latent variable. We will explore this model in more detail in subsequent chapters. What is interesting to note at the present time is that the use of latent variables rather than measured variables increased the estimate of the effect of Homework on Grades from .15 (from the path analysis) to above .20 (in the latent variable SEM; the value is not shown in the figure). Again, the latent variable analysis has the advantage of removing measurement error from consideration in the model and thus getting closer to the level of the constructs we are really interested in (e.g., Homework and Grades). The latent variable estimate of this model should thus be the more accurate one.

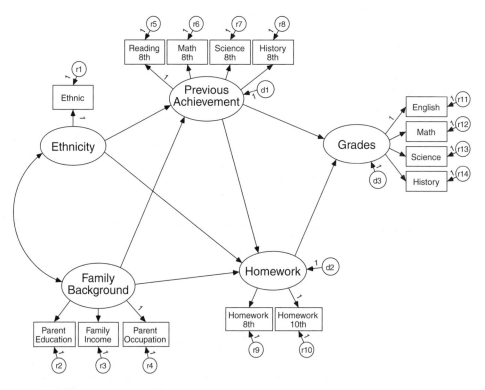

**FIGURE 13.15   Latent variable version of the Homework model.
We will examine and estimate this model in Chapter 16.**

We will explore this example in more depth in subsequent chapters. First, however, we will take a minor detour in the next chapter into confirmatory factor analysis, or the measurement model portion of latent variable SEM.

Before leaving this chapter, I reiterate that the problems discussed here—the effects of imperfect measurement in research—apply to all research. Here I have focused on the effects of measurement error in nonexperimental research–path analysis–structural equation modeling because this is our focus. But measurement error affects all research, experimental and nonexperimental, whether analyzed through ANOVA, correlations, multiple regression, or SEM.

SUMMARY

One assumption required to interpret regression (path) coefficients in a causal fashion is that the exogenous variables be measured without error. We rarely satisfy this assumption and thus need to know the effect of this violation on our estimates of the effects of one variable on another. To expand this discussion, I noted that unreliability and invalidity affect *all* types of research, not just path analysis and multiple regression. Problems in measurement in both the independent and dependent variables affect our research results.

Reliability is the converse of error. Error-laden measurements are unreliable, and reliable measurements contain little error. We can consider reliability from the standpoint of variance by thinking of true score variance as the total variance in a set of scores minus the error variance. In path analytic form, we can think of a person's score on a measurement as being affected by two influences: their true score on the measure and errors of measurement. The true score and error influences are latent variables, whereas the actual score the person earns on the measurement is a measured variable. These concepts are important for research purposes, because other variables generally correlate with the true score, but not the error. For this reason, the reliability of a measurement places an upper limit on the correlation a variable can have with any other variable. Unreliable measurements can make large effects look small and statistically significant effects look nonsignificant.

The path models we have been discussing so far assume that the variables in our models are measured with perfect reliability. In a series of models, I demonstrated what would happen when we recognized and quantified the unreliability of these measurements. When unreliability was taken into account in these models, the apparent effects of one variable on another changed and usually increased. Taking unreliability into account in our research will improve our estimates of the effects of one variable on another.

Reliability is not the only aspect of measurement that needs to be considered, however; there is also validity. I demonstrated that a measurement may be reliable, but may focus on some unique skill, rather than the central skill we are interested in. Said differently, a measurement may be reliable, but may not be a valid measure of our construct of interest. As it turns out, validity is a subset of reliability. We can get closer to valid measurement, closer to the constructs of interest in our research, by using multiple measures of constructs.

Latent variable structural equation modeling seeks to move closer to the constructs of interest in our research by using such multiple measures. With latent variable SEM, we simultaneously perform a confirmatory factor analysis of the measured variables in our research to get at the latent variables of true interest, along with a path analysis of the effects of these latent variables on each other. In the process, latent variable SEM removes the effects of unreliability and invalidity from consideration of the effects of one variable on another and avoids the problem of imperfect measurement. In the process, latent variable SEM gets closer to the primary questions of interest: the effect of one construct on another.

Although our discussion focused on the effects of imperfect measurement in multiple regression and path analysis, it is worth remembering that measurement affects every type of research, however that research is analyzed. With the addition of latent variables to SEM, we are able to take measurement problems into account and thus control for them.

EXERCISES

1. Pick a research study in your area of interest. Describe the latent variables, the constructs the authors were interested in. What was the construct of interest underlying the independent variable(s)? What was the construct of interest underlying the dependent variable(s)? What measured variables were used to approximate these constructs?

2. How could you convert this research from a measured variable study into a latent variable study? Think of ways to include multiple measures of the researchers' independent and dependent variables. Draw a model incorporating both measured and latent variables.

3. What is the advantage of moving from a measured to a latent variable approach? What might happen to the estimates of effects with this transition?

4. Find an article in your area of interest that uses latent variable structural equation modeling (it may be referred to as structural equation modeling or covariance structures analysis). Read the article. Do the authors discuss reasons for using latent over measured variables? Do they link latent variables with reliability and validity? How do they label the disturbances? The error and unique variances of the measured variables?

NOTES

1. Some of these examples are actually systematic errors rather than random errors and are thus not considered unreliability. I include them because I want you to consider the errors that can be included in even such a straightforward item.

2. The results are equivalent only because the example is so simple. With more items and multiple factors, the results of a confirmatory analysis will be different from those of an "exploratory" factor analysis (from SPSS), and even the results of an exploratory analysis will differ depending on the method used and the assumptions made. The example is useful for heuristic purposes, however, as a conceptual illustration of what factor analysis is.

CHAPTER FOURTEEN

CONFIRMATORY FACTOR ANALYSIS

FACTOR ANALYSIS OR THE MEASUREMENT MODEL

This chapter will focus in more detail on the *measurement model* of latent variable structural equation modeling, more generally known as *confirmatory factor analysis*. At its most basic level, factor analysis is a reduction technique, a method of reducing many measures into fewer measures. The methodology works by placing tests or items that correlate highly with each other on one factor, while placing items that correlate at a low level with each other on different factors. Because one primary reason items correlate highly with one another is that they measure the same construct, factor analysis provides insights as to the common constructs measured by a set of tests or items. Because it helps answer questions about the constructs measured by a set of items, factor analysis is a major method of establishing the validity of tests, questionnaires, and other measurements. You can also think of factor analysis as a method of establishing convergent and divergent validity: items that measure the same thing form a factor (converge), whereas items that measure different constructs form a separate factor (diverge).

With *exploratory* factor analysis (not covered in this text), one analyzes a set of items or scales that presumably measures a smaller set of abilities, traits, or constructs. Decisions are made concerning the method of factor extraction to use, the method for deciding the number of factors to retain, and the method of factor rotation to use. Given these choices and the data, the results of the analysis will suggest that the items measure a smaller number of factors. For example, factor analysis of 13 scales may suggest that these scales measure four separate constructs. The output from the analysis will include factor loadings of each scale on the four factors and, if oblique rotation is used, the correlations of the factors with each other. The researcher then decides on names for the factors based on the constructs they presumably reflect, a decision based on the loadings of the variables on the factors, relevant theory, and previous research.

With *confirmatory* factor analysis one uses previous research and relevant theory to decide in advance what the factors or constructs are that underlie the measures. Just as in path analysis, we propose a model that underlies the variables of interest. The fit statistics then provide feedback concerning the adequacy of the model in explaining the data. I hope it is obvious why the methods are termed exploratory versus confirmatory factor analysis. With the first, we examine the results and decide what the various scales are measuring, whereas with the second we decide what the various scales are measuring and then examine the results to find out how accurate our predictions were. This dichotomy is an obvious simplification—we can use exploratory factor analysis in a confirmatory fashion and can use confirmatory factor analysis in an exploratory fashion—but it is still a useful distinction.

The development of factor analysis is inexorably linked with development of theories of intelligence and intelligence tests. Early intelligence researchers developed the methods of factor analysis to understand the nature and measurement of intelligence tests, and factor analysis continues to be a major method of supporting and challenging the validity of intelligence tests. For this reason, I will illustrate the method of confirmatory factor analysis using intelligence test data.

AN EXAMPLE WITH THE DAS

The Differential Ability Scales (DAS; Elliott, 1990) is among the most commonly administered individual intelligence tests for children. The DAS includes a series of short verbal and nonverbal subtests and is appropriate for children and youth ages 2½ through 18. The DAS is a common portion of a broader psychological evaluation for children and adolescents who are having learning, behavioral, or adjustment problems. It may be used to help place children in special programs (e.g., those for children with learning disabilities and gifted programs); diagnose learning, behavioral, and neurological problems; or provide information relevant to an intervention to ameliorate such problems.

Structure of the DAS

For school-aged children and youth, the DAS includes nine subtests that supposedly assess three or more underlying constructs. The test names and the theoretical structure of the DAS are shown in Figure 14.1 (one subtest is excluded from the figure). Although I will not describe the subtests in detail, they measure a variety of verbal and nonverbal skills. For example, the Similarities subtest requires children to explain the construct shared by three words. In contrast, Pattern Construction requires the child to construct, from pictures, geometric designs using two-colored blocks. According to the author, the DAS measures verbal reasoning (Verbal Ability), nonverbal, inductive reasoning (Nonverbal Reasoning), and visual–spatial reasoning (Spatial). The figure shows which subtests are designed to measure which skills. This structure is reflected in the actual scoring of the test: the top six subtests shown in the figure are added together in pairs to form Verbal, Nonverbal Reasoning, and Spatial composite scores. The final two subtests are not actually added together into a Memory composite score, but I have added a Memory factor to the figure for the purposes of our analyses in this chapter. One DAS subtest (Speed of Information Processing) is not analyzed here.

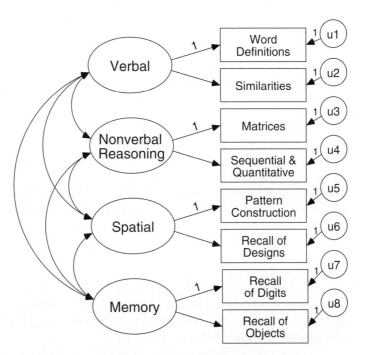

**FIGURE 14.1   DAS model. Does the DAS measure verbal,
nonverbal, and spatial reasoning, along with memory skills?**

The Initial Model

Figure 14.1 is also the setup for a confirmatory factor model (indeed, the figure is the input for analysis in Amos), with the constructs underlying the DAS shown in ovals as latent variables and the eight subtests (the actual measurements we obtain) shown in rectangles as measured variables. The arrows in the figure make explicit the causal assumptions underlying such testing and models. The paths point from the constructs to the subtests in recognition of the implicit assumption that each person's level of verbal reasoning ability is the primary influence on his or her score on the Word Definitions subtest, for example, whereas each person's level of Spatial ability is the primary influence on his or her score on the Pattern Construction subtest. Although the constructs the test is designed to measure are the primary influence on individuals' scores on the subtests, you know from the last chapter that individuals' scores on each subtest are also influenced by unreliability and by the unique characteristics of each test. This latter statement also makes sense intuitively as well. Although Pattern Construction and Recall of Designs (in which children draw complex designs from memory) obviously both require visual and spatial skills, they also both obviously require different specific skills, such as the mental translation of a two-dimensional picture into three-dimensional form versus visual and spatial memory skills. These unique skills and unreliability are represented by the small latent variables pointing to each subtest labeled u1 through u8. u5, for example, represents all influences on children's scores on the Pattern Construction subtest other than Spatial Ability.

You will recall that latent variables have no set scale, and we must set the scale of each latent variable to estimate the model. Recall also that one way to set the scale of a latent variable is to set a path from each latent variable to one measured variable at 1.0. This is done in Figure 14.1. The Verbal factor's scale is set to be the same as that for the Word Definitions subtest. The choice of which measured variable to use is arbitrary; I have simply set the scale of each factor to be the same as the first variable that measures this factor. Likewise, the scales for the unique–error variances are set to the same scale as their corresponding subtests: u1 is set to have the same scale as Word Definitions, u2 as Similarities, and so on. Alternatively, we could also set the scale of the factors by setting the variance of each factor to 1.0.

The model shown in Figure 14.1 also includes correlations among each construct thought to be measured by the DAS. It is commonly recognized that cognitive tests and cognitive factors are positively correlated (Carroll, 1993). The model shown in the figure is on the Web site (www.ablongman.com/keith1e) under the name "DAS first 1.amw."

The DAS manual includes tables of correlations among the subtests for each of 21 age levels 2½ through 17 (along with means and standard deviations). The averaged covariance matrix for school-aged children is shown in Table 14.1 (the average matrix was produced as a by-product of CFA analyses designed to determine whether the DAS measures the same constructs across its age levels; see Keith, 1990). The matrix of covariances among the eight subtests was used to estimate the model shown in Figure 14.1 The covariance matrix is also contained in the Excel file "das.xls" and the SPSS file "das.sav." The sample size for the analyses was set at 200 (the n for each of the 12 age groups 6 to 17).

Standardized Results: The Initial Model

Figure 14.2 shows standardized results of the initial analysis of the DAS model. First, focus on the fit statistics. The Root Mean Square Residual was 0, lower (better) than our rule of thumb for good models of .05. The TLI and CFI were above our target for a good model (.95). By these criteria, it appears that the DAS model fits the data well. In other words, the model that underlies the DAS indeed could produce the correlations and covariances we observe among the DAS subtests, and the theoretical structure of the DAS is supported. Focusing on the model itself, it appears that most subtests provided relatively strong

TABLE 14.1 Average Covariance Matrix for the DAS for Ages 6 through 17

SUBTEST NAME	PATTERN CONSTRUCTION	RECALL OF DESIGNS	WORD DEFINITIONS	MATRICES	SIMILARITIES	SEQUENTIAL AND QUANTITATIVE REASONING	RECALL OF DIGITS	RECALL OF OBJECTS
Pattern Construction	99.800							
Recall of Designs	56.487	100.032						
Word Definitions	40.946	37.688	98.354					
Matrices	54.051	44.874	43.809	104.337				
Similarities	44.207	38.49	63.859	45.71	101.225			
Sequential and Quantitative Reasoning	53.699	43.859	51.083	59.431	51.397	99.214		
Recall of Digits	20.663	19.218	28.109	25.167	27.012	29.007	100.799	
Recall of Objects	21.351	26.097	24.01	22.941	25.42	22.921	18.389	104.555

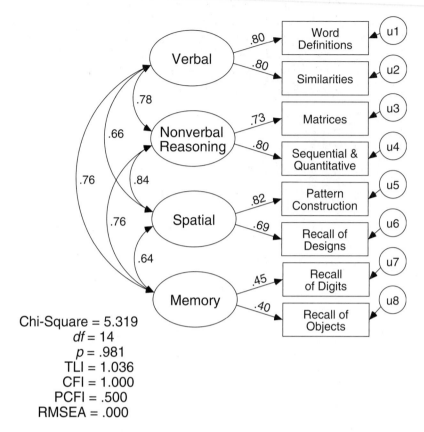

FIGURE 14.2 Standardized solution for the initial DAS four-factor model.

measures of the appropriate ability or construct; the factor loadings for the Verbal, Nonverbal Reasoning, and Spatial factors were all .69 or higher. The exceptions to these substantial loadings were the two subtests that were indicators of the Memory factor (loadings of .40 and .45). Although the detailed printout shows that these loadings were statistically significant, they are lower than for the other factors. Within factors, most subtest pairs had fairly equivalent loadings on the factor they supposedly measure. Word Definitions and Similarities had equivalent loadings on the Verbal factor, for example, suggesting that they are equally good measures of this construct. The exception to this statement was for the Spatial factor, for which Pattern Construction had a somewhat higher loading than did Recall of Designs. This difference in loadings suggests that the common construct measured by these two tests is better measured by Pattern Construction than by Recall of Designs. The results also show that the latent factors correlate substantially with each other, with factor correlations ranging from .64 to .84.

Figure 14.3 shows the unstandardized estimates of the factor loadings, standard errors, and z values, along with the standardized loadings. Note that all estimated paths (factor loadings) and covariances were statistically significant ($z \geq 2$).

Regression Weights

	Estimate	S.E.	C.R.	P
Word <--- Verbal	1.000			
Similar <--- Verbal	1.027	.107	9.609	***
Matrices <--- NonVerbal_Reasoning	1.000			
Seq_Quan <--- NonVerbal_Reasoning	1.056	.108	9.738	***
Pattern <--- Spatial	1.000			
R_Design <--- Spatial	.848	.100	8.447	***
R_Digits <--- Memory	1.000			
R_Object <--- Memory	.908	.260	3.491	***

Standardized Regression Weights

	Estimate
Word <--- Verbal	.795
Similar <--- Verbal	.805
Matrices <--- NonVerbal_Reasoning	.734
Seq_Quan <--- NonVerbal_Reasoning	.795
Pattern <--- Spatial	.817
R_Design <--- Spatial	.692
R_Digits <--- Memory	.448
R_Object <--- Memory	.400

Covariances

			Estimate	S.E.	C.R.	P
Verbal	<-->	NonVerbal_Reasoning	46.139	7.404	6.231	***
Verbal	<-->	Spatial	42.533	7.228	5.884	***
Verbal	<-->	Memory	26.909	6.553	4.106	***
NonVerbal_Reasoning	<-->	Spatial	51.401	7.777	6.610	***
NonVerbal_Reasoning	<-->	Memory	25.520	6.366	4.009	***
Spatial	<-->	Memory	23.536	6.432	3.659	***

Correlations

			Estimate
Verbal	<-->	NonVerbal_Reasoning	.784
Verbal	<-->	Spatial	.664
Verbal	<-->	Memory	.762
NonVerbal_Reasoning	<-->	Spatial	.844
NonVerbal_Reasoning	<-->	Memory	.760
Spatial	<-->	Memory	.644

FIGURE 14.3   Unstandardized output for the initial DAS four-factor model.

Testing a Standardized Model

It is also possible to set the scale of the latent factors in the model by setting the factor variances to 1.0 (instead of setting one factor loading per factor to 1.0). The setup for such a standardized model for the DAS is shown in Figure 14.4. Although less common, and less consistent with SEM, than the method of setting factor loadings, the factor variance method has the advantage of producing *standardized* covariances (i.e., correlations) among the factors. Recall that a correlation matrix is a standardized covariance matrix, the result of standardizing the variables in the matrix (i.e., setting their variances to 1.0). Alternatively, you can think of a correlation matrix as just another variance–covariance matrix, but with all variances set to 1.0. Thus, when we set the variances of the factors in a CFA to 1.0, we have standardized the covariance matrix of factors. Figure 14.5 shows the *unstandardized* output for the factor-variance-set-to-1 analysis just described. Note that the covariances (correlations) in this figure are the same as the correlations from the standardized output shown in Figure 14.2. The factor loadings, however, are still in an unstandardized metric.

The advantage of having the factor covariances standardized comes into play when we wish to compare competing models. Note the high correlation between the Nonverbal

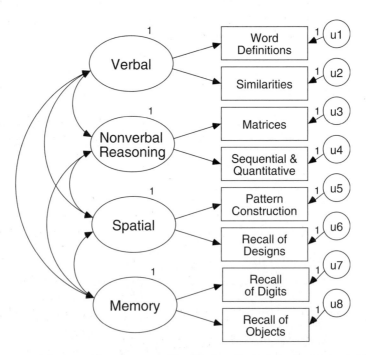

FIGURE 14.4 Alternative standardized method of specifying the initial DAS model. With this method, we set the scale of the latent variables by setting their variances to 1 instead of constraining a factor loading.

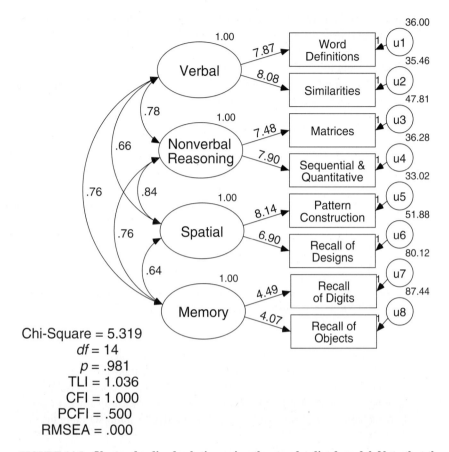

FIGURE 14.5   Unstandardized solution using the standardized model. Note that the factor covariances are now equivalent to the factor correlations from Figure 14.2.

Reasoning and Spatial factors (.84). We may wonder if this correlation is statistically significantly different from 1.0, meaning that the factors may be inseparable. We could test this supposition by setting the factor correlation to 1.0 and comparing the fit of this model with the original model. However, model constraints apply to the *unstandardized* model only. Thus, if we wish to set a factor correlation to 1.0 (or some other value), we need to make the factor correlations equivalent to the factor covariances, using this standardized model.

Although the primary results of a CFA—notably the fit indexes and the standardized output—will generally be the same whichever method is used, some results may change slightly depending on whether the standard (factor loading set to 1) or the standardized (factor variance set to 1) method is used. In particular, the unstandardized parameter estimates and the standard errors may change across the two methods, and the resulting z values (critical ranges) may change as well. What this means is that it is possible for a factor loading or factor covariance to be statistically significant using one method, but not statistically significant using the other. (For more information, see Millsap, 2001. This article also shows that with complex models, where tests load on multiple factors, the fit of models can change depending on which factor to test path is set to 1.0.)

Before moving to the next topic, notice the numbers beside the unique and error variances: 36.00 for u1, 35.46 for u2, and so on. These numbers are the estimates of the combined unique and error variances of the various subtests. You can compare them to the variances of the variables shown in the diagonals of the variance–covariance matrix (Table 14.1). It appears that a little more than one-third of the variation in the Word Definitions subtest is error and unique variance.

TESTING COMPETING MODELS

This initial example has tested the adequacy of a single confirmatory model. As in SEM, however, a more powerful use of the methodology is to compare alternative and competing models. I will briefly illustrate this method using the DAS example.

Although I have argued that the DAS should measure four underlying constructs, the actual structure of the DAS for school-aged children and youth includes only three corresponding composites: Verbal, Nonverbal, and Spatial. The two tests I have used as indicators of a Memory factor are actually stand-alone diagnostic measures that are not added together into a composite. Thus, the DAS was *intended* to measure Verbal, Nonverbal, and Spatial skills, and a model specifying that the DAS measures three, rather than four, underlying constructs is a reasonable alternative model for understanding the DAS.

A Three-Factor, No-Memory Model

A plausible three-factor model of the DAS is shown in Figure 14.6. Consistent with DAS theory and structure, this model has the Recall of Digits and Recall of Objects as stand-alone tests, rather than as reflections of an underlying Memory ability. These two tests are correlated with the three factors and with each other, but the model does not assert any reason for these correlations. Because there are no arrows pointing to the Recall of Digits and Recall of Objects subtests, there are no longer any unique–error variances associated with these subtests. Said differently, because the model does not assert any causes of these subtests, we no longer need to include the latent residual variable reflecting all *other* causes from outside the model. The fit statistics associated with the model and the standardized solution are also shown in the figure.

The DAS three-factor model fits the data well. Our primary stand-alone fit index, the RMSEA, suggests that the two-factor model explains well the test standardization data. The other stand-alone fit indexes (TLI, CFI) also suggest a good fit of the model to the data. If we focus only on the fit of each model in isolation, we conclude that this model fits well, as does the earlier four-factor model. Our primary interest, however, is *relative* fit of the two models. In particular, we are interested in how this three-factor model compares to

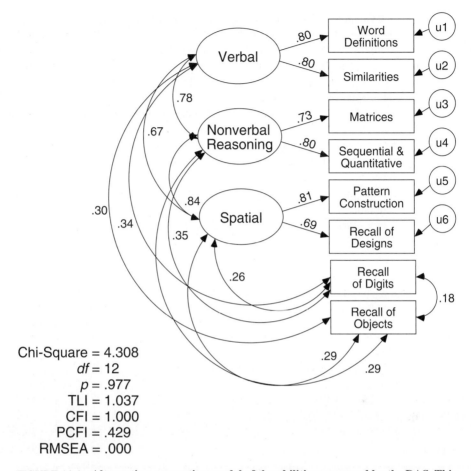

FIGURE 14.6   Alternative, competing model of the abilities measured by the DAS. This model suggests that the Recall of Digits and Recall of Objects tests do not measure the same underlying ability, but instead measure separate abilities. This model is more consistent with the actual structure of the DAS than is the initial model.

the initial four-factor model explaining the DAS. The three-factor model is less parsimonious than the four-factor model. The three-factor model has 12 as opposed to 14 degrees of freedom. Degrees of freedom represent parameters that are constrained to some value, rather than freely estimated, and thus each additional degree of freedom means an increase in parsimony. Thus, if the two models fit equally well, we will prefer the four-factor (more parsimonious) model. Do the models fit equally well? To answer this question, we need to focus on the fit indexes appropriate for comparing competing models.

In Chapter 12 I argued that $\Delta\chi^2$ was a good method for comparing competing models that were nested, that is, when one model can be derived from the other by fixing one or more parameters. In the current example, it is not possible to get from one model to another by fixing parameters, and thus the two models are not nested. With nonnested models, I suggested focusing on the AIC as a method of comparing competing models (other related fit indexes, such as the BIC or the Expected Cross-Validation Index, ECVI, are also appropriate). Table 14.2 shows this and other fit indexes for these two models. The rule of thumb with the AIC is that the smaller the value the better; using this criterion, it appears our original four-factor model provides a better explanation of the DAS than does the three-factor model. This means that, even though the two subtests in question (Recall of Digits, Recall of Objects) do not load highly on a Memory factor, this explanation of their intercorrelations makes more sense than considering them as not measuring some common, underlying characteristic. (It is worth noting, before moving on, that we would have reached the same conclusion if we had considered the models nested and had used $\Delta\chi^2$ as the method of comparing competing models.)

TABLE 14.2   Comparison of Fit Indexes for Alternative Models of the Structure of the Differential Ability Scales

MODEL	χ^2	df	$\Delta\chi^2$	Δdf	p	AIC	BIC	PCFI
Initial Four Factor	5.319	14				49.319	167.630	.500
Three Factor 1 (No Memory)	4.308	12				52.308	181.374	.429
Three Factor 2 (Combined Nonverbal)	16.172	17	10.853	3	.013	54.172	156.349	.607
Hierarchical	7.491	16	2.172	2	.338	47.491	155.046	.571

The $\Delta\chi^2$ compared the alternative models to the initial four-factor model.

A Three-Factor Combined Nonverbal Model

We could easily argue that the Spatial and the Nonverbal Reasoning subtests should be considered as measuring a single underlying ability. After all, all these tests require some degree of spatial awareness and nonverbal reasoning; why separate the two factors? This argument is bolstered by the high correlation (.84) between the factors in Figure 14.2. Thus, we have both a priori logical as well post hoc data-driven reasons for suggesting another plausible model, one that combines these two factors. Figure 14.7 shows such a plausible three-factor model. Although it is not obvious, the model *is* nested with the model in Figures 14.1 through 14.5. This three-factor model is equivalent to the model shown in Figure 14.4 (the standardized model) with the following constraints:

1. Set the Nonverbal Reasoning–Spatial correlation to 1.0. This constraint essentially equates the factors.

2. Constrain other factor correlations to be equal to one another across these factors. That is, constrain the Memory–Spatial factor to be equal to the Memory–Nonverbal Reasoning correlation, and then do the same with the Verbal–Spatial and the Verbal–Nonverbal. The way to do this in Amos is to constrain the correlations to an alphabetical value (e.g., *a* for the first two correlations and *b* for the second two). The result of this constraint is that the values will be freely estimated, but all values with the same letter will be constrained to be equal.

Because the models are nested, $\Delta\chi^2$ can be used to compare the competing models. Unlike the earlier three-factor model, this model is more parsimonious that the initial four-factor model. (Make sure you understand why this three-factor model is more parsimonious

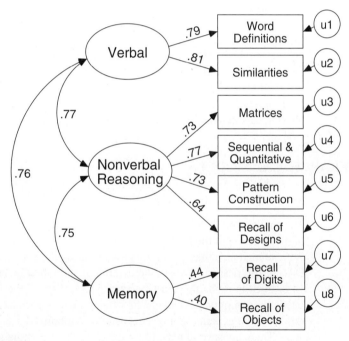

Chi-Square = 16.172
df = 17
p = .512
TLI = 1.003
CFI = 1.000
PCFI = .607
RMSEA = .000

FIGURE 14.7 Another competing model of the DAS. This model combines the Nonverbal Reasoning and Spatial factors into a single Nonverbal factor.

and the earlier three-factor model was less parsimonious than the initial model.) Thus, if the two models have an equivalent fit, we will favor the more parsimonious three-factor model with the Combined Nonverbal factor.

As shown in Figure 14.7, the three-factor Combined Nonverbal model showed a good fit to the data according to the stand-alone fit indexes, yet the χ^2 also increased for this model. The four-factor model had a χ^2 of 5.319 ($df = 14$) versus 16.172 ($df = 17$) for the three-factor Combined Nonverbal model. Change in $\chi^2 = 10.853$ ($df = 3$), a value that is statistically significant ($p = .013$). This means that the Combined Nonverbal model, although more parsimonious than the four-factor model, does not explain the relations among the DAS subtests, the DAS structure, as well as does the four-factor model. The models shown in Figures 14.1 through 14.4 provide a better "theory" for understanding the DAS than does the model shown in Figure 14.7. Both of these analyses suggest that the DAS should be interpreted as measuring four, rather than three, underlying abilities. The fit indexes for this model are also shown in Table 14.2.

Although $\Delta\chi^2$ is our primary method for comparing competing, nested models, it is also worth noting the other fit indexes we discussed as useful for comparing (not nested) models, the AIC, the BIC, and the PCFI. The rule of thumb for the AIC (and BIC) is that they favor the model with the lower value; again the four-factor model appears superior if we use the AIC or BIC to compare models. In contrast, the PCFI (the larger the value the better) favors the three-factor Combined Nonverbal model. In my experience, the PCFI places too great a premium on parsimony. Again, according to our primary criteria, the four-factor model provides a better fit than do either of the three-factor models. I did not include the RMSEA in the table because all values were zero.

HIERARCHICAL MODELS

Model Justification and Setup

The analyses so far have pointed to the model in Figure 14.1 as a more valid representation of the structure of the DAS than the models in Figures 14.6 and 14.7. But the model in 14.1 is not complete, either. In addition to measuring the four abilities shown in Figure 14.1, the DAS is also designed to measure overall general intelligence. The model shown in Figure 14.8, then, is probably a more accurate reflection of the intended structure of the DAS: rather than simply having the first-order factors correlated, these factors are shown as reflections of general intelligence, usually symbolized as g, in a hierarchical model.

There are several reasons for developing and estimating such hierarchical models. In the arena of intelligence, hierarchical models are more consistent with commonly accepted theories of intelligence (e.g., three-stratum or Cattell–Horn–Carroll theory, Carroll, 1993) and are more consistent with the actual structure of most intelligence tests. Hierarchical models may be equally relevant in many other areas of research. Hierarchical models can also lead to a better understanding of the first level of factors. Just as the first level of factors helped us understand what the subtests measured, the second-order factor may help us better understand the first-order factors.

The mechanics of estimating a hierarchical CFA also need comment. Note that the scale of the second-order factor (g) is set in the same way as the first-order factors, by fixing one path from it to one of the first-order factors to 1.0. We could also set the scale by fixing the variance of g to 1.0 (we will still need to set the scale of the first-order factors by setting a path to 1.0, and thus the first-order factor solution will not be standardized). The hierarchical model differs from the first-order model in that the first-order factors have small latent variables pointing toward them, labeled uf1 through uf4 (for unique factor variance). These latent variables have the same essential meaning as other disturbances–residuals: they represent all influences on the first-order factors (Verbal, Nonverbal Reasoning, etc.) other than g. To put it another way, *any variable—whether measured or latent—that has an arrow pointing to it must also include a latent disturbance/unique variable to represent all other influences on the variable.* Finally, the model shown here includes three levels—measured variables, first-order factors, and a second-order factor—but additional levels are possible and are capable of estimation using these same methods.

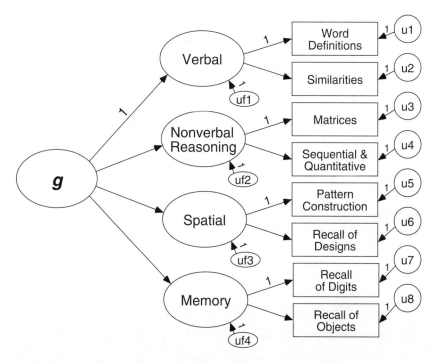

FIGURE 14.8   Hierarchical model of the DAS. The model specifies that the DAS measures general intelligence in addition to the four less general factors.

Hierarchical Model Results

Figure 14.9 shows the fit statistics and standardized estimates for the hierarchical analysis. Note that the first-order factor loadings are almost the same as they were for the initial, nonhierarchical analysis. The equivalence is because the essential difference between the hierarchical and the first-order model is that the hierarchical model explains the correlations–covariances among the factor correlations. The first-order factor model helps explain why the *subtests* correlate with each other: because there are four abilities that partially cause students to perform at a certain level on the eight subtests. The second-order model adds to that a possible explanation of the reason for the correlations among the four *factors*: because there is one general intellectual ability that influences, in part, the four more narrow abilities. Conceptually, the factor analysis of latent variables (second-order) is equivalent to the factor analysis of measured variables (first-order).

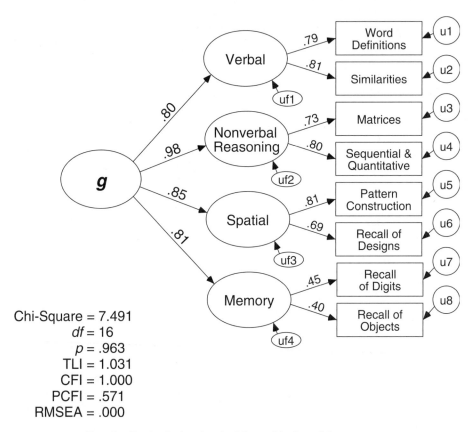

Chi-Square = 7.491
df = 16
p = .963
TLI = 1.031
CFI = 1.000
PCFI = .571
RMSEA = .000

FIGURE 14.9   Standardized solution for the hierarchical model.

Given this similarity across models, it should be clear, then, that the hierarchical model may be considered a more constrained, more parsimonious version of the first-order model. The first-order model places no constraints on the factor correlations, whereas the hierarchical model says that these correlations are the product (in this case) of another latent variable, *g*. Given this similarity, I consider the two models as nested (although I recognize that not everyone will agree with me; I also think such models are justified on purely theoretical grounds, without reliance on fit indexes). Since the models are nested, we can compare the models using $\Delta\chi^2$ ($\Delta\chi^2 = 2.172$, *df* = 2, *p* = .338). The hierarchical model is more parsimonious and fits as well as does the first-order model. It appears that a single general intelligence factor may be a plausible explanation for the correlations among the first-order factors.

Note where these two extra degrees of freedom come from as you look over the model. For the first-order model, there were six correlations among the first-order factors (number of correlations $= [v \times (v - 1)]/2 = (4 \times 3)/2$, where v equals the number of variables). The hierarchical model uses up four of these free parameters to estimate three of the second-order to first-order factor loadings (recall that one path was set to 1) along with the variance of g factor, leaving two extra df. This means that if there are only three first-order factors the hierarchical portion of the model will be just-identified; the two models will then have identical fit and cannot be compared statistically. If we try to add a hierarchical factor to a model with only two first-order factors, the hierarchical portion of the model will be underidentified and estimation will be impossible unless we were to make additional constraints (e.g., constraining the two second-order loadings to be the same). You need to pay attention to the identification status of the hierarchical portions of such models (identification was discussed in Chapter 10).

Recall that one reason for investigating hierarchical models is to help understand the first-order factors. Indeed, the second-order factor loadings are interesting. The highest loading (near unity) was by the Nonverbal Reasoning factor. Nonverbal Reasoning thus appears to be the most intellectually laden of the first-order factors. This finding suggests that the inductive reasoning that underlies the tasks on this factor is close to the essence of general intelligence.

Total Effects.   Psychometric researchers are often also interested in understanding which of the subtests are most highly related to the global general intelligence factor. We can calculate these loadings of the subtests on the second-order factor by multiplying paths (e.g., the loading of Word Definitions on g would equal $.80 \times .79 = .63$). If this process sounds familiar, it should; we are simply calculating the indirect effect of g on each subtest. Because there are no direct effects, these indirect effects are also the total effects. Figure 14.10 shows the total standardized effects of g on the first-order factors and subtests (for some reason, the order of subtests in the table is reversed from the order of the subtests in the figure). The total effects from g to subtests are shown in boldface. As shown in the figure, the Sequential and Quantitative Reasoning subtest had the highest total effect from g (.782). Thus, this subtest is most closely related to g, or g has a stronger effect on this subtest that on any of the other subtests.

MODEL FIT AND MODEL MODIFICATION

A common response when a model does not fit well is to examine more detailed aspects of fit with an eye toward modifying the model. I won't try to dissuade you from this practice, because it is indeed useful and necessary, but I encourage you to do so sparingly, unless you are primarily involved in model development and exploration (as opposed to testing predetermined models). I am not alone in this ambivalence concerning model modification: "As a statistician, I am deeply suspicious of modification indices. As a data analyst, however, I find they are really great" (Dag Sörbom, one of the authors of LISREL, quoted in Wolfle, 2003, p. 32). There are several aspects of the printout that may help in this process.

Standardized Total Effects

	g	Memory	Spatial	NonVerbal_Reasoning	Verbal
Memory	.809	.000	.000	.000	.000
Spatial	.848	.000	.000	.000	.000
NonVerbal_Reasoning	.981	.000	.000	.000	.000
Verbal	.804	.000	.000	.000	.000
R_Object	**.325**	.401	.000	.000	.000
R_Digits	**.361**	.446	.000	.000	.000
R_Design	**.589**	.000	.695	.000	.000
Pattern	**.690**	.000	.814	.000	.000
Seq_Quan	**.782**	.000	.000	.797	.000
Matrices	**.719**	.000	.000	.733	.000
Similar	**.648**	.000	.000	.000	.806
Word	**.638**	.000	.000	.000	.794

FIGURE 14.10   Total effects (standardized) for the hierarchical model. The lower portion of the first column essentially shows the loading of the subtests on the hierarchical *g* variable.

Modification Indexes

To illustrate the use of the more detailed fit statistics, we need to return to the three-factor Combined Nonverbal model from Figure 14.7 (all the other models fit too well!). Figure 14.11 shows the modification indexes from the Amos output for this model. With some programs, all modification indexes are printed; with Amos you can request modification indexes above a certain level. The figure shows indexes greater in magnitude than 4.0. When models do not fit well, you may be able to improve the fit by freeing parameters in the model. Recall that freeing a parameter reduces the degrees of freedom (parsimony) of the model and improves the $\Delta\chi^2$ to some degree. The question we ask with such relaxations in the model is whether the decrease in $\Delta\chi^2$ is worth the reduction in the *df*. The modification indexes estimate the minimum decrease in χ^2 that will result from freeing the listed parameter. Note the modification index for the covariance between u5 and u6: a value of 8.822. This modification index suggests that χ^2 can be reduced by at least 8.822 by freeing the covariance between u5 and u6. Although this is a statistically significant decrease in $\Delta\chi^2$ with a Δdf of 1, we need to consider whether this change makes theoretical sense. The variables u5 and u6 represent the unique variances of Pattern Construction and Recall of Designs. Freeing this covariance–correlation suggests that we think the unique variances of the Pattern Construction and Recall of Designs subtests are related above and beyond the effect of Nonverbal Reasoning on each subtest. The factors correlate with each other because they are both affected by Nonverbal Reasoning, but could they be correlated for other reasons, as well? Stated differently, do Pattern Construction and Recall of Designs measure something in common other than the factor Nonverbal Reasoning? Given our other analyses, it is fairly easy to answer this question: yes, these two subtests likely measure Spatial skills, as separate from Nonverbal Reasoning. If we had started with this three-factor (Combined Nonverbal) model and if we were skilled in reading the modification indexes, they may have suggested to us to split these four tests into two factors. This example also illustrates that the modification indexes are not always easy to interpret! The other column in the table of modification indexes (Par Change) shows the likely value for the unstandardized parameter if we make the suggested change.

Modification Indices

Covariances

	M.I.	Par Change
u5 <-->u6	8.822	12.609

Regression Weights

	M.I.	Par Change
Pattern <--- R_Design	4.764	.116

FIGURE 14.11   Modification indexes for the model shown in Figure 14.7. The indexes suggest that the Pattern Construction and Recall of Designs subtests measure something in common other than overall Nonverbal Reasoning.

The other modification index greater than 4.0 shown in Figure 14.11 suggests that freeing the path between Recall of Design to Pattern Construction will result in a decrease in χ^2 of at least 4.764. This specific change does not make much sense, but again may indirectly suggest that Recall of Designs and Pattern Construction have something in common beyond the Nonverbal factor.

Here are common rules of thumb for using modification indexes. Examine the larger values of the modification indexes. Note that in actual practice you will likely have many more modification indexes to examine than the few shown for this model. What is large? Modification indexes, like χ^2, are sample-size dependent; if our model fit much worse or if we had a larger sample size, we would have larger modification indexes and more modification indexes greater than 4.0. Thus, you should examine the larger values of the modification indexes relative to the other values. Again, the modification indexes show the expected minimum reduction in χ^2 if the listed parameter is freed, at a cost of 1 *df*. You should consider whether each change is justifiable through theory and previous research. Make the single change that makes the most theoretical sense and results in the largest improvement in model fit, and reestimate the model. You can then repeat the process. Don't use the modification indexes to make several changes at a time, because with each additional change the modification indexes are likely to differ. I remind you to use the modification indexes cautiously. You will find it is all too easy to justify model modifications *after* examining modification indexes; do so sparingly and with an eye toward theory and previous research.

Standardized Residuals

Another aspect of fit to examine to understand why a model does not fit well is the matrix of standardized residuals (Standardized Residual Covariances) shown in Figure 14.12 (this matrix is also from the results of the model analyzed in Figure 14.7). Recall from Chapter 12 that the various fit statistics examine the consistency between the actual covariance matrix and the covariance matrix implied by the model. The difference between these two matrices is the matrix of residual covariances; the matrix of standardized residual covariances simply puts these residuals on the same standardized scale so that they can be compared. The matrix is shown in Figure 14.12.

Standardized Residual Covariances

	R_Object	R_Digits	R_Design	Pattern	Seq_Quan	Matrices	Similar	Word
R_Object	.000							
R_Digits	.000	.000						
R_Design	.835	-.311	.000					
Pattern	−.198	-.538	1.212	.000				
Seq_Quan	−.125	.451	-.667	-.313	.000			
Matrices	−.019	.038	-.333	-.046	.309	.000		
Similar	−.018	-.072	-.214	-.223	.428	-.097	.000	
Word	−.107	.188	-.168	-.475	.578	-.166	.000	.000

FIGURE 14.12   Matrix of standardized residual covariances. These too may be used to modify models. In this case (but not always) they suggest essentially the same modifications as do the modification indexes.

For this matrix, as well, we are looking for relatively larger values, regardless of sign. One rule of thumb suggests examining standardized residuals greater in absolute magnitude than 2.0; but the standardized residuals are also sample-size dependent, so with larger samples you may have many values greater than 2, whereas with smaller samples (like the present example) there may be few or no standardized residuals that reach this level. Again, focus on the relatively larger values. For the present example, the Combined Nonverbal DAS model, there is in fact only one value greater than 1.0, between the Recall of Designs and Pattern Construction subtests (1.212).

What does this value mean? Recall how this matrix is created: the implied covariance matrix is subtracted from the actual covariance matrix to create the residuals. The residuals are then standardized to create this matrix. This means that for positive values the *actual* correlation between two measured variables is larger than the *implied* correlation. For negative residuals, just the opposite is the case: the implied correlation is larger than the actual correlation. This means that positive standardized residuals suggest that the model does not adequately account for the observed correlation between two variables, whereas for negative residuals the model more than accounts for the original correlation between variables. Positive residuals are thus generally more informative for purposes of model modification in that they suggest ways the model can be modified to improve the fit.

In the current example, the highest value, 1.212, is between Recall of Designs (R_Design) and Pattern Construction (Pattern). The value is positive, which suggests that the model does not adequately account for the correlation between Pattern Construction and Recall of Designs. The standardized residuals thus seem to hint at the same thing as the modification indexes, that the three-factor model in Figure 14.7 does not account adequately for the relation between the two Spatial tests.

To use the standardized residuals to modify models, focus on the larger relative values. Models rarely fit as well as this one, and often you will find a number of high values for the standardized residuals. Consider whether the larger positive values share some characteristic in common (you can do the same for the larger negative values, which may suggest additional constraints to the model). Although the standardized residuals are somewhat more difficult to interpret than the modification indexes, they also sometimes show a pattern, and thus may be very useful in suggesting additional paths, correlations, or even minor factors to add to a model.

Adding Model Constraints and z Values

You can modify a model by relaxing constraints to the model (estimating a parameter that was previously set to zero), as discussed above. Model relaxations will always improve χ^2, but will make the model less parsimonious. Sometimes the relaxation of constraints is worth the improvement in fit. Another direction in modifying models is to add constraints, generally by constraining a previously estimated value to zero (or some other value). If, for example, some of the factor loadings had been statistically not significant according to the critical ranges (z values), we might have constrained these values to zero (i.e., removed the path) in subsequent models. Adding constraints to the model will always lead to a larger (worse) χ^2, but a more parsimonious model. If the $\Delta\chi^2$ is not statistically significant, the constraint makes sense. These same rules apply to many other fit statistics, as well: relaxations will improve fit, constraints will degrade fit. The exception to this rule is with fit indexes that take model parsimony into account; these indexes may improve with constraints and degrade with relaxations. We have already noted that the Parsimonious CFI (or GFI) works in this way, but the TLI, RMSEA, and AIC also take parsimony into account (although much less so than the PGFI or PCFI). Indeed, the AIC and related fit indexes (e.g., BIC) are designed to prevent "overfitting," or making small, sample-specific changes solely to improve fit.

Cautions

I again encourage you to be cautious when making model modifications. Extensive model modifications will take you far afield from the supposedly confirmatory, theory-testing nature of SEM and CFA and can even lead to erroneous models (MacCallum, 1986). Some authors make the useful distinction between the use of SEM and CFA in a theory testing versus a more exploratory matter (Joreskog & Sorbom, 1993). I believe this is a useful distinction, and encourage you to know where you are along this continuum. If you make more than minor changes to your model, you should not think of what you are doing as theory testing without confirmation with new data.

ADDITIONAL USES OF CFA

Occasionally, it is useful to be able to specify single-indicator factors. This may seem impossible, given that we earlier noted that we needed to have multiple measures of each construct to have a latent variable model. As you will see, with single indicators the portion of the measurement model is underidentified, but there are ways of working around this problem.

The school-aged version of the DAS in fact includes nine subtests; this additional subtest is called *Speed of Information Processing* and is designed to measure processing speed, or the speed with which one can perform basic mental processes. If we want to build this construct (Processing Speed) into the model, we can do so in several ways. One method is to develop a new, five-factor model, with the Speed of Processing test on a Processing Speed factor; we now have a latent variable with only a single indicator (see Figure 14.13). This sort of model is more difficult to estimate because, without further constraints, this portion of the model is underidentified. The common method for estimating a single-indicator latent variable in SEM is to fix the value of the unique–error variance. If we constrain the value to zero, this suggests that we believe the measured variable is measured without error, that the measured variable and the factor are exactly the same. A more common approach is to use information about the estimated *reliability* of the measured variable in the model, if we know it or can estimate it. One minus the reliability provides an estimate of the proportion of error in the measured variable; if this value is multiplied by the variance of the variable, the result is the variance in the measured variable that can be attributed to error. Figure 14.13 shows a model that uses this methodology. The estimated reliability for the Speed of Processing test, across school ages, is .91 (Elliott, 1990), and the variance of Speed of Processing for the present sample is 98.463. The estimate used for the error variance for Speed of Processing (u9) is thus 8.862:

$$V_e = (1 - r_{tt})V = (1 - .91) \times 98.463 = 8.862$$

Study this portion of the model. As for all other factors, one path from the latent to the measured variable is set to 1 in order to set the scale. The only difference is that there is only one path from the factor to the measured variable. The path from the subtest to unique variance to the subtest is also set to 1, again to set the scale. Recall when we discussed estimating path models via SEM programs that we noted we can either estimate the path from the disturbance or estimate the variance of the disturbance. It is the same with the unique and error variances. Normally, we set the path from the unique–error variance to 1 and estimate the unique and error variance. With only a single measured variable, we have to fix the unique–error variance as well as the path to allow model estimation. The value 8.862 beside u9 shows that we have done so, and with this constraint we can estimate the model successfully. Again, this is a common method for dealing with single-indicator latent variables; for more detail, see Hayduk (1987, chap. 4). In fact, this was the method I used to estimate the models showing the effects of different degrees of error in the previous chapter. It is also possible to use estimates of validity to account for both error and unreliability.

The results of this analysis are shown in Figure 14.14. The Processing Speed factor had a considerably lower loading on the g factor than did the other first-order factors. Although this method allows us to estimate a model with single-indicator factors, it obviously provides less information about these factors than do factors defined by multiple measured variables. For the current example, the model tells us the relative effect of g on Processing Speed (with Processing Speed defined as closely related to the Speed of Pro-

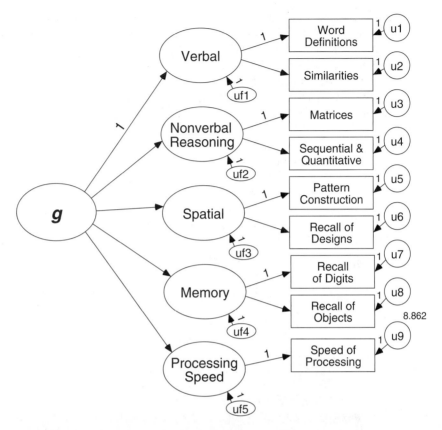

FIGURE 14.13   Modeling a single-indicator factor. The processing speed factor has only a single measured variable.

cessing subtest), but provides little additional information concerning the nature of the Speed of Processing test or the Processing Speed factor.

Another, more powerful method of better answering the questions of the constructs being measured by the DAS Processing Speed factor (and other factors) is to factor analyze the DAS with another test that includes known measures of processing speed along with other related factors. For example, Stone (1992) analyzed the DAS along with another intelligence test, the Wechsler Intelligence Scale for Children—Revised (Wechsler, 1974) to better understand the constructs measured by both tests.

The examples in this chapter have focused on testing the validity of existing measures. CFA can also be used to test theories. I have mentioned three-stratum theory in the area of intelligence. The DAS, it appears, measures several important constructs from three-stratum theory, and thus we can use three-stratum theory to develop a better understanding of what the DAS measures. We can turn this process around, as well, to examine the validity of the guiding theory. If we develop multiple measures of the constructs in three-stratum theory, CFA can be used to determine whether a three-stratum-derived model fits the data better than do plausible alternative theories (cf. Keith, 2005).

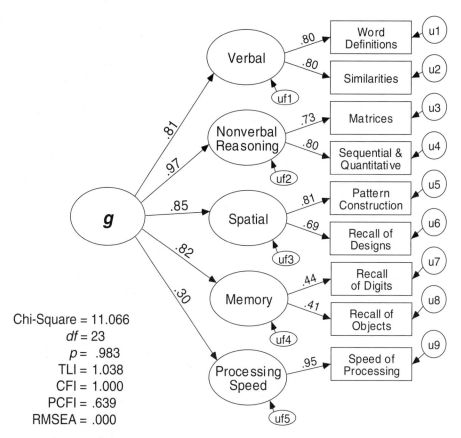

FIGURE 14.14   Standardized solution for the model with a single indicator for a Processing Speed factor.

SUMMARY

In the preceding chapter we introduced the full latent variable SEM model. In this chapter we focused on the measurement portion of this model. As it turns out, the measurement model portion of SEM is a useful methodology of its own, generally termed Confirmatory Factor Analysis (CFA). Because the history of factor analysis is so intertwined with the history of intelligence testing, the chapter illustrated CFA through the analysis of a common measure of intelligence, the Differential Ability Scales (DAS).

The eight subtests of the DAS supposedly measure four underlying constructs. We drew a model that shows the relations among the factors and subtests (latent and measured variables) (Figure 14.1). The model specifies, with paths drawn from factors to subtests, which subtests load on, or measure, which factors. Consistent with our rules for other path models, each subtest also has a small latent variable pointing to it that represents all other influences on the subtest beyond the four latent factors. With CFA–measurement models, these other influences represent errors and unique or specific influences. With just a few changes—the addition of constraints to set the scales of the latent factors and the unique variances and correlations among the factors—the conceptual model supposedly underlying the DAS is a testable confirmatory factor model.

We estimated the DAS model with averaged data derived from the DAS standardization sample. The initial model fit the data well according to the stand-alone fit indexes that we have used in previous chapters (e.g., RMSEA = .000), and most of the subtests appear to measure their corresponding factors strongly. That is, the paths from factors to measured variables, or factor loadings, are generally high. Another way of interpreting these loadings is that the latent constructs (e.g., verbal ability, spatial ability) have strong effects on the corresponding subtests. The factors, or latent constructs, also correlate substantially with each other; all correlations are greater than .60. This finding suggests that these latent, broad abilities are substantially related to each other.

The common method of setting the scale of latent variables is to set one path from each latent variable to 1, which sets the scale of the variable to be the same as that of the measured variable. An alternative method is to set the variance of the latent variable to 1. When done with first-order factors, this method turns the factor covariances in the unstandardized solution into factor *correlations*, because a correlation matrix is simply a covariance matrix among standardized variables. This methodology may be useful to test hypotheses about factor correlations.

Just as we can test competing path models using fit statistics, so can we test alternative competing CFA models. We illustrated the testing of competing models by comparing the initial four-factor DAS model with two alternative three-factor models. In both cases, the initial model fit the data better than did the competing models.

We are often interested in hierarchical models. The field of intelligence is replete with hierarchical models, but such models may be relevant in other fields, as well. For the DAS example, we hypothesized that a more general factor, often symbolized as *g* for general intelligence, affects each of the four latent variables, which, in turn, affect the subtests. Said differently, our hierarchical model explains that the correlations among the latent factors is a product of their each being affected, in part, by another, more general factor. The fit of this model compared favorably with the first-order factor models in earlier figures: the hierarchical model had an equivalent fit, but was more parsimonious.

When we wish to use information from the model results to revise the model, several aspects of the SEM program may be useful. Modification indexes and standardized residual covariances may suggest relaxations in the model that will lead to a better fit. Using these data for model modifications will result in less parsimonious, but presumably better fitting models. Using the *t* (or *z*) values may lead to values that can be constrained, and thus should lead to more parsimonious, but equivalent fitting models. You should use such methods to modify models sparingly or else recognize that you are using CFA in an exploratory rather than a theory testing manner.

It is possible to model latent variables or factors when some of these latent variables include only a single measured variable by constraining the unique–error variance (i.e., u9 in Figure 14.13) to some value. A common method of estimating that unique–error variance uses estimates of the reliability of the measured variable (and thus really only models the error variance). This may prove a useful method when we only have a single indicator, but recognize that the variables are not error free. The method can be used in both CFA and SEM models. The chapter ended with a hint of some other uses of CFA.

EXERCISES

1. Conduct the analyses outlined in this chapter. If you have a student version program that only allows a certain number of variables, you may be able to estimate a portion of the models. The Amos student version allows eight measured variables, which means you should be able to estimate all models except the final one. The initial four-factor model is on the accompanying Web site (www.ablongman.com/keith1e) as the file "DAS first 1.amw," and the data are in the file labeled "das.xls" or "das.sav."

2. The NELS data include a series of items (ByS44a to ByS44m) designed to assess students' self-esteem and locus of control. Choose several or all of these items that you believe best measure self-esteem and locus of control and subject them to confirmatory factor analysis. First use SPSS (or another general statistical program) to create a matrix for analysis in Amos (or one of the other programs). Then analyze your model using this matrix.

3. The files "DAS simulated.sav" and "DAS simulated.xls" include 500 cases of simulated data for the DAS.

   a. Conduct the first-order factor analyses from this chapter using the simulated data. Interpret the findings. How do the results compare with those in this chapter (and in Exercise 1)? Would you come to different conclusions following these analyses than we did in the chapter?

   b. Note the fit indexes. Which changed the most from the analyses in the chapter? Why do you think this may be?

   c. As you examine your analyses, are any other hypotheses or models suggested by the findings? If so, conduct these analyses and interpret the findings.

■ ■ ■ ■ ■ ■

CHAPTER FIFTEEN

PUTTING IT ALL TOGETHER: INTRODUCTION TO LATENT VARIABLE SEM

Let's review our progress in our adventures beyond MR. You know how to conduct path analysis using MR. This experience includes the estimation of standardized and unstandardized paths, the calculation of disturbances ($\sqrt{1 - R^2}$), and the calculation and comparison of direct, indirect, and total effects using two different methods. We transitioned into estimating path models using Amos and other SEM programs and focused again on the estimation of both standardized and unstandardized effects and direct, indirect, and total effects. With Amos, we switched from the estimation of the paths from disturbances to estimating the variances of the disturbances, although either is possible. We have defined just-identified, overidentified, and underidentified models, and I suggested that you use a SEM program to estimate overidentified models, but use either MR or an SEM program if your models are just-identified. We have examined fit indexes for overidentified models and have highlighted a few that are useful for evaluating a single model and those that are useful for comparing competing models. We briefly focused on equivalent models, nonrecursive models, and longitudinal data. We focused on the effects of measurement error on path analysis, MR, nonexperimental research, and research in general and began considering the use of latent variables as a method of obviating this threat. We expanded our knowledge of latent variables, their meaning, and estimation via confirmatory factor analysis.

PUTTING THE PIECES TOGETHER

In this chapter, we will begin putting all these pieces together in latent variable structural equation modeling. As noted in Chapter 13, you can consider latent variable SEM as a confirmatory factor analysis of the constructs involved in the research project, along with a path analysis of the effects of these constructs on each other. For this reason, many writers refer to these as the measurement model and the structural model, respectively (e.g., Mulaik & Millsap, 2000), to denote the conceptual distinctions between components of latent variable SEMs. Kline (1998) refers to latent variable structural equation models as "hybrid models" to denote the conceptual merging of these components. Although this separation of measurement and structural portions is not necessary statistically, it can be very useful conceptually, especially at this stage of learning.

Figure 15.1 displays, for review, the components of a latent variable SEM. The measurement model consists of the estimation of the four latent variables from eight measured variables. The structural model consists of four paths and one correlation among the four latent variables. Note that each variable that has a path pointing to it also has a residual–disturbance–error term pointing to it, representing all other influences on the variable other than the variables pointing to it. Some of these residuals represent the unique and error variances of measured variables, the remaining influences on these measured variables other than the latent variable underlying it. Some residuals represent disturbance terms for latent

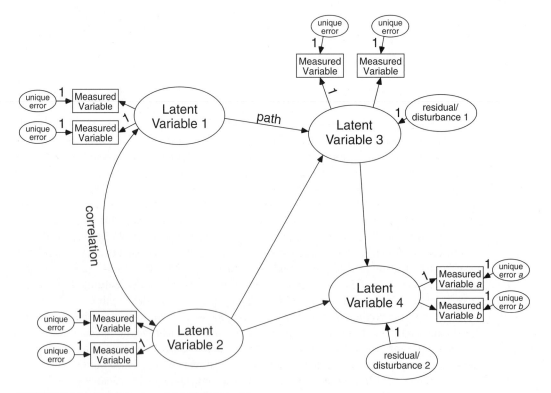

FIGURE 15.1   Full latent variable SEM model.

variables, meaning all remaining influences on these latent variables other than the other latent variables. Although I refer to some of these as unique–error variances and others as disturbances, the terms error and residual are used fairly interchangeably.

Why, you may wonder, doesn't Latent Variable 1 have a disturbance pointing to it? Because Latent Variable 1 has no paths pointing to it; it is exogenous. Note also that each latent variable (including the unique–error variances and the disturbances) has its scale set by fixing a single path from it to another variable to 1. So, for example, the latent variable labeled residual/disturbance 2 has its scale set to the same value as the latent variable labeled Latent Variable 4, which in turn is set to the same value as Measured Variable *a*. Note that the biggest difference between this model and the CFA models from the last chapter is that some correlations among latent variables are replaced by paths. As a result, the latent variables with paths pointing to them also have disturbances pointing to them. Of course, this is akin to the difference between a correlation matrix of variables and a path model specifying that one variable influences another. Take some time studying the model to make sure you understand it.

AN EXAMPLE: EFFECTS OF PEER REJECTION

Overview, Data, and Model

Eric Buhs and Gary Ladd used SEM to examine the effects of peer rejection on Kindergarten students' academic and emotional adjustment (2001). A portion of the model they analyzed is shown in Figure 15.2. The latent variables in the model, along with the measured variables used to estimate them, were these:

1. Rejection was indexed by averaged sociometric ratings for each child by the other children in the class (Averaged Rating; the scale of this variable was reversed) and by the number of times each child was nominated negatively (as someone other children did not want to play with; Negative Nominations).
2. Change, from a previous rating, in Classroom Participation. This variable was estimated from teacher ratings of Cooperative Participation (e.g., accepts responsibility) and Autonomous Participation (e.g., self-directive).
3. Achievement, which the authors considered one aspect of adjustment, was estimated from the Language and Quantitative subtests from a standardized readiness test (the Metropolitan Readiness Test, Nurss & McGauvran, 1986).
4. Emotional Adjustment, as indexed by self-ratings of students' Loneliness at school and their desire to avoid school (School Avoidance). These two variables were reversed to make the latent variable consistent with the positive name (Adjustment).

Buhs and Ladd's article included an additional intervening variable (Negative Peer Treatment) and an additional indicator of Rejection. These variables were not included here to simplify the model. The model is longitudinal; the Rejection variables were collected in the fall, the other variables in the spring (for more detail, see Buhs & Ladd, 2001).

Recall that with our earlier path models (e.g., the homework models in Chapter 12) many of the variables in the model were composites (e.g., Achievement was a composite of

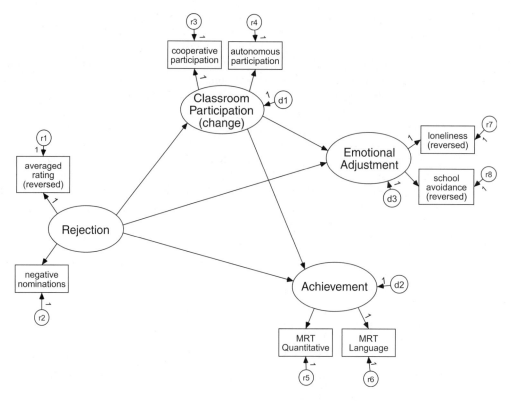

FIGURE 15.2   Effects of peer rejection on Academic and Emotional Adjustment, initial model. The model was derived from Buhs and Ladd, 2001.

four scores). Buhs and Ladd (2001) could have done the same thing here, but instead of adding Quantitative and Language into an achievement *composite* variable, for example, the authors used these two measures as indicators of an Achievement latent variable. Recall our discussion in Part 1 about multiple regression predicting an outcome variable from an *optimally weighted combination* of the independent variables. Conceptually, the latent variables in SEM are similar: they are optimally weighted combinations of the measured variables.

The model will be estimated from the *measured* variables. A portion of the data is shown in Table 15.1 (and is saved as data files on the Web site under the label "buhs & ladd data.sav" and "buhs & ladd data.xls"). Note there are no variables in the data file corresponding to the latent variables. This is because the latent variables, or factors, are estimated from the measured variables. If this is still confusing, think of the latent variables as *imaginary variables* that we estimate from the measured variables. (In the actual data file, the variable names are shortened versions of the variable labels used in the table and the Amos model, but they should be self-explanatory. Note that the data included here and on the Web site are not the actual data, but rather simulated data created to be consistent with the correlation matrix, means, and standard deviations reported in the actual article. $N = 399$. Three of the measured variables were reversed to make them consistent with the variable names and thus more easily interpretable.)

TABLE 15.1   Sample Data: Measured Variables for the Peer Rejection Example

CHILD	AVER-AGED RATING	NEGATIVE NOMINA-TIONS	COOPERATIVE PARTICIPATION	AUTONOMOUS PARTICIPATION	QUANTI-TATIVE	LAN-GUAGE	LONELI-NESS	SCHOOL AVOIDANCE
1	1.57	−1.09	1.19	.69	7.47	6.30	.93	1.62
2	−1.08	.55	−.13	−.07	2.72	2.76	1.60	1.94
3	.88	−1.09	−.29	−1.26	6.40	5.39	1.43	2.72
4	−1.18	−.36	−.19	−.56	.99	1.05	2.08	1.97
5	−.34	−.01	−.36	−.13	2.80	3.56	2.66	1.90
6	1.44	−1.51	.04	.07	7.07	7.79	1.65	2.07
7	−.18	.39	−.25	.40	3.68	3.47	.94	1.10
8	.64	−.81	.78	1.03	7.03	4.94	.99	1.49
9	−1.75	1.89	−.45	−.66	1.51	5.08	2.36	3.11

For the current model, I have symbolized the unique–error variances of the measured variables as r1 through r8 and the disturbances of the latent variables as d1 through d3. Recall that we can consider the unique–error variances as all other influences on the measured variables beyond the influence of the latent variable, just as the disturbances are all other influences on a latent variable beyond those of the other latent variables.

Measurement Model.   For the sake of clarity, the measurement model, without the structural model, is shown in Figure 15.3. Except for its placement of variables (in a circular fashion instead of in a line), the model is similar to the confirmatory factor models from the last chapter. The model simply delineates the estimation of the four latent variables (Rejection, Adjustment, etc.) from the eight measured variables (Averaged Rating, Negative Nominations, etc.).

Note that each latent variable had its scale set by a single factor loading (path from the latent to measured variable) set to 1. Each error–unique (residual) variable had its scale set by setting the path from it to its corresponding measured variable to 1.

Structural Model.   The structural portion of the model is shown in Figure 15.4, a figural representation of the hypotheses of the effects of one latent variable on another, and includes the disturbances for the endogenous latent variables in the model. The model examines the effect of Rejection on Adjustment, both directly and indirectly, through the class participation of the students.

The full SEM model (Figure 15.2) has 15 degrees of freedom. Fourteen degrees of freedom are from the measurement portion of the model (Figure 15.3). Note that all the factor loadings that could be included in the model (e.g., a path from Rejection to Cooperative Participation or Loneliness) are not included; these constraints are the source of this 14 *df*. The structural model (Figure 15.4) includes one additional *df*, resulting from the omission of a path between Achievement and Adjustment. The model is saved on the Web site (www.ablongman.com/keith1e) in the file "Buhs & Ladd model 1.amw."

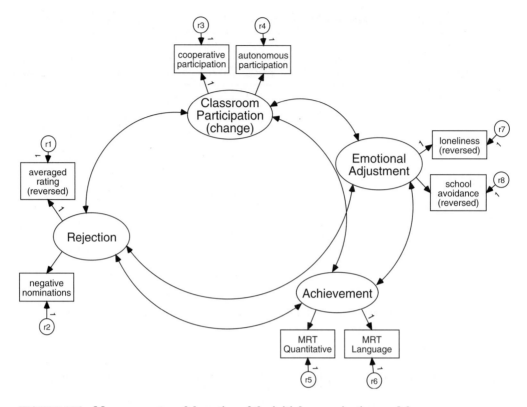

FIGURE 15.3   Measurement model portion of the initial peer rejection model.

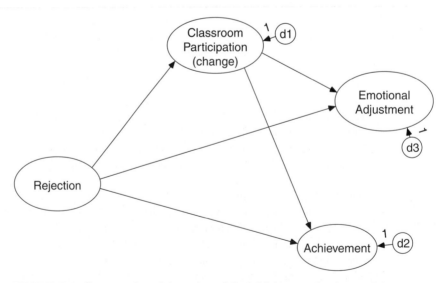

FIGURE 15.4   Structural model portion of the initial peer rejection model.

Results: The Initial Model

The model (Figure 15.2) was analyzed using the raw data (Table 15.1 and the file "buhs & ladd data.sav" or "buhs & ladd data.xls") via Amos. Figure 15.5 shows relevant fit indexes, along with the standardized output. The model shows an adequate, but not good, fit to the data. The RMSEA was above .05 (.067, 90% confidence interval = .043 to .092), but was below .08. The SRMR was below the cutoff of .08 (.046). The CFI was above .95, but the TLI was below the cutoff for a good fit of .95. Again, the model shows an adequate, but not good, fit. The full array of fit indexes is shown in Figure 15.6. Because the model had an adequate fit, we'll first interpret these results. Later in the chapter we'll take a look at the more detailed fit information and consider how the model might be modified.

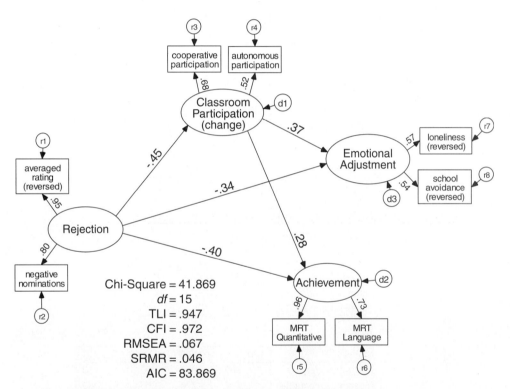

FIGURE 15.5   Standardized estimates from the initial peer rejection model. The model had an adequate, but not good, fit to the data.

Figure 15.7 shows more detail concerning the paths and factor loadings, including the unstandardized coefficients, their standard errors, and critical ranges (z statistics). All the parameters that were estimated were statistically significant (z greater than approximately 2).

Standardized Results.   Let's now focus on the meaning of the results (Figure 15.5). Our primary interest was in the effects of Rejection on kindergarten students' academic and

Model Fit Summary

CMIN

Model	NPAR	CMIN	DF	P	CMIN/DF
Default model	21	41.869	15	.000	2.791
Saturated model	36	.000	0		
Independence model	8	972.032	28	.000	34.715

RMR, GFI

Model	RMR	GFI	AGFI	PGFI
Default model	.047	.974	.938	.406
Saturated model	.000	1.000		
Independence model	.504	.574	.453	.447

Baseline Comparisons

Model	NFI Delta1	RFI rho1	IFI Delta2	TLI rho2	CFI
Default model	.957	.920	.972	.947	.972
Saturated model	1.000		1.000		1.000
Independence model	.000	.000	.000	.000	.000

Parsimony-Adjusted Measures

Model	PRATIO	PNFI	PCFI
Default model	.536	.513	.520
Saturated model	.000	.000	.000
Independence model	1.000	.000	.000

FMIN

Model	FMIN	F0	LO 90	HI 90
Default model	.105	.068	.028	.126
Saturated model	.000	.000	.000	.000
Independence model	2.442	2.372	2.125	2.637

RMSEA

Model	RMSEA	LO 90	HI 90	PCLOSE
Default model	.067	.043	.092	.110
Independence model	.291	.276	.307	.000

AIC

Model	AIC	BCC	BIC	CAIC
Default model	83.869	84.841	167.637	188.637
Saturated model	72.000	73.666	215.603	251.603
Independence model	988.032	988.403	1019.944	1027.944

FIGURE 15.6   Fit indexes for the initial rejection model.

Regression Weights

			Estimate	S.E.	C.R.	P
Classroom_Participation_(change)	<---	Rejection	-.205	.034	-6.055	***
Emotional_Adjustment	<---	Classroom_Participation_(change)	.289	.098	2.944	.003
Achievement	<---	Rejection	-.578	.105	-5.526	***
Achievement	<---	Classroom_Participation_(change)	.886	.274	3.236	.001
Emotional_Adjustment	<---	Rejection	-.118	.034	-3.430	***
NEG_NOM	<---	Rejection	.802	.057	14.157	***
AVE_RAT	<---	Rejection	1.000			
COOP	<---	Classroom_Participation_(change)	1.000			
AUTO	<---	Classroom_Participation_(change)	.788	.141	5.596	***
LONE	<---	Emotional_Adjustment	1.000			
SCHAVOID	<---	Emotional_Adjustment	1.140	.223	5.104	***
LANG	<---	Achievement	1.000			
QUANT	<---	Achievement	1.465	.134	10.901	***

Standardized Regression Weights

			Estimate
Classroom_Participation_(change)	<---	Rejection	-.451
Emotional_Adjustment	<---	Classroom_Participation_(change)	.372
Achievement	<---	Rejection	-.403
Achievement	<---	Classroom_Participation_(change)	.281
Emotional_Adjustment	<---	Rejection	-.335
NEG_NOM	<---	Rejection	.803
AVE_RAT	<---	Rejection	.949
COOP	<---	Classroom_Participation_(change)	.682
AUTO	<---	Classroom_Participation_(change)	.520
LONE	<---	Emotional_Adjustment	.567
SCHAVOID	<---	Emotional_Adjustment	.540
LANG	<---	Achievement	.726
QUANT	<---	Achievement	.957

FIGURE 15.7   Unstandardized and standardized paths and loadings, standard errors, and critical ratios.

Emotional Adjustment. The standardized direct effect of Rejection on Achievement was −.40, whereas the direct effect on Emotional Adjustment was −.34. Both effects were statistically significant and large. Given the adequacy of the model, for each *SD* change in the latent Rejection variable, Emotional Adjustment should decrease by .34 of a standard deviation, and Achievement should decrease by .40 of a *SD,* other things being equal. These findings, in turn, suggest strong effects for Rejection on kindergarteners' subsequent Adjustment, both academically and emotionally. Obviously, Rejection can have deleterious effects.

Unstandardized Findings.   Focus on the unstandardized coefficients (Figure 15.7). The unstandardized direct effect of Rejection on Adjustment was –.118, meaning that for each 1-unit change in the latent Rejection variable Emotional Adjustment decreased by .118 points. To understand the meaning of this statement, we need to understand the scales involved. The Rejection latent variable was set to have the same scale as the measured Averaged Ratings variable, whereas the Emotional Adjustment latent variable was set to the same scale as the Loneliness scale. The Averaged Ratings variable was originally based on a 3-point scale, but was each child's average rating on this 3-point scale by all of his or her classmates. In addition, these ratings were standardized separately by classroom (Buhs & Ladd, 2001). This seems a good approach, but it means that the Averaged Ratings unstandardized metric and thus the metric of the Rejection latent variable are not readily interpretable. According to the authors, the Loneliness scale is a five-item composite (Buhs & Ladd). Although not explained further, it appears from the means and standard deviations that this scale is also a mean of the item scores. Without further detail, the unstandardized metric of this variable and thus the Emotional Adjustment latent variable are also not interpretable. The unstandardized coefficients, although useful for other purposes (e.g., comparisons with other research), are not readily interpretable, and thus the previous interpretation of the standardized paths is probably our best approach.

Mediation.   Many more interesting findings are contained in the model beyond the direct effects. One primary interest of the researchers was to determine whether classroom participation *mediated* the effect of Rejection on Adjustment. In other words, what were the *indirect* effects of Rejection on Adjustment through Classroom Participation? Note in Figure 15.7 that Rejection had a powerful effect on Participation (–.45): rejected children showed less participation than did their nonrejected peers. Classroom Participation, in turn, had a strong effect on both Achievement (.28) and on Emotional Adjustment (.37); children who participated evidenced higher achievement and better adjustment. Thus, it certainly seems that the indirect effects of Rejection on the two adjustment variables were also substantial and that Classroom Participation partially mediates the effects of Rejection on Adjustment.

Total Effects.   Figure 15.8 shows the standardized direct, indirect, and total effects of the latent variables on each other. Rejection had moderate and negative indirect effects on Achievement (–.126) and Emotional Adjustment (–.168). Although not shown in the figure, these effects were also statistically significant. Although these effects are smaller than the direct effect of Rejection on each variable, they are meaningful and show that students' participation in class partially mediates the effects of rejection on adjustment. Children who are rejected by their peers show less participation, which, in turn, results in lower levels of school emotional adjustment and achievement. Because the direct and indirect effects of Rejection on the academic (Achievement) and Emotional Adjustment variables were both negative, the total effects were even larger (–.529 on Achievement; –.503 on Emotional Adjustment). (Of course we could have calculated these indirect and total effects by hand. For example, the indirect effect of Rejection on Achievement via Participation = –.451 × .281 = –.127. The total effect = –.126 – .403 = –.529 [the same value as the figure, within errors of rounding]. With more complex figures, of course, such calculations become considerably more complex.)

Standardized Total Effects

	Rejection	Classroom_Participation _(change)	Achievement	Emotional_ Adjustment
Classroom_Participation_(change)	-.451	.000	.000	.000
Achievement	-.529	.281	.000	.000
Emotional_Adjustment	-.503	.372	.000	.000

Standardized Direct Effects

	Rejection	Classroom_Participation _(change)	Achievement	Emotional_ Adjustment
Classroom_Participation_(change)	-.451	.000	.000	.000
Achievement	-.403	.281	.000	.000
Emotional_Adjustment	-.335	.372	.000	.000

Standardized Indirect Effects

	Rejection	Classroom_Participation _(change)	Achievement	Emotional_ Adjustment
Classroom_Participation_(change)	.000	.000	.000	.000
Achievement	-.126	.000	.000	.000
Emotional_Adjustment	-.168	.000	.000	.000

FIGURE 15.8   Standardized total, direct, and indirect effects for the initial rejection model.

COMPETING MODELS

We may wonder if the model, as drawn, is correctly specified. Is it reasonable, for example, to assume that the *only way* Achievement and Adjustment are related to each other is by their both being affected by Rejection and Participation? Or does Achievement affect Adjustment, as well (or Adjustment affect Achievement)?

Figure 15.9 shows an alternative model in which Achievement affects Adjustment. The logic behind this competing model is simple: children who are successful academically, a major component of the orientation of kindergarten, will, as a result, be better emotionally adjusted than will children who have difficulty with the academic aspects of kindergarten. As shown in the figure, this model had a good fit to the data. In particular, the RMSEA was .048, and the TLI and CFI were above .95.

More directly, we can compare the fit of this model with the initial model. Because the two models are nested, we can use $\Delta\chi^2$ to compare the two models. The fit statistics for this Achievement Effect model are shown in Table 15.2, along with those from the initial model. As can be seen in the table, the model in which Achievement was allowed to affect Adjustment resulted in a smaller χ^2 than did the initial model, and this $\Delta\chi^2$ was statistically significant ($\Delta\chi^2$ [1 *df*] = 15.095, $p < .001$). Although the initial model was more parsimonious, our rule of thumb is that when $\Delta\chi^2$ is statistically significant we will reject the more parsimonious model in favor of the better fitting model. In this case, the model shown in

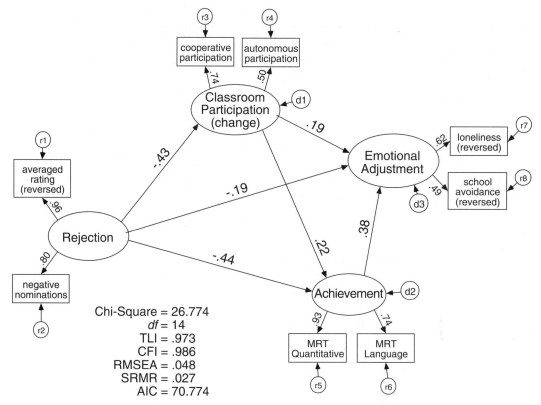

FIGURE 15.9   Alternative Achievement Effect model of the effects of rejection on educational and emotional adjustment. The model includes a path from Achievement (educational adjustment) to Emotional Adjustment.

Figure 15.9 is the better fitting model; the decrease in parsimony is worth the decrease in χ^2.

Given our acceptance of the Achievement Effect model over the Initial Model, what are the implications for this new model? The results shown in Figure 15.9 suggest that Achievement has a powerful effect on Emotional Adjustment ($\beta = .38$). If this model is correct, then it appears that Achievement is an important mediating variable between Rejection and Adjustment: children who are rejected suffer academically, and this academic difficulty, in turn, results in lower levels of adjustment in school.

TABLE 15.2   Comparison of the Fit of Alternative Peer Rejection Models

MODEL	χ^2	df	$\Delta\chi^2$	Δdf	p	AIC	PCFI	RMSEA (90% CI)
Initial	41.869	15				83.869	.520	.067 (.043–.092)
Achievement Effect	26.774	14	15.095	1	.001	70.774	.493	.048 (.018–.075)

This change in the model also substantially reduced the direct effect of both Rejection and Participation on Emotional Adjustment (compare the models shown in Figures 15.5 and 15.9). If you compare the total effects for Rejection on Adjustment in the two models, however, you will find them to be similar. Take a few minutes to consider why this is the case.

Other Possible Models

You may question why I drew the path from Achievement to Adjustment rather than the reverse. The decision was based primarily on logic. I reasoned that the types of skills and abilities assessed by the Achievement measured variables are more stable than the ratings of loneliness and school avoidance assessed by the Adjustment latent variable. Given what is meant by these two latent variables, it seemed to me that it was more likely that Achievement would affect Adjustment than it was that Adjustment would affect Achievement. What do you think? Should the path go in this direction or the reverse? It is interesting to conduct this exercise, but if we examine this model as more than an exercise, we will need to examine relevant theory and previous research to see which of these possibilities is more likely. We would use such theory and research to design the study and to draw the path in the appropriate direction.

Why not, you may wonder, just estimate a model with the path drawn in the opposite direction and see how that model fits? Recall the rules for equivalent models in Chapter 12. Unfortunately, these two models are statistically equivalent; their fit is identical. Although this alternative Adjustment Effect model will have very different implications for interpretation, the data cannot tell us which model is correct. It is also inappropriate to run this alternative model, interpret it, and then decide which interpretation we like more. Perhaps, then, we can draw the paths in both directions, a nonrecursive model, and see which path is stronger? This solution will not work either; the structural model will be underidentified. If differentiation between these two models is one of the purposes of the research, the researchers could build in noncommon causes of the two outcome variables and thus test nonequivalent or nonrecursive models; likewise, longitudinal data will help. With the current model and data, we must rely on theory and previous research to make this decision.

What if theory and previous research do not inform this decision; what if you cannot decide in which direction to draw the path? One option, an agnostic option, is shown in Figure 15.10. In this model, we have allowed the disturbances of Achievement and Adjustment to be correlated. Note that this model is also equivalent to the model in Figure 15.9; the fit indexes are therefore the same, and the data cannot tell us which of the two models is correct. But consider what this model with the correlated disturbances says about our assumptions of the causal process underlying these variables. The disturbances are all other influences on the latent variables other than the variables in the model that are pointing to the latent variable. To allow the disturbances to be correlated means that we recognize that these other causes may be related. In other words, we recognize that Emotional Adjustment and Achievement may be related in other ways beyond the paths shown in the model, but we're not really sure what these other relations may be. Practically, these correlated disturbances may mean that the two variables are causally related, but we don't know the direction. The correlated disturbances may also mean that there is some other variable, not included in the model, that affects both Adjustment and Achievement (an unmeasured common cause). If you think about it, this correlation means what any correlation may mean: *a* may cause *b*, *b* may cause *a*, or there may be a third variable, *c*, that causes both *a* and *b*. Again, the models are equivalent, so we can't decide which is correct based on the data. As a general rule, however, I prefer to make the causal statement (Figure 15.9) than to be noncommittal (Figure 15.10), but want a more solid grounding in relevant theory and research than I now have before making the decision of causal direction. We will return to the topic of causal direction in the next chapter.

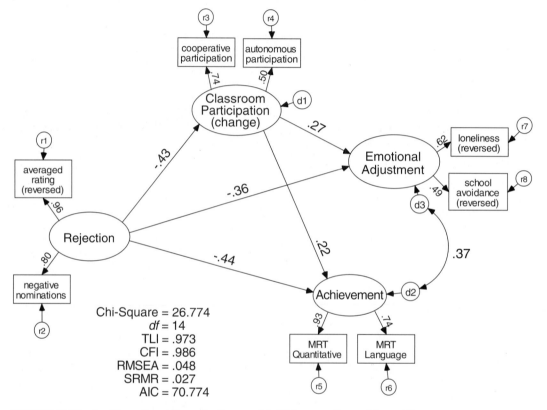

FIGURE 15.10   Another alternative rejection model. This agnostic model specifies an unknown causal relation between Emotional Adjustment and Achievement. The model is equivalent to and statistically indistinguishable from the previous Achievement Effect model.

MODEL MODIFICATIONS

The competing model discussed above was developed based on logic rather than analysis of the detailed fit information. You may wonder, if we had not thought of this competing model, would the modification indexes (MIs) or the standardized residuals have hinted at it? Figure 15.11 shows the modification indexes greater than 4.0 for the initial model (from Figure 15.5). Although many of the modification indexes do not make a lot of sense, several are worth noting. The largest index suggests that χ^2 could be reduced by at least 16.425

by freeing the correlation–covariance between the residual for Loneliness (r7) and the disturbance for Achievement (d2). This modification makes little sense. The next largest modification index (12.075 for the covariance between d3 and d2) does, however. This MI suggests that the model will fit statistically significantly better if this covariance is freed. Focus on the MIs for the regression weights (the paths). Although they are not the largest MIs, the first two listed also suggest that the fit of the model could be improved by focusing on the relation between Achievement and Emotional Adjustment. Thus, although the modification indexes do not point directly to our Achievement Effect model, they certainly hint in that direction.

Modification Indices

Covariances

	M.I.	Par Change
d3 <--> d2	12.075	.086
r7 <--> d2	16.425	.120
r7 <--> r5	4.590	.073
r4 <--> r5	7.147	.101
r4 <--> r6	10.334	-.117

Regression Weights

		M.I.	Par Change
Achievement	<--- Emotional_Adjustment	4.714	.522
Emotional_Adjustment	<--- Achievement	7.159	.046
QUANT	<--- AUTO	5.448	.250
LANG	<--- AUTO	8.107	-.294
LONE	<--- Achievement	9.785	.065
LONE	<--- QUANT	9.925	.041
LONE	<--- LANG	9.972	.046
AUTO	<--- LANG	4.345	-.033

FIGURE 15.11 Modification indexes for the initial rejection model.

Figure 15.12 shows the standardized residual covariances among the variables. These residuals show that the Initial Model did not adequately account for the correlations between Loneliness and the MRT Quantitative and Language scores and also, to a lesser extent, between Language and School Avoidance. Again, the standardized residuals *might* lead you in the direction of the Achievement Effect model if you had not thought of it previously.

As long as we are cleaning up our models, we might reexamine the statistical significance of the various parameter estimates to see if all paths are statistically significant, with the idea that if any are not it will be okay to remove them. As shown earlier in Figure 15.7, all paths were statistically significant. Although not shown here, all paths are also statistically significant in the Achievement Effect model. It is worth reiterating a previous point: Models that are extensively modified based on modification indexes and other tools for model modification should be considered exploratory, tentative models until tested against new data.

Standardized Residual Covariances

	QUANT	LANG	SCHAVOID	LONE	AUTO	COOP	AVE_RAT	NEG_NOM
QUANT	.000							
LANG	.000	.000						
SCHAVOID	.682	1.260	.000					
LONE	2.968	3.096	.000	.000				
AUTO	.321	-1.821	-.008	-1.089	.000			
COOP	-.608	-.488	-.128	-.444	.313	.000		
AVE_RAT	.006	-.235	.236	-.053	.760	-.286	.000	
NEG_NOM	.433	-.104	-.536	.741	.333	-.983	.014	.000

FIGURE 15.12   Standardized residual covariances for the initial rejection model.

SUMMARY

This chapter is the first to focus on latent variable structural equation models. Such SEM models may be considered as a confirmatory factor analysis of the various constructs involved in the research, with a simultaneous path analysis of the effects of these constructs on each other. The chapter reviewed the components of latent variable SEMs and illustrated the methodology with an extended example from the research literature.

Conceptually, you may consider latent variable SEM as a confirmatory factor analysis of the constructs underlying the measured variables in the research, along with a path analysis of the latent variables. The measurement model includes the latent variables, constructs, or factors that underlie the measured variables in the research as causes of these measured variables. The measurement model also includes latent variables, one per measured variable, representing the unique and error variances of each variable, or all other causes of that measured variable other than the construct–latent variable. The structural model includes the paths and covariances among the latent variables, along with the disturbances for the endogenous latent variables (all other causes of the latent variables other than those with arrows pointing to the latent variables). It is often confusing to those new to the SEM methodology to know which variables require latent variables representing disturbances or unique–error variances. At the most mechanical level, any variable that has an arrow pointing to it must also include a latent variable representing all other influences on this variable. For measured variables, these other influences are unique and error variances. For latent variables, these other influences generally represent disturbances along the lines of the disturbances from path analysis or the residuals from multiple regression analysis. In fact, you can, and some methodologists recommend that you do, analyze the model separately as a measurement (confirmatory factor) model, and then add the structural model. We have not used this process here, but it can be useful, especially for complex models or in the beginning stages of research.

The research example used in the chapter was based on research on the effects of peer rejection on kindergarten students' academic and emotional adjustment (Buhs & Ladd, 2001). The example analyzed models similar to (but smaller than) those analyzed in the actual research, with data simulated to mimic the actual data. The initial model included four latent variables with two measured variables indexing each latent variable (more good measures per latent variable are preferable in practice, but our interest was in a smaller, more manageable example). We split apart the measurement model from the structural model for conceptual purposes, but not for analysis. The initial model was fairly parsimonious (15 *df*), with most of the degrees of freedom a result of constraints (undrawn paths on factor loadings) in the measurement model.

The initial model had an adequate fit to the data and suggested that Rejection by peers resulted in lower subsequent Achievement and school-related Emotional Adjustment. A portion of these effects were indirect, or mediated, through Class Participation: rejected students had lower rates of participation, which resulted in lower achievement and adjustment. Thus, all three types of effects—direct, indirect, and total—were interesting and interpretable.

An alternative model, which included an additional path from Achievement to Emotional Adjustment, was also estimated. This change resulted in a statistically significant improvement in χ^2, which we interpreted as meaning that the alternative Achievement Effect model was a better explanation of the data than the initial model. The alternative model led to different interpretations of direct, indirect, and total effects. As an aside, this change (in the structural portion of the model) used up the 1 degree of freedom that was due to the structural portion of the model.

Any complacency we may have garnered that we had now found the correct model was quickly shattered, however. The chapter discussed two alternative models that are equivalent to our preferred Achievement Effect model. Although these two models are statistically indistinguishable from the Achievement Effect model, they have very different interpretations and implications. The chapter included the standardized figural output from one of these alternative models to demonstrate its statistical, but not conceptual, equivalence to the Achievement Effect model. This fuzziness served as another reminder of the importance of theory, logic, and previous research in the construction of models. The equivalent models also served as a reminder of the importance of planning the research so that you can indeed answer the questions of interest.

In the final section of the chapter we examined some of the more detailed fit statistics from the SEM program output. The modification indexes and the standardized residual covariances for the initial model hinted at the change we made in the Achievement Effect model (although they also suggested the other equivalent, indistinguishable models). Although we might have arrived at the same place had we constructed the alternative Achievement Effect model based on these hints, alternative models devised prior to the examination of the data and results should generally be given more credence than models derived from extensive data-driven model modifications. There were no statistically not-significant paths or factor loadings that we might have constrained in subsequent models.

Although not discussed in detail, there are always equivalent possible models, and their veracity must be tested against these (theory, etc.) standards, not through complex statistical analysis. We can test and reject some models, but we can rarely (maybe never) test and evaluate all possible models that would result in alternative interpretations. Some we don't think of, and some are indistinguishable. At the most basic level, our models always come back to this need for theory, thought, and previous research. "The study of structural equation models can be divided into two parts: the easy part and the hard part" (Duncan, 1975, p. 149). The hard part is developing sound, theory-grounded models. Again, welcome to the dangerous world of SEM.

EXERCISES

1. Analyze the simulated Buhs and Ladd data ("Buhs & Ladd data.sav" or Buhs & Ladd data.xls") using a structural equation modeling program (if you are using Amos, the initial model is saved as "Buhs & Ladd model 1.amw").

   a. Estimate the models discussed in this chapter. Study the parameter estimates and standard errors, the fit statistics, modification indexes, and standardized residuals.

   b. Interpret the model. Be sure to interpret the indirect and total effects in addition to the direct effects.

   c. Compare the initial model with the competing model discussed in this chapter (the Achievement Effect model). Do you agree that this model is a better alternative? What theoretical, logical, and research evidence can you offer in support of this model? What evidence argues against this model?

   d. Are there other alternative models that you are interested in testing? Do so; be sure to evaluate the relative fit of the model and to interpret your findings.

   e. Are there any common causes that the authors may have neglected? How could you investigate the possibility of unmeasured common causes more completely?

2. Figure 15.13 shows a model to test the effects of participation in Head Start on children's cognitive ability. This example is a classic reanalysis of a controversial quasi-experiment; I have seen variations of it presented in Kenny (1979) and Bentler and Woodward (1978), among others. The measured background variables in the model include measures of mother's and father's educational attainment, father's occupational status, and family income. Head Start was hoped to improve participants' cognitive skills, and the latent Cognitive Ability outcome was indexed by scores on two tests: the Illinois Test of Psycholinguistic Abilities (ITPA) and the Metropolitan Readiness Test (MRT). The Head Start variable is a dummy variable coded 1 for those who participated in Head Start and 0 for children in the control group. The data are shown in Table 15.3. These are data from 303 children from an early Head Start evaluation, 148 who attended Head Start in the summer and 155 who did not. To understand why the example is so controversial, note the correlation between Head Start and the two cognitive outcomes: both are negative (–.10, –.09), suggesting that Head Start may have negative effects on Ability! The model is one of several possible models designed to determine what the outcomes of Head Start are after taking the family's background characteristics into account. The correlations and *SD*s are also included in the Excel file "head start.xls." All continuous variables are standardized.

   a. Draw (set up) and estimate the model. Is the structural portion of the model just-identified or overidentified? Evaluate the fit of the model and, if adequate, focus on parameter estimates. Interpret the model. According to these results, does Head Start have a positive effect on cognitive ability, a negative effect, or no effect at all? Interpret the other aspects of the model.

   b. Fix the path from Head Start to Cognitive Ability to zero; compare the fit of this model to the initial model. Do you still come to the same conclusion as before?

   c. Are there other alternative models that you are interested in testing? Are they equivalent to the initial model? Test these models; be sure to evaluate the relative fit of the model and to interpret your findings.

   d. Are there any common causes that the research may have neglected? How could you investigate the possibility of unmeasured common causes more completely?

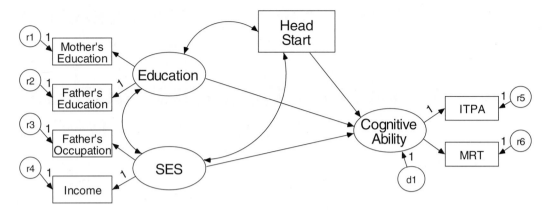

FIGURE 15.13   Model testing the potential effects of Head Start participation on children's cognitive ability.

TABLE 15.3   **Head Start Correlations**

VARIABLES	MOMED	POPED	POPOCC	INCOME	HEAD START	ITPA	MRT
MomEd	1						
PopEd	.47	1					
PopOcc	.24	.28	1				
Income	.30	.21	.41	1			
Head Start	−.12	−.08	−.22	−.18	1		
ITPA	.26	.25	.22	.12	−.10	1	
MRT	.28	.22	.26	.19	−.09	.65	1

N = 303.

■ ■ ■ ■ ■

LATENT VARIABLE MODELS: MORE ADVANCED TOPICS

In the previous chapter we introduced and explored latent variable structural equation models. This chapter will review and consolidate that learning by reviewing another example. We will continue our exploration with several more advanced topics and an assessment of where we stand in our efforts to conduct meaningful nonexperimental research. The chapter will begin with a model that incorporates two complexities that we have hinted at previously: single-indicator variables and correlated errors.

SINGLE INDICATORS AND CORRELATED ERRORS

A Latent Variable Homework Model

Figure 16.1 shows a latent variable version of our earlier Homework model from Chapter 12. The primary variables in the model are Homework, indexed by student reports of average time spent on homework in 8th (Homework 8th) and 10th (Homework 10th) grades, and students' overall Grades in high school, a latent variable estimated by students' high school GPAs in English, Math, Science, and History–Social Studies (from students' transcripts at graduation). Other measured variables in the model were as follows:

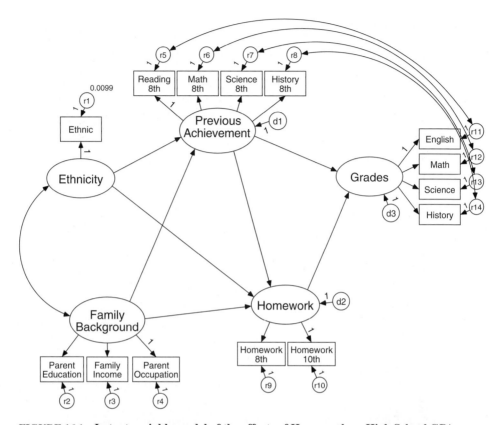

FIGURE 16.1   Latent variable model of the effects of Homework on High School GPA.

1. Achievement test scores, from 8th grade, in Reading, Math, Science, and History–Social Studies
2. Parent Educational attainment, Family Income, and Parent Occupational status. These variables were generally taken from the parent file; Parent Occupation and Parent Education were each based on the higher value reported for either the father or the mother.
3. Ethnic orientation, coded 1 for White and 0 for other.

Recall that with the earlier homework model most of the variables were composites of some sort; Previous Achievement, for example, was a composite of the four 8th-grade achievement tests. In the current model, these components were not added together as composites, but appear in the model as measured variables. Instead of adding the four tests together to create a Previous Achievement *composite* variable, for example, the four 8th-grade tests are used as indicators of a Previous Achievement *latent* variable.

The model will be estimated from the covariance matrix of the measured variables. The covariance matrix is recovered from the correlation matrix and standard deviations, shown in Table 16.1, and on the accompanying Web site (www.ablongman.com/keith1e) under the label "hw latent matrix.xls." The variable names are the variable names (rather than the

TABLE 16.1   Correlations, Means, and Standard Deviations among Measured Variables in the Latent Variable Homework Model

VARIABLE	ETHNIC	BYPARED	BYFAMINC	PAROCC	BYTXRSTD	BYTXMSTD	BYTXSSTD	BYTXHSTD	HW_8	HW_10	ENG_12	MATH_12	SCI_12	SS_12
ETHNIC	1.000													
BYPARED	0.169	1.000												
BYFAMINC	0.278	0.526	1.000											
PAROCC	0.242	0.629	0.524	1.000										
BYTXRSTD	0.204	0.386	0.288	0.339	1.000									
BYTXMSTD	0.161	0.430	0.335	0.362	0.714	1.000								
BYTXSSTD	0.231	0.384	0.293	0.322	0.717	0.719	1.000							
BYTXHSTD	0.210	0.396	0.308	0.346	0.731	0.675	0.728	1.000						
HW_8	0.003	0.168	0.075	0.105	0.226	0.271	0.221	0.168	1.000					
HW_10	0.056	0.208	0.155	0.173	0.219	0.286	0.206	0.207	0.271	1.000				
ENG_12	0.098	0.334	0.243	0.260	0.524	0.565	0.450	0.491	0.204	0.313	1.000			
MATH_12	0.071	0.285	0.220	0.218	0.418	0.587	0.415	0.409	0.173	0.289	0.761	1.000		
SCI_12	0.083	0.294	0.209	0.231	0.484	0.576	0.493	0.476	0.192	0.282	0.803	0.759	1.000	
SS_12	0.111	0.328	0.253	0.265	0.519	0.567	0.485	0.519	0.181	0.284	0.851	0.745	0.795	1.000
SD	0.445	1.284	2.523	21.599	10.290	10.380	10.318	10.182	1.131	1.903	2.674	2.747	2.682	2.873
Mean	0.728	3.203	9.917	51.694	51.984	52.545	51.883	51.653	1.731	3.381	6.250	5.703	5.952	6.418

variable labels) from the Amos model and should either be familiar to you or self-explanatory. The data are 1000 cases chosen at random from the 8th- through 12th-grade NELS data, including information from students' transcripts. For the current model, I have symbolized the unique–error variances of the measured variables as r1 through r14 and the disturbances of the latent variables as d1 through d3.

Note that each latent variable has its scale set by a single factor loading (path from the latent to measured variable) set to 1. Each error–unique (residual) variance has its scale set by constraining the path from it to its corresponding measured variable to 1.

The model examines the effect of time spent on homework on subsequent GPA while controlling for students' previous school performance. Two background variables, Ethnic background and Family Background, are also controlled, although the model specifies that both background variables affect Grades only indirectly through Previous Achievement and Homework. Note that the model is simply a latent variable version of the path model from Chapter 12 and, like that model, is supported by theory and previous research.

Single-Indicator Latent Variable.   The model included several less common characteristics, as well. First, notice the value associated with the residual (r1) of the Ethnic variable (.0099). The latent variable Ethnicity is indexed by a single measured variable (Ethnic), and this portion of the measurement model would be underidentified without further constraints. As discussed in Chapter 14, a common method for dealing with single-indicator factors is to constrain the error–unique variance of that measured variable to some value, often a value of 1 minus the estimated reliability of the measured variable. Why, you may ask, would a variable as clear-cut as ethnic background be unreliable? Students' reports of their ethnic identity should be very, but not completely, reliable. Students may misread the questionnaire item or might decide on a whim to mark it incorrectly. Students of mixed ethnic background can only chose one group when they belong to more than one. Those who enter the data into the computer may make transcription errors. All these possibilities add small amounts of error. For these reasons, I estimated the reliability of the Ethnic variable at approximately .95. Thus 5% of the variability of the Ethnic measured variable is due to unreliability, or error. The variance of Ethnic is .198 (from Table 16.1, $SD^2 = .445^2 = .198$), and 5% of this variance is .0099; the error variance of the Ethnic variable was constrained to this value.

Correlated Errors.   The model also includes correlations between the error and unique variances of the Achievement test scores and later Grades. The model, for example, specifies that the unique and error variance of the 8th-grade Math achievement test score is correlated with the unique and error variance of the 12th-grade Math GPA. Conceptually, this correlated error means that we believe that the Math test score and Math Grades share something in common above and beyond the effect of general Previous Achievement on overall Grades. If you think about it, this makes sense, and we can even label that "something" that Math test scores and Math grades share in common: specific Math achievement. The model also includes correlated errors between Reading–English, Science test and grades, and History–Social studies test and grades. Such correlated errors are common in longitudinal models in which a single measure is administered more than once or (as in the present model) when closely related measures are administered at two different times. Indeed, the ability to take the possibility of correlated unique and error variances into account is an important advantage of SEM.

The full SEM model (Figure 16.1) has 66 degrees of freedom. Sixty-four degrees of freedom are from the measurement portion of the model. Simply note all the factor loadings that could be included in the model that are not included (e.g., a path from Homework to Reading 8th or Parent Occupation); these constraints are the source of this 64 *df*. The structural model produces the other 2 *df*, resulting from the paths from Ethnicity and Family Background to Grades that are constrained to zero.

Results.   The model (Figure 16.1 and in the file "hw latent 1.amw") and the data (Table 16.1 and the file "hw latent matrix.xls") were analyzed via Amos. Figure 16.2 shows relevant fit indexes, along with the standardized output. The model showed a good fit to the data. The RMSEA was below .05 (.046, 90% confidence interval = .039–.052), and the GFI, TLI, and CFI were all above .95. Although not shown in the figure, the SRMR for this model was .029, meaning that the matrix implied by the model differed from the actual correlation matrix, on average, by only .029. The full array of fit indexes is shown in Figure 16.3. Because the model generally fits well, we'll first interpret the results. Later in the chapter we will take a look at the more detailed fit information to see how the model might be modified.

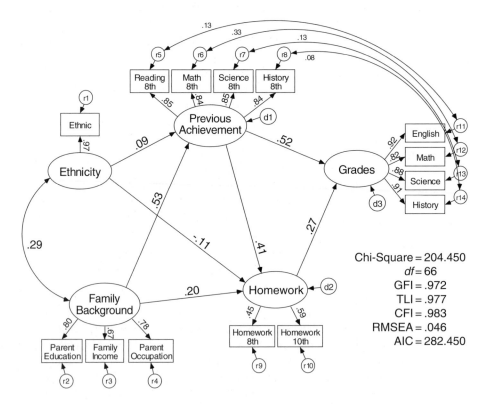

FIGURE 16.2   Standardized output for the latent variable homework model.

Figure 16.4 shows more detail concerning the paths and factor loadings, including the unstandardized coefficients, their standard errors, and critical ranges (*z* statistics). All the parameters that were estimated were statistically significant (*z* greater than approximately 2). Figure 16.5 shows the covariances, correlations, and variances. Note that covariances

Model Fit Summary

CMIN

Model	NPAR	CMIN	DF	P	CMIN/DF
Default model	39	204.450	66	.000	3.098
Saturated model	105	.000	0		
Independence model	14	8383.652	91	.000	92.128

RMR, GFI

Model	RMR	GFI	AGFI	PGFI
Default model	1.389	.972	.955	.611
Saturated model	.000	1.000		
Independence model	24.569	.310	.204	.269

Baseline Comparisons

Model	NFI Delta1	RFI rho1	IFI Delta2	TLI rho2	CFI
Default model	.976	.966	.983	.977	.983
Saturated model	1.000		1.000		1.000
Independence model	.000	.000	.000	.000	.000

Parsimony-Adjusted Measures

Model	PRATIO	PNFI	PCFI
Default model	.725	.708	.713
Saturated model	.000	.000	.000
Independence model	1.000	.000	.000

FMIN

Model	FMIN	F0	LO 90	HI 90
Default model	.205	.139	.099	.186
Saturated model	.000	.000	.000	.000
Independence model	8.392	8.301	8.003	8.605

RMSEA

Model	RMSEA	LO 90	HI 90	PCLOSE
Default model	.046	.039	.053	.825
Independence model	.302	.297	.308	.000

AIC

Model	AIC	BCC	BIC	CAIC
Default model	282.450	283.639	473.852	512.852
Saturated model	210.000	213.201	725.314	830.314
Independence model	8411.652	8412.079	8480.361	8494.361

FIGURE 16.3   Fit indexes for the initial homework model.

were also statistically significant, with the exception of the covariance between r8 and r14. The correlated error between 8th-grade History test scores and 12th-grade History grades was not statistically significant; we could, if desired, remove this parameter in subsequent models, presumably without any noticeable loss of fit.

Regression Weights

			Estimate	S.E.	C.R.	P
Previous_Achievement	<---	Family_Background	.278	.020	13.649	***
Previous_Achievement	<---	Ethnicity	1.774	.646	2.748	.006
Homework	<---	Family_Background	.013	.004	3.120	.002
Homework	<---	Previous_Achievement	.053	.008	6.640	***
Homework	<---	Ethnicity	-.281	.123	-2.292	.022
Grades	<---	Previous_Achievement	.145	.012	12.574	***
Grades	<---	Homework	.601	.132	4.566	***
Ethnic	<---	Ethnicity	1.000			
parocc	<---	Family_Background	1.000			
byfaminc	<---	Family_Background	.100	.005	19.214	***
bypared	<---	Family_Background	.062	.003	21.607	***
bytxrstd	<---	Previous_Achievement	1.000			
bytxmstd	<---	Previous_Achievement	.997	.030	33.737	***
bytxsstd	<---	Previous_Achievement	.990	.030	33.520	***
bytxhstd	<---	Previous_Achievement	.967	.029	32.909	***
eng_12	<---	Grades	1.000			
Math_12	<---	Grades	.896	.024	37.813	***
Sci_12	<---	Grades	.957	.022	43.683	***
ss_12	<---	Grades	1.062	.022	48.194	***
hw10	<---	Homework	1.000			
hw_8	<---	Homework	.453	.060	7.549	***

Standardized Regression Weights

			Estimate
Previous_Achievement	<---	Family_Background	.529
Previous_Achievement	<---	Ethnicity	.087
Homework	<---	Family_Background	.198
Homework	<---	Previous_Achievement	.413
Homework	<---	Ethnicity	-.108
Grades	<---	Previous_Achievement	.518
Grades	<---	Homework	.274
Ethnic	<---	Ethnicity	.975
parocc	<---	Family_Background	.776
byfaminc	<---	Family_Background	.667
bypared	<---	Family_Background	.805
bytxrstd	<---	Previous_Achievement	.855
bytxmstd	<---	Previous_Achievement	.844
bytxsstd	<---	Previous_Achievement	.846
bytxhstd	<---	Previous_Achievement	.837
eng_12	<---	Grades	.924
Math_12	<---	Grades	.820
Sci_12	<---	Grades	.878
ss_12	<---	Grades	.914
hw10	<---	Homework	.592
hw_8	<---	Homework	.451

FIGURE 16.4 Unstandardized and standardized factor loadings and paths for the initial latent variable homework model.

Covariances

		Estimate	S.E.	C.R.	P
Family_Background <--> Ethnicity		2.136	.277	7.705	***
r5	<-->r11	.704	.248	2.842	.004
r6	<-->r12	2.856	.342	8.346	***
r7	<-->r13	.920	.285	3.225	.001
r8	<-->r14	.533	.277	1.926	.054

Correlations

		Estimate
Family_Background <--> Ethnicity		.294
r5	<--> r11	.128
r6	<--> r12	.331
r7	<--> r13	.130
r8	<--> r14	.082

Variances

	Estimate	S.E.	C.R.	P
Family_Background	280.913	21.615	12.996	***
Ethnicity	.188	.009	21.232	***
d1	53.163	3.516	15.122	***
d2	.915	.182	5.017	***
d3	3.150	.202	15.596	***
r1	.010			
r4	185.127	13.024	14.215	***
r3	3.528	.193	18.267	***
r2	.580	.046	12.691	***
r5	28.555	1.718	16.617	***
r6	31.233	1.822	17.145	***
r7	30.165	1.768	17.059	***
r8	30.864	1.775	17.390	***
r11	1.052	.075	14.108	***
r12	2.378	.122	19.536	***
r13	1.653	.094	17.617	***
r14	1.364	.090	15.125	***
r10	2.352	.202	11.633	***
r9	1.018	.058	17.553	***

FIGURE 16.5   Covariances, correlations, and variances for parameters estimated in the initial homework model.

Interpretation.   Let's now focus on the meaning of the results. First, our primary interest was in the effects of Homework on GPA. The standardized coefficient was .27, meaning that for each *SD* change in the latent Homework variable Grades should change by .27 of a standard deviation, other things being equal. This finding, in turn, suggests a strong effect of time spent on homework on subsequent GPA (given the adequacy of the model). This effect is larger than in our previous path analyses using only measured variables (even though we are focusing on a longer time span—through 12th grade, rather than 10th grade) and larger than the effect shown in Part 1 when we examined the effect of homework on learning using multiple regression. As noted in Chapter 13, our measures of variables in research are always error laden. Latent variable SEM removes unreliability and invalidity from the estimates of the effects of one variable on another. The most common effect of removing measurement error from our estimation process is to increase the apparent effect of one variable on another. This effect is illustrated well by comparing the present homework model with previous versions. The current, latent variable model is a more accurate representation of the true effects of homework on learning, because it gets closer to the level of the constructs of true interest.

Unstandardized Coefficients.   Focus on the unstandardized coefficients (Figure 16.6). The unstandardized effect of Homework on Grades was .60, meaning that for each 1-unit change in the latent homework variable Grades increase .60 point. To understand the meaning of this statement, we need to understand the scales involved. The Homework latent variable was set to have the same scale as the measured Homework 10th variable, whereas the Grades latent variable was set to the same scale as the English GPA measured variable. If Homework 10th had been measured on a simple hour scale and English GPA on a standard 4.0 scale, interpretation would be relatively straightforward. Unfortunately, the underlying scales for both variables are not that meaningful, which is one reason I am focusing more on the interpretation of standardized as opposed to unstandardized coefficients. The Homework 10th measured variable was a mean of two questions, F1S36A1 and F1S36A2 (average time spent on homework in school and time spent on homework out of school). I changed the scale of each of these items so that they ranged from 0 (none) to 9 (over 15 hours a week; I changed the scale from a 0 to 7 scale so that it would be consistent with the scale used for the 8th-grade homework question). The homework scales in NELS are presumably designed to take into account the curvilinear nature of the effect of homework on learning. The English GPA scale ranged from 0 (an F average) to 12 (A+). Again, the unstandardized coefficients are less interpretable than would be ideal.

Effects on Homework, Indirect and Total Effects.   Many more interesting findings are contained in the model, as well. The analysis has shown that Homework affects Grades, but this raises another question. Which other variables in the model affect Homework? That is, who spends more time on homework? Previous Achievement had a strong effect (.41, standardized) on Homework. Students who achieve at a higher level spend more time on homework than those who achieve at lower levels; this increase in Homework time subsequently results in higher Grades as well. The coefficients from Family Background suggest that students from more advantaged backgrounds have higher 8th-grade achievement (.53) and complete more homework (.20). Students' Ethnic background had only a small effect on 8th-grade Achievement (.09). Ethnicity had a negative effect on Homework (–.11). Given the coding of the Ethnic variable, this means that students from minority ethnic backgrounds report higher levels of homework time than majority (White) students. The unstandardized coefficient for the Ethnicity–Homework path (–.28) shows that minority students report .28 points higher on the Homework time scale than do majority students when the other variables in the model are controlled.

Figure 16.7 shows the standardized indirect and total (as well as the direct) effects of the latent variables on each other. Note that, because there are no paths from Ethnicity or

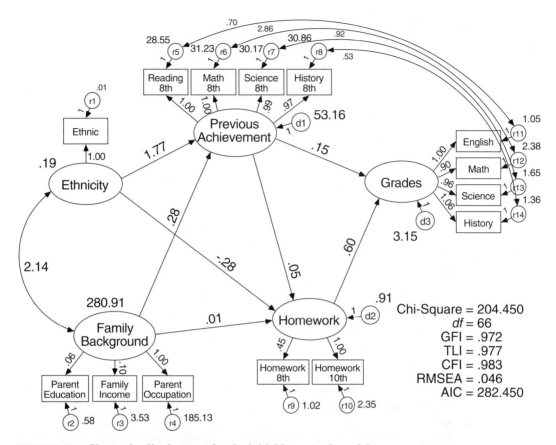

FIGURE 16.6 Unstandardized output for the initial homework model.

Family Background to Grades, there are, of course, no direct effects for these variables on Grades. Family Background, however, had a large indirect effect on Grades (.388), primarily through its effect on Previous Achievement (.529 times the total effect of Previous Achievement on Grades, .631 = .334). The indirect effect of Family Background on Grades through Homework was smaller, but still meaningful (.198 × .274 = .054). Because there are no direct effects of Family Background on Grades, the total effects are the same as the indirect effects. In contrast, the total effect of Ethnicity on Grades is very small (.025), and I would probably consider it nonmeaningful. The reason this effect is so small is that the positive indirect effect of Ethnicity through Previous Achievement is canceled out by the negative indirect effect through Homework.

With the use of a single indicator accounting for the likely error in the measured variable, the latent variable Ethnicity behaves like all the other latent variables in the model. Note that the loading of Ethnic on Ethnicity (standardized) was .97 (Figure 16.2). This value is simply a function of the reliability estimate used to fix the error variance (the standardized loading is equal to $\sqrt{r_{tt}}$, with r_{tt} equal to the estimate of the reliability used to constrain the error). Another option is to simply have Ethnic appear as a measured, rather than latent variable, an option that does not recognize the error inherent in the

Standardized Total Effects

	Ethnicity	Family_Background	Previous_Achievement	Homework	Grades
Previous_Achievement	.087	.529	.000	.000	.000
Homework	-.072	.417	.413	.000	.000
Grades	.025	.388	.631	.274	.000

Standardized Direct Effects

	Ethnicity	Family_Background	Previous_Achievement	Homework	Grades
Previous_Achievement	.087	.529	.000	.000	.000
Homework	-.108	.198	.413	.000	.000
Grades	.000	.000	.518	.274	.000

Standardized Indirect Effects

	Ethnicity	Family_Background	Previous_Achievement	Homework	Grades
Previous_Achievement	.000	.000	.000	.000	.000
Homework	.036	.219	.000	.000	.000
Grades	.025	.388	.113	.000	.000

FIGURE 16.7 Standardized direct, indirect, and total effects for the initial homework model.

variable. As a result of building error into this variable, the standardized estimates of the effects from Ethnicity are slightly larger than they would have been without recognition of this error.

Note that I simply made an educated guess as to the likely reliability of the Ethnic variable. If reliability estimates are available for a variable, or a similar variable, use them, but sometimes a guess is the best you can do. In such cases, it may be worthwhile to try different values for the reliability (e.g., .90 or .98 versus .95) to make sure you have a good understanding of what happens to the parameters of interest when you make these changes.

If you return to Figure 16.2 and focus on the correlated errors, you will see that the correlated error between the Math test and subsequent Math grades is substantial (.33), suggesting that these measures indeed share something in common (specific math achievement) above and beyond the effect of general achievement on overall grades. The other correlated errors are smaller, but all except one (History 8th–History) are statistically significant. The expectation for the existence of correlated errors is probably reasonable.

Competing Models

We may wonder if, indeed, Ethnicity and Family Background *really* only affect Grades indirectly, only through Previous Achievement and Homework. We could test this hypothesis by comparing the initial model to one in which paths are estimated from Ethnicity and Family Background to Grades. The fit statistics for this model are shown in Table 16.2

under the label Direct Background Effects. The model in which the background variables affect Grades directly results in a smaller χ^2 (202.263), but the change in χ^2 is not statistically significant ($\Delta\chi^2 = 2.187$, $df = 2$, $p = .335$). When $\Delta\chi^2$ is not statistically significant, our rule of thumb is to prefer the more parsimonious model, which is the initial model in Figure 16.2. In other words, yes, it appears that Ethnicity and Family Background only affect Grades indirectly, not directly.

TABLE 16.2 Comparison of the Fit of Alternative Homework Models

MODEL	χ^2	df	$\Delta\chi^2$	Δdf	p	AIC	PCFI	RMSEA (90% CI)
Initial	204.450	66				282.450	.713	.046 (.039–.053)
Direct Background Effects	202.263	64	2.187	2	.335	284.263	.692	.047 (.039–.054)
No Correlated Errors	319.412	70	114.962	4	<.001	389.412	.746	.060 (.053–.066)
No Homework Effect	235.867	67	31.417	1	<.001	311.867	.721	.050 (.043–.057)

Was the assumption that the error–unique variances are correlated across similar tests and grades really necessary? To test the veracity of this assumption, we can delete these correlated errors from the model and compare the fit of this No Correlated Errors model with the initial model. This new model is more parsimonious than the initial model because it includes four fewer parameters to be estimated (the four correlated errors), so if the models fit equally well, we would prefer the more parsimonious No Correlated Errors model. The fit indexes for the model are also shown in Table 16.2. The deletion of the correlated errors resulted in a $\Delta\chi^2$ of 114.962, with four df. This increase in χ^2 is statistically significant, meaning that the No Correlated Errors model, although more parsimonious, resulted in a statistically significantly worse fit to the data than did the initial model. Our rule of thumb is that if the $\Delta\chi^2$ is statistically significant we prefer the less parsimonious model. The increase in parsimony is not worth the cost of additional misfit; the initial model appears a better representation of the effect of these variables on Grades; the correlated errors are needed. [It is also worth noting that the RMSEA for this model is not particularly good, and even its 90% CI does not include our cutoff for a good model (.05). We might have rejected this model even based on the RMSEA used as a stand-alone fit index.]

We may also want to test directly the statistical significance of the effect of Homework on Grades by comparing the initial model to one in which the path from Homework to Grades is set to zero. The previous two competing models essentially tested assumptions underlying the initial model, whereas this competing model tests the substantive research question guiding the research: whether homework affects high school grades. The fit of this model is also summarized in Table 16.2. When this No Homework Effect model is compared to the initial model, the $\Delta\chi^2$ is 31.417 ($df = 1$, $p < .001$). Although the No Homework Effect model is more parsimonious, the parsimony (the extra df) resulted in too great a cost in model fit; the χ^2 increase is statistically significant. Yes, Homework indeed has a strong and statistically significant effect on students' high school GPA. Of course, we would come to this same conclusion through examination of the statistical significance of the Homework to Grades path in the original model (Figure 16.4).

Model Modifications

Should we consider other, post hoc model modifications? One possible modification was already discussed: constraining the correlated error between History test scores and History GPA to zero, thus specifying that these error and unique variances are not correlated. This additional constraint results in a worse fit of the model (increase in χ^2), but this change will likely not be statistically significant.

We may wonder if there are model modifications we can make that will *improve* the fit of the model. Because our initial model fit well, this change may have lower priority than it would have if the model did not fit well; but it is still worth exploring if for no other reason than to reinforce the concepts presented in previous chapters. Figure 16.8 shows the modification indexes greater than 4 (not all are listed for space reasons). The largest modification index is for the covariance between r6 and d2 and suggests that χ^2 can be lowered by at least 28.05 by freeing the correlation between the error of measurement for the 8th-grade Math test and the disturbance for Homework. Allowing such a change suggests that the Math Test and Homework share something in common, or have a common cause, other than those shown in the model. Although we could probably make up all sorts of reasons why this might be if we tried hard enough, there is no real theoretical or research-based reason to allow such a correlation. Another possibility is to free the covariance between the Math test unique–error variance and the disturbance for Grades (modification index = 21.132), but this change also makes little sense. In a related fashion, the modification indexes for regression weights suggest that we consider allowing a path from Homework to Math Achievement test scores (20.912) or from Science grades to Math test scores (21.287). Again, these modification indexes make little sense, other than to suggest that the 8th-grade Math test score seems to be a general source of misfit in the model.

Figure 16.9 shows the standardized residual covariances, our other method of isolating sources of misfit in the model. There are no especially large standardized residuals, which is consistent with our overall satisfaction with the model fit. If we arbitrarily pick a value of ± 2 as representing a larger standardized residual, there are three large values in the matrix. Consistent with the speculation that the Math test score is something of a source of misfit, two of these large values are with the 8th-grade Math test (bytxmstd). They suggest that the model does not adequately account for the correlation between the math test and 8th-grade homework time (hw_8) or 12th-grade science GPA. The third large standardized residual suggests that the model does not completely account for the correlation between the Ethnic measured variable and Family Income. Again, we are not slapping ourselves on the head, thinking "I can't believe I did not think of that before (and build it into the model)!" There are no really compelling reasons to relax any of the constraints in the model to improve the fit.

MULTISAMPLE MODELS

Our previous homework models included the variable Ethnicity. This variable was included for the simple reason that it is often included as a background variable in such models,

Covariances

	M.I.	Par Change
r9 <-->d3	5.461	-.155
r14<-->d2	4.042	-.133
r12<-->r13	10.441	.222
r8 <-->d2	6.712	-.769
r8 <-->r9	6.483	-.531
r7 <-->Ethnicity	6.788	.216
r7 <-->d3	10.663	-1.230
r7 <-->r11	11.075	-.794
r7 <-->r8	6.160	2.866
r6 <-->Ethnicity	9.522	-.251
r6 <-->Family_Background	8.285	9.729
r6 <-->d2	28.050	1.526
r6 <-->d3	21.132	1.688
r6 <-->r9	7.955	.571
r6 <-->r13	6.817	.697
r6 <-->r8	13.541	-4.148
r2 <-->Ethnicity	17.664	-.053
r2 <-->d1	5.900	.564
r3 <-->Ethnicity	17.316	.115
r1 <-->r7	5.743	.197
r1 <-->r6	6.493	-.205
r1 <-->r2	18.380	-.053
r1 <-->r3	17.347	.114

Regression Weights

	M.I.	Par Change
hw_8 <--- bytxmstd	4.546	.007
Sci_12 <--- Math_12	5.365	.038
Sci_12 <--- bytxmstd	5.329	.010
eng_12 <--- bytxsstd	6.293	-.010
bytxhstd <--- hw_8	7.752	-.479
bytxsstd <--- Ethnicity	4.822	1.004
bytxsstd <--- Grades	6.760	-.209
bytxsstd <--- Sci_12	4.924	-.159
bytxsstd <--- eng_12	11.603	-.246
bytxsstd <--- Ethnic	4.891	.961
bytxmstd <--- Ethnicity	5.668	-1.065
bytxmstd <--- Homework	20.912	1.024
bytxmstd <--- Grades	16.586	.321
bytxmstd <--- hw_8	15.356	.655
bytxmstd <--- hw10	9.556	.307
bytxmstd <--- ss_12	11.112	.219
bytxmstd <--- Sci_12	21.287	.324
bytxmstd <--- Math_12	10.536	.228
bytxmstd <--- eng_12	16.159	.284
bytxmstd <--- bypared	5.130	.334
bytxmstd <--- Ethnic	5.737	-1.018
bypared <--- Ethnicity	15.925	-.277
bypared <--- Homework	5.914	.084
bypared <--- Grades	4.378	.026
bypared <--- hw_8	4.089	.053

FIGURE 16.8   Modification indexes for the initial homework model.

although our analyses suggested that Ethnicity did not need to be considered to make the model valid. The results of the Ethnicity variable are interesting, however, in that our analyses suggested that Ethnicity has no effect on high school GPA and that minority students spend more time on homework than do majority students. Perhaps more importantly for our purpose, its inclusion allowed the illustration of the use of a single-indicator latent variable.

A Multisample Homework Model across Ethnic Groups

Now I want you to consider another possibility. Our explorations so far have suggested that Ethnicity has no effect on GPA. It could be the case, however, that Homework has different effects on GPA depending on students' ethnic group membership. Previous research, for example, has suggested that homework may have larger effects on learning outcomes for minority, as opposed to majority, students (Keith, 1993; Keith & Benson, 1992). If this is the case, it means that a teacher or school that increased homework demands can expect this homework to pay off in increased learning for all students, but to result in an even larger increase in learning for minority students. If this sort of speculation sounds methodologically familiar, it should.

Standardized Residual Covariances

	hw_8	hw10	ss_12	Sci_12	Math_12	eng_12	bytxhstd	bytxsstd	bytxmstd	bytxrstd	bypared	byfaminc	parocc	Ethnic
hw_8	.000													
hw10	.136	.000												
ss_12	-1.180	-.105	-.027											
Sci_12	-.580	.137	-.284	-.176										
Math_12	-.623	1.109	.212	1.243	.813									
eng_12	-.531	.681	.141	-.303	.399	-.044								
bytxhstd	-.618	-1.204	.014	-.180	-.919	-.424	.051							
bytxsstd	.969	-1.310	-.582	-.781	-.878	-1.714	.537	.038						
bytxmstd	2.508	1.122	1.704	2.482	1.129	1.509	-.846	.095	-.149					
bytxrstd	1.047	-.997	.216	-.280	-.959	-.530	.373	-.162	-.265	-.067				
bypared	.768	.619	1.130	.391	.894	1.206	.685	.190	1.551	.105	.000			
byfaminc	-1.382	-.031	.346	-.721	.237	-.038	-.055	-.606	.639	-.854	-.318	.000		
parocc	-1.037	-.263	-.490	-1.202	-.915	-.735	-.427	-1.259	-.064	-.891	.105	.165	.000	
Ethnic	-.598	.851	-.421	-1.147	-1.233	-.871	.378	.960	-1.223	.041	-1.908	2.684	.590	.000

FIGURE 16.9   Standardized residual covariances for the initial homework model.

What we are talking about is the possibility of testing an *interaction* between Ethnic background and Homework in their effects on Grades. Another way of stating this is that we are interested in whether Ethnic background *moderates* the effect of Homework on Grades.

Conceptually, we can test this hypothesis by analyzing a homework model separately for minority and majority students and then comparing the effect of homework on grades for the two groups. Such a model is illustrated in Figure 16.10; we can analyze the model for majority students and find the unstandardized value for the path from Homework to Grades (denoted with a question mark in the figure). We can then analyze the model for minority students and examine the same path. We might even put a 95% confidence interval around one of the coefficients and see if the other value was within this interval, as we did with regression coefficients in Chapter 2.

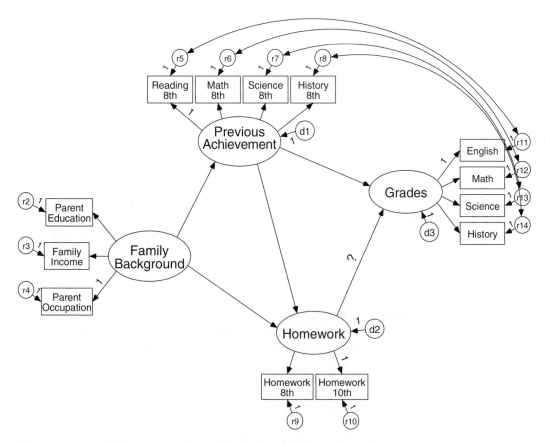

FIGURE 16.10   Multisample analysis of the effects of Homework on Grades for majority and minority students. This model makes no constraints across groups.

Before moving on, make sure you understand why Ethnicity does not appear in the model (because it is the variable on which the sample is divided into subsamples). Also, make sure you understand why I said to use the unstandardized paths (review the reasons in Chapter 2).

Constraining Parameters across Groups.   Although this method will work, there is a better method for testing the equivalence of this path, and other parts of the model, across groups. Within Amos and other SEM programs, it is possible to test *multisample* models, which generally means the same model tested across two or more groups. With such models, it is possible to constrain parameters to be equal across groups and compare the fit of these constrained models to models without constraints. An example will illustrate.

Figure 16.10 also illustrates the basic, or initial, model for the multisample analysis. The identical model is specified for each group (minority and majority), and each group's model is estimated from its own data matrix. Both models are estimated within a single analysis. Thus, Figure 16.10 represents the input model for one group; the model for the other group is identical. In Amos, this is accomplished using the Manage Groups option under the Model-Fit menu. The manuals of other SEM programs will detail their method for conducting multisample analyses. The file "initial multi sample model.amw" shows this initial model, and the files "majority matrix.xls" and "minority matrix.xls" contain Excel versions of the correlation matrices, means, and standard deviations necessary to estimate the models.[1] If you are using the student version of Amos, you can still view the model, although it contains too many variables to estimate with the student version.

This initial model has no constraints across the two groups; the path from Homework to Grades is not constrained to be equal for minority and majority students, nor are there any other constraints. The reason is that this represents the baseline model to which we will compare models with such constraints. The fit statistics for the multisample analysis represent the fit of "*all* models in all groups" (Jöreskog & Sörbom, 1993, p. 54). With no constraints across groups, the χ^2 and degrees of freedom for the multisample analysis are the same as if we had analyzed the majority model and minority model separately and added together the values (the χ^2 is not always identical, but should be quite close).

Figures 16.11 and 16.12 show the unstandardized output for the unconstrained multisample model for minority and majority students, respectively. First note the fit indexes. The χ^2 for the initial multisample analysis was 219.576, with 112 degrees of freedom. In contrast, separate analyses showed χ^2 equal to 92.097 (56 *df*) for minority students and 127.401 (56 *df*) for majority students, which sums to 219.498 (112 *df*); the initial model, with no constraints across groups, has essentially the same fit (χ^2) as the two groups analyzed separately. The RMSEA for the multisample analysis was .031, suggesting a good fit. Steiger (1998) has argued that the RMSEA should be adjusted in multisample analyses, however, by multiplying it by the square root of the number of groups analyzed:

$$RMSEA_{adjusted} = RMSEA \times \sqrt{numbergroups}$$
$$= .031 \times \sqrt{2}$$
$$= .044$$

This adjusted value, .044, is closer to the average of the RMSEAs when the two groups are analyzed separately (.041 and .049), but also suggests a good fit of the models to the data across the two groups.[2] The other stand-alone fit indexes (GFI, TLI, CFI) also suggest a good fit of the model to the data across groups, as does the SRMR (.041; not shown in the figure). The initial model appears to fit well and should serve as a good baseline for comparing subsequent models.

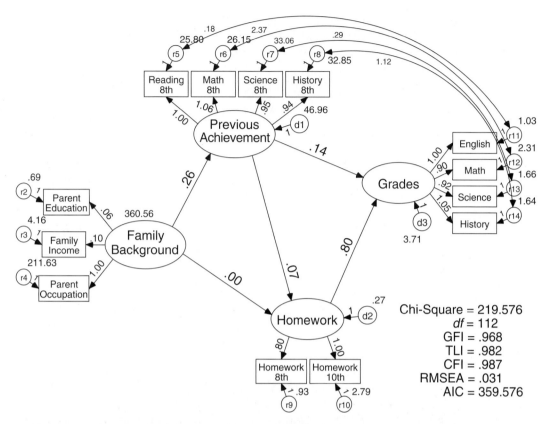

FIGURE 16.11   Unstandardized output for the unconstrained multisample homework model. These results are for minority students.

Our primary interest, of course, is whether the path from Homework to Grades is the same across groups. For minority students, the unstandardized effect was .80, versus .47 for majority students. Perhaps homework does have different effects for the two groups! Although if we use standard errors (.637 minority and .114 majority), we will be tempted to say that the two parameters are not different from one another, we will make such tests more directly in just a minute. Interestingly, the standardized paths for minority and majority students are nearly identical (.24 and .25), illustrating again the fact that the standardized and unstandardized coefficients may produce different answers to the question of equivalence across groups (again, the reasons for focusing on unstandardized as opposed to standardized coefficients for such comparisons are spelled out in Chapter 2).

Our baseline model fits well; let's now compare it to several models in which we add constraints across groups. In Amos, the way to add constraints across groups is to fix the relevant parameters to some alphabetic (not numeric) label. We can, for example, set the path from Homework to Grades to a value of *a* for both groups (or "path1" or some other label). This constraint will allow the parameter to be estimated, but will constrain the (unstandardized) estimate to be identical across the two groups.

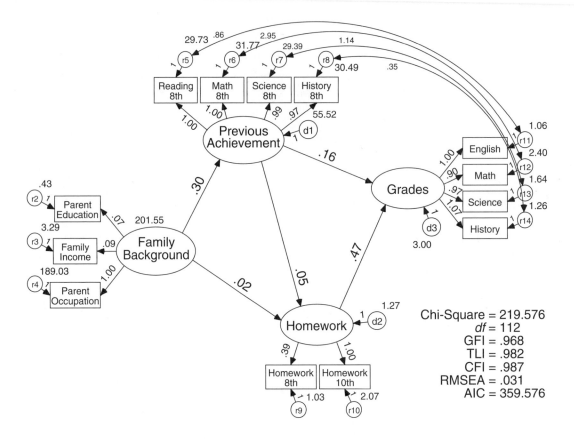

FIGURE 16.12   Unstandardized output for the unconstrained multisample homework model. These results are for majority students.

Measurement Constraints.   Although our primary interest is in comparing the Homework to Grades path across groups, the first model to be compared actually involves a different set of constraints. The model shown in Figure 16.13 sets the factor loadings from all latent to measured variables to be the same across groups. The model shown is the setup for minority students. As in all previous models, note that one factor loading from each latent variable is set to 1.0. In addition, however, the other factor loadings are set to specific labels (fl2, for factor loading, through fl14). The model for majority students, if displayed, will show the same constraints for the factor loadings, thus constraining these loadings to be equal for minority and majority students.

Why start with constraints on factor loadings? Basically, this constraint specifies that the latent variables (Homework, Grades, etc.) are the same across the two groups. This specification means that we are measuring the same thing across groups, that our variables of interest mean the same thing for minority students as for majority students. Consider for a minute what it would mean if Homework meant something different for one group compared to the other. If Homework has one meaning for one group and a different meaning for another, then it really doesn't make much sense to ask whether Homework has the same

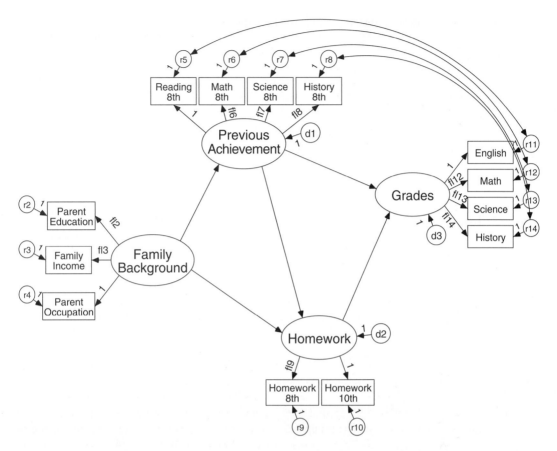

FIGURE 16.13   Multisample homework model with factor loadings constrained to be equal across groups. Model specification for minority students.

effect across the two groups, does it? Differences in the measurement model (factor structures) across groups suggest a difference in the constructs being measured. You will also hear this step of comparisons referred to as testing the invariance of the factor or measurement model across groups.

Table 16.3 shows the fit statistics for this Compare Loadings model in comparison to the initial model. There are 9 additional degrees of freedom for this model, representing the 9 factor loadings that were constrained to be equal across groups (one factor loading per latent variable was already set to 1 for both groups). The model is more parsimonious than the initial model, and thus χ^2 is larger. However, the $\Delta\chi^2$ was not statistically significant, meaning that the additional constraints are justified. The specification that the factor loadings of the latent variables be identical across groups cannot be rejected; the measured variables represent the same constructs for minority and majority youth; the latent variables have the same meaning across groups. Given that we are measuring the same constructs across groups, we can now determine whether these latent constructs have the same *effects* on each other across groups.

TABLE 16.3   Comparison of Multisample Homework Models

MODEL	χ^2	df	$\Delta\chi^2$	Δdf	p	AIC	PCFI	RMSEA
Initial	219.576	112				359.576	.708	.044
Compare Loadings	235.591	121	16.015	9	.067	357.591	.765	.042
Compare Homework Effect	236.522	122	.931	1	.335	356.522	.771	.042
Compare All Effects	241.323	126	4.801	4	.308	353.323	.796	.042
Compare Errors	288.262	147	46.939	21	<.001	358.262	.926	.044

Does Homework Have the Same Effect across Groups?   The next step in model comparison answers the question in which we are most interested: whether Homework has the same effect on Grades across groups. The model specification for minority students is shown in Figure 16.14. For this model, all the constraints from the last model (Compare Loadings) are retained, and one new constraint is added. For both groups, the path from Homework to Grades was set to a value of *a*, meaning that the path will be freely estimated, but that the unstandardized path will be constrained to be equal across groups.

The $\Delta\chi^2$ and other fit indexes for this Compare Homework Effect model are also shown in Table 16.3. As you can see, the $\Delta\chi^2$ was not statistically significant. The additional constraint specifying that the effect of Homework on Grades be identical for minority and majority students did not lead to a statistically significant degradation in the fit of the model. It appears, then, that homework has about the same effect on high school students' grades whether they come from minority ethnic backgrounds or not. When students spend time on homework it will have approximately the same effect on grades whatever their ethnic background (at least for the gross division of majority–minority). Another way of saying this is that there is no interaction between Ethnic background and Homework in their effects on high school Grades, or that Ethnicity does not appear to *moderate* the effect of Homework on Grades.

Other Effects.   There may be several other comparisons of interest to pursue in these multisample analyses. Although it appears that Homework has the same effect on Grades for both groups, we may wonder if the other variables in the model have the same effects on each other across groups. In essence, we are asking if *any* of the variables interact with Ethnicity in their effects on other variables in the model. To test this possibility, we can simply set all other paths (Family Background to Previous Achievement, and so on) in the model to be the same across groups. For this model, four additional constraints are required beyond those for the Compare Homework Effect model. The results of this Compare All Effects model are also shown in Table 16.3. Again, this more constrained model did not lead to a statistically significant $\Delta\chi^2$. It appears that all the effects of one latent variable on another in the model are consistent across groups; the variables in the model have the same effects on each other for minority as for majority youth.

None of the models so far has made constraints on the errors of measurement or the disturbances. Both of these types of parameters represent errors of some sort, either errors

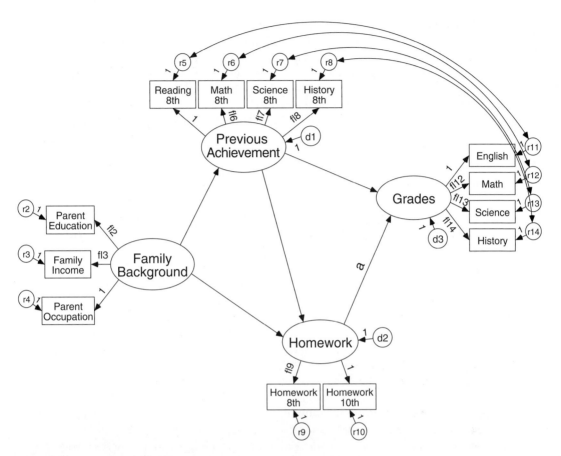

FIGURE 16.14   Multisample homework model testing the equivalence of the effects of Homework on high school GPA across groups.

of measurement (r2 through r14) or the variance left unexplained by the other variables in the model (d1 through d3). These parameters do not really represent substantive portions of the model, and thus it is probably not reasonable to expect them to be invariant across groups (Marsh, 1993). Likewise, I can think of no substantive reason why the variance of the exogenous variable (Family Background) or the correlated errors (between the test scores and corresponding grades) should be expected to be equal across groups. For these reasons, these "errors" were not constrained to be equal across groups in any of the models, and we could reasonably stop our model testing without such constraints. For our present purposes, however, it will be instructive to see if these nonsubstantive parameters are indeed equivalent across groups.

The results for the Compare Errors model are shown in the bottom row of Table 16.3. For this model, 13 measurement errors (r2 through r14), three disturbances, the variance of the Family Background latent variable, and the four correlated errors are constrained to be the same for the two groups. These 21 additional constraints resulted in a statistically significant increase in $\Delta\chi^2$. Taken together, these equality constraints across the two groups resulted in a considerable degradation in model fit. The errors and other nonsubstantive aspects of the models, as expected, are not identical across groups. If desired, we can fix or free these parameters in smaller blocks to see exactly where the differences are (less formally, we can compare the unstandardized parameters for the models shown in Figures 16.11 and 16.12 to look for differences).

Figures 16.15 and 16.16 show the standardized estimates for the Compare All Effects model for minority and majority students, respectively. Of course, for this model the factor loadings and paths are set to be equal across groups, so in the *unstandardized* estimates they will be the same for majority and minority youth. Note the minor differences, however, for the standardized estimates across groups. Again, the unstandardized coefficients should be used to compare across groups; standardized estimates should only be used for interpretations within each group. Nevertheless, our interpretation of effects will be similar within each group and also consistent with the estimates for the overall model given earlier in the chapter.

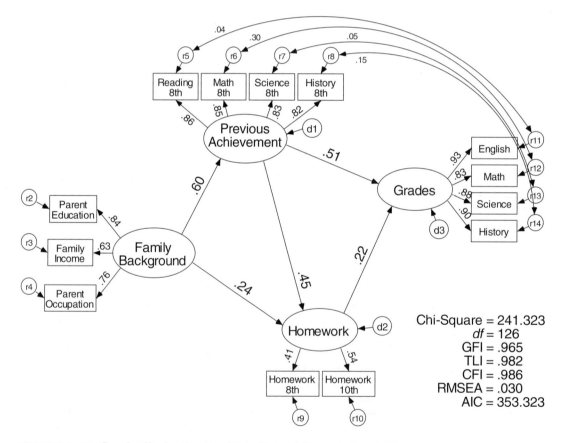

Chi-Square = 241.323
df = 126
GFI = .965
TLI = .982
CFI = .986
RMSEA = .030
AIC = 353.323

FIGURE 16.15   Standardized estimates of the effects of Homework and other influences on GPA for minority students. These results pertain to the model in which all influences were constrained to be equal across groups.

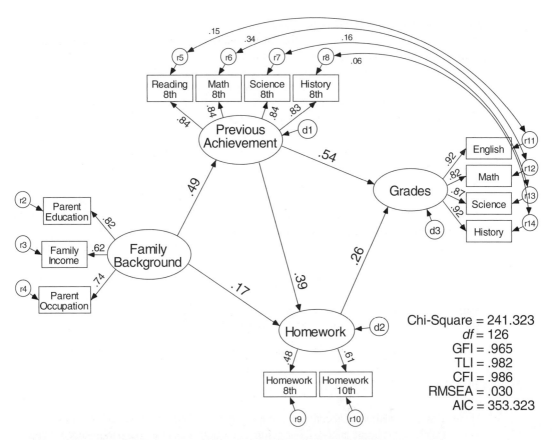

FIGURE 16.16   Standardized estimates for the fully constrained model for majority students. The *standardized* estimates differ across groups because constraints were made for unstandardized parameters.

Summary: Multisample Models.   This series of analyses has illustrated a method for conducting tests of interactions in SEM via the comparison of nested, multisample models. The method can be used to test for an interaction between a single categorical variable and a single continuous variable or, more broadly, between one categorical variable and *all* other variables in the model. This broader orientation (e.g., the Compare All Effects model) essentially asks if entire models are comparable across groups and may be of interest when you have questions such as "Are the variables that influence the learning of Whites also important for minority students?" Such questions are common. For example, in the 1980s, one outcome of the controversial report *A Nation at Risk* (National Commission on Excellence in Education, 1983) was a proposal for an ideal, academic high school curriculum (Bennett, 1987). Columnist William Rasberry (1987) agreed that such a curriculum should work well for White and middle-class youth, but wondered if it would work equally well for minority youth. One way to test this question would be to test a multisample school learning model across various ethnic groups (e.g., Keith & Benson, 1992).

    There is nothing sacred about the order in which I tested successive models. It is just as defensible to begin with the most constrained model and gradually free parameters.

Different groupings of constraints will also work well. For example, I could have constrained parameters one at a time, rather than as a block, in going from the Compare Homework Effect model to the Compare All Effects model. The main considerations in this process of model comparison should be that you do them in a logical, systematic fashion and that you understand exactly what is and what is not being tested at each step.

There is also one additional model that is sometimes tested in such analyses. We could also compare the overall covariance matrix for majority youth with that of minority youth. Consider that all the models that we have estimated are derived from the covariance matrices. Thus, if we specify that the two covariance matrices be identical across groups, this means that we are specifying that *all* aspects of the model be identical across groups, but without specifying a model. In essence, this comparison says, "I don't know (or don't care) what the model is, but whatever it is, it's the same across groups." This model is thus nested with, but less constrained than the Compare Errors model, and the difference between the two represents the cost of specifying a *particular* model.

This example has illustrated multisample models as a method of testing for an interaction between a categorical variable and other variables in a SEM. There are also methods of testing for interactions between continuous variables in SEMs, but they are beyond the scope of this book. Schumacker and Marcoulides (1998) is a good resource for more information about this method. In tests of invariance of structures across groups, it is also possible to test for invariance in means and intercepts; this topic is also beyond the scope of this book, but is covered in most SEM program manuals.

REPLICATION AND CROSS-VALIDATION

There is another method of accomplishing essentially the same purpose as with multisample models. With multisample analysis, our guiding question is whether the parameters of interest (e.g., paths, factor loadings) are the same across two or more groups. Another way of approaching this problem is to first estimate the model for one group and then estimate a model for a second group in which the parameters of interest are constrained to the values for the first group.

Using One Sample to Set Constraints in Another

As an example, I first estimated the earlier model for majority students alone; the unstandardized parameter estimates are shown in Figure 16.17. In a second analysis, the unstandardized factor loadings and paths were constrained to the majority group values during the estimation of the same model for minority youth. The model used as the *input* for this analysis is shown in Figure 16.18. The relevant fit indexes for this constrained minority model are adequate to good (e.g., RMSEA = .052, CFI = .977, SRMR = .055). Of greater interest, this constrained model may be compared to alternative models with fewer constraints. Table 16.4 shows several such comparisons. Interestingly, using this method, constraining factor loadings resulted in a statistically significant increase in $\Delta\chi^2$ and thus, if this is our primary criterion for model fit, we conclude that the constructs in the model in fact measure something different for minority as compared to majority students. The next step is to isolate the particular area of difference. The restriction of the equivalence of the paths, however, resulted in $\Delta\chi^2$ that was not statistically significant.

Regression Weights (Majority)

			Estimate	S.E.	C.R.	P
Previous_Achievement	<---	Family_Background	.299	.027	11.056	***
Homework	<---	Family_Background	.022	.006	3.655	***
Homework	<---	Previous_Achievement	.046	.009	4.914	***
Grades	<---	Previous_Achievement	.156	.012	13.213	***
Grades	<---	Homework	.468	.114	4.116	***
parocc	<---	Family_Background	1.000			
byfaminc	<---	Family_Background	.094	.007	14.103	***
bypared	<---	Family_Background	.072	.004	16.226	***
bytxrstd	<---	Previous_Achievement	1.000			
bytxmstd	<---	Previous_Achievement	.997	.036	28.003	***
bytxsstd	<---	Previous_Achievement	.987	.035	28.085	***
bytxhstd	<---	Previous_Achievement	.970	.035	27.506	***
eng_12	<---	Grades	1.000			
Math_12	<---	Grades	.901	.028	32.133	***
Sci_12	<---	Grades	.972	.026	37.541	***
ss_12	<---	Grades	1.065	.026	41.649	***
hw10	<---	Homework	1.000			
hw_8	<---	Homework	.389	.063	6.176	***

Covariances (Majority)

	Estimate	S.E.	C.R.	P
r5 <--> r11	.859	.289	2.969	.003
r6 <--> r12	2.949	.400	7.382	***
r7 <--> r13	1.138	.327	3.481	***
r8 <--> r14	.349	.310	1.126	.260

Variances (Majority)

	Estimate	S.E.	C.R.	P
Family_Background	201.550	20.393	9.883	***
d1	55.518	4.256	13.045	***
d2	1.269	.275	4.620	***
d3	3.001	.215	13.969	***
r4	189.029	14.130	13.378	***
r3	3.294	.197	16.690	***
r2	.430	.056	7.681	***
r5	29.735	2.044	14.546	***
r6	31.774	2.135	14.880	***
r7	29.387	2.009	14.631	***
r8	30.494	2.046	14.907	***
r11	1.059	.085	12.488	***
r12	2.398	.141	17.003	***
r13	1.643	.108	15.251	***
r14	1.260	.099	12.762	***
r10	2.070	.282	7.350	***
r9	1.026	.066	15.441	***

FIGURE 16.17 Testing the equivalence across groups using a replication methodology. These results are for majority students analyzed alone.

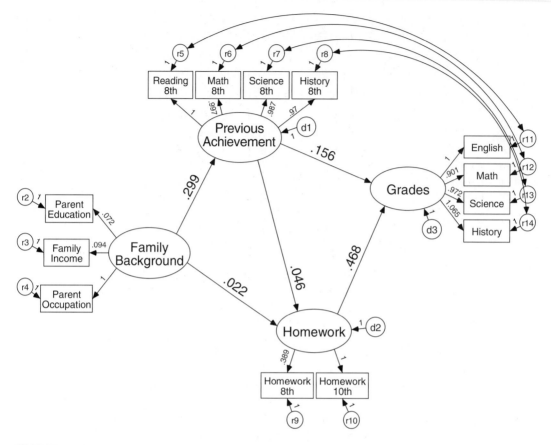

FIGURE 16.18   Unstandardized estimates from Figure 16.17 were used to make these constraints in the input model for minority students.

TABLE 16.4   Homework Model Comparisons for Minority Students with Values Fixed to Those for Majority Students

MODEL	χ^2	df	$\Delta\chi^2$	Δdf	p	AIC	PCFI	RMSEA
All Free	92.097	56				197.401	.709	.041
Fixed Loadings	113.957	65	21.860	9	.009	165.957	.815	.053
Fixed Loadings and Paths	121.571	70	7.614	5	.179	163.571	.877	.052

This difference in findings depending on the method used is disconcerting. And although I have presented this method as an alternative to the multisample method, you should recognize that the questions asked by the two methods are subtly different. For the multisample method, we are asking whether the parameters are the same for the two groups.

With the current method, we are asking whether the parameters for one group (in this case, minority students) are the same as those we obtained when the model was freely estimated for a different group. It may help to think of it this way: for the first method, the misfit is essentially spread out across two groups, whereas with the second all the misfit is confined to the second group. Thus, if given the choice, I will likely use the multisample method rather than the constrain-the-second group method.

Multisample versus Replication Models.   In certain circumstances, the method of constraining parameters in one group to values found for another group can be very useful, such as in questions of replication. Suppose that, instead of having data for both majority and minority students, your data were for minority students only. You might then reasonably ask if the parameters and influences for minority youth are the same as for those found in a previously published article. That is, consider the values for majority youth as the "previously published" findings. As you conduct your research with minority youth, you might reasonably ask, as one of your research questions, whether the same parameters and influences hold for majority youth. In earlier chapters we discussed the issue of replication in multiple regression analysis; the ability to set parameters to previously obtained values is a powerful method of testing for replication in SEM. (This example also illustrates the importance of publishing, or otherwise making available, unstandardized results. Of course, if the previous research published a covariance matrix, it would also be possible to conduct a multisample analysis.)

There are other instances when this method of replication may be useful. Suppose that two researchers conduct research to address the same question (e.g., the effect of homework on learning), but define the constructs in their models differently (e.g., by using different measures of learning, or homework, or previous achievement). We can use this method to determine whether the effects are consistent across samples, even with different definitions of the constructs (by constraining paths only). We might wonder whether the effect of homework is the same for this generation as for previous or (subsequent) generations, and thus we could compare the results of these homework models with those from research using High School and Beyond, an earlier national longitudinal data base (cf. Keith, 1982; Wolfle & List, 2004).

Model Development.   With large data sets such as the full NELS data, we almost have an abundance of data. One option, especially in preliminary research in which we expect to make considerable model modifications, is to split the sample into several subsamples. With this approach, it is possible to use an initial subsample in an exploratory fashion or to fine-tune a model, and then use the other subsamples to cross-validate the initial findings, test hypotheses, and so on. The comparison can be informal or, more formally, by constraining parameters. Thus, this method of using one sample to fix parameters in a new sample can be used for cross-validation in SEM, as well (cf. Keith et al., 1998).

DANGERS, REVISITED

Recall that in Chapter 11 we discussed the dangers of path analysis in particular and nonexperimental research in general. Given that I have argued for the advantages of overidentified models (in Chapter 12) and latent variable models in the last few chapters, you may wonder if the fit statistics that result from using SEM programs to analyze overidentified models or the advantages of latent variables somehow obviate these dangers. Let's find out.

Omitted Common Causes

Throughout this book, I have argued that the biggest danger in nonexperimental research is the possibility of neglecting to include in the analysis an important common cause of the presumed cause and the presumed effect. As shown, a neglected common cause will result in inaccurate estimates of the effects of one variable on another. Do fit indexes and latent variables control this danger; do SEM programs alert you when you have neglected a common cause? Unfortunately, no.

Figure 16.19 shows the homework model analyzed at the beginning of this chapter. It is obvious that Previous Achievement is an important common cause of Grades and Homework. Previous Achievement had a large effect on both Homework ($\beta = .41$) and Grades (.52). What will happen if we delete it from the model? Will the fit statistics or some other aspect of feedback alert us to the deletion?

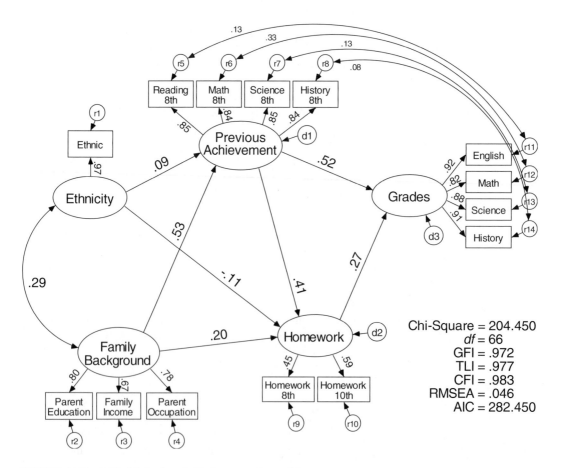

FIGURE 16.19   Initial, latent variable homework model.

Figure 16.20 shows the results of an analysis without Previous Achievement in the model. As expected and consistent with previous analyses, the apparent effect of Homework on Grades changed dramatically from the previous analysis. Also consistent with previous discussions, the omission of this important common cause led to an inflated estimate of the effect of Homework on Grades. In this model, the standardized effect of homework was .66, much inflated from the .27 value in earlier figures.

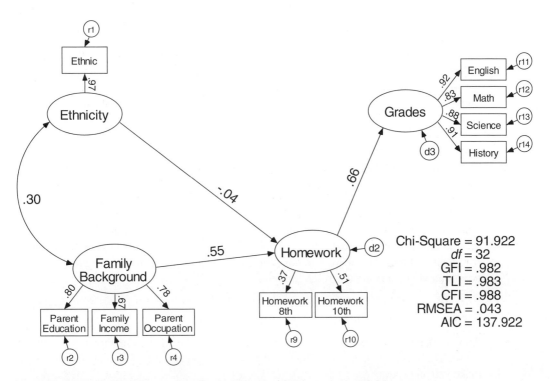

FIGURE 16.20   Homework model with the Previous Achievement variable omitted. The fit statistics do not alert us to the fact that we have not included an important common cause of Homework and GPA.

Notice the fit indexes accompanying the model. Obviously, it is not the case that the omission of an important common cause resulted in a worse fit; in fact, the model fits better without Previous Achievement in the model! (Of course, with different variables in the model, you can't compare the models formally, but at an informal level the model without the common cause shows a better fit.) Likewise, there is nothing in the more detailed fit information that suggests to you, the researcher, that you have done something wrong, such as neglecting an important variable. As this example illustrates, the fit statistics of latent variable SEM do not protect against the danger of omitted common causes; they do not alert us to any errors. If you think about it, this makes sense. The fit statistics can only tell us about the fit of the variables *in* the model; they can't inform us about things that are *not* included in the model.

In contrast, if we want to find out if Previous Achievement is indeed a common cause of Homework and Grades, we can put the variable in the model and set the path from Previous Achievement to either Homework or Grades (or both) to zero. In this case, the fit statistics will show a statistically significant degradation. But the common cause must be in the model to test it.

Path in the Wrong Direction

What about the other major danger in nonexperimental analysis: assuming a variable is an effect when it is really a cause (or vice versa)? Figure 16.21 shows the results of a model that is misspecified, with a path drawn in the wrong direction. In fact, unlike many models, we can be certain that this model is incorrect, because the Grades variable occurs in time mostly after the Homework variable. More importantly, using the rules for generating equivalent models from Chapter 12, this model is not equivalent with the original model from Figure 16.2. The Homework and Grades variables do not have the same variables pointing to them, and the path cannot be reversed and still have an equivalent model. The two models are not nested, however, because they have the same degrees of freedom. Thus, the two models should be comparable via fit statistics (e.g., the AIC) that do not require nested models. It is gratifying to see that the model with the path drawn in the correct direction (Figure 16.2) indeed had the lower AIC and thus the better fit. In this example, we would have chosen the model with the path drawn in the correct direction even without prior knowledge of the correct order of the variables. Yes, under the right conditions, with overidentified models that are also nonequivalent we *may* be able to guard against the danger of drawing paths in the wrong direction.

Incomplete Knowledge

Another danger is related to the complexity of SEM. Like all such methods, it is open to abuse. These few chapters constitute a very basic introduction to SEM and by no means make you an expert.

If you have read, understood, and worked through this section of the book, you should be fairly well equipped to be a good consumer of SEM research. You understand the primary dangers of nonexperimental methods and SEM; these dangers (e.g., omitted common causes) constitute the most likely serious problems with nonexperimental and SEM studies that you will encounter. You also have a beginning understanding of what you, and the researchers, should be looking for in SEM studies.

It is easy, however, to suspend critical judgment as you read research using complex statistical methods. The authors, after all, are the experts. Can't we assume they know what they are doing? Don't be "seduced by sophistication" (Wampold, 1987, p. 311). Yes, it may be harder to be a savvy consumer of SEM research, but just as necessary. Of course, you should also keep in mind that there is no perfect research; no study is immune to criticism, and your standard should not be unrealistically high.

These cautions are even more important for those conducting SEM research. SEM is not magic. No matter how sophisticated our analyses, they cannot turn bad data into good

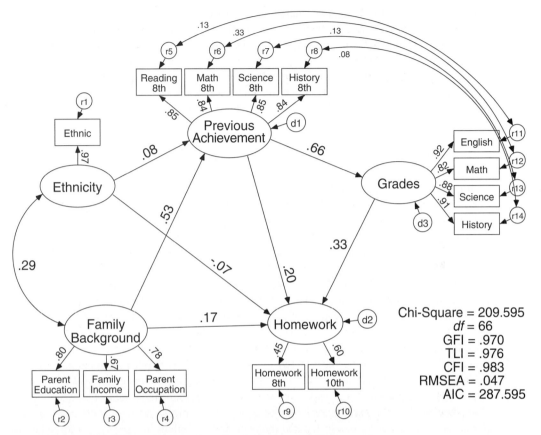

FIGURE 16.21   Path from Homework to Grades is incorrectly reversed in this model. The model has a worse fit than the initial model.

or a poor design into a powerful one. Even SEM cannot create a silk purse from a sow's ear. As with other research methods, "the manipulation of statistical formulas is no substitute for knowing what one is doing" (Blalock, 1972, p. 448).

For those who wish to conduct SEM research, these few chapters may have provided just enough information to make you dangerous. I hope these few chapters have excited you about the power and possibilities of SEM and to try out the method to test research questions of interest to you. If you want to play around with the method, you should, but I encourage you to work with someone who is more knowledgeable and experienced. If you plan to use SEM on a regular basis, further reading is needed. The next chapter will discuss the topics incompletely covered in this introduction and sources for further study.

SUMMARY

This chapter reviewed and built on the previous chapter and covered several more complex topics in latent variable SEM. We estimated a latent variable version of our earlier homework model. This model included two interesting features: a latent variable estimated from a single measured variable and correlations among the unique and error variances.

The latent variable homework model included one latent variable (Ethnicity) that was indexed by a single measured variable (Ethnic). The primary reason for doing this, rather than simply using only a measured variable, is to build into the model estimates of the error inherent in the measured variable and to take this error into account in the analysis. In the example, we estimated the Ethnic variable to have a reliability of .95, and thus 5% of the variance in Ethnic is attributable to error. To use this information in the model, we constrained the error variance of the measured Ethnic variable to be 5% of its total variance.

The homework model also included the specification of correlations between the unique and error variances of the 8th-grade Achievement test scores and high school Grades in related areas. The reason for specifying these correlated errors was to recognize that Grades and tests in a particular area (e.g., Mathematics) may share more than simply the effect of general achievement on general Grades. Our initial and subsequent comparative analyses showed that these correlated errors are indeed important and that removing them from the model resulted in a statistically significantly worse fit to the model.

We explored multisample models as a method of testing interactions between categorical and other variables in SEMs. To illustrate the method, we analyzed the homework model separately for majority (White) and minority youth in an effort to determine whether the effects of Homework on Grades are the same for both groups. The example gradually constrained parameters to be the same across groups and used $\Delta\chi^2$ to test the viability of these constraints. In the example, we showed that the constructs (latent variables) are equivalent across groups and that the variables in the model have the same effects on each other across groups. Homework, it appears, has the same effect on the learning of minority and majority youth.

The chapter also illustrated a method of replicating the results of one sample to another by using the parameters from one group to set constraints with another group. We analyzed the model for one group and then constrained values in a second group to be the same as the unstandardized values in the first group. This method can be used as a method of replicating the findings from one study to another. When large samples are available, the method can also be used to explore and modify a model in one subset of the data and then cross-validate the modified model in another subsample.

The final section of the chapter revisited some of the dangers we discussed previously in connection with structural equation modeling, path analysis, and nonexperimental research. Do the fit statistics and other advantages of SEM obviate these dangers? We showed that there is nothing in the fit statistics or other aspects of a latent variable SEM that will alert us when we neglect an important common cause in our models. In contrast, the measures of fit did alert us when we estimated a model with a path drawn in the wrong direction. This was only the case because we were working with an overidentified model and comparing the fit of two nonequivalent models. Latent variable SEM methodology does not protect against the danger of an omitted common cause; but if you plan carefully to construct nonequivalent models, you may be able to guard against the danger of a path drawn in the wrong direction.

A final danger, dealing with the complexity of SEM, was also raised. I encourage you to be intelligent consumers and educated conductors of SEM research. Explore the method, but to use it wisely, you will need to expand your knowledge of the method beyond the introduction provided by this book. Resources for further exploration will be discussed in the next, final chapter.

EXERCISES

1. If you have a full-featured SEM program, analyze the series of full homework models starting with the model shown in Figure 16.1. Make sure your results match those presented here. If you are using a student version of a program that places a limit on the number of variables you can analyze, try eliminating the Ethnicity variables, Family Income, and the Science and History Test and Grades variables. Estimate this smaller model; compare your results to those presented in this chapter. Are the results similar?

   a. Study the parameter estimates and standard errors, the fit statistics, modification indexes, and standardized residuals. Are there changes that you might make to the model? Are they theoretically justifiable?

   b. Interpret the model. Be sure to interpret the indirect and total effects in addition to the direct effects.

   c. Compare the model with the two competing models discussed in this chapter (the Direct Background Effects model and the No Homework Effect model).

2. Nancy Eisenberg and colleagues (2001) conducted research to determine the effects of mothers' emotions on their young children's behavior problems and social competence. One interest in the research was whether these effects are mediated by children's own emotional regulation. Figure 16.22 shows a model patterned after those in this article. It includes fewer variables, but still includes many interesting aspects of the original research. Mother's Positive Expressivity represents mothers' expression of positive emotions with their children, both as rated by the mothers and as observed during their work on a task. Child's Regulation, Externalizing, and Social Competence are latent variables representing these child characteristics, and each was rated both by the mothers and by teachers. The model includes correlated errors between the child ratings by the mother and the child ratings by the teacher. The model is contained in the Amos file "Eisenberg et al 1.amw." Simulated data designed to mimic the relevant portions of the correlation matrix presented in the article are contained within the Excel file "Eisenburg et al 2001.xls" and the SPSS file "Eisenburg et al 2001.sav"

TABLE 16.5 Variable Names and Variable Labels for the Eisenberg and Colleagues Model

VARIABLE NAME (EISENBERG ET AL 2001.XLS)	VARIABLE LABEL (FROM FIGURE 16.22)
Exp_mo	Expressivity Observed
Exp_msr	Expressivity Self-Report
Reg_mr	Mother Report (Child's Regulation latent variable)
Reg_tr	Teacher Report (Child's Regulation)
Exter_mr	Mother Report (Externalizing Problems)
Ext_tr	Teacher Report (Externalizing Problems)
Soc_mr	Mother Report (Social Competence)
Soc_tr	Teacher Report (Social Competence)

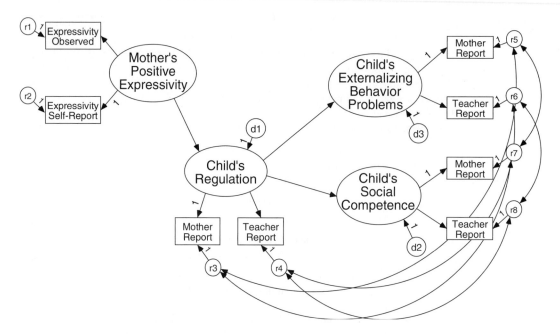

FIGURE 16.22   Model testing the effects of Mother's emotional expression on child outcomes. The model is drawn from Eisenberg et al., 2001.

on the accompanying Web site. The variable names in the data and the corresponding labels from the model are shown in Table 16.5.

a. Estimate the model as shown. Focus on the fit indexes and, if you judge them to be adequate, interpret the model.

b. Estimate a model without the correlated errors. What happens to the fit of the model? Were these parameters justified?

c. Compare the fit of this model with one in which Mother's Expressivity is also allowed to have direct effects on the two child outcomes. Based on the change in fit, would you say that children's Regulation completely or partially mediates the effect of Mother's Expressivity on Behavior Problems and Social Competence?

d. Calculate and interpret direct, indirect, and total effects for your accepted model.

e. Test any additional alternative models that are of interest.

N O T E S

1. Most SEM programs, including Amos, also allow the analysis of a single, raw data file, with some selection or grouping variable used to separate the two groups. We will not delve that deeply into program specifics here, but it is good to know that this option is available.

2. Some programs, such as Steiger's SEPATH, have the correction already built in, as do recent versions of LISREL.

CHAPTER SEVENTEEN

SUMMARY: PATH ANALYSIS, CFA, AND SEM

SUMMARY
  Path Analysis
  Error
  Confirmatory Factor Analysis
  Latent Variable SEM

ISSUES INCOMPLETELY OR NOT COVERED
  Maximum Likelihood Estimation
  Missing Values
  Sample Size, Number of Parameters, and Power

Differences across Programs
Longitudinal Models
Causality and the Veracity of Models

ADDITIONAL RESOURCES
  Introductory Texts
  More Advanced Resources
  Books about Specific SEM Programs
  Reporting SEM Results
  Cautions

Part 1 discussed multiple regression as a research tool. Part 2 has been concerned with the "And Beyond" portion of the title of the book and has focused on path analysis, confirmatory factor analysis, and structural equation modeling. This final chapter will begin with a review and summary of Part 2. I will then briefly discuss several topics about which you should be aware, but which are not covered in this text.

SUMMARY

Path Analysis

Basics. Throughout this book I have assumed that we are primarily interested in estimating the effects of one variable on another. We became even more explicit in this assumption in Part 2, where we focused on variations of structural equation modeling. The journey of SEM discovery started with path analysis, the simplest form of SEM.

If, through previous research, relevant theory, and logic, you can specify the likely causal relations among a set of variables, you can (given a few other conditions) estimate these effects using the correlations among the variables and simple algebra. Figure 17.1

shows such a model with the likely causal relations among the variables represented by paths. The paths represent a weak causal ordering, meaning that they do not assert that one variable directly affects another, but rather that if the two variables are causally related the influence is in the direction shown, rather than the reverse. If this model includes a one-way causal flow, we can forgo the algebra and use multiple regression to estimate the effects of one variable on another. These estimates, or paths, are estimated by the standardized and unstandardized coefficients in multiple regression. The paths to Achievement are estimated by the simultaneous regression of Achievement on Family Background, Ability, Motivation, and Coursework; the paths to Coursework are estimated using the regression coefficients from the regression of Coursework on Family Background, Ability, and Motivation; and so on. The standardized paths from disturbances, represented by the variables in ovals labeled d1 through d4, are estimated as $\sqrt{1 - R^2}$ from each regression equation. The disturbances represent all other influences on these variables beyond the variables in the model; many writers use the term residuals (consistent with MR) or errors instead of disturbances. We interpret the paths in much the same way as we did explanatory regressions in Part 1. The standardized paths (β's) represent the change in standard deviation units in the outcome for each standard deviation change in the influence, and the unstandardized paths (b's) represent the amount of change in the outcome for each 1-unit change in the influence.

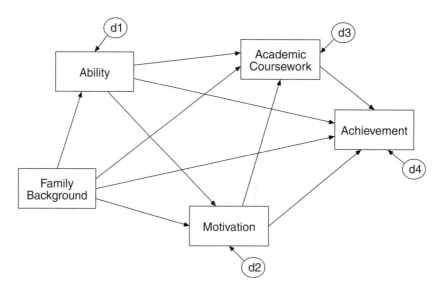

FIGURE 17.1   Path model; the paths represent the presumed effects of one variable on another.

We dealt with some of the jargon and symbols you are likely to encounter in structural equation modeling. Measured variables, the variables actually measured in your research, are symbolized by rectangles. Unmeasured, or latent, variables are symbolized by circles or ovals. Disturbances–residuals represent unmeasured variables not considered in the model. Recursive models have arrows pointing in one direction only, whereas nonrecursive models have feedback loops, or arrows pointing in two directions. Just-identified models are those for which we have just enough information to solve for the paths, and overidentified models are those for which we have more information than we need and can thus estimate some of the paths in more than one way. Underidentified models are those for which we have more paths than we have information to estimate the paths; they are, therefore, not solvable without additional constraints. The causes of exogenous variables come from outside the model; exogenous variables have no paths pointing toward them. Endogenous variables are effects; they have paths pointing to them in the model. Most of this jargon is summarized in Figure 10.17.

The paths provide estimates of the direct effects of one variable on another. It is also possible to estimate indirect effects, such as the effect of Motivation on Achievement through Coursework in Figure 17.1. We can estimate the indirect effects by multiplying the paths involved. Indirect effects are also referred to as mediation: we may be interested in the extent to which Coursework *mediates* the effect of Motivation on Achievement. When the indirect and direct effects of one variable on another are added together, they provide an estimate of the total effect of one variable on the other. We can also calculate total effects directly using the regression coefficients from a series of sequential regressions. We finished Part 1 with questions about which type of MR to use. Although we had discussed direct versus total effects, these distinctions became much clearer with the development of path analysis: simultaneous regression focuses on direct effects, whereas sequential regression focuses on total effects. If nothing else, path analysis provides a valuable heuristic device for understanding and organizing the results of multiple regressions. I argued that path analysis should be the method of choice for those interested in MR for explanatory, nonexperimental research.

One noteworthy aspect of this process is how we made decisions concerning the influence of one variable on another: through logic, theory, and previous research. The correlations did not inform these decisions, they merely provided fuel for the calculations once we developed the causal model. To make a valid inference of cause and effect, there must be a functional relation between the variables, the cause must precede the effect in time, and the relation must not be spurious. For multiple regression to provide valid estimates of paths, we must be able to assume that there are no omitted common causes of the presumed cause and presumed effect, that there is no reverse causation, and that the exogenous variables are perfectly measured.

Dangers.   The biggest danger of path analysis is that of omitted common causes. When a common cause (a variable that affects both the presumed cause and the presumed effect) is omitted from the model, we get inaccurate estimates of the effects of one variable on another. We showed that the problem of omitted common causes is at the heart of the dreaded spurious correlation, which is, in turn, the reason for the admonition that we should not infer causation from correlations. When common causes are accounted for, paths provide accurate estimates of the effects of one variable on another. True experiments provide powerful evidence of cause and effect because the process of random assignment to groups rules out the possibility of common causes. The problem of common causes is not unique to path analysis, but is paramount in any nonexperimental (and most quasi-experimental) research. Omitted common causes are one likely reason for variability in findings from such research. If you disagree with the results of nonexperimental research, focus on the possibility of the research having omitted a common cause of the presumed cause and effect. You need to go beyond mere armchair analysis, however, and provide *evidence* of an omitted common cause.

The danger of common causes does not mean that *all* possible causes of every variable must be included in a model. If a variable, for example, affects an endogenous variable in research, but not an exogenous variable, it does not necessarily need to be included. Likewise, it is not necessary to include intervening or mediating variables in models for the results to be valid. Intervening variables are valuable, however, in that they can help us understand *how* one variable goes about influencing another. Noncommon causes and intervening variables may both be valuable in helping devise nonequivalent overidentified models, however.

Another danger in path analysis occurs when you draw a path in the wrong direction, although the extent to which this is a problem depends on the paths involved. You should not use reciprocal paths (nonrecursive models) to avoid making decisions concerning the direction of causation. Nonrecursive models are much more complex than recursive models and cannot be estimated through ordinary multiple regression. Even worse is to estimate a model via MR with a path drawn in one direction, and then the other direction; the results will *not* tell you which direction is correct.

The solution to both of these dangers is to have a good understanding of relevant theory and previous research. Think about the variables in your model, how they are related to one another. If necessary, bolster causal assumptions (e.g., *a* affects *b* rather than *b* affects *a*) through the use of longitudinal data. Think about possible common causes, and investigate them in the research literature. If necessary, test common causes in the research itself. In fact, most of what you should do to ensure the adequacy of your model boils down to the same advice for developing a model in the first place: theory, previous research, and logic. One advantage of path analysis over ordinary MR is that the figural display of the model makes your assumptions, and also any errors, very obvious.

Path Analysis Using SEM Programs.   There are special computer programs for analyzing structural equation models, including path models. In Chapter 12 I illustrated their use for path analysis. Although the example used the computer program Amos, the concepts generalize to other SEM programs, and Appendix C illustrates the use of several other such programs.

Your knowledge of MR and path analysis translates directly into SEM programs. Although there are differences in the look and labeling of output, the output from SEM programs will list unstandardized paths, standard errors, statistical significance, along with standardized paths, correlations, covariances, and variances. Most programs will also provide tables of direct, indirect, and total effects (both standardized and unstandardized), along with their standard errors, an advantage for such programs over MR.

SEM programs become even more valuable in the analysis of overidentified models. When models are overidentified (when we have more information than we need to estimate the paths), they have positive degrees of freedom. The covariance matrix implied by the solved model will also differ to some extent from the covariance matrix that was used to solve the model when models are overidentified, and the extent of the similarity or dissimilarity of these two matrices can be used to assess the fit of the model to the data. There are a plethora of fit indexes for SEM, all of which are designed to assess the fit of the model to the data, or the likelihood that the solved model could have produced the data. We focused on RMSEA, SRMR, GFI, CFI, and TLI as measures of the fit of a single model to the data. Although we talk of the fit of the model, strictly speaking, what is really assessed is the veracity of the overidentifying restrictions (e.g., paths constrained to zero or some other value) in the model.

A major advantage of SEM programs is that they may be used to compare the fit of competing theoretical models. When two models are nested (one is a more constrained version of the other), the change in χ^2 between the two models can be used to determine which model better explains the data. When $\Delta\chi^2$ is statistically significant (when compared to Δdf), we favor the better fitting, but less parsimonious, model. When $\Delta\chi^2$ is not statistically significant, we favor the more parsimonious model (the model with the larger df). The AIC and parsimony fit indexes (e.g., PCFI) can be used to compare nonnested, competing models.

Any overidentified model will likely have a number of models that are equivalent to it, models that cannot be differentiated from it based on fit. Such models may have paths reversed or replaced by correlations. We discussed rules for developing equivalent models; these rules are also useful for developing nonequivalent models, models that *can* be differentiated based on their fit. We saw that carefully designed nonequivalent models may be able to obviate one of the threats we encountered with models estimated through MR: a path drawn in the wrong direction. SEM programs can also analyze nonrecursive models.

If you can develop overidentified models, there are advantages to using an SEM program instead of a MR program. If you are using MR to estimate path models, there are few reasons to strive for overidentified models. If, however, you are using an SEM program, you should see if you can develop an overidentified model prior to estimation. Whichever method is used, be aware of the threat of equivalent models.

Error

One assumption required to interpret regression (path) coefficients in a causal fashion is that the exogenous variables be measured without error. We rarely satisfy this assumption, and thus we need to know the effect of this violation on our estimates of the effects of one variable on another. To expand this discussion, I noted that unreliability and invalidity affect *all* types of research, not just path analysis and multiple regression. Problems in measurement in both the independent and dependent variables affect our research results.

Reliability is the converse of error. Error-laden measurements are unreliable, and reliable measurements contain little error. We can consider reliability from the standpoint of variance, by thinking of true score variance as the total variance in a set of scores minus the error variance. In path analytic form, we can think of a person's score on a measurement as being affected by two influences: their true score on the measure and errors of measurement. The true score and error influences are *latent variables,* whereas the actual score the person earns on the measurement is a *measured variable.* These concepts are important for research purposes because other variables generally correlate with the true score, but not the error. For this reason, the reliability of a measurement places an upper limit on the correlation a variable can have with any other variable. Unreliable measurements can make large effects look small and statistically significant effects look nonsignificant.

MR and path models assume that the variables in our models, and especially the exogenous variables, are measured with perfect reliability. We demonstrated that if the variables in our models were unreliable (but we assumed perfect reliability) our estimates of the effects of one variable on another were inaccurate and were often underestimates of true effects. Given the complexity of path models, unreliability can also result in the overestimation of true effects.

Reliability is not the only aspect of measurement that needs to be considered, however; there is also validity. As it turns out, validity is a subset of reliability. We can get closer to valid measurement, closer to the constructs of interest in our research, by using multiple measures of constructs.

Latent variable structural equation modeling seeks to move closer to the constructs of interest in our research by using such multiple measures. With latent variable SEM, we simultaneously perform a confirmatory factor analysis of the measured variables in our research to get at the latent variables of true interest, along with a path analysis of the effects of these latent variables on each other. In the process, latent variable SEM removes the effects of unreliability and invalidity from consideration of the effects of one variable on another and avoids the problem of imperfect measurement. In the process, latent variable SEM gets closer to the primary questions of interest: the effect of one *construct* on another.

Although our discussion focused on the effects of imperfect measurement in multiple regression and path analysis, it is worth remembering that measurement affects every type of research, however that research is analyzed. With the addition of latent variables to SEM, we are able to take measurement problems into account and thus control for them.

Confirmatory Factor Analysis

We spent a chapter focused on confirmatory factor analysis, the measurement portion of the latent variable SEM model. CFA focuses on and tests hypotheses about the constructs measured in our research. For example, the CFA model in Figure 17.2 asserts that the eight *measured* variables (subtests from the Differential Ability Scales) are really reflections of four broader abilities or constructs: Verbal, Nonverbal, Spatial, and Memory abilities. The fit statistics associated with the estimation of this model will tell us whether it is indeed reasonable to assume that these eight measured variables are indicators of four such general latent abilities. We can interpret the factor loadings (the paths from the latent to the measured variables) in two ways. First, we can compare the effects as evidence of the relative validity of each test in measuring the corresponding factor (a CFA-type interpretation). We can also consider these paths as the effect of the latent variables on the measured variables (an SEM-type interpretation).

With path models, we added disturbances to account for all other influences on endogenous variables besides the variables in the model. We do something similar with the CFA–measurement models and add latent variables reflecting all other influences on each measured variable beyond its corresponding latent variable. These "all other influences"

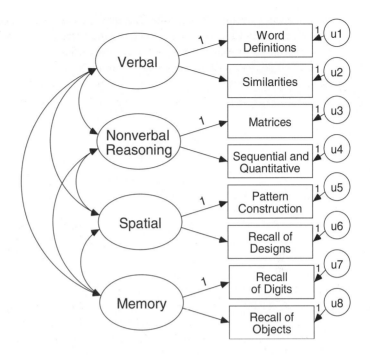

FIGURE 17.2   Confirmatory factor analysis model.

are, in fact, unreliability and invalidity, or errors of measurement. The latent variable u1 (for unique), for example, symbolizes all other influences on the Word Definitions test beyond Verbal Ability. Such influences include measurement error and specific–unique influences, such as specific vocabulary knowledge.

As in other types of SEM, with CFA we can use fit indexes to compare competing models, models that hypothesize different constructs or different compositions of these constructs. The SEM programs also provide more detailed fit statistics that may be useful for modifying poorly fitting models. Hierarchical models are also possible; for example, we tested a model in which we hypothesized that the four latent factors in Figure 17.2 were, in turn, reflections of a single general intellectual ability factor.

Latent Variable SEM

In Chapters 15 and 16, we combined path analysis and CFA into latent variable SEM. With multiple measures of the constructs of interest, SEM performs simultaneous confirmatory factor analysis of the constructs in a model and path analysis of the effects of these constructs on each other. Figure 17.3 shows such a model, designed to determine the effects of peer rejection on kindergarten students' academic and emotional adjustment. The model included eight measured variables (in rectangles) designed to measure four constructs (in large ovals). We hypothesized that the constructs affected each other as shown by the paths connecting each latent variable. The model tested whether peer rejection affects academic and emotional adjustment and whether this effect is partially mediated (indirect effect) by children's classroom participation. We found that all three types of effects—direct, indirect, and total effects—were meaningful and interesting.

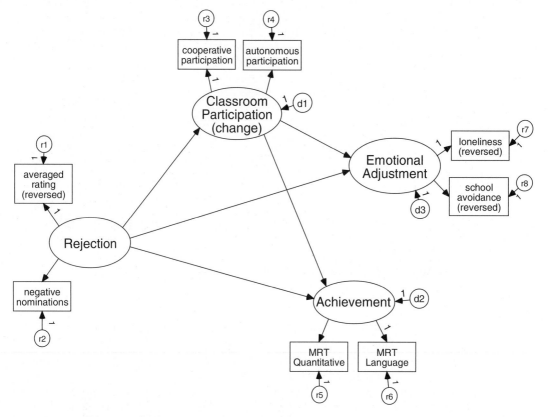

FIGURE 17.3   Latent variable structural equation model.

It is generally preferable in all three variations of SEM (path analysis, CFA, and latent variable SEM) to test hypotheses about models by comparing competing models. "The fact that one model fits the data reasonably well does not mean that there could not be other, different models that fit better. At best, a given model represents a tentative explanation of the data. The confidence with which one accepts such an explanation depends, in part, on whether other, rival explanations have been tested and found wanting" (Loehlin, 2004, p. 61). We did so with this example and found another model that both made sense and had a better fit than the initial model. We also discussed two equivalent alternatives to this model that had different interpretations, but which were statistically indistinguishable from our accepted model.

We can easily build more complex models than that shown in Figure 17.3. Figure 17.4, for example, shows a model in which one latent variable is indexed by a single measured variable. The model also includes correlated errors, the specification that the unique aspects of the measures of one construct share something in common with those of another construct beyond the effect of one construct on another. Such specifications are common in longitudinal research in which the same measures are obtained at several times or when different respondents are asked to provide assessments of multiple constructs. In the exercises for Chapter 16, for example, both parents and teachers provided feedback concerning multiple constructs. Correlated errors were used to control for respondent variance and remove it from consideration of the effects of one variable on another.

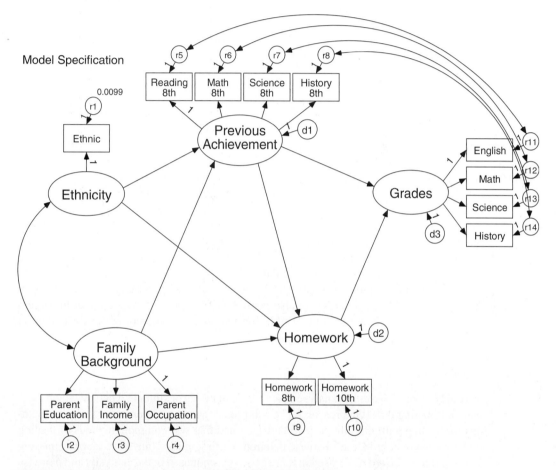

FIGURE 17.4   More complex latent variable SEM. This model includes a single-indicator latent variable and correlated errors.

It is possible to test for interactions between categorical and other variables in SEM through multisample SEM. We analyzed the homework model separately for minority and majority students, for example. By constraining various parameters to be equivalent across groups and comparing the fit of these models to models without constraints, we were able to determine that Homework (and other variables in the model) had the same effect on Achievement for one group as for the other. That is, we found that Homework and Ethnic orientation did not interact in their effect on Achievement.

A conceptually similar technique is to take the unstandardized results from one group and constrain parameters to these same values in another group. This method may be useful to determine whether findings from one group, sample, or population replicate in another.

It is worth reiterating one more time that the fit statistics from SEM, while providing some feedback as to the quality of the model, are no panacea. In particular, the fit statistics do not help with the biggest dangers in nonexperimental research. They do not warn you when you have left out a common cause from your model.

ISSUES INCOMPLETELY OR NOT COVERED

Maximum Likelihood Estimation

In Part 1 we focused on least squares estimation; we showed that MR works by minimizing the errors of prediction around the regression line. SEM programs generally use a different approach by default, maximum likelihood estimation. Rather than minimizing errors, ML is designed to provide estimates that most likely would have resulted in the sample data. Simplistically, for each set of possible parameters, the probability that these estimates could have produced the data is computed. The estimates with the highest probability are used.

With simple, just-identified path models, maximum likelihood and least squares estimates are equivalent, and thus MR and SEM programs provide the same estimates. The two methods will also generally yield very similar results for overidentified path models. The interpretation of the coefficients is also the same.

Maximum likelihood estimation is the default for SEM programs, but other methods (e.g., generalized least squares) are also possible. For more information about maximum likelihood estimation, see Eliason (1993); for additional information about estimation in SEM, see Bollen (1989) or Loehlin (2004).

Missing Values

Throughout Part 2 we either analyzed covariance matrices or simulated data in which there were no missing data. One reason for this approach was to postpone discussion of methods for dealing with missing data. In Part 1 I noted that two common methods of dealing with missing data in MR are listwise deletion of missing data (any case that has missing information on the variables used in the regression is not used in the analysis) and pairwise deletion of missing data (a case that has a missing value on a variable is not used to calculate the correlations with this variable, but the case is used to calculate other correlations). These methods are also available for calculating the matrices we use in SEM analyses. If Amos is used to analyze raw data in which data are missing, however, it uses *full information maximum likelihood* estimation to deal with the missing data (other SEM programs are increasingly using this method, as well). ML methods (which include expectation–maximization or EM methods) for dealing with missing data are generally recognized as superior to other methods (Arbuckle, 1996) and thus should be used when available.

Unfortunately, many of the more detailed aspects of fit that we examined are not available in Amos when there are missing data. Thus, when the data to be analyzed (e.g., NELS) included missing data, I estimated a covariance matrix (or correlation matrix and *SD*s) using the EM methodology (using SPSS Missing Values Analysis) for subsequent analysis in SEM.

In practice, with data like NELS, I have found only minor differences using different methods of dealing with missing data. The estimates and standard errors change slightly, but the conclusions one draws from the model rarely change when using different methods of dealing with missing data, including SPSS EM, Amos FIML, listwise deletion, or—methodologists will shudder to read this—even pairwise deletion (the approach most criticized by methodologists). I'm not suggesting that this will always be the case, but rather that this has been my experience with large extant data sets of the quality of NELS, and I often double-check. This consistency may have something to do with the generally low level of missing data in NELS. With more missing data and with missing data that is less random, real differences can result from using different methods. Pairwise deletion can be especially problematic, and maximum likelihood and related methods are recommended. I often conduct initial analyses using an EM-estimated covariance matrix to get all the detailed fit information available, but reanalyze final models using Amos with the raw data. For more information about the problem of missing data, see Arbuckle (1996), Schafer and Graham (2002), or Wothke (2000).

Sample Size, Number of Parameters, and Power

In the summary for Part 1, we briefly reviewed issues of samples size and power in MR. MR, and to a greater extent SEM, are large-sample techniques, and one good rule of thumb is the more the better. But many students and researchers struggling to collect data often wonder about minimum sample sizes in SEM, just as in MR. In Part 1, we examined several of our analyses using a power analysis program to determine the sample sizes needed to have a reasonable chance of rejecting a false null hypothesis in MR.

For SEM research, MacCallum, Browne, and Sugawara (1996) showed how to calculate power for the RMSEA using the sample size and *df*, or how to calculate the sample size given the *df* and desired power (see also Kaplan, 1995, for a discussion of power). Briefly, the larger the sample size and the larger the degrees of freedom, the higher the power is. Thus, complex, highly constrained models are more powerful than models with fewer *df*. As of this writing, several free, downloadable programs will do such calculations. Muthén and Muthén (2002) illustrated the use of Monte Carlo studies to answer such questions.

The other issue with SEM gets at the accuracy and stability of findings. A common rule of thumb is that SEM studies should include a minimum sample size of 100; this rule of thumb is based on simulation studies that show problems with results below this level (e.g., Boomsma, 1985; see also Loehlin, 2004, for a summary).

Another important consideration in SEM studies is the number of indicators per factor. Although here I have presented models that include two indicators per factor (to allow their estimation on free versions of SEM software), another good SEM rule of thumb is to try for three or more indicators per factor. This rule becomes more important with smaller sample sizes. Including more indicators should lead to more stable estimates of factors, and (because more indicators generally result in greater *df*) more power. For a dissenting view, however, see Hayduk, 1996.

Differences across Programs

If you have run our examples on a software program other than Amos, you may have found minor differences in your estimates versus those presented in this book (see, for example, differences in output in Appendix C). One likely reason for this difference is that different programs calculate covariances differently. Amos, for example, uses N in the denominator (the maximum-likelihood estimate), whereas LISREL uses $N - 1$ (the unbiased estimate). The differences should be minor, however, especially with large samples. If you get substantially different results, double-check your analyses, because one of us is in error!

Longitudinal Models

I have hinted that longitudinal models can help bolster your guesses about causal ordering by building in an actual time component in your analysis. If X is measured prior to Y, it is less likely that you are committing an error when you draw a path from X to Y. Longitudinal models are no panacea for the danger of confused time precedence, however. Consider, for example, if you measure Self-Concept in 2000 and Sex in 2002. Despite the longitudinal nature of the data collection, you will still be mistaken if you draw the path from Self-Concept to Sex. Sometimes logical time precedence takes precedence over actual time precedence. Longitudinal data are probably most useful in instances where reciprocal effects are plausible. They are also useful in instances like the Homework model, where we controlled for previous achievement. It is likely that by doing so we controlled for many likely common causes, because most influences on current achievement will likely flow through previous achievement. Longitudinal models are also useful for understanding the effects of variables on the change in some other variable (e.g., change in achievement).

Causality and the Veracity of Models

I have tried to find a middle ground on the issue of causality and the degree to which we can make valid inferences of causality with nonexperimental research methods. No doubt some readers will think I've gone too far, overstating the degree to which we can make such inferences. Others will think I've understated the case. This issue will continue to be debated and is certainly not settled in this text. Nevertheless, you should be aware of some fascinating developments in this realm. Pearl (2000), for example, details advances in understanding and demonstrating causality; see also Shipley (2000) for some of these issues translated to biology. Other researchers are working on methods other than fit statistics for testing the verisimilitude (truth) of causal models (Meehl & Waller, 2002).

ADDITIONAL RESOURCES

These last few chapters have provided only a brief introduction to SEM, perhaps just enough to make you dangerous. This introduction may be sufficient to make you a good reader of SEM studies, but to actually do structural equation analysis yourself will likely require further reading. I hope you have enjoyed this adventure into the fascinating world of nonexperimental analysis via SEM (and MR). I hope you will experiment with these methods and seek to develop your initial skills more completely. The sources listed next are good starting points.

Introductory Texts

I have mentioned several introductory textbooks that are worth your review:

Hoyle, R. H. (Ed.). (1995). *Structural equation modeling: Concepts, issues, and applications.* Thousand Oaks, CA: Sage.
Kline, R. B. (1998). *Principles and practices of structural equation modeling.* New York: Guilford.
Loehlin, J. C. (2004). *Latent variable models: An introduction to factor, path, and structural analysis* (4th ed.). Hillsdale, NJ: Erlbaum.

See also:

Maruyama, G. M. (1998) *Basics of structural equation modeling.* Thousand Oaks, CA: Sage.
Raykov, T., & Marcoulides, G. A. (2000). *A first course in structural equation modeling.* Mahwah, NJ: Erlbaum.
Schumacker, R. E., & Lomax, R. G. (1996). *A beginner's guide to structural equation modeling.* Mahwah, NJ: Erlbaum.

For an excellent, historically oriented annotated bibliography of path analysis and SEM literature, see:

Wolfle, L. M. (2003). The introduction of path analysis to the social sciences, and some emergent themes: An annotated bibliography. *Structural Equation Modeling, 10,* 1–34.

More Advanced Resources

If you want to advance your knowledge about SEM beyond the basics, I recommend the journal *Structural Equation Modeling,* published by Lawrence Erlbaum Associates. You may also be interested in joining the SEMnet listserve. For information, go to www.gsu .edu/~mkteer/semnet.html. Some worthwhile books include:

Bollen, K. A. (1989). *Structural equations with latent variables.* New York: Wiley.
Bollen, K. A., & Long, J. S. (Eds.). (1993). *Testing structural equation models.* Newbury Park, CA: Sage.

Hancock, G. R., & Mueller, R. O. (in press). *A second course in structural equation modeling.* Greenwich, CT: Information Age.

Kaplan, D. (2000). *Structural equation modeling: Foundations and extensions.* Newbury Park, CA: Sage.

Marcoulides, G. A., & Schumacker, R. E. (Eds.). (1996). *Advanced structural equation modeling.* Mahwah, NJ: Erlbaum.

Marcoulides, G. A., & Schumacker, R. E. (Eds.). (2001). *New developments and techniques in structural equation modeling.* Mahwah, NJ: Erlbaum.

Schumacker, R. E., & Marcoulides, G. A. (Eds.). (1998). *Interactive and nonlinear effects in structural equation modeling.* Mahwah, NJ: Erlbaum.

Books about Specific SEM Programs

Several texts are program specific and are valuable if you want to go beyond the examples presented in the user's guide to your program:

Byrne, B. M. (1994). *Structural equation modeling with EQS and EQS/Windows: Basic concepts, applications, and programming.* Thousand Oaks, CA: Sage.

Byrne, B. M. (1998). *Structural equation modeling with LISREL, PRELIS, and SIMPLIS: Basic concepts, applications, and programming.* Mahwah, NJ: Erlbaum.

Byrne, B. M. (2001). *Structural equation modeling with Amos: Basic concepts, applications, and programming.* Mahwah, NJ: Erlbaum.

Mueller, R. O. (1995). *Basic principles of structural equation modeling: An introduction to LISREL and EQS.* New York: Springer-Verlag.

Reporting SEM Results

SEM results are obviously complex, and writing up SEM results is often a challenge. You need to provide enough detail so that other researchers can reproduce your results, but it is easy to go overboard and report too much detail, resulting in a research report that is too long and uninteresting. How do you decide what you should report? First, model exemplary research in your area of interest. Then, turn to these references:

Boomsma, A. (2000). Reporting analyses of covariance structures. *Structural Equation Modeling, 7,* 461–483.

Hoyle, R. H., & Panter, A. T. (1995). Writing about structural equation models. In R. H. Hoyle (Ed.), *Structural equation modeling: Concepts, issues, and applications* (pp. 158–176). Thousand Oaks, CA: Sage.

McDonald, R. P., & Ho, M.-H. R. (2002). Principles and practice in reporting structural equation analyses. *Psychological Methods, 7,* 64–82.

Cautions

Finally, several references to remind you to be cautious in your use and reporting of SEM results:

Cliff, N. (1983). Some cautions concerning the application of causal modeling methods. *Multivariate Behavioral Research, 18,* 115–126.

Freedman, D. A. (1987). As others see us: A case study in path analysis. *Journal of Educational Statistics, 12,* 101–128.

MacCallum, R. (1986). Specification searches in covariance structure modeling. *Psychological Bulletin, 100,* 107–120.

Steiger, J. H. (2001). Driving fast in reverse: The relationship between software development, theory, and education in structural equation modeling. *Journal of the American Statistical Association, 96,* 331–338.

Don't let the need for vigilance deter you from exploring further, however. SEM is a fascinating and powerful methodology. Experiment with it!

On my office door, I have the SEM model shown in Figure 17.5, along with the caption "Happiness Is a Latent Variable." I trust by now you understand the various meanings of this statement. At the most basic level, in the model, the variable Happiness is, in fact, a latent variable. More broadly, in the real world, happiness is a latent variable: it's not something we can measure exactly, but we do get indicators of it from many different behaviors. Finally, the statement is meant to say something about latent variable SEM. It is challenging, humbling, fascinating, and satisfying. I hope you experience some of the same enjoyment I have from learning and applying the method!

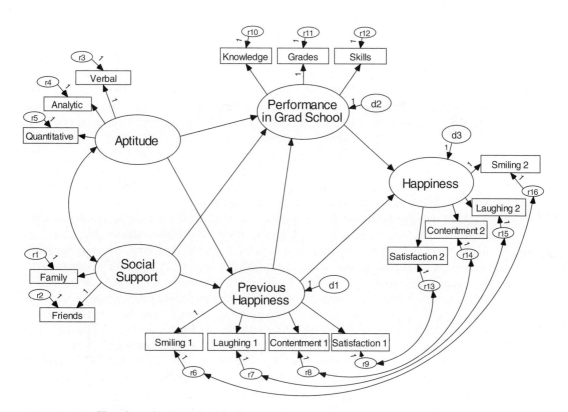

FIGURE 17.5   Happiness is a latent variable.

DATA FILES

The Web site that accompanies this book (www.ablongman.com/keith1e) includes the data used as research examples throughout the book. It includes a folder for each chapter in the book; the smaller data sets are included in the folder that corresponds to the chapter in which they appear. Most files appear in several formats, including an SPSS ".sav" file, Excel format, and as plain text files (usually with the extension ".txt" or ".dat"). If you can use the SPSS files, they generally have the most information (e.g., value labels, missing values). My second choice is to use the Excel files (except for the large NELS data set).

NELS DATA

The NELS data set used throughout the book is included in the folder labeled "NELS." I have converted the original SPSS file to several different formats: SYSTAT, SAS Transport, and plain text. The conversions were done using the program DBMS/COPY. If you can use the SPSS files, I recommend doing so because it is the original form of the data. The file is also saved as an SPSS portable file (extension .por). The SYSTAT and SAS files are also clean and easily usable (although users of both programs should be able to use the SPSS file as well). For more information about the NELS data, including how to obtain a CD with the full data set, visit the National Center for Education Statistics Web site (nces.ed.gov/ surveys); you'll be amazed at all the data available to you!

The variable labels for all the variables in the NELS file are listed next (using the DIS-PLAY LABELS command in SPSS). A quick perusal of these labels should give you an idea of the power and scope of these amazing data. The format of the listing is the variable name, its position in the file, and the variable label. Variable names that start with BY are from the base year, when the students were in the 8th grade. The prefix BYS means the variable is from the student file; BYP means the variable is from the Parent File. Composite variables created by NELS generally do not have the S or P designation. Composites that I created start with variable 1379, ParentEd. Variables that start with F1 are from the first follow-up, when students were in the 10th grade. The abbreviation R in the variable labels refers to the respondent. Thus, the variable BYS8A, labeled R LIVES IN HOUSEHOLD WITH FATHER, means that the respondent lives in a household with his or her father. The variables are listed in the order in which they appear in the data set. If you want to, once you get the data in your statistics program, you should be able to output the variables in alphabetic order.

National Education Longitudinal Study (NELS)
List of variable names (file order)

Base year (8th grade) student data
First follow-up (10th grade) student data
Base year parent data

LIST OF VARIABLES ON THE WORKING FILE

Name	Position	Label
STU_ID	1	Student Public Release Id
SCH_ID	2	School Public Release Id
SSTRATID	3	Superstratum Public Release Id
BYS2A	4	Is Mother/Female Guardian Living
BYS4A	5	Mother/Female Guardian Employment Status
BYS4OCC	6	Mother/Female Guardian's Occupation
BYS5A	7	Is Father/Male Guardian Living
BYS7A	8	Father/Male Guardian Employment Status
BYS7OCC	9	Father/Male Guardian's Occupation
BYS8A	10	R Lives In Household With Father
BYS8B	11	R Lives In Hh With Other Male Guardian
BYS8C	12	R Lives In Household With Mother
BYS8D	13	R Lives In Hh With Other Female Guardian
BYS8E	14	R Lives In Household With Brother(S)
BYS8F	15	R Lives In Household With Sister(S)
BYS8G	16	R Lives In Household With Grandparent(S)
BYS8H	17	R Lives In Household W/Other Relative(S)
BYS8I	18	R Lives In Household W/ Non-Relative(S)
BYS12	19	Sex Of Respondent
BYS14	20	Sector Of High School R Plans To Attend
BYS15	21	Is There Another H.S. R May Attend Instd
BYS16	22	Sector Of 2Nd Choice High School
BYS17	23	R Speak Any Lang Oth Thn English Bfr Sch
BYS18	24	1St Lang R Learned To Speak As A Child
BYS19	25	Other Lang R Spoke Before Starting Schl
BYS20	26	Language R Usually Speaks Now
BYS21	27	Any Other Language Spoken In R's Home
BYS22	28	Lang Usually Spokn By People In R's Home
BYS23	29	Other Language Spoken In R's Home
BYS24	30	Lang Other Thn English R Uses Most Often
BYS25A	31	How Well R Understands That Language
BYS25B	32	How Well R Speaks That Language
BYS25C	33	How Well R Reads That Language
BYS25D	34	How Well R Writes That Language
BYS26A	35	How Often R Speaks Language To Mother

BYS26B	36	How Often R's Mother Speaks Lang To R
BYS26C	37	How Often R Speaks Language To Father
BYS26D	38	How Often R's Father Speaks Lang To R
BYS26E	39	How Often Parents Speak Lang To Each Oth
BYS26F	40	How Often Grandparents Speak Lang To R
BYS26G	41	How Often Siblings Speak Language To R
BYS26H	42	How Oft Speaks Lang To Neighbrhd Friends
BYS26I	43	How Often R Speaks Lang To Schl Friends
BYS27A	44	How Well R Understands Spoken English
BYS27B	45	How Well R Speaks English
BYS27C	46	How Well R Reads English
BYS27D	47	How Well R Writes English
BYS28A1	48	Math Taught In English: 1St 2Yrs In U.S.
BYS28A2	49	Math Taught In Oth Lang:1St 2Yrs In U.S.
BYS28A3	50	Math Not Taught: 1St 2 Yrs In U.S.
BYS28B1	51	Science Taught In Eng:1St 2Yrs In U.S.
BYS28B2	52	Science Taught Oth Lang:1St 2Yrs In U.S.
BYS28B3	53	Science Not Taught: 1St 2 Yrs In U.S.
BYS28C1	54	U.S. Lit Taught In Eng:1St 2Yrs In U.S.
BYS28C2	55	U.S. Lit Taught Oth Lang:1St 2Yrs U.S.
BYS28C3	56	U.S. Lit Not Taught: 1St 2Yrs In U.S.
BYS28D1	57	U.S. His,Gov,S. S. Taught In Eng:1St 2Yrs
BYS28D2	58	U.S. His,Gov,S. S. In Other Lang:1St 2Yrs
BYS28D3	59	U.S. His,Gov,S. S. Not Taught: 1St 2Yrs
BYS28E1	60	Own Lit/Lang Arts Taught In Eng:1St 2Yrs
BYS28E2	61	Own Lit/Lang Arts In Other Lang:1St 2Yrs
BYS28E3	62	Own Lit/Lang Arts Not Taught: 1St 2Yrs
BYS28F1	63	Own His,Gov,S. S. Taught In Eng:1St 2Yrs
BYS28F2	64	Own His,Gov,S. S. In Other Lang:1St 2Yrs
BYS28F3	65	Own His,Gov,S. S. Not Taught:1St 2Yrs
BYS29	66	R Ever In A Language Assistance Program
BYS30A	67	Enrolled In Lang Assistance Pgm 1St Grd
BYS30B	68	Enrolled In Lang Assistance Pgm 2Nd Grd
BYS30C	69	Enrolled In Lang Assistance Pgm 3Rd Grd
BYS30D	70	Enrolled In Lang Assistance Pgm 4Th Grd
BYS30E	71	Enrolled In Lang Assistance Pgm 5Th Grd
BYS30F	72	Enrolled In Lang Assistance Pgm 6Th Grd
BYS30G	73	Enrolled In Lang Assistance Pgm 7Th Grd
BYS30H	74	Enrolled In Lang Assistance Pgm 8Th Grd
BYS31A	75	R's Race/Ethnic Background
BYS31B	76	Asian Or Pacific Islander Subdivision
BYS31C	77	Hispanic Subdivision
BYS31D	78	Hispanic Race
BYS32	79	Number Of Siblings R Has
BYS33	80	Number Of Siblings Older Than R

BYS34A	81	Father's Highest Level Of Education
BYS34B	82	Mother's Highest Level Of Education
BYS35A	83	R's Family Has Specific Place For Study
BYS35B	84	R's Family Has A Daily Newspaper
BYS35C	85	R's Family Has Regularly Rec'd Magazine
BYS35D	86	R's Family Has An Encyclopedia
BYS35E	87	R's Family Has An Atlas
BYS35F	88	R's Family Has A Dictionary
BYS35G	89	R's Family Has A Typewriter
BYS35H	90	R's Family Has A Computer
BYS35I	91	R's Family Has An Electric Dishwasher
BYS35J	92	R's Family Has A Clothes Dryer
BYS35K	93	R's Family Has A Washing Machine
BYS35L	94	R's Family Has A Microwave Oven
BYS35M	95	R's Family Has More Than 50 Books
BYS35N	96	R's Family Has A Vcr
BYS35O	97	R's Family Has A Pocket Calculator
BYS35P	98	R Has Own Bedroom
BYS36A	99	Discuss Programs At School With Parents
BYS36B	100	Discuss School Activities With Parents
BYS36C	101	Discuss Thngs Studied In Class Wth Prnts
BYS37A	102	R's Parents Attended A School Meeting
BYS37B	103	R's Parents Spoke To Teacher/Counselor
BYS37C	104	R's Parents Visited R's Classes
BYS37D	105	R's Parents Attended A School Event
BYS38A	106	How Often Parents Check On R's Homework
BYS38B	107	How Often Parents Require Chores Done
BYS38C	108	How Often Parents Limit Time Watching Tv
BYS38D	109	How Oftn Prnts Limit Going Out Wth Frnds
BYS39A	110	Parents Trust R To Do What They Expect
BYS39B	111	Often Dk Why I Am To Do What Parents Say
BYS39C	112	Often Count On Parents To Solve Problems
BYS40A	113	Mother Home When R Returns From School
BYS40B	114	Father Home When R Returns From School
BYS40C	115	Othr Adult Rel Home Whn R Retrns Frm Sch
BYS40D	116	A Sitter Home When R Returns From School
BYS40E	117	Adult Neighbr Home Whn R Retrns Frm Schl
BYS40F	118	Older Sibling Home When R Retrns Fr Schl
BYS40G	119	Youngr Sibling Home Whn R Retrns Fr Schl
BYS40H	120	No One Is Home When R Returns From Schl
BYS41	121	Time Spent After Schl Wth No Adult Prsnt
BYS42A	122	Tv Viewing
BYS42B	123	No. Of Hours R Watches Tv On Weekends
BYS43	124	No. Of Cigarettes R Smokes Per Day
BYS44A	125	I Feel Good About Myself

BYS44B	126	I Don't Have Enough Control Over My Life
BYS44C	127	Good Luck More Important Than Hard Work
BYS44D	128	I'm A Person Of Worth, Equal Of Others
BYS44E	129	I Am Able To Do Things As Well As Others
BYS44F	130	Every Time I Get Ahead Somethng Stops Me
BYS44G	131	Plans Hardly Work Out, Makes Me Unhappy
BYS44H	132	On The Whole, I Am Satisfied With Myself
BYS44I	133	I Certainly Feel Useless At Times
BYS44J	134	At Times I Think I Am No Good At All
BYS44K	135	Whn I Make Plans I Can Make Them Work
BYS44L	136	I Feel I Do Not Have Much To Be Proud Of
BYS44M	137	Chance And Luck Important In My Life
BYS45	138	How Far In Sch Do You Think You Will Get
BYS46	139	How Sure That You Will Graduate From H. S
BYS47	140	How Sure R Is To Go Further Than H. S.
BYS48A	141	How Far In Schl R's Father Wants R To Go
BYS48B	142	How Far In Schl R's Mother Wants R To Go
BYS49	143	Which Program R Expects To Enroll In H. S
BYS50A	144	Talk To Father About Planning H. S. Prog
BYS50B	145	Talk To Mother About Planning H. S. Prog
BYS50C	146	Talk To Counslr About Planning H. S. Prog
BYS50D	147	Talk To Teachers About Plannng H. S. Prog
BYS50E	148	Talk To Relatvs About Planning H. S. Prog
BYS50F	149	Talk To Friends About Planning H. S. Prog
BYS51AA	150	Talk To Counselor About H. S. Programs
BYS51AB	151	Talk To Teacher About H. S. Programs
BYS51AC	152	Talk To Other Adult About H. S. Programs
BYS51BA	153	Talk To Counselor Abt Jobs/Career Aft Hs
BYS51BB	154	Talk To Teacher About Jobs/Career Aft Hs
BYS51BC	155	Talk To Oth Adult Abt Jobs/Career Aft Hs
BYS51CA	156	Talk To Counselor Abt Improving Sch Work
BYS51CB	157	Talk To Teacher About Improving Sch Work
BYS51CC	158	Talk To Othr Adult Abt Improving Sch Wrk
BYS51DA	159	Talk To Counselor About Courses At Schl
BYS51DB	160	Talk To Teacher About Courses At School
BYS51DC	161	Talk To Other Adult About Courses At Sch
BYS51EA	162	Talk To Counselor About Studies In Class
BYS51EB	163	Talk To Teacher About Studies In Class
BYS51EC	164	Talk To Other Adult Abt Studies In Class
BYS51FA	165	Talk To Counselor About Discipline Probs
BYS51FB	166	Talk To Teacher Abt Discipline Problems
BYS51FC	167	Talk To Other Adult Abt Discipline Probs
BYS51GA	168	Talk To Counselor Abt Drug/Alcohol Abuse
BYS51GB	169	Talk To Teacher About Drug/Alcohol Abuse
BYS51GC	170	Talk To Oth Adult Abt Drug/Alcohol Abuse

BYS51HA	171	Talk To Counselor Abt Personal Problems
BYS51HB	172	Talk To Teacher About Personal Problems
BYS51HC	173	Talk To Othr Adult Abt Personal Problems
BYS52	174	Kind Of Work R Expects To Do At Age 30
BYS53	175	No. Of Hours R Works For Pay Per Week
BYS54	176	Kind Of Work R Does For Pay Current Job
BYS55A	177	R Sent To Office For Misbehaving
BYS55B	178	R Sent To Office With Schl Work Problems
BYS55C	179	Parents Received Warning Abt Attendance
BYS55D	180	Parents Received Warning About Grades
BYS55E	181	Parents Received Warning About Behavior
BYS55F	182	R Got Into Fight With Another Student
BYS56A	183	Students In Class See R As Popular
BYS56B	184	Students In Class See R As Athletic
BYS56C	185	Students In Class See R As Good Student
BYS56D	186	Students In Class See R As Important
BYS56E	187	Students In Class See R As Trouble-Maker
BYS57A	188	R Had Something Stolen At School
BYS57B	189	Someone Offered To Sell R Drugs At Schl
BYS57C	190	Someone Threatened To Hurt R At School
BYS58A	191	Student Tardiness A Problem At School
BYS58B	192	Student Absenteeism A Problem At School
BYS58C	193	Students Cutting Class A Problem At Schl
BYS58D	194	Physical Conflicts Among Stud A Problem
BYS58E	195	Robbery Or Theft A Problem At School
BYS58F	196	Vandalism Of School Property A Problem
BYS58G	197	Student Use Of Alcohol A Problem At Schl
BYS58H	198	Student Use Of Illegal Drugs A Problem
BYS58I	199	Student Possession Of Weapons A Problem
BYS58J	200	Physical Abuse Of Teachers A Problem
BYS58K	201	Verbal Abuse Of Teachers A Problem
BYS59A	202	Students Get Along Well With Teachers
BYS59B	203	There Is Real School Spirit
BYS59C	204	Rules For Behavior Are Strict
BYS59D	205	Discipline Is Fair
BYS59E	206	Other Students Often Disrupt Class
BYS59F	207	The Teaching Is Good
BYS59G	208	Teachers Are Interested In Students
BYS59H	209	Teachers Praise My Effort
BYS59I	210	In Class I Feel Put Down By My Teachers
BYS59J	211	Most Of My Teachers Listen To What I Say
BYS59K	212	I Don't Feel Safe At This School
BYS59L	213	Student Disruptions Inhibit Learning
BYS59M	214	Misbehaving Studs Often Get Away With It
BYS60A	215	R's Ability Group For Mathematics

BYS60B	216	R's Ability Group For Science
BYS60C	217	R's Ability Group For English
BYS60D	218	R's Ability Group For Social Studies
BYS61	219	Talk To Tchr/Cnslr About Taking Algebra
BYS62	220	Did Prnts/Grdns Want R To Take Algebra
BYS63	221	Friends Encrg/Discrg R From Taking Algbr
BYS64	222	Asked By Principal If Wntd To Take Algbr
BYS65	223	Who Had The Mst To Say Abt R Tkng Algbr
BYS66A	224	In Advanced,Enriched,Accelerated English
BYS66B	225	In Advancd,Enrichd,Accelertd Soc. Studies
BYS66C	226	In Advanced,Enriched,Accelerated Science
BYS66D	227	In Advanced,Enriched,Accelerated Math
BYS67A	228	Attend Remedial Math At Least Once A Wk
BYS67B	229	Attend Regular Math At Least Once A Week
BYS67C	230	Attend Algebra At Least Once A Week
BYS67AA	231	Attend Laboratory At Least Once A Week
BYS67AB	232	Attend Science At Least Once A Week
BYS67AC	233	Attend Biology At Least Once A Week
BYS67AD	234	Attend Earth Science At Least Once A Wk
BYS67BA	235	Attend English At Least Once A Week
BYS67BB	236	Attend Remedial Eng At Least Once A Week
BYS67BC	237	Attend History At Least Once A Week
BYS67BD	238	Attend Social Studies At Least Once A Wk
BYS67BE	239	Attend Foreign Lang At Least Once A Week
BYS67BF	240	Attend Art At Least Once A Week
BYS67BG	241	Attend Music At Least Once A Week
BYS67BH	242	Attend Computer Ed At Least Once A Week
BYS67CA	243	Attend Home Economics At Least Once A Wk
BYS67CB	244	Attend Shop At Least Once A Week
BYS67CC	245	Attend Typing At Least Once A Week
BYS67CD	246	Attend Consumer Ed At Least Once A Week
BYS67CE	247	Attend Agriculture At Least Once A Week
BYS67DA	248	Attend Drama/Speech At Least Once A Week
BYS67DB	249	Attend Religious Ed At Least Once A Week
BYS67DC	250	Attend Physical Ed At Least Once A Week
BYS67DD	251	Attend Sex Education At Least Once A Wk
BYS68A	252	Enrolled In Classes For Gifted Students
BYS68B	253	Enrolled In Bilingual Education
BYS69A	254	Usually Look Forward To Math Class
BYS69B	255	Afraid To Ask Questions In Math Class
BYS69C	256	Math Will Be Useful In My Future
BYS70A	257	Usually Look Forward To English Class
BYS70B	258	Often Afraid To Ask Questions In English
BYS70C	259	English Will Be Useful In My Future
BYS71A	260	Look Forward To Social Studies Class

BYS71B	261	Afraid To Ask Question In Social Studies
BYS71C	262	Soc. Studies Will Be Useful In My Future
BYS72A	263	Usually Look Forward To Science Class
BYS72B	264	Afraid To Ask Question In Science Class
BYS72C	265	Science Will Be Useful In My Future
BYS73	266	Ever Feel Bored When You Are At School
BYS74	267	Ever Held Back A Grade In School
BYS74A	268	Ever Repeat Kindergarten
BYS74B	269	Ever Repeat Grade 1
BYS74C	270	Ever Repeat Grade 2
BYS74D	271	Ever Repeat Grade 3
BYS74E	272	Ever Repeat Grade 4
BYS74F	273	Ever Repeat Grade 5
BYS74G	274	Ever Repeat Grade 6
BYS74H	275	Ever Repeat Grade 7
BYS74I	276	Ever Repeat Grade 8
BYS75	277	# Of Days Missed From Schl Past 4 Weeks
BYS76	278	How Often Do You Cut Or Skip Classes
BYS77	279	# Of Times Late For School Past 4 Weeks
BYS78A	280	How Often Come To Class W/O Pencil/Paper
BYS78B	281	How Often Come To Class Without Books
BYS78C	282	How Often Come To Class Without Homework
BYS79A	283	Time Spent On Math Homework Each Week
BYS79B	284	Time Spent On Science Homework Each Week
BYS79C	285	Time Spent On English Homework Each Week
BYS79D	286	Time Spent On Soc Studies Homewk Each Wk
BYS79E	287	Time Spent On All Oth Subjects Each Week
BYS80	288	Reading On Own
BYS81A	289	English88-Grade
BYS81B	290	Math88-Grades
BYS81C	291	Science88-Grades
BYS81D	292	Sstudies88-Grades
BYS82A	293	Participated In Science Fairs
BYS82B	294	Participated In School Varsity Sports
BYS82C	295	Participated In Intramural Sports
BYS82D	296	Participated In Cheerleading
BYS82E	297	Participated In Band Or Orchestra
BYS82F	298	Participated In Chorus Or Choir
BYS82G	299	Participated In Dance
BYS82H	300	Participated In History Club
BYS82I	301	Participated In Science Club
BYS82J	302	Participated In Math Club
BYS82K	303	Participated In Foreign Language Club
BYS82L	304	Participated In Othr Subject Matter Club
BYS82M	305	Participated In Debate Or Speech Team

BYS82N	306	Participated In Drama Club
BYS82O	307	Participated In Academic Honors Society
BYS82P	308	Participated In Student Newspaper
BYS82Q	309	Participated In Student Yearbook
BYS82R	310	Participated In Student Council
BYS82S	311	Participated In Computer Club
BYS82T	312	Participated In Religious Organization
BYS82U	313	Participated In Voc. Education Club
BYS83A	314	Participated In Scouting
BYS83B	315	Participated In Religious Youth Groups
BYS83C	316	Participated In Hobby Clubs
BYS83D	317	Participated In Neighborhood Clubs/Progs
BYS83E	318	Participated In Boys' Or Girls' Clubs
BYS83F	319	Participated In Non-School Team Sports
BYS83G	320	Participated In 4-H
BYS83H	321	Participated In Y Or Other Youth Groups
BYS83I	322	Participated In Summer Programs
BYS83J	323	Participated In Any Other Activities
BYQWT	324	Base Year Questionnaire Weight
BYTEQFLG	325	At Least One Teacher Quex Available
BYPAQFLG	326	Parent Questionnaire Available
BYTXPAFG	327	Student Tests & Parent Quex Available
BYTEPAFG	328	Parent & At Least 1 Teacher Quex Avail
BYTXFLG	329	Student Tests Available
BYADMFLG	330	School Administrator Quex Available
BYIEPFLG	331	Individualized Education Program Flag
G8TYPE	332	Grade Span Of School
G8CTRL	333	School Control Composite
BYSCENRL	334	Total School Enrollment Composite
G8ENROL	335	8Th Grade Enrollment Composite
G8URBAN	336	Urbanicity Composite
G8REGON	337	Composite Geographic Region Of School
G8MINOR	338	Percent Minority In School
G8LUNCH	339	Percent Free Lunch In School
NOMSECT	340	Sector Of 1St Nominated 10th Grade Schl
SEX	341	Composite Sex
RACE	342	Composite Race
HISP	343	Hispanic Subgroups
API	344	Asian/Pacific Islander Race Composite
HEARIMP	345	Hearing Impairment Composite
HANDPAST	346	Past Handicap Program Recipient
BYHANDPR	347	Parent-Reported Handicap Pgm Recipient
BYHANDTR	348	Teacher-Reported Handicap
BIRTHMO	349	Month Of Birth
BIRTHYR	350	Year Of Birth

BYLOCUS1	351	Locus Of Control 1
BYLOCU1T	352	Tertile Coding Of Variable Bylocus1
BYLOCUS2	353	Locus Of Control 2
BYLOCU2T	354	Tertile Coding Of Variable Bylocus2
BYCNCPT1	355	Self Concept 1
BYCNCP1T	356	Tertile Coding Of Variable Bycncpt1
BYCNCPT2	357	Self Concept 2
BYCNCP2T	358	Tertile Coding Of Variable Bycncpt2
BYSES	359	Socio-Economic Status Composite
BYSESQ	360	Quartile Coding Of Byses Variable
BYPARED	361	Parents' Highest Education Level
BYFAMSIZ	362	Family Size
BYFCOMP	363	Family Composition Composite
BYPARMAR	364	Parents' Marital Status
BYFAMINC	365	Yearly Family Income
BYHMLANG	366	Home Language Background
BYPSEPLN	367	Post-Secondary Education Plans
BYHOMEWK	368	Number Of Hrs Spent On Homework Per Week
BYLEP	369	Limited English Proficiency Composite
BYLM	370	Language Minority Composite
BYGRADS	371	Grades Composite
BYGRADSQ	372	Quartile Coding Of Bygrads Composite
BYTXRNR	373	Reading Number Right
BYTXRNW	374	Reading Number Wrong
BYTXRNNA	375	Reading Number Not Attempted
BYTXRFS	376	Reading Formula Score
BYTXRSTD	377	Reading Standardized Score
BYTXRIRR	378	Reading Irt-Estimated Number Right
BYTXRIRS	379	Reading Irt-Estimated Formula Score
BYTXRQ	380	Reading Quartile (1=Low)
BYTXMNR	381	Mathematics Number Right
BYTXMNW	382	Mathematics Number Wrong
BYTXMNNA	383	Mathematics Number Not Attempted
BYTXMFS	384	Mathematics Formula Score
BYTXMSTD	385	Mathematics Standardized Score
BYTXMIRR	386	Mathematics Irt-Estimated Number Right
BYTXMIRS	387	Mathematics Irt-Estimated Formula Score
BYTXMQ	388	Mathematics Quartile (1=Low)
BYTXSNR	389	Science Number Right
BYTXSNW	390	Science Number Wrong
BYTXSNNA	391	Science Number Not Attempted
BYTXSFS	392	Science Formula Score
BYTXSSTD	393	Science Standardized Score
BYTXSIRR	394	Science Irt-Estimated Number Right
BYTXSIRS	395	Science Irt-Estimated Formula Score

BYTXSQ	396	Science Quartile (1=Low)
BYTXHNR	397	History/Cit/Geog Number Right
BYTXHNW	398	History/Cit/Geog Number Wrong
BYTXHNNA	399	History/Cit/Geog Number Not Attempted
BYTXHFS	400	History/Cit/Geog Formula Score
BYTXHSTD	401	History/Cit/Geog Standardized Score
BYTXHIRR	402	History/Cit/Geog Irt-Estimated No. Right
BYTXHIRS	403	History/Cit/Geog Irt-Est'd Formula Score
BYTXHQ	404	History/Cit/Geog Quartile
BYTXCOMP	405	Stndrdized Test Composite (Reading,Math)
BYTXQURT	406	Standardized Test Quartile (1=Low)
BYTXRPRO	407	Overall Reading Proficiency
BYTXMPRO	408	Overall Math Proficiency
F1S7A	409	Students Get Along Well With Teachers
F1S7B	410	There Is Real School Spirit
F1S7C	411	Rules For Behavior Are Strict At School
F1S7D	412	Discipline Is Fair At School
F1S7E	413	Studnts Friendly With Othr Racial Groups
F1S7F	414	Other Students Often Disrupt Class
F1S7G	415	The Teaching Is Good At School
F1S7H	416	Teachers Are Interested In Students
F1S7I	417	When R Works Hard Teachers Praise Effort
F1S7J	418	In Class Often Feel Put Down By Teachers
F1S7K	419	Often Feel Put Down By Students In Class
F1S7L	420	Most Teachers Listen To R
F1S7M	421	R Doesn't Feel Safe At This School
F1S7N	422	Disruptions Impede R's Learning
F1S7O	423	Misbehaving Stdns Often Get Away With It
F1S8A	424	R Has Not Won Any Awards
F1S8B	425	R Elected Officer Of A School Class
F1S8C	426	R Won An Academic Honor
F1S8D	427	R Participated In A Science Or Math Fair
F1S8E	428	Received Recognition For Good Attendance
F1S8F	429	Received Recognition For Good Grades
F1S8G	430	Received Recognition For Writing Essay
F1S8H	431	Named Most Valuable Player On Sport Team
F1S8I	432	Received A Community Service Award
F1S8J	433	Participated In Voc/Tech Competition
F1S9A	434	Had Something Stolen At School
F1S9B	435	Someone Offered To Sell R Drugs At Schl
F1S9C	436	Someone Threatened To Hurt R At School
F1S9D	437	Got Into A Physical Fight At School
F1S10A	438	How Many Times Was R Late For School
F1S10B	439	How Many Times Did R Cut/Skip Classes
F1S10C	440	How Many Times R Got In Trouble

F1S10D	441	How Many Times Put On In-Schl Suspension
F1S10E	442	How Many Times R Suspended From School
F1S10F	443	R Transferred For Disciplinary Reasons
F1S10G	444	How Many Times Was R Arrested
F1S11A	445	It's Ok To Work Hard For Good Grades
F1S11B	446	It's Ok To Ask Challenging Questions
F1S11C	447	It's Ok To Solve Problms Using New Ideas
F1S11D	448	It's Ok To Help Students With Schoolwork
F1S12A	449	Feel It's Ok To Be Late For School
F1S12B	450	Feel It's Ok To Cut A Couple Of Classes
F1S12C	451	Feel It's Ok To Skip School A Whole Day
F1S12D	452	Feel It's Ok To Cheat On Tests
F1S12E	453	Feel It's Ok To Copy Someone's Homework
F1S12F	454	Feel It's Ok To Get Into Physical Fights
F1S12G	455	Feel It's Ok To Belong To Gangs
F1S12H	456	Feel It's Ok To Make Racist Remarks
F1S12I	457	Feel It's Ok To Make Sexist Remarks
F1S12J	458	Feel It's Ok To Steal Belongings Frm Sch
F1S12K	459	Feel It's Ok To Destroy School Property
F1S12L	460	Feel It's Ok To Smoke On School Grounds
F1S12M	461	Feel It's Ok To Drink Alcohol At School
F1S12N	462	Feel It's Ok To Use Drugs At School
F1S12O	463	Feel It's Ok To Bring Weapons To School
F1S12P	464	Feel It's Ok To Abuse Teachers
F1S12Q	465	Feel It's Ok To Talk Back To Teachers
F1S12R	466	Feel It's Ok To Disobey School Rules
F1S13	467	How Many Days Was R Absent From School
F1S14	468	Main Reason For R's Last Absence Frm Sch
F1S15A	469	When Absent School Did Not Do Anything
F1S15B	470	When Absent School Called R's Home
F1S15C	471	When Absent The School Visited R's Home
F1S15D	472	When Absent The Schl Sent A Letter Home
F1S15E	473	When Absent R Had To See A Counselor
F1S16A	474	Aft Being Absent Teacher Helped R Do Wrk
F1S16B	475	After Being Absent Stus Helped R Do Work
F1S16C	476	After Being Absent Someone Else Helped R
F1S16D	477	After Being Absent R Didn't Need Help
F1S16E	478	After Being Absent The Teacher Got Mad
F1S16F	479	After Being Absent, Asked Where R Was
F1S16G	480	After Being Absent R Fell Behind
F1S17	481	How Many Yrs Will It Take R To Graduate
F1S18A	482	R Sure To Graduate From High School
F1S18B	483	R Sure To Further Education After H. S
F1S19A1	484	Attend First Two Wks Of Sch Fall Of 1988
F1S19B1	485	Enroll In A Special Program Fall 1988

F1S19C1	486	Pass To The Next Term/Grade Fall Of 1988
F1S19A2	487	Attend First Two Wks Of Schl Spring 1989
F1S19B2	488	Enroll In Special Program Spring Of 1989
F1S19C2	489	Pass To The Next Term/Grade Spring 1989
F1S19A3	490	Attend First Two Wks Of Sch Fall Of 1989
F1S19B3	491	Enroll In A Special Program Fall Of 1989
F1S19C3	492	Pass To The Next Term/Grade Fall Of 1989
F1S20	493	Describe Present High School Program
F1S21A	494	Main Reason R Taking Math
F1S21B	495	Main Reason R Taking Science
F1S21C	496	Main Reason R Taking English
F1S21D	497	Main Reason R Taking History
F1S22A	498	How Much Coursework In General Math
F1S22B	499	How Much Coursework In Pre-Algebra
F1S22C	500	How Much Coursework In Algebra I
F1S22D	501	How Much Coursework In Geometry
F1S22E	502	How Much Coursework In Algebra Ii
F1S22F	503	How Much Coursework In Trigonometry
F1S22G	504	How Much Coursework In Pre-Calculus
F1S22H	505	How Much Coursework In Calculus
F1S22I	506	How Much Coursework In Business Math
F1S22J	507	How Much Coursework In Other Math
F1S23A	508	How Much Coursework In General Science
F1S23B	509	How Much Coursework In Physical Science
F1S23C	510	How Much Coursework In Biology
F1S23D	511	How Much Coursework In Earth Science
F1S23E	512	How Much Coursework In Chemistry
F1S23F	513	How Much Coursewrk In Principles Of Tech
F1S23G	514	How Much Coursework In Physics
F1S23H	515	How Much Coursework In Other Science
F1S24A	516	How Much Coursework In English
F1S24B	517	How Much Coursework In World History
F1S24C	518	How Much Coursework In U.S. History
F1S24D	519	How Much Coursework In Geography
F1S24E	520	How Much Coursework In Government/Civics
F1S24F	521	How Much Coursework In Economics
F1S24G	522	How Much Coursework In Foreign Language
F1S24H	523	How Much Coursework In Art
F1S24I	524	How Much Coursework In Music
F1S24J	525	How Much Coursework In Drama
F1S24K	526	How Much Coursework In Religious Ed
F1S24L	527	How Much Coursework In Physical Ed
F1S24M	528	How Much Coursework In Sex Education
F1S24N	529	How Much Coursework In Psychology
F1S24O	530	How Much Coursework In Computer Science

F1S25A	531	How Much Coursework In Computer Ed
F1S25B	532	How Much Coursework In Consumer Ed
F1S25C	533	How Much Coursework In Home Economics
F1S25D	534	How Much Coursework In Shop Class
F1S25E	535	How Much Coursework In Typing Class
F1S25F	536	How Much Coursework In Agriculture Class
F1S25G	537	How Much Coursewrk In Career Exploration
F1S25H	538	How Much Coursework In Computer Literacy
F1S26A	539	Often Asked To Show Understand Math
F1S26B	540	Often Asked To Show Understand English
F1S26C	541	Often Asked To Show Understand History
F1S26D	542	Often Asked To Show Understand Science
F1S27A	543	Often Work Hard In Math Class
F1S27B	544	Often Work Hard In English Class
F1S27C	545	Often Work Hard In History Class
F1S27D	546	Often Work Hard In Science Class
F1S28A	547	Often Feel Challenged In Math Class
F1S28B	548	Often Feel Challenged In English Class
F1S28C	549	Often Feel Challenged In History Class
F1S28D	550	Often Feel Challenged In Science Class
F1S29	551	Respondent Has Not Taken A Science Class
F1S29A	552	Review Science Work From Previous Day
F1S29B	553	Make Choice Of Science Topic To Study
F1S29C	554	Copy Teacher's Notes In Science Class
F1S29D	555	Write Rpts Of Laboratory Work In Science
F1S29E	556	Use Books To Show How Experiment Works
F1S29F	557	Make Up Methods To Solve Science Problem
F1S29G	558	Conduct Own Experiments In Science
F1S29H	559	Use Computers To Write Science Reports
F1S29I	560	Use Computers For Collectng Science Data
F1S29J	561	Use Computers For Science Calculations
F1S29K	562	Use Computers For Science Models
F1S29L	563	Listen To The Teacher Lecture In Science
F1S29M	564	Discuss Careers In Scientific Fields
F1S29N	565	Watch The Tchr Demonstrate An Experiment
F1S30A	566	Emphasis On Increasing Science Interest
F1S30B	567	Emphasis On Learning Science Facts/Rules
F1S30C	568	Emphasis On Further Study In Science
F1S30D	569	Emphasis On Ways To Solve Sci. Problems
F1S30E	570	Emphasis On Science Importance In Life
F1S31	571	Respondent Has Not Taken Math Class
F1S31A	572	Emphasis On Increasing Interest In Math
F1S31B	573	Emphasis On Learning Math Facts/Rules
F1S31C	574	Emphasis On Further Study In Math
F1S31D	575	Emphasis On Ways To Solve Math Problems

F1S31E	576	Emphasis On Importance Of Math In Life
F1S32A	577	Often Review Math Work From Previous Day
F1S32B	578	Often Use Books Othr Thn Math Text Books
F1S32C	579	Often Copy Teacher's Notes In Math Class
F1S32D	580	Often Do Problem-Solving In Math
F1S32E	581	Often Use Computers In Math Class
F1S32F	582	Often Use Hands-On Materials In Math
F1S32G	583	Often Use Calculators In Math Class
F1S32H	584	Often Participate In Student Discussions
F1S32I	585	Often Explain Math Work In Class Orally
F1S33	586	R Has Not Taken A Vocational Course
F1S33A	587	Emphasis On Teaching Skills To Use Now
F1S33B	588	Emphasis On Teaching Voc Facts, Rules
F1S33C	589	Emphasis On Undrstndng Sci. Ideas At Wrk
F1S33D	590	Emphasis On Ways To Solve Problems
F1S33E	591	Emphasis On Understndng Math & Sci Ideas
F1S34A	592	Ever Been In A Remedial English Class
F1S34B	593	Ever Been In A Remedial Math Class
F1S34C	594	Ever Been In Bilingual/Bicultural Class
F1S34D	595	Ever Been In English As Second Lang Prog
F1S34E	596	Ever Been In Advanced Placement Program
F1S34F	597	Ever Been In Educationally Handicap Prog
F1S34G	598	Ever Been In Physically Handicapped Prog
F1S34H	599	Ever Been In Dropout Prevention Program
F1S35A	600	Received Information On Sex Education
F1S35B	601	Received Information On Aids Education
F1S35C	602	Received Information On Alcohol/Drugs Ed
F1S36A1	603	Time Spent On Homework In School
F1S36A2	604	Time Spent On Homework Out Of School
F1S36B1	605	Time Spent On Math Homework In School
F1S36B2	606	Time Spent On Math Homework Out Of Schl
F1S36C1	607	Time Spent On Science Homework In School
F1S36C2	608	Time Spent On Science Homewrk Out Of Sch
F1S36D1	609	Time Spent On English Homework In School
F1S36D2	610	Time Spent On English Homewrk Out Of Sch
F1S36E1	611	Time Spent On History Homework In School
F1S36E2	612	Time Spent On History Homewrk Out Of Sch
F1S36F1	613	Time Spent On All Oth Subjects In School
F1S36F2	614	Time Spent On All Oth Subjects Out Schl
F1S37	615	# Of Class Periods R Spent In Study Hall
F1S38	616	How Important Are Good Grades To R
F1S39A	617	Describe Respondent's Math Grades
F1S39B	618	Describe Respondent's English Grades
F1S39C	619	Describe Respondent's History Grades
F1S39D	620	Describe Respondent's Science Grades

F1S40A	621	Often Go To Class Without Pencil/Paper
F1S40B	622	Often Go To Class Without Books
F1S40C	623	Often Go To Class Without Homework Done
F1S41AA	624	Played Baseball/Softball At School
F1S41AB	625	Played Basketball At School
F1S41AC	626	Played Football At School
F1S41AD	627	Played Soccer At School
F1S41AE	628	Participated On Swim Team At School
F1S41AF	629	Played Other Team Sport
F1S41AG	630	Played An Individual Sport
F1S41AH	631	Participated In Cheerleading
F1S41AI	632	Participated On Pom-Pom, Drill Team
F1S41BA	633	Participated In School Band, Orchestra
F1S41BB	634	Participated In School Play Or Musical
F1S41BC	635	Participated In Student Government
F1S41BD	636	Participated In Academic Honor Society
F1S41BE	637	Participated In Schl Yearbook, Newspaper
F1S41BF	638	Participated In School Service Clubs
F1S41BG	639	Participated In School Academic Clubs
F1S41BH	640	Participated In School Hobby Clubs
F1S41BI	641	Participated In School Fta, Fha, Ffa
F1S42	642	Time Spent On Extracurricular Activities
F1S43	643	Reading Done Per Week On Own Outside Sch
F1S44A	644	Visit With Friends At Local Hangout
F1S44B	645	How Often Does R Use Personal Computers
F1S44C	646	How Often Does R Work On Hobbies
F1S44D	647	How Often Does R Read For Pleasure
F1S44E	648	How Often Does R Go To The Park,Gym,Pool
F1S44F	649	How Often Does R Play Ball Or Oth Sports
F1S44G	650	How Often Does R Attend Youth Groups
F1S44H	651	How Often R Performs Community Services
F1S44I	652	How Often Does R Drive Or Ride Around
F1S44J	653	How Often R Talks On Phone With Friends
F1S44K	654	How Often R Does Things W/Mother/Father
F1S44L	655	How Often R Talks With Other Adults
F1S44M	656	How Oftn R Takes Music, Art, Dance Class
F1S44N	657	How Often R Takes Sports Lessons
F1S44O	658	How Often R Attends Religious Activities
F1S45A	659	How Many Hours On Weekdays R Watches Tv
F1S45B	660	How Many Hours On Weekends R Watches Tv
F1S46A	661	Important Being Successful In Line Work
F1S46B	662	Important Finding Right Person To Marry
F1S46C	663	Important Having Lots Of Money
F1S46D	664	Important To Have Strong Friendships
F1S46E	665	Important To Be Able To Find Steady Work

F1S46F	666	Important To Help Others In Community
F1S46G	667	Give My Children Better Opportunities
F1S46H	668	Important Living Close Parents,Relatives
F1S46I	669	Important Getting Away From This Area
F1S46J	670	Working To Correct Economic Inequalities
F1S46K	671	Important Having Children
F1S46L	672	Important Having Leisure Time
F1S46M	673	Important Getting Away From Parents
F1S47A	674	Father's Desire For R After High School
F1S47B	675	Mother's Desire For R After High School
F1S47C	676	Friend's Desire For R After High School
F1S47D	677	Close Relative's Desire For R After H. S.
F1S47E	678	School Counselor's Desire For R After Hs
F1S47F	679	Favorite Teacher's Desire For R After Hs
F1S47G	680	Coach's Desire For R After High School
F1S48A	681	How Far In School Father Wants R To Go
F1S48B	682	How Far In School Mother Wants R To Go
F1S49	683	How Far In School R Thinks He Will Get
F1S50A	684	Does R Plan To Take The Pre-Sat Test
F1S50B	685	R Plans To Take College Board Sat Test
F1S50C	686	Does R Plan To Take The Act Test
F1S50D	687	R Plans To Take Advanced Placement Test
F1S50E	688	Does R Plan To Take The Asvab
F1S50F	689	Does R Plan To Take The Pact Test
F1S51	690	Does R Plan To Go To College After H. S.
F1S52A	691	How Important Are College Expenses
F1S52B	692	How Important Is Financial Aid
F1S52C	693	How Important Are Specific Courses
F1S52D	694	How Important Is College Athletic Progrm
F1S52E	695	How Important Is Social Life At College
F1S52F	696	How Impt Attend College And Live At Home
F1S52G	697	How Impt Attend College & Not Live At Hm
F1S52H	698	How Important Is A Religious Environment
F1S52I	699	How Important Is A Low Crime Environment
F1S52J	700	How Important Is College Job Placement
F1S52K	701	How Important Is Reputation Of College
F1S52L	702	How Important Easy Admission Standards
F1S53A	703	Occupation R Expects To Have After H. S
F1S53B	704	Occupation R Expects To Have At Age 30
F1S54	705	Language Besides English Spoken At Home
F1S55	706	What Other Language Is Spoken At Home?
F1S55A	707	R's Native Language Spoken At Home
F1S55BA	708	How Well Does R Understand Native Lang
F1S55BB	709	How Well Does R Speak Native Language
F1S55BC	710	How Well Does R Read Native Language

F1S55BD	711	How Well Does R Write Native Language
F1S56	712	R Talks To Parents In English Abt Hmwrk
F1S57A	713	How Well R Understands Spoken English
F1S57B	714	How Well Does R Speak English
F1S57C	715	How Well Does R Read English
F1S57D	716	How Well Does R Write English
F1S58	717	Special Help In Reading,Writing English
F1S59A	718	Help In Form Of Individual Tutoring
F1S59B	719	Help In Form Of A Small Group
F1S59C	720	Special Help In Form Of A Large Group
F1S59D	721	Help In Form Of English Second Language
F1S59E	722	Help In Form Of Bilingual Education
F1S60A	723	How Often Did R Listen To English Tapes
F1S60B	724	How Often Did R Improve English Speaking
F1S60C	725	How Often Was R Reading English
F1S60D	726	How Often Was R Writing English
F1S60E	727	How Often Did R Work On Other Activities
F1S61A	728	Understandng Spoken English Has Improved
F1S61B	729	Speaking English Improved By Spec. Class
F1S61C	730	Reading English Improved By Spec Classes
F1S61D	731	Writing English Improved By Spec Classes
F1S62A	732	R Feels Good About Him/Herself
F1S62B	733	R Doesn't Have Enough Control Over Life
F1S62C	734	Good Luck More Important Than Hard Work
F1S62D	735	R Feels S/He Is A Person Of Worth
F1S62E	736	R Able To Do Things As Well As Others
F1S62F	737	When Gettng Ahead Somebody/Thing Stops R
F1S62G	738	R Feels Plans Hardly Ever Work Out
F1S62H	739	On The Whole, R's Satisfied With Self
F1S62I	740	R Feels Useless At Times
F1S62J	741	At Times, R Thinks He Is No Good At All
F1S62K	742	When Makes Plans R's Certain They Work
F1S62L	743	R Does Not Have Much To Be Proud Of
F1S62M	744	Chance,Luck Very Important For R's Life
F1S62N	745	Feel Emotionally Empty Most Of The Time
F1S63A	746	R's Parents Treat R Fairly
F1S63B	747	Learn Things Quickly In English Classes
F1S63C	748	R Has Friends Who Are Members Of Own Sex
F1S63D	749	Mathematics Is One Of R's Best Subjects
F1S63E	750	English Is One Of R's Best Subjects
F1S63F	751	R Does Not Like His Parents Very Much
F1S63G	752	R Gets Good Marks In English
F1S63H	753	Gets Lots Of Attention From Opposite Sex
F1S63I	754	R Gets Along Well With His/Her Parents
F1S63J	755	R Has Always Done Well In Mathematics

F1S63K	756	R Makes Friends Easily With Girls
F1S63L	757	R Makes Friends Easily With Boys
F1S63M	758	Parents Disappointed With What R Does
F1S63N	759	R Hopeless In English Classes
F1S63O	760	R Does Not Get Along Well With Girls
F1S63P	761	R Does Not Get Along Well With Boys
F1S63Q	762	R Gets Good Marks In Mathematics
F1S63R	763	Can't Make Friends W/Members Of Own Sex
F1S63S	764	R Does Badly In Tests Of Mathematics
F1S63T	765	R Not Very Popular With Opposite Sex
F1S63U	766	R's Parents Understand Him/Her
F1S64A	767	Chances That R Will Graduate From H. S.
F1S64B	768	Chances That R Will Go To College
F1S64C	769	Chances R Will Have A Job That Pays Well
F1S64D	770	Chances That R Will Be Able To Own Home
F1S64E	771	Chances R Will Have A Job That He Enjoys
F1S64F	772	Chances R Will Have A Happy Family Life
F1S64G	773	Chances R Will Stay In Good Health
F1S64H	774	Chances R Will Be Able To Live Anywhere
F1S64I	775	Chances R Will Be Respected In Community
F1S64J	776	Chances R Will Have Friends To Count On
F1S64K	777	Chances R's Life Better Than Parents
F1S64L	778	Chance R's Children Life Better Than R's
F1S65A	779	Courses Were Harder In High School
F1S65B	780	Teachers Were Stricter In High School
F1S65C	781	Schl Rules Were Strictly Enforced In Hs
F1S65D	782	More Difficult To Make Friends In H. S.
F1S65E	783	R Felt More Alone In High School
F1S66A	784	R Thinks The Classes Are Interesting
F1S66B	785	Satisfaction Doing What Expectd In Class
F1S66C	786	R Has Nothing Better To Do
F1S66D	787	Educatn Is Important To Get A Job Later
F1S66E	788	School Is A Place For R To Meet Friends
F1S66F	789	Goes To Schl Because He Plays On A Team
F1S66G	790	Teachers Expect R To Succeed In School
F1S67A	791	Students Think Of R As Being Popular
F1S67B	792	Students Think Of R As Being Athletic
F1S67C	793	Students Think R Is Socially Active
F1S67D	794	Students Think R Is A Good Student
F1S67E	795	Students Think Of R As Being Important
F1S67F	796	Students Think Of R As A Trouble-Maker
F1S67G	797	Think Of R As Part Of The Leading Crowd
F1S67H	798	Think Of R As Not Fitting In Any Group
F1S68	799	Close Friends Now Friends In 8Th Grade
F1S69	800	Number Of Close Friends Who Dropped Out

F1S70A	801	Important To Attend Classes Regularly
F1S70B	802	Among Friends,How Important To Study
F1S70C	803	Among Friends,How Important Play Sports
F1S70D	804	Among Friends How Imp To Get Good Grades
F1S70E	805	Important To Be Popular With Students
F1S70F	806	Among Friends How Important To Finish Hs
F1S70G	807	Important To Have Steady Boy/Girlfriend
F1S70H	808	Important To Be Willing To Party
F1S70I	809	Important To Continue Education Past Hs
F1S70J	810	Imp To Participate In Religious Activity
F1S70K	811	Important To Do Community Work,Volunteer
F1S70L	812	Among Friends,How Important To Have Job
F1S71A	813	Person R Admires The Most Is Popular
F1S71B	814	Person R Admires The Most Is Honest
F1S71C	815	Person R Admires The Most Dresses Well
F1S71D	816	Person R Admires The Most Is Intelligent
F1S71E	817	Person R Admires The Most Understands R
F1S71F	818	Person R Admires Most Drives A Nice Car
F1S71G	819	Person R Admires The Most Has A Job
F1S71H	820	Person R Admires Makes A Lot Of Money
F1S71I	821	Person R Admires Most Is Good At Sports
F1S71J	822	Admired Person Thinks The Way R Does
F1S71K	823	R Does Not Admire Anyone
F1S72	824	R's Relationship To The Admired Person
F1S73A	825	People R Spends Time With 13Yrs/Younger
F1S73B	826	People R Spends Time With 14–15Yrs Old
F1S73C	827	People R Spends Time With 16–17Yrs Old
F1S73D	828	People R Spends Time With 18–19Yrs Old
F1S73E	829	People R Spends Time With 20–21Yrs Old
F1S73F	830	People R Spends Time With 22–25Yrs Old
F1S73G	831	People R Spends Time With 26Yrs And Oldr
F1S74	832	Important To Be Married Before Sex
F1S75	833	Consider Having A Child Before Marriage
F1S76	834	R Have Any Children Of (His/Her) Own
F1S77	835	How Many Cigarettes Does R Smoke Per Day
F1S78A	836	In Lifetime,# Times Had Alcohol To Drink
F1S78B	837	Last 12 Mos, # Of Times R Drank Alcohol
F1S78C	838	Last 30 Days, # Times R Drank Alcohol
F1S79	839	# Times R Had 5 Drinks Or More In A Row
F1S80AA	840	In Lifetime, # Of Times R Used Marijuana
F1S80AB	841	Last 12 Months, # Times Used Marijuana
F1S80AC	842	Last 30 Days, # Times Used Marijuana
F1S80BA	843	In Lifetime, # Of Times Taken Cocaine
F1S80BB	844	Last 12 Months, # Of Times Taken Cocaine
F1S80BC	845	Last 30 Days, # Times Taken Cocaine

F1S81	846	What Is R's Religious Background
F1S82	847	How Often R Attend Religious Services
F1S83	848	R Thinks He Is A Religious Person
F1S84	849	R Currently Employd Or Ever Been Employd
F1S85	850	How Many Hrs Does R Usually Work A Week
F1S86	851	How Many Of Those Hrs Are On The Weekend
F1S87	852	Type Of Work R Does On Current Job
F1S88	853	How Much Does/Did R Earn Per Hour On Job
F1S89	854	Does R Have A Twin Brother Or Sister
F1S90A	855	How Many Older Brother(S) Does R Have
F1S90B	856	How Many Older Sister(S) Does R Have
F1S91A	857	How Many Younger Brother(S) Does R Have
F1S91B	858	How Many Younger Sister(S) Does R Have
F1S92A	859	Father Lives In Same Household As R
F1S92B	860	Stepfather Lives In Same Household As R
F1S92C	861	Oth Adult Male Lives In Same Hsehld As R
F1S92D	862	Mother Lives In Same Household As R
F1S92E	863	Stepmother Lives In Same Househld As R
F1S92F	864	Othr Adult Female Lives In Same Househld
F1S92G	865	Spouse Lives In Same Household As R
F1S92H	866	Boy/Girlfriend Lives In Same Household
F1S92I	867	R's Child/Childrn Lives In Same Househld
F1S93A	868	No. Brother(S) Living In Same Household
F1S93B	869	No. Sister(S) Living In Same Household
F1S93C	870	Number Of Grandparents In Same Household
F1S93D	871	No. Oth Relative(S) Under 18 In Househld
F1S93E	872	No. Othr Relative(S) 18 & Over In Hsehld
F1S93F	873	No. Non-Relatives Under 18 In Household
F1S93G	874	No. Non-Relatives 18 & Over In Household
F1S94	875	Number Of Dropout Siblings
F1S95	876	Does R Babysit Own Child, Or Siblings
F1S96	877	Hours Per Day Spent Babysitting
F1S97	878	Number Of School Days Missed To Babysit
F1S98A	879	R Gets Along With All Family Members
F1S98B	880	R Doesn't Get Along With His/Her Father
F1S98C	881	Doesn't Get Along With Oth Male Guardian
F1S98D	882	R Doesn't Get Along With His/Her Mother
F1S98E	883	Doesn't Get Along With Step/Fostermother
F1S98F	884	R Doesn't Get Along With Brothers
F1S98G	885	R Doesen't Get Along With Sisters
F1S98H	886	R Doesn't Get Along With Grandparent(S)
F1S98I	887	R Doesn't Get Along With Other Relatives
F1S99A	888	In Last 2 Yrs Family Moved To A New Home
F1S99B	889	Last 2Yrs One Of R's Parents Got Married
F1S99C	890	In Last 2 Years R's Parents Got Divorced

F1S99D	891	In Last 2 Yrs R's Mother Lost Her Job
F1S99E	892	In The Last 2Yrs R's Father Lost His Job
F1S99F	893	In Last 2Yrs R's Mother Started To Work
F1S99G	894	In Last 2 Yrs R's Father Started To Work
F1S99H	895	In The Last 2 Yrs R Became Seriously Ill
F1S99I	896	In The Last 2Yrs R's Father Died
F1S99J	897	In The Last 2Yrs R's Mother Died
F1S99K	898	In Last 2Yrs A Close Relative Died
F1S99L	899	Last 2Yrs Unmarried Sister Got Pregnant
F1S99M	900	Last 2Yrs R's Brother/Sister Dropped Out
F1S99N	901	In Last 2Yrs R's Family Went On Welfare
F1S99O	902	In Last 2Yrs R's Family Went Off Welfare
F1S99P	903	In Last 2 Yrs Family Stayed On Welfare
F1S99Q	904	Family Member Became Ill In Past 2 Yrs
F1S99R	905	In Past 2 Years R's Family Was Homeless
F1S99S	906	None Of The Above Applies To R
F1S100A	907	How Often Parents Check R's Homework
F1S100B	908	How Often Parents Help R With Homework
F1S100C	909	Special Privileges Given For Good Grades
F1S100D	910	Parents Limit Privileges Due Poor Grades
F1S100E	911	R Required To Work Around The House
F1S100F	912	Parents Limit Tv Watching Or Video Games
F1S100G	913	Parents Limit Time With Friends
F1S101	914	Latest R Can Stay Out On School Nights
F1S102A	915	Parents Try To Find Out Who Friends Are
F1S102B	916	Parent Try To Find Where R Goes At Night
F1S102C	917	Parents Try To Find How R Spends Money
F1S102D	918	Try To Find What R Does With Free Time
F1S102E	919	Parents Try Find Where R Is After School
F1S103	920	R's Parents Know Closest Friends Parents
F1S104A	921	Who Decides How Late R Can Stay Out
F1S104B	922	Who Decides Friends R Spends Time With
F1S104C	923	Who Decides Which Classes R Will Take
F1S104D	924	Who Decides If R Can Have A Job
F1S104E	925	Who Decides The Age R Can Leave School
F1S104F	926	Who Decides How R Will Spend His Money
F1S104G	927	Who Decides Whether R Can Date
F1S104H	928	Who Decides If R Goes Out For Schl Sport
F1S104I	929	Decides If R Should Be In Sch Activities
F1S104J	930	Who Decides If R Should Go To College
F1S105A	931	Discussed School Courses With Parent
F1S105B	932	Discussed School Activities With Parent
F1S105C	933	Discuss Things Studied In Class W/Parent
F1S105D	934	How Often Discussed Grades With Parents
F1S105E	935	Discussed Transferring To Another School

F1S105F	936	Discussed Prep For The Act/Sat Test
F1S105G	937	Discussed Going To College With Parents
F1S106A	938	How Often Parents Attend School Meetings
F1S106B	939	How Often Parent Phoned Teachr,Counselor
F1S106C	940	How Often Parents Attended School Event
F1S106D	941	Parents Acted As Volunteer At R's School
F1S107A	942	Parents Rec'd Warning About R Attendance
F1S107B	943	Parent's Rec'd Warning About R's Grades
F1S107C	944	Parents Rec'd Warning About R's Behavior
F1S108A	945	Parents Trust R To Do What They Expect
F1S108B	946	R Doesn't Know Why He Should Obey Parent
F1S108C	947	Often Count On Parents To Solve Problems
F1S108D	948	R Will Be A Source Of Pride To Parents
F1S108E	949	R's Parents Get Along Well With Each Oth
F1S108F	950	R's Family Will Be Similar To His Own
F1S109	951	Did R Run Away From Home In Last 2Yrs
F1S110MO	952	Month Respondent Completed Interview
F1S110DA	953	Day Respondent Completed Interview
F1S110YR	954	Year Respondent Completed Interview
F1QWT	955	1Fu Questionnaire Weight
F1PNLWT	956	1Fu Panel Weight
F1QFLG	957	First Follow-Up Questionnaire Available
F1BYQFLG	958	Base Year Questionnaire Available
F1PANFLG	959	Base Year & 1Fu Questionnaires Available
F1TXFLG	960	Student Tests Available
F1NSSFLG	961	New Student Supplement Available
F1ADMFLG	962	School Questionnaire Available
F1TRNFLG	963	Student Transfer Flag
F1SEQFLG	964	Enrolled 10Th Gr. When Quex Administered
F1SMPFLG	965	Sample Member Flag
F1STAT	966	Status Of Sample Member
F1SRVMTH	967	Method Used To Gather Data
F1DOSTAT	968	Dropout Status
F1SEX	969	Composite Sex
F1RACE	970	Composite Race
F1API	971	Asian Pacific Islander Race Composite
F1SES	972	Socio-Economic Status Composite
F1SESQ	973	Socio-Economic Quartile
F1PARED	974	Parents' Highest Education Level
F1LOCUS1	975	Locus Of Control 1
F1LOCUS2	976	Locus Of Control 2
F1LOCU2Q	977	Quartile Coding Of Variable F1locus2
F1CNCPT1	978	Self-Concept 1
F1CNCPT2	979	Self-Concept 2
F1CNCP2Q	980	Quartile Coding Of Variable F1cncpt2

F1BIRTHM	981	Birth Month Of Sample Member
F1BIRTHY	982	Birth Year Of Sample Member
F1DRPS89	983	Studnt Dropped Out During Spring 89 Term
F1DRPF89	984	Student Dropped Out During Fall 89 Term
F1DRPS90	985	Studnt Dropped Out During Spring 90 Term
F1HSPROG	986	Hs Program In Which R Is/Was Enrolled
FAMCOMP	987	Adult Composition Of The Household
G8CTRL1	988	Eighth Grade School Composite 1
G8CTRL2	989	Eighth Grade School Composite 2
G10CTRL1	990	School Classification Reported By School
G10CTRL2	991	School Classification
G10URBAN	992	Urbanicity Of The Student's School
G10REGON	993	Region Of The Country (4 Census Regions)
F1SCENRL	994	Entire School Enrollment
G10ENROL	995	Tenth Grade Enrollment
F1TXRIRR	996	Reading Irt-Estimated Number Right
F1TXRSTD	997	Reading Standardized Score
F1TXRQ	998	Reading Quartile (1=Low)
F1TXRG	999	Reading Irt-Estimated Gain By To Fu1
F1TXMIRR	1000	Math Irt-Estimated Number Right
F1TXMSTD	1001	Math Standardized Score
F1TXMQ	1002	Math Quartile (1=Low)
F1TXMG	1003	Math Irt-Estimated Gain By To Fu1
F1TXSIRR	1004	Science Irt-Estimated Number Right
F1TXSSTD	1005	Science Standardized Score
F1TXSQ	1006	Science Quartile (1=Low)
F1TXSG	1007	Science Irt-Estimated Gain By To Fu1
F1TXHIRR	1008	Hist/Cit/Geog Irt Estimated Number Right
F1TXHSTD	1009	Hist/Cit/Geog Standardized Score
F1TXHQ	1010	Hist/Cit/Geog Quartile (1=Low)
F1TXHG	1011	Hist/Cit/Geog Irt-Est. Gain By To Fu1
F1TXCOMP	1012	Standardizd Test Composite (Readng,Math)
F1TXQURT	1013	Standardized Test Quartile (1=Low)
F1TXRPL1	1014	Reading Proficiency—Level 1
F1TXRPL2	1015	Reading Proficiency—Level 2
F1TXRPRO	1016	Overall Reading Proficiency
F1TXRPP1	1017	Reading Level 1: Probability Of Prof.
F1TXRPP2	1018	Reading Level 2: Probability Of Prof.
F1TXRGP1	1019	Reading Level 1: Gain In Probability
F1TXRGP2	1020	Reading Level 2: Gain In Probability
F1TXMPL1	1021	Math Proficiency—Level 1
F1TXMPL2	1022	Math Proficiency—Level 2
F1TXMPL3	1023	Math Proficiency—Level 3
F1TXMPL4	1024	Math Proficiency—Level 4
F1TXMPRO	1025	Overall Math Proficiency

F1TXMPP1	1026	Math Level 1: Probability Of Prof. Ful
F1TXMPP2	1027	Math Level 2: Probability Of Prof. Ful
F1TXMPP3	1028	Math Level 3: Probability Of Prof. Ful
F1TXMPP4	1029	Math Level 4: Probability Of Prof. Ful
F1TXMGP1	1030	Math Level 1: Gain In Probability
F1TXMGP2	1031	Math Level 2: Gain In Probability
F1TXMGP3	1032	Math Level 3: Gain In Probability
F1TXMGP4	1033	Math Level 4: Gain In Probability
F1SCHLID	1034	1Fu School Id
F1N2	1035	What Is Respondent's Sex
F1N4	1036	Is Respondent's Mother Living
F1N5A	1037	Is R's Mother's Working/Unemployed
F1N5B	1038	What Is R's Mother's Occupation:
F1N6	1039	Is Respondent's Father Living
F1N7A	1040	Is R's Father Working/Unemployed Etc.
F1N7B	1041	What Is R's Father's Occupation:
F1N8A	1042	Which Best Describes R's Race
F1N8B	1043	Describe R's Api Background
F1N8C	1044	Describe R's Hispanic Background
F1N9	1045	What Is Hispanic R's Race
F1N10	1046	Respondent's 8Th Grade School Type
F1N11	1047	Did R Speak A Language Oth Than English
F1N12	1048	1St Language R Learned To Speak
F1N13	1049	Other Language R Spoke Before School
F1N14	1050	What Language Does R Usually Speak Now
F1N15	1051	Language Other Than English R Uses Now
F1N16A	1052	R Understand Language When Spoken By Oth
F1N16B	1053	How Well Does R Speak That Language
F1N16C	1054	How Well Does R Read That Language
F1N16D	1055	How Well Does R Write That Language
F1N17A	1056	R Understands English When Spoken By Oth
F1N17B	1057	How Well Does R Speak English
F1N17C	1058	How Well Does R Read English
F1N17D	1059	How Well Does R Write English
F1N18	1060	Did R Ever Receive Special Help In Schl
F1N19A	1061	R Enrolled In This Program In 1St Grade
F1N19B	1062	R Enrolled In This Program In 2Nd Grade
F1N19C	1063	R Enrolled In This Program In 3Rd Grade
F1N19D	1064	R Enrolled In This Program In 4Th Grade
F1N19E	1065	R Enrolled In This Program In 5Th Grade
F1N19F	1066	R Enrolled In This Program In 6Th Grade
F1N19G	1067	R Enrolled In This Program In 7Th Grade
F1N19H	1068	R Enrolled In This Program In 8Th Grade
F1N19I	1069	R Enrolled In This Program In 9Th Grade
F1N19J	1070	R Enrolled In This Program In 10Th Grade

F1N20A	1071	How Far In School Did R's Father Go
F1N20B	1072	How Far In School Did R's Mother Go
F1N21A	1073	Family Has A Specific Place For Study
F1N21B	1074	Does Family Receive A Daily Newspaper
F1N21C	1075	Does Family Regularly Receive A Magazine
F1N21D	1076	Does Family Have An Encyclopedia
F1N21E	1077	Does Family Have An Atlas
F1N21F	1078	Does Family Have A Dictionary
F1N21G	1079	Does Family Have A Typewriter
F1N21H	1080	Does Family Have A Computer
F1N21I	1081	Does Family Have An Electric Dishwasher
F1N21J	1082	Does Family Have A Clothes Dryer
F1N21K	1083	Does Family Have A Washing Machine
F1N21L	1084	Does Family Have A Microwave Oven
F1N21M	1085	Does Family Have More Than 50 Books
F1N21N	1086	Does Family Have A Vcr
F1N21O	1087	Does Family Have A Pocket Calculator
F1N21P	1088	Does R Have Own Room
F1N22	1089	Has R Ever Been Held Back A Grade In Sch
F1N22A	1090	R Repeated Kindergarten
F1N22B	1091	R Repeated Grade 1
F1N22C	1092	R Repeated Grade 2
F1N22D	1093	R Repeated Grade 3
F1N22E	1094	R Repeated Grade 4
F1N22F	1095	R Repeated Grade 5
F1N22G	1096	R Repeated Grade 6
F1N22H	1097	R Repeated Grade 7
F1N22I	1098	R Repeated Grade 8
F1N22J	1099	R Repeated Grade 9
F1N22K	1100	R Repeated Grade 10
BYP1A1	1101	R's Relationship To Eighth Grader
BYP1A2	1102	Partner's Relationship To 8Th Grader
BYP1B	1103	Amt Of Time Student Lives W/Respondent
BYP2	1104	Number Of People Dependent Upon R
BYP3A	1105	Number Of Siblings 8Th Grader Has
BYP3B	1106	Number Of Siblings Presently In Home
BYP4	1107	No. Of Childrn Older Than R's 8Th Grader
BYP5A	1108	Number Of Children In High School
BYP5B	1109	Number Of Children Graduated From H. S.
BYP6	1110	Number Of Children Who Dropped Out Of Hs
BYP7	1111	R's Current Marital Status
BYP8	1112	R's Year Of Birth
BYP9	1113	Spouse's Year Of Birth
BYP10	1114	R's Race/Origin
BYP10A	1115	Asian Ethnic Background

BYP10B	1116	Hispanic Ethnic Background
BYP10C	1117	Hispanic Race
BYP11	1118	8Th Grader's Mother's Birthplace
BYP12	1119	Number Of Years Ago Mother Came To U.S.
BYP13	1120	Mother's Occupatn Before Coming To U.S.
BYP14	1121	8Th Grader's Father's Birthplace
BYP15	1122	Number Of Years Ago Father Came To U.S.
BYP16	1123	Father's Occupatn Before Coming To U.S.
BYP17	1124	8Th Grader's Birth Place
BYP18	1125	No. Of Yrs Ago 8Th Grader Came To U.S.
BYP19	1126	8Th Grader Attend School Outside U.S.
BYP20A	1127	8Th Gr Completd Kindergartn Outside U.S.
BYP20B	1128	8Th Grdr Completd 1St Grade Outside U.S.
BYP20C	1129	8Th Grdr Completd 2Nd Grade Outside U.S.
BYP20D	1130	8Th Grdr Completd 3Rd Grade Outside U.S.
BYP20E	1131	8Th Grdr Completd 4Th Grade Outside U.S.
BYP20F	1132	8Th Grdr Completd 5Th Grade Outside U.S.
BYP20G	1133	8Th Grdr Completd 6Th Grade Outside U.S.
BYP20H	1134	8Th Grdr Completd 7Th Grade Outside U.S.
BYP20I	1135	8Th Grdr Completd 8Th Grade Outside U.S.
BYP20J	1136	No Grades Completed Outside U.S.
BYP21	1137	Grade 8Th Gr In When Began Schl In U.S.
BYP22A	1138	Lang Othr Thn English Spoken In R's Home
BYP22B	1139	Is English Also Spoken In R's Home
BYP22C2	1140	Spanish Spoken In R's Home
BYP22C3	1141	Chinese Spoken In R's Home
BYP22C4	1142	Japanese Spoken In R's Home
BYP22C5	1143	Korean Spoken In R's Home
BYP22C6	1144	A Filipino Language Spoken In R's Home
BYP22C7	1145	Italian Spoken In R's Home
BYP22C8	1146	French Spoken In R's Home
BYP22C9	1147	German Spoken In R's Home
BYP22C10	1148	Greek Spoken In R's Home
BYP22C11	1149	Polish Spoken In R's Home
BYP22C12	1150	Portuguese Spoken In R's Home
BYP22C13	1151	Other Language Spoken In R's Home
BYP22D	1152	Language Spoken Most Often At Home
BYP23	1153	Main Language Usually Spoken In R's Home
BYP24	1154	Language R Currently Uses Most Often
BYP25A	1155	How Well R Understands Language In 22D
BYP25B	1156	How Well R Speaks Language In 22D
BYP25C	1157	How Well R Reads Language In 22D
BYP25D	1158	How Well R Writes Language In 22D
BYP26A	1159	How Well R Understands Spoken English
BYP26B	1160	How Well R Speaks English

BYP26C	1161	How Well R Reads English
BYP26D	1162	How Well R Writes English
BYP27	1163	Lang Usually Spoken To 8Th Grdr At Home
BYP28	1164	Language 8Th Grdr Usually Speaks At Home
BYP29	1165	Religious Background
BYP30	1166	Highest Level Of Education R Completed
BYP31	1167	Spouse's Highest Level Of Educ Completed
BYP32	1168	During The Past 4 Weeks Were You Working
BYP33A	1169	Current Work Status
BYP33B	1170	Have You Ever Held A Regular Job
BYP34A	1171	Self-Employed Or Do You Work For Someone
BYP34B	1172	Description Of Current Job
BYP35	1173	During Past Week Was Spouse Working
BYP36A	1174	Spouse's Current Work Status
BYP36B	1175	Spouse/Partner Ever Held A Regular Job
BYP37A	1176	Spouse Self-Employed/Works For Someone
BYP37B	1177	Description Of Spouse's Current Job
BYP38A	1178	Did 8Th Grader Attend Day Care Program
BYP38B	1179	Did 8Th Grader Attend Nursery/Pre-School
BYP38C	1180	Did 8Th Grader Attend Head Start Program
BYP38D	1181	Did 8Th Grader Attend Kindergarten Pgm
BYP39	1182	No. Of Yrs 8Th Grader At Present Schl
BYP40	1183	No. Of Times 8Th Grader Changed Schools
BYP41	1184	8Th Gradr Ever Skipped A Grade In School
BYP42A	1185	Skipped Grade Because Of Parent Request
BYP42B	1186	Skipped Grade Because Of School Request
BYP42C	1187	Skipped Grade Because Of Other Reason
BYP43A	1188	8Th Grader Skipped Kindergarten
BYP43B	1189	8Th Grader Skipped First Grade
BYP43C	1190	8Th Grader Skipped Second Grade
BYP43D	1191	8Th Grader Skipped Third Grade
BYP43E	1192	8Th Grader Skipped Fourth Grade
BYP43F	1193	8Th Grader Skipped Fifth Grade
BYP43G	1194	8Th Grader Skipped Sixth Grade
BYP43H	1195	8Th Grader Skipped Seventh Grade
BYP44	1196	8Th Grader Ever Held Back A Grade
BYP45A	1197	Held Back Because Of Parental Request
BYP45B	1198	Held Back Because Of School Request
BYP45C	1199	Held Back Because Of Other Reason
BYP46A	1200	8Th Grader Repeated Kindergarten
BYP46B	1201	8Th Grader Repeated First Grade
BYP46C	1202	8Th Grader Repeated Second Grade
BYP46D	1203	8Th Grader Repeated Third Grade
BYP46E	1204	8Th Grader Repeated Fourth Grade
BYP46F	1205	8Th Grader Repeated Fifth Grade

BYP46G	1206	8Th Grader Repeated Sixth Grade
BYP46H	1207	8Th Grader Repeated Seventh Grade
BYP46I	1208	8Th Grader Repeated Eighth Grade
BYP47A	1209	Child Has Visual Handicap
BYP47B	1210	Child Has Hearing Problem
BYP47C	1211	Child Has Deafness
BYP47D	1212	Child Has Speech Problem
BYP47E	1213	Child Has Orthopedic Problem
BYP47F	1214	Child Has Other Physical Disability
BYP47G	1215	Child Has Specific Learning Problem
BYP47H	1216	Child Has Emotional Problem
BYP47J	1217	Child Has Any Other Health Problem
BYP48A	1218	Child Recvd Services For Visual Handicap
BYP48B	1219	Child Recvd Services For Hearing Problem
BYP48C	1220	Child Received Services For Deafness
BYP48D	1221	Child Recvd Services For Speech Problem
BYP48E	1222	Child Recvd Services For Orthopedic Prob
BYP48F	1223	Child Recvd Services For Physcl Disabil
BYP48G	1224	Child Recvd Services For Learning Problm
BYP48H	1225	Chld Recvd Services For Emotionl Problem
BYP48J	1226	Child Recvd Services For Oth Health Prob
BYP49A	1227	Child In Bilingual/Bicultural Ed Prog
BYP49B	1228	Child Enrolled In English 2Nd Lang Prog
BYP49C	1229	Child Rec Orthopedicly Handicpd Services
BYP49D	1230	Child In Spec Ed For Learning Disabled
BYP50	1231	Child Ever Had Behavior Problem At Schl
BYP51	1232	Child Enrolled In Gifted/Talented Prog
BYP52A	1233	How Important Child Complete Schl Faster
BYP52B	1234	How Import Gaining Deepr Underst Of Subs
BYP52C	1235	How Import Chld W/Oth Hi Ability Chldren
BYP52D	1236	How Imprtnt Greater Intellectl Challenge
BYP52E	1237	How Important Devel Music/Artistic Abil
BYP53	1238	Child Enrolled In Algebra Course This Yr
BYP54	1239	Most Influential In Child Taking Algebra
BYP55	1240	Child Enrolled In Foreign Lang Course
BYP56	1241	Influential In Child Taking Foreign Lang
BYP57A	1242	Contacted About Academic Performance
BYP57B	1243	Contacted About Academic Program
BYP57C	1244	Contacted About H. S. Course Selection
BYP57D	1245	Contacted About Placemnt Dec Re H. S. Pgm
BYP57E	1246	Contacted About Behavior In School
BYP57F	1247	Contacted About School Fund Raising
BYP57G	1248	Contacted About Info For School Records
BYP57H	1249	Contacted About Volunteer Work At School
BYP58A	1250	Contacted Schl About Academic Performanc

BYP58B	1251	Contacted School About Academic Program
BYP58C	1252	Contacted School About Behavior
BYP58D	1253	Contacted School About Fund Raising
BYP58E	1254	Contactd Schl About Info For Sch Records
BYP58F	1255	Contacted Sch Abt Doing Volunteer Work
BYP59A	1256	Belong To Parent-Teacher Organization
BYP59B	1257	Attend Parent-Teacher Organiztn Meetings
BYP59C	1258	Take Part In Parent-Teach Org Activities
BYP59D	1259	Act As A Volunteer At The School
BYP59E	1260	Belong To Any Other Organization
BYP60A	1261	Child Study Art Outside Regular School
BYP60B	1262	Child Study Music Outside Regular School
BYP60C	1263	Child Study Dance Outside Regular School
BYP60D	1264	Child Study Language Outside Regular Sch
BYP60E	1265	Child Study Religion Outside Regular Sch
BYP60F	1266	Child Study History Outside Regular Schl
BYP60G	1267	Child Study Computer Outside Regular Sch
BYP60H	1268	Child Study Other Skills Outside Reg Sch
BYP61AA	1269	R Borrows Books From Public Library
BYP61AB	1270	8Th Grader Borrows Books Fr Pub Library
BYP61BA	1271	R Attends Concerts/Other Musical Events
BYP61BB	1272	8Th Grdr Attnds Concerts/Musical Events
BYP61CA	1273	R Goes To Art Museums
BYP61CB	1274	8Th Grader Goes To Art Museums
BYP61DA	1275	R Goes To Science Museums
BYP61DB	1276	8Th Grader Goes To Science Museums
BYP61EA	1277	R Goes To History Museums
BYP61EB	1278	8Th Grader Goes To History Museums
BYP62	1279	R Knows 1St Name Of 8Th Grader's Friends
BYP62A1	1280	1St Friend Attends Same School
BYP62B1	1281	R Knows Parent(S) Of Child's 1St Friend
BYP62A2	1282	2Nd Friend Attends Same School
BYP62B2	1283	R Knows Parent(S) Of Child's 2Nd Friend
BYP62A3	1284	3Rd Friend Attends Same School
BYP62B3	1285	R Knows Parent(S) Of Child's 3Rd Friend
BYP62A4	1286	4Th Friend Attends Same School
BYP62B4	1287	R Knows Parent(S) Of Child's 4Th Friend
BYP62A5	1288	5Th Friend Attends Same School
BYP62B5	1289	R Knows Parent(S) Of Child's 5Th Friend
BYP63A	1290	Child Ever Involved In Boy/Girl Scouts
BYP63B	1291	Child Ever Invlvd In Cub Scouts/Brownies
BYP63C	1292	Chld Ever Involved In Campfire/Bluebirds
BYP63D	1293	Child Ever Involved In Boys-Girls Club
BYP63E	1294	Child Ever Involved In Religious Group
BYP63F	1295	Child Ever Involved In Ymca, Ywca, Jcc

BYP63G	1296	Child Ever Involved In Sports Teams
BYP63H	1297	Child Ever Involved In 4-H Club
BYP63I	1298	Child Ever Involved In Community Group
BYP64A	1299	Family Rule About Pgms Child May Watch
BYP64B	1300	Family Rule How Early/Late Chld Watch Tv
BYP64C	1301	Family Rule How Many Hrs Child Watch Tv
BYP64D	1302	Fmly Rule How Mny Hrs Wtch Tv On Sch Dys
BYP65A	1303	Family Rule About Maintaining Grade Avg
BYP65B	1304	Family Rule About Doing Homework
BYP65C	1305	Family Rule About Doing Household Chores
BYP66	1306	How Oftn Talks To Chld Abt Schl Experncs
BYP67	1307	How Oftn Talks To Child About H. S. Plans
BYP68	1308	How Oft Talks To Chld Re Post H. S. Plans
BYP69	1309	How Often Help Child With Homework
BYP70	1310	Computer In Home Used For Ed Purposes
BYP71	1311	Does Child Come Home Directly After Schl
BYP72A	1312	Mother Home When Child Returns From Schl
BYP72B	1313	Father Home When Child Returns From Schl
BYP72C	1314	Adult Rltv Home Whn Chld Retrns Frm Schl
BYP72D	1315	Sitter Home When Child Returns From Schl
BYP72E	1316	Adlt Nghbr Home Whn Child Return Frm Sch
BYP72F	1317	Older Sib Home When Child Retrns Frm Sch
BYP72G	1318	Younger Sib Home When Chld Rtrns Frm Sch
BYP72H	1319	No One Is Home Whn Chld Returns From Sch
BYP73	1320	Where Does Child Usually Go After Schl
BYP74A	1321	The Sch Places High Priority On Learning
BYP74B	1322	Homework Assigned Is Worthwhile
BYP74C	1323	My Child Is Challenged At School
BYP74D	1324	My Child Is Working Hard At School
BYP74E	1325	My Child Enjoys School
BYP74F	1326	Standards Set By The Schl Are Realistic
BYP74G	1327	Schl Is Preparing Students Well For H. S.
BYP74H	1328	Sch Preparing Students Well For College
BYP74I	1329	The School Is A Safe Place
BYP74J	1330	Parents Have Adequate Say In Schl Policy
BYP74K	1331	Parents Wk Togethr Supporting Sch Policy
BYP75	1332	How Satisfied With Ed Child Has Received
BYP76	1333	How Far In School R Expect Child To Go
BYP77	1334	Who Will Decide Child's H. S. Courses
BYP78	1335	Child Has Parent Who Lives Outside Home
BYP79	1336	Oth Parent's Part In Education Decisions
BYP80	1337	Total Family Income Frm All Sources 1987
BYP81	1338	# Of Earners Contributd To Family Income
BYP82A	1339	Any Edctnl Expenses For Religious School
BYP82B	1340	Any Edctnl Expenses For Private School

BYP82C	1341	Any Edctnl Expenses For College Tuition
BYP82D	1342	Any Educational Expenses For Tutoring
BYP82AA	1343	Educational Expenses For 1987–88 Sch Yr
BYP82BA	1344	Current Earnings Covered Ed Expenses
BYP82BB	1345	Savings/Sale Assets Covered Ed Expenses
BYP82BC	1346	Second Mortgage Covered Ed Expenses
BYP82BD	1347	Personal Loan Covered Ed Expenses
BYP82BE	1348	Alimony/Chld Support Covered Ed Expenses
BYP82BF	1349	Chld Earning/Savings Covered Ed Expenses
BYP82BG	1350	Trust Fund Covered Educational Expenses
BYP82BH	1351	Relatives Covered Educational Expenses
BYP82BI	1352	Scholarships/Grants Covered Ed Expenses
BYP82BJ	1353	State/Federal Loans Covered Ed Expenses
BYP82BK	1354	Social Security/Va Covered Ed Expenses
BYP82BL	1355	Other Sources Covered Ed Expenses
BYP83	1356	Expect Child Will Go On To Additional Ed
BYP84	1357	Saved Any Money For Child Ed After H. S.
BYP84AA	1358	Started A Savings Account
BYP84AB	1359	Bought An Insurance Policy
BYP84AC	1360	Bought U.S. Savings Bonds
BYP84AD	1361	Made Investments In Stocks/Real Estate
BYP84AE	1362	Set Up A Trust Fund
BYP84AF	1363	Started Working/Taken An Additional Job
BYP84AG	1364	Established Another Form Of Savings
BYP84B	1365	Money R Set Aside For Child's Future Ed
BYP84C	1366	Money R Expect To Set Aside For Child Ed
BYP84D	1367	Expect Amount To Cover Cost Of Child Ed
BYP85A	1368	Child Will Be Able To Earn Money For Ed
BYP85B	1369	Can Pay For Child Ed Without Assistance
BYP85C	1370	Family Not Willing Go Into Debt For Ed
BYP85D	1371	Family Income Too High For Loan/Schlrshp
BYP85E	1372	Child Grades Not High Enough To Qualify
BYP85F	1373	Chld Test Scores Not Good Enough Qualify
BYP85G	1374	Too Much Work To Apply For Financial Aid
BYP85H	1375	Not Much Information On Financial Aid
BYP85I	1376	Don't See Way To Get Money For College
BYP85J	1377	Reltvs Will Help Pay Child Coll Expenses
BYSPANFG	1378	Base Year Spanish Parent Quex Flag
PARENTED	1379	Parents' Highest Education Level
INCOME	1380	
PAROCC	1381	Parent Occ Status Composite
ETHNIC	1383	Ethnicity
ZF1S36A1	1384	Zscore: Time Spent On Homework In Schoo
ZF1S36A2	1385	Zscore: Time Spent On Homework Out Of S
ZF1S36B1	1386	Zscore: Time Spent On Math Homework In

ZF1S36B2	1387	Zscore: Time Spent On Math Homework Out
ZF1S36C1	1388	Zscore: Time Spent On Science Homework
ZF1S36C2	1389	Zscore: Time Spent On Science Homewrk O
ZF1S36D1	1390	Zscore: Time Spent On English Homework
ZF1S36D2	1391	Zscore: Time Spent On English Homewrk O
ZF1S36E1	1392	Zscore: Time Spent On History Homework
ZF1S36E2	1393	Zscore: Time Spent On History Homewrk O
ZF1S36F1	1394	Zscore: Time Spent On All Oth Subjects
ZF1S36F2	1395	Zscore: Time Spent On All Oth Subjects
BYHOME	1396	Base Year Homework
FFUHW1	1397	Overall Hw Out Of School
FFUHW2	1398	Mean Hw Out Of School
ZBYHOME	1399	Zscore(Byhome)
ZFFUHW2	1400	Zscore(Ffuhw2)
HOMEWK	1401	By & Ffu Homework
FFUHOME2	1402	Mean Of Ffuhw1,2
FFUGRAD	1403	Ffu Grades
STUDASP	1404	
STUDTALK	1405	
PARTALK	1406	
ZSTUDASP	1407	Zscore(Studasp)
ZBYP76	1408	Zscore: How Far In School R Expect Chil
ZSTUDTAL	1409	Zscore(Studtalk)
ZPARTALK	1410	Zscore(Partalk)
ASPIRE	1411	
TALK	1412	
BYTESTS	1413	Eighth Grade Achievement Tests (Mean)
ZASPIRE	1414	Zscore(Aspire)
ZTALK	1415	Zscore(Talk)
PAR_INV	1416	Parent Involvement

SAMPLE STATISTICAL PROGRAMS AND MULTIPLE REGRESSION OUTPUT

This appendix presents brief examples of MR output from three different general statistical analysis programs: SPSS, SAS, and SYSTAT. This quick overview will not make you an expert in these programs, but will show the similarities among programs to allow you to translate mentally the examples in this text into whichever program you are using. If you need basic information about running these programs, numerous books are available to help with this goal, including the manuals that accompany each program. These books present the intricacies of using these statistical programs much more completely than this book or appendix. The statistical programs are updated regularly, so the samples presented here may not be identical to the results you get with the most current version of each program. This is another good reason to accompany this book with a book or manual devoted to the program you are using.

For each program I will illustrate a simultaneous regression using the data from Chapter 2 (the simplest of our multiple regressions): "chap 2, hw grades" in one of the forms presented on the accompanying Web site www.ablongman.com/keith1e. Next, I will illustrate sequential regression using the NELS data and the example used throughout Chapter 5.

STATISTICAL PACKAGE FOR THE SOCIAL SCIENCES: SPSS

SPSS for Windows or Mac uses three windows:

1. A data editor window, in spreadsheet style, as shown in Figure B.1. These are the data on which we perform operations; when you save or open these data, they are stored with an extension of .sav.
2. An output window that includes output tables and graphs. Output files are stored with the extension .spo.
3. A syntax window. Although SPSS is primarily a menu-driven program, you can also run various SPSS procedures the old-fashioned way, using a series of written commands in the syntax. A few operations can only be performed using syntax (e.g.,

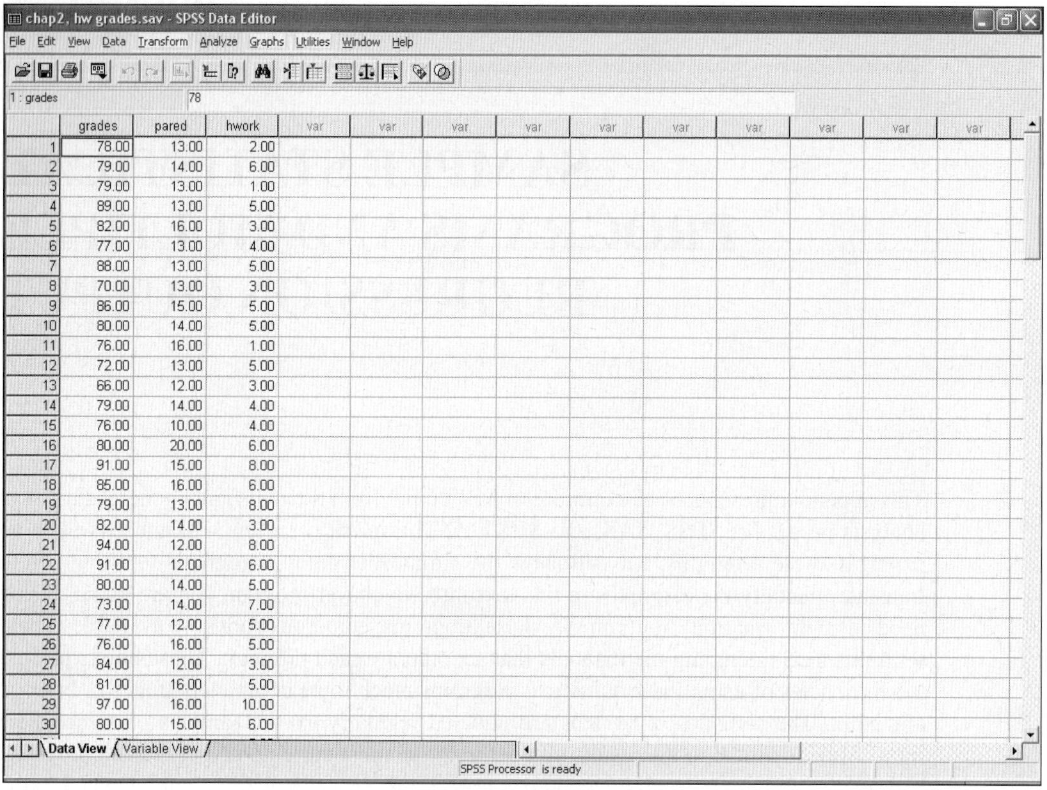

	grades	pared	hwork
1	78.00	13.00	2.00
2	79.00	14.00	6.00
3	79.00	13.00	1.00
4	89.00	13.00	5.00
5	82.00	16.00	3.00
6	77.00	13.00	4.00
7	88.00	13.00	5.00
8	70.00	13.00	3.00
9	86.00	15.00	5.00
10	80.00	14.00	5.00
11	76.00	16.00	1.00
12	72.00	13.00	5.00
13	66.00	12.00	3.00
14	79.00	14.00	4.00
15	76.00	10.00	4.00
16	80.00	20.00	6.00
17	91.00	15.00	8.00
18	85.00	16.00	6.00
19	79.00	13.00	8.00
20	82.00	14.00	3.00
21	94.00	12.00	8.00
22	91.00	12.00	6.00
23	80.00	14.00	5.00
24	73.00	14.00	7.00
25	77.00	12.00	5.00
26	76.00	16.00	5.00
27	84.00	12.00	3.00
28	81.00	16.00	5.00
29	97.00	16.00	10.00
30	80.00	15.00	6.00

FIGURE B.1 Data Editor window in SPSS. The data are from the regression of Grades on Parent Education and Homework from Chapter 2.

"Display labels" to obtain a list of variables and their names is, I think, one of these), and some operations are easier to perform using syntax than using the menus (e.g., complex IF statements). It is also possible to use the menus to generate syntax. All procedures (in the Analyze or Graph pull-down menus) have a "Paste" button that will write the syntax for you to conduct an analysis. This function is useful if you need to perform a lot of similar analyses. If you want the syntax window to open automatically when you start SPSS, you need to request this option under the "Edit" menu at the top of the data editor window; next click on "Options."

Simultaneous Multiple Regression

To conduct the MR from Chapter 2 using these three variables, first open the data file "chap 2, hw grades.sav." Click on "Analyze," then "Regression," then "Linear" in the menu at the top of the data editor window. These steps will result in the Linear Regression window shown in Figure B.2. In this window, click on the variable Grades and then use the arrow button to move it to the "Dependent" slot; move ParEd and HWork to the "Independent(s)" section. The method defaults to "Enter," which enters all variables into the regression equation at one time, a method we will refer to as simultaneous regression. (If you are using the Macintosh version of SPSS, you will find minor differences with some of the menus, commands, or output, but these should be easy to figure out.)

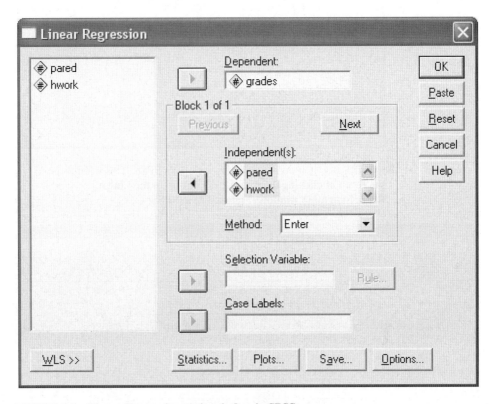

FIGURE B.2   Linear Regression main window in SPSS.

Click on the "Statistics" button at the bottom of the window, which will produce the window shown in Figure B.3. Here, we will generally check "Confidence Intervals" and "Descriptives" ("Estimates" and "Model Fit" should already be selected). For some chapters, we will also want "R squared change" or "Part and partial correlations." Click continue, which takes you back to the original window (Figure B.2).

We don't need to make changes to any other defaults, but if we did, the "Options" button allows you to change, among other things, the criteria for dealing with missing data. In Chapter 3, we used the "Save" button to save residuals and predicted values. Again, we will generally not make changes to these options. Click on "OK" in the Linear Regression window, and you should get output in the output window that looks like that shown in Figure B.4 (you will actually get more output than this, but this is the primary output of interest). The left

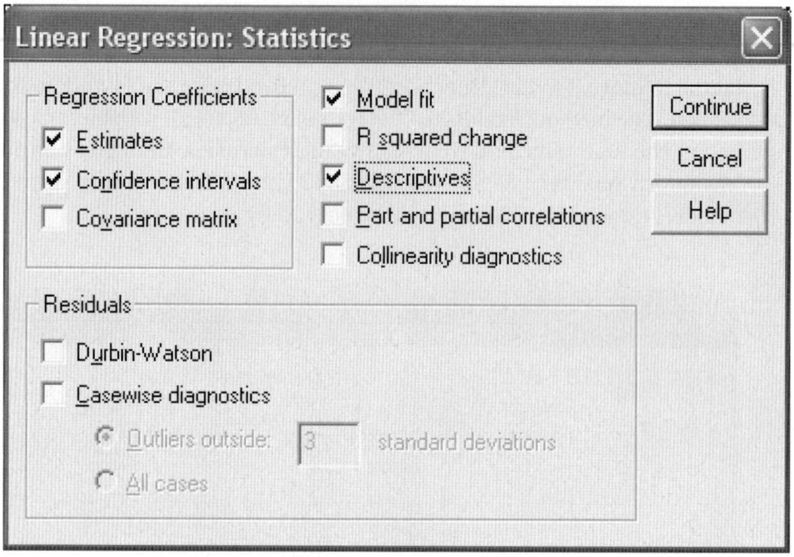

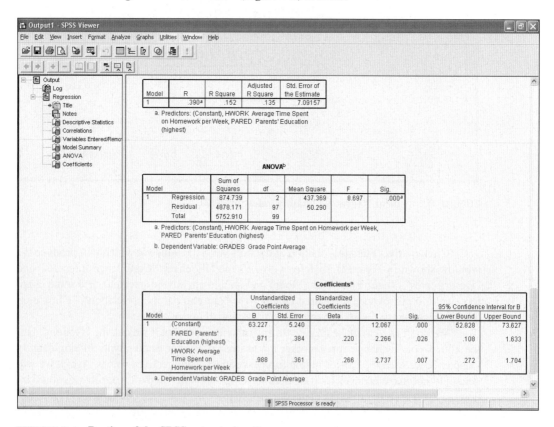

FIGURE B.3 Changing statistics options in SPSS. This window is the result of clicking the "Statistics" button in the Linear Regression main window (Figure B.2) in SPSS.

Model	R	R Square	Adjusted R Square	Std. Error of the Estimate
1	.390[a]	.152	.135	7.09157

a. Predictors: (Constant), HWORK Average Time Spent on Homework per Week, PARED Parents' Education (highest)

ANOVA[b]

Model		Sum of Squares	df	Mean Square	F	Sig.
1	Regression	874.739	2	437.369	8.697	.000[a]
	Residual	4878.171	97	50.290		
	Total	5752.910	99			

a. Predictors: (Constant), HWORK Average Time Spent on Homework per Week, PARED Parents' Education (highest)

b. Dependent Variable: GRADES Grade Point Average

Coefficients[a]

Model		Unstandardized Coefficients		Standardized Coefficients	t	Sig.	95% Confidence Interval for B	
		B	Std. Error	Beta			Lower Bound	Upper Bound
1	(Constant)	63.227	5.240		12.067	.000	52.828	73.627
	PARED Parents' Education (highest)	.871	.384	.220	2.266	.026	.108	1.633
	HWORK Average Time Spent on Homework per Week	.988	.361	.266	2.737	.007	.272	1.704

a. Dependent Variable: GRADES Grade Point Average

FIGURE B.4 Portion of the SPSS output, simultaneous regression.

portion of this window essentially shows an outline of all the output (very valuable when you have done many analyses) and the right side shows the tables, graphs, and so on, produced by SPSS. This output is similar to that shown throughout this text, so I won't comment on it further.

Syntax.   If you are analyzing several regressions or when using data sets with many variables (like NELS), it is often worthwhile to run the regression using Syntax rather than the pull-down menus. You can also start this process using the pull-down menus. If, instead of clicking "OK" after selecting all options, you had clicked "Paste" (Figure B.2), the syntax shown in Figure B.5 would have been pasted into the Syntax window. Note the last two lines of the syntax, which delineates the Dependent variable (Grades) and the independent variables (ParEd and HWork), entered simultaneously. You can then select the regression syntax (or a portion of a multijob syntax) using the mouse, and click the "Run" menu, then "Selection" to run the regression. The potential advantage of this approach is that when you have several regressions to run it is easy to simply change the variables in the Dependent or Method line and rerun the regression.

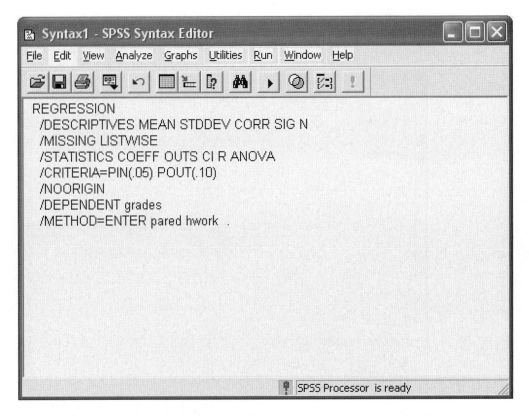

FIGURE B.5   Running regression in SPSS using Syntax. This syntax was generated by clicking on the "Paste" button in the Main Regression window. We could now highlight this syntax, and click on "Run" and "Selection" to run the regression.

Scatterplot

Throughout the text there are scatterplots and regression lines; here's a simple way to produce these in SPSS. From the pull-down menus, select "Graphs," then "Scatter," "Simple," and "Define." This series of steps generates the Window shown in Figure B.6. Move the variable "grades" to the "Y Axis" box, and the variable "hwork" to the box labeled "X Axis," which produces the output shown in Figure B.7. If you now double-click on the actual graph in the output, you will be able to add to and modify this graph, via the "Chart Editor" window that will pop up as a result of that double-click (Figure B.8). If you now click on one of the data points and wait a few seconds, all of the data points should be highlighted. Click on "Chart" in the menu, and "Add Chart Element," and then "Add Fit Line at Total." This will give you the window shown in Figure B.9; select "Linear" and "Apply," and you will get a regression line for the scatterplot. In later chapters, we will fit more than one regression line by adding another variable to the "Set Markers by" box in the initial Scatterplot Window (Figure B.6). We will also add curves or "lowess" lines under "Fit Line at Total." You can also change the labels or scales of the axes or the color or texture of the data point and line and use many other options to improve the graph. After you have finished editing the graph, close the Chart Editor window to return to the SPSS output. You can also copy and paste these graphs into your word processing document.

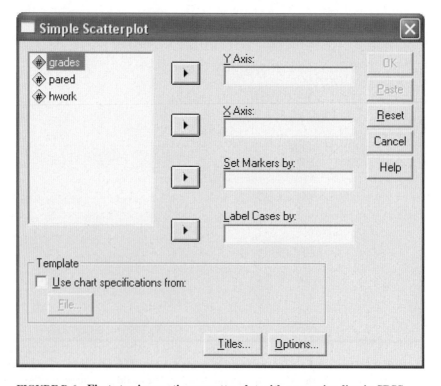

FIGURE B.6   First step in creating a scatterplot with regression line in SPSS.

```
GRAPH
 /SCATTERPLOT(BIVAR)=hwork WITH grades
 /MISSING=LISTWISE .
Graph
```

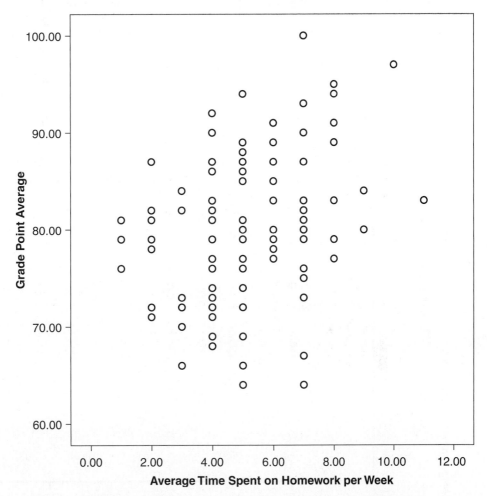

FIGURE B.7 Output from running the scatterplot command. If you double-click on the graph, the Chart Editor window (Figure B.8) appears.

Sequential Multiple Regression

In Chapter 5 we began using sequential MR, in which variables are entered sequentially in blocks, rather than all at once. Figures B.10 and B.11 illustrate how to conduct sequential regression in SPSS, using the example from that chapter. In the "Linear Regression" window, we add the first independent variable (BYSES) in the "Independent(s)" box (Figure

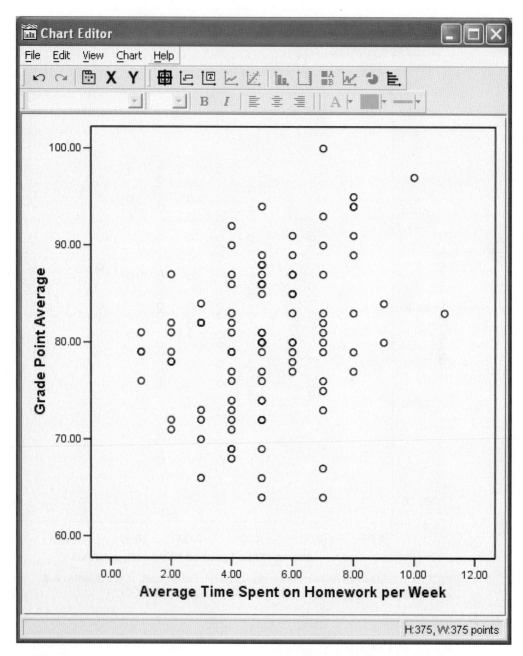

FIGURE B.8 **SPSS Chart Editor window. From this window you can add a regression line (by clicking on "Chart," then "Options) and make changes and improvements in the look of the graph.**

FIGURE B.9 Click on "Linear" under Fit Line to add a regression line to the scatterplot.

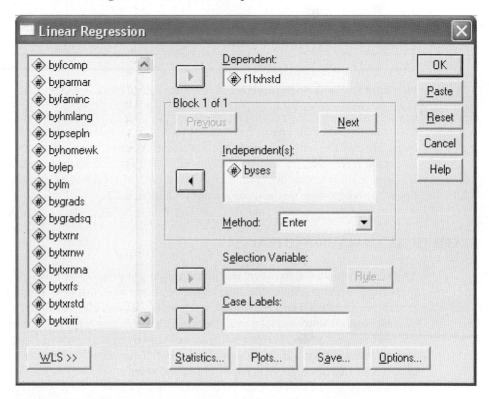

FIGURE B.10 Block 1 of the sequential regression example from Chapter 5. BYSES is entered as an independent variable; then click on "Next" to add a second block of independent variables.

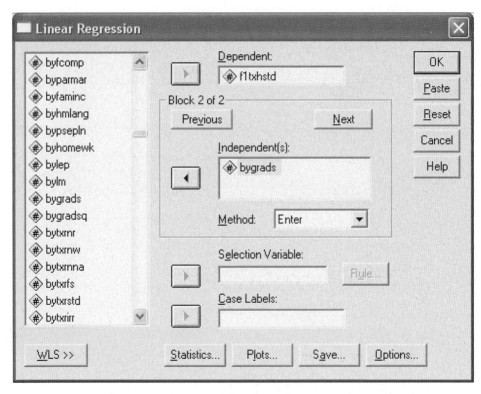

FIGURE B.11   Variable ByGrads is entered in the second block in a sequential regression.

B.10) and then click the "Next" button to add a new block to the regression. In this second block, we add the second independent variable (BYGrads, Figure B.11), and so on. In sequential regression, we also generally click the "R squared change" (shown in Figure B.3) option after clicking the "Statistics" box in the main Linear Regression window. A portion of the output from this analysis is shown in Figure B.12.

STATISTICAL ANALYSIS SYSTEM (SAS)

SAS is a very powerful statistical and data management program that runs on a variety of operating systems. SAS, like the other programs shown here, displays several windows at startup (see Figure B.13). The leftmost window shows available SAS libraries, which are essentially shortcuts to data locations. The top right screen shows the log of run commands; when procedures are run, this screen will show whether they ran correctly; if not, it will help you to understand what the errors were. The lower right screen is the Editor, where you type in commands to create, get, or manipulate data and to run statistical procedures. These commands can be saved (with the extension .sas) for rerunning or editing. Although it is possible to run many procedures in SAS interactively and using menus, my experience is that most SAS users use this Editor to run procedures from syntax. I will use that approach here. When you actually run an analysis, the leftmost window will change to a Results window,

Model Summary

Model	R	R Square	Adjusted R Square	Std. Error of the Estimate	R Square Change	F Change	df1	df2	Sig. F Change
					Change Statistics				
1	.430[a]	.185	.184	8.91132	.185	200.709	1	885	.000
2	.573[b]	.328	.327	8.09549	.143	188.361	1	884	.000
3	.577[c]	.333	.330	8.07265	.005	6.009	1	883	.014
4	.582[d]	.339	.336	8.04121	.006	7.918	1	882	.005

a. Predictors: (Constant), BYSES SOCIO-ECONOMIC STATUS COMPOSITE

b. Predictors: (Constant), BYSES SOCIO-ECONOMIC STATUS COMPOSITE, BYGRADS GRADES COMPOSITE

c. Predictors: (Constant), BYSES SOCIO-ECONOMIC STATUS COMPOSITE, BYGRADS GRADES COMPOSITE, F1CNCPT2 SELF-CONCEPT 2

d. Predictors: (Constant), BYSES SOCIO-ECONOMIC STATUS COMPOSITE, BYGRADS GRADES COMPOSITE, F1CNCPT2 SELF-CONCEPT 2, F1LOCUS2 LOCUS OF CONTROL 2

Coefficients[a]

Model		Unstandardized Coefficients B	Std. Error	Standardized Coefficients Beta	t	Sig.	95% Confidence Interval for B Lower Bound	Upper Bound
1	(Constant)	51.090	.299		170.745	.000	50.503	51.677
	BYSES SOCIO-ECONOMIC STATUS COMPOSITE	5.558	.392	.430	14.167	.000	4.788	6.328
2	(Constant)	34.793	1.218		28.561	.000	32.402	37.183
	BYSES SOCIO-ECONOMIC STATUS COMPOSITE	3.875	.377	.300	10.280	.000	3.135	4.615
	BYGRADS GRADES COMPOSITE	5.420	.395	.400	13.724	.000	4.645	6.195
3	(Constant)	35.138	1.223		28.734	.000	32.738	37.538
	BYSES SOCIO-ECONOMIC STATUS COMPOSITE	3.798	.377	.294	10.068	.000	3.057	4.538
	BYGRADS GRADES COMPOSITE	5.291	.397	.391	13.318	.000	4.512	6.071
	F1CNCPT2 SELF-CONCEPT 2	1.016	.414	.069	2.451	.014	.203	1.829
4	(Constant)	35.517	1.226		28.981	.000	33.112	37.923
	BYSES SOCIO-ECONOMIC STATUS COMPOSITE	3.690	.378	.285	9.772	.000	2.949	4.431
	BYGRADS GRADES COMPOSITE	5.150	.399	.380	12.910	.000	4.367	5.933
	F1CNCPT2 SELF-CONCEPT 2	.218	.501	.015	.436	.663	-.764	1.201
	F1LOCUS2 LOCUS OF CONTROL 2	1.554	.552	.097	2.814	.005	.470	2.638

a. Dependent Variable: F1TXHSTD HIST/CIT/GEOG STANDARDIZED SCORE

FIGURE B.12 Portion of the output from the sequential regression example from SPSS.

outlining the output (output is saved with the extension .lst). The top right window is replaced with an output window, showing the output from your analyses. You can switch back and forth between these various windows using the tabs at the bottom of the screen. SAS can read data in a variety of formats, including SPSS portable files and Excel files.

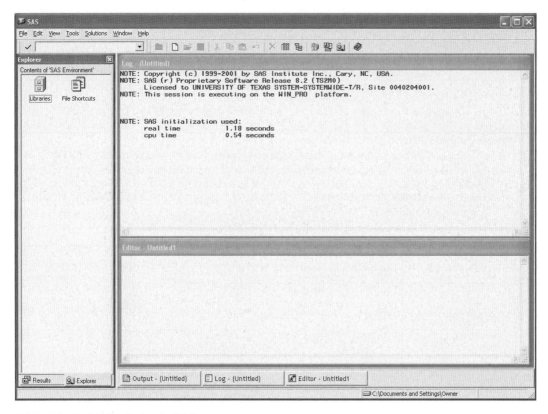

FIGURE B.13   Main window in SAS.

Simultaneous Regression

To conduct the homework regression from Chapter 2, I imported the Excel version of the data saved on the Web site under Chapter 2. Enter the commands

```
proc reg;
model grades=pared hwork
/stb clb;
run;
```

in the Editor, select this syntax, and click on the "Run" icon (the small running person icon at the top of the screen). In the syntax, the "Model" statement spells out the regression equation; the options "stb" and "clb" request standardized regression coefficients and confidence intervals for these coefficients.

The output from these commands is shown in Figure B.14. Although the output looks different from that presented throughout the text, it contains the same information. The Analysis of Variance section shows the test of the statistical significance of the overall regression and matches that shown in the SPSS output. It is followed by the R^2 and the mean of the dependent variable. The section labeled Parameter Estimates shows the same

The REG Procedure
Model: MODEL1
Dependent Variable: GRADES GRADES

Analysis of Variance

Source	DF	Sum of Squares	Mean Square	F Value	Pr > F
Model	2	874.73870	437.36935	8.70	0.0003
Error	97	4878.17130	50.29043		
Corrected Total	99	5752.91000			

Root MSE	7.09157	R-Square	0.1521	
Dependent Mean	80.47000	Adj R-Sq	0.1346	
Coeff Var	8.81269			

Parameter Estimates

Variable	Label	DF	Parameter Estimate	Standard Error	t Value	Pr > |t|	Standardized Estimate
Intercept	Intercept	1	63.22702	5.23978	12.07	<.0001	0
PARED	PARED	1	0.87062	0.38423	2.27	0.0257	0.22047
HWORK	HWORK	1	0.98785	0.36088	2.74	0.0074	0.26634

Parameter Estimates

Variable	Label	DF	95% Confidence Limits	
Intercept	Intercept	1	52.82750	73.62655
PARED	PARED	1	0.10803	1.63322
HWORK	HWORK	1	0.27159	1.70410

FIGURE B.14 SAS output for the simultaneous regression using the Grades–Homework example from Chapter 2.

information as did the Coefficients table in SPSS (Figure B.4): the intercept of the regression equation, the unstandardized regression coefficients (in the column labeled Parameter Estimate), the standard errors of these coefficients, the t statistic and associated probability, and the standardized regression coefficients, or β. The second section under parameter estimates shows the 95% confidence intervals for the unstandardized regression coefficients.

Sequential Regression

SAS has a multitude of procedures, and one blessing (or perhaps a curse, if you are novice) is that you can often do any procedure in a variety of ways. One simple method of conducting a sequential regression in SAS is

```
proc reg;
model f1txhstd=byses bygrads f1cncpt2 f1locus2
/stb clb scorr1(seqtests);
run;
```

This example uses the NELS data (either the SAS transport file or the SPSS Portable file) and the variables from Chapter 5. The "scorr1 (seqtests)" option on the third line produces the change in R^2 statistics often of interest in sequential regression. The output resulting from this syntax is shown in Figure B.15. The top section (Analysis of Variance) shows the test of the final regression equation, with all variables entered. The primary results of interest are contained in the remainder of the output. The column labeled Squared Semi-partial Corr Type 1 (in the second section of Parameter Estimates) shows the increase in ΔR^2 as each variable is added to the regression equation; compare these to the R Square Change column in the Model Summary section of the SPSS output in Figure B.12. The columns labeled DF, F Value, and Pr > F in the third section of parameter estimates show the degrees of freedom associated with each block of variables added to the regression, the F associated with the change in R^2 with each addition, and the statistical significance of this F.

```
                    The REG Procedure
                      Model: MODEL1
        Dependent Variable: F1TXHSTD HIST/CIT/GEOG STANDARDIZED SCORE

                   Analysis of Variance
```

Source	DF	Sum of Squares	Mean Square	F Value	Pr > F
Model	4	29187	7296.72118	112.85	<.0001
Error	882	57031	64.66104		
Corrected Total	886	86218			

Root MSE	8.04121	R-Square	0.3385	
Dependent Mean	51.11351	Adj R-Sq	0.3355	
Coeff Var	15.73206			

```
                   Parameter Estimates
```

Variable	Label	DF	Parameter Estimate	Standard Error	t Value	Pr > |t|
Intercept	Intercept	1	35.51738	1.22556	28.98	<.0001
BYSES	SOCIO-ECONOMIC STATUS COMPOSITE	1	3.69033	0.37764	9.77	<.0001
BYGRADS	GRADES COMPOSITE	1	5.15020	0.39892	12.91	<.0001
F1CNCPT2	SELF-CONCEPT 2	1	0.21832	0.50069	0.44	0.6629
F1LOCUS2	LOCUS OF CONTROL 2	1	1.55383	0.55219	2.81	0.0050

```
                   Parameter Estimates
```

Variable	Label	DF	Standardized Estimate	Squared Semi-partial Corr Type I	Cumulative R-Square
Intercept	Intercept	1	0	.	0
BYSES	SOCIO-ECONOMIC STATUS COMPOSITE	1	0.28547	0.18486	0.18486
BYGRADS	GRADES COMPOSITE	1	0.38024	0.14318	0.32804
F1CNCPT2	SELF-CONCEPT 2	1	0.01474	0.00454	0.33259
F1LOCUS2	LOCUS OF CONTROL 2	1	0.09684	0.00594	0.33852

```
                   Parameter Estimates
```

Variable	Label	DF	-Sequential Type I- F Value	Pr > F	95% Confidence Limits	
Intercept	Intercept	1	.	.	33.11203	37.92273
BYSES	SOCIO-ECONOMIC STATUS COMPOSITE	1	200.71	<.0001	2.94916	4.43150
BYGRADS	GRADES COMPOSITE	1	188.36	<.0001	4.36726	5.93315
F1CNCPT2	SELF-CONCEPT 2	1	6.01	0.0144	-0.76436	1.20100
F1LOCUS2	LOCUS OF CONTROL 2	1	7.92	0.0050	0.47007	2.63760

FIGURE B.15   Sequential regression output from SAS. These results are from the example from Chapter 5, using the NELS data.

SYSTAT

SYSTAT is another general-purpose statistical analysis program. One strength of SYSTAT is its excellent graphing features. SYSTAT can read data in a variety of formats, including SPSS files, SAS files, Excel files, and, of course, SYSTAT files (SYSTAT data files have an extension of .syd). One version of the NELS data on the Web site is as a SYSTAT file. When you open SYSTAT, you will find a screen like that shown in Figure B.16; the contents of this main window are similar to those for SPSS and SAS. On the left portion of the screen is the Output Organizer, which shows an outline of the output. The actual output is shown in the top right pane of the window (the Output Pane); output files are saved with the extension ".syo." The lower portion of the screen is the Command Pane, where you can type in and run commands and check the log to see which commands have been run successfully (or errors). Note the three tabs for this pane; these allow you to enter commands interactively (Interactive), run a saved series of commands (Untitled), and view the command log (Log). When you open a data set, a data window will also appear in standard spreadsheet format.

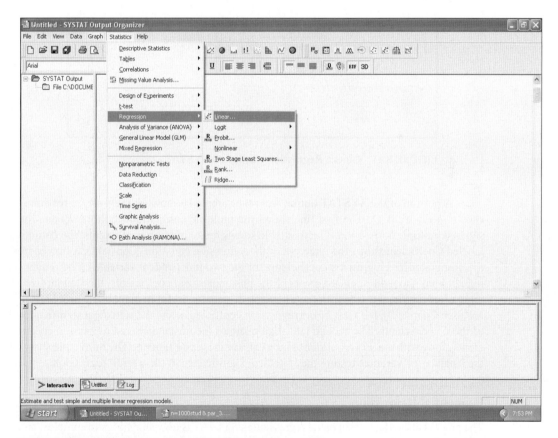

FIGURE B.16 Main window from SYSTAT. The figure also shows the steps to conduct multiple regression.

Simultaneous Regression

Running a simultaneous regression in SYSTAT is straightforward. After opening the "chap 2, hw grades" data in the Chapter 2 directory of the Web site (I used the SPSS file: "chap 2, hw grades.sav"), click on the Statistics menu, then Regression, then "Linear." These steps are illustrated in Figure B.16 and result in the Linear Regression window shown in Figure B.17. We enter Grades as the dependent variable and ParEd and HWork as the independent variables. No options need to be changed, so simply click OK to complete the multiple regression and produce the output.

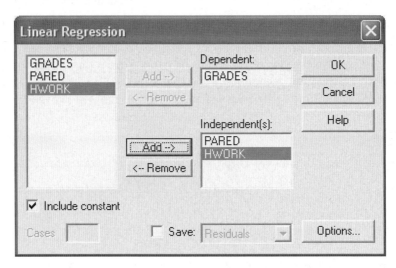

FIGURE B.17   Linear Regression window in SYSTAT.

A portion of the SYSTAT output from the sample Homework multiple regression is shown in Figure B.18. The first line shows the multiple correlation (multiple R) and the squared multiple correlation. The first table shows the regression coefficients: the column labeled Coefficient shows the intercept of the regression equation (Constant), followed by the unstandardized regression coefficients for the two independent variables. The remaining columns show the standard errors of the unstandardized coefficients, the standardized regression coefficients (the β's), the tolerance (a statistic useful in diagnosing problems in MR; see Chapter 9), the t test of the regression coefficients, and the statistical significance of these coefficients. The second table again shows the unstandardized regression coefficients along with the 95% confidence intervals for these coefficients. The third table shows the Analysis of Variance testing the statistical significance of the overall regression.

Sequential Regression

The process to conduct a sequential regression in SYSTAT is only slightly more complex, and requires the use of the interactive command pane at the bottom of the main window. To conduct sequential regression (using the NELS data and the example from Chapter 5), enter the dependent and all independent variables in the main Linear Regression window. Then click on the

```
Dep Var: GRADES   N: 100   Multiple R: 0.390   Squared multiple R: 0.152

Adjusted squared multiple R: 0.135   Standard error of estimate: 7.092
```

Effect	Coefficient	Std Error	Std Coef	Tolerance	t	P(2 Tail)
CONSTANT						
	63.227	5.240	0.000	.	12.067	0.000
PARED						
	0.871	0.384	0.220	0.923	2.266	0.026
HWORK						
	0.988	0.361	0.266	0.923	2.737	0.007

Effect	Coefficient	Lower 95%	Upper 95%
CONSTANT	63.227	52.828	73.627
PARED	0.871	0.108	1.633
HWORK	0.988	0.272	1.704

```
Analysis of Variance
```

Source	Sum-of-Squares	df	Mean-Square	F-ratio	P
Regression					
	874.739	2	437.369	8.697	0.000
Residual					
	4878.171	97	50.290		

```
Durbin-Watson D Statistic        1.750
First Order Autocorrelation      0.123
```

FIGURE B.18   SYSTAT output for the simultaneous regression of Grades on Parent Education and Homework example from Chapter 2.

"Options" button at the bottom of this window, which will produce a new window, illustrated in Figure B.19. In this window, change the estimation method from "Complete" to "Stepwise." Under the heading "Stepwise Options," click on "Forward" and "Interactive." Click "Continue" and then "OK." This will produce the first step in output, shown at the top of Figure B.20. Essentially, nothing has entered the regression equation at this step, but the table shows the four independent variables ready to enter the equation on your command. To enter the variables one at a time in a particular order, you next go to the Command Pane at the bottom of the main window and click on the "Interactive" tab. Then type in

```
>step byses
>step bygrads
>step f1cncpt2
>step f1locus2
>
```

Each time you enter one of these commands and hit Enter, SYSTAT produces a new section of printout. I have skipped over the output for Steps 1 and 2 in the figure, but show the results of the third and fourth steps.

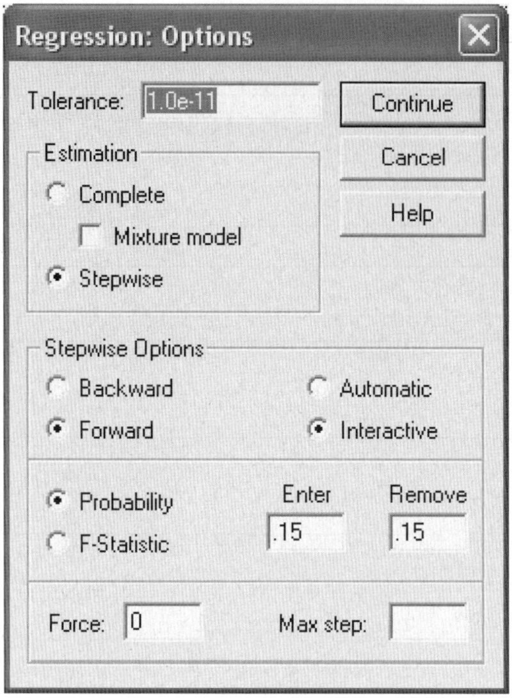

FIGURE B.19   Click on the "Options" button in the Main Regression window in SYSTAT to conduct sequential regression. Click "Stepwise," "Forward," and "Interactive." The variables are then entered one at a time using the Interactive Command pane.

Focus on the output from Step 3 (the second table). The first portion of the table is consistent with the output from the simultaneous regression. The last three columns are of particular interest for sequential regression, however. These show the F tests for each block of variables. The F for the variable entered in a particular block shows the statistical significance of the change in R^2 resulting from this block. Thus, for Step 3 the addition of F1Cncpt2 to the regression equation resulted in a statistically significant increase in ΔR^2 ($F = 6.009$ [1, 883], $p = .014$). This information is consistent with that presented in the Model Summary portion of the SPSS output (Figure B.12). Focus also on the lower portion of this same table, on the column labeled Part. Corr. The value reported here represents the partial correlations of each variable with the outcome, with the effects of the variables already in the equation statistically removed. Thus, for Step 3 the partial correlation of F1Locus2 with F1TxHStd, with the effects of BYSES, BYGrads, and F1Cncpt2 removed, is .094. Partial correlations are discussed in more detail in Appendix D. Note also the values listed under Part. Corr for Step 0. Because at Step 0 there are no other variables in the equation, the coefficients are simply the Pearson correlations between each variable and the outcome (F1TxHStd).

```
Step # 0 R =  0.000 R-Square =  0.000
```

	Effect	Coefficient	Std Error	Std Coef	Tol.	df	F	'P'
In								
1	Constant							
Out		Part. Corr.						
2	BYSES	0.430	.	.	1.00000	1	200.709	0.000
3	BYGRADS	0.498	.	.	1.00000	1	291.410	0.000
4	F1CNCPT2	0.173	.	.	1.00000	1	27.207	0.000
5	F1LOCUS2	0.248	.	.	1.00000	1	57.867	0.000

```
Step # 3 R =  0.577 R-Square =  0.333
Term entered: F1CNCPT2
```

	Effect	Coefficient	Std Error	Std Coef	Tol.	df	F	'P'
In								
1	Constant							
2	BYSES	3.798	0.377	0.294	0.88787	1	101.371	0.000
3	BYGRADS	5.291	0.397	0.391	0.87847	1	177.372	0.000
4	F1CNCPT2	1.016	0.414	0.069	0.96531	1	6.009	0.014
Out		Part. Corr.						
5	F1LOCUS2	0.094			0.63325	1	7.918	0.005

	Effect	Coefficient	Std Error	Std Coef	Tol.	df	F	'P'
In								
1	Constant							
2	BYSES	3.690	0.378	0.285	0.87883	1	95.495	0.000
3	BYGRADS	5.150	0.399	0.380	0.86459	1	166.677	0.000
4	F1CNCPT2	0.218	0.501	0.015	0.65604	1	0.190	0.663
5	F1LOCUS2	1.554	0.552	0.097	0.63325	1	7.918	0.005
Out		Part. Corr.						
	none							

FIGURE B.20 **Portion of the results from sequential regression in SYSTAT.**

In Chapter 5, I rail against stepwise multiple regression, in which the computer decides the order of entry of variables into the regression equation. Note that, despite the labeling in SYSTAT, what we are doing here is *not* this type of stepwise regression, because we, not the computer, decide the order of entry.

SAMPLE OUTPUT
FROM SEM PROGRAMS

This appendix presents brief examples of the output from several statistical programs designed to analyze structural equation models (SEMs) and confirmatory factor analyses (CFAs). The primary purpose of this appendix is to allow you to translate the SEM results presented in this text into whichever program you are using. I also briefly demonstrate how to run these programs, but keep in mind that these are complex programs and this quick overview will not make you an expert on running these programs! If you need basic information about running these programs, see the manual associated with your software, the publisher's Web site, and the other resources mentioned in Chapters 12 and 17. The programs illustrated are updated regularly, so the output shown here may not be identical to what you will get with the most recent versions of these programs. This change in programs is another good reason to accompany this book with the manual for the SEM program you are using!

For each program, I illustrate a simple path analysis from Chapter 12; this example provides enough output to allow you to understand the similarities and differences in output for the various programs. The example uses the data set contained on the accompanying Web site (under Chapter 12, the files "homework overid 1.sav" or "homework overid 1.xls").

AMOS (ANALYSIS OF MOMENT STRUCTURES)

Like most SEM programs, Amos is known by its acronym rather than its longer name. It is the program I used to produce the SEM results in Part 2 and also the program used to produce the path and SEM models throughout the book. Amos is probably the easiest SEM program to learn and use, especially if you understand SEM input and output best via path models as presented in this book. In Amos, you generally specify SEM models by drawing them, and this drawing, along with the data, allows the program to produce the results. (You can also specify models through commands.) The output of Amos includes high-quality, publishable figures. Amos can read raw data or matrix data in a variety of formats. Other notable features of Amos are that it allows bootstrapping to estimate standard errors of parameters, uses sophisticated methods for dealing with missing data (full information maximum likelihood), and can automatically compare variations of models (a more exploratory approach).

Amos was developed by James Arbuckle and is licensed through SPSS, Inc. As this is written, Amos is currently in version 5.0 for Windows (Arbuckle, 2003; Arbuckle &

Wothke, 1999); there is no Macintosh version of Amos. Amos can be purchased from SPSS and currently comes as part of the SPSS Grad Pack. As noted in Chapter 12, the Amos Web site (www.amosdevelopment.com) includes several brief, useful tutorials (under the Student Version link). The Amos manual and program include numerous examples that you can run.

The Homework Path Analysis

When you first start up Amos, the screen should look like that shown in Figure C.1. The right-hand portion of the figure represents a piece of paper on which you will draw your model to specify it; this drawing surface can be in portrait or landscape orientation. The left side of the figure shows the most common tools used in Amos for drawing and modifying figures, analyzing data, viewing output, and so on. These and other tools are also included in the pull-down menus at the top of the window. The middle column in the figure allows you to switch from your input to output model (buttons at the top) among groups for multi-sample analyses (see Chapter 16) and between standardized and unstandardized output. The bottom section of this column shows all the different Amos models in the current subdirectory.

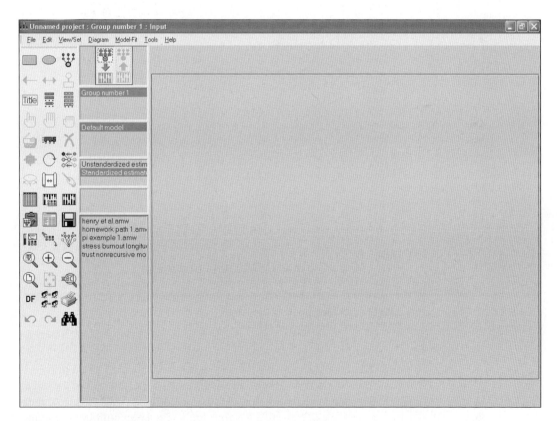

FIGURE C.1   Initial layout upon opening the Amos program.

We can start using Amos either by drawing the model or selecting the data to be analyzed. We'll start by specifying the "homework overid 1.xls" data on the Web site (www .ablongman.com/keith1e) under Chapter 12. Amos can read and analyze data in a variety of file formats (SPSS, Excel, and text files are common). It can also read both raw data and matrix data (the matrix can be in a variety of file formats—SPSS, Excel, ASCII—but needs to be in the same layout as SPSS; an example is shown in Table 12.2). Click on the "File" menu, then "Data Files," then "File Name." Go to the Chapter 12 subdirectory and select the type of file you want to use at the bottom of the window (in this case, an Excel file; see Figure C.2). Next select "homework overid 1.xls," click on "Open," "Sheet 1," "OK," and "OK." You have now specified the data to be used in the analysis.

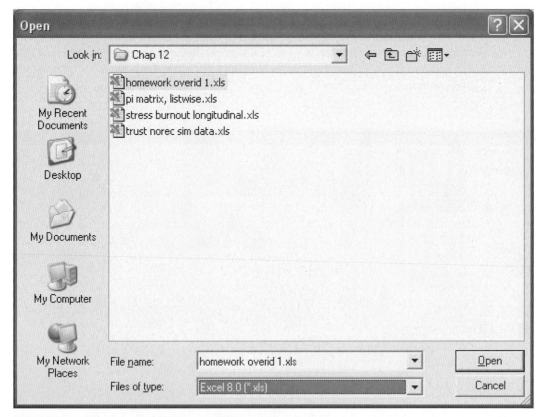

FIGURE C.2   Choosing the data file and filetype in Amos. Amos can analyze SPSS, Excel, and ASCII text files, among others.

Next, we draw the model to look like the one shown in Chapter 12 and reprinted in Figure C.3. The basic tools for drawing models are in the tools menu at the left of the screen (Figure C.4); note the rectangle and ellipse on the first line of tools, used to denote measured and unmeasured variables, respectively. (Your tools may be in a different arrangement from mine. Therefore, whenever I refer to a tool as being in a specific location, refer to the figures in this appendix. You can also hold the cursor over any of the tools for a sec-

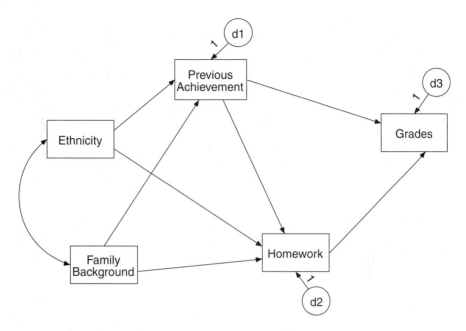

FIGURE C.3   Homework path model from Chapter 12.

ond or two to find out what they do.) Start by clicking on the rectangle, move the mouse to the "paper," and click and drag to draw the first measured variable (Figure C.4). You can draw the other measured variables in the model in the same way, or you can copy this initial rectangle using the copy machine button shown in the first column of tools. Next draw the disturbances using the ellipse button, the paths using the single-headed arrow in the second row of tools, and the correlation between the two exogenous variables using the two-headed arrow. You can move these objects using the small moving van tool (middle column) and touch up aspects of the figure using the magic wand (toward the middle of the think column of tools). Your figure should now look something like Figure C.5.

You can name the variables in the path model two different ways. First, you can double-click on each variable (rectangle or circle). This will open the Object Properties window, where you can type in the name of the variable (in the "Variable name" section). It is important that you use the same variable names in the model that are used in the data set. Second, if you have specified the data file first, you can click on the "list variables in the data set" button (third row, third column). This will produce a small window showing all the variables in your data set, which you can then drag to the appropriate rectangle (Figure C.6). If you want to use the longer, more explanatory names shown in Figure C.3, you can now double-click on the variables and type the longer names in as "Variable Labels" in the Object Properties window (make sure the "Text" tab is selected). Double-click on the circles to type in the names of the three disturbances (d1, d2, d3, in the "variable names" section). Constrain the path from each disturbance to the corresponding variable by double-clicking on the arrow. Click on the "Parameters" tab, and then type in the value "1" as the regression weight. This sets the scale of the disturbance to be the same as that of the measured variable.

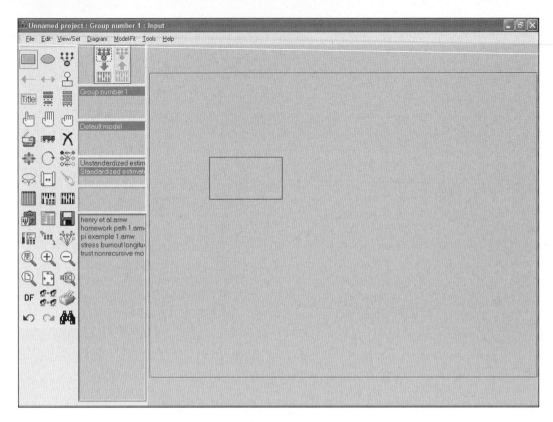

FIGURE C.4 Using the rectangle tool to draw the first measured variable in Amos.

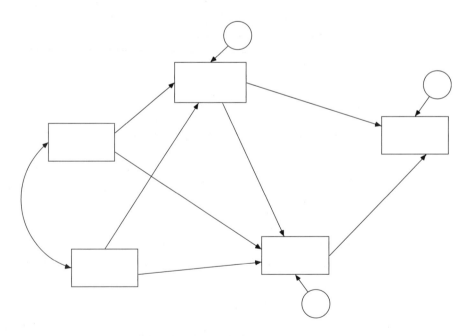

FIGURE C.5 Results of drawing the model in Amos.

456

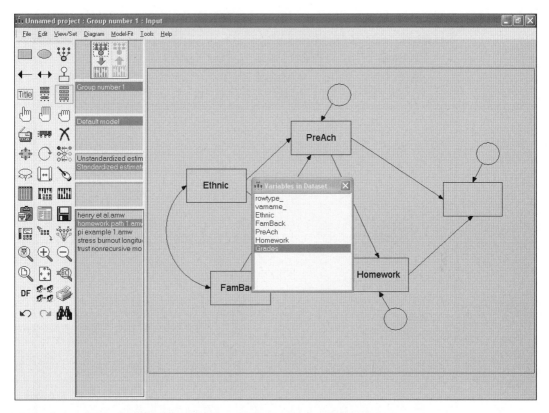

FIGURE C.6   You can drag the names of variables in the chosen data set to their corresponding measured variables in the Amos path model.

The model is now specified in enough detail to perform the analysis, but you will want to request a few aspects of output beyond what Amos provides by default. Click on the top "View/Set" menu, "Analysis Properties," and "Output" (see Figure C.7). You will want the standardized estimates, sample moments (the original correlation and covariance matrices), all implied moments, and the indirect, direct, and total effects. For model modification, you may be interested in residual moments and modification indexes. Squared multiple correlations may be of interest (although I did not request these for the examples in this book), and if you are analyzing raw data, tests for normality and outliers may also be of interest.

Begin the analysis by clicking on the abacuslike tool toward the middle of the third column of tools. If the analysis is successful, you will get the message "OK: Default model" in the second column. Click on the second button in the top section of the second column to get the unstandardized graphic output, and click on "Standardized estimates" farther down in this column to get the standardized graphic output (shown in Figure C.8). You can easily copy and paste this figure into a variety of applications (as I have done throughout this book). To view the text output, click on the tool that looks like

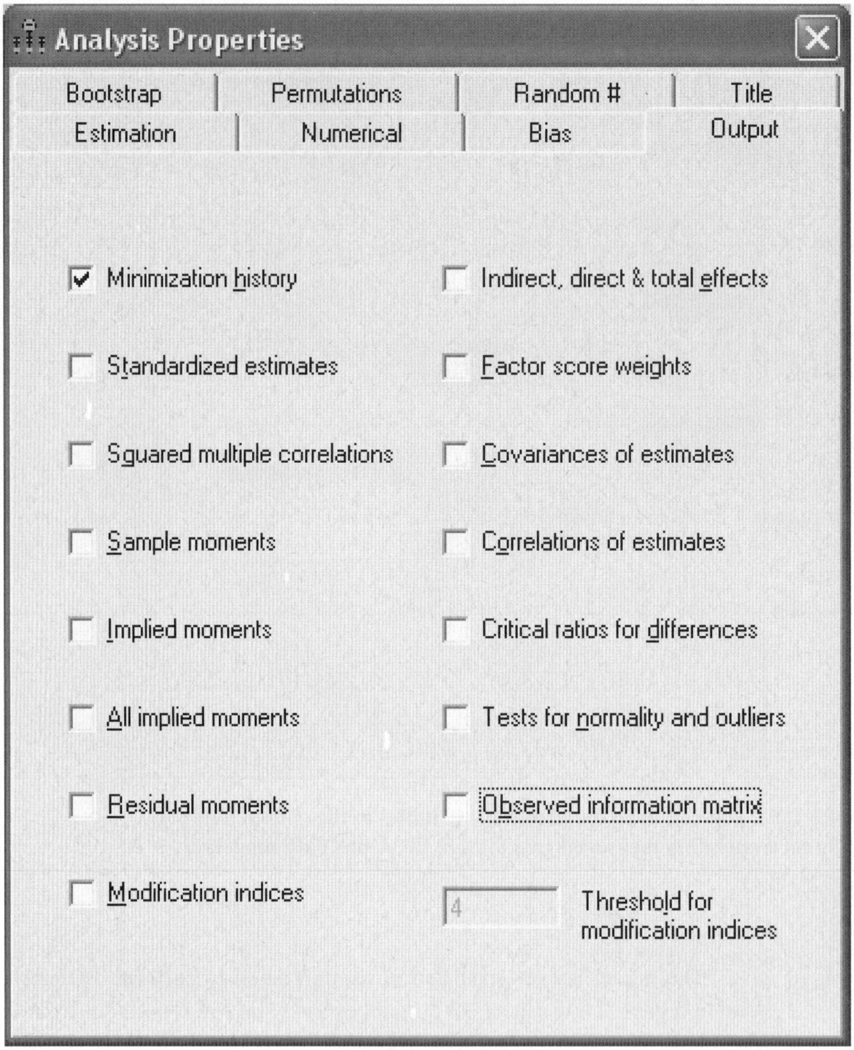

FIGURE C.7   Options for output in Amos. Here we will choose standardized estimates, sample moments, all implied moments, and indirect, direct, and total effects.

a piece of paper with three columns of text in the lower half of the middle column of tools. Click on this tool and the detailed text output will appear in its own window. The output window is similar to that from most general statistical programs in that an outline of the output is shown on the left, allowing you to navigate quickly to the portions of the analysis of interest. A portion of the output showing the unstandardized and standardized path coefficients is shown in Figure C.9. A portion of the output showing the fit indexes is shown in Figure C.10. I won't discuss the Amos output in any detail because

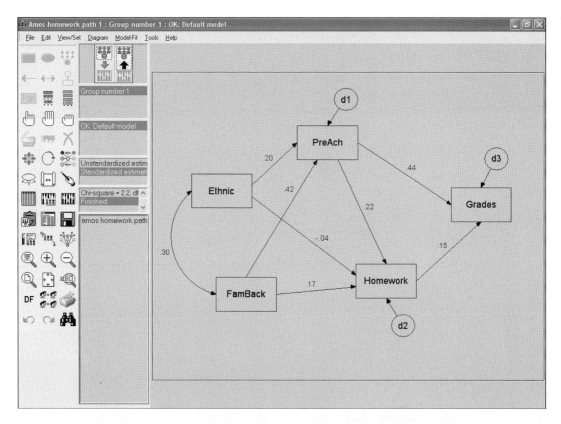

FIGURE C.8   Graphic output from Amos; the standardized solution is shown here.

Amos output was used extensively throughout the main body of this text (starting in Chapter 12).

LISREL (LINEAR STRUCTURAL RELATIONS)

LISREL was developed by Karl G. Jöreskog and Dag Sörbom and, as this is written, is in version 8.7. It is published by Scientific Software International; extensive information about the program is included at their Web site (www.ssicentral.com), including a free, downloadable student edition that differs from the commercial program in that it allows the analysis of up to only 12 variables. The current version of LISREL uses maximum-likelihood methods to deal with missing data and allows the analysis of multilevel models (e.g, the effects of homework at both the individual and classroom level).

LISREL was the first structural equation modeling program, and in many ways it still defines such analyses. Some people refer to SEM as LISREL analyses, and many textbooks

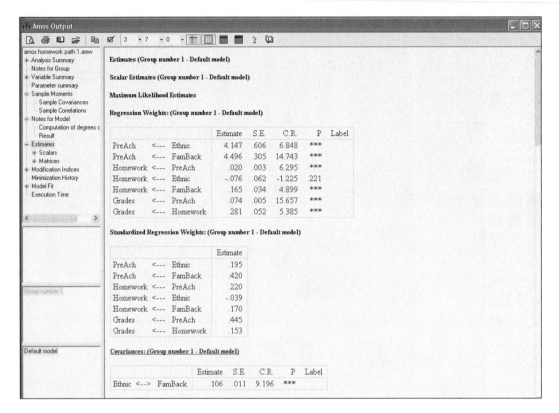

FIGURE C.9   Portion of the detailed text output from Amos. The unstandardized and standardized path coefficients are shown.

and discussions refer to portions of models using the original LISREL notation, in which models were specified as matrices. So, for example, the paths from exogenous to endogenous variables constitute the gamma matrix, whereas paths from endogenous to exogenous variables are part of the beta matrix.

Users of LISREL can run the program using the original command language (in which the paths and other parameters are specified as matrices) or using SIMPLIS, a closer-to-English command language in which models are specified as equations. Either LISREL or SIMPLIS can be run interactively or by using commands in a syntax file. I will run the example using SIMPLIS and using syntax. LISREL also includes a preprocessor (PRELIS), which can be used to manipulate data, calculate matrices, and conduct non-SEM analyses.

After starting LISREL, click the "File" menu, "New," and "SIMPLIS Project" (see Figure C.11). You will be prompted for a location for saving the file (in my experience, LISREL does not always handle multiname subdirectories well; therefore I used the directory C:\temp). I chose the name "Homework Path 1," and SIMPLIS used the extension ".spj."

Model Fit Summary

CMIN

Model	NPAR	CMIN	DF	P	CMIN/DF
Default model	13	2.166	2	.338	1.083
Saturated model	15	.000	0		
Independence model	5	817.868	10	.000	81.787

RMR, GFI

Model	RMR	GFI	AGFI	PGFI
Default model	.008	.999	.994	.133
Saturated model	.000	1.000		
Independence model	1.998	.715	.572	.477

Baseline Comparisons

Model	NFI Delta1	RFI rho1	IFI Delta2	TLI rho2	CFI
Default model	.997	.987	1.000	.999	1.000
Saturated model	1.000		1.000		1.000
Independence model	.000	.000	.000	.000	.000

Parsimony-Adjusted Measures

Model	PRATIO	PNFI	PCFI
Default model	.200	.199	.200
Saturated model	.000	.000	.000
Independence model	1.000	.000	.000

RMSEA

Model	RMSEA	LO 90	HI 90	PCLOSE
Default model	.009	.000	.064	.854
Independence model	.284	.268	.301	.000

AIC

Model	AIC	BCC	BIC	CAIC
Default model	28.166	28.324	91.967	104.967
Saturated model	30.000	30.181	103.616	118.616
Independence model	827.868	827.929	852.407	857.407

FIGURE C.10 Fit statistics from the Amos text output (the output is edited; not all statistics are shown).

Figure C.12 shows the syntax used to analyze this example in LISREL. Briefly, the syntax lists the title of the analysis and then lists the observed (measured) variables. Since this is a path analysis, all variables are observed (there are no latent variables). We can use longer, multiword versions of the variable names, but will need to enclose them in single quotes to tell LISREL that the two words represent one variable (e.g., 'Family Background'). We tell LISREL the sample size, and that we are inputting correlations and

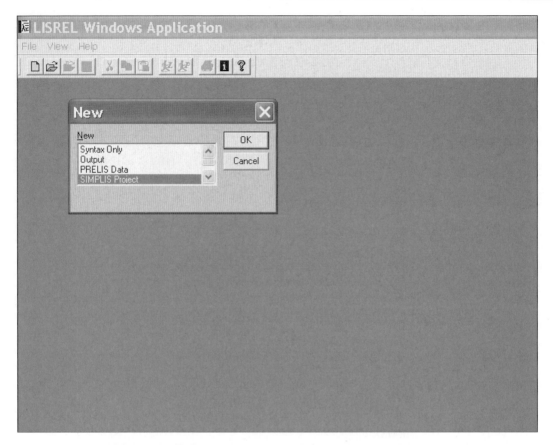

FIGURE C.11   Creating a new SIMPLIS set of commands in LISREL.

standard deviations. Alternatively, we could have input a covariance matrix, and we could also include means. LISREL can access all these as external files and read *raw* data from a variety of formats, including SPSS, Excel, and ASCII files. The free student version has limitations in the types of files that can be imported, however. With this simple example (and because we are using a matrix as input), it is easy to include the matrix data as a part of the syntax.

The section that starts with the word "relationships" essentially spells out the path model in equation format. Thus, Grades is a product of Previous Achievement and Homework; no other variables are included because our path model did not include paths to Grades from Ethnicity and Family Background. Alternatively, we could have specified the model using path-type symbols in the syntax (Ethnic -> PreAch Homework), under the heading Paths.

The final section of syntax spells out the options for the analysis and output. We request three decimal places for the output (ND=3) and LISREL-style, rather than SIM-PLIS-style, output. The reason for this request is that we can get more of the information that we are interested in with the LISREL-style output. With this output, we request the standardized solution (SC, or standardized completely), total and indirect effects (EF), and

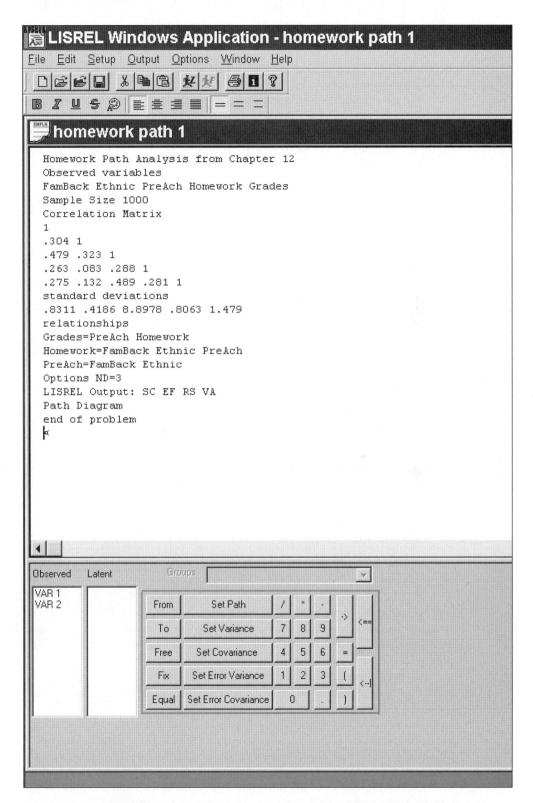

FIGURE C.12   SIMPLIS commands to analyze the Homework path model from Chapter 12.

the actual (VA), predicted, and residual matrices (RS). Finally, we request that LISREL produce a path diagram and end the syntax.

You can run the SIMPLIS syntax by pressing the button with the little running figure on it at the top of the window (Figure C.12) or by clicking on "Run" in the File menu. Running the syntax should produce two extra windows besides the Syntax window: one showing the text output and one, the path diagram.

Figures C.13 though C.18 show portions of the LISREL output. I will present the output in the order it appears in the printout, but will skip over portions of this output. Figure C.13 shows the unstandardized estimates from a portion of the LISREL text output, under the heading LISREL Estimates (Maximum Likelihood). The first table in the figure shows the beta matrix, which shows the effects of the endogenous variables (variables affected by other variables in the model) on each other. The table lists the unstandardized paths, their standard errors, and their t (z) values; values greater than approximately 2 are statistically significant. In these tables, the columns are the causes and the rows the effects. Thus, the first value (.020) shows the effect of Previous Achievement on Homework. The next matrix is the gamma matrix, listing the effect of the exogenous variables (variables not affected by other variables in the model) on the endogenous variables. The phi matrix is the variance–covariance matrix of the exogenous variables, and the psi matrix is the variance–covariance matrix of the disturbances. In the present example, only variances (a diagonal matrix) are shown for psi because we did not specify any covariances among disturbances.

Figure C.14 shows the variety of fit statistics output by LISREL. I'll mention these in the order listed, but will skip over some fit statistics. These include most of the fit measures discussed in this book, including the df, χ^2 and probability, RMSEA and 90% CI for RMSEA, AIC (Model AIC), the TLI (listed as the nonnormed fit index, or NNFI), CFI, the standardized RMR, and the GFI. These various fit measures are discussed in Chapter 12 and subsequent chapters.

Figure C.15 shows the covariance matrix implied by the model (called the fitted covariance matrix), the residuals (the actual matrix minus the fitted matrix), and the standardized residuals. Figure C.16 shows the standardized solution from LISREL. These tables are read the same way as the unstandardized coefficients (from column to row). Next are the unstandardized total and indirect effects, their standard errors, and z values (Figure C.17) and the standardized total and indirect effects (Figure C.18). The transition from this output to that shown in this book should be relatively painless.

Finally, Figure C.19 shows the path model produced by LISREL. LISREL will produce the unstandardized model by default, but you can obtain the standardized solution by changing the Estimates box at the top right of the screen (not shown in the figure). I also moved the boxes and paths around in the model shown to improve its looks. It is also possible to run LISREL by drawing a figure, rather than using syntax.

If you have compared the LISREL output with that from Amos, you will notice slight differences in standardized and unstandardized coefficients (at the third decimal place). The reason for these inconsistencies is discussed in Chapter 17. For now, you should simply know that you are likely to get minor differences. The differences are minor enough so that the figural output from the two programs, showing only two decimals, matches (Figures C.8 and C.19). There are also differences in the fit statistics for the two programs. It appears that LISREL uses different rules for generating the null, or independence, model, resulting in a different value for χ^2 for the null model. This difference should also result in minor differences in the fit statistics that use the null model, such as CFI and TLI.

```
LISREL Estimates (Maximum Likelihood)

    BETA

              PreAch    Homework    Grades
              --------  --------    --------

PreAch         - -        - -        - -

Homework      0.020       - -        - -
             (0.003)
              6.279

Grades        0.074      0.280       - -
             (0.005)    (0.052)
             15.647      5.375

    GAMMA

              FamBack    Ethnic
              --------   --------
PreAch        4.492      4.154
             (0.305)    (0.606)
             14.713      6.853

Homework      0.165     -0.076
             (0.034)    (0.062)
              4.897     -1.228

Grades         - -        - -


    PHI

              FamBack    Ethnic
              --------   --------
FamBack       0.691
             (0.031)
             22.327

Ethnic        0.106      0.175
             (0.012)    (0.008)
              9.184     22.327

    PSI
    Note: This matrix is diagonal.

              PreAch    Homework    Grades
              --------  --------    --------
             58.261      0.582      1.618
             (2.609)    (0.026)    (0.072)
             22.327     22.327     22.327
```

**FIGURE C.13   Unstandardized path coefficients
in the format presented in LISREL.**

Goodness of Fit Statistics

Degrees of Freedom = 2
Minimum Fit Function Chi-Square = 2.133 (P = 0.344)
Normal Theory Weighted Least Squares Chi-Square = 2.131 (P = 0.345)
Estimated Non-centrality Parameter (NCP) = 0.131
90 Percent Confidence Interval for NCP = (0.0 ; 8.133)

Minimum Fit Function Value = 0.00214
Population Discrepancy Function Value (F0) = 0.000131
90 Percent Confidence Interval for F0 = (0.0 ; 0.00816)
Root Mean Square Error of Approximation (RMSEA) = 0.00810
90 Percent Confidence Interval for RMSEA = (0.0 ; 0.0639)
P-Value for Test of Close Fit (RMSEA < 0.05) = 0.857

Expected Cross-Validation Index (ECVI) = 0.0282
90 Percent Confidence Interval for ECVI = (0.0281 ; 0.0362)
ECVI for Saturated Model = 0.0301
ECVI for Independence Model = 1.008

Chi-Square for Independence Model with 10 Degrees of Freedom = 995.323
Independence AIC = 1005.323
Model AIC = 28.131
Saturated AIC = 30.000
Independence CAIC = 1034.861
Model CAIC = 104.931
Saturated CAIC = 118.616

Normed Fit Index (NFI) = 0.998
Non-Normed Fit Index (NNFI) = 0.999
Parsimony Normed Fit Index (PNFI) = 0.200
Comparative Fit Index (CFI) = 1.00
Incremental Fit Index (IFI) = 1.00
Relative Fit Index (RFI) = 0.989

Critical N (CN) = 4315.198

Root Mean Square Residual (RMR) = 0.00790
Standardized RMR = 0.00843
Goodness of Fit Index (GFI) = 0.999
Adjusted Goodness of Fit Index (AGFI) = 0.994
Parsimony Goodness of Fit Index (PGFI) = 0.133

FIGURE C.14   Fit statistics for the Homework model in LISREL.

Homework Path Analysis from Chapter 12

Fitted Covariance Matrix

	PreAch	Homework	Grades	FamBack	Ethnic
PreAch	79.171				
Homework	2.066	0.650			
Grades	6.435	0.335	2.187		
FamBack	3.542	0.176	0.311	0.691	
Ethnic	1.203	0.028	0.097	0.106	0.175

Fitted Residuals

	PreAch	Homework	Grades	FamBack	Ethnic
PreAch	- -				
Homework	- -	- -			
Grades	- -	0.000	- -		
FamBack	0.000	0.000	0.027	- -	
Ethnic	- -	0.000	-0.015	- -	- -

Standardized Residuals

	PreAch	Homework	Grades	FamBack	Ethnic
PreAch	- -				
Homework	- -	- -			
Grades	- -	- -	- -		
FamBack	- -	- -	0.916	- -	
Ethnic	- -	- -	-0.947	- -	- -

FIGURE C.15 Fitted (implied) covariance matrix, residuals, and standardized residuals in LISREL.

EQS

EQS, developed by Peter Bentler and published by Multivariate Software (www.mvsoft .com), was the second major SEM program. EQS, sometimes pronounced X, is a contraction of "equations." When initially published in the mid-1980s, EQS models were specified through a series of equations, which made the program somewhat easier to learn than LISREL, which required consideration of multiple matrices. In its current form, EQS can still be executed via a series of commands that specify the model using equations (Bentler, 1995). One can also specify the model by drawing it, however, after which the program generates the EQS commands needed to run the analysis (Bentler & Wu, 1995).

EQS is available for Windows and mainframe operating systems and has been available in Macintosh versions in the past. EQS offers extensive simulation capabilities. It can

```
Standardized Solution

  BETA

                PreAch     Homework      Grades
                --------   --------     --------
       PreAch     - -         - -          - -
     Homework    0.219        - -          - -
       Grades    0.445       0.153         - -

  GAMMA

                FamBack     Ethnic
                --------   --------
       PreAch    0.420       0.195
     Homework    0.170      -0.040
       Grades     - -         - -


  PSI
  Note: This matrix is diagonal.

                PreAch     Homework      Grades
                --------   --------     --------
                 0.736      0.895        0.739
```

FIGURE C.16   Standardized solution in LISREL.

import *raw* data in several formats, including SPSS and ASCII (text) formats. The soon to be released version 6 will allow the analysis of multilevel models, uses maximum likelihood methodology to deal with missing data, and allows bootstrapping/resampling to generate standard errors. Although a downloadable demo version of EQS is available on the Web site, you cannot save or print the results of the analyses.

For the sake of simplicity and because my primary purpose is to illustrate program output, I will here demonstrate EQS (version 5.7) by running commands via syntax. Figure C.20 shows the series of EQS commands needed to analyze the Homework path analysis from Chapter 12. Assuming that you are using EQS for Windows, when you open the program up, it expects you to enter data or open a data file. You can also open or enter a simple text file like the one shown here.

The commands are relatively straightforward. Each command begins with a forward slash, and subcommands end with a semicolon. The /Specifications command defines the data set (to be read as part of the syntax), with 1000 cases, in the form of a correlation matrix. The "Analysis=cov" subcommand means that we will analyze the covariance, rather than the correlation, matrix. In the /Specifications command we could also have directed EQS to an external data set, either in raw format or in the form of a covariance matrix. EQS refers to measured variables as V1, V2, . . . ; disturbances for the measured variables as E1, E2, . . . (for "error"); latent variables as F1, F2, . . . (for "factor"); and disturbances for latent variables as D1, D2, ... It is worth noting that EQS labels disturbances for latent

```
Total and Indirect Effects

          Total Effects of X on Y

                  FamBack     Ethnic
                  --------    --------
    PreAch         4.492       4.154
                  (0.305)     (0.606)
                  14.713       6.853

  Homework         0.254       0.006
                  (0.031)     (0.062)
                   8.168       0.105

    Grades         0.404       0.309
                  (0.034)     (0.055)
                  12.017       5.648

        Indirect Effects of X on Y

                  FamBack     Ethnic
                  --------    --------
    PreAch          - -         - -

  Homework         0.089       0.083
                  (0.015)     (0.018)
                   5.775       4.630

    Grades         0.404       0.309
                  (0.034)     (0.055)
                  12.017       5.648

          Total Effects of Y on Y

                  PreAch    Homework    Grades
                  --------  --------   --------
    PreAch          - -       - -        - -

  Homework         0.020      - -        - -
                  (0.003)
                   6.279

    Grades         0.080     0.280       - -
                  (0.005)   (0.052)
                  17.200     5.375

        Indirect Effects of Y on Y

                  PreAch    Homework    Grades
                  --------  --------   --------
    PreAch          - -       - -        - -
  Homework          - -       - -        - -
    Grades         0.006      - -        - -
                  (0.001)
                   4.083
```

FIGURE C.17 Unstandardized total and indirect effects in the LISREL output.

469

```
Homework Path Analysis from Chapter 12

Standardized Total and Indirect Effects

        Standardized Total Effects of X on Y

              FamBack        Ethnic
            --------      --------
   PreAch      0.420         0.195
 Homework      0.262         0.003
   Grades      0.227         0.087

        Standardized Indirect Effects of X on Y

              FamBack        Ethnic
            --------      --------
   PreAch       - -           - -
 Homework      0.092         0.043
   Grades      0.227         0.087

        Standardized Total Effects of Y on Y

              PreAch    Homework       Grades
            --------    --------     --------
   PreAch       - -         - -          - -
 Homework      0.219         - -          - -
   Grades      0.479       0.153          - -

        Standardized Indirect Effects of Y on Y

              PreAch    Homework       Grades
            --------    --------     --------
   PreAch       - -         - -          - -
 Homework       - -         - -          - -
   Grades      0.034         - -          - -
```

FIGURE C.18 **Standardized total and indirect effects from the LISREL output.**

variables as disturbances, but refers to both the disturbances (for path models) and the unique–error variances (for latent variable models) of measured variables as error. There's nothing wrong with this, but new users of EQS should be aware of this inconsistency in labeling between this text and the program. The /Labels command simply provides labels for the variables; they are listed in the order they appear in the subsequent matrix.

The /Equations command is where the model is specified. V5 (Grades) has paths from V3 (PreAch) and V4 (Homework), as well as from a disturbance (E3; recall that any variable that has arrows pointing to it must also have a disturbance or error term pointing to it). Thus, the equation for V5 is V3 + V4 + E3. The asterisk before each variable tells EQS

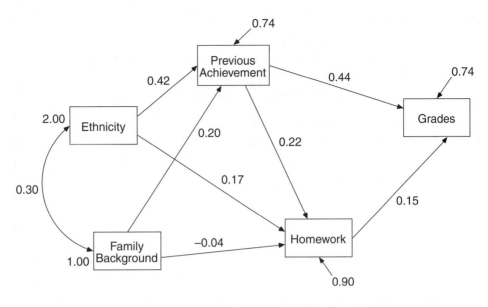

Chi-Square = 2.13, df = 2, P-value = 0.34461, RMSEA = 0.008

FIGURE C.19   Standardized path diagram produced as a part of the LISREL analysis.

```
/Title
  Homework Path Analysis from Chapter 12
/Specifications
  Cases=1000; Vars=5; Matrix=Cor; Analysis=cov;
/Labels
  V1=FamBack; V2=Ethnic; V3=PreAch; V4=Homework; V5=Grades;
/Equations
  V5=          *V3+*V4+E3;
  V4=*V1+*V2+*V3     +E2;
  V3=*V1+*V2         +E1;
/Variances
  E1 to E3 = *;
  V1 to V2 = *;
/Covariances
  V1,V2=*;
/Print
  effect=yes; covariance=yes; correlation=yes; fit=all;
/Matrix
  1
  0.3041     1
  0.3228     0.4793     1
  0.0832     0.2632     0.2884      1
  0.1315     0.2751     0.489 0.2813       1
/Standard Deviations
  0.4186     0.8311     8.8978      0.8063      1.479
/end
```

**FIGURE C.20   EQS commands needed to conduct
the Homework path analysis from Chapter 12.**

that these parameters are free (unconstrained) and thus need to be estimated. Similar to Amos, the paths from the disturbances are fixed in EQS, but we need to estimate the variances of the disturbances. We also estimate the variances of the exogenous variables; both of these occur in the /Variances command. The model includes a covariance between the two exogenous variables (Ethnicity and Family Background, V2 and V1); we tell EQS to estimate this covariance with the /Covariances command. In the /Print command we request the sample correlation and covariance matrix, as well at the indirect and total effects (EF). The fit = all portion of the /Print command ensures that the output includes all, rather than just a few, fit indexes. The correlations and standard deviations are read in via the /Matrix and /Standard Deviations commands.

Figures C.21 through C.26 show portions of the EQS output. These appear in the same order as in the printout, but portions of the printout have been skipped. After mirroring the command input, the covariance and correlation matrices, EQS provides information

```
MAXIMUM LIKELIHOOD SOLUTION (NORMAL DISTRIBUTION THEORY)
PARAMETER ESTIMATES APPEAR IN ORDER,
NO SPECIAL PROBLEMS WERE ENCOUNTERED DURING OPTIMIZATION.



RESIDUAL COVARIANCE MATRIX  (S-SIGMA) :


                        FAMBACK    ETHNIC     PREACH     HOMEWORK   GRADES
                        V  1       V  2       V  3       V  4       V  5
        FAMBACK   V  1   0.000
        ETHNIC    V  2   0.000      0.000
        PREACH    V  3   0.000      0.000      0.000
        HOMEWORK  V  4   0.000      0.000      0.000      0.000
        GRADES    V  5  -0.015      0.027      0.000      0.000      0.000


                    AVERAGE ABSOLUTE  COVARIANCE  RESIDUALS    =      0.0028
            AVERAGE OFF-DIAGONAL ABSOLUTE  COVARIANCE  RESIDUALS    =      0.0042



STANDARDIZED RESIDUAL MATRIX:


                        FAMBACK    ETHNIC     PREACH     HOMEWORK   GRADES
                        V  1       V  2       V  3       V  4       V  5
        FAMBACK   V  1   0.000
        ETHNIC    V  2   0.000      0.000
        PREACH    V  3   0.000      0.000      0.000
        HOMEWORK  V  4   0.000      0.000      0.000      0.000
        GRADES    V  5  -0.025      0.022      0.000      0.000      0.000


                    AVERAGE ABSOLUTE STANDARDIZED RESIDUALS    =      0.0031
            AVERAGE OFF-DIAGONAL ABSOLUTE STANDARDIZED RESIDUALS    =      0.0046
```

FIGURE C.21   Residuals and standardized residuals from the EQS output.

```
TITLE:    Homework Path Analysis from Chapter 12              08/18/03
MAXIMUM LIKELIHOOD SOLUTION (NORMAL DISTRIBUTION THEORY)


GOODNESS OF FIT SUMMARY

INDEPENDENCE MODEL CHI-SQUARE =        817.868 ON    10 DEGREES OF FREEDOM

INDEPENDENCE AIC =   797.86828   INDEPENDENCE CAIC =    738.79073
       MODEL AIC =    -1.83351         MODEL CAIC =    -13.64902

CHI-SQUARE =        2.166 BASED ON    2 DEGREES OF FREEDOM
PROBABILITY VALUE FOR THE CHI-SQUARE STATISTIC IS      0.33850
THE NORMAL THEORY RLS CHI-SQUARE FOR THIS ML SOLUTION IS          2.164.

BENTLER-BONETT NORMED    FIT INDEX=       0.997
BENTLER-BONETT NONNORMED FIT INDEX=       0.999
COMPARATIVE FIT INDEX (CFI)       =       1.000
BOLLEN (IFI)            FIT INDEX=       1.000
McDonald (MFI)         FIT INDEX=       1.000
LISREL GFI             FIT INDEX=       0.999
LISREL AGFI            FIT INDEX=       0.994
ROOT MEAN SQUARED RESIDUAL (RMR)  =       0.008
STANDARDIZED RMR                  =       0.008
ROOT MEAN SQ. ERROR OF APP.(RMSEA)=       0.009
90% CONFIDENCE INTERVAL OF RMSEA (       0.000,        0.064)
```

FIGURE C.22   Fit statistics produced by EQS for the Homework path analysis.

about residuals; the residuals and standardized residuals are shown in Figure C.21. The Goodness of Fit Summary in Figure C.22 shows the χ^2 for the independence or null model; the AIC for the model ("Model AIC"); χ^2, *df*, and probability for the model analyzed; and the TLI (listed as the Bentler–Bonett Nonnormed Fit Index), the CFI, and the GFI (listed as "LISREL GFI"). This is followed by the SRMR (Standardized RMR), the RMSEA, and the 90% confidence interval of the RMSEA (I've listed these in their order of appearance, but have skipped over some fit statistics).

The section titled Measurement Equation with Standard Errors and Test Statistics shows the unstandardized paths, their standard errors, and the *t* (*z*) values (Figure C.23). Thus, the paths to Grades are .074 from Previous Achievement (V3) and .281 from Homework (V4). Both are statistically significant ($z > 2$). Also shown are the variances of the exogenous variables and the disturbances. The section titled "Covariances among Independent Variables" shows, as you might expect, the covariance between Ethnicity and Family Background, its standard error, and *z*. The sections titled "Decomposition of Effects . . . " show the unstandardized total and indirect effects, followed by the standardized total and indirect effects (Figure C.24). Next comes the "Standardized Solution," which shows the standardized paths to each endogenous variable, again in equation format (Figure C.25). For Grades, the standardized effects are .445 from Previous Achievement (V3) and .153 from Homework (V4). Finally, Figure C.26 shows a path model created with the EQS/Windows diagrammer. As noted earlier, this diagram could have been used as a starting point for EQS and could have been used to create syntax. The program would then have also output a solved version of the model, including parameter estimates for paths and covariances.

```
MAXIMUM LIKELIHOOD SOLUTION (NORMAL DISTRIBUTION THEORY)

MEASUREMENT EQUATIONS WITH STANDARD ERRORS AND TEST STATISTICS


PREACH   =V3   =    4.147*V1    + 4.496*V2    + 1.000 E1
                     .606          .305
                    6.848        14.743

HOMEWORK=V4    =     .020*V3    -  .076*V1    +  .165*V2     + 1.000 E2
                     .003          .062          .034
                    6.295        -1.225         4.899

GRADES   =V5   =     .074*V3    +  .281*V4    + 1.000 E3
                     .005          .052
                   15.657         5.385


VARIANCES OF INDEPENDENT VARIABLES
----------------------------------

                      V                         F
                     ---                       ---
V1   -FAMBACK              .175*I                              I
                          .008 I                              I
                        22.349 I                              I
                               I                              I
V2   -ETHNIC              .691*I                              I
                          .031 I                              I
                        22.349 I                              I


VARIANCES OF INDEPENDENT VARIABLES
----------------------------------

                      E                         D
                     ---                       ---
E1   -PREACH           58.249*I                              I
                         2.606 I                              I
                        22.349 I                              I
                               I                              I
E2   -HOMEWORK            .582*I                              I
                          .026 I                              I
                        22.349 I                              I
                               I                              I
E3   -GRADES            1.617*I                              I
                          .072 I                              I
                        22.349 I                              I


COVARIANCES AMONG INDEPENDENT VARIABLES
---------------------------------------

                      V                         F
                     ---                       ---
V2   -ETHNIC              .106*I                              I
V1   -FAMBACK             .012 I                              I
                         9.196 I                              I
```

FIGURE C.23   Unstandardized path coefficients, variances, and covariances from the EQS output. Also shown are the standard errors and *t* values.

```
DECOMPOSITION OF EFFECTS WITH NONSTANDARDIZED VALUES

PARAMETER TOTAL EFFECTS
-----------------------

PREACH  =V3  =    4.147*V1    + 4.496*V2   + 1.000 E1

HOMEWORK=V4  =     .020*V3    +  .007*V1   +  .254*V2   +  .020 E1
                 1.000 E2

GRADES  =V5  =     .080*V3    +  .281*V4   +  .309 V1   +  .404 V2
                   .080 E1    +  .281 E2   + 1.000 E3


DECOMPOSITION OF EFFECTS WITH NONSTANDARDIZED VALUES

PARAMETER INDIRECT EFFECTS
--------------------------

HOMEWORK=V4  =     .083*V1    +  .090*V2   +  .020 E1
                   .018          .015         .003
                  4.634         5.789        6.295

GRADES  =V5  =     .006*V3    +  .309 V1   +  .404 V2   +  .080 E1
                   .001          .055         .034         .005
                  4.092         5.644       12.036       17.216

                   .281 E2
                   .052
                  5.385


DECOMPOSITION OF EFFECTS WITH STANDARDIZED VALUES

PARAMETER TOTAL EFFECTS
-----------------------

PREACH  =V3  =     .195*V1    +  .420*V2   +  .858 E1

HOMEWORK=V4  =     .220*V3    +  .003*V1   +  .262*V2   +  .188 E1
                   .946 E2

GRADES  =V5  =     .478*V3    +  .153*V4   +  .087 V1   +  .227 V2
                   .410 E1    +  .145 E2   +  .860 E3


DECOMPOSITION OF EFFECTS WITH STANDARDIZED VALUES

PARAMETER INDIRECT EFFECTS
--------------------------

HOMEWORK=V4  =     .043*V1    +  .092*V2   +  .188 E1

GRADES  =V5  =     .034*V3    +  .087 V1   +  .227 V2   +  .410 E1
                   .145 E2
```

FIGURE C.24   Total and indirect effects from EQS, both unstandardized and standardized.

```
STANDARDIZED SOLUTION:                                          R-SQUARED


PREACH  =V3 =     .195*V1    +  .420*V2    +  .858 E1                      .264
HOMEWORK=V4 =     .220*V3    -  .039*V1    +  .170*V2    +  .946 E2        .105
GRADES  =V5 =     .445*V3    +  .153*V4    +  .860 E3                      .261



CORRELATIONS AMONG INDEPENDENT VARIABLES
----------------------------------------

                    V                        F
                    ---                      ---
V2  -ETHNIC        .304*I                          I
V1  -FAMBACK        I                              I
                    I                              I
```

FIGURE C.25   Standardized solution from the EQS output.

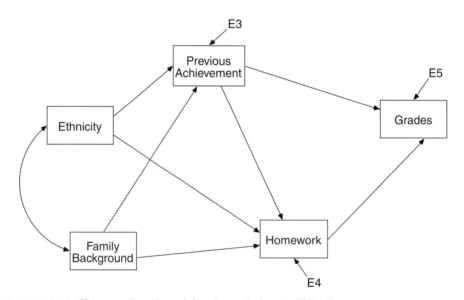

FIGURE C.26   Homework path model as drawn using the EQS diagrammer.

There are very few differences between the numerical values produced by EQS compared to those produced by Amos. The one practical difference is the value of the AIC fit statistic (–1.83 for EQS versus 28.166 for Amos). There are several different ways to calculate the AIC. Although the values differ, you would use them in the same way for either program by comparing the AIC values for competing models, with the lower AIC value suggesting a better fitting model.

MPLUS

Mplus is a powerful SEM program developed and published by Bengt Muthén and Linda Muthén (Muthén & Muthén, 2000). In addition to the standard SEMs discussed here, Mplus is capable of analyzing models with categorical outcome variables. It also can analyze multilevel models and be used to conduct simulation studies. You can download a free demonstration version of Mplus at www.statmodel.com. The demonstration version of Mplus is limited to two exogenous and six endogenous variables.

Mplus is run via syntax, which is fairly simple and straightforward. When you open Mplus, a window pops up into which you can enter this syntax. Figure C.27 shows the commands used to run the current example in Mplus; each command is followed with a colon, and each subcommand ends with a semicolon. The Data: command lists the name of the ASCII (text) file containing the data (these data should be in the directory with the program or a path needs to be specified). If the data are in some form other than raw data, you should also specify the nature of the data (here the file included a correlation matrix and a line of standard deviations, in that order). The Variable: command lists the variables in the file; if this is a large file, you can choose (through a "Usevariables" subcommand) a subset of the variables in the file. The Model: command lists, in regressionlike language, the equations that make up the model. For example, "Grades on Homework PreAch" means regress Grades on Homework and Previous Achievement. The "with" portion of the command on the final line of the model command asks for the covariance–correlation between the two exogenous variables (these are correlated by default in Mplus). The Output: command asks for the statistics (covariance matrix, etc.) associated with the sample data (Sampstat), the standardized solution, and residuals. You can also request modification indexes and confidence intervals.

To run the analysis, click on the "Run" button at the top of the screen or select the Mplus menu at the top of the screen and then "Run Mplus." Portions of the output are shown in Figures C.28 through C.30. The output is shown in the same order as the printout, but portions of the printout have been skipped. Figure C.28 shows the fit statistics produced by MPlus. These include the χ^2, df, and associated probability, CFI and TLI, the AIC and BIC, the RMSEA and its 90% confidence interval, and the SRMR (along with other fit statistics not discussed here).

Figure C.29 shows the unstandardized coefficients, standard errors, and t (z) values. The final column (StdYX) shows the standardized coefficients for the model. With latent variable models, the Std and the StdYX columns show two different types of standardized coefficients. Finally, Figure C.30 shows the covariances implied by the model ("Model Estimated Covariances . . . ") and the unstandardized residuals ("Residuals for

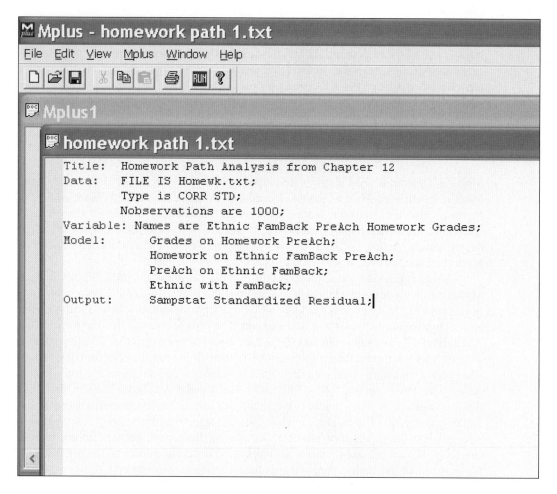

FIGURE C.27 Commands needed to conduct the Homework path analysis from Chapter 12 using Mplus. The standard deviations and correlations are in an external ASCII text file (Homewk.txt).

Covariances . . . "). Again, the output differs in form from that used in the main body of the text, but it is easy to translate from one into the other.

The numerical values of parameters and fit statistics match well those produced by Amos. The two exceptions are the AIC and the χ^2 for the null model (called the Baseline Model in Mplus). As noted in the discussion of EQS, there are several different ways to calculate the AIC, so this difference is understandable. Although the values differ, you use

```
TESTS OF MODEL FIT

Chi-Square Test of Model Fit

          Value                              2.169
          Degrees of Freedom                     2
          P-Value                           0.3345

Chi-Square Test of Model Fit for the Baseline Model

          Value                            721.651
          Degrees of Freedom                     9
          P-Value                           0.0000

CFI/TLI

          CFI                                1.000
          TLI                                0.999

Loglikelihood

          H0 Value                        -7989.958
          H1 Value                        -7988.874

Information Criteria

          Number of Free Parameters             13
          Akaike (AIC)                    16005.917
          Bayesian (BIC)                  16069.718
          Sample-Size Adjusted BIC        16028.429
             (n* = (n + 2) / 24)

RMSEA (Root Mean Square Error Of Approximation)

          Estimate                           0.009
          90 Percent C.I.                    0.000   0.064
          Probability RMSEA <= .05           0.854

SRMR (Standardized Root Mean Square Residual)

          Value                              0.008
```

FIGURE C.28   Fit statistics from the Mplus output.

```
MODEL RESULTS

                     Estimates    S.E.   Est./S.E.    Std    StdYX

GRADES    ON
     HOMEWORK          0.281     0.052     5.387     0.281    0.153
     PREACH            0.074     0.005    15.665     0.074    0.445

HOMEWORK ON
     ETHNIC           -0.076     0.062    -1.225    -0.076   -0.039
     FAMBACK           0.165     0.034     4.902     0.165    0.170
     PREACH            0.020     0.003     6.298     0.020    0.220

PREACH    ON
     ETHNIC            4.147     0.605     6.852     4.147    0.195
     FAMBACK           4.496     0.305    14.750     4.496    0.420

ETHNIC    WITH
     FAMBACK           0.106     0.011     9.200     0.106    0.304

Variances
     ETHNIC            0.175     0.008    22.361     0.175    1.000
     FAMBACK           0.690     0.031    22.361     0.690    1.000

Residual Variances
     PREACH           58.190     2.602    22.361    58.190    0.736
     HOMEWORK          0.581     0.026    22.361     0.581    0.895
     GRADES            1.616     0.072    22.361     1.616    0.739


R-SQUARE

     Observed
     Variable  R-Square

     PREACH      0.264
     HOMEWORK    0.105
     GRADES      0.261
```

FIGURE C.29   Unstandardized path coefficients, their standard errors and associated
t values from Mplus. The last column (StdYX) shows the standardized paths.

```
RESIDUAL OUTPUT


     ESTIMATED MODEL AND RESIDUALS (OBSERVED - ESTIMATED)


         Model Estimated Covariances/Correlations/Residual Correlations
              PREACH       HOMEWORK     GRADES       ETHNIC       FAMBACK
              _____     _____     _____     _____     _____


  PREACH       79.092
  HOMEWORK      2.067       0.649
  GRADES        6.429       0.335       2.185
  ETHNIC        1.201       0.028       0.097       0.175
  FAMBACK       3.541       0.176       0.311       0.106       0.690


         Residuals for Covariances/Correlations/Residual Correlations
              PREACH       HOMEWORK     GRADES       ETHNIC       FAMBACK
              _____     _____     _____     _____     _____


  PREACH        0.000
  HOMEWORK      0.000       0.000
  GRADES        0.000       0.000       0.000
  ETHNIC        0.000       0.000      -0.015       0.000
  FAMBACK       0.000       0.000       0.027       0.000       0.000
```

FIGURE C.30 Covariance matrix implied by the model and residuals from the Mplus output.

them in the same way for either program by comparing the AIC values for competing models, with the lower AIC value suggesting a better fitting model. Concerning the difference in the null model ($\chi^2 = 817.868$ with 10 df for Amos versus $\chi^2 = 721.651$ with 9 df for Mplus), it is clear that Mplus uses a different null–independence model than does Amos (or the other programs). For the Amos null model, all variables are assumed to be unrelated. In contrast, it appears that with Mplus the two exogenous variables are allowed to correlate in the baseline model. This difference in null–independence–baseline models will also have a small effect on the other fit statistics that use the null model, such as the TLI and CFI.

PARTIAL AND SEMIPARTIAL CORRELATION

In earlier chapters we touched on the topic of semipartial correlations and noted how they are related to ΔR^2 and to t. I also mentioned partial and semipartial correlation when we first raised the issue of the meaning of "controlling for" in Chapter 2. In this appendix, we will focus in more detail on the topics of partial and semipartial correlation. I have placed this topic in an appendix for several reasons. It does not really fit in with the flow of the other chapters, and it is a topic that will not be of interest to all readers of the text. In addition, although the topic fits better in Part 1 of the text, it will be more understandable following an introduction to path and SEM models.

PARTIAL CORRELATIONS

Partial correlations are correlations between two variables, with other variables taken into account. You may also hear partial correlations described as the correlation between two variables with the effects of other variables removed or other variables controlled. Let's use an example to illustrate.

Example: Optimism and Locus of Control

Figure D.1 shows the correlations among several variables from the NELS data. Optimism is a composite I created from a series of questions about students' outlook toward the future (F1S64A through F1S64K): "Think about how you see the future. What are the chances that:

> You will graduate from high school?
> You will go to college?
> You will have a job that pays well?
> You will be able to own your own home?
> You will have a job that you enjoy doing?
> You will have a happy family life?
> You will stay in good health most of the time?
> You will be able to live wherever you want in the country?

You will be respected in your community?
You will have good friends you can count on?
Life will turn out better for you than it has for your parents?
Your children will have a better life than you had?

Students with high scores on the composite had a fairly optimistic view of the future, whereas those with low scores were more pessimistic about the future. F1Locus2 is a locus of control scale; students with an internal locus of control had high scores, whereas those with an external locus had low scores. Par_Inv is a measure of parent involvement in education, defined as the educational aspirations parents have for their children along with the extent that they communicate with their children about school and education. BySES and ByGrads are the SES (Family Background) and GPA composites we have used previously.

Previously, I noted that simple Pearson correlation coefficients are sometimes called zero-order correlations. Thus, the output shown here (from the SPSS Partial Correlation procedure) labels these correlations as zero-order partials. This simply means that these are

Partial Corr

Zero Order Partials (Simple Correlations)

	OPTIMISM	F1LOCUS2	PAR_INV	BYSES	BYGRADS
OPTIMISM	1.0000	.3635	.3146	.2036	.2987
	(0)	(799)	(799)	(799)	(799)
	P= .	P= .000	P= .000	P= .000	P= .000
F1LOCUS2	.3635	1.0000	.2430	.2028	.2529
	(799)	(0)	(799)	(799)	(799)
	P= .000	P= .	P= .000	P= .000	P= .000
PAR_INV	.3146	.2430	1.0000	.4187	.3909
	(799)	(799)	(0)	(799)	(799)
	P= .000	P= .000	P= .	P= .000	P= .000
BYSES	.2036	.2028	.4187	1.0000	.3420
	(799)	(799)	(799)	(0)	(799)
	P= .000	P= .000	P= .000	P= .	P= .000
BYGRADS	.2987	.2529	.3909	.3420	1.0000
	(799)	(799)	(799)	(799)	(0)
	P= .000	P= .000	P= .000	P= .000	P= .

(Coefficient / (D.F.) / 2-tailed Significance)

FIGURE D.1   Zero-order correlations among Optimism, Locus of Control, Parent Involvement, SES, and Grades.

correlations with no other variables controlled. The primary correlation of interest is between the variables Optimism and Locus of Control: .36. Adolescents who have a more internal locus of control are also more optimistic. Note also, however, that these primary variables of interest also show small to moderate correlations with the other variables, in the .2 to .3 range. Thus, it is likely that once we control for, or remove the effects of, these variables the correlation between Optimism and Locus will decrease.

Figure D.2 shows the partial correlation between Optimism and Locus, controlling for Parent Involvement, SES, and base year GPA. As expected, once these background variables are controlled, the partial correlation is lower than the zero-order correlation (.28). I'll symbolize this partial correlation as $pr_{\text{Optimism–Locus}\cdot\text{Parent,SES,Grades}}$ = .28 with the pr symbolizing partial correlation and the dot symbolizing "controlling for. . . ." If this sounds a lot like regression coefficients, it should. We spoke of the coefficients in MR as representing the effect of one variable on another, controlling for one or more background variables. These regression coefficients are sometimes also referred to as *partial* regression coefficients. The difference is that partial correlations are correlations; that is, they have no directional quality, no implication of cause and effect or the prediction of one variable from another. In the introduction to path analysis, I referred to an agnostic model; partial correlations are like agnostic regression coefficients.

```
- - -  P A R T I A L    C O R R E L A T I O N    C O E F F I C I E N T S  - - -

Controlling for..     PAR_INV    BYSES      BYGRADS

              OPTIMISM    F1LOCUS2

OPTIMISM       1.0000       .2843
              (     0)     (  796)
              P= .        P= .000

F1LOCUS2        .2843      1.0000
              (   796)     (    0)
              P= .000     P= .

(Coefficient / (D.F.) / 2-tailed Significance)
```

FIGURE D.2   Partial correlation between Optimism and Locus of Control, controlling for Parent Involvement, SES, and Grade Point Average.

Understanding Partial Correlations

If you recall our initial discussions of multiple regression, the phrase "with the effects of . . . removed" should also sound familiar. Recall that in Chapter 3 we used this phrase to describe the residuals. There we described the residual from the regression of Grades on Homework and Parent Education as representing Grades with the effects of Homework and Parent Education removed. Are partial correlations, then, related to the residuals in some way? Yes. One way of calculating partial correlations is to regress each variable of interest (Optimism and Locus) on the control variables (Parent Involvement, SES, and Grades) and to save the residuals. These residuals then represent Optimism and Locus of Control with the effects of the control variables removed. The correlation between these two residuals is then equivalent to the partial correlation of Optimism with Locus, with the effects of Parent Involvement, SES, and Grades removed. The correlation between the Optimism and Locus residuals (with the effects of SES, Parent Involvement, and Grades removed from each) is shown in Figure D.3; the value (.28) is consistent with the partial correlations in Figure D.2.

Correlations[a]

		OPT_RES Optimism Unstandardized Residual	LOC_RES Locus Unstandardized Residual
OPT_RES Optimism Unstandardized Residual	Pearson Correlation	1	.284**
	Sig. (2-tailed)	.	.000
LOC_RES Locus Unstandardized Residual	Pearson Correlation	.284**	1
	Sig. (2-tailed)	.000	.

**. Correlation is significant at the 0.01 level (2-tailed).

a. Listwise N=801

FIGURE D.3   The correlation of Optimism and Locus residuals (controlling for SES, Grades, and Parent Involvement) is equal to the partial correlation between Optimism and Locus, controlling for these background variables.

Figure D.4 demonstrates the relation between residuals and partial correlations using path analysis. Recall that the disturbances in path analysis are the same as the residuals in MR. Thus the disturbance d3 represents Optimism with SES, Parent Involvement, and GPA controlled; d4 represents Locus with these three background variables controlled. The correlation between these disturbances, then, is the partial correlation of Optimism with Locus of Control, with SES, Grades, and Parent Involvement taken into account, or controlled. Figure D.5, the solved path model, shows that the value .28 is again equivalent to the partial correlations from the partial correlation procedure and from the correlations between residuals.

Uses of Partial Correlations

Why would you use partial correlations? One potential reason is when you want to take obvious control variables into account without making causal statements about the two variables of interest. Alternatively, you may be interested in whether the correlation between two variables is spurious, the product of each being affected by one or more common causes. To use the present example, you may be interested in whether the correlation between students' levels of optimism and their locus of control is nonspurious or the extent to which the correlation remains after taking into account the background variables (potential common causes)

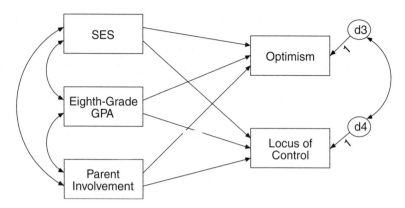

FIGURE D.4   Partial correlation in path analytic form. The correlation between the disturbances (residuals) is a partial correlation.

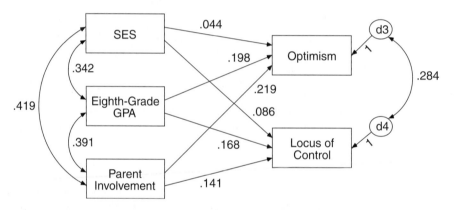

FIGURE D.5   Solved path model shows the equivalence to the partial correlation with the estimates in previous figures.

of SES, Parent Involvement, and Grades. From an explanatory standpoint, you might be interested in the effects of all these variables on each other, but be unable to decide whether optimism affects locus of control or the reverse. Although the model shown in Figures D.4 and D.5 will not help you decide which variable was the cause and which the effect, it will allow you to determine that the variables are still related in some way, after controlling for other relevant variables (assuming these are *the* relevant variables). Another possible meaning of partial correlations in the path models is that we recognize that there may also be other common causes of these two variables not taken into account in the model.

Partial correlations are also used in research on mediation (cf., Baron & Kenny, 1986). I think most questions of mediation are more easily tested via the indirect effects in path analysis and structural equation modeling, however.

SEMIPARTIAL CORRELATIONS

With semipartial correlations (also known as *part* correlations), the effects of the background or control variables have been removed from only *one* variable of interest. An example is shown in Figure D.6, which illustrates the semipartial correlation of Locus with Optimism, with the effects of SES, Parent Involvement, and GPA removed from Optimism (but not removed from Locus of Control). The correlation between the disturbance–residual of Optimism and the variable Locus of Control is equivalent to this semipartial correlation; $sr_{\text{Locus–(Optimism·Parent,SES,Grades)}} = .27$. (In this method of representation, the parentheses around both Optimism and the control variables illustrates that the control variables are partialed from Optimism, but not Locus of Control; the *sr* stands for semipartial correlation.)

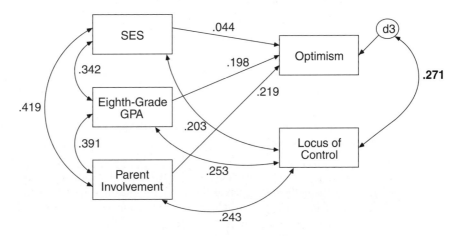

FIGURE D.6   Semipartial, or part, correlation in path analytic form. The effects of the control variables have been removed only from Optimism, not Locus of Control. The semipartial correlation is equal to the correlation between the Optimism disturbance and the Locus variable.

Given this description of semipartial correlations, it should also be possible to compute them using the residuals from multiple regression. It is. Again, our interest is in the correlation between Locus of Control and Optimism, with the background variable effects removed from Optimism. This means that we should correlate the Optimism residuals (SES, Grades, and Parent Involvement controlled) with the original Locus of Control variable. The value .268 is shown in Figure D.7. This value is the same as that shown in the path model, within errors of rounding.

Many statistics programs do not compute semipartial correlations directly; there is, for example, no semipartial correlation procedure in SPSS. In Chapter 5, however, you saw several methods of getting semipartial correlations as a result of MR output. It is possible in some programs, for example, to request semipartial correlations as a part of the MR

Correlations

		OPT_RES Optimism Unstandardized Residual	F1LOCUS2 LOCUS OF CONTROL 2
OPT_RES Optimism Unstandardized Residual	Pearson Correlation	1	.268**
	Sig. (2-tailed)	.	.000
	N	818	801
F1LOCUS2 LOCUS OF CONTROL 2	Pearson Correlation	.268**	1
	Sig. (2-tailed)	.000	.
	N	801	940

**. Correlation is significant at the 0.01 level (2-tailed).

FIGURE D.7   Calculating semipartial correlations via residuals. The Locus of Control variable is correlated with the Optimism residual.

output. Recall, also, that *squared* semipartial correlations are equivalent to the unique variance of a variable entered last in a regression equation, that is, ΔR^2.

The only tricky part about using MR to calculate semipartial correlations is understanding which of the two variables being correlated has background variables controlled and which does not. Unlike partial correlations, semipartial correlations are not symmetric. That is, $sr_{\text{Locus–(Optimism·Parent,SES,Grades)}} \neq sr_{\text{Optimism–(Locus·Parent,SES,Grades)}}$. When using MR to calculate semipartial correlations, the outcome or dependent variable is uncontrolled (or outside the parentheses), whereas the variable controlled is considered one of the predictor variables. From Chapter 5: "Conceptually, a semipartial correlation is the correlation of Y with X_1, with the effects of X_2, X_3, etc., removed from X_1. It may be symbolized as $sr_{y(1.23)}$, with the parentheses showing that the effects of X_2 and X_3 are removed from X_1, but not from Y." Thus, to calculate $sr_{\text{Locus–(Optimism·Parent,SES,Grades)}}$, we would need to regress Locus of Control on SES, Parent Involvement, Grades, and Optimism.

I regressed Locus of Control on SES, Parent Involvement, and Grades in a simultaneous regression and then sequentially added Optimism to the regression. Figure D.8 shows that the change in R^2 for the addition of Optimism was .073. Recall that the semipartial correlation is equivalent to $\sqrt{\Delta R^2}$, or $\sqrt{.073} = .270$, again consistent with other estimates within errors of rounding. Think about what this means: The semipartial correlation squared is equal to the unique variance that Optimism explains in Locus of Control, after the other variables have been taken into account. This should make sense when you focus on Figure D.6 as well. We've already removed any effects that SES, Grades, and Parent Involvement have on Optimism; what then is the unique aspect that Optimism can explain in Locus of Control?

Figure D.9 shows the table of coefficients from the second part of this same regression. The final three columns of the table list the original correlation between each of the four variables (SES, Grades, Parent Involvement, and Optimism) and Locus; the partial cor-

Model Summary

Mode l	R	R Square	Change Statistics				
			R Square Change	F Change	df1	df2	Sig. F Change
1	.307[a]	.094	.094	27.664	3	797	.000
2	.409[b]	.167	.073	69.982	1	796	.000

a. Predictors: (Constant), PAR_INV Parent Involvement, BYGRADS GRADES COMPOSITE, BYSES SOCIO-ECONOMIC STATUS COMPOSITE

b. Predictors: (Constant), PAR_INV Parent Involvement, BYGRADS GRADES COMPOSITE, BYSES SOCIO-ECONOMIC STATUS COMPOSITE, OPTIMISM Level of optimism, 10th grade

FIGURE D.8 **Calculating semipartial correlations using multiple regression. The square root of the change in R^2 when Optimism is entered last in a regression is equal to its semipartial correlation with Locus, with the effects of the background variables removed from Optimism.**

relation between each variable with Locus, with the other three variables partialed out of both the dependent and respective independent variables, and the semipartial (part) correlation of each variable with Locus, with the other three variable removed only from the independent variable side of the equation. Thus, the final part correlation (Optimism, .271), shows the semipartial correlation of Optimism with Locus of Control, with the effects of SES, Grades, and Parent Involvement removed from Optimism. The coefficient for Parent Involvement, in turn, shows the semipartial correlation of Parent Involvement with Locus of Control, with SES, Grades, and Optimism removed from Parent Involvement, and so on.

Coefficients[a]

	Unstandardized Coefficients		Standardized Coefficients			Correlations		
	B	Std. Error	Beta	t	Sig.	Zero-order	Partial	Part
(Constant)	-1.530	.167		-9.186	.000			
BYSES SOCIO-ECONOMIC STATUS COMPOSITE	6.02E-02	.030	.073	2.007	.045	.203	.071	.065
BYGRADS GRADES COMPOSITE	9.64E-02	.032	.111	3.018	.003	.253	.106	.098
PAR_INV Parent Involvement	6.11E-02	.030	.078	2.042	.041	.243	.072	.066
OPTIMISM Level of optimism, 10th grade	.310	.037	.291	8.366	.000	.364	.284	.271

a. Dependent Variable: F1LOCUS2 LOCUS OF CONTROL 2

FIGURE D.9 **Additional output from the multiple regression. Some programs (e.g., SPSS) will produce semipartial correlations on request. It is also possible to calculate semipartial correlations from the t values.**

Finally, and as noted in Chapter 5, it is possible to calculate the semipartial correlations from the values of t given in the output for each coefficient:

$$\left(sr_{y(1\cdot234)} = t\sqrt{\frac{1 - R^2}{N - k - 1}} \right)$$

For the Locus of Control–Optimism semipartial correlation, the value of t (from Figure D.9) is 8.366, and the equation is

$$sr_{\text{Locus(Optimism}\cdot\text{SES,Grades,Parent)}} = t\sqrt{\frac{1 - R^2}{N - k - 1}}$$

$$= 8.366\sqrt{\frac{1 - .167}{801 - 4 - 1}}$$

$$= .271$$

(with R^2 and df from Figure D.8).

Uses of Semipartial Correlations

In my experience, the most common use of semipartial correlations is in attempts to describe the unique variance of a predictor in accounting for some outcome. Given the adequacy of the variables in the model, the squared semipartial correlations provide estimates of the unique variance of each independent variable in explaining the outcome. The sr^2 values are equal to the ΔR^2 values obtained when each variable is added last in the regression equation.

Semipartial correlations (not squared) can also be used to describe the relative importance of the variables in a regression. In such usage (and, again, given the adequacy of the regression model), they are interpreted in much the same way as β's, as representing the *relative* direct effects of each variable on the outcome. Indeed, some authors recommend the semipartial correlations over regression coefficients for this purpose (e.g., Darlington, 1990).

CONCLUSION

Partial and semipartial correlations are useful adjuncts to multiple regression analysis and can be useful procedures by themselves. Although the primary focus of this book has been on using multiple regression and related methods in an explanatory fashion, research questions do not always fit this mold. We sometimes are interested in the extent to which a set of background variables explains the existing correlation between two variables, that is, the extent to which the relation may be spurious. Alternatively, we may be interested in demonstrating that a correlation still exists after controlling for such background variables or that a key variable predicts an outcome after controlling for background effects. Partial and semipartial correlations are useful in these cases. In this short appendix we have approached these concepts from several different orientations; it is not necessary that you understand all these different methods of obtaining and explaining partial and semipartial correlations. One or two of them should resonate so that you feel comfortable with and understand these concepts.

REVIEW OF BASIC
STATISTICS CONCEPTS

This appendix is intended as a brief review of some basic statistics concepts that are assumed in this book. It skims the surface of a broad range of material and is intended as a conceptual overview and memory jogger, not an in-depth treatment. If you need more background or review, a number of excellent introductory textbooks are available. One of my favorites is Howell's *Statistical Methods for Psychology* (2002).

Why do we need statistics? You may have wondered about that as you signed up for or sat in a statistics course, but reconsider the question now. Suppose you were to conduct an experiment in which you examined the effect of a specific type of therapy on the depressive symptoms of depressed adolescents (compared to those in a no-treatment control group). Assume that you used random assignment to treatment groups and that the random assignment was effective. After six months of treatment, you collect data on a measure of depression. Why calculate statistics? Why not just eyeball the data to determine whether your treatment worked?

If almost every person in the experimental group performed better on this posttest than did every member of the control group, there is indeed no reason to calculate statistics. You simply graph the data (e.g., Figure E.1) and any reasonable person will agree that you have demonstrated the efficacy of the treatment. Your data will pass the "interocular trauma test"; the data will hit you between the eyes.

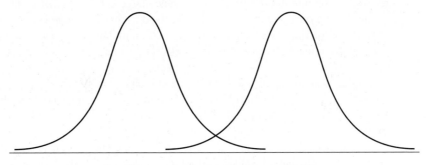

FIGURE E.1 A large difference between groups. If data always looked like this, we'd rarely need statistical significance tests.

Social science research is rarely this clear, however. What is more common is considerable overlap between the two groups so that reasonable people eyeballing the data will likely disagree as to whether the treatment was effective or not (e.g., Figure E.2). That's why we need statistics: to help us determine whether the difference between groups is big enough, unusual enough, so that we can say with assurance that the treatment worked or, more generally, that the relation between two variables (in this case, treatment and outcome) is large enough so that we can assume it did not happen by chance.

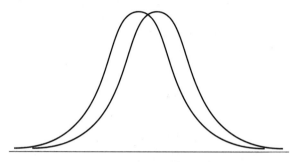

FIGURE E.2   Data more commonly look like this. Without statistical tests, it's difficult to tell whether the two groups are really different.

This sort of reasoning is related to the notion of null hypothesis significance testing. A little more formally, when we test to determine whether two groups are statistically significantly different, the underlying logic goes something like this. First, we assume that in the population the groups are not, in fact, different. We then calculate the statistic of interest (e.g., the difference between the two means) and ask this question: If, in fact, the two groups are not different in the population, what is the probability of getting a difference this large by chance alone, given the size of the sample? If the chance of getting a difference that large is, say, 25%, few researchers will be willing to say the groups differed; that is, they will say you could not reject chance as the cause of the differences between groups. Many researchers require that we obtain a difference large enough so that it occurs less than 5% of the time by chance. Others require that the difference be large enough so that it occurs only 1% of the time by chance. These rules of thumb are, of course, the values of $p < .05$ and $p < .01$, commonly used as benchmarks for deciding that something is statistically significant. When we say something is statistically significant, what we are saying is "it would be very unusual to get this kind of difference if chance variation were the only thing going on. We'd only get a difference this large five times (or one time) out of a hundred. Therefore, there must be something other than chance operating. Since I used random assignment to form groups, that other thing can only be the treatment; therefore, I can conclude that the treatment probably worked." The same logic applies to tests of correlation coefficients, regression coefficients, F values, and so on.

This logic is not always pretty and has been criticized for years (e.g., Cohen, 1994), but it works fairly well and has served the social sciences well. It definitely should be augmented, however, with a focus on *effect sizes* and *confidence intervals,* as discussed later in this appendix and throughout this book.

BASIC STATISTICS

Mean

How would you describe a set of scores? Suppose your professor tells you that you got a score of 123 on an exam for which the total possible points were 140. Would you be happy or upset? Unless your professor always uses a 90%-equals-an-A type scale, you'd probably want more information. You'd want to know what the average score was on the test. In statistics, we generally define "the average" as the mean. The mean of a set of measures is the simple arithmetic average: Sum the scores and divide by the number of scores to get the mean. Here, I will symbolize the mean using the symbol M.

Variance and Standard Deviation

Suppose the mean of scores on this test was 110. Now are you happy or disappointed? Probably happy; you scored above the mean, but how much above the mean? Is your score just above the average or well above the average? In addition to needing some idea of what the average is, you need some idea as to what the variability is in a set of scores. If 99% of people in the class scored between 100 and 120, you'd probably be pretty happy; you scored well above the mean. The range of scores is indeed one measure of variability, but in statistics we more commonly use the variance as the measure of variability in the set of scores.

Conceptually, the variance (V) is the average, squared, variation in a set of scores. Subtract the mean score from every score in the set. If you sum this number $\left[\sum (X - M)\right]$, you get a value of zero because the negative values for those who scored below the mean cancel out the values for those who scored above the mean. To get around this problem, we can square each deviation prior to summing and then, to get the average, divide by the number of scores:

$$V = \frac{\sum (X - M)^2}{N}$$

In fact, with variance, as with many statistics, we generally divide by the number of scores *minus 1* $(N - 1)$, rather than N. The reason is that we are generally calculating a *sample* variance, and using $N - 1$ gives us a better estimate of the population variance than we get using N. The new formula is

$$V = \frac{\sum (X - M)^2}{N - 1}$$

The variance, although useful, is not in the original unit of measurement, because we had to square the deviations from the mean to calculate the variance. To convert back to the original metric, it is easy to take the square root of the variance; this new measure of variability is referred to as the standard deviation ($SD = \sqrt{V}$). The standard deviation is useful in measurement, because it is a measure of variability that is in the original units of measure-ment. If you know that your score on the statistics test was 123 and that the mean and *SD* of the test were 110 and 5, respectively, you now know that you scored more than 2 standard deviations above the mean.

z scores are scores transformed into standard deviation units. If my score was 2 stan-dard deviation units below the mean, my z score will be –2; a z score of 1.5 means a score 1½ *SD*s above the mean; a z score of zero corresponds to a score exactly at the mean. z scores are the parent of all other types of standard scores, and you can easily convert from z scores to other types of standard scores.

Distributions

As you know, many natural and social phenomena have frequency distributions that con-form to a normal, or bell, curve. Figure E.3, for example, shows the frequency distribution for students' scores on the base year Science test in the NELS data on the accompanying Web site (www.ablongman.com/keith1e). Each bar on the histogram represents a 2.5-range of scores on the test, and the height of the bars represents the number of students with scores in this range. As you can see, the data conform fairly closely to the normal curve superim-posed over the histogram.

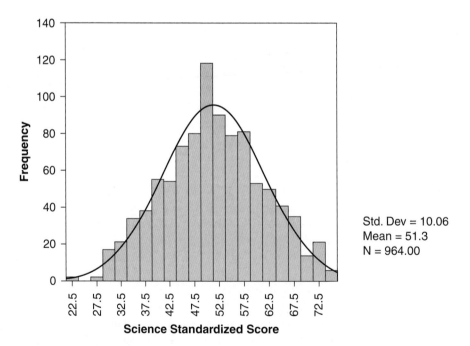

Std. Dev = 10.06
Mean = 51.3
N = 964.00

FIGURE E.3   Frequency distribution of scores on the Base Year Science test from the NELS data. The data conform well to a normal curve.

When data conform to a normal curve, this curve can be described fairly accurately using the mean and standard deviation of the data. [You can improve this description further by focusing on skew (whether the distribution has an extended tail in one direction or the other) and kurtosis (the flatness or peakedness of the distribution.)] When data conform to a normal curve, there are also well-defined relations between the distribution and statistics that describe the distribution. So, for example, approximately 68% of people will score between 1 *SD* above the mean and 1 *SD* below the mean (as shown in Figure E.4); approximately 96% will score between 2 *SD*s below and 2 *SD*s above the mean (Figure E.5), and so on. You can also use this information to determine the percentile rank of a particular

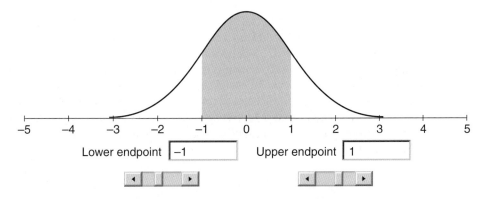

Highlighted area: 68.3%

FIGURE E.4 **Sixty-eight percent of cases fall between negative and positive 1 *SD* around the mean in a normal curve.**

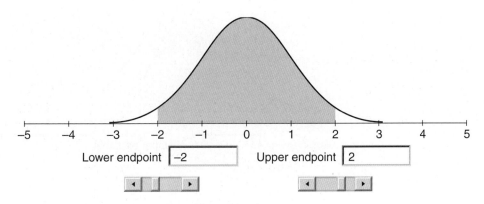

Highlighted area: 95.5%

FIGURE E.5 **+2 *SD*s around the mean encompass approximately 96% of cases in a normal curve.**

score. Say you scored 1 *SD* above the mean on another test. Fifty percent of people score below the mean, and 34% score between the mean and 1 SD above the mean (68% divided by 2). You therefore scored higher than 84% of people on this test (50 + 34). This information is summarized in Figure E.6. (These normal curves were drawn using P. B. Stark's SticiGui tools, at stat-www.berkeley.edu/users/stark/Java.) Thus it appears that your score on the statistics test—more than 2 *SD*s above the mean—was very good!

This is nice, but you may want to know the percentage corresponding to, say, 1.75 *SD*s above the mean. Alternatively, you may want to know where on the normal curve (in standard deviation units) a score at the 98th percentile will be. For this purpose, you can turn to the *z* distribution or a *z* table (or a variety of tools available on the Web). There you can look up a *z* of 1.75, and you will find a value of .9599, meaning that a *z* of 1.75 is higher than 95.99% of other scores. In this book, I have encouraged you to use electronic versions of such tables. For example, click on a cell in Excel and then click on "Insert" and "Function." Find the function called "NORMSDIST" (for normal, standard distribution) and use it. Type in 1.75 and Excel will return a value of .9599. I also recommend a probability calculator you can download free of charge from www.ncss.com, or the SticiGui tools mentioned above (see Figure E.7). Return to your score of 123 on the statistics exam, which was 2.6 *SD* above the mean. What is the corresponding percentile rank? According to Excel, this value corresponds to a percentile rank of 99.53. Nice work!

Standard Error

Suppose you take a random sample of five cases from NELS for the base year Science test scores and compute the mean of these five scores. Will the mean be identical to the mean for the full sample of 1000? No, it will vary to a certain extent, because we took a small

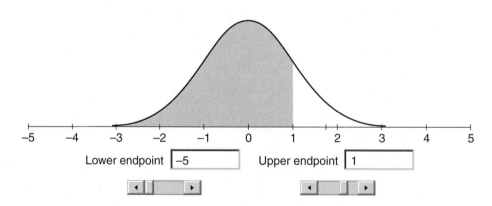

Highlighted area: 84.1%

FIGURE E.6   One *SD* above the mean corresponds to the 84th percentile. That is, 84% of people score at or below a standard deviation above the mean.

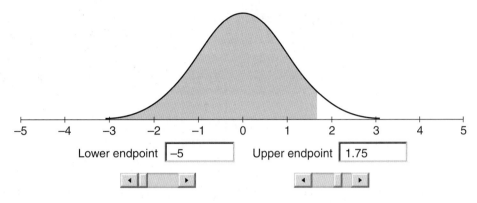

Lower endpoint −5   Upper endpoint 1.75

Highlighted area: 96%

FIGURE E.7   **The 96th percentile corresponds to 1.75 *SD*s above the mean.**

sample from a larger group. The first time I did this the mean of the five cases was 53.50, the second sample of 5 had a mean on the Science test of 51.47, and the third sample had a mean of 47.55. If I do this over and over, what do you think we will find? If we plot these means in a frequency distribution, what will it look like? If you answered "a normal curve," good for you! Yes, we will get a normal curve of means. The frequency distribution and normal curve for 200 such samples is shown in Figure E.8. It's more narrow than the normal curve of original scores because means are more stable than individual scores. The *SD* of the normal curve of means was 4.59 versus 10.6 for the distribution of individual scores.

The reason for this exercise is that when we select a sample from a population we are assuming that the sample information (in this case, the sample mean) reflects the population. You can see from the histogram, however, that this assumption is sometimes more accurate and sometimes less accurate. Not all of our five-person-sample means were close to the overall mean. What is interesting is that the *SD* of this distribution of means provides useful information about the amount of variability (the amount of error) in the distribution of means. A narrow curve with a small *SD* tells us that most of our samples provide fairly accurate estimates of the real mean. A wide curve with a large *SD* tells us that many of our estimates will be error laden. Because this standard deviation reflects the error likely inherent in any estimate of the mean, it has a special name: the standard error of the mean.

In practice, we don't repeatedly take smaller samples from a larger population. Instead, we can estimate the standard error from the characteristics of a single sample and the size of the sample. Other things being equal, the larger the *n* for each subsample is, the more narrow the curve of means. Thus, as sample size increases, the standard error decreases. In addition, we can estimate the standard error of many different statistics, regression coefficients, for example, and use this information to test these parameters for statistical significance.

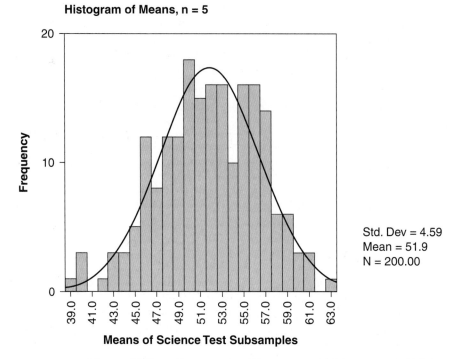

Histogram of Means, n = 5

Std. Dev = 4.59
Mean = 51.9
N = 200.00

Means of Science Test Subsamples

FIGURE E.8   Means of 200 random samples of five cases each, Science test, NELS data.

Confidence Intervals and Statistical Significance.   Because our normal curve of means has the same properties as other normal curves, we can apply our knowledge of normal curves to this one. Because 68% of cases are between –1 and +1 SD around the mean, we know that 68% of the means in our sample of means are between 47.31 and 56.49 (the overall mean of means $\pm$ the *SE,* or 51.9 $\pm$ 4.59). Now, if we were to sample a single mean only, we could use this information in reverse. Our first mean that we sampled was 53.50. I could add and subtract the *SE* from this value and make a statement about the likely value of the overall mean, something like "if we were to collect repeated samples from this population, two-thirds of the time (68% is slightly more than two-thirds) the mean will be between 48.91 and 58.09 (*M* $\pm$ *SE,* or 53.50 $\pm$ 4.59). " Or "there is a 68% chance that the true mean is between 48.91 and 58.09." (In reality, if we sample a single mean, we will likely get a slightly different estimate of the *SE* of the mean, but we will continue to use the value 4.59 for this illustration.)

Sixty-eight percent isn't the most convenient number to use. It would be more convenient to talk about 90% of the time (or 95%). Because we know the properties of a normal curve, however, it is easy to make this transformation. To encompass 90% of the curve, we multiply the SE by 1.65; to encompass 95% of the normal curve around the mean, we multiply the SE by 1.96. We call these bands of error around our means (or any other statistic) *confidence intervals,* the 90% confidence interval (CI), or the 95% CI. CIs are extremely useful for giving you an estimate of the likely range of a parameter and how error laden our estimate of the parameter likely is.

The standard error of a statistic can also be used to test its statistical significance in a variation of the *t* test. You may be most familiar with the *t* test as a test of differences between group means (discussed later in this appendix), but the *t* test is also a general statistical formula, in which a statistic (e.g., a regression coefficient) is divided by its standard error: $t = \text{statistic}/SE_{\text{statistic}}$. We can test all sorts of questions with the *t* test. The *t* in the *t* test is actually a series of distributions depending on sample size (with large sample sizes, the *t* distribution mirrors the *z* distribution), and we can look up in a table (or Excel or a probability calculator) the probability of obtaining a given *t* with a certain sample size. If the probability of obtaining a *t* by chance is small (say less than a 5% chance), we say that the parameter is statistically significant.

Degrees of Freedom

Most statistics that we use are accompanied by degrees of freedom (*df*). Conceptually, degrees of freedom are what the name suggests, the degree to which a given parameter is free to vary. Return to the example where we drew five cases from the NELS data (the Science test) and calculated a mean. The values of the five cases were 45.23, 47.66, 47.38, 60.39, and 66.84, and the mean was 53.50. *Given* the value of this mean, how many of the five cases could have different values? Say the first value was 44.23 instead of 45.23. Could we still get the same mean? Yes, we could if, for example, the final value is 65.84 instead of 66.84. In fact, four of the five scores ($N - 1$) could change and we could still get the same mean (by adjusting the final score). This is the essence of degrees of freedom— how much maneuvering room you have in your data or the number of independent pieces of information in your data—and the reason we often use $N - 1$ in formulas instead of N. As you will see in Part 2, SEM is the exception to the use of N for calculating degrees of freedom.

CORRELATIONS

Correlation coefficients describe the degree to which two variables are related, that is, the degree to which they are co-related. Correlation is one of the most fundamental concepts in statistics, and it underlies everything presented in this text. But think for a minute, if the correlation coefficient did not exist, how could you come up with such an index, a single number that accurately describes the degree to which two variables are related?

You'd probably start by graphing the two variables together. Figure E.9 shows a scatterplot, a graph of a group of high school students' scores on two variables: scores on an intelligence test and scores on an achievement test. Note the data point in the upper-right corner of the plot. This point belongs to the 24th individual in the data set; that person obtained a score of 145 on the Intelligence test (the horizontal or *X*-axis), and a score of 86 on the Achievement test (the vertical or *Y*-axis). Each other data point represents one person's scores on the two measures. Would you say that these two variables are fairly highly co-related? Yes; it is apparent that people who obtain a high score on the Intelligence test also generally earn a high score on the Achievement test, and those who score at a low level on one test generally score at a low level on the other test. This, then, is one aspect we might look for in a correlation coefficient: it should tell us the degree to which the rank order stays the same for the two variables, whether high scores on one variable are matched with high scores on the other, and so on.

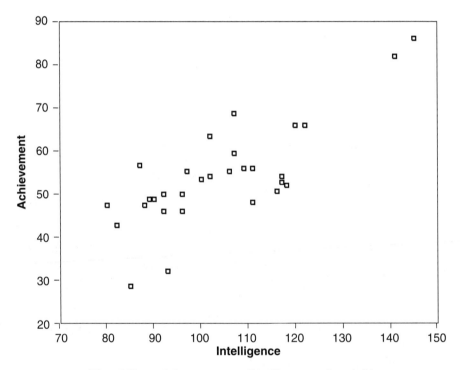

FIGURE E.9 **Plot of 30 people's scores on an Intelligence and an Achievement test. The scatterplot shows that the two tests are closely related.**

We could get a little more sophisticated and a little clearer, however, by making sure our two variables are on the same scale. Figure E.10 shows a scatterplot of the same two variables, after converting them to *z* scores. Now the two scales are directly comparable. And we can now ask the degree to which the *z* scores stay the same on the two tests. This reasoning is likely similar to that of Karl Pearson when he invented what we now know as the Pearson product moment correlation: To what extent do the *z* scores for two different measures stay the same versus the extent to which they differ?

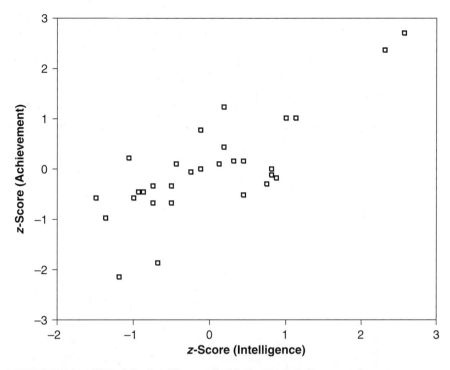

FIGURE E.10 **Plot of the Intelligence–Achievement data in z score format.**

Given this description of the correlation coefficient, let's develop a formula. The kind of formula we're talking about would index the degree to which two sets of z scores stay the same versus differ. In other words, we are interested in the *average* difference in these scores. We could subtract each person's z score on one instrument from his or her z score on the other to get an idea of this degree of difference. Then square these values (because if we were simply to sum them, the negatives would cancel out the positives), sum them, and divide by $N - 1$ (see the discussion of variance for the use of $N - 1$ instead of N). Our formula is now

$$\sum \frac{(z_x - z_y)^2}{N - 1}$$

(Cohen et al., 2003). If you calculate this coefficient for the data shown in the scatterplot, you obtain a value of .44 (the data for this example are contained in the files "IQ Achieve.sav" and "IQ Achieve.xls" on the Web site under Appendix Basics).

What does this value mean? If the two measures are perfectly related, that is, there is no difference at all in the z scores, our formula returns a value of zero. If, in contrast, the two scales are perfectly inverted so that every person who scored high on the first test scored low on the second test (and vice versa), we obtain a value close to 4. Finally, if the two tests are unrelated, with scores on the Intelligence test providing no information whatsoever for scores on the Achievement test, then our formula produces a value around 2. Our scale ranges from 0 to 2 to 4. Although we are getting close, this is not a very logical scale, so let's make a few adjustments.

We can easily transform the scale into one that makes more sense:

$$r = 1 - \frac{1}{2}\left(\sum \frac{(z_x - z_y)^2}{N - 1}\right)$$

We divide the previously obtained coefficient by 2 and subtract that value from 1. With these changes, our correlation coefficient is .778 ($r = .778$). Furthermore, our new correlation coefficient is much more logical. It ranges from 0, meaning that the two variables are unrelated, to 1, meaning that the two variables have the *exact same z* scores. In addition, the scale tells the direction of the relation. If it is positive, this means that high scores on one scale are paired with high scores on the other scale. If it is negative, high scores on one scale go with negative scores on another scale.

Another formula for r that also makes it obvious that we are comparing z scores is

$$r = \frac{\sum z_x z_y}{n - 1}$$

We will not normally calculate r using either of these formulas (there is a formula that allows some computational short-cuts), but they make it obvious that we are looking for similarities and differences in the z scores of the two scales (for more detail, see Cohen et al., 2003). Even better, we can calculate the correlation coefficient using a statistical program. Let's check the value above against the value calculated by SPSS. This value is also .778, as shown in Figure E.11.

Correlations

		IQ	ACHIEVE
IQ	Pearson Correlation	1	.778**
	Sig. (2-tailed)	.	.000
	N	30	30
ACHIEVE	Pearson Correlation	.778**	1
	Sig. (2-tailed)	.000	.
	N	30	30

**. Correlation is significant at the 0.01 level (2-tailed).

FIGURE E.11 Correlation (and its statistical significance) of Intelligence and Achievement scores.

The Pearson correlation ranges from -1.0, suggesting a perfect relation, but with high scores on one scale paired with negative scores on the other scale, to +1.0, suggesting a perfect positive relation. A correlation of zero between the two scales would suggest no relation between the z scores; that is, the z scores between the two tests are unrelated. These relations are illustrated in Figures E.12 through E.14, which show scatterplots of large negative (E.12, $r = -.905$), near zero (E.13, $r = -.067$), and large positive (E.14, $r = .910$) correlations.

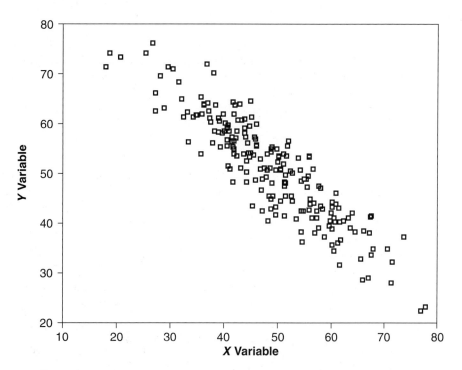

FIGURE E.12 Scatterplot of a high negative correlation ($r = -.905$).

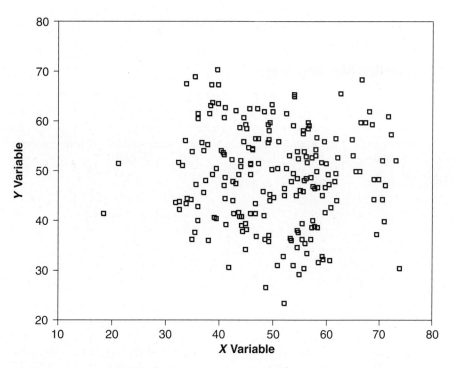

**FIGURE E.13 Scatterplot of a near zero correlation (r = -.067).
The two scales are virtually unrelated.**

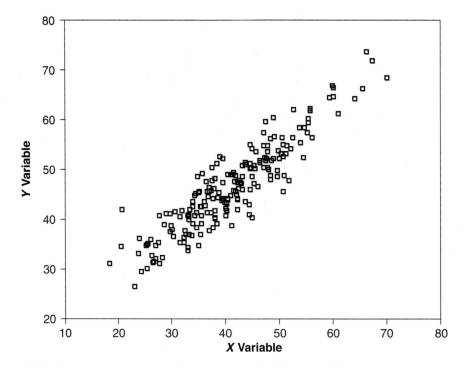

FIGURE E.14   **Scatterplot of a high positive correlation ($r = .910$).**

Statistical Significance of r

Correlation coefficients can be tested for statistical significance using the formula $t = r\sqrt{N - 2}/\sqrt{1 - r^2}$. You then look up the value of t with $N - 2$ *df* to determine how likely it is to get a value of this size given a "true" population value of zero. Using the current example, the correlation between an Intelligence and an Achievement test, we obtain a t value of 6.56.

$$t = \frac{r\sqrt{N - 2}}{\sqrt{1 - r^2}}$$

$$= \frac{.778\sqrt{30 - 2}}{\sqrt{1 - .778^2}}$$

$$= \frac{4.117}{.628}$$

$$= 6.56$$

with 28 *df*. The correlation is indeed statistically significantly different from zero ($p < .001$).

In your reading, you will come across other varieties of correlation coefficients, such as Spearman's rho and the point–biserial correlation. Spearman's rho is appropriate when the variables are rankings; the point–biserial correlation is appropriate when one variable is continuous and the other dichotomous. How are they calculated? In fact, these two types of correlations (along with phi, a correlation with two dichotomous variables) are simply short-cuts for the correlation coefficient we derived above, Pearson's *r*. They are holdovers from the days when we calculated statistics by hand and, given the nature of the data (e.g., dichotomous), one could take a few short-cuts in the calculation. In this era of computers, you can calculate these three types of correlations just as easily using the standard *r*. Stated differently, these three types of correlations are really no different than Pearson *r*. For more information, see Howell (2002).

t Tests

If you come to this book with a background in psychology or education, you may well have more experience with *t* tests and analyses of variance than with regression. It is likely, for example, that much of the research you read uses these methods. It is easy to think that these methods that are so appropriate for experimental research do something fundamentally different than does regression. This is not the case; the *t* test and ANOVA are simply subsets of multiple regression. Here I will briefly review the use of these methods and illustrate them with computer output.

These statistical analyses (*t* tests and ANOVA) are especially useful in experimental research, in which participants are assigned to one group or another and given different experimental treatments. The primary difference between the *t* test and ANOVA is that a *t* test is appropriate when there is only one independent variable and there are only two groups, whereas ANOVA can be used with more than two groups and more than one IV.

As an example, suppose you were interested in the effects of cognitive behavior therapy (CBT) on the depressive symptoms of adolescent girls. Perhaps you set up an experiment in which each girl from a sample of 40 depressed girls is assigned, at random, to a CBT group or to a waiting list (members of which will receive treatment following the experiment if the treatment proves effective). The simulated data are included in the dataset "t test.sav" and "t test.xls" on the Web site. Some of the cases are shown in Table E.1. The first column shows the group (1 = experimental, or CBT, and 0 = control, or wait list), and the second column shows the girls' scores on a measure of depressive symptoms following treatment (a high score represents more depressive symptomology and thus is bad).

Figure E.15 shows a portion of the results of a *t* test conducted on these data using SPSS. After treatment, the average score for the control group was 59.65 on the measure of depressive symptoms versus an average score of 49.25 for the experimental group. Given that a high score on the measure represents greater depression, the experimental group indeed showed less depression than the control group. Is this difference between groups statistically significant? The second table in the figure shows the results of the *t* test. The *t* associated with the difference between groups was 3.20. With 38 ($N - 2$) degrees of freedom, the probability of obtaining a *t* this large by chance is .003, or 3 out of 1000. Using common rules of thumb for statistical significance, the difference between groups was

TABLE E.1 Portion of the Data from the *t* Test Example

GROUP	DEPRESS
0	66
0	63
0	44
0	56
0	62
0	65
0	35
0	62
0	76
.	.
.	.
.	.
1	60
1	56
1	59
1	47
1	47
1	49
1	45
1	63
1	57
1	30

Group Statistics

	GROUP Treatment group	N	Mean	Std. Deviation	Std. Error Mean
DEPRESS Depressive symptoms	0 Control	20	59.65	9.599	2.146
	1 CBT, Experimental	20	49.25	10.915	2.441

Independent Samples Test

		t-test for Equality of Means					95% Confidence Interval of the Difference	
		t	df	Sig. (2-tailed)	Mean Difference	Std. Error Difference	Lower	Upper
DEPRESS Depressive symptoms	Equal variances assumed	3.200	38	.003	10.40	3.250	3.820	16.980

FIGURE E.15 Test results for the simulated CBT therapy experiment.

indeed statistically significant. Because girls were assigned at random to the two groups, we have effectively ruled out other plausible explanations for the difference (e.g., that girls who received treatment were less depressed to start with) and can conclude that the CBT treatment was probably indeed effective. (In this book we will come to call such ruling out of alternative explanations by a different name: ensuring that there are no common causes of the presumed cause and the presumed effect.)

The general formula for a t test is $t = (M_e - M_c)/SE_{e-c}$, or the difference in means between the experimental and control group divided by the standard error of that difference. It really doesn't matter which group is subtracted from which, because you are primarily interested in the absolute value of t. The df are $N - 2$.

Although this process of comparing means seems very different from the process of correlating two variables, they are, in fact, the same process. As I will show in the main text, you will get the same essential results if you correlate the two variables (group and depressive symptoms scores) that we got with the t test.

Effect Sizes

It is interesting to know that the two groups are statistically significantly different, but is the difference large, small, or somewhere in between? This is, in my opinion, one advantage of regression approaches: with multiple correlation and standardized regression coefficients, we automatically get an index of the magnitude of the effect. There are a number of measures of effect size that are common for two-group experimental research; the most common is likely d. The formula for d is $d = (M_e - M_c)/SD$ or the difference between the two groups divided by the overall standard deviation (think of d as somewhat like a z score). For the present example, d is .910 [$d = (49.25 - 59.65)/11.431$]; ignore the sign). According to common rules of thumb, d's above .80 are considered large (small = .20, medium = .50, large = .80; Cohen, 1988), although it is possible and desirable to have different rules of thumb for specific areas of research. According to these generic rules of thumb, CBT therapy in our simulated data had a large effect on depressive symptoms.

ANOVA

Analysis of variance is appropriate when there are more than two groups in an experiment or when there is more than one independent variable. It can also be used to analyze data from experiments with one IV and only two groups and will give the same results as the t test.

Consistency with the t Test

Figure E.16 shows the results of an ANOVA for the therapy–depression example above. The lower table shows that for the ANOVA, like the t test, the difference between the two groups on the posttest was statistically significant. The F statistic was 10.239 with 1 and 38 degrees of freedom; such an F is unlikely to occur if there are no real differences between groups ($p = .003$). The F is equal to t^2 and shows the same level of statistical significance as does the results of the t test.

The general formula for F is $F = \dfrac{V_{\text{between group}}}{V_{\text{within group}}}$, the variation between groups divided by the average variation within groups. You can literally calculate the variance of the group means (times the n in each group) to get the V_{between} and take a weighted average of the variances of the groups to obtain the V_{within}. F statistics require two values for degrees of

Between-Subjects Factors

		Value Label	N
GROUP Treatment group	0	Control	20
	1	CBT, Experimental	20

Descriptive Statistics

Dependent Variable: DEPRESS Depressive symptoms

GROUP Treatment group	Mean	Std. Deviation	N
0 Control	59.65	9.599	20
1 CBT, Experimental	49.25	10.915	20
Total	54.45	11.431	40

Tests of Between-Subjects Effects

Dependent Variable: DEPRESS Depressive symptoms

Source	Type III Sum of Squares	df	Mean Square	F	Sig.	Partial Eta Squared
GROUP	1081.600	1	1081.600	10.239	.003	.212
Error	4014.300	38	105.639			
Corrected Total	5095.900	39				

FIGURE E.16   ANOVA results for the simulated CBT therapy experiment.
The results are the same as for the t test, although $F = t^2$.

freedom, generally corresponding to the treatment and error (within group). The total df for the ANOVA is equal to $N - 1$. The df for the treatment is the number of groups minus 1, and the df for the error term is equal to the $df_{total} - df_{group}$.

It may seem that we are doing something different with a t test, which compares group means, versus ANOVA, which analyzes variances. But the general formula for F above shows that the variance in the numerator of the equation is the variance of *group means*. Yes, the processes are essentially the same. I will demonstrate in the text that ANOVA can be accomplished through multiple regression. As you read the text itself, you should note the general similarity of the formula for F in ANOVA and that for F for regression. Both divide the variance explained by the independent variable by the variance left unexplained.

Effect Sizes, η^2

A number of measures of effect size are available for ANOVA. Shown in Figure E.16 is eta squared ($\eta^2 = .212$). η^2 is a great measure of effect size for our purposes, because as we will see, it is equal to R^2 from a regression solution to the same problem. Common rules of thumb for η^2 are small = .01, medium = .10, and large = .25.

Factorial ANOVA

To take our therapy–depression example a little further, suppose you were interested in whether CBT had positive effects for depressed adolescent boys as well as girls. You could conduct a new experiment using both boys and girls. You are not sure, however, whether CBT will have the same effect for both sexes, so you add Sex as a second independent variable. In the parlance of ANOVA, you now have a design appropriate for analysis via a 2×2 factorial ANOVA. The analysis will determine the effect of CBT, the effect of Sex, and whether there are differential effects of CBT for boys and girls (the interaction between Group and Sex in their effects on Depressive Symptoms).

Figure E.17 shows some of the output from the 2×2 ANOVA. The data are in the files "cbt 2way.sav" and "cbt 2way.xls" on the Web site. As shown in the bottom table of the figure, Group (CBT versus Control) had a medium to large effect on Depressive Symptoms in these simulated data and this effect was statistically significant ($\eta^2 = .192$, $F = 18.091$

Between-Subjects Factors

		Value Label	N
GROUP CBT vs Control	.00	Control	40
	1.00	CBT	40
SEX Girls vs Boys	.00	Girls	40
	1.00	Boys	40

Descriptive Statistics

Dependent Variable: DEPRESS Depressive Symptoms

GROUP CBT vs Control	SEX Girls vs Boys	Mean	Std. Deviation	N
.00 Control	.00 Girls	60.500	11.4455	20
	1.00 Boys	54.650	13.0557	20
	Total	57.575	12.4754	40
1.00 CBT	.00 Girls	48.850	8.2798	20
	1.00 Boys	45.800	9.7257	20
	Total	47.325	9.0480	40
Total	.00 Girls	54.675	11.4900	40
	1.00 Boys	50.225	12.2149	40
	Total	52.450	11.9936	80

Tests of Between-Subjects Effects

Dependent Variable: DEPRESS Depressive Symptoms

Source	Type III Sum of Squares	df	Mean Square	F	Sig.	Partial Eta Squared	Noncent. Parameter	Observed Power[a]
GROUP	2101.250	1	2101.250	18.091	.000	.192	18.091	.987
SEX	396.050	1	396.050	3.410	.069	.043	3.410	.446
GROUP * SEX	39.200	1	39.200	.337	.563	.004	.337	.088
Error	8827.300	76	116.149					
Corrected Total	11363.800	79						

a. Computed using alpha = .05

FIGURE E.17   Results of a factorial ANOVA to compare the effects of CBT versus no therapy on the depressive symptoms for boys and girls.

[1, 76], $p < .001$). An examination of the means shows that adolescents in the experimental (CBT) group had fewer depressive symptoms at posttest than did the control group. Sex had a small effect that was not statistically significant ($p = .069$); nor was the interaction statistically significant ($p = .563$).

The data are graphed in Figure E.18, an excellent way to summarize data from this type of experiment. It is clear that both boys and girls in the experimental group benefited from the CBT therapy. It appears that boys in both groups show somewhat fewer symptoms than do girls, but the ANOVA tells us that this difference is not statistically significant. The fact that the two lines are basically parallel reaffirms the nonsignificant interaction term from the ANOVA and shows that CBT had similar effects for both boys and girls.

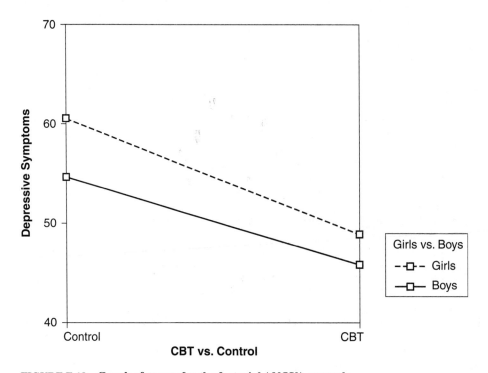

FIGURE E.18   Graph of means for the factorial ANOVA example.

I hope this quick review has gotten your mind back into statistics so that you are ready to begin exploring multiple regression and structural equation modeling. If you need additional review, Howell (2002) is excellent. For an even more gentle review, Kranzler (2002) is an excellent resource.

REFERENCES

■ ■ ■ ■ ■ ▬▬▬▬▬▬▬▬▬▬▬▬▬▬▬▬▬▬▬▬▬▬▬▬▬▬▬▬▬

Aiken, L. S., & West, S. G. (1991). *Multiple regression: Testing and interpreting interactions.* Thousand Oaks, CA: Sage.

Alexander, R. A., & DeShon, R. P. (1994). Effect of error variance heterogeneity on the power of tests for regression slope differences. *Psychological Bulletin, 115,* 308–314.

Allison, P. D. (1999). *Multiple regression: A primer.* Thousand Oaks, CA: Pine Forge.

American Psychological Association. (2001). *Publication manual of the American Psychological Association* (5th ed.). Washington, DC: Author.

Arbuckle, J. L. (1996). Full information estimation in the presence of incomplete data. In G. A. Marcoulides & R. E. Schumacker (Eds.), *Advanced structural equation modeling* (pp. 243–278). Mahwah, NJ: Erlbaum.

Arbuckle, J. L. (2003). *Amos 5.0 update to the Amos user's guide.* Chicago: Smallwaters.

Arbuckle, J. L, & Wothke, W. (1999). *Amos 4.0 user's guide.* Chicago: Smallwaters.

Baron, R. M., & Kenny, D. A. (1986). The moderator–mediator variable distinction in social psychological research: Conceptual, strategic, and statistical considerations. *Journal of Personality and Social Psychology, 51,* 1173–1182.

Begley, S. (1998, March 30). Homework doesn't help. *Newsweek,* 50–51.

Bennett, W. J. (1987). *James Madison high school: A curriculum for American students.* Washington, DC: U.S. Department of Education.

Bentler, P. M. (1995). *EQS structural equations program manual.* Los Angeles: Multivariate Software.

Bentler, P. M., & Woodward, J. A. (1978). A Head Start reevaluation: Positive effects are not yet demonstrable. *Evaluation Quarterly, 2,* 493–510.

Bentler, P. M., & Wu, E. J. C. (1995). *EQS for Windows user's guide.* Encino, CA: Multivariate Software.

Berry, W. D. (1993). *Understanding regression assumptions.* Thousand Oaks, CA: Sage.

Birnbaum, M. H. (1979). Procedures for the detection and correction of salary inequities. In T. H. Pezzullo & B. E. Brittingham (Eds.), *Salary equity* (pp. 121–144). Lexington, MA: Lexington Books.

Blalock, H. M. (1972). *Social statistics* (2nd ed.). New York: McGraw-Hill.

Bollen, K. A. (1989). *Structural equations with latent variables.* New York: Wiley.

Bollen, K. A., & Long, J. S. (Eds.). (1993). *Testing structural equation models.* Newbury Park, CA: Sage.

Boomsma, A. (1985). Nonconvergence, improper solutions, and starting values in LISREL maximum likelihood estimation. *Psychometrika, 50,* 229–242.

Boomsma, A. (2000). Reporting analyses of covariance structures. *Structural Equation Modeling, 7,* 461–483.

Borenstein, M., Rothstein, H., & Cohen, J. (2003). *SamplePower 2.0.* Chicago: SPSS, Inc.

Bradley, D. R. (1988). *DATASIM.* Lewiston, ME: Desktop.

Brady, H. V., & Richman, L. C. (1994). Visual versus verbal mnemonic training effects on memory-deficient and language-deficient subgroups of children with reading disability. *Developmental Neuropsychology, 10,* 335–347.

Bremner, J. D., Shobe, K. K., & Kihlstrom, J. F. (2000). False memories in women with self-reported childhood sexual abuse: An empirical study. *Psychological Science, 11,* 333–337.

Browne, M. W., & Cudeck, R. (1993). Alternative ways of assessing model fit. In K. A. Bollen & J. S. Long (Eds.), *Testing structural equation models* (pp. 136–162). Newbury Park, CA: Sage.

Bryk, A. S., & Raudenbush, S. W. (1992). *Hierarchical linear models.* Thousand Oaks, CA: Sage.

Buhs, E. S., & Ladd, G. W. (2001). Peer rejection as an antecedent of young children's school adjustment: An examination of mediating processes. *Developmental Psychology, 37,* 550–560.

Butler, J. K. (2001). Reciprocity of dyadic trust in close male–female relationships. *Journal of Social Psychology, 126,* 579–591.

511

Byrne, B. M. (1994). *Structural equation modeling with EQS and EQS/Windows: Basic concepts, applications, and programming.* Thousand Oaks, CA: Sage.

Byrne, B. M. (1998). *Structural equation modeling with LISREL, PRELIS, and SIMPLIS: Basic concepts, applications, and programming.* Mahwah, NJ: Erlbaum.

Byrne, B. M. (2001). *Structural equation modeling with Amos: Basic concepts, applications, and programming.* Mahwah, NJ: Erlbaum.

Carroll, J. B. (1963). A model for school learning. *Teachers College Record, 64,* 723–733.

Carroll, J. B. (1993). *Human cognitive abilities: A survey of factor-analytic studies.* New York: Cambridge University Press.

Christenson, S. L., Rounds, T., & Gorney, D. (1992). Family factors and student achievement: An avenue to increase students' success. *School Psychology Quarterly, 7,* 178–206.

Cleary, T. A. (1968). Test bias: Prediction of grades of Negro and white students in integrated colleges. *Journal of Educational Measurement, 5,* 115–124.

Cliff, N. (1983). Some cautions concerning the application of causal modeling methods. *Multivariate Behavioral Research, 18,* 115–126.

Cohen, J. (1968). Multiple regression as a general data-analytic system. *Psychological Bulletin, 70,* 426–443.

Cohen, J. (1978). Partialed products *are* interactions; partialed powers *are* curve components. *Psychological Bulletin, 85,* 114–128.

Cohen, J. (1983). The cost of dichotomization. *Applied Psychological Measurement, 7,* 249–253.

Cohen, J. (1988). *Statistical power analysis for the behavioral sciences* (2nd ed.). Hillsdale, NJ: Erlbaum.

Cohen, J. (1994). The earth is round ($p < .05$). *American Psychologist, 49,* 997–1003.

Cohen, J., & Cohen, P. (1983). *Applied multiple regression/correlation analysis for the behavioral sciences* (2nd ed.). Hillsdale, NJ: Erlbaum.

Cohen, J., Cohen, P., West, S. G., & Aiken, L. S. (2003). *Applied multiple regression/correlation analysis for the behavioral sciences* (3rd ed.). Hillsdale, NJ: Erlbaum.

Coleman, J. S., Hoffer, T., & Kilgore, S. (1981). *Public and private schools.* Washington, DC: U.S. Department of Education.

Cooper, H. (1989). *Homework.* New York: Longman.

Cronbach, L. J., & Snow, R. E. (1977). *Aptitudes and instructional methods: A handbook for research on interactions.* New York: Irvington.

Cudek, R. (1989). Analysis of correlation matrices using covariance structure models. *Multivariate Behavioral Research, 27,* 269–300.

Darlington, R. B. (1990). *Regression and linear models.* New York: McGraw-Hill.

Duncan, O. D. (1975). *Introduction to structural equation models.* New York: Academic Press.

Duncan, O. D., Haller, A. O., & Portes, A. (1971). Peer influences on aspirations: A reinterpretation. In H. M. Blalock (Ed.), *Causal models in the social sciences* (pp. 219–244). New York: Aldine-Atherton.

Eberhart, S. W., & Keith, T. Z. (1989). Self-concept and locus of control: Are they causally related in secondary students? *Journal of Psychoeducational Assessment, 7,* 14–30.

Eisenberg, N., Gershoff, E. T., Fabes, R. A., Shepard, S. A., Cumberland, A. J., Losoya, S. H., et al. (2001). Mothers' emotional expressivity and children's behavior problems and social competence: Mediation through children's regulation. *Developmental Psychology, 37,* 475–490.

Eliason, S. R. (1993). *Maximum likelihood estimation: Logic and practice* (Sage University Paper series on Quantitative Applications in the Social Sciences, series no. 07–096). Newbury Park, CA: Sage.

Elliott, C. D. (1990). *Differential Ability Scales: Introductory and technical manual.* San Antonio, TX: Psychological Corporation.

Fan, X., Thompson, B., & Wang, L. (1999). Effects of sample size, estimation methods, and model specification on structural equation modeling fit indexes. *Structural Equation Modeling, 6,* 56–83.

Fox, J. (1997). *Applied regression analysis, linear models, and related methods.* Thousand Oaks, CA: Sage.

Fredrick, W. C., & Walberg, H. J. (1980). Learning as a function of time. *Journal of Educational Research, 73,* 183–204.

Freedman, D. A. (1987). As others see us: A case study in path analysis. *Journal of Educational Statistics, 12,* 101–128.

Gage, N. L. (1978). *The scientific basis of the art of teaching.* New York: Teachers College Press.

Green, S. B. (1991). How many subjects does it take to do a regression analysis? *Multivariate Behavioral Research, 26,* 499–510.

Hancock, G. R., & Mueller, R. O. (in press). *A second course in structural equation modeling.* Greenwich, CT: Information Age.

Hayduk, L. A. (1987). *Structural equation modeling with LISREL: Essentials and advances.* Baltimore: Johns Hopkins University Press.

Hayduk, L. A. (1996). *LISREL issues, debates, and strategies.* Baltimore: Johns Hopkins University Press.

Henry, D. B., Tolan, P. H., & Gorman-Smith, D. (2001). Longitudinal family and peer group effects on violence and nonviolent delinquency. *Journal of Clinical Child Psychology, 30,* 172–186.

Hintze, J. L. (2002). *PASS 2002: User's guide.* Kaysville, UT: NCSS.

Hintze, J. M., Callahan, J. E., III, Matthews, W. J., Williams, S. A. S., & Tobin, K. G. (2002). Oral reading fluency and prediction of reading comprehension in African American and Caucasian elementary school children. *School Psychology Review, 31,* 540–553.

Howell, D. C. (2002). *Statistical methods for psychology* (5th ed.). Pacific Grove, CA: Brooks/Cole.

Hoyle, R. H. (Ed.). (1995). *Structural equation modeling: Concepts, issues, and applications.* Thousand Oaks, CA: Sage.

Hoyle, R. H., & Panter, A. T. (1995). Writing about structural equation models. In R. H. Hoyle (Ed.), *Structural equation modeling: Concepts, issues, and applications* (pp. 158–176). Thousand Oaks, CA: Sage.

Hu, L., & Bentler, P. M. (1998). Fit indices in covariance structure modeling: Sensitivity to underparametrized model misspecification. *Psychological Methods, 3,* 424–453.

Hu, L., & Bentler, P. M. (1999). Cutoff criteria for fit indexes in covariance structure analysis: Conventional criteria versus new alternatives. *Structural Equation Modeling, 6,* 1–55.

Huberty, C. J. (2003). Multiple correlation versus multiple regression. *Educational and Psychological Measurement, 63,* 271–278.

James, L. R., Mulaik, S. A., & Brett, J. M. (1982). *Causal analysis: Assumptions, models, and data.* Beverly Hills: Sage.

Jensen, A. R. (1980). *Bias in mental testing.* New York: Free Press.

Jensen, A. R. (1998). *The g factor: The science of mental ability.* Westport, CT: Praeger.

Jöreskog, K. G., & Sörbom, D. (1993). *LISREL 8: Structural equation modeling with the SIMPLIS command language.* Hillsdale, NJ: Erlbaum.

Jöreskog, K. G., & Sörbom, D. (1996). *LISREL 8 user's reference guide.* Lincolnwood, IL: Scientific Software.

Kaplan, D. (1995). Statistical power in structural equation modeling. In R. H. Hoyle (Ed.), *Structural equation modeling: Concepts, issues, and applications* (pp. 100–117). Thousand Oaks, CA: Sage.

Kaplan, D. (2000). *Structural equation modeling: Foundations and extensions.* Newbury Park, CA: Sage.

Keith, T. Z. (1982). Time spent on homework and high school grades: A large-sample path analysis. *Journal of Educational Psychology, 74,* 248–253.

Keith, T. Z. (1990). Confirmatory and hierarchical confirmatory analysis of the Differential Ability Scales. *Journal of Psychoeducational Assessment, 8,* 391–405.

Keith, T. Z. (1993). Causal influences on school learning. In H. J. Walberg (Ed.), *Analytic methods for educational productivity* (pp. 21–47). Greenwich, CT: JAI Press.

Keith, T. Z. (1999). Structural equation modeling in school psychology. In C. R. Reynolds & T. B. Gutkin (Eds.), *The handbook of school psychology* (3rd ed., pp. 78–107). New York: Wiley.

Keith, T. Z. (2005). Using confirmatory factor analysis to aid in understanding the constructs measured by intelligence tests. In D. P. Flanagan & P. L. Harrison (Eds.), *Contemporary intellectual assessment: Theories, tests, and issues* (2nd ed., pp. 581–614). New York: Guilford.

Keith, T. Z., & Benson, M. J. (1992). Effects of manipulable influences on high school grades across five ethnic groups. *Journal of Educational Research, 86,* 85–93.

Keith, T. Z., & Cool, V. A. (1992). Testing models of school learning: Effects of quality of instruction, motivation, academic coursework, and homework on academic achievement. *School Psychology Quarterly, 7,* 207–226.

Keith, T. Z., Hallam, C. D., & Fine, J. G. (2004). Longitudinal effects of in-school and out-of-school homework on high school grades. *School Psychology Quarterly, 19,* 187–211.

Keith, T. Z., Keith, P. B., Quirk, K. J., Sperduto, J., Knowles, S. S., & Killings, S. (1998). Longitudinal effects of parent involvement on high school grades: Similarities and differences across gender and ethnic groups. *Journal of School Psychology, 36,* 335–363.

Keith, T. Z., Keith, P. B., Troutman, G. C., Bickley, P. G., Trivette, P. S., & Singh, K. (1993). Does parental involvement affect eighth grade student achievement? Structural analysis of national data. *School Psychology Review, 22,* 474–496.

Keith, T. Z., Kranzler, J. H., & Flanagan, D. P. (2001). What does the Cognitive Assessment System (CAS) measure? Joint confirmatory factor analysis of the CAS and the Woodcock–Johnson Tests of Cognitive Ability (3rd ed.). *School Psychology Review, 30,* 89–119.

Keith, T. Z., Reimers, T. M., Fehrmann, P. G., Pottebaum, S. M., & Aubey, L. W. (1986). Parental involvement, homework, and TV time: Direct and indirect effects on high school achievement. *Journal of Educational Psychology, 78,* 373–380.

Kenny, D. A. (1979). *Correlation and causality.* New York: Wiley.

Kerlinger, F. N. (1986). *Foundations of behavioral research* (3rd ed.). New York: Holt, Rinehart & Winston.

Kirk, R. E. (1995). *Experimental design: Procedures for the behavioral sciences* (3rd ed.). Pacific Grove, CA: Brooks/Cole.

Klecka, W. R. (1980). *Discriminant analysis.* Thousand Oaks, CA: Sage.

Kline, R. B. (1998). *Principles and practices of structural equation modeling.* New York: Guilford.

Kling, K. C., Hyde, J. S., Showers, C. J., & Buswell, B. N. (1999). Gender differences in self-esteem: A meta-analysis. *Psychological Bulletin, 125,* 470–500.

Kraemer, H. C., & Theimann, S. (1987). *How many subjects? Statistical power analysis in research.* Newbury Park, CA: Sage.

Kranzler, J. H. (2002). *Statistics for the terrified* (3rd ed.). Upper Saddle River, NJ: Prentice Hall.

Kranzler, J. H., Miller, M. D., & Jordan, L. (1999). An examination of racial/ethnic and gender bias on curriculum-based measurement of reading. *School Psychology Quarterly, 14,* 327–342.

Krivo, L. J., & Peterson, R. D. (2000). The structural context of homicide: Accounting for racial differences in process. *American Sociological Review, 65,* 547–559.

Lee, S., & Hershberger, S. (1990). A simple rule for generating equivalent models in covariance structure modeling. *Multivariate Behavioral Research, 25,* 313–334.

Lindsay, D. S., & Read, J. D. (1994). Psychotherapy and memories of childhood sexual abuse: A cognitive perspective. *Applied Cognitive Psychology, 8,* 281–338.

Loehlin, J. C. (2004). *Latent variable models: An introduction to factor, path, and structural analysis* (4th ed.). Hillsdale, NJ: Erlbaum.

Lott, J. R. (1998). *More guns, less crime: Understanding crime and gun-control laws.* Chicago: University of Chicago Press.

MacCallum, R. C. (1986). Specification searches in covariance structure modeling. *Psychological Bulletin, 100,* 107–120.

MacCallum, R. C., Browne, M. W., & Sugawara, H. M. (1996). Power analysis and determination of sample size for covariance structure modeling. *Psychological Methods, 1,* 130–149.

MacCallum, R. C., Wegener, D. T., Uchino, B. N, & Fabrigar, L. R. (1993). The problem of equivalent models in applications of covariance structure analysis. *Psychological Bulletin, 114,* 185–199.

MacKinnon, D. P., Lockwood, C. M., Hoffman, J. M., West, S. G., & Sheets, V. (2002). A comparison of methods to test mediation and other intervening variable effects. *Psychological Methods, 7,* 83–104.

MacKinnon, D. P., Warsi, G., & Dwyer, J. H. (1995). A simulation study of mediated effect measures. *Multivariate Behavioral Research, 30,* 41–62.

Marcoulides, G. A., & Schumacker, R. E. (Eds.). (1996). *Advanced structural equation modeling.* Mahwah, NJ: Erlbaum.

Marcoulides, G. A., & Schumacker, R. E. (Eds.). (2001). *New developments and techniques in structural equation modeling.* Mahwah, NJ: Erlbaum.

Marsh, H. W. (1993). The multidimensional structure of academic self-concept: Invariance over gender and age. *American Educational Research Journal, 30,* 841–860.

Maruyama, G. M. (1998). *Basics of structural equation modeling.* Thousand Oaks, CA: Sage.

McDonald, R. P., & Ho, M.-H. R. (2002). Principles and practice in reporting structural equation analyses. *Psychological Methods, 7,* 64–82.

McManus, I. C., Winder, B. C., & Gordon, D. (2002). The causal links between stress and burnout in a longitudinal study of UK doctors. *Lancet, 359,* 2089–2090.

Meehl, P. E., & Waller, N. G. (2002). The path analysis controversy: A new statistical approach to strong appraisal of verisimilitude. *Psychological Methods, 7,* 283–300.

Menard, S. (1995). *Applied logistic regression analysis.* Thousand Oaks, CA: Sage.

Millsap, R. E. (2001). When trivial constraints are not trivial: The choice of uniqueness constraints in confirmatory factor analysis. *Structural Equation Modeling, 8,* 1–17.

Morris, W. (Ed.). (1969). *The American Heritage dictionary of the English language.* Boston: Houghton Mifflin.

Mueller, R. O. (1995). *Basic principles of structural equation modeling: An introduction to LISREL and EQS.* New York: Springer-Verlag.

Mulaik, S. A., & Millsap, R. E. (2000). Doing the four-step right. *Structural Equation Modeling, 7,* 36–73.

Muthén, L. K., & Muthén, B. O. (1998). *Mplus user's guide* (2nd ed.). Los Angeles: Muthén & Muthén.

Muthén, L. K., & Muthén, B. O. (2002). *How to use a Monte Carlo study to decide on sample size and determine power.* Retrieved March 26, 2003, from www.statmodel.com/index2.html.

National Commission on Excellence in Education. (1983). *A nation at risk: The imperative for educational reform.* Washington, DC: U.S. Government Printing Office.

Neale, M. C., Boker, S. M., Xie, G., & Maes, H. H. (1999). *Mx: Statistical modeling* (5th ed.). Box 126 MCV, Richmond, VA 23298: Department of Psychiatry. Downloadable from www.vcu.edu/mx/executables.html.

Nurss, J. R., & McGauvran, M. E. (1986). *The Metropolitan Readiness Tests.* New York: Psychological Corporation.

Page, E. B., & Keith, T. Z. (1981). Effects of U.S. private schools: A technical analysis of two recent claims. *Educational Researcher, 10*(7), 7–17.

Pearl, J. (2000). *Causality: Models, reasoning, and inference.* New York: Cambridge University Press.

Pedhazur, E. J. (1997). *Multiple regression in behavioral research: Prediction and explanation* (3rd ed.). New York: Holt, Rinehart & Winston.

Quirk, K. J., Keith, T. Z., & Quirk, J. T. (2001). Employment during high school and student achievement: Longitudinal analysis of national data. *Journal of Educational Research, 95,* 4–10.

Raju, N. S., Bilgic, R., Edwards, J. E., & Fleer, P. F. (1999). Accuracy of population validity and cross-validity estimation: An empirical comparison of formula-based, traditional empirical, and equal weights procedures. *Applied Psychological Measurement, 23,* 99–115.

Rasberry, W. (1987, December 30). Learn what the smart kids learn? *Washington Post,* p. A23.

Ratnesar, R. (1999, January 25). The homework ate my family. *Time, 153,* pp. 55–56, 59–63.

Raykov, T. & Marcoulides, G. A. (2000). *A first course in structural equation modeling.* Mahwah, NJ: Erlbaum.

Reibstein, D. J., Lovelock, C. H., & Dobson, R. DeP. (1980). The direction of causality between perceptions, affect, and behavior: An application to travel behavior. *Journal of Consumer Research, 6,* 370–376.

Rigdon, E. E. (1994). Demonstrating the effects of unmodeled random measurement error. *Structural Equation Modeling, 1,* 375–380.

Rigdon, E. E. (1995). A necessary and sufficient identification rule for structural models estimated in practice. *Multivariate Behavioral Research, 30,* 359–383.

Rosenthal, R., & Rubin, D. B. (1979). A note on percent variance explained as a measure of the importance of effects. *Journal of Applied Social Psychology, 9,* 395–396.

Salzinger, S., Feldman, R. S., Ng-Mak, D. S., Mojica, E., & Stockhammer, T. F. (2001). *Development and Psychopathology, 13,* 805–825.

Schafer, J. L., & Graham, J. W. (2002). Missing data: Our view of the state of the art. *Psychological Methods, 7,* 147–177.

Schumacker, R. E., & Lomax, R. G. (1996). *A beginner's guide to structural equation modeling.* Mahwah, NJ: Erlbaum.

Schumacker, R. E., & Marcoulides, G. A. (Eds.). (1998). *Interactive and nonlinear effects in structural equation modeling.* Mahwah, NJ: Erlbaum.

Sethi, S., & Seligman, M. E. P. (1993). Optimism and fundamentalism. *Psychological Science, 4,* 256–259.

Shinn, M. R. (1989). *Curriculum-based measurement: Assessing special children.* New York: Guilford.

Shipley, B. (2000). *Cause and correlation in biology.* Cambridge, UK: Cambridge University Press.

Shrout, P. E., & Bolger, N. (2002). Mediation in experimental and nonexperimental studies: New procedures and recommendations. *Psychological Methods, 7,* 442–445.

Simon, H. A. (1954). Spurious correlation: A causal interpretation. *Journal of the American Statistical Association, 48,* 467–479.

Stapleton, L. M. (in press). Using multilevel structural equation modeling techniques with complex sample data. In G. R. Hancock & R. Mueller (Eds.), *A second course in structural equation modeling.* Greenwich, CT: Information Age.

Steiger, J. H. (1998). A note on multiple sample extensions of the RMSEA fit index. *Structural Equation Modeling, 5,* 411–419.

Steiger, J. H. (2001). Driving fast in reverse: The relationship between software development, theory, and education in structural equation modeling. *Journal of the American Statistical Association, 96,* 331–338.

Stelzl, I. (1986). Changing the causal hypothesis without changing the fit: Some rules for generating equivalent path models. *Multivariate Behavioral Research, 21,* 309–331.

Stone, B. J. (1992). Joint confirmatory factor analyses of the DAS and WISC-R. *Journal of School Psychology, 30,* 185–195.

Tanaka, J. S. (1993). Multifaceted conceptions of fit in structural equation models. In K. S. Bollen & J. S. Long (Eds.), *Testing structural equation models* (pp. 10–39). Newbury Park, CA: Sage.

Teigen, K. H. (1995). Yerkes–Dodson: A law for all seasons. *Theory and Psychology, 4,* 525–547.

Thompson, B. (1998, April). *Five methodology errors in educational research: The pantheon of statistical significance and other faux pas.* Invited address presented at the annual meeting of the American Educational Research Association, San Diego. (ERIC Document Reproduction Service No. ED 419 023).

Thompson, B. (1999, April). *Common methodology mistakes in educational research, revisited, along with a primer on both effect sizes and the bootstrap.* Invited address presented at the annual meeting of the American Educational Research Association, Montreal. (ERIC Document Reproduction Service No. ED 429 110).

Thompson, B. (2002). What future quantitative social science research could look like: Confidence intervals for effect sizes. *Educational Researcher, 31*(3), 25–32.

Tiggeman, M., & Lynch, J. E. (2001). Body image across the life span in adult women: The role of self-objectification. *Developmental Psychology, 37,* 243–253.

Walberg, H. J. (1981). A psychological theory of educational productivity. In F. H. Farley & N. Gordon (Eds.), *Psychology and education* (pp. 81–110). Berkeley: CA: McCutchan.

Walberg, H. J. (1986). Synthesis of research on teaching. In M. C. Wittrock (Ed.), *Handbook of research on teaching* (3rd ed., pp. 214–229). New York: Macmillan.

Wampold, B. E. (1987). Covariance structures analysis: Seduced by sophistication? *Counseling Psychologist, 15,* 311–315.

Wechsler, D. (1974). *Manual for the Wechsler Intelligence Scale for Children—Revised.* New York: Psychological Corporation.

Williams, P. A., Haertel, E. H., Haertel, G. D., & Walberg, H. J. (1982). The impact of leisure-time television on school learning: A research synthesis. *American Educational Research Journal, 19,* 19–50.

Wolfle, L. M. (1979). Unmeasured variables in path analysis. *Multiple Linear Regression Viewpoints, 9*(5), 20–56.

Wolfle, L. M. (1980). Strategies of path analysis. *American Educational Research Journal, 17,* 183–209.

Wolfle, L. M. (2003). The introduction of path analysis to the social sciences, and some emergent themes: An annotated bibliography. *Structural Equation Modeling, 10,* 1–34.

Wolfle, L. M., & List, J. H. (2004). Temporal stability in the effects of college attendance on locus of control, 1972–1992. *Structural Equation Modeling, 11,* 244–260.

Wothke, W. (2000). Longitudinal and multi-group modeling with missing data. In T. D. Little, K. U. Schnabel, & J. Baumert (Eds.), *Modeling longitudinal and multilevel data: Practical issues, applied approaches, and specific examples* (pp. 219–240). Mahwah, NJ: Erlbaum.

SUBJECT INDEX

Note: Page numbers followed by the letters *f, t,* and *n,* indicate figures, tables, and notes, respectively.